The Writing of History in the Middle Ages

Essays Presented to Richard William Southern

EDITED BY

R. H. C. DAVIS & J. M. WALLACE-HADRILL

with the assistance of

R. J. A. I. CATTO & M. H. KEEN

CLARENDON PRESS · OXFORD
1981

Oxford University Press, Walton Street, Oxford OX2 6DP
London Glasgow New York Toronto
Delhi Bombay Calcutta Madras Karachi
Kuala Lumpur Singapore Hong Kong Tokyo
Nairobi Dar es Salaam Cape Town
Melbourne Auckland
and associate companies in
Beirut Berlin Ibadan Mexico City

Published in the United States by
Oxford University Press, New York

British Library Cataloguing in Publication Data

The Writing of history in the Middle Ages.
  1. Historiography—History—Addresses, essays,
lectures
  I. Davis, Ralph Henry Carless
  II. Wallace-Hadrill, John Michael
  III. Southern, Sir Richard William
  907.2   D13   80–41708

ISBN 0–19–822556–3

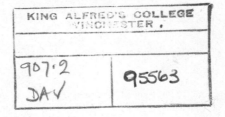

Set and Printed in Monotype Bembo by
Latimer Trend & Company Ltd, Plymouth

Foreword

SIR RICHARD SOUTHERN is, like Bede, a Northumbrian. Had he been born the other side of the Channel, his seventieth birthday would have been marked by the presentation of a multi-volume Festschrift, reflecting all the facets of his learning. We beg him to accept this single volume in place of several and in the name of many. Even had its contributors been limited to all of his pupils over the full range of matters in which he has been their inspiration, the volume would have been little less bulky than the Codex Amiatinus. We therefore decided to limit contributions to one major theme dear to his heart: the historiography of the Middle Ages. By this we have understood not only the writing of history by medieval men but the way they looked at the past and the influences that led to that looking. We hope, perhaps vainly, that our contributions may have coherence both by reason of the theme and through our common upbringing by one whose mind has never ceased to range majestically over the deep issues of men's sense of their past. We offer him what we have written in gratitude and affection.

Contents

Plates

Abbreviations

AABB	*Analecta Bollandiana*
A. Cl.	*Annals of Clonmacnoise*
AI	*Annals of Innisfallen*
AT	*Annals of Tigernach*
AU	*Annals of Ulster*
BEC	*Bibliothèque de l'École des chartes*
BIHR	*Bulletin of the Institute of Historical Research*
BN	Bibliothèque nationale
BRUO	*A Biographical Register of the University of Oxford to A.D. 1500* by A. B. Emden, 3 vols (Oxford, 1957–9)
BT	Bayeux Tapestry
Bury	*Chronicle of Bury St. Edmunds*, ed. Antonia Gransden (NMT, 1964)
CDS	*Die Chroniken der deutschen Städte vom 14 bis im 16 Jahrhundert* (Hist. Komm. der Bayerischen Akademien der Wissenschaften, Leipzig, 1862–00)
Chron. John	*The Chronicle of John of Worcester*, ed. J. R. H. Weaver (Anecdota Oxoniensia, 4th series, xiii, 1908)
Cotton	*Bartholomaei de Cotton Historia Anglicana*, ed. H. R. Luard (RS, 1859)
DNB	*Dictionary of National Biography* (London and Oxford, 1885 ff.)
Dunstable	*Annales Prioratus de Dunstaplia* in *Annales Monastici*, ed. H. R. Luard, iii (RS, 1866)
EHR	*English Historical Review*
Flores	*Flores Historiarum*, ed. H. R. Luard, 3 vols (RS, 1890)
Flor. Wig.	*Florentii Wigorniensis Chronicon ex Chronicis*, ed. B. Thorpe (English Hist. Soc., 2 vols, 1848–9)
GP	*Willelmi Malmesbiriensis monachi de Gestis Pontificum Anglorum libri quinque*, ed. N. E. S. A. Hamilton (RS, 1870)
GR	*Willelmi Malmesbiriensis monachi de Gestis Regum Anglorum libri quinque*, ed. W. Stubbs, 2 vols (RS, 1887–9)
Guisborough	*Chronicle of Walter of Guisborough*, ed. Harry Rothwell (Camden Third Series, lxxxix, 1957)

HE	*Baedae: Historia Ecclesiastica Gentis Anglorum*
HN	*Eadmeri Historia Novorum in Anglia*, ed. M. Rule (RS, 1884)
JEH	*Journal of Ecclesiastical History*
JTS	*Journal of Theological Studies*
KKES	*Kings and Kingship in Early Scotland* by M. O. Anderson (Edinburgh, 1973)
Knighton	*Chronicon Henrici Knighton*, ed. J. R. Lumby, 2 vols (RS, 1889–95)
Lanercost	*Chronicon de Lanercost*, ed. J. Stevenson (Edinburgh, 1839)
Langtoft	*Chronicle of Pierre de Langtoft*, ed. T. Wright, 2 vols (RS, 1866–8)
London	*Annales Londonienses* in *Chronicles of the Reigns of Edward I and Edward II*, ed. W. Stubbs (RS, 1882), i. 1–251
MARS	*Medieval and Renaissance Studies*
MGH	*Monumenta Germaniae Historica*
NMT	*Nelson's Medieval Texts*
OMT	*Oxford Medieval Texts*
Oseney	*Annales de Oseneia* in *Annales Monastici*, ed. H. R. Luard, 5 vols (RS, 1864–9), iv. 1–352
OV	*The Ecclesiastical History of Orderic Vitalis*, ed. Marjorie Chibnall, 6 vols (OMT, 1969–80)
PG	*Patrologia Graeca*, ed. J. P. Migne
PL	*Patrologia Latina*, ed. J. P. Migne
Reg.	*Regesta Regum Anglo-Normanorum, 1066–1154*, ed. H. W. C. Davis *et al.* 4 vols (Oxford, 1913–69)
Rev. belge	*Revue belge de Philologie et d'histoire*
Rev. bén	*Revue bénédictine*
Rev. celt	*Revue celtique*
Rishanger	*Willelmi Rishanger Chronica et Annales*, ed. H. T. Riley RS, 1865)
RS	Rolls Series
Scalacronica	*Scalacronica by Sir Thomas Gray of Heton, Knight*, ed. J. Stevenson (Edinburgh, 1838)
SD	*Symeonis monachi opera omnia*, ed. T. Arnold, 2 vols (RS, 1882–5)
Settimane	*Settimane di Studio: Centro Italiano di Studi sull' alto Medioveo*
SHF	Société de l'histoire de France
SHN	Société de l'histoire de Normandie

SHR   *Scottish Historical Review*

Trevet   *F. Nicholai Triveti Annales*, ed. T. Hog (English Hist. Soc., 1845)

TRHS   *Transactions of the Royal Historical Society*

VCH   Victoria History of the Counties of England

WJ   *Guillaume de Jumièges: Gesta Normannorum*, ed. Jean Marx (SHN, 1914)

Worcester   *Annales de Wigornia* in *Annales Monastici*, ed. H. R. Luard (RS, 1869), iv. 353–564

WP   *Guillaume de Poitiers: Histoire de Guillaume le Conquérant*, ed. Raymonde Foreville (Paris, 1952)

Bede, Iona, and the Picts

ARCHIBALD A. M. DUNCAN

'HIS capacious mind was seldom swayed by prejudice, firm in its judgments, well fitted to deal with a large mass of disorderly material and to present it systematically and succinctly.' Most historians would hope to measure up to this, R. W. Southern's perception of his fellow Northumbrian, Bede, whose 'simple and grand' aims were 'to make the raw new nation . . . at home in the past . . . of the Latin learning of the Christian church'.[1] One fragment of Christian Latin learning, Gildas, was Bede's sole authority for the three Pictish incursions into late Roman Britain; yet Gildas is cited only once (I, 22), not as a source, but as a repository of further details omitted by Bede, whose frankness about his informants in the dedicatory epistle is thus shown to be selective. Modern students have understandably followed the trail laid by Bede in identifying his sources in England and at Rome,[2] but they have scarcely pondered the lesson of his treatment of Gildas: that he used sources of Celtic provenance without disclosing his debt. C. W.

[1] R. W. Southern, *Medieval Humanism and Other Studies* (1970), pp. 3, 5. Over thirty years ago R. W. Southern introduced me to Bede the Latin scholar; and I wondered how he came by his northern information. This study was prompted by questions from my pupils at the University of Glasgow and encouraged by my colleague Mr C. P. Wormald, whom I wish particularly to thank for many critical comments on various drafts and not a few suggestions which are incorporated in it; he is not responsible for such errors as remain.

[2] For example, it is now agreed that additional material on Augustine and Gregory came to Bede's hand after his work had been drafted; see the useful review in H. Mayr-Harting, *The Coming of Christianity to Anglo-Saxon England* (1972), Appendix 1. For Gildas see M. Miller, 'Bede's Use of Gildas', *EHR*, xc (1975), pp. 241–61.

Jones remarked perceptively in 1947 that 'Bede had no direct access to Irish records, but did work from a digest of such records'; but this has been ignored. Indeed C. W. Jones's fine book passes almost unnoticed in the 1969 edition of the *HE*.[1] Again, Dr Mayr-Harting suggests that Wilfrid's speeches at the Synod of Whitby were composed by Bede with the letter of Cummian (probably abbot of Clonfert) to Segene abbot of Iona, 'or something like it' in front of him.[2]

The evidence that Bede did have Irish materials in front of him is not slight, though it has been generally ignored because, until Dr A. P. Smyth's brilliant paper of 1972, historians had to regard the early Irish annals as sources of uncertain date, provenance, and value. Thanks to Drs Bannerman and Smyth we know now that the earliest annals in these islands were written in the monastery of St. Columba in Iona (although when begun between 550 and 650 is not agreed).[3] This paper first reviews the northern information in the *HE* arguing that it was partly drawn from the Iona annals and was mediated to Bede with a distinctly Pictish view of events; secondly identifies the mediator as the writer of a letter from King Nectan of the Picts to Ceolfrith, abbot of Jarrow, a writer anxious to reform the Easter observance at Iona; and thirdly, arguing that Cummian's letter and three other letters relating to the Irish church which appear in Bede were similarly transmitted to Ceolfrith, it suggests the consequences of these identifications for the understanding of Bede's impulse to historiography.

---

[1] C. W. Jones, *Saints' Lives and Chronicles in Early England* (1947), pp. 47, 178, 180; *Bede's Ecclesiastical History of the English People*, ed. B. Colgrave and R. A. B. Mynors (1969).

[2] Mayr-Harting, *Coming of Christianity*, p. 112. Cf. Jones, *Saints' Lives and Chronicles*, pp. 181–2, 197–9; Gabriele Isenberg, *Die Würdigung Wilfrieds von York in der Historia Ecclesiastica Gentis Anglorum Bedas und der Vita Wilfridi des Eddius* (1978), pp. 33–58.

[3] A. P. Smyth, 'The Earliest Irish Annals', *Proc. Royal Irish Academy*, lxxii, section C (1972), pp. 1–48; J. Bannerman, *Studies in the History of Dalriada* (1974), pp. 132–46. But see now K. Harrison, 'Epacts in Irish Chronicles', *Studia Celtica*, xii/xiii (1977–8), pp. 17–32.

I

We meet the problem of the north at the very beginning of the *HE* where Bede provides a general survey of the languages and races of the island of Britain (I, 1): first, and briefly, the Britons, then, at much greater length, the Picts and finally the *Scotti* led by Reuda, who 'won lands among the Picts by either friendship or the sword' and also settled in Britain; they are called after their leader *Dalreudini* 'for in their language *daal* means "a part" '. We are so accustomed to the name 'Dalriada' cast across Argyll on historical maps of Scotland that the very slender basis for this attribution for early times scarcely registers. Adomnan knows Scots of Britain but not a Scottish Dal Riada: Bede, apart from this mention, is in like case, and seems on occasion to use *Scottia* for Argyll. In the annals of the seventh century, Dal Riada was certainly a people of north-eastern Ireland, and their kings, although they ruled in Ireland and Kintyre, seem to occur in annals in an Irish context. Only with a battle of Dal Riada and Britons in 704 do we have a certain use in the annals for the Scots in Britain, and further uses occur between 704 and 741 and from 781. The extension of the name to Argyll was relatively recent when Bede wrote; it would come to him from Ireland or Iona and it was certainly not widely known or understood in Britain. The spelling of *daal* shows that it came from an Irish source, written not oral.

According to Bede the race of Picts from Scythia, 'as they say', entered the ocean in a few long ships, sailing round Britain to Northern Ireland. The Picts were refused lands by the *Scotti* and advised to go easterly to another island which the *Scotti* would help them to conquer; the Picts seized northern Britain, and sought wives from the *Scotti*, who agreed only if, when in doubt, the Picts would choose their kings from the female and not the male line, a custom still observed. The source for this elaborate tale was probably reflecting Pictish custom in the accounts of Pictish exogamy and of the succession. But Bede's explanation—and it is an *explanation*—of exogamy, having recourse to Ireland, is not Pictish; and Irish legend had no need of an explanation of Pictish exogamy and succession.

[3]

Thus the explanation is Irish in its stress on the links between Ireland and the Picts and on the priority of Ireland in Pictish settlement-intentions; but it is Pictish in what it is concerned to explain. It is therefore not derived from Irish or Pictish legend, but is an original composition. Probably Isidore of Seville provided the name of the Scythians, but if there already existed a pseudo-etymology it was surely of the '*Scotti* from Scythia' nature; '*Picti* from Scythia' must be an invention for the purpose of Bede's source, to explain the Picts in terms of the *Scotti*.[1]

The Pictish slant recurs with events known otherwise to us from the Irish annals, most notably with the account of Columba, who is seen not as the early monks of Iona saw him, sanctified by his pilgrimage, through life, and particularly overseas, but as a missionary (an Anglian view) to the Picts (III, 4; V, 9, 24). The primary Iona annal for Columba is the obit best represented by *AI*: 'Quies Coluimb cille, nocte Dominica hi.u.id. Iuin anno xx°xu° peri-grinationis suae, aetate autem lxxui'[2] with which *AT* is in close

---

[1] H. M. Chadwick and G. S. MacEoin have discussed the Pictish origin legend especially in relation to the *Cruithni* who, by the mid-ninth century, were identified with the Picts. It is quite possible that Bede's informant was influenced by the story of the *Cruithni* (who married Irish wives) and that he borrowed this for the Picts. Subsequently the identity was noticed and the equation of Picts and *Cruithni* made, perhaps under influence of Isidore's *Etymologiae* where both Picts and Scots are said to derive from 'tattooed', the Scots in a name which they have in their own language—a name assumed from the ninth century until the nineteenth to be *Cruithni*. But in Adomnan and the early annals the *Cruithni* are an Irish people who have nothing whatever to do with the Picts. H. M. Chadwick, *Early Scotland* (1949), chapter vi; G. S. MacEoin, 'On the Irish legend of the origin of the Picts', *Studia Hibernica*, iv (1964), pp. 138–55; K. H. Jackson, in F. T. Wainwright, *The Problem of the Picts* (1955), pp. 158–9; *Adomnan's Life*, pp. 63–5, and index under Picts, Cruithni. Isidore, *Etymologiae*, xix, 23, 7 (Picts); ix, 2, 103 (Scots).

[2] *The Annals of Inisfallen*, ed. S. MacAirt (1951), pp. 80–1. 'hi' = on Iona. Dr A. P. Smyth has shown that *AI* is derived from the 'earliest stratums' underlying *AU* up to the middle of the eighth century (*Proc. Roy. Irish Acad.*, lxxii, C, p. 31), i.e. from the Iona annals. *AI* seems to be particularly valuable for Iona entries. On pilgrimage see K. Hughes, 'The changing theory and practice of Irish pilgrimage', *JEH*, xi (1960), pp. 143–51; T. M. Charles-Edwards, 'The social background to Irish *peregrinatio*', *Celtica*, xi (1976), pp. 43–59.

agreement, showing only insertion of an incorrect association with Whitsunday and a different but still correct way of expressing his age: 'Quies Coluim cille in nocte Dominica Pentecostes. u. edh Iuin anno perigrinacionis sue. xxxu. etatis uero. lxx. uii' (*AT*).[1] Columba died in his seventy-seventh year on Sunday, 9 June 597.[2]

The annals are also agreed on the 35th year for the pilgrimage and this would yield an Iona annal for Columba's voyage, again best represented by *AI*: 'Columcille i n-ailithre. Prima nox eius in Albain in Pentecosten' (Columba in pilgrimage; his first night in Britain in Whitsun). The Iona chronicle may have been in Latin, when the opening phrase would have been *Nauigatio Coluimcille* as in *AT*; *AT*, however, having transferred Whitsun to his death, replaces it by a calculation of his age (42) at the time of the pilgrimage;[3] this age-figure has no independent value.

This information must also have been known to the authors of lives of Columba. When Bishop Colman left Lindisfarne in 664 and returned to Iona, he may have prompted Cummian, abbot of Iona (*c*. 657–69), to write his book of the powers, *virtutes*, of Columba to answer the challenges thrown out at Whitby; only a brief extract survives of this,[4] apparently the earliest Irish hagiographic writing, but it would certainly agree with the annals in dating Columba's

[1] The best edition is by Whitley Stokes in *Rev. celt.*, xvii (1896), p. 160. All 'Scottish' annals are very carefully translated (with the unfortunate exception of 'Picts' for *Cruithni*) under 'corrected' years by A. O. Anderson in his *Early Sources of Scottish History*, i (1922); the text may also be consulted in *Chronicles of the Picts and Scots*, ed. W. F. Skene (1867), where however the extracts from the Annals of Ulster are particularly unreliably given.

[2] *AU* has a late short entry without the year of pilgrimage and with an error of transcription, *anno . . . etatis lxxui*; *AU*, i. ed. W. M. Hennessy (1887), p. 64. Note that *AI* and *AT* are not in conflict over Columba's age at death, despite the assertions of modern commentators.

[3] *Ann. Inisfallen*, ed. MacAirt, p. 74; *Rev. celt.*, xvii. p. 144, printing *quadragesimo quinto* (for xluᵒ); this is a misreading by Stokes of *xlii*, a good example of the difficulty of distinguishing *u* and *ii*. *AU*, i. p. 60; Skene, *Picts-Scots Chronicles*, p. 344.

[4] *Adomnan's Life of Columba*, ed. A. O. and M. O. Anderson (1961), pp. 91 475–6; it is possible that Cogitosus' Life of Brigit was earlier than Cummian's work.

arrival to Whitsun—an Easter-related and therefore suspect feast. That it had reference to the Easter controversy is suggested by its disappearance and the circulation of a new Life written by Adomnan, the first abbot of Iona (*c.* 679–704) to accept the Roman Easter. Adomnan wrote out of Columba's life all reference to his arrival on Whitsunday, and tells of his death very shortly after the 34th anniversary of his arrival (563 + 34 = 597, when Whitsun fell on 26 May) in a last illness which began in May—an oblique but deliberate way of avoiding mention of the Whitsuntide anniversary which must surely have been commented on in Cummian's life. The most natural reading of Adomnan's Life is that Columba's death occurred early in the 35th year of his pilgrimage; Adomnan also places the pilgrimage in his 42nd year.[1] These figures agree with the annals, but, like the annalist, Adomnan must have begun not with an age at pilgrimage, but with an age at death which must have been the 77th year as in the annals.

Now Bede dates Columba's 'mission' in four or five ways; AD 565, the accession of Justin II (this is derived from Bede's imperial *fasti* and need not detain us), the ninth year of Bridei king of Picts, and 32 years before Columba's death at the age of 77 (III, 4); in addition he notes that Iona observed the pseudo-AnatolianEaster for 150 years up to AD 715.

The statement that Columba died *lxxvii annorum* can derive from no other source than the Iona obit, although it is slightly misrepresented. The shortened stay of 'about' 32 years in Iona is a simple misreading by Bede or his source of a kind very common in Iona–Irish annals: *xxxu* and *xxxii*. As with the age at death, an annalistic 'in the 35th [32nd] year' has become Bede's 'for 32 years' this time with the saving grace of 'about'. The obit agreed by Iona sources, with death in the 77th year of age, 35th of pilgrimage, gives the information given to Bede. But the date of death, Sunday, 9 June (which would have yielded a year date) was clearly unknown

---

[1] *Adomnan's Life*, pp. 186–7, 514–17; the editors summate to 75 years of age at death, p. 66.

to Bede, and this is further evidence that the obit came to him through an intermediary.

It is generally accepted that there is a relationship between Bede's ninth year of King Bridei for the donation of Iona, and the statement found in the List P group of the Pictish King Lists that Bridei was baptized in the eighth year of his reign by St. Columba. Elaborate scenarios to take account of these dates (e.g. *nauigatio* 563, conversion 564, donation 565) assume a chronological record of Columba's activity which is highly improbable in kind, is unknown to Adomnan, and is unnecessary. Of course we could assume a King List whose *uiiii* was misread as *uiii* by Bede or his sources—but that would not explain the different events ascribed to that year by List P and by Bede.

Recently Dr Molly Miller has shown that the pseudo-historical portion of List P gives reign lengths adding up to 14 years or multiples thereof, showing derivation from pseudo-Anatolian Easter tables. In my view the reigns immediately before Bridei belong to this pseudo-historical section with reigns in List P of 15 (amended from 12) + 5 + 7 + 1 = 28, and 11 + 1 + 2 = 14.[1] Bridei is therefore the earliest king whose thirty-year reign length is independent of these computational fictions and was within historical memory when the historical kings were entered retrospectively in a set of Easter-table annals (containing also Columba's *nauigatio*) in the form of obits and reign lengths. The relevant annal

---

[1] For the King Lists see M. O. Anderson, *KKES*, where the texts are critically edited and discussed. M. Miller, 'The disputed historical horizon of the Pictish King Lists', *SHR*, lviii (1979), pp. 7–14, is an important further discussion. The emendation I propose is in accord with Dr Miller's emendations. Her Drest III and Drest IV together have 5 years in one P MS, 12 in the other; I read 15. Dr Miller tells me she is reluctant to admit this emendation since it interferes with her calculations equating Patrick's arrival in 19 Drest I with 432. This calculation, in my view, begins from the wrong date (587 instead of 584) and ignores the 'control' indicated by Dr Miller, of the death of Drest I in 449 according to *A.Cl.* The attempt to transfer any of these fifth-century events including the foundation-legend of Abernethy (sheer fiction) into AD dates is bound to fail because sparse annals were readily misplaced in a chronography which had no consecutive numbering.

would have something like: [584] *Bruide mac Meilochon regnauit xxx annis*; this places Columba's *nauigatio* of 563 in the ninth year of Bridei: such a set of annals was known to Bede's source.

However, at a later date which need not concern us, some at least of the pseudo-historical kings were added to the Pictish Easter table annals with Galam Cennaleph preceding Bridei with a two-year reign. His reign survives in List P manuscripts in two lengths: *G.C. vno anno/iiii annis regnauit cum Briduo i° anno*, while the generally later List Q gives simply 4 years, having no year of joint-reign. These variants are instructive not of some partition of kingdoms, but of a chronographer's slip. The reign was originally *ii* years misread as *u*, and the division shows that it was placed in the annals not in 554, but in 555, only 29 years before Bridei's death. This attracted the subsequent gloss noting the overlap: *cum Briduo i° anno*. Counting from the death of Galam, Columba's *nauigatio* occurred in the eighth year of Bridei.

First stage	Second stage adds	Third stage adds gloss
[584] *Bruide mac Meilochon re' xxx annis*		
[563] *Nauigatio Coluimcille*		
	[555] *Galam C. re' ii annis*	*cum Briduo i° anno*
[554 Implied accession of Bridei]		

When the ambiguous obit for 555 was turned into King Lists, P turned 2 (or 5) — 1 into 1 (or 4) + 1, whereas Q subtracted, 5 — 1, and gave 4.[1] The Pictish obits of the first stage were also borrowed

---

[1] *KKES*, pp. 247–8, 262 (List P); 266, 272, 280, 287 (List Q). *AU*, i. p. 70, for Bridei's death. *AT* gives the death of Bridei *rig Cruithneach* under f.n. 6 = 581; the Irish title represents a late entry. The earliest obit for him in *AT* is probably that among events of 752, of a battle among Picts in Circinn *in quo cecidit Bruidhi mac Maelchon*; *Rev. celt.*, xvii. pp. 154, 253. As Dr I. Henderson points out, this entry must have been made on an 84-year Easter table: 752 — 168 = 584. One List Q version, Fordun, gives Bridei a reign length of 19 years, an error for 29 years—a different way of solving the overlap between Bridei and Galam.

by the Iona annals adding a word for 'death' and dropping the reign lengths; the date of this borrowing is likely to have been 705 × 730 but Bede's source must have used the Pictish version.

There was only one Columban annal for the arrival in Britain, that for the *nauigatio* in 563: without Galam this fell in the ninth year of Bridei, with Galam it was in the eighth year. To Bede's source it signified the arrival of the man who converted the Picts; to the compiler of List P he was the man who baptized Bridei, to the compiler of List Q the man who converted Bridei—and so [563] expressed as a regnal year appears in Bede and List P in those guises.[1] By the early eighth century Columba was accepted by the Picts as apostle to the Picts.

Nowhere does Bede claim explicitly that Bridei was converted or that Bridei gave Iona to Columba, and in this regard he is in accord with Adomnan's *Life of Columba* which records a number of Pictish baptisms by Columba but not Bridei's nor a general conversion of Picts. However, Bede's claim that Columba went first to the Picts, and that the Picts gave him Iona is contradicted by the Iona annals which state that King Connall (of Dal Riada) gave Iona,[2] and by Adomnan who is clear that Columba went first to Iona and that all land west of Drumalban was Scottish not Pictish. That Bridei (like the rulers of other barbarian peoples dealing with missionaries) tolerated Columba's mission to the Picts is in accord with the evidence of both Adomnan and Bede. Bede was misinformed by someone who accepted the view of Columba also embodied in the

---

[1] The King List entries of the conversion/baptism of Bridei cannot have been derived from Bede who makes no such statement. They are in the same form as the arrival of Patrick in the nineteenth year of Drest and the foundation of Abernethy also dated by a regnal year; all are therefore taken from an annalistic source. Of the List Q texts, List I states 'Bridei son of Maelchon. St. Columba converts him. Coming of St. Columba to the Picts in 565, and he lived 32 years with them. In the time of Bridei, 597 Columba died.' In this passage the sentence 'Coming . . .' is clearly derived from Bede and is unique to List I; but the preceding statement 'St. Columba converts him' is common to List Q texts, and is independent of Bede.

[2] *Rev. celt.*, xvii. p. 151; *AU*, i. p. 64. This was doubtless recorded later, perhaps a century later, but it remains an early Iona statement of Iona's history.

King Lists, a Pictish view that Columba came to convert Picts and that the Picts gave him Iona for a monastery, a point twice reiterated by Bede (III, 4; V, 9, 24). And Bede's informant was close enough to the Picts to give the king's name as an accurate *Bridius filius Meilochon* and to flatter him as 'a most powerful king' (III, 4).

Since the annals yield only the date 563 for Columba's *nauigatio*, persistence of the erroneous Easter among Columba's successors 'for a very long time, that is up to the year of the incarnation 715 for 150 years' was not computed by Bede as 715 — 565 = 150. On the contrary, as others have pointed out,[1] Bede must have calculated 565 by deducting 150 from 715. This was based upon a misunderstanding which I hope to explain later (for Iona followed the 'erroneous' Easter tables for 152 years (563–715)), but it establishes that Bede provided '565' (and hence the accession of Justin II) and that his source provided him with '150 years'.

The Pictish and Irish elements in Bede's account are prominent in the rest of III, 4. Columba was the founder of Iona, of Durrow, and first teacher, *primus doctor* of the northern Picts. From Durrow and Iona 'sprang many monasteries established in Britain and Ireland by his disciples, in all of which the island monastery holds *principatus*'. This is the only use of *principatus* in the *HE* and *princeps* is used in Irish sources (annalistic and in canon law) consistently of the abbot, *principatus* of his authority. Bede here reflects a source familiar with the Irish monastic *paruchia* and expressing the authority of the abbot of Iona within the *paruchia*. At this point the new paragraph in modern editions is most misleading,[2] for Bede expands the nature of its *principatus* in the next sentence: 'but the island has a ruler, always an

---

[1] C. W. Jones, *Saints' Lives and Chronicles*, p. 35; rejected by P. Grosjean in *AABB*, lxxviii (1960), 387 n. C. Plummer (*Venerabilis Baedae Opera Historica*, 1966, ii. p. 130) claims that Bede's 715 is a mistake for 716; but Bede is correct, 715 *was* the last year in which the pseudo-Anatolian Easter *ratio* was followed in Iona.

[2] There is no break at this point in the Moore MS (*The Moore Bede*, ed. P. Hunter Blair and R. A. B. Mynors, Copenhagen, 1959, fo. 46v), but something like a paragraph break occurs in *The Leningrad Bede*, ed. O. Arngart (Copenhagen, 1952), 51b.

abbot priest, to whose authority [*ius*] the whole province and even
the bishops must be subject in an unusual structure [*ordo*], according
to the example of that first teacher who was not a bishop but a
priest and a monk'. This stress on primacy of the authority of the
successor abbots, over bishops, where Columba was first teacher, in
Pictland, is surely not fortuitous and the 'priest-abbot' reflects a
defensive attitude to the claims of any other church claiming primacy
whose first teacher and his successors were bishops.

Bede is reflecting his Pictish-inclined source in asserting the
independence of the whole *paruchia* of Columba, the monasteries
founded by him and founded by his followers or claiming to have
been founded by either. Twice Iona is described as the chief authority
(*arx*) of monasteries, Scottish and Pictish, and in relation to the
missions to England.[1] The first occurrence is at the sending of
Bishop Aidan to Lindisfarne; Bishop Finan is also said to be 'ab Hii
Scottorum insula et monasterio' (III, 17); Bishop Ceollach returned
to Iona, the second use of *arx* (III, 21). Colman, a bishop from
Ireland, left Britain (taking 'part of the bones' of Aidan, in III, 26)
after the Synod of Whitby with the Irish and thirty English from
Lindisfarne. He went to Iona, whence he had been sent to England,
then to a small island off Ireland, Inishbofin, that is 'insula uitulae
albae', where he built a monastery (construxit monasterium) (IV, 4).
That the source of this was ultimately the Iona annals is shown by
the wording of *AT*'s annal: 'Nauigatio Colmani episcopi cum
reliquis sanctorum ad Insulam Vacce Albe in qua fundauit ecclesiam.'[2]
Bede goes on to narrate the circumstances of the foundation by the
thirty English monks of the monastery of Mayo called *Mag eo* or
Muig eo, under its canonical abbot, a narrative derived from a source
familiar with that monastery, an Irish source.

---

[1] *Arx* is used for Hadrian's Wall in I. 12, and quoted in the phrase *in arce poli*
(in Heaven's citadel) from two inscribed epitaphs in v. 7, 8—a metaphorical
use of the word. I wonder whether Bede or his source pronounced *Hii* or
Hiienses in such a way as to suggest the OE word *hyge* [hyje] 'mind' 'heart'
'soul', the governing authority in the body and hence its citadel, *arx*.

[2] *Rev. celt.*, xvii. p. 200; also in *AU*, i. p. 122, where the bishop is misnamed
Columbani.

These passages are important in another respect: Bede's name for Iona. Adomnan's Life consistently uses *Ioua insula* even when, in referring to the beach or the sound, *insula* seems redundant. The reason was probably the difficulty of finding a Latin declension for Io or *Iou.[1] Bede's usual *Hii insula* is only once replaced by an indeclinable *Hii*. In V, 15 Abbot Adomnan visited Aldfrith, the learned and pious king of Northumbria, and returned but failed to convert the stubborn monks *in Hii* to the catholic Easter. This failure is also recorded in the letter (preserved in Bede's *HE*, V, 21) from Abbot Ceolfrith of Jarrow to Nectan king of Picts, where the phrase used is *in Hii insula*. Now this fact would not be a matter of recollection at Jarrow and must have reached Ceolfrith and Bede from another, probably common, source, using, I suggest, *in Hii* which is possible written Irish, with nasalization following the preposition *i* (= in) and the dative of the name *hI*, or rather it is a Latin preposition, *in*, followed by the name in the correct Irish case, the dative. The common source used, I suggest, *in Hii*, altered by Ceolfrith in order to avoid the solecism of *in* followed by an apparent genitive, *Hii*. Ceolfrith's solution, *in Hii insula* was otherwise generally adopted by Bede from Ceolfrith's letter, but once (V, 15) Bede kept *in Hii* and he also had recourse to a neologism, *Hiienses monachos* (V, 22, 24 at 716). In III, 4 where Iona is absolutely central to the discussion, it is not named once (as Grosjean noticed)[2] but the anonymous 'island' or 'monastery' was required in the nominative or accusative case and Bede was clearly reluctant to use *Hii* in that way and unable to provide Latin case-endings. It remains a puzzle why he did not use *Hii insula(m)*.

In the account of the visit to Aldfrith in V, 15, Bede adds that Adomnan withdrew to Ireland where he persuaded almost all to 'catholic unity', but in the last year of his life returned to Iona and

[1] In the anonymous life of Cuthbert, Aldfrith was living in 684 *in insula quam Ii nominant*, which Bede, in his prose life, renders as *in insulis Scottorum*; Bede usually omits unfamiliar names. *Two Lives of St. Cuthbert*, ed. B. Colgrave (1940), pp. 104, 236. The modern name, Iona, is a ghost name, a misreading of *Ioua insula*.

[2] *AABB*, lxxviii (1960), p. 387.

failed again. Adomnan himself in his *Life of Columba* tells of two visits in two years to Aldfrith and the annals (which may be using the *Life* here) ascribe two visits to 686 and 688, Adomnan returning captives on both occasions.[1] Moreover the annals seem to record two journeys by Adomnan to Ireland in 691 or 692 ('Adomnanus xiiii anno post pausam Failbe Ea ad Hiberniam pergit') and in 697, apparently telling against Bede's version, and against the annals as a source for Bede's source.

Much, however, depends upon the original text of the annal for 697. Two versions, although written in Irish are evidently independent translations from Latin:

Adhomnan tuc recht lecsa i nErind in bliadain sea (*AT*)
(Adomnan brought a law into Ireland this year)
Adomnan do chor chana for Erind (*AI*)
(Adomnan imposed a law on Ireland).

The sense of these two is very similar and the *lecsa* in *AT* points to a Latin original in which *lex* was glossed *recht*. This Latin annal also lay behind the version in *AU*:

Adomnanus ad Hiberniam pergit et dedit legem innocentium populis.
(Adomnan went to Ireland and gave a law of innocents to the peoples).[2]

On the evidence of *AT* and *AI* the original annal would have only one verb, whose meaning evidently puzzled the compilers of all three annals, driving two to Irish translations, the third to an expanded version which made clear reference to the Cáin Adomnáin. I suggest that reading was close to 'Adomnan*i* lex pergit ad Hiberniam' ('the law of Adomnan went to Ireland'), first misread as 'Adomnanus lex . . .', whence the confusion of the later Irish annals.[3] But the original did not mean that Adomnan went to

[1] *Adomnan's Life*, pp. 460–3, 103b; *AU*, i. p. 136; *Rev. celt.*, xvii. pp.210– 11.
[2] *Rev. celt.*, xvii. pp. 212 (691/2), 215 (697); *AI*, p. 100 (697 only); *AU*, i. pp. 140 (691/2), 144–6 (697).
[3] *Cáin Adomnáin*, ed. Kuno Meyer (Anecdota Oxoniensia, Mediaeval and Modern series, 12, 1905) has no discussion of this later text. James F. Kenney. *The Sources for the Early History of Ireland, Ecclesiastical* (1929), pp. 245–6, and K. Hughes, *Church in Early Irish Society*, p. 150, have useful discussions,

Ireland, and the annals of 691/2 and 697 were not in conflict with Bede; on the contrary, if Adomnan's law were interpreted (tendentiously, perhaps) as 'catholic unity' the annals could well have been his informant's source. On the other hand Bede's knowledge that Adomnan returned to Iona at the end of his life must have come from a source familiar with Iona but not from the annals; Abbot Ceolfrith also knew of this return (V, 21) another indication that he and Bede were drawing on the same source.

The use made of the annals for the northern battles in Bede is a more complex matter. Bede knows three battles between the Picts and the Angles in 685, 698, and 711; these three and these three alone occur also in the Irish annals, with differences which if anything strengthen the case for the annals as his source at one remove. In 684, according to Bede, King Egfrith sent an invasion to Ireland under ealdorman Berct, though he was warned to desist by the Anglian-Irish monk Egbert. Egfrith was punished in the next year when the Picts defeated and killed him in a battle among their mountains on 20 May in the fifteenth year of his reign: the Picts and Scots recovered territory (IV, 26). A Northumbrian source is usually assumed for this narrative, but the Iona annals have the invasion of the plain of Brega in Ireland, and the battle of Dunnichen on 20 May in the following year, when Egfrith after completing the fifteenth year of his reign, was defeated by Brude son of Bile, king of Fortriu.[1]

The agreement over the invasion of Ireland and the month-date is as striking as the difference over the regnal year which Bede has evidently corrected. The Iona annals noted the death of Oswy in 670 which was evidently reckoned the first regnal year of Egfrith, and 684 therefore the fifteenth.[2] As Mr Harrison has shown, Egfrith

---

Professor F. J. Byrne confirms to me that an Irish scribe would normally omit the nom. and gen. case endings for a name ending in -nan.

[1] *AU*, i. pp. 134–6; *Rev. celt.*, xvii. pp. 208–9.

[2] *AU*, i. p. 124; *Rev. celt.*, xvii. p. 201. Note the implication of this argument, that when the annal for 684 was entered, that for 670 was already there; these annals are not far from being contemporaneous.

succeeded only after an eight-month struggle, and Bede was well familiar with his correct regnal years and death soon after the consecration of Jarrow, which still has an inscription carrying the record of that event on 23 April in Egfrith's fifteenth year.[1] The most likely link with the annals is a narrative used by Bede, based upon the annals, but adding the name of the ealdorman Berct and the mission of the monk Egbert.

The battles of 698 and 711 with the Picts are recorded by Bede in his *recapitulatio* (V, 24). In 698, the ealdorman Berctred was killed; the Irish annals give the battle and add Berctred's patronymic. In 711, however, the annal for 'a slaughter of Picts in the plain of Mano by the Saxons and there Finguine son of Deleroith fell' is paralleled by Bede's 'Ealdorman Berctfrith fought against Picts'.[2] It is unlikely that Bede would have ignored the defeat of the Picts so his silence probably derived from his immediate source, a Pictish-mediated account, which might also have added the names of Berct (685) and Berctfrith (711).

The Anglo-Saxon Chronicle for these years is largely extracted from Bede, but the 'northern' recension, represented by MSS E and (from 693) D, preserves some additional information in ten entries, including the location of the battles of 685 and 711. It is surely significant that the Irish annals give no location for the battle of 698, and neither does the Chronicle; that the annal for 685 gives 'Dunnichen' and 'king of Fortriu' where the Chronicle has 'benorth the sea' (i.e. the Forth) and that the annal for 711 gives 'the plain of Mano' where the Chronicle has the equivalent 'between *Haefe* and *Caere*'.[3] These forms for Avon and Carron are scarcely Anglo-Saxon,

[1] K. Harrison, *The Framework of Anglo-Saxon History to 900* (1976), chapter 5; K. Harrison, 'The reign of King Ecgfrith of Northumbria', *Yorks. Arch. Journ.*, xliii (1971), pp. 79–84. Mr Harrison does not consider the Irish annal. The Jarrow stone is figured in P. Hunter Blair, *An Introduction to Anglo-Saxon England* (1977), plate VI.

[2] *Rev. celt.*, xvii. pp. 216, 222; *AU*, i. pp. 146, 158–60.

[3] *Two of the Saxon Chronicles Parallel*, ed. J. Earle and C. Plummer, i. (1892), pp. 39, 41, 43. These additions are discussed by P. Hunter Blair, 'The Northumbrians and their Southern Frontier', *Archaeologia Aeliana*, 4th ser. xxvi (1948), pp. 106–11.

and the intrusive initial in *Haefe* together with the incorrect endings, presumably misread signs of contraction, suggest that they came from Irish. In other words the source of these locations was using Iona-related annals as did Bede's source; Bede and the Chronicle may have been employing the same intermediary.

At the fourth northern battle, Degsastan, according to Bede, Aedan, the Scottish king, was defeated with heavy losses though King Aethelfrith's brother, Theobald, and his army were slaughtered. He adds that Aethelfrith completed the war in 603 (it is not certain whether this means that Aethelfrith fought in the battle) and that no later king of the Scots has dared to make war against the English (I, 34).[1] The annals seem to differ:

Cath Saxanum la hAedan ubi cecidit Eanfraich frater Etalfraich la Maeluma macBaedain in quo uictus erat (*AT*)
(A battle of the English with Aedan in which Aethelfrith's brother Eanfrith was killed by Maelumai, Beatan's son, in which he was conquered).[2]

Who was conquered? Aedan according to *AU*, which give us the date 599=600 for the event; contrariwise *A. Cl.* give the victory to Aedan. Plainly the original annal could (and *AT* can) be interpreted in either way: but common sense suggests the annal meant to convey that Eanfrith was both killed and defeated. Bede's battle in which Aedan was defeated but both sides had heavy losses reflects this ambiguity.

The northern version of the Anglo-Saxon Chronicle again expands on the *HE* with the statement that Aedan fought with *Deolreda* (evidently thought to be a personal name) and with Aethelfrith at *Degsanstan* (*sic*), adding that 'Hering son of Hussa led the army thither'.[3] The appearance of Dal Riada, a name known only

[1] C. W. Jones, *Saints Lives and Chronicles*, pp. 34–5, has argued persuasively that this chapter was a late addition to book I.

[2] *Rev. celt.*, xvii. p. 163. Also in *AU*, i. p. 78. *A. Cl.*, p. 97. For Aedan mac Gabrain see Bannerman, *Studies in the History of Dalriada*, pp. 80–90. Note that Bede has the same form as the annalist (*Aedan*) for the king, although for the bishop he has *Aidan*, the form used by Adomnan for the king.

[3] Earle and Plummer, *Two of the Saxon Chronicles*, i. p. 21. This material is

to Bede and this chronicle among non-Celtic sources, makes a common source likely, and suggests that this source described a battle of Aedan with the Dal Riada (*cum Daalreuda*), meaning his war-band, taken correctly by Bede when he comments on the size and fate (*uictus*, the word used in *AT*) of Aedan's army.

There are four difficulties in the way of deriving Bede's chapter and the Chronicle additions from the Iona annal: the rhetoric about Aethelfrith's mighty achievements as a new Saul: the name of the battle (Degsastan); the name (Theobald) for Aethelfrith's brother; and the treason of Hering son of Hussa in the Chronicle. All these difficulties belong, I suggest, to another battle, with the Welsh and not the Scots. In the rhetoric of I, 34, Aethelfrith is the 'greatest slayer of the Britons', which should direct our attention to Bede's account of his battle with the Welsh at Chester (II, 2); it has three parts. It seems plain that the first part, the meeting of Augustine with Welsh bishops at Augustine's Oak (the name is given in English) had an English, presumably Canterbury, source, but that the second meeting, depicting Augustine as a proud prelate who would not stand to greet his fellow bishops and the massacre of 1,300 Bangor monks at the Battle of Chester (given its Welsh name, Carlegion) where Aethelfrith is the enemy of Christ, must be Welsh in origin. The source of these latter parts would have been a British Latin lament in the manner of Gildas for the miseries inflicted upon monks, written probably at Bangor.[1] The description of Aethelfrith in I, 34 fits well into such a context; like Saul he conquered

---

discussed by P. Hunter Blair, 'The Bernicians and their Northern Frontier', *Studies in Early British History*, ed. N. K. Chadwick (1954), pp. 156-8, unfortunately discounting the Irish annals.

[1] Mayr-Harting, *Coming of Christianity*, 72, sees that the account of the second meeting 'may originally have come from the British themselves'. The Irish annals, probably also familiar with the Welsh lament, record the battle of Cair Legion where the saints were slain and where Solan, Conan's son, king of the Britons (and King Cetula, *AT*) fell; Aethelfrith died immediately afterwards. On the relationship of the *Annales Cambriae*, which also record the battle, with the Irish annals see K. Hughes, 'The Welsh Latin chronicles', *Proc. Brit. Acad.*, lix (1973), pp. 236-42.

land and subjected or killed the natives, and of him it could be said that he 'shall ravin as a wolf . . . devour the prey . . . divide the spoil'. His repute as *gloriae cupidissimus* echoes not a heroic poem, as Dr Colgrave thought, but Paul's words 'Let us not be desirous of vain glory' ('inanis gloriae cupidi') (Gal. 5: 26).[1]

I see the death of Theobald at Degsastan as part of the same British lament, explaining Aethelfrith's hostility to the Britons; Bede found the names in this source. The compilation underlying the E Chronicle also obtained from it the information that Hering son of Hussa led the army against Theobald, as well as the variant name-form *Degsanstan*. It also obtained the number of slain monks at Chester as 200 (*cc*) not Bede's 1,200 (*mcc*), and 605, its date for that battle, presumably derives from an indication that it was fought two years after Degsastan. In sum, the northern versions of the Anglo-Saxon Chronicle (D and E) incorporated additional material from an earlier Northumbrian chronicle which up to 731 was largely based on Bede, but also had access to some of his sources; it may well, therefore, have been written at Jarrow or Wearmouth.

Since Chester is datable 613 × 616, we may date Degsastan to 611 × 614, long after the death of Aedan in 608. This interval between Degsastan and Chester may explain Bede's ambiguity over Aethelfrith's participation at the former, compromising on a statement that he 'completed the war' (I, 34). Degsastan had nothing to do with Aedan. It was a battle fought 611 × 614 between Britons, guided by Hering son of Hussa, and Theobald brother of Aethelfrith in which the latter was killed; two years later Aethelfrith took his revenge at Chester.

Bede was also given a distorted version of an ambiguous Iona annal for 600; he was told of a defeat of Aedan and his army and the slaughter of Aethelfrith's unnamed brother and his army, so

---

[1] Bede, *HE*, ed. Colgrave and Mynors, 116 n. See the comments in J. M. Wallace-Hadrill, *Early Germanic Kingship in England and on the Continent* (1971), pp. 76–8. For Bede and heroic poetry see C. P. Wormald, 'Bede "Beowulf" and the Conversion of the Anglo-Saxon Aristocracy', in *Bede and Anglo-Saxon England*, ed. Robert T. Farrell (1978), pp. 32–95.

that no later Dalriadic king dared to attack the English. As the same source told him of Columba's death aged 77 after 35 years' pilgrimage (correctly in the 77th and 35th year), so it would tell of the battle with Aedan 38 years after Columba's *nauigatio* in 563 (correctly in the 38th year, 600). Bede calculated 565 + 38 to arrive at 603.

For the battles of 600/603, 685, 698, and 711, as for Columba's mission, Bede's ultimate source was annals now represented by the Irish annals but it is neither needful nor desirable to assume more than one mediating informant. That informant gave to the battles themselves a significant slant which survives in Bede: because of Aedan's defeat no king of Scots has since dared to make war on the English, but the English king Egfrith who attacked *Scottia* despite Egbert's pleas for peace, was defeated and killed by the Picts, and in consequence both the Scots and the Picts recovered lost territory. The peaceability of the Scots was stressed (through the agency of Egbert in 684) and a Pictish protectorate of Dal Riada's interests was implied, while the battles of 698 and 711 (the Pictish defeat suppressed) underlined the strength of the Picts in facing Northumbria.

A number of additional points may be noted. The interest in derivation, so characteristic of Irish scholarship and shown by Bede's explanation of *Dalreudini*, is found also in the etymology of Durrow (*campus roborum*) (III, 4) and of Columcille (*columba* and *cella*) (V, 9) and in the two forms given for Mayo, all matters whose common link is Iona.[1] We may note too that in the phrase 'the example of that first teacher' (III, 4) the word *illius* looks to an earlier use of *primus doctor* which in fact we find later in a short account of

---

[1] Bede places the foundation of Durrow before that of Iona, Adomnan (who is more likely to be correct) after. However Bede's text may reveal how he was misled: '[Iona] quam successores eius usque hodie tenent ubi et ipse sepultus est, cum esset annorum lxxvii, post annos xxx et duos ex quo ipse Brittaniam praedicaturus adiit. Fecerat autem, priusquam Brittaniam ueniret, ... [Durrow]'. I suggest that Bede's source told of the foundation of Durrow *prius* (i.e. before his death), and that Bede misunderstood the reference. If I am correct, then Bede's informant knew at least the substance of the matter as recorded in Adomnan.

Columba (V, 9). This suggests that Bede is using a Latin account from which he has taken these phrases, while reversing them. Moreover, a double account is found not only with Columba (III, 4; V, 9) but also with Aidan (III, 3), Finan (III, 17, 25) Colman (III, 26, 27 and Ceollach (III, 21, 24). The significance of this duplication is not obvious but it surely points to a common source for these passages.

But there is also an English element in the passages so far discussed. It is obvious in the narrative of the English monastery at Mayo, but is also there in the brief description of Iona: 'Neque enim magna est, sed quasi familiarum quinque iuxta aestimationem Anglorum' ('It is some five hides in size according to the reckoning of the English'). Now Dal Riada had a system in which lands were assessed at 120, 60, 30, 20, and 5 'houses', and the 'house' probably had the same nature as the hide—the land needed to support a family.[1] If Bede had been told Iona had land of five houses, he might have transmuted these to hides, but he must then give the reckoning as *Scottorum* 'of the Irish'. It follows from 'English reckoning' that Bede's source was familiar with Iona and with the English hide.

2

Why, how, and by whom was all this information mediated to Bede? By a source influenced by Irish learning and familiar with the Irish *paruchia* of Columba, with access to the Iona annals and also to Pictish Easter tables, concerned with Pictish history to present the Picts in a favourable light, and also knowing the English hide? If, instead of a multiplicity of faulty recollections and written sources of uncertain provenance, we seek a single source for Bede's information, we cannot do better than follow the suggestion first made by A. O. and M. O. Anderson, and more fully by that sadly missed scholar, Kathleen Hughes: 'surely the most likely people to give him his account of Columba's settlement at Iona . . . were the messengers sent by King Nectan to Ceolfrith of Jarrow' (between 709 and

---

[1] Bannerman, *Studies in the History of Dalriada*, pp. 132–46.

716).[1] An oral communication by these messengers (*legatarios*) which included *inter alia* the year of Columba's *nauigatio* the duration of his *peregrinatio* and his age at death, as well as the meaning of the name Durrow and the fact that Nectan already had catholic Easter tables seems very unlikely. Moreover Bede's account puts all the requests as Nectan's: *he* asked for a confutation of the wrong Easter, information about the tonsure, for architects to build a church of stone 'among the people' in the Roman fashion, to be dedicated to St. Peter; he and all his people would always follow the customs of the Roman Church so far as they could learn them 'remote as they were from the speech and nation of Romans'. Only Easter and the tonsure could be deduced from Ceolfrith's reply, and the rest is too detailed, and too specific to Nectan, to be the result of an oral request recollected at Jarrow. Ceolfrith's reply gives the king's name as Naitan, very close to the Pictish form, but Bede twice gives Naiton, which seems to be even more correct (V, 21); both must have been using a written source from Pictland, which Bede saw independently of Ceolfrith.[2] If Jarrow preserved Ceolfrith's reply it also preserved a letter from Nectan of which Bede made extensive and unacknowledged use. This is the common source which gave Ceolfrith and Bede their accounts of Adomnan's visit to King Aldfrith and his subsequent failure to convert Iona to catholic Easter and tonsure. And having reported this, Ceolfrith's reply bursts out 'But now I urge you, oh king, to strive to keep in every way, along with your people, these observances.' Evidently the

---

[1] *Adomnan's Life*, p. 77; K. Hughes, *Celtic Britain in the Early Middle Ages* (1980), p. 77 (reprinted from her Jarrow lecture of 1970); cf. pp. 9–10.

[2] K. H. Jackson, 'The Pictish Language', in *The Problem of the Picts*, ed. F. T. Wainwright (1955), p. 145; K. H. Jackson, *Language and History in Early Britain* (1953), pp. 410–11. Plummer pointed out the stylistic similarities of Ceolfrith's letter to Bede's computistic works (*Baedae Opera Historica*, ii. 332–4) but C. W. Jones 'can see no justification for Plummer's notion that Bede wrote the letter. Verbal similarities come from using common sources and a common computistical jargon.' (*Bedae Opera de Temporibus*, ed. C. W. Jones, 1943, 104 n. 4.) But Jones himself identified one curious unique feature (pp. 126–7).

reform of Iona was linked to or part of Nectan's proposal that he would introduce correct observances among the Picts.

The assumption behind Nectan's move, that the regulation of ecclesiastical affairs is a natural concern for a king, would be perfectly acceptable in Anglian Northumbria where the Synod of Whitby is only the most famous such intervention. But Irish clergy would have none of such Erastianism, reserving their synods for their own number, and sternly rejecting royal intervention.[1] An Irish mission in Pictland, therefore, would turn neither to the king, nor, surely, to a Northumbrian abbot. A Northumbrian mission would, however, turn to the king for help, and might well direct his enquiries to Abbot Coelfrith. For the disturbing of Nectan's view of Easter we must look to an Englishman or Englishmen at Nectan's court. But this mission can scarcely have come from England because it was unprovided with the arguments in favour of the canonical Easter. Moreover, since the reply was written between 709 and 716 (when Abbot Ceolfrith set out for Rome), Nectan's letter presumably lies between the same years. But as the battles of 685, 698, and 711 show, however fair the weather in 731, it was very unsettled twenty years earlier.

The annals, however, are clear that Easter was changed in Iona in 716, and Bede supports this date, ascribing the conversion to the man of God, Egbert, of whom he has much to tell in the course of the *HE*. Egbert died in 729 at the age of 90 (so was born about 640); as a young Englishman in the 660s he had gone to Ireland, became a monk in the monastery of *Rathmelsigi*, and had vowed he would not return to Britain. He became a bishop, living a life of great holiness and brought much blessing both to his own race and to those among whom he lived in exile, the Scots and Picts. He had been visited by various English churchmen and warned King Egfrith against aggression. In the 690s Egbert planned to undertake the conversion of the Germans; a monk had a vision warning him not to do so, but instead to give instruction in the monasteries of Columba. Egbert

[1] F. J. Byrne, *Irish Kings and High Kings* (1973), pp. 34–5.

then stimulated other Anglo-Saxon missions, to the Frisians. In 716 he went to Iona and taught the monks under Abbot Duncan the true date of Easter, thereafter remaining for thirteen years on Iona until his death at Easter 729.[1]

Egbert is of greater interest than even Bede realized, for he provides us with an author who fits neatly some of the specifications for Bede's informant about Columba and the Picts: he is English and knows hidages as well as the authority of an English king in the church. He has lived long enough in Ireland to acquire a foreigner's knowledge of the language and the interest in the etymology of words or names, characteristic of Irish scholarship. And, as Nora Chadwick suggested, Mayo would be a 'natural centre' for the activities of Egbert—whence his knowledge of its foundation. But the reasons why Egbert should leave Ireland to convert Iona must have been more immediate and political than Bede's suggestion of an academic or theological interest in the Easter question.

In Ireland the Easter problem evidently reached its first crisis about 630 when a synod of Irish ecclesiastics agreed to follow the catholic Easter. According to the letter of Cummian (probably abbot of Clonfert) to Segene abbot of Iona 'not long after there arose a certain whited wall pretending that he was maintaining the traditions of the elders' who caused dissension so that a mission was sent to Rome, returning about 632.[2]

The 'whited wall', 'paries dealbatus', has been tentatively identified with various prelates, but without regard to the origin of the phrase. In Acts 23: 3, when Paul appeared before the priests, Ananias, the high priest ('princeps sacerdotum') commanded that he be struck, provoking Paul's curse 'God shall smite thee, thou whited wall . . .'.

---

[1] *HE*, III, pp. 4, 27; IV, p. 3; V, pp. 9, 10, 22, 23, 24. See further, for Egbert's connections with Northumbria, Aethelwulf, *De Abbatibus*, ed. A. Campbell (1967), pp. 10–13. *Rathmelsigi* has not been identified.

[2] For Cummian's letter, *PL*, 87 cols, pp. 969–78; *AU*, iv. pp. cxxv–cxlii. It is discussed in Harrison, *The Framework of Anglo-Saxon History to A.D. 900*, pp. 58–62; Hughes, *Church in Early Irish Society*, pp. 105–7, Plummer, *Baedae Opera Historica*, ii. pp. 112–14. The identity of Cummian was suggested to me by Mr C. P. Wormald.

The bystanders protested at this reviling of the high priest ('summus sacerdos') and Paul (ironically) claimed ignorance of Ananias's standing ('nesciebam, fratres, quia princeps est sacerdotum'). The intention of Cummian was surely to identify his opponent ironically as one who claimed to be *princeps sacerdotum* (abbot of bishops) and *summus sacerdos* (chief bishop), though others might not recognize him as chief: and this can be no other than the bishop-abbot of Armagh, already intent upon pressing his claims as Patrick's successor over the whole Irish church.

A papal letter of John IV in 640 shows that Armagh and Iona were then in the traditionalist party (I shall discuss this letter later), from which Cummian's letter represents an attempt to detach Iona. It failed, but at an unknown date, perhaps in the third quarter of the century, Armagh accepted the Dionysiac Easter and became the protagonist of conformity in conflict with the traditionalism of Columba's *paruchia*. If this had ever been a north-south conflict, it now ceased to be so. Working with the secular claims of the northern Ui Neill kings of Tara, the successors of Patrick advanced claims to ecclesiastical supremacy buttressed assiduously by hagiography, by relics of Roman martyrs Peter, Paul, Stephen, and Laurence, and by the papal origin of the early mission to Ireland. There was appeal from all Ireland to Armagh, and from Armagh to Rome only; Armagh claimed the authority of Rome for the position of Armagh. A distinction was drawn between the *terminus*, an area over which the abbot-bishop of Armagh exercised direct rule, and the *paruchia*, over which he had indirect suzerainty. The heirs of other saints too had a *terminus* and a *paruchia* of daughter houses, but the latter was now challenged by the heir of Patrick with a claim of hegemony: all Ireland is his *paruchia*. In Tirechan's work of the late seventh century the *paruchiae* of Clonmacnoise and Iona were explicitly attacked as usurpations; since Columba was of the Ui Neill, a conflict between his heirs and Patrick's would seem especially likely.[1]

[1] Hughes, *Church in Early Irish Society*, chs 8–10 and pp. 275–81; D. A. Binchy, 'Patrick and his biographers, ancient and modern', *Studia Hibernica,*

In Columba's *paruchia* Patrick himself was respected; in Cummian's letter he is 'our father' and he is mentioned with reverence in Adomnan's *Life of Columba*.[1] But the Easter controversy might drive a wedge between Iona and other houses of Columba's *paruchia* such as Durrow, and indeed the monasteries converted by Adomnan in the 690s are most likely to have been these Irish Columban houses—including Mayo. The obits of several eighth-century bishops make it clear that 'Mayo of the Saxons' preserved the order used at Lindisfarne where the abbot as head of the community was either bishop or subordinate to the bishop—'canonical abbot' as Bede has it (IV, 4).[2] One more piece of the evidence falls into place if we see Egbert as bishop and protector of this Columban house. He would then have particular reason to comment upon this subordination of bishops to the abbot of Iona, and to cite the bishops of Lindisfarne as well as to relate the foundation of Mayo; he would also have cause to be defensive about the priest-abbot of Iona before the bishop-abbot of Armagh.

Much more, he would have reason to visit Columba's heir if his house was subject to the swelling pretensions of another bishop—Armagh—for it would be vital to win Iona's support, and vital, too, to persuade Iona to abandon the pseudo-Anatolian Easter which now weakened its position in the Irish church. In these circumstances lie the reasons for Egbert's departure to Iona with the claim that it was chief, *arx*, of northern Irish monasteries, a sharp retort to the claims of Armagh. His devotion to the cult of St. Columba is surely proved by the last thirteen years of his life, spent in Iona, years for which Bede had no account of his activities, but he would also find it necessary to urge that the *paruchia* of Columba was no less devoted to the see of St. Peter than the *paruchia* of Armagh whence the

---

ii (1962), pp. 7–173, especially 59–69, 149–50, 164–73. The texts of Muirchu, Tirechan and the Liber Angeli are in *The Book of Armagh*, ed. J. Gwynn (1913).

[1] *Adomnan's Life*, pp. 182–3; St. Mochte is a pupil *sancti Patricii episcopi*, where *sancti* is not a merely conventional epithet.

[2] Nora K. Chadwick, 'Bede, St. Colman and the Irish Abbey of Mayo', *Celt and Saxon*, p. 195, citing the *Historia Regum* attributed to Symeon of Durham for Bishops Hadwine, Leuthfrith, and Aldulf.

'Roman' promises in Nectan's letter to which I come later. For Egbert was surely the author of that letter.

Because Iona had so long resisted the arguments of catholicity it would be remarkable if between Christmas 715 and Easter 716, a migrant Anglo-Irish monk-bishop stepped inside the vallum of Iona and carried all before him. We must surely envisage a longer process and more compelling reasons than were known to Bede, and the statement that Egbert came from Ireland to Iona in 716 must be discounted as synchronizing on Bede's part. The multiplicity of abbots of Iona after Adomnan's death (704), implies perhaps schism, certainly controversy. The annals speak of a single 'chair' of Columba and imply only one abbot of Iona at a time; we must interpret accordingly: Conamail resigned, voluntarily or compulsorily in 707 (died 710), and was replaced by Duncan, who in his turn lost 'the chair' to Dorbene a month or two after Easter in 713, evidently a crisis in the abbey's affairs since he was restored after Dorbene's death five months later. On 19 April 716 the Iona monks celebrated the Roman Easter 'under Abbot Duunchad' as Bede noted, reproducing the Irish form of his name from an Iona source which must have seen Duncan as favouring change. By August 716 Duncan (died, May 717) had yielded to a new abbot, Faelchu.[1]

It seems likely that between 664 and 720 the Celtic and Dionysiac

---

[1] The annals are readily found in *AU* and *AT*. They have been collected and discussed many times, including a discussion by Dr J. Bannerman in an appendix to an article by K. Hughes. Dr Bannerman argues that the many abbacies between 704 and 801 reflect the civil wars of Dal Riada. This is not unlikely, but it is a concurrent explanation not an alternative one. If the cenel Loairn sought to oust abbots of the house of Conall Gulban, they would find replacements most readily among opponents of those abbots over the Easter question. *Irish Historical Studies*, xiii (1962–3), pp. 113–16. See also the discussions in *Adomnan's Life*, pp. 98–9, 102; and in W. F. Skene, *Celtic Scotland*, ii (1887), pp. 175–8.

For Dorbene as abbot (not bishop, as A. O. and M. O. Anderson argue) see Paul Grosjean, 'Virgile de Salzbourg en Irlande', *AABB*, lxxviii (1960), pp. 92–7; *Martyrology of Tallaght*, ed. R. I. Best and H. J. Lawlor (Henry Bradshaw Society, 1931), 85 under 28 October; *Rev. celt.*, xvii. 225; *KKES*, 7 n. 29. Dr Hughes consistently used 'the chair' of the abbot's position, and in this is reflecting Irish usage.

Easters diverged only in 671, 672, 675, 691, 692, 695, 702, 712, and 716.[1] Clearly the Easter issue could scarcely be forced in the 680s but from 690 to Adomnan's death in 704 it arose five times—and his struggle for the Roman Easter is then recorded. The matter would then rest until 712 when the isolation of Columba's *paruchia* would again be plain. In consequence, I suggest, Egbert came in 712–13 from Ireland where he was bishop, probably of Mayo, to persuade the monks of Iona to celebrate the Dionysiac Easter in 716. Abbot Duncan supported him and lost office; frustrated, Egbert left Iona for the court of Nectan, king of Picts. Bede records this visit when he says that Egbert lived in exile among the Scots *and Picts* and that he lived in Iona from 716 until his death (V, 22): he visited the Picts before 716. He persuaded Nectan of the need to reform the observance of Easter among the Picts and to convince Iona to follow suit. As an Englishman, he understandably chose Ceolfrith to supply him with the authority he must deploy. In 713–14 he wrote in the name of King Nectan a long letter to Ceolfrith which presented Columba as apostle to the Picts, Iona, chief of monasteries among the northern Scots and Picts, as a Pictish gift, and the Scots as a people protected by the Picts—all to justify Nectan's interference in Iona's affairs. This letter was the only source of Bede's account of Columba, the Picts, and Ninian.

We can now consider the oft-glossed words in which Bede describes the conversion of southern Picts by Ninian, relegating Columba to conversion of the northern Picts (III, 4):

For the southern Picts who have their seats to this side of the same mountains had, as they relate, a long time before forsaken the error of idolatry and received the faith of truth, when the word was preached to them by Ninian a most reverend bishop and very holy man of the race of the Britons; and one who had been regularly trained at Rome in the faith and the mysteries of truth. And even now the English nation obtains the see of his episcopate notable for the name and church of the bishop St. Martin; and there also

[1] For Celtic Easter tables see D. J. O'Connell, 'Easter Cycles in the Early Irish Church', *Journ. Royal Soc. Antiq. Ireland*, lxvi (1936), pp. 67–106. This article has very useful tables, but we must exclude many of O'Connell's possible dates. A divergence of Easters was only occasional.

[Ninian] rests in the body, along with very many saints. And this place, pertaining to the province of the Bernicians, is commonly called *ad Candidam Casam*, because he made there a church of stone, after a custom strange to the Britons.

If we examine this passage without any commitment to its accuracy, the influence under which it was written is clear. Few now accept Bede's statement that Ninian was taught at Rome; his source desired to establish that in ecclesiastical matters Ninian was a Roman. In the later seventh century Muirchu was establishing the same regularity for Patrick (also a bishop, also responsible for a conversion) by writing a biography in which the saint visited the apostolic see for study and stayed also with St. Germanus at Auxerre.[1] Ninian too had supposed links with Gaulish experience in his church of the name of Martin of Tours, a saint of particular authority in Ireland, where his cult was far stronger than in Britain —the Book of Armagh contains the Life of Patrick, the New Testament, and Sulpicius's Life of Martin. Bede's details about Ninian betray their Irish origin. On quite other grounds Professor J. MacQueen has shown that there once existed an Irish Life of Ninian, now lost, and this we may take as ultimately a source of some of Bede's information.[2]

The most difficult phrase in the whole passage is the church of stone. In the Cumbrian and Irish world to which Galloway belonged, this is a possibility in the mid-seventh century, but surely very improbable in the remote sub-Roman culture of Galloway in the fifth or sixth.[3] Yet Bede's statement must reflect the fame of a relatively early stone church associated with Ninian. In Bede this

---

[1] *The Book of Armagh*, ed. J. Gwynn (1913), 44a: 'egressus ad sedem apostolicam uisitandam et honorandam ad caput itaque omnium ecclesiarum totius mundi ut sapiens iam diuina sanctaque misteria adquae uocauit illum deus ut disceret atque intellegeret et inpleret et ut praedicaret et donaret diuinam gratiam innationibus externis conuertens ad fidem Christi.'

For a (generally accepted) rejection of Ninian's education at Rome, see P. Grosjean, 'Les Pictes apostats dans l'Epitre de S. Patrice', *AABB*, lxxvi (1958), pp. 354–63 and 376–8.

[2] J. MacQueen, *St. Nynia* (1966), pp. 1–6.

[3] A. C. Thomas, *The Early Christian Archaeology of North Britain* (1971), *passim*.

association has a point: Ninian, a Briton, was accustomed to things British; at Rome he was taught *regulariter*; he then built a stone church. The anticipation of the request by Nectan, king of the Picts, for masons and a stone church, to be dedicated to St. Peter with the promise to follow Roman customs, is clear, and we can place Ninian in the letter written on Nectan's behalf by Egbert.

But of course, *casa*, 'an estate', 'a brothel', cannot be traced in any context which implies stonework. Isidore's *Etymologiae* which would not only reflect Vulgar Latin usage but would be a source for the learned Latin of seventh-century Ireland and Britain give: '*Casa* is a rural shelter [*habitaculum*] made of stakes and wattle . . .'[1] Bede's words and form (III, 4) *uulgo ad Candidam Casam* demand a translation for which we need not look beyond *æt thæm Hwitan Ærne*. In place names *ærn* 'is always combined with a significant word' and there seem to be few uses of the word by itself or in translation e.g. of *domus*.[2] It seems therefore that Candida Casa must be a translation of *Hwitærn* and (since we might have expected e.g. *ad Casam Albam*) a very literary translation, which achieved a striking alliterative effect built on *casa*, a reasonable translation of *ærn*.

Moreover there is a logic behind the translation. The word *casa* occurs once in the Vulgate: 'et in locis desertis fixerunt casas' (*Lib. Sap.*, xi, 2). And the Holy Land, in whose deserts these houses were fixed, provided another model—that of the walls and streets of Jerusalem: 'ex lapidi candido . . . sternuntur' (*Tobit*, xiii. 22). The adjective *candidus* is more usually applied to cloth but the use for stone here provided the translator of *Hwitærn* with his model, where the most holy (*sanctissimo*) Ninian and many saints (*sanctis*) rested— a holy place. The stone church was linked to the use of *candidus* in Adomnan's *De Locis Sanctis* where the tombs of the three patriarchs in Hebron are covered with three white stones: *tribus superpositis*

---

[1] Isidore, *Etymologiae*, xv. 12, 1. The other meanings are from Cassiodorus and Augustine. See the discussion in MacQueen, *St. Nynia*, pp. 13–17, which easily withstands the critique of R. P. C. Hanson, *Saint Patrick* (1966).

[2] A. H. Smith, *English Place-Name Elements*, i (English Place Name Society, 1956), p. 4. Bosworth and Toller, *Anglo-Saxon Dictionary*, s.v. 'aern'.

candidis lapidibus.[1] The phrase is fragmented in Bede's summary of Adomnan's work, but *lapidibus . . . candidis* is also there in the last of the paragraphs about the holy places selected by Bede for quotation in his *HE* (V, 17). *Candida Casa* was a translation of *Hwitærn* made by a biblical scholar familiar with Adomnan's or Bede's *De Locis Sanctis* and seeking alliteration. The same alliteration is found in Bede's translation of Gateshead as *ad Capræ Caput* (III, 21), and the author of *Candida Casa* was surely Bede. The difficult statement that the place was commonly (*uulgo*) called by a Latin name would best be explained if Bede had originally written the vernacular name and later substituted his translation. The strangeness of Britons building in stone is also Bede's contribution, an echo of their building of Antonine's wall not in unaccustomed stone but in useless turf (I, 12); this Bede obtained from Gildas.

For Bede's source for Ninian, most have looked to Whithorn itself, some specifically to Bishop Pecthelm of Whithorn, Bede's contemporary, a pupil of Aldhelm of Malmesbury. Bede twice gives Pecthelm as his authority for miracles (V, 13, 18), the second time fairly briefly with the parenthesis 'of whom something will be said in the following [pages] in its place'. Yet that intention seems to have changed for the only 'following' passage (in the penultimate chapter) lists Pecthelm among current Northumbrian bishops 'at the church called Candida Casa, which, the number (*plebibus*) of the faithful having lately multiplied, has become an episcopal see with Pecthelm as its first bishop' (V, 23). In a history of conversions, bishoprics, and bishops, following the vagaries of Northumbrian sees with particularly close attention, the striking weakness of this undated statement may be explained by the contradictory assertion in III, 4, that Ninian's see had been *Candida Casa*. The church bearing St. Martin's name is another inherent contradiction, for the medieval dedication of Whithorn was to Ninian and this can scarcely have ousted an earlier Martin dedication. The explanation of these

---

[1] *Adamnan's De Locis Sanctis*, ed. D. Meehan (*Scriptores Latini Hiberniae*, 1958), p. 80; *Itinera Hierosolymitana*, ed. P. Geyer (*Corpus Scriptorum Ecclesiasticorum Latinorum* vol. 39, 1898), p. 260.

contradictions is the hybrid character of the Ninianic passage in
III, 4, bringing together the mission of Ninian, a Roman-trained
Briton, and his stone church of Martin's name, all derived by way
of Egbert's letter from an Irish source, probably the lost Irish life,
with what Bede learned from Pecthelm, that Whithorn, a Northumbrian see, was dedicated to Ninian. Bede identified the stone
church with Whithorn (wrongly), and invented a Latin name and
explanation to cement the union.

Without Egbert's letter we cannot be sure what Bede learned of
Ninian's missionary work, but he has surely improved upon it,
introducing another contradiction—that the Picts were ignorant of
the true Easter calculation, although the southern Picts had been
converted by the 'regular' Ninian. Pictish sources, albeit exiguous,
have no knowledge of Ninian. Egbert must surely have portrayed
Ninian as missionary to a non-Pictish people.

It has been suggested, I think rightly, that Bede invented the name
'*North*umbrians' for the people hitherto known as *Humbrenses* or
Transhumbrana gens.[1] Similarly, given the structure of the Irish
monastic *paruchia*, Bede's adoption of the Dionysiac Easter by the
southern Irish while the northern remained obdurate was surely an
over-simplification. Bede was too ready to turn an indication that
something was northerly or southerly into a structure with northern
and southern divisions. So it was with the Picts. Bede took the
horrid mountains in the midst of Pictland where Nechtansmere
was fought together with a statement that Ninian converted people
in southern regions, and, wrongly understanding that Ninian had
converted southern Picts, he adjusted Columba's achievement,
whence the northern Picts. Egbert had doubtless intended that
Ninian converted Britons, in Galloway and Southern Scotland, but

[1] The evidence of *Nordanhymbri* is reviewed by J. N. L. Myres, 'The
Teutonic Settlement of Northern England', *History*, xx (1935–6), pp. 250–8,
who sees the name as Bede's invention, and by P. Hunter Blair, 'The Northumbrians and their Southern Frontier', *Archaeologia Aeliana*, 4th ser. xxvi
(1948), pp. 98–104, who argues that it was a translation from Anglo-Saxon,
made fashionable by Bede. Bede divides the Mercians into northern and
southern by the river Trent (III, 24).

this would have created more problems for Bede, never well disposed towards the Britons, and possessed of knowledge of an Anglian see of Whithorn dedicated to St. Ninian and responsible for the recent spread of Christianity in that region. It was more consistent to apply Ninian's endeavours to southern Picts, and, since Ninian was apparently a bishop at Whithorn, to reduce the intended account of the more recent conversion of Galloway to a mere note.

Whereas Southern Pictland has only long-cist burials confirming its links with Christianity in Lothian and the see of Abercorn, the Upper Tweed region has yielded early Christian memorial stones to confirm a link with Whithorn. A lost cross-slab recorded by a mid-fifteenth-century chronicler as having been dug up in 1261 at the Cross Kirk of Peebles bore, he claims, an inscription: *Locus Sancti Nicholai Episcopi*. The word *Locus* takes us back unmistakeably to the enclosed cemeteries of the sub-Roman centuries, whereas *Nicholai* belongs to medieval cults, and must be a misreading. The nearest likely name-form is Ninian, the inscription reading 'niniaui' or more probably 'NINIA/'.[1] With this emendation we have at Peebles the only early association with Ninian outside Whithorn. A recently published stone, probably from the churchyard of the same kirk, is inscribed NEITANO SACERdOS. Epigraphically it has been dated to the late seventh century but it could be somewhat earlier or later. The name Neitan is British or Pictish; *sacerdos*

---

[1] For long-cist oriented graves on the east coast as far north as Arbroath see the map in A. C. Thomas, 'The evidence from North Britain', *Christianity in Britain, 300–700* (1968), ed. M. W. Barley and R. P. C. Hanson, p. 107. Essentially these seem to be a Lothian (seventh-century Anglian) phenomenon with outliers; the one near Largo recalls Cuthbert's journey to the Niuduera Picts whom I have associated with Nithbren = Newburn near Largo (A. A. M. Duncan, *Scotland, The Making of the Kingdom*, 1975, p. 78). Memorial stones are mapped in *Christianity in Britain, 300–700*, pp. 102, 104. I regard the later eighth-century poem *Miracula Nynie Episcopi* as a Whithorn production, which, so far as it mentions the Picts, is based on the *HE*. Of 503 lines, 21 are devoted in vague generalities to Ninian's Pictish achievement; the one detail, the *Naturae* Picts, is in a chapter heading and is borrowed from the *Niduari* of Bede's prose *Life of Cuthbert*.

Note that if the lost inscription used capitals, N could well be misread as H and the ligatured A/ would be read as A; hence NIHIAI.

probably means bishop.[1] It seems that Peebles was a British Christian centre of some importance, possibly an episcopal see in the seventh century; it is the most likely candidate to be the missionary centre to which Ninian came to preach the faith to Britons.[2]

It is now, I hope, possible to reconstruct convincingly the elements of Nectan's letter though their order must remain uncertain; it might have gone something like this:

The Picts came from Scythia to Ireland, then settled in Britain taking their wives from the Scots, whence their succession custom. Their first teacher, in the eighth year of Bridei, was Columba, sometimes called Columcille from *Columba* and *cella*. Scots under Reuda, called *Dalreudini* [? or *Dal Riada*] also settled in Britain and [thirty-eight years after Columba's coming to Britain] King Aedan [with the Dal Riada] fought a battle with Aethelfrith's brother in which he was defeated so that the Scots have subsequently kept peace with the English. Yet King Egfrith sent his army under Berct against [the Scots in] Ireland (although warned by Bishop Egbert not to do so), and as divine retribution he was killed by Picts in the following year on 20 May, the fifteenth year of his reign, at a battle fought in the mountains which divide the Picts; the Picts, Scots and Britons recovered territory from the English. [Thirteen years later] the Picts defeated the ealdorman Berctred, and [thirteen further years later] fought again with the English [?between Avon and Carron] so that their power waned. The Picts gave to that first teacher an island (?hI) about five hides in English reckoning in which to found a monastery. His disciples are said to have preserved writings about him. After 32/35 years there, he died aged 77. Before [this] he also founded Durrow meaning 'field of oaks', in Ireland and from these monasteries his disciples established others among the Picts and Scots, over which the island monastery in which his body lies held authority (*principatus*). This island (?hI) has as ruler an abbot-priest to whose authority the whole province and even bishops, by his example, are subject. Thus four bishops were sent

[1] *Johannis de Fordun Scotichronicon*, ed. W. Goodall (1759), ii. pp. 96–7. K. A. Steer, 'Two unrecorded early Christian stones', *Proc. Soc. Antiq. Scot.*, ci (1968–9), pp. 127–9. The cult of St. Nicholas first appears in the western church in the ninth century and spread to Britain in the eleventh; C. W. Jones, *The St. Nicholas Liturgy* (1963), especially chapter ix.

[2] The name Peebles in British with an English plural in -s. A 'dedication' there to Ninian could have been lost during a period of pagan Anglian occupation. In my view Ninian came from an established ('Martin') church to (?) Peebles and returned to move his original see to Whithorn.

from this *arx* of northern Irish and Pictish monasteries to the English: Aidan, Finan, Ceollach and Colman; Colman returned to the island and then to Ireland with relics to found a monastery of Irish at Inishbofin meaning 'isle of the white cow' and of English at Mayo (*Mag eo* or *Muig eo*) which has a canonical abbot. Whatever Columba was, his successors were good men who in ignorance continued to use obsolete Easter tables; when Abbot Adomnan visited King Aldfrith of the English and learned the correct Easter, he returned but was unable to convert the monks in hI, so withdrew to Ireland where he persuaded almost all to catholic unity. At the end of his life he went back to the island where he failed once again. The island has now persisted in celebrating Easter erroneously for 150 years. Now, however, the king desires that he and his people follow the customs of the Roman church, and therefore seeks masons to build a church of stone after the Roman fashion to be dedicated to St. Peter [following the example of] Ninian, a Briton, who long ago preached the Word to southern [regions], was taught at Rome and built a church of stone at his see, celebrated for its church of St. Martin. He also seeks the *ratio* of the catholic observance of Easter as learned from the apostolic see and of the tonsure, to confute the erroneous observance at hI.

(Passages in square brackets are my suggestions; I have used 'English' for what might have been 'Saxons' or 'Angles'; the rest is in Bede.)

The letter would have been undated but its statement that Iona had observed Easter wrongly for 150 years was absolutely correct between Easter 713 and Easter 714. Bede erroneously applied the statement to 715–16 and deduced 565 as the date of Columba's *nauigatio*. Where had Nectan obtained the catholic Easter tables with which according to Bede he was already supplied? He had no known correspondence with Northumbria before this letter, none known to Ceolfrith. As Bede implies, Egbert took catholic tables to Iona; he surely purveyed them also to Nectan. Moreover, we may note that none would be better placed than Egbert to add to the annal for 684 the name of Berct and the peace-mission of Egbert. The names of the Anglian leaders of 685, 698, and 711, all beginning Berct, show that they were perhaps related to one another; it is not impossible that they were also related to Egbert.

Egbert offered unity with the church of St. Peter whose successor kept the keys of heaven and the gift of a church of St. Peter among the Picts, built in prestigious stone; Nectan was prepared to listen. In 714–15 Ceolfrith replied, and Northumbrian architects duly built a church of St. Peter at Restennet (whose tower is strikingly reminiscent of that at Monkwearmouth). As Wilfrid swayed his Oswy, so Egbert won over Nectan and then repaired to Iona with the authority of Nectan, demanding that the abbey accept 'catholic truth'. Bede in due course transcribed Ceolfrith's response because it paraded the Dionysiac Easter-argument; he plundered Nectan's letter (whose true author, Egbert, he did not recognize) without acknowledgement because it contained so much useful 'history' that it could readily be broken up, and did not copy it because it did not deploy useful ecclesiology, and indeed was diffuse and perhaps in imperfect Latin—whence comment upon the inadequate Latin of the Picts (V, 21).

The conversion of 716 was not complete. Adomnan had been a convert to the Roman Easter, but Ceolfrith's letter makes it clear that he retained the tonsure of his predecessors. In accepting the change of Easter in 716, the monks of Iona would have remained committed to the tonsure of their elders (stigmatized as that of Simon magus (V, 21)) so that Abbot Duncan, an advocate of change, was replaced a few months after Easter by Faelchu. By 717 someone, perhaps Egbert, had persuaded Nectan to act again and in that year the community (*familia*) (or the stubborn part of it) was expelled by him across Drumalban into Pictland. In 718, 'the [Roman] tonsure-crown was put upon the family of Iona' (*AT*).[1] This interpretation requires not a Pictish conquest of Dal Riada but a naval raid—the Picts lost '150' ships in 729—milder than that which devastated Dal Riada and took Dunadd in 737. It also requires that Nectan, who entered religion in 724, was powerfully influenced by

---

[1] *Expulsio familie Ie trans dorsum Britannie a Nectano rege*; *Rev. celt.*, xvii. pp. 225–6; *AU*, i. pp. 166–7. For the *familia* of Iona slain by the Vikings in 806 see *AU*, i. pp. 290–1. This and other examples make it certain that this annal cannot refer to the expulsion of clergy of the Columban *paruchia* from Pictland—the usual interpretation.

the clergy—as Ceolfrith's letter bears out.[1] Bede knew only that both Easter and tonsure were changed, concluding wrongly that both took place in 716; his source must have been written a few years after the events of 716–18 so that they were telescoped into one glorious conversion.

How Egbert could have made use of Iona annals in Pictland can only be conjectured: he may have taken the annals with him; more probably he transcribed matter from them to his own Easter tables; and very probably he added Pictish royal obits when in Pictland, transmitting these to Iona and eventually Ireland. From 713 to *c.* 740 (when our knowledge of Iona annals ceases because of transmission to Ireland) the Pictish and Iona content of these annals greatly increases and we can distinguish domestic Pictish annals in 713 and from 724 until August 729, with one or two jejune notes up to 741.[2] It can scarcely be coincidence that the annals fit so neatly with the career of Egbert outlined here, with a visit to Pictland in 713–14 and Egbert's death in April 729. The annal for August 729 suggests that news was sent from a Pictish monastery to Egbert in Iona in a letter written in ignorance of his death; the inspiration of that letter (and of others), even its author, may be identified by the first entry in the group for 724–9: 'the entry into religion of Nectan king of Picts'.

3

The background essential to an understanding of Bede's debt to Egbert is an Irish one with two elements: the radical pretensions of Armagh and the conservatism of Iona in the matters of Easter and the tonsure. But Bede's understanding of the Irish church was incomplete as his selective quotations from three letters to Ireland, to which he ascribed a Paschal emphasis, show. The beginning of a

---

[1] It is usual to follow the King Lists in assuming that this King Nectan (*c.* 705–24) was Nectan mac Derile, restored *c.* 728–9. I believe that the King Lists are based upon the annals at this period, and the annals show (under 713) that he was Nectan mac Drostan and that the sons of Derile were his rivals.

[2] The long 'Pictish' annals for 734 and 736 concern attacks upon Dal Riada and are not domestic.

petulant letter (1) from Laurence, (arch)bishop of Canterbury, and his episcopal colleagues (datable *c.* 610) to the Irish church, about Irish discourtesy, described by Bede as an exhortation to keep Catholic peace and unity; he does not say that the letter referred to Easter, which was scarcely an issue outside Gaul in 610, and Laurence's reported disquiet over Irish paschal customs is merely Bede's disquiet (II, 4).[1] This letter was sent to Ireland, for Laurence and his colleagues are named in the Stowe Missal;[2] Bede therefore received its text from an Irish source.

Having quoted in full a letter of Honorius I (625–38) giving the pallium to Canterbury (II, 18), Bede merely summarized a letter (2) of Honorius to the Irish urging them not to think themselves wiser than the rest of the church, and not to observe a different Easter from that decided by an ecumenical council [the Dionysiac Easter]. In the same chapter (II, 19) Bede quotes from the reply (3) of Roman prelates, including John (IV), pope-elect, in 640 to five Irish prelates (including those of Armagh and Iona) whose writings to the late pope were understood, quite wrongly, to mean that some Irish were celebrating Easter on *luna xiv*. Bede's quotation is introduced with his statement that the reply is an argument in favour of the Dionysiac Easter; it ends abruptly with his gloss that the quartodeciman is clearly asserted to have been a recent and partial heresy—for Bede knew that the Irish did not celebrate Easter on 14 Nisan without regard to the day of the week. Then, remarking that the reply went on to expound the *ratio* of Easter, he quotes its condemnation of Irish Pelagianism (II, 19); again Rome was probably quick to misunderstand whatever the Irish had said.

Rome in 631, as Cummian's letter shows, used the Victorine tables, not the Dionysiac; the only evidence in favour of a change to the Dionysiac in the 630s is not the papal letters (2) and (3) but

[1] Bede also mentions a letter from Laurence and his fellow bishops to the Welsh about Catholic unity. He probably knew of this because of reference to it in the letter to the Irish.

[2] Plummer, *Bedae Opera Historica*, ii. p. 81; *The Stowe Missal*, ed. G. F. Warner (Henry Bradshaw Society), i (1906), fo. 32v; ii (1915), p. 16; P. Grosjean in *AABB*, lxiv (1946), p. 232 n. 3.

Bede's summaries of them, and it is truly remarkable that Bede, if really provident with papal arguments for the Dionysiac *ratio*, should have avoided quoting them. He excised from a papal letter of 667 for the Northumbrian King (III, 29) a passage in favour of uniformity following the Dionysiac *ratio*, whose intent was close to that claimed for letter (2). In borrowing thus, Bede was not deliberately falsifying. As C. W. Jones has argued, because 'the Roman see was constantly embarrassed by its own changes in Paschal observance' and by the adherence of Gaul to the Victorine *ratio*, papal letters (2) and (3) would not be explicit in favour of either the Victorine or the Dionysiac *ratio*, and Bede provided his (in my view erroneous) Dyonisiac interpretation of their 'cloud of traditional remarks'.[1] Letters (2) and (3) in Bede's summaries should not be used as evidence of a papal shift to the Dionysiac *ratio*, which more probably occurred under Greek influence at Rome after 653.

Letters (2) and (3), it is generally agreed, lie on either side of Cummian's letter to Segene of Iona of 632–6, the text of which came to England—it is preserved in a single eleventh-century English manuscript. Dr Mayr-Harting has already commented that 'almost every one of' the points made by Bede's Wilfrid at the Synod of Whitby (III, 25) 'can be found in some form in Cummian's letter'. Both deal with the appeal of Catholicity (the opposition absurdly holds that everyone is wrong except the Britons and the Irish

---

[1] On these letters see Harrison, *Framework of Anglo-Saxon History*, pp. 59–63, with whom I have regretfully disagreed. As he points out, the Dionysiac *ratio* was unknown in Kent in 654 (ibid. 64)—and therefore not prescribed by the pope. For other arguments see Jones, *Bedae Opera de Temporibus*, pp. 99–104. The Dionysiac passage from the bull of 667 omitted from III, 29, is quoted ibid. p. 104: 'Numquam enim celebrare sanctum pascha nisi secundum apostolicam et catholicam fidem, ut in toto celebratur orbe a Christiana plebe, id est secundum apostolicam regulam CCCXVIII sanctorum patrum ac computum sancti Cyrilli et Dionysii. Nam in toto terrarum orbe sic Christi una columba, hoc est ecclesia immaculata, sanctum paschae resurrectionis diem celebrat. Nam Victoris sedes apostolica non adprobavit regulam paschae, ideo nec sequitur dispositionem eius pro pascha. Kenney, *Sources for the Early History of Ireland, Ecclesiastical*, pp. 218–23, commenting also on the fact that Bede does not quote the 'essential part' of the texts of these letters (223).

(Cummian), the Picts and the Britons (Bede)), with the example of John the Evangelist, with the forgery attributed to Anatolius, and with Columba, whose simple ignorance is no excuse for the obduracy of his later followers.[1] The *Acta Synodi Cæsareæ* and Aldhelm's letter to Geruntius may have influenced the writing of III, 25, as Jones and Isenberg respectively argued;[2] a role at least as important should not be denied to Cummian's letter—indeed would long have been recognized if the letter had dealt with a British and not an Irish situation. The fact that it must have come to Bede from Iona does not, however, make it any less likely as a source for the *HE*, since in Egbert we have his anonymous Iona informant, a source also for the texts of letters (1)–(3).

The author of the English paschal crisis was Wilfrid of Ripon and we can be fairly sure that he left computistical material, perhaps even accompanying annals, at Ripon. Wilfrid had two important pupils there: Willibrord who became a pupil of Egbert in Ireland and was sent by him to christianise the Frisians; and Ceolfrith later abbot of Jarrow. The possibility, suggested by these links, that Egbert was also a Ripon cleric is surely confirmed by the statement of the tenth-century *Resting Places of the Saints*, that Saint Egbert rested at Ripon.[3] Although not buried there, relics must have been transferred from Iona because of his roots at Ripon, perhaps in 757 when the abbot of Iona visited Ripon to ascertain the date of the Saxons' arrival in Britain.[4] Iona looked for annals there; the man most likely to have inspired them to do so was Egbert, for Egbert was interested in Easter and in annals.

In Ripon we have an explanation why Nectan's letter was directed

[1] For Cummian's letter see above, p. 23, n. 2; Mayr-Harting, *Coming of Christianity*, p. 112.

[2] Jones, *Chronicles and Annals*, pp. 181–2, 197–9; Gabriele Isenberg, *Die Würdigung Wilfrieds* (see p. 2, n. 2), pp. 35–7, 119–20.

[3] *Die Heiligen Englands*, ed. F. Liebermann (1889), pp. 9–10. This treatise is discussed by D. W. Rollason in *Anglo-Saxon England*, vii (1978), pp. 61–93.

[4] The evidence for the visit to Ripon is the Chartres MS of the *Historia Brittonum*, discussed by P. Grosjean in *AABB*, lxxviii. pp. 381–90, and in Harrison, *Framework of Anglo-Saxon History*, p. 99. The significance of Ripon was pointed out to me by Mr C. P. Wormald.

to Ceolfrith, but also a possible explanation for other features of the *HE*. The emphasis upon the Paschal controversy seems to have passed from Wilfrid and Ripon to Egbert who collected in Ireland and on Iona a dossier of letters from Archbishop Laurence and his colleagues, Honorius I, Cummian, and John IV. In these he found what his Ripon background—and his opponents—told him was no longer adequate, exhortations to unity embedded in unhelpful, even irrelevant, traditional remarks. Hence his request, in Nectan's name to another Ripon-trained cleric, Ceolfrith, for arguments 'from the apostolic see' for the catholic Easter (V, 21). This was surely a request not for an extended lecture from Ceolfrith but for the text of an authoritative and unambiguous papal pronouncement—for, like Oswy and Pippin, Nectan was convinced of the unique *virtutes* of Peter. It would also have been accompanied by the dossier of four Irish letters,[1] which explains why Bede thought Nectan 'not a little informed' on the matter of Easter (V, 21).

Between Bede's *De Temporibus* of 703 and the *De Temporum Ratione* of 725 his concern with the Paschal controversy clearly increased greatly, presumably towards the later date. The *Chronica Majora*, part of the *De Temporum Ratione*, although it makes no reference to Columba or the Lindisfarne mission, does summarize the papal letters (2) and (3) to Ireland and includes the conversion in 716 of 'several provinces of the Scots'.[2] Nectan's letter, the Irish dossier, and Ceolfrith's reply may have been in Bede's hands since 713, or they may have lain forgotten until 725 when he certainly had the Irish dossier. But there is a strong probability that in 724 or 725 Bede learned for the first time of Egbert's success at Iona in 716, and that this turned him first to an academic exposition of the Dionysiac Easter, the *De Temporum Ratione*, and then to these Irish and Pictish materials. Thus the *Chronica Majora* of 725 under a

---

[1] It is possible that Egbert collected all these letters in Iona, whose abbot is addressed by name in two of them.

[2] *MGH, Auctores Antiquissimi*, xiii (1898), p. 319, and *Bedae Opera Omnia*, ed. J. A. Giles, vi (1843), contain the *Chronica Majora*. For its date see Jones, *Bedae Opera de Temporibus*, pp. 136–7.

reign (at Byzantium) datable 716 records the conversion of 'several Scottish provinces' to the canonical Easter, by Egbert *vir sanctus*, 'a pilgrim for the heavenly life' in '716'.[1] Egbert the saint we shall meet in the *HE*; Egbert the pilgrim is there twice (IV, 3; V, 9) in this phrase, used also for missions from Ireland by Willibrord (*Chronica* and *HE*, III, 13) and Fursey (III, 19). The close relationship between the *Chronica* and *HE* for Egbert's conversion of Iona suggested by these identical phrases is surely strengthened by the use of the year of the Incarnation. This form of dating is found in the *Chronica* only twice, 532, the first year of the Dionysiac cycle, and 716; it arose from the use of the Dionysiac Easter cycle, and was particularly appropriate to record the adoption of that cycle. But may it not be that this adoption by Iona suggested or encouraged the idea that a history might be written whose framework was the era of the Incarnation? For there seems to be no earlier example than this of the use of the year of the Incarnation in historical writing.[2]

If the conversion of Iona brought the seed (in the *Chronica Majora*) of historical dating by the year of the Incarnation, the flowering of that seed (the *HE*) was, I suggest, brought about by news of the death of Egbert in 729. In III, 4, Egbert's 'long and holy life' perhaps implies his death; in III, 27, the contrast between Egbert's vow never to return to Britain and his death (on Iona) is avoided by not mentioning the place of death. His death is recorded in IV, 3 (as a pilgrim, not in Ireland as Colgrave's translation mistakenly states), in V, 22, and V, 23. Finally in the chronological summary he has the unique distinction of epithets, *uir domini* under 716, *sanctus* at his death in 729; no other prelate, not Augustine, Gregory I, Hadrian, or Wilfrid, shares this mark of esteem (V, 24). Clearly, Egbert was pre-eminent in Bede's eyes, because he had brought about the conversion of Iona, a pre-eminent event in the ecclesiastical history of Britain.

[1] *MGH, Auct. Ant.*, xiii. p. 319; *Bedae Opera Omnia*, vi. pp. 330–1.
[2] These matters are discussed in Harrison, *Framework of Anglo-Saxon History*, chapters 3–5.

In books III–IV of the *HE* the whole of the English race was brought to catholic observances by the Synod of Whitby and the work of Archbishop Theodore. The headings of books I–IV record that this is the 'ecclesiastical history of the English race' and these are also the last words of the *HE*. Book V, less well structured, has no such heading and in his epilogue Bede describes his work as the 'ecclesiastical history of the Britains and especially of the English race' (V, 24) because book V was written to bring the Picts and Scots of Britain to the rule 'of the catholic faith' (V, 22). He had precious little material on the Picts and Scots before 716 to put in book V, and created a narrative of sorts with miracles, pilgrimages to Rome, episcopal successions (all evidence of catholicity), the Frisian mission, and an obituary of Wilfrid. But the absence of English 'history' apart from episcopal successions was quite deliberate, for the English theme was concluded in book IV. It follows that book V was planned to end in 716, and the concluding narrative chapter (V, 23) is indeed no more than a few desultory annals to lead up to 'the present state of the English race or of all Britain'. These annals begin in 725; they are memorabilia noted down after the conclusion of the *Chronica Majora* and as Bede worked on the *HE* between 729 and 731.

Bede, it has been said, was providing the English race with a history. The importance of this theme, and of Canterbury and York in Bede's view of the theme, cannot be overestimated. These pages suggest no more than that a letter about the conversion of Iona may have proved a catalyst to Bede, that, ignoring the obdurate Britons, he should write a history of the progress of catholic truth on the framework of the era of the Incarnation. For the conversion of Iona is the *consummatum est* of the *HE* and it was brought about by two Englishmen, Ceolfrith and Egbert; the working of God's will for the whole island of Britain through the *gens Anglorum* was worthy of—demanded—written history.[1]

---

[1] Cf. J. N. Stephens, 'Bede's Ecclesiastical History', *History*, lxii (1977), pp. 12–14.

History in the mind of Archbishop Hincmar

J. M. WALLACE-HADRILL

IN the massive *œuvre* of Hincmar[1] we find no history; not, that is, history as conceived by Gregory of Tours, Paul the Deacon or Bede, who, for all their differences, had had in common the compulsion to look attentively at large tracts of the past and out of them to make a world, full of people. Hincmar, who knew both his Gregory and his Bede, was not like that. In his own way, however, he did imagine and use the past. Like Hugh of St. Victor, 'his historical thoughts came to him not through writing history';[2] they came to him as allies in his long life's search for secure foundations. The purpose of this essay is to disentangle some of these thoughts.

The beginnings were sunny. Born into a substantial family, perhaps in northern Francia and probably in about 805,[3] Hincmar emerges some eight years later as a boy at the great abbey of Saint-Denis, admission to which may argue some family influence. Certainly by 830 he was playing a part in public affairs under the eye of the abbot Hilduin, his mentor and teacher. There, and at the court of Louis the Pious at Aachen,[4] he learnt to know some of the men who had surrounded Charlemagne in his declining years as

[1] Substantially in Migne, *PL*, vols. 125–6, which reproduces Sirmond's edition with many typographical errors.

[2] R. W. Southern, *TRHS*, 5th series, 21 (1971), p. 164.

[3] So Jean Devisse, *Hincmar, archevêque de Reims, 845–882* (Geneva, 1975), pp. 1096 ff., to whom I am indebted for much that follows.

[4] On the contribution of Saint-Denis in the way of notaries, etc., to the chancellery, see Otto Gerhard Oexle, *Forschungen zu monastischen und geistlichen Gemeinschaften im westfränkischen Bereich* (*Münstersche Mittelalter-Schriften*, 31, 1978), pp. 31, 43.

well as the *novi homines* of Charlemagne's son. Among them was Adalhard of Corbie. He wrote of these beginnings in July 867 to Pope Nicholas I. He was, he said, educated as a child in the rudiments at Saint-Denis, *sub canonico habitu*, and taken thence for further instruction to the palace of the Emperor Louis, 'where I remained a considerable time'.[1] He goes on to say that he became a monk at the abbey, where he had been brought up and which he never had any wish to leave for a bishopric. Rather belatedly it seems, he took some part in the reform of the community.[2] It may have been of more significance for his future that he held the office of *custos sacrorum pignerum*.[3] Relics were always for him the irreplaceable link with spiritual patrons. Whether at Saint-Denis or Aachen he became a broadly educated man, if not a scholar in the mould of Servatus Lupus. Bookishness he counted *avaritia*.

Both at Aachen—which still housed a remarkable library under Louis the Pious[4]—and at Saint-Denis itself Hincmar had access to much literature that opened up the past to him;[5] not only histories, chronicles, and annals but also what speaks of the past in the Bible, patristic writings, saints' Lives, theology, liturgy, law, the liberal arts, and charters. Moreover, he moved among men who used the past. We can take an example of the use that plainly affected his thinking in years to come. St. Dionysius, first bishop of Paris, was martyred with his companions in the mid-third century. To Gregory of Tours, writing towards the end of the sixth century, the martyr was already a Gallic hero.[6] In 626 King Dagobert moved his

[1] *MGH, Epist. Karo. Aevi*, i, 1, ed. E. Perels (Berlin, 1939), 198, p. 210.

[2] According to Flodoard, *Historia Remensis Ecclesiae*, iii, 1 (*MGH Scriptores*, xiii. p. 475). But see Oexle, pp. 32, 112 ff., 118.

[3] Flodoard, ibid.

[4] See Bernhard Bischoff, 'Die Hofbibliothek unter Ludwig dem Frommen', *Medieval learning and literature: essays presented to Richard William Hunt* (Oxford, 1976), pp. 3–22.

[5] Discussed by Devisse, pp. 1056 ff. and by H. Schrörs, *Hinkmar Erzbischof von Reims* (Freiburg, 1884), pp. 444 ff.

[6] *Libri Historiarum*, i, 30, *MGH S(cript.) R(er) M(ero.)*, i, 1, ed. Krusch and Levison (Hanover, 1951), p. 23; *Liber in Gloria Martyrum*, ch. 71 (*MGH SRM*, i, 2, ed. Krusch, 1885), p. 535 (p. 85 in reprint).

remains to the abbey, of which the king was a munificent patron.[1]
Thereafter, the liturgical cult of the saint developed naturally, and
with it the conviction that he shared with St. Martin the patronage
of the Merovingians and in due course the Carolingians. The details
need not concern us. In 827 the Byzantine Emperor Michael the
Stammerer sent to Louis the Pious a copy of the Greek writings of
Pseudo-Dionysius.[2] Abbot Hilduin was required by Louis to prepare a Latin translation (in a few years to be replaced by a better
translation from the pen of John Scotus Eriugena).[3] To Hilduin it
was clear that Dionysius of Paris, Pseudo-Dionysius, and even
Dionysius the Areopagite were one and the same man. Out of this
fruitful confusion emerged a Frankish patron who was at once the
pupil of St. Paul, the first bishop of Paris, and the author of a great
corpus of mystical theology. Such was Hilduin's belief. It was
shared by his pupil Hincmar.[4] It also intrigued the Emperor Louis
and after him his son, Charles the Bald.[5] There survives a letter from
Louis to Hilduin[6] which plainly follows upon some discussion

[1] Fredegar, *Chronicon*, iv, 79; ed. Krusch, *MGH SRM*, ii (Hanover, 1887),
p. 161; ed. Wallace-Hadrill (London, 1960), pp. 67–8. The implications are
examined by L. Levillain, 'Études sur l'abbaye de Saint-Denis à l'époque
mérovingienne', ii, *BEC*, 86 (1925), pp. 22 ff. Paul Lehmann, *Erforschung des
Mittelalters*, iv (Stuttgart, 1961), p. 201, prints the Saint-Denis epitaph of
Dagobert from the Wolfenbüttel MS of Hinricus Token's *Rapularius*, of the
mid-fifteenth century.

[2] Now in Paris: BN MS gr. 437. Between 758 and 763 Pope Paul I had
sent to Pippin III certain books, 'geometricam, orthografiam, grammaticam,
omnes Greco eloquio scriptas', which he attributed to Dionysius the Areopagite. (*MGH Epist. Mero. et Karo. Aevi*, i. p. 529.)

[3] The problems facing a Carolingian scholar translating from Greek into
Latin are clarified by R. Le Bourdellès, 'Connaissance du grec et méthodes
de traduction dans le monde carolingien jusqu'à Jean Scot Erigène', *Jean Scot
Erigène et l'histoire de la philosophie: Colloques internationaux du Centre National
de la recherche scientifique*, 561 (Paris, 1977), esp. p. 121.

[4] Many years later Hincmar confirmed this, adding some interesting details,
in a prefatory letter to Charles the Bald, introducing Anastasius' translation of
a Life of the Areopagite (*PL* 126, cols 153–4).

[5] See Max Buchner, 'Die Areopagitika des Abtes Hilduin von St Denis und
ihr kirchenpolitischer Hintergrund', *Hist. Jahrbuch*, 56 (1936), pp. 441–80, and
Das Vizepapsttum des Abtes von St Denis (Paderborn, 1928).

[6] *MGH Epist. Karo. Aevi*, iii, no. 19, pp. 326–7.

between the two men, perhaps after the emperor's restoration at the abbey in 834. Louis rehearses the benefits his predecessors (not simply his ancestors) had derived from the saint, and the reciprocal benefits the abbey had enjoyed from Frankish rulers.[1] He begins with Dagobert, 'one of the old Frankish kings', who honoured the saint exceptionally and who, in consequence, was freed by the saint from the punishment of his sins and taken to eternal life 'sicut divina ac celebris ostensio perhibet'. Charles Martel, Pippin III, and Charlemagne, men of his own blood, had similarly benefited from the saint's patronage. Therefore he asks Hilduin to compose a book about the saint from the records, both Greek and Latin, available to him. Hilduin replies very quickly:[2] he has, he says, put together all that he can find about the life and martyrdom of St. Denis and has added his proof that the saint was the Areopagite. Those that disbelieve this betray lack of patriotism.[3] There were obviously doubters. He also writes to the Church in general on the subject.[4] The correspondence is elaborate and learned. It witnesses to an advance in historical criticism since the days of Charlemagne.[5] Hilduin can raise in an historical context problems of textual transmission; he can discuss the authenticity of sources and of manuscripts; and he can face the arguments of those who disagree with him. He and his king are looking back over many centuries. They are not interested in the contrast between Merovingians and Carolingians that had struck Einhard when he wrote his *Vita Karoli Magni* not so long before. Frankish kings of both dynasties and the abbey of Saint-Denis are by long usage dependent on each other. Hilduin commands a wide range of sources, historical and other, and, exceptionally, some material that bears the imprint of fabrication. One may instance the *revelatio* of Pope Stephen in conjunction with the restoration of the emperor at the abbey: what

---

[1] This résumé may well have influenced Hincmar when he attempted something of the same for Reims. See Buchner, *Areopagitika*, p. 446.

[2] *MGH Epist. Karo. Aevi*, iii, no. 20, pp. 328 ff.

[3] Ibid., p. 334.

[4] Ibid., no. 21, pp. 335 ff.

[5] See Buchner, *Areopagitika*, p. 456.

ought to have existed, but did not, could be provided for in the interests of a higher truth.

The outcome of the correspondence between emperor and abbot was Hilduin's Life of the saint;[1] and associated with this heightened interest are two further productions of Saint-Denis which are difficult to place in chronological order: the *Miracula* of the saint[2] and the *Gesta Dagoberti*.[3] It was the opinion of Léon Levillain, later somewhat revised, that Hincmar was the author of both.[4] This no longer seems likely,[5] though the possibility remains of collaboration between Hilduin and Hincmar,[6] more particularly with the *Miracula*. What is certain is that Hincmar, now responsible for the treasures and relics of the abbey,[7] must have been intimately aware of what was being done by his master. We can at least suppose him to have been one of those who would have dug out material for Hilduin. It was from Hilduin that Hincmar learnt how to use Frankish history and to Hilduin that he owed his introduction to Dagobert and to the beginnings of Carolingian rule under Charles Martel and Pippin III. To learn to use Frankish history was, moreover, to learn how to select and present material in the context of a patron-saint. There is no attempt at a full-length account of Dagobert in the *Gesta*, 'maxime ob fastidientium lectorum vitandum tedium',[8] nor would details of the king's life be relevant in the *Miracula*.[9] Hincmar had learnt, too, the value of archival material and of liturgical resources. The *Gesta Dagoberti* were among the Saint-Denis hagiographical sources that followed Hincmar to

---

[1] *PL* 106, cols 23–50.

[2] Ed. Mabillon, *Acta Ord. Sancti Ben. saec.* 3, pars 2.

[3] *MGH SRM*, ii. pp. 396–425 (see also ibid. vii. pp. 778–82); Wattenbach-Levison, *Deutschlands Geschichtsquellen im Mittelalter*, i (Weimar, 1952), p. 113, n. 254, do not commit themselves as to authorship; Devisse, p. 1007, follows Buchner on this (see below, n. 5).

[4] 'Etudes', i (*BEC*, 82, 1921), pp. 88 ff., and in *Moyen Age*, 30 (1929), p. 95.

[5] See Buchner, *Areopagitika*, pp. 445 ff.

[6] Devisse, p. 1092.

[1] See note 2, p. 44, above.

[8] *MGH SRM*, ii, ch. 42, p. 419.

[9] *Miracula*, p. 359.

Reims.[1] He considered himself the heir of Hilduin (who died in 840)[2] in what amounted to a hagiographical mission. Without this background, emotional as much as intellectual, it is scarcely possible to imagine Hincmar's subsequent career.

Saint-Denis and Reims had been linked in an association of prayer for the sick and the dead since 838.[3] The clergy of Reims knew what they were doing when in 845 they joined forces with the bishops and the king in urging Hincmar to accept their great and troubled archbishopric. The tragedy of his deposed predecessor and the ensuing vacancy must greatly have weakened the standing of the see and its ability to resist spoliation. Hincmar was to Reims more than a proved man of powerful character and administrative experience. He, if anyone, would know how to bring the past of an ancient church to life, how to find strength in what lay buried. Though one was a monastery and the other an archbishopric, Saint-Denis and Reims had much in common. Both housed splendid libraries and rich archives; both looked back to the patronage of illustrious holy men; both had had long experience of kings, whether as benefactors or despoilers. Benefactions in particular tied both to the Merovingians as much as to the Carolingians. The cult of St. Remigius was already venerable and elaborate[4] when Hincmar arrived at Reims though, as in other matters, he seems to have been in no hurry to explore its possibilities. He liked to work systematically through his evidence. Only at the end of his career did he feel able to assemble all that he knew about the saint in a Life of extraordinary complexity. It is best left, as Hincmar left it, to the end.

Many a ninth-century bishop fought for his own with historical

---

[1] Cf. Devisse, p. 1092, n. 174.

[2] It is not known what, if anything, Hincmar owed to Hilduin's successor, the Abbot Louis, grandson of Charlemagne, archchancellor of Charles the Bald, and long a monk at Saint-Denis (cf. Oexle, *Forschungen*, pp. 29–30, 33). Flodoard records three letters from Hincmar to Louis (*MGH Epist. Karo. Aevi*, i, 1, p. 202).

[3] The initiative for this association came from Reims.

[4] The general development of ninth-century cults is in part investigated by Oexle, notably for St. Martin's of Tours (esp. 120 ff.).

weapons that lay to hand: he could find them in the Old Testament and its commentators, and in canon law.[1] Hincmar was no exception, unless indeed his use of them was conditioned, as M. Devisse believes, by an awareness of the purposes of Christian society that was beyond the grasp of most of his contempories.[2] He saw the world of the Old Testament kings and prophets much as they did. It was an exemplary world.[3] Read the Books of the kings, he urges, the *sacra regum historia*, and there you will find examples of a nation's prosperity resulting from its ruler's conformity to God's purpose—or the reverse. In the matter of the making of kings he had a special interest, to which we will come. But in general the world of the Israelites stood for him as a prototype. It raised no chronological problems. Other historical weapons lay in the Roman past. Hincmar used these, if sparingly. Alexander and Trajan, Constantine and the two Theodosii came naturally to his mind; and of other emperors he had some knowledge. But this is not to say that he had a steady view of Antiquity. Orosius, and increasingly Augustine, gave him no favourable impression of the Roman world and its emperors. Rome left him cold: it was not the home of any golden age. Genuine as was his respect for papal authority, when

[1] Hincmar's struggle with what may be called the historicity of canon law is discussed by Devisse, and by C. Brühl, 'Hinkmariana', *Deutsches Archiv*, 20 (1964), pp. 48–77. Civil and canon law can come neatly together in Hincmar's mind, as thus: 'lege librum XVI legis Romanae, lege decreta Damasi, percurre Leonis epistolas et ceterorum pontificum de diversis conciliis ad imperatores transmissas, revolve augustorum edicta . . . scrutare caesarum nostrorum capitula . . .' (*MGH Epist. Karo. Aevi, i*, 1, pp. 84–5).

[2] Chs 6 and 8 in particular.

[3] M. Devisse seems to me to make no very significant distinction when he writes (p. 675) of Hincmar's O.T. citations 'ceux-ci ne sont cités que comme des exemples, rarement comme des prototypes totalement transportables'. He further considers (p. 1322) that Hincmar made less use than did some of his contemporaries of the Pentateuch and the historical books of the O.T. In terms of citations this is true. Yet there are many. A fairer estimate of Hincmar's approach to the O.T. may be that of P. E. Schramm, 'Das Alte und das Neue Testament in der Staatslehre und Staatssymbolik des Mittelalters', *Settimane*, x (1963), pp. 233–7. See also H. H. Anton, *Fürstenspiegel und Herrscherethos in der Karolingerzeit* (Bonn, 1968), pp. 318, 347.

not exercised to the detriment of his own, the reading of the *Liber Pontificalis*[1] had not stirred his imagination nor left him with any love of papal Rome as the historical nursery of western Christianity. Rome and its past seemed of small account as he surveyed useful beginnings.

What mattered was the Franks. They did not matter to Hincmar in the way that the Anglo-Saxons mattered to Bede; or, if they did, he felt no urge to write about them as a regenerate people with the world at their feet. Yet for a century they had learnt to see themselves so; it was the lesson of the prologue to the Carolingian recension of *Lex Salica* as also of the *Liber Historiae Francorum*, of the continuators of Fredegar's Chronicle, and of much liturgical acclamation. With all this, as with Gregory of Tours, the harbinger, Hincmar was familiar. He could nearly always find strength and justification and consolation in the Frankish past. It was by no means a story of uninterrupted progress. The Franks had had their ups and downs. Sometimes they had lost sense of direction under wicked rulers. Hincmar noted these losses and made use of them. He was not short of historical material from which to sum up royal relations with Reims from the beginning.[2] Reverence for Charlemagne is there, naturally; indeed, it increases as the years pass; but it is not blind reverence. Charles Martel was to him a villain; the deposition of Louis the Pious a traumatic experience; and the quarrels of his sons a terrible warning. But, when all is said, the whole Frankish past was a living experience; it was active, where that of the Israelites and Romans was passive.

The sense of the active past is vividly alive in the long letter of rebuke to Louis the German, written by Hincmar on behalf of his colleagues in November 858, after Louis's invasion of Charles the Bald's kingdom.[3] The archbishop is outraged at this unbrotherly and unkingly act, exacerbated as it is by Viking attack. Moreover,

---

[1] Cf. 'ad episcopos', *PL* 126, col. 190.

[2] See for example *PL* 126, cols 200 ff. for a neat summary with special reference to the troubles of Reims in the lifetime of St. Boniface.

[3] *MGH Capit.* ii, 2, pp. 428 ff.

the Church and its lands are threatened. Let Louis consider the fate of Charles Martel, 'qui primus inter omnes Francorum reges ac principes res ecclesiarum ab eis separavit atque divisit'; and for this, 'signis manifestatur eventibus',[1] he had lost eternal life. Louis is treated to an account of the vision of Eucher, bishop of Orleans under Pippin III—an account well calculated to alarm even the formidable Louis because it was a piece of family history. It was not the only *visio* of a Carolingian in trouble. The monk Wetti had already seen Charlemagne punished for his shortcomings.[2] Nor was it the last; for Hincmar, near his end, was to report Bernold's *visio* of Charles the Bald in purgatory.[3] But it was the first appearance of Eucher's *visio*, which, briefly, was his account of witnessing Charles Martel's torments in hell and of his further assurance that Charles's tomb at Saint-Denis would on investigation be found empty. The news had taken St. Boniface and the Abbot Fulrad to the tomb. This they opened. Out of its smouldering interior flew a dragon. 'And I myself', adds Hincmar, 'have known those who lived into my time but were present on that occasion, and they assured me to my face of the truth of what they heard and saw.' Clearly he is reporting an incident familiar to the monks of Saint-Denis when he was one of them. He cannot be the inventor of it but certainly he is the first to make use of it; and he does so in a formal synodical letter from the bishops of two provinces, Reims and Rouen, to the great-great-grandson of Charles Martel. Moreover, he adds that Pippin III and Charlemagne took due note of it, or implies that they did so. Louis should remember that his brother Charles was an anointed king. Hincmar glances back into the biblical past: 'legite libros regum'—as so often—'et invenietis quanta reverentia rebrobatum et abiectum a Domino Saul ducere dignum

---

[1] Ibid., p. 432.
[2] Heito's prose version, *MGH Poet. Lat.*, ii. pp. 271 ff.; Walahfrid's verse version, ibid. v. pp. 460 ff. There is a more recent edition by David Traill (Bern, 1974) which I have not seen. See also B. de Gaiffier, 'La Légende de Charlemagne: le péché de l'empereur et son pardon', *Études critiques d'hagiographie et d'iconologie* (Brussels: *Subsidia Hagiographica*, 43, 1967), pp. 260–75.
[3] *PL* 125, cols 1115–20.

C   [51]

duxit sanctus Samuhel, cuius locum in ecclesia nos licet indigni tenemus'. St. Boniface and his colleagues had once written to King Aethelbald of Mercia[1] to rebuke him for his loose living and his seizure of church property; nor did they hesitate to draw his attention to the fate of his own predecessor, Ceolred. It was a classic in the genre of *Mahnschreiben*. But between him and them lay the Channel and Francia. Hincmar and Louis the German were separated by a few miles. It was a risky letter.

'I conceive it will be a great service to posterity to commit to writing the deeds of the present for the use of the future.' The words are Eadmer's.[2] Only a man with a lively sense of the past could have written them. Hincmar would have understood. The Royal Frankish Annals had been composed in the imperial chapel at Aachen till the death of Louis the Pious in 840,[3] latterly by the court cleric Prudentius who took refuge with the Empress Judith at Poitiers during the troubles. When she rejoined her son Charles at Châlons in 841, Prudentius seems to have accompanied her. The King then asked him to continue the Annals, although at about the same time he asked his kinsman Nithard to write a personal history of his reign as it developed. Prudentius did his best (better than his predecessors) until his death, as bishop of Troyes, in 861. At this point Hincmar borrowed Prudentius' Annals from the king and presumably had a copy taken before returning them. From 861 to the day of his death in 882 he kept his record at Reims. His Annals, then, were not official. But he was often at the centre of events and could incorporate official material of great importance; and he had an unrivalled knowledge of the men who took decisions. His record is unlike any other. His contemporary, the Fulda annalist,

---

[1] M. Tangl, *Die Briefe des heiligen Bonifatius und Lullus* (*MGH Epist. Select.* i, Berlin, 1955), 73, pp. 146–55. See also W. Levison, 'Die Politik in den Jenzeitsvisionen des frühen Mittelalters', *Aus rheinischer und fränkischer Frühzeit* (Düsseldorf, 1948), pp. 240 ff.

[2] *Historia Novorum*, ed. M. Rule, (RS 1884), p. 1. The translation is that of R. W. Southern, *TRHS*, 5th series, 23 (1973), p. 252.

[3] See L. Levillain, in *Annales de Saint-Bertin*, ed. F. Grat, J. Vielliard, and S. Clémencet (*SHF*, Paris, 1964), pp. xii ff.

pursues with skill the orthodox path; that is, he recounts what he
selects of events in a strictly East-Frankish interest. His canvas was
sufficiently wide. Hincmar is less content with his own West
Franks. His province of Reims straddled two Frankish kingdoms and
his Church had possessions far beyond them. The world he looks out
upon has its centre in Reims, not in the court of Charles the Bald.
He will have had in mind the interests of his successors, and the
difficulties with kings, colleagues, and magnates that he had had to
face and that they might face in their turn.[1] But his Annals are more
than a *vade mecum*. They are a personal record, a justification of his
own actions, and an investigation of the reasons for and aims of
political decisions.[2] Beyond that, he intends to leave a picture of
public life in the widest sense, the triumphs, betrayals, and misunderstandings of the men he knew. And all this he views against
the purposes of God for the society he belonged to. We should
expect him to be fairly full on matters that involved him directly:
for example, the restoration of Bishop Rothad,[3] the case of Wulfad,[4]
the quarrel with Hincmar of Laon,[5] the overshadowing horror of
the Vikings. Where possible, letters and documents needed to be
recorded. No man of the ninth century was more convinced of the
necessity for written proof. Hence the refrain 'exemplar habemus',[6]
'libellum quem habemus',[7] 'synodum ipsam habemus'.[8] But then,
there are surprises in the Annals. We might not expect from the pen
of so sophisticated a political observer the account of the miracle
of the bloodstained shirt at Thérouanne,[9] nor the fascinating story
of how Satan tempted Charles, son of Louis the German, and of how

[1] There is no manuscript of Hincmar's Annals at Reims today but Flodoard
and Richer used one there, and it was presumably Hincmar's own.

[2] Cf. Schrörs, p. 456.

[3] *Ann. Bert.*, s.a. 865, p. 118.

[4] Ibid., s.a. 866, p. 129; s.a. 867, p. 137.

[5] Ibid., s.a. 868, pp. 150 ff.

[6] *MGH Epist. Karo. Aevi*, i, 1, 198, p. 211.

[7] Ibid., 198, p. 208.

[8] *PL* 126, col. 15.

[9] *Ann. Bert.* s.a. 862, p. 92.

his father dealt with the situation.[1] We might expect Hincmar's growing disillusionment with his own king, Charles the Bald. Like Bede, Hincmar is difficult to see behind. Yet we know enough to imagine a rather different Charles: violent and ambitious certainly, but also very clear about the duties of a Christian king, intensely pious, and always aware of the history of his dynasty. To Hincmar he must have seemed in retrospect a big man in the light of the youngsters who followed him. Even the victory of Louis III at Saucourt in 881 is only grudgingly acknowledged.[2] Early medieval annals are customarily dry records of events. Hincmar's are not like that. His concern is with motives and reasons, and the entire account of public life as he sees it over more than twenty years betrays the historian's instinctive control of material. He writes for his own satisfaction, often with bitterness, sometimes with injustice. He writes also for the Church of Reims, perhaps as a warning.

Under the year 869 the annalist records at length a momentous occasion: the unction and coronation at Metz of Charles the Bald as successor to his nephew Lothar in Lorraine. Whatever part Hincmar may have played in the events leading up to this blatant *coup*, he was certainly the organizer of the coronation. The protocol for the *Ordo*, which survives, was his work,[3] as doubtless the *Ordo* itself. There are interesting innovations about it. What concerns us here is one feature only. In his own allocution Hincmar dwells on the past in this manner: first, the famous Frankish king, Clovis, had been baptized at Reims by St. Remigius with heaven-sent oil, some of which he, Hincmar, now has with him to anoint Charles.[4]

---

[1] Ibid., s.a. 873, p. 190.

[2] Ibid., s.a. 881, p. 244. The estimates of the Annals of Saint-Vaast and of Fulda, as well as that of Regino of Prüm, are very different.

[3] *MGH Capit.*, ii, 2, pp. 456–7. See C. A. Bouman, *Sacring and Crowning* (Groningen, 1957), pp. 8–9.

[4] It is worth noting that the account in the Annals, s.a. 848, of Charles's unction at Orleans speaks of 'sacroque crismate delibutum'. Hincmar in his letter of 858 to Louis the German refers to this unction and adds that the chrism used was 'divina traditione' (*MGH Capit.*, ii, 2, p. 439). Was this, too, the oil of St. Remigius?

Secondly, the Carolingians are descended from the Merovingians through St. Arnulf of Metz.[1] As to the second claim, Hincmar perhaps had in mind the link alleged in the anonymous poem 'Origo et exordium gentis Francorum',[2] also addressed to Charles the Bald; namely, that Ansbert, grandfather of St. Arnulf, was husband of Blithildis, daughter of Chlotar I. (The poem is important evidence that Hincmar was not alone in the search for sustaining links with the Merovingian past.) There is no supporting evidence for this claim.[3] Hincmar seeks a Carolingian link with Clovis, and so with Remigius, and finds one through St. Arnulf, the great forebear and bishop of the Carolingian stronghold in which Charles was about to be consecrated. We shall come in due course to the reasons for the overwhelming significance of St. Remigius in Hincmar's eyes. What matters immediately is that the whole past of Frankish kingship is subsumed by Hincmar in solemn liturgical form. Only thus can Charles hope to command Lotharingian loyalty. Only thus will Lothar's bishops be persuaded to accept him. Louis the German, Charles's elder brother, was just as much a Merovingian as he was; but nobody suggested that the holy oil of Reims was available to Louis. Hincmar's coronation *Ordines* are a large subject and have been much studied.[4] They seem to have owed nothing directly to Anglo-Saxon or Visigothic precedent. Hincmar looks to Reims and, beyond that, to the Old Testament.[5] The prefiguration was in far-off Israel, the impetus in Reims.

[1] See O. G. Oexle, 'Die Karolinger und die Stadt des heiligen Arnulf', *Frühmittelalterliche Studien*, i (1967), esp. 351 ff.

[2] *MGH Poet. Lat.*, ii. pp. 141–5.

[3] See Eduard Hlawitschka, 'Merowingerblut bei den Karolingern?, *Adel und Kirche*, ed. J. Fleckenstein and Karl Schmid (Freiburg, 1968), pp. 66–91.

[4] e.g. by P. E. Schramm, *Der König von Frankreich* (Weimar, 1960), and *Herrschaftszeichen und Staatssymbolik* (Stuttgart, 1954); Bouman, op. cit.; Janet L. Nelson, 'National synods, kingship as office, and royal anointing', *Studies in Church History*, 7 (Cambridge, 1971), pp. 41–59, and 'Inauguration rituals', *Early medieval kingship*, ed. P. H. Sawyer and I. N. Wood (Leeds, 1977), pp. 50–71; A. Sprengler, 'Die Gebete der Krönungsordinen Hinkmars von Reims für Karl den Kahlen und für Ludwig den Stammler', *Zeitschrift für Kirchengeschichte* lxiii (1950–1), pp. 245–67.

[5] See Schramm, *Settimane*, x, pp. 235 ff., and, as to background, R. Kottje,

The field in which one would most expect to find Hincmar looking to the past is the series of his admonitory letters and treatises, especially those addressed to kings. We have seen what he could do for Louis the German in 858, when a comparatively young metropolitan. Relevant texts came easily to him, some obvious and others not. In 873 he presented Charles with a contribution to the genre of Mirrors of Princes; one of four such in the ninth century.[1] It was meant as a consolation, probably for the revolt of Carloman, the worst of the king's unhappy sons. If it is exemplary[2] it reassures the king that he has been following the right path, not that he has been straying from it: 'talem in benignitate ac bonitate, sicut ipsae describunt sententiae, vos esse et sic agere scio'.[3] The *sententiae* are collected from the Fathers and mostly from Augustine, though sometimes direct from the Old Testament: 'timeat princeps quod in regum historia legitur . . .'. This is country trodden by many who sought to put kings right or justify them; by Smaragdus, Sedulius Scottus, Jonas of Orleans, and Agobard among others. But what can Hincmar adduce from the secular past for a worried Carolingian? He will not go so far as Augustine in denying that the state, Roman or other, is a *respublica* as Christians should conceive it but is sufficiently impressed by Augustine not to proffer examples from among the Roman emperors. Still less would he have agreed with the view shortly to be expressed at Troyes by Pope John VIII that Rome of the popes had created all kings, judges, and priests throughout the world.[4] Hincmar remained a Gelasian.[5] But there

---

Studien zum Einfluss des Alten Testamentes auf Recht und Liturgie des frühen Mittelalters (Bonn, 1970).

[1] Cf. Anton, op. cit., and Otto Eberhardt, *Via Regia* (Munich, 1977).

[2] It is not easy to understand why Devisse writes (p. 675) of Hincmar's O.T. *exempla* that they were used rarely 'comme des prototypes totalement transportables'.

[3] *De regis persona et regio ministerio, PL* 125, col. 833. See also G. Laehrs, 'Ein karolingischen Konzilsbrief und des Fürstenspiegel Hinkmars von Reims', *Neues Archiv*, xv (1933), pp. 106–34.

[4] Mansi, *Amplissima Collectio*, xvii, A, p. 347.

[5] See e.g. *De fide Karolo regi servanda*, ch. 39, *PL* 125, col. 982.

were secular pickings. So we find him recording this, among his six kinds of ruler, in his long treatise on the divorce of Lothar and Theutberga: 'successione etiam paterna quidam regnant, sicut de his omnibus in historiis et chronicis et etiam in libro qui inscribitur *Vita Caesarum*, invenitur'.[1] This nestles in among citations and examples from the Old Testament. When he wishes to illustrate how fewness of numbers should not deter a king from battle if God is with him, he refers him first to the story of Gideon, then to the Books of Maccabees, and finally to Orosius' account[2] of how Leonidas faced Xerxes in the passes of Thermopylae. The story of bravery in the face of hopeless odds appeals so strongly to Hincmar that he reproduces most of Orosius' chapter.[3] It is the virtue that he often urges on kings who prefer to buy off Vikings when they ought to be fighting them. He does not ask himself whether they had the means to do what he wanted.[4]

Only rarely does Hincmar state what reading lies behind his writing. One instance of this is his *De fide Karolo regi servanda* of 875.[5] Among much else he has been searching saints' Lives for examples of resistance to the injustice of the powerful. He has found what he needed in the Lives of Hilary of Poitiers, Paulinus of Trier, Dionysius of Milan, Eusebius of Vercelli, John of Constantinople *et multi alii*. But he has also read the Lives of Lupus of Troyes, Martin of Tours, and Basil of Caesarea, to say nothing of others he used on this and other occasions.[6] He can also draw on the Tripartite History for an imperial *exemplum*. This piece, addressed to the bishops of his province, cannot have been long in the making, for it is an urgent appeal to their loyalty on the second invasion of West Francia by Louis the German during the absence of Charles in Italy. The historical material is, then, at his finger-tips; he knows the library of Reims. Saints' Lives are what he requires for his purpose,

---

[1] *De divortio Lotharii et Tetbergae*, PL 125, col. 758.
[2] *Adversum Paganos*, ii, ch. 9.
[3] PL 125, cols 843–4.
[4] Anton, pp. 298 ff. has a useful discussion of Hincmar's *Kriegstheologie*.
[5] PL 125, col. 969.
[6] Cf. Devisse, p. 1012, where they are listed.

and his examples are deftly employed. Such Lives are historical sources.

Another kind of historical material that Hincmar can use with real mastery is law, both civil and canon. One can see how his mind works in his long dissertation to Charles the Bald *pro ecclesiae libertatum defensione*,[1] inspired by the quarrel between the king, Hincmar of Laon, and himself. The immediate trouble is confiscation of church property. Hincmar looks back to Constantine, *magnus imperator*, and his legislation, and thence to succeeding Christian emperors, and cites their decisions on immunity. Moreover, *moderni reges Francorum* have followed their example: 'itaque cum aliis memorabilibus imperatoribus ac regibus loquimur, avi vestri, magni imperatoris Caroli non est praetereunda memoria'.[2] Charlemagne had acted swiftly on a complaint from the Patriarch Paulinus, 'sicut vobis bene notum esse cognosco'. Canons, patristica, and capitularies can then be exhibited in order to the same effect. Above all, let Charles remember the example of Theodosius when faced by St. Ambrose: 'et ideo exaltatus est, et merito et nomine, et sanctitatis insigne super omnes post Constantinum Romanos imperatores'.[3] Justification lies in the past, the right texts can be assembled, and their authority is cumulative. The balance between the kind of texts used will depend on the issue. For example, *De coercendo raptu viduarum, puellarum ac sanctimonialium*[4] relies more heavily on the Old Testament than is usual with Hincmar, though Roman Law is not overlooked: 'testentur hoc publicae Romanorum leges'.[5] Augustine had approved the 'lex Antonini pagani imperatoris',[6] though in the end 'nec Romanis, nec Salicis, nec Gundobadis sed divinis et apostolicis legibus judicandos'.[7]

What seems remarkable is Hincmar's capacity to view the whole

---

[1] *PL* 125, cols 1035–70.
[2] Ibid., col. 1040.
[3] Ibid., col. 1056.
[4] Ibid., cols 1017–36.
[5] Ibid., col. 1021.
[6] Ibid., col. 1024.
[7] Ibid., col. 1026.

of the useful past as a continuum. There is no point at which its authority ceases. If Charles the Bald needed frequent reminders of this, much more did his youthful successors, Louis the Stammerer, Carloman, and Charles the Fat. Hincmar's *Novi regis instructio*[1] is a straight lesson in Frankish history for Louis the Stammerer on his accession. The young man must know that royal accessions are commonly occasions of discord: 'legimus in antiquis historiis'.[2] Much depends on sensible advisers and wise provision for the future. Thus, 'de recentioribus historiis vobis proponam exempla':[3] Pippin III on his death-bed at Saint-Denis had arranged for the peaceful accession of his two sons; and Louis the Pious had succeeded Charlemagne peacefully. But alas, 'causa emergente quam non oportet nunc dicere', dissensions later broke out among Louis's sons and their magnates that have never died down. For a start there had been the terrible battle of Fontenoy, than which no such battle had been fought between Christians since the first Charles (Martel) fought with Ragamfred at Vinchy.[4] Young Louis will be well aware of the ensuing troubles. So Hincmar's advice is 'ut de antiquis historiis quantum potestis attendatis'. Let the king observe the reasons for the peaceful accession after Pippin III and avoid what happened at the death of Louis the Pious. His father Charles the Bald had done his best to make this possible. In the end, all he has to do is to ensure that 'solicite ambulatis cum seniore vestro rege regum'.[5] The right advisers, as always in the past, are essential. This too is the message for the Emperor Charles the Fat, whom he saw as the natural protector of Louis's sons.[6] Charles will recall that Alexander the Great suffered from the sad example of Leonides, his tutor; that Solomon fell under the sway of youthful, and therefore bad, advisers; that on the other hand Jehoash, king of Judah, benefited when young from the counsel of the priest Jehoida; and that

[1] Ibid., cols 983–90.
[2] Ibid., col. 984.
[3] Ibid., col. 985.
[4] Ibid., col. 986.
[5] Ibid., col. 988.
[6] Ibid., cols 989–94.

Gregory the Great had given sound advice to the tutors of the Greek emperor's sons. Hincmar jumps about chronologically but it does not matter. There is a cumulative effect. A more serious effort is Hincmar's advice to Carloman. This, the *De ordine palatii*,[1] written in the last years of his life, is his most impressive attempt to bring the experience of the past to the help of yet another young king. Hincmar was now a very old man. To his nostalgia for the Carolingian past he seems to add an increasing reliance on the wisdom of old men of ripe experience. It is not surprising.[2] But *De ordine* is by no means the leisurely memoir of a retired statesman. It is hard, urgent advice. Charlemagne as Hincmar sees him is now the much-needed exemplar of mature rulership, balancing between the Charlemagnes of Einhard's *Vita* and Notker's *Gesta*. He is set on course for the *chansons de geste*. But Hincmar is not content with his own memories. He draws upon the earlier work of Adalhard, supplementing where he sees fit.[3] The outcome is a manual of Christian government which makes its true impact only when read in conjunction with the advice offered to the king by the bishops at the Council of Fismes (Ste Macre) in the preceding year.[4] Hincmar now has the task, imposed on him by his colleagues, of telling Carloman what he recalls or has read of life under Charlemagne and Louis the Pious.[5] 'These, then, are the additions to be made to ancestral decisions confirmed at the recent synod of Ste Macre and presented to the late King Louis (III). They are the provisions that I gathered from the writings and words of our predecessors that were still current in my youth.'[6] He is the only channel through which the experience of the Carolingian past can now reach

[1] Ed. M. Prou, *Hincmari Remensis archiepiscopi epistola de ordine palatii* (*Bibl. de l'école des hautes études*, 58, 1885) and, better, by V. Krauze, *MGH Fontes . . . in usum scholarum*, v (1894).

[2] See Devisse, p. 998.

[3] For the breakdown of chapters see Devisse, pp. 992 ff.

[4] *PL* 125, cols 1069–86, and especially the final *capitulum, ad regem*.

[5] *De ordine palatii* is not solely concerned with the palace and its officials. The title, which is Sirmond's and not Hincmar's, is to this extent misleading.

[6] Ed. Krauze, ch. 37, p. 25.

Carloman, 'for I know well that none survives of those I once knew of the great men of the palace and of the kingdom under the Emperor Louis'.[1] Probably the advice proffered is disinterested. Hincmar must have known that his days of power were over and his own life near its end. His own recollections and his received account of the men and offices of an earlier time may not have been wholly accurate. He measures the instability of 882 against what seem the moral certitudes and calm control of the palace of his youth. It is not change he dreads so much as fluctuation and uncertainty, the natural result of short reigns, youthful inexperience, and bad advisers. Thus he can bid young Louis go to Compiègne: 'inclinate oculos ubi jacet pater vester'.[2] Old men find solace in their pasts. Hincmar does more than this. He shows Carloman in an exemplary way the principles by which his own family had ruled. He reminds him, too, that far away in the background was Clovis.[3] It is a new kind of family history, concerning itself not with chronological details but with principles distilled from them. Moreover, he means what he says. The men he admired are dead indeed, but they have heirs and successors: 'I know that the fathers have left sons of noble blood to take their place though I cannot tell what standards and qualities they may have.'[4] These sons, young as they are and surrounded by difficulties, must above all learn to preserve their *mores*, their *virtus*. The past eighty years yield the great lesson of moral discipline for all who hold office and bear social responsibility.

This last *aperçu* of Carolingian glory was preceded by Hincmar's most significant piece of writing, both in his own eyes and for those who wish to see what he made of the past: his *Vita Remigii*. We must go back a little. In 845 Hincmar had left one patron for another, St. Denis for St. Remigius. He took with him some at least of the Dionysian compositions for which Hilduin had been responsible.

---

[1] Ibid.
[2] Letter 20 (of 881), *PL* 126, col. 120.
[3] Ed. Krauze, ch. 14, p. 14.
[4] Ibid., ch. 37, p. 25.

They were not without effect on what he himself was later to compose.[1] Perhaps more important was his knowledge of what had been made of St. Denis in a few years. A Parisian saint had emerged as, an admittedly composite, national patron: the apostle of Gaul, a martyr, and the author of a body of philosophy; a patron, moreover, whose shrine near Paris had been lavishly endowed by Dagobert and subsequently honoured by Merovingians and Carolingians alike. No saintly confection was ever more potent, unless perhaps the Irish St. Brigid—whose Life Hincmar knew. But St. Remigius, to whom Hincmar now came, was not like that. He was a historical figure: son of aristocratic parents, bishop of Reims for some seventy years, a leader of the Gallo-Roman clergy who welcomed the first Merovingians, a respectable landowner who knew how to dispose of his property in a sensible will.[2] But his reputation after death was largely confined to his own locality. Gregory of Tours, in whose History the baptizer of Clovis first appears, had certainly read a Life of him which we no longer have,[3] and, a century or more later, there came another Life, attributed wrongly to Venantius Fortunatus. This second Life at least was at Reims for Hincmar's inspection and use.[4] It formed part of the

[1] See L. Levillain, 'Études', *BEC*, 82, (1921), pp. 91 ff.

[2] The will appears in Hincmar's *Vita Remigii*, ch. 32 (ed. Krusch, *MGH SRM*, iii (1896), pp. 336–40). See A. H. M. Jones, P. Grierson, and J. A. Crook, 'The authenticity of the Testamentum S. Remigii', *Révue belge*, 35, ii (1957), pp. 356–73. The will is good incidental evidence that Clovis was baptized at Reims. It was personally inspected by Charles the Bald (Flodoard, *Hist. Rem. Eccl.*, ch. 4, *MGH SS*, 13, p. 477, who also provides a longer version of the will, ibid., ch. 19, pp. 428–34).

[3] *Hist. Libri*, ii, 31, *MGH SRM*, i, 1, p. 77.

[4] What Hincmar says of this Life is worth notice as an instance of his care with documents: 'This is what I heard old men say who had been the contemporaries of Archbishop Tilpin [of Reims, 753–9] ... Their seniors told them that they had seen a large book, written in an antique hand, which related the history of the birth, life, miracles and death of our most holy patron, St. Remigius. This book later perished in the following circumstances. Egidius, fourth successor of Remigius, asked the celebrated poet Fortunatus ... to excerpt certain miracles that people could understand and enjoy ... This was done, and the reader is thus formally appraised of its origin: *studeamus pauca disserere, plurima praeterire*. It happened that this résumé, because of its brevity

material collected over the years by the clergy of Reims for the liturgical cult of Remigius; in fact, it was the Legend attached to the Office, correct in nine lessons.[1] Along with this Life went the cathedral's *Liber Responsalis* (on which Gottschalk commented rather sourly without impugning its authenticity)[2] and the preface for the Gallican mass of St. Remigius, discontinued in favour of the Roman rite by Hincmar's time. A fragment of the preface survives.[3] MS 1395 of the Bibliothèque de la ville de Reims, of the ninth century, is a hagiographical collection which contains Gregory of Tours on St. Remigius, the so-called Fortunatus Life, and the preface to the mass. This collection, apart from the Office itself, suggests that someone was interested in St. Remigius's history. Baix wondered whether it was compiled by or for Hincmar. In short, the new archbishop, fresh from Saint-Denis, found enough writing on his new patron to cause him to meditate on the possibilities of what was still a local cult. Above all, he would have learnt from the liturgy that Remigius had not only baptized Clovis but had used for the purpose a heaven-sent ampulla of chrism.[4] Later, at the coronation and unction of Charles the Bald at Metz, Hincmar was to use a phrase from the Office—'coelitus sumpto chrismate'—which he

---

and popular nature, enjoyed rapid dissemination, whereas the original—too long and bulky—was increasingly neglected. And so to the troubles of Charles Martel's time . . . when the few priests remaining at Reims made ends meet by trading in a small way, frequently wrapping up the money they took in pages torn from books. Thus the book of St. Remigius, already rotted by damp and gnawed by mice, lost the greater part of its remaining pages. It has been hard work to find a few of the dispersed pages, here and there.' (*MGH SRM*, iii. pp. 250 ff.) Obviously what remained was of very limited use to Hincmar.

[1] See the important study of F. Baix, 'Les Sources liturgiques de la Vita Remigii de Hincmar', *Miscellanea Historica in honorem Alberti de Meyer* Louvain, Brussels, 1946), i. p. 220.

[2] Ibid., pp. 213, 218–19.

[3] Ibid., pp. 222–6.

[4] Marc Bloch, *Les rois thaumaturges* (Strasbourg, Paris, 1924), pp. 224–9, suspected something of this before Baix. See also the conjectures, not in themselves implausible, of Sir Francis Oppenheimer, *The legend of the Ste. Ampoule* (London, 1953), on the survival of an ampulla at Reims.

recorded in the Annals of St. Bertin.[1] Over his years as archbishop Hincmar seems to have been collecting material for a *Vita Remigii*. He did not need to invent what he called his *pitaciolae*[2] and *schedulae*.[3] But he did need to consult others, as for instance Ado of Vienne,[4] and a certain Lantard who was asked for further information beyond what was already available in ancient writings at Reims.[5] As so often, Hincmar was slow and thorough in accumulating evidence. If, as seems probable, he quite soon conceived the idea of writing an authoritative *Vita Remigii*, he took a long time to bring it to completion.

One stage in the promotion of St. Remigius was the translation of his relics to a new crypt. This happened in the king's presence in 852.[6] Hincmar's intention seems to have been to add solemnity to the protective power of his miracle-working patron, who alone could shield the properties of his Church from devastation and alienation. His aim was practical, as always. He did not hope to substitute St. Remigius for St. Denis or St. Martin as royal patron.[7] For any sign that St. Remigius had a bigger role in Hincmar's eyes we have to wait for the unction of Charles the Bald in 869. Yet even then the publication of the *Vita Remigii* was delayed for a further eight or nine years.

Old men do not necessarily expect to die, but Hincmar was conscious of his age and of the slipping away of power. It must therefore be asked why the *Vita Remigii* was finished only in 877 or 8, when he had less than four years of life left to him. It was perhaps less a matter of being finished than of the author feeling that circumstances compelled him to publish. The *Vita* appears at a time when Charles the Bald had turned from him to find support in a younger

---

[1] *Ann. Bert.*, s.a. 869, pp. 162–3; also *MGH Capit.*, ii, 2, p. 340.

[2] *MGH SRM*, iii. p. 253.

[3] Ibid.

[4] Flodoard, *Hist. Rem.*, 3, ch. 21, p. 515.

[5] Ibid., ch. 28, p. 552.

[6] Ibid., ch. 9, pp. 482 ff. The king was also present at the dedication of the new cathedral in 862.

[7] See his letter of 857–8 to the king, *MGH Epist. Karo. Aevi*, vi, i, 1, 108,

metropolitan, Ansegisus of Sens, who shared his master's enthusiasm for the imperial crown and saw nothing to fear in papal pretensions in Francia.[1] The Synod of Ponthion marks the turning-point.[2] It must be allowed that Reims had some justification in fighting for her position. The challenge came not only from Rome but from Sens, whose rivalry with Reims begins with Ansegisus,[3] and still nearer home from the claims to greater antiquity of the prestigious suffragan see of Laon.[4] Moreover, the building-up of the claims of Saint-Denis proceeded smoothly through the ninth century. A new version of the *Miracula* was produced in 876–7.[5] It is likely enough that in the 870s St. Denis and St. Martin were more generally appreciated than was St. Remigius.[6] A few months after Ponthion Charles himself was dead and Carolingian strength shattered. The *Vita* places St. Remigius in a position of new strength. It stakes out his historical claims to defend his own. It aims to save Reims from disorder, from Viking attack, from the disruptions caused by seizure of lands and from challenges to metropolitical authority such as it had recently faced from its suffragans.[7]

The *Vita Remigii* is an elaborate composition; few saints' Lives are more so. Its framework is broadly liturgical. We still lack a satisfactory edition, Krusch[8] having missed much, including the

---

pp. 52–5. Charles' favours to and interest in Saint-Denis, of which he became lay-abbot, extended throughout his reign. (*Ann. Bert.*, s.a. 867 (p. 135), s.a. 869 (pp. 152, 167), s.a. 876 (p. 200), s.a. 877 (p. 211), s.a. 878 (p. 228) are examples.)

[1] Hincmar's idiosyncratic views on the special primatial position of Reims as derived from St. Remigius are explained in letters to Pope Leo IV (*MGH Epist. Karo. Aevi*, vi, i, 1, 62, p. 34; Flodoard *Hist. Rem.*, 3, ch. 10, p. 483) and to Pope Nicholas I (ibid., 169, p. 158; ibid., 3, chs 12–14).

[2] *MGH Capit.*, ii, 2, 279, pp. 348–53; *Ann. Bert.*, s.a. 876, p. 201.

[3] See Schramm, *König von Frankreich*, p. 41.

[4] See Devisse, pp. 1006, 1044.

[5] See Levillain, 'Études', *BEC*, 82, p. 60.

[6] See Devisse, p. 1005.

[7] I hesitate to accept the more metaphysical motives for the composition of Life enumerated by Devisse, p. 1004.

[8] *MGH SRM*, iii, pp. 239–341.

significance of Hincmar's directions in his text; but with the help of
M. Devisse[1] we can now see how Hincmar meant the Life to be
used. We need not concern ourselves with his numerous models,[2]
none of which he follows at all closely; and of his sources for St.
Remigius enough has been said. He adopted a traditional pattern
for his hero's career, from birth through virtues and miracles of a
foretelling kind to a career of public service much like that of any
Gallo-Roman aristocrat-bishop of the fifth century,[3] and so to his
death, subsequent miracles and translation. It thus harks back to a
firm past. It was the long, fruitful life of a saintly prelate and not
simply a setting for the conversion and baptism of a king. Because
he was the apostle of the Franks he was the more powerful in
Reims. M. Devisse believes that it is not the re-creation of a career
but a work of edification for a province and a kingdom.[4] If it were
indeed edification for a kingdom it was not immediately successful;
if for a province, it was. Let Hincmar speak for himself. He echoes
the words of Bede, himself echoing Jerome,[5] on the true law of
history: 'vera est lex hystoriae simpliciter ea que fama vulgante
colligitur ad instructionem posteritatis litteris commendare'.[6] Like
Bede, Hincmar's aim is *instructio*; but unlike Bede he does not
address a king or a people but a local saint and his faithful men:
'dilectis fratribus ac comministris nostris, huius sanctae Remensis
aecclesiae filiis'.[7] His *historia* is a saint's Life, not an ecclesiastical
history of a people; and because it is a saint's Life, and therefore
edificatory in a special sense, his critical principles are not Bede's.

---

[1] Who is preparing a new edition.

[2] Discussed by Devisse, pp. 1011 ff.

[3] His career is summarized by K. F. Stroheker, *Der senatorische Adel im
spätantiken Gallien* (Tübingen, 1948), pp. 207–8, and fits in comfortably with
those careers discussed by M. Heinzelmann, *Bischofsherrschaft in Gallien*
(Munich, 1976).

[4] op. cit., pp. 233–54, 1018.

[5] *Bede's Ecclesiastical History of the English People*, ed. B. Colgrave and
R. A. B. Mynors (Oxford, 1969), *praefatio*, p. 6; Jerome, *PL* 23, cols 187–8.

[6] *Vita Rem.*, p. 253.

[7] Ibid., p. 250.

But the *Vita* is none the less the re-creation of a career that had been continuously active from the fifth to the ninth century.

Liturgical? Certainly; but in no simple fashion. The author provides a reader's guide to explain his intentions.[1] The Life is not to be read right through by all. Different parts are designed for different occasions, and are so marked by him. Some of the readings are straightforward *lectiones* or popular instruction through the liturgy, others are pastoral meditations for clergy, and others again are disquisitions on vital topics for the pondering of the learned. Prolixity cannot be avoided, even though Hincmar observes a career-structure:[2] namely, Remigius' life before the arrival of the Franks—his predestination, his dawning sense of mission, his education, election, and early miracles, all as preparing him to deal with the pagan Franks without unduly troubling himself with the Gallo-Romans or Rome; then, his career as a Frankish bishop and the central feature of the conversion and baptism of Clovis; and finally, his career after death as the protector of his flock.

The account of the conversion and baptism of Clovis is marked by Hincmar for general reading within the liturgy. All who hear or read it at Reims will be edified by the incident of the chrism brought down from heaven for the king's baptism by a dove in an ampulla[3] and, further, by the account of the king's victories that were the consequence.[4] The grip of Remigius's successors may thus be strengthened[5]—always supposing that kings were to make a habit of attending St. Remigius's mass in person. Similarly, Hincmar's detailed account of St. Remigius's disposal of the gifts and properties bestowed on Reims by Clovis might be taken as a warning to Carolingian poachers; but on the other hand is likelier to impress local gentry with their eyes on quite small Church properties. Remigius defends all his properties, great and small, and does so

---

[1] Ibid., pp. 258–9.
[2] As Devisse shows, pp. 1037 ff.
[3] *Vita Rem.*, p. 297.
[4] e.g. ibid., pp. 310–11.
[5] As Devisse argues, p. 1044.

miraculously when need arises. *Exempla* of menace and retribution are not spared. The inhabitants of the village of Sault refused to obey the saint's order: the men were forthwith stricken with gout and the women with goitre—and their children had inherited the curse to the present day.[1] Pippin III was chastised in his sleep for seizing the property of Anizy from the suffragan see of Laon.[2] Louis the German was defeated in 858 because he had installed himself in a villa of Reims—'in Luliaco mansit'—before giving battle.[3] There is much more to the same effect. If all this were to worry a Carolingian, how much more would it impress the regular attendants at the celebration of the saint?

St. Remigius prepares for death and makes his will. Hincmar reflects upon his great age and saintly character: 'triumphator in gentibus egregius, confessor offitio, martyr quoque studio'[4] and so on. Does Hincmar see himself in the dying bishop, and a Carolingian in Clovis?[5] It may be so. But if it is so, he is still providing the faithful of Reims with what is essentially a local saint strengthened in his dealings with local problems by his exceptional connection with national affairs. Always Remigius defends his own. The last words Hincmar ever wrote, the final entry in the St. Bertin Annals for 882, record the delivery of Reims from the Vikings: 'sed civitatem, quam nec murus nec humana manus defendit, Dei potentia et sanctorum merita nec illam ingrederentur defenderunt'[6] *Sanctorum*: St. Remigius had companions in the protection of Reims. In particular he interceded with the Virgin for his Church and its servants.[7] The more that is known of the author of the *Vita Remigii*, the more careful he appears in his search for evidence, the more scrupulous in recording it. The historical content of the *Vita* is unusually large.

[1] *Vita Rem.*, pp. 315–16.
[2] Ibid., pp. 321–2.
[3] Ibid., p. 322.
[4] Ibid., p. 318.
[5] As conjectured by Devisse, p. 1052.
[6] *Ann. Bert.*, p. 250.
[7] For Hincmar's veneration of the Virgin and her cult at Reims see Flodoard, *Hist. Rem.*, 3, chs 5–6, pp. 478–80.

This does not make it other than a saint's Life. But, unlike St. Denis, St. Remigius is grounded in fact. He is and remains a Gallo-Roman bishop about whom much was known and round whom stories of venerable age had gathered. To such beginnings Hincmar recalls his readers and hearers. The Franks and St. Remigius came together; their prosperity had been linked over the centuries. Whatever might be true about St. Denis and the conversion of the Gauls, there was a fresh start with Remigius in the fifth century. A century after Hincmar's death, Flodoard copied the inscription on his tomb:

> Nomine non merito, praesul Hincmarus, ab antro
> Te, lector, tituli, quaeso, memento mei.
> Quem grege pastorem proprio Dyonisius olim
> Remorum populis, ut petiere, dedit.[1]

The two phases of his life, the Dionysian and the Remegian, come together without any sense of incongruity or mutual challenge in the mind of Flodoard. They were equally contributions from the past of Hincmar's career. In a long justificatory treatise to his nephew of Laon, the exasperated Hincmar writes: 'Si ergo, frater, immemor beneficiorum a me tibi impensorum oblitus, adversum me rebellare non times, time tamen rebellare adversus beatum Remigium.'[2] The saint matters most in the end, not so much because of any alleged claim to a special apostolic position in his own day[3] as because of his sanctity. This it was that had left traces through history. Conformist in his view of the historical process, Hincmar accepts the providential message of the past and uses what he finds there in an exemplary way. There are no surprises. With the Franks, however, his mind enters the active past that conditions the world he lives in: there had been nearly four centuries of it. Over it broods the patronage of holy men, intercessors with heaven for the Frankish people. We may find it hard to imagine what it

---

[1] *PL* 135, cols 261–2.
[2] *PL* 126, col. 337.
[3] The import of Hincmar's fabricated letter from Pope Hormisdas to St. Remigius is ably discussed by Devisse, pp. 651 ff.

was like to live as a member of a venerable community under the protection of one's own saint, the records of whose doings stretched back to the beginnings. One was indeed his man, now and in eternity. But, once imagined, it will tell one more about Archbishop Hincmar and the Carolingian reformation than any number of administrative documents.

William of Poitiers and his History of William the Conqueror

R. H. C. DAVIS

THE WORK

AS we have it, the *History of William the Conqueror* by William of Poitiers is incomplete. The manuscript which André Duchesne used for his edition in 1619 has been lost, but he stated that it was already lacking at both the beginning and the end.[1] No other manuscript has yet been found, and consequently all subsequent editions have been based on Duchesne's printed text.[2] What we have, therefore, is a torso; it has no account of William's parentage, birth, or accession, but starts in mid-sentence with an account of English affairs on the death of King Cnut (1035); and it breaks off in mid-sentence among the events of 1067–8, though there are good reasons for thinking that it originally extended to 1071–2.[3] None the less it is an essential source for the Conqueror's career.

The surviving text is impressive. It is impossible to read it without appreciating that its author was a classical scholar and stylist of distinction, intent on producing a work of great literature. Though

---

[1] André Duchesne, *Historiae Normannorum scriptores antiqui* (Paris, 1619), pp. 178–213. For a discussion of the manuscript, see below pp. 98–100.

[2] By Francis Maseres (London, 1783 and 1807), J. A. Giles (London, 1845), and J. P. Migne in *PL*, 149 (Paris, 1853). The standard edition is Raymonde Foreville, *Guillaume de Poitiers: Histoire de Guillaume le Conquérant* (Paris, 1952), henceforth cited as WP, which has a full scholarly apparatus and a French translation. Like Duchesne she divides the text into two 'books', but chooses a different (and better) point of division. This is important, since it means that references to the *chapters* of Book II are different in the various editions. For this reason the references in this paper are to the *pages* in WP.

[3] For the lost beginning, see Appendix, pp. 98–100.

Orderic stated that his style was modelled on that of Sallust, WP himself demonstrates that he was capable of imitating the style of quite a number of ancient authors, choosing for each of his themes the model which seemed most suitable, and often interrupting his narrative for a passage of pure rhetoric. Sometimes it even happens that the rhetorical interludes are piled on top of each other, or strung together like a series of exercises on given themes—on obedience in the manner of Cicero, on victory in the manner of Caesar or Sallust, or on the sailing of a fleet in the manner of Virgil. One of his pieces, on the temperance and prudence of William's government, pleased him so much that he used it twice over.[1] He was not a plagiarist, nor was he merely a purveyor of apt quotations. He thought himself into the relevant style and used it boldly; in his comparison between the invasions of Julius Caesar and William the Conqueror, which naturally favours the latter, he moves about Caesar's *Gallic Wars* with the ease of a master, using its facts solely as they are relevant to his purpose.

This classical view is important and sets the tone of the whole work. Some commentators have emphasized that WP's prime aim was to flatter the Conqueror, but this is only half the truth; he was also flattering himself, demonstrating to his readers that he was a real man of letters, capable of extolling a monarch who could be likened to the heroes of old. The conquest of England was by any standard a major event—a whole country conquered as the result of one day's battle—and it merited not just a history but a panegyric. Just as Einhard had modelled his *Life of Charlemagne* on the lives of earlier emperors, as written by Suetonius, so WP also sought classical models for the history of a conquest. Naturally his thoughts turned to the Trojan War as the most famous of sea-borne invasions, but he made considerable use also of Caesar's *Gallic* and *Civil Wars*, Sallust's *Conspiracy of Catiline*, Lucan's *Pharsalia*, Statius's *Thebaid* and Virgil's *Aeneid*. We can only guess the extent to which these models may have taken hold of his

[1] WP, pp. 152 and 262.

imagination. It may be, and probably was, that the Conqueror's fleet was becalmed at Saint Valèry as Agamemnon's had been at Aulis, and that in each case a divinity had to be placated.[1] But had there also been shipwrecks, and had the Conqueror attempted, like Xerxes, to conceal the extent of the disaster by burying the dead secretly?[2] When we are told that the Conqueror, realizing that his ship had lost contact with the rest of his fleet, subdued the crew's alarm by settling down to a banquet, we cannot help wondering whether WP was not too conscious that that was what Aeneas had done when he was shipwrecked on the coast of Africa.[3] Similarly when the Conqueror is made to refuse Harold's mother permission to bury her son, even though she offered his weight in gold, one cannot help feeling that the reality was WP's memory of Achilles and the body of Hector.[4]

If the literary *topos* offers one caution against accepting everything in WP as historically true, another is offered by the formal structure of the work. It is no mere chronicle relating events in the order in which they happened. It collects information about particular topics, so that here we have rebellions, there Angevin wars, and in yet another place all the virtues of the Norman Church. It is a sensible arrangement, but there is no denying that it endows the narrative with a plot, particularly since the early part is punctuated with 'advance notices' of English affairs. The surviving text opens with an account of England at the death of Cnut (pp. 2–12), and reverts to England for the accession of Edward the Confessor (pp. 28–32),

[1] WP, p. 160. The story of Troy was known in various Latin versions, and WP specifically refers to Agamemnon in this context (WP, p. 162) and again later (WP, p. 208). Most of these classical allusions were noted by E. A. Freeman in his *History of the Norman Conquest* (2nd ed., Oxford, 1875), iii. pp. 390, 394, 397, 400, 407, 437, 439, 473, 476, 483, 484, 491, 493, 498, 512, etc., though it is often hard to tell whether he regarded them as literary *topoi* or as examples of history repeating itself.

[2] WP, p. 160, Herodotus, vii. 146.

[3] WP, p. 16 and *Aeneid*, i. 195–222. As in many other cases, I owe the reference to Foreville's footnote. Aeneas's banquet was in fact on land, like that shown in the Bayeux Tapestry.

[4] *Iliad*, xxiii. 351–4.

Harold's embassy and oath to Duke William (pp. 100–4 and 114), and his final seizure of the English throne (p. 146), while the history of the conquest itself occupies most of the last half of the book. WP may have been composing a literary work worthy of the ancients, but he was also writing propaganda to show that the conquest of England was just and inevitable.

How much trust, then, can we put in his history? The question is difficult because there is very little means of controlling it from the English side, and such control as can be exercised depends on the other Norman sources, which are equally problematic. But we can start by attempting to fix the date at which WP was writing. It cannot have been earlier than 1071 because, according to Orderic Vitalis whose text of the work was fuller than ours, WP's narrative extended to the death of Earl Edwin in that year.[1] It also refers to the dedication of St. Stephen's abbey in Caen, which is now accepted as having taken place on 13 September 1077,[2] but it is possible that this reference is due to a late revision, since WP's panegyric of Hugh bishop of Lisieux suggests that he was still alive, though he died on 17 July 1077.[3] We cannot be very far out, however, if we date the completion of WP *c.* 1077.

The alternative Norman sources, if we exclude the controversial *Carmen de Hastingae proelio*,[4] are the Bayeux Tapestry (BT) and the

[1] Below, p. 85.

[2] Foreville (pp. xix and 128 n. 2) noted that Orderic had given this date for the dedication, but followed Lemarignier in thinking he was mistaken. Subsequently Lucien Musset has confirmed Orderic's date from the cartulary of St. Stephen's, Caen. (Lucien Musset, *Les Actes de Guillaume le Conquérant et de la reine Mathilde pour les abbayes caennaises* (Méms. de la Soc. des antiquaires de Normandie, xxxvii (1967), pp. 14–15, n. 15) and OV, ii. p. 148 n. 3.) It should perhaps be added that Foreville's attempt to date WP by reference to the career of Roussel de Bailleul in the Byzantine Empire (1073–4) has been invalidated by the criticism of Marguerite Mathieu in her edition of *Guillaume de Pouille: La Geste de Robert Guiscard* (Palermo, 1961), p. 339.

[3] WP, pp. 136–42.

[4] I have explained why I think the *Carmen de Hastingae Proelio* a twelfth-century composition, in *EHR*, xciii (1978), pp. 241–61. Catherine Morton and Hope Muntz, who edited the work (Oxford, 1972), consider it to have been composed before 11 May 1068 as a reliable narrative. Others, like Frank

Gesta Normannorum Ducum of William of Jumièges (WJ).[1] Of these the more difficult to date is the Bayeux Tapestry. Since it glorifies the part played by Bishop Odo of Bayeux, it is generally thought to have been made before his fall (1082) and perhaps also before the consecration of his new cathedral (1077), but Dr N. P. Brooks[2] has recently pointed out that later dates are possible, even if they are less likely.

WJ extends to the first months of 1070. Louis Halphen considered the composition later than, and in some places an abbreviation of, WP, but most commentators have held the opposite view, believing that WP used, and enlarged upon, WJ. In support of this latter view I have argued elsewhere that WJ's treatment of Robert Curthose gives added weight to the view favoured by most scholars that it dates from 1070–1.[3]

Halphen's view, though originally based on a mistaken view of the lordship of Domfront, opened up a lengthy and fruitful controversy about the chronology of Duke William's campaigns between 1047 and 1054.[4] We need not rehearse the various arguments in detail, but it is important to realize that the root cause of

Barlow (in *Studies in International History presented to W. Norton Medlicott*, ed. K. Bourne and D. C. Watt (London, 1967), pp. 35–67, and L. J. Engels (in *Proceedings of the Battle Conference 1979*), consider it early but so full of poetic licence as to make its account of such major incidents as the death of Harold incredible.

[1] The editions cited are: *The Bayeux Tapestry*, ed. Sir Frank Stenton (London, 1957) and *Guillaume de Jumièges: Gesta Normannorum Ducum*, ed. Jean Marx (SHN, 1914).

[2] N. P. Brooks and the late H. E. Walker, 'The authority and interpretation of the Bayeux Tapestry', *Proceedings of the Battle Conference on Anglo-Norman Studies*, i (1978), pp. 1–34, particularly 9–10.

[3] Louis Halphen, *Le Comté d'Anjou au xi siècle* (Paris, 1906), pp. xii–xiii and 72 n. 4. See also his review of Marx's edition in *Revue historique*, cxxi (1916), pp. 317–20. Marx's reply is in *Mélanges d'histoire du moyen âge offerts à Ferdinand Lot* (Paris, 1925), pp. 543–8. I have outlined my own views in 'William of Jumièges, Robert Curthose and the Norman Succession', *EHR*, xcv (1980).

[4] Halphen, *Comté d'Anjou*, pp. 70–80; R. Latouche, *Histoire du Comté du Maine pendant les xe et xie siècles* (Paris, 1910), pp. 27–32; Henri Prentout, *Histoire de Guillaume le Conquérant—Le duc de Normandie* (*Méms. acad. nat. de*

WP's subject-matter and its order in WJ compared

WP (refs. to pages)		WJ (refs. to pages)
2–12	England 1035–40	120–1
12–20	Revolt of Guy of Brionne and Battle of Val-és-dunes (1047)	122–4
20–8	William's glory; Henry I's growing jealousy	
28–32	England: accession of Edward the Confessor (1042)	**122**
32–44	War against Anjou: campaign of Domfront and Alençon	124–7
44–50	William's marriage	127–8
50–64	Revolt of William of Arques	**119–20**
64–74	Henry I's invasion: battle of Mortemer (1054)	129–30
74–8	Angevin war: building of the castle of Ambrières	**127**
80–2	Invasion of Normandy and battle of Varaville	131–2
82–4	Death of Henry I (1060) and Geoffrey Martel (1060)	132
86–98	Submission of Le Mans and revolt of Geoffrey of Mayenne	**130–1**
100–6	Harold Godwinson's embassy to Normandy: oath of Bonneville	132–3
106–12	War against Brittany	
114	Harold's return	
114–46	Panegyric of Duke William, Normandy, the Norman Church, and the Duke's alliances	
146–242	Story of the conquest of England from the death of Edward the Confessor to William's coronation (1066)	133–6
242–62	William's return to Normandy Panegyrics of the Conqueror and of his government	137
262–70	Revolts in England (1067): Eustace of Boulogne and Copsi	138–40

Note: figures in heavy type show where the order of events in WJ is different from that in WP.

the controversy was that though WJ and WP narrate many of the same events, they place them in a different order. Since WJ's narrative reads like a series of annals and WP's is highly literary, it would be natural to assume that it was WP who had tampered with the true sequence of events. But this does not seem to have been the case. Modern scholars, in spite of their disagreements on other points, are unanimous in thinking that the main fault lies with WJ, since it is he who has misplaced the revolts of William of Arques and Geoffrey of Mayenne. It is hard to believe that WJ was abbreviating WP's material and reorganizing it in order to fit a theme, because it is impossible to see what that theme could have been. But there is no difficulty in supposing that WP had sufficient independent knowledge to correct WJ's chronology.

So far as information is concerned, WP and WJ have a great deal in common for the period before 1066, but if one reads them side by side to see which is deriving his knowledge from the other, one is constantly baffled by the way in which it is first one, then the other, who seems the better informed. Thus in his account of the rebellion of Guy of Burgundy, WP gives more facts than WJ, mentioning that Guy held the castle of Vernon in addition to Brionne, and that amongst his accomplices were Ranulf the vicomte of Bayeux and Hamo Dentatus.[1] But WJ is rather better than WP on the battles of Val-és-dunes[2] and Varaville,[3] in each case mentioning that the French King's approach was through the county of

---

Caen, viii (1936), pp. 136–52; J. D. Dhondt, 'Les Relations entre la France et la Normandie sous Henri I' (Normannia, xii (1939), pp. 465–86) and 'Henri I, l'empire et l'anjou' (Rev. belge, xxv (1946), pp. 87–109); finally, David C. Douglas, William the Conqueror (London, 1964), pp. 383–90, who is generally in agreement with Prentout, should be compared with Olivier Guillot, Le Comté d'Anjou et son entourage au xi siècle (Paris, 1972), i. pp. 69–79 and 82–6, who on many points makes a very effective counter-case.

[1] WP, p. 16, WJ, pp. 122–3.
[2] WP, pp. 14–18, WJ, pp. 123–4.
[3] WP, pp. 80–2, WJ, p. 131. It should be added, however that WP did appreciate that it was the tide which prevented Duke William from pursuing the defeated French. There may also be a verbal similarity in the use of alacriter superveniens, sub regis oculis by the two authors.

Exmes, and in each case making the course of the battle more intelligible, stating, for example, that the reason why half the French
army was caught on the wrong side of the ford at Varaville was that
the tide had risen. When it comes to the conquest of England the
two works diverge completely, WP being full and detailed while
WJ is perfunctory and (so far as he gives any details at all) at
variance with WP, considering that Harold fell in the *first* Norman
attack at Hastings, and that London did not surrender peacefully
but was captured after a skirmish in the main square.[1] But just as
one is concluding that the two works must have lost contact with
each other completely, one finds striking similarities in their
accounts of the revolt of Eustace of Boulogne at Dover (1067).[2]

. The verbal parallels between the two texts have been carefully
studied by Foreville.[3] She points out that they are confined to six
episodes, mostly in the early part of WP, and that, except in the
account of the English expedition of the athelings Edward and
Alfred, they are not particularly striking. She argues that if one
author was borrowing from the other, the borrower was probably
WP, since words and phrases which are grouped in WJ have been
tastefully dispersed through longer passages in WP. This is a fair
observation, but a similar result could also have been obtained if

[1] WJ, pp. 135, 136.

[2] WJ, p. 138, WP, p. 266. There are many verbal similarities in the two
passages, but while WJ latinizes Dover as *Dorobernia*, WP uses the more usual
Dovera. *Dorobernia* normally indicates Canterbury, but William of Malmesbury (*GR*, i. pp. 155, 279) and *Flor. Wig.*, i. p. 201 use it, like WJ, for Dover.
But elsewhere *GR*, i. p. 241, and Eadmer's *HN*, 7, use *Dovera* and *Dofris*.

[3] WP, pp. xxv–xxxv. The principal passages, which she discusses in detail,
are:
(i) The English expedition of the athelings Alfred and Edward (WP,
pp. 4–10; WJ, pp. 120–2).
(ii) The battle of Val-és-dunes (WP, pp. 14–18; WJ, pp. 122–4).
(iii) The building of the castle of Arques (WP, p. 54; WJ, p. 119).
(iv) The submission of Le Mans and Mayenne (WP, pp. 88–92, and 96–100;
WJ, pp. 130–1).
(v) The capture of Harold by Guy of Ponthieu (WP, p. 100; WJ, p. 132).
(vi) The revolt of Eustace of Boulogne at Dover (WP, pp. 264–8; WJ
p. 138).

both authors had been using a common source which is now lost.

Such a hypothesis was indeed propounded by Gustav Körting as long ago as 1875,[1] but he weakened his case by insisting that the lost source must have been a national epic (*Volkspoesie*), thus enabling Marx to reply that 'If there had been such a source, Orderic would have known it and cited it.'[2] In fact there is no reason why the lost source should have been a national epic, and it is clear that Orderic does not name all the sources which he used; he mentions those which he found particularly important, especially if they were by well-known writers, but he obviously thought that the general run of monastic annals and saints' lives could be taken for granted.[3]

It seems clear that WJ was using written sources of some sort. In his account of the capture of Alençon (1048 × 51), he says that the Conqueror 'ordered all the jokers [*illusores*] to have their hands and feet cut off in full view of all the inhabitants of Alençon',[4] but he does not explain who these 'jokers' were or what they had done wrong. To find the explanation we have to turn to Orderic's edition of WJ where he continues as follows: 'without delay 32 men were maimed at his command, for they had beaten on pells and hides to insult the duke, disrespectfully calling him a tanner because his mother's relatives were tanners [*polinctores*]'.[5] Since WJ was dedicating his history to the Conqueror, it is understandable that he should have censored remarks about his illegitimate birth, but it is hard to see why he had included even part of the story, unless he had begun copying it before he realized how unsuitable was its end. For Orderic, writing in the early years of the twelfth century, the joke was no longer dangerous. But how had he known it?

It is clear that WP also was following some earlier work or

---

[1] Gustav Körting, *Willhelms von Poitiers Gesta Guillelmi Ducis Normannorum et Regis Anglorum: Ein Beitrag zur anglo-normannischen Historiographie* (Separatabdrück aus dem Programm der Kreuzschule zu Dresden vom Jahre 1875) (Dresden, 1875).

[2] WJ, pp. xvii–xviii.

[3] Cf. Chibnall in OV, ii. p. xxii.

[4] WJ, p. 126.

[5] WJ, p. 171.

works. In one of his references to Arques he refers to 'the whole part of Normandy next to it which is situated on this side of the River Seine [*citra flumen Sequanam*]',[1] though one would have expected him to describe it as 'on the other side' (*ultra*) of the river, since he lived to the south of it and Arques was a long way north of it. In his account of the accession of Edward the Confessor he seems to follow two different sources. At first he implies what WJ explicitly states, that Harthacnut, being a son of Emma's facilitated his half-brother's succession by inviting him back to England to reside at his court.[2] But when it comes to Harthacnut's death, WP states that Edward was not in England but in Normandy, that it was because of representations by the Duke of Normandy that he was elected King, and that when he did cross the channel he was provided with a Norman escort.[3] The first story suggests that the Norman claim to England would stem from the marriage of Emma, daughter of Duke Richard I, to Kings Ethelred and Cnut; the second that it would stem simply from military might; and it looks as if, in constructing his narrative, WP had borrowed from two sources, one of which had also been used by WJ, and the other not.

As they approach the conquest of England, the narratives of WJ and WP become much less similar, and the comparison which has to be made is between WP and the Bayeux Tapestry. For example, WJ's account of Duke Harold's visit to Normandy is very brief; it says that Harold was sent to Normandy by Edward the Confessor, that he was blown on to the coast of Ponthieu and imprisoned by Count Guy, and that he was eventually rescued by Duke William, to whom he did 'fealty concerning the Kingdom', and by whom he was rewarded before returning to England.[4] BT and WP enlarge

---

[1] WP, p. 52. It is true that Nithard (*Histoire des fils de Louis le Pieux*, ed. Ph. Lauer, Paris, 1926, pp. 18, 44) uses *citra* to indicate 'the other side of', but WP's own use of it is both consistent and correct (e.g. WP, pp. 82, 216, 262).

[2] WP, p. 12, WJ, p. 122. This is also the story given in *The Anglo-Saxon Chronicle*, C and D, s.a. 1041, and in *Encomium Emmae Reginae*, ed. Alistair Campbell (Camden 3rd series, lxxii, 1949), p. 52.

[3] WP, pp. 28–30.

[4] WJ, pp. 132–3.

the story considerably. First, on a point of detail, they both name the place where Harold's oath was taken, but whereas BT says it was Bayeux, WP says it was Bonneville.[1] Secondly they both add that Harold accompanied Duke William on an expedition against Brittany, though once again the details are significantly different. BT shows that when the army was passing Mont-Saint-Michel, Harold rescued two men from the quicksands, dragging one of them by the hand while he carried the other on his back.[2] It then shows how Duke Conan was attacked in Dol but escaped from the castle by sliding down a rope, after which the Normans advanced past Rennes to Dinant, which surrendered to them.[3] It may be unimportant that WP tells nothing of the march past Mont-Saint-Michel or the incident of the quicksands, but when it comes to Dol he is quite specific that Conan was not inside the castle but besieging it. The castle was held, he says, by an ally of Duke William's called Ruallus, and when William approached, Conan raised the siege and retreated. He is also specific in stating that William did not advance beyond Dol because of the unknown and inhospitable country, and because he learnt that Geoffrey of Anjou had joined forces with Conan. He stayed near Dol in order to confront his enemies, but this upset Ruallus because Duke William, though his ally, was living off his land. William therefore promised compensation, forbad further foraging, and awaited battle against Conan and Geoffrey, though in the event they did not dare to confront him.[4]

A further difference of detail, this time about the battle of Hastings may have some bearing on the dates of the two works, for in the Tapestry Eustace of Boulogne is shown as something of a hero and in WP as rather a coward.[5] The reason for WP's unfavourable

[1] BT, pls 28–9; WP, pp. 102–4.
[2] BT, pl. 22.
[3] BT, pls 23–6. In an interesting passage Brooks and Walker (*op. cit.*, p. 3) claim that the Tapestry's inscription, *Venerunt ad Dol et Conan fuga vertit*, is correct but has been misunderstood by the artist. None the less, the continuation of the inscription, telling how the duke marched past Rennes to Dinant, which surrendered to him, is unambiguously in opposition to WP's account.
[4] WP, pp. 110–12.
[5] BT, pls 68–9; WP, pp. 202–4.

view is almost certainly connected with Eustace's revolt against King William in 1067, as a result of which Eustace was condemned to forfeit his fiefs.[1] WP adds that Eustace was subsequently restored to favour (as is confirmed by the Domesday Survey), but his tone suggests that this was only recently, since his misdeeds were still fresh in the memory. In this case the Bayeux Tapestry, unless it was completed in the first months of 1067, would have to be later than WP's account of *c*. 1077.

The real difficulty, however, is that neither BT nor WP is wholly convincing. BT, which was probably made for Bayeux Cathedral, places Harold's oath at Bayeux, while WP, who was an archdeacon of Lisieux and a native of Préaux, places it at Bonneville, the ducal palace nearest to him. BT's description of Harold's rescue of two men from the quicksands looks like a piece of Herculean folklore, while Conan's escape down a rope from the castle at Dol suggests a standard medieval joke which was subsequently to be repeated, for example, with regard to the *funambuli* or 'rope-trick men' who escaped from the siege of Antioch.[2] WP, on the other hand, has (as befits a Norman from Poitiers) a fixation about Geoffrey of Anjou as the chief enemy of Duke William, while his account of the Duke's measures to protect the crops of his allies is surely a classical *topos*. As for his story of Conan announcing the precise day of his invasion, it is one of the commonplaces of chivalric literature, which WP himself had already employed twice with regard to Duke William in his wars against Anjou.[3]

Fabulous stories are by no means uncommon in WP. Some of them are little more than the literary conventions of the panegyric, as when Duke William with four companions is said to have routed 15, 300, or 500 of Count Thibaud's cavalry, or with a group of 50 knights to have defeated an Angevin force of 300 cavalry and

---

[1] WP, pp. 266–8.

[2] OV, v. p. 98.

[3] WP, p. 108, cf. pp. 40 and 74–6. But Eric John in 'Edward the Confessor and the Norman succession', *EHR*, xciv (1979), p. 260 n. 2, is disposed to accept WP more literally.

700 infantry.[1] These events were supposed to have occurred some twenty-five years before. But others which seem equally legendary or folkloric concern the conquest of England and could only have had ten or eleven years to develop before WP wrote them down. They include the banquet at sea which, as we have already remarked, may have been inspired by the *Aeneid*; the story of Duke William carrying fitz Osbern's cuirass when they both returned on foot from an exhausting reconnoitre;[2] William putting his armour on back to front;[3] and probably the story of Harold's burial.[4]

Raymonde Foreville was rightly struck by the fact that such fabulous tales could have been told so soon after the actual conquest. Considering that there could not have been sufficient time for popular imagination to work up a 'spontaneous collective poetry', she argued that the epic legends could not have contributed to WP, but on the contrary must have been derived from him. 'Born in court chapels and addressed to an educated world ... the *Gesta Guillelmi* show that propaganda organized by clerks round recent events was able to give birth to an epic legend.'[5] Expressed in this way, Foreville's view has not won general favour. Quite apart from a general reluctance to believe that the medieval epics originated in Latin prose, it has been pointed out that the circulation of WP was extremely limited, and that there is nothing to suggest it was sufficiently well known to inspire a popular literature. Foreville was unwilling to believe that popular imagination could create new legends within ten years of the historical event to which they referred, but the truth of the matter is surely that the legends were not new, but old ones adapted to new circumstances. WP would have accepted them as cheerfully as he accepted the legends of classical

---

[1] WP, pp. 24–6, 36.

[2] WP, p. 168.

[3] WP, p. 182. Cf. 'le bon roi Dagobert portait ses pantalons à l'envers'.

[4] WP, p. 204.

[5] Raymonde Foreville, 'Aux Origines de la légende épique: les *Gesta Guillelmi ducis Normannorum et Regis Anglorum* de Guillaume de Poitiers', *Moyen Age*, 56 (1950), pp. 195–219 (esp. 218). It should be added, however, that she then believed that WP was writing in 1073–4 rather than *c.* 1077.

antiquity, and used them in a very similar way, as a natural part of his literary apparatus.[1]

For this reason any editor of WP has to be an expert not only on the classics but also on the vernacular literature of the period, so as to identify the *topoi* and the stock-in-trade of contemporary poets. In this respect Kurt-Ulrich Jäschke has performed a useful service in his analysis of the burial of Harold and accession of William the Conqueror.[2] But the question remains whether men acted as they did because they modelled their lives on the legends which they had learnt in infancy, or whether an author asserted that they had behaved in a particular way because that was what his literary models demanded.

THE AUTHOR

In his *Ecclesiastical History* Orderic Vitalis has three passages bearing on the career of WP, the first two probably written in 1114–15 and the third in 1125:

(i) William of Poitiers, an archdeacon of Lisieux, who has published a book wonderfully polished in style and mature in judgement. He was for many years the King's chaplain, and he set out to describe authentically, in detail, the events which he had seen with his own eyes, and in which he had taken part, although he was unable to continue the book to the King's death because he was prevented by unfavourable circumstances (*adversis casibus impeditus*)[3]

---

[1] It is interesting to see which of WP's stories reappear in Wace and which in Benoît. Neither has the banquet at sea or Duke William carrying fitz Osbern's cuirass. Wace (iii. 7500–7520) has William putting on his armour back to front, but the story is not in Benoît. On the other hand Benoît has William striking Eustace of Boulogne (396949 ff.) and the same Eustace's revolt (40449–40558). The fact that Benoît places Harold's oath at Bonneville, while Wace places it at Bayeux (of which he was a canon), suggests that Benoît must have known WP, because we know of no other source from which he could of got this information. See *Le Roman de Rou de Wace*, ed. A. J. Holden (3 vols, Soc. des anciens textes de France, Paris, 1970–3); and *Chronique des ducs de Normandie par Benoît*, ed. C. Fahlin (3 vols, Uppsala, 1951–67).

[2] Kurt-Ulrich Jäschke, *Willhelm der Eroberer; sein doppelter Herrschaftsantritt im Jahre 1066* (Vorträge und Forschunger, Sonderband 24) (Sigmaringen, 1977).

[3] OV, ii. p. 184.

(ii)   William of Poitiers has brought his history up to this point [1071], eloquently describing the deeds of King William in a clever imitation of the style of Sallust. He was by birth a Norman from the village of Préaux where he had a sister who was the superior of the nuns in the monastery of St. Léger. He was called 'of Poitiers' because he had drunk deeply of the fountain of philosophy at Poitiers. When he came back to his own people he was distinguished by being more learned than all his friends and neighbours, and in ecclesiastical affairs he helped bishops Hugh [1049–77] and Gilbert [1077–1101] in the office of archdeacon. Before he became a cleric he lived a rough life in the affairs of war and put on knightly arms to fight for his earthly prince, so that he was all the better able to describe the battles he had seen, through having himself some experience of the dire perils of war. In his old age he gave himself up to silence and prayer, and spent more time composing prose and poetry than in dicosurse. He published many subtly linked verses intended for declamation, and was so free from jealousy that he invited his juniors to criticize and improve them.[1]

(iii)   The books of William called Calculus of Jumièges and William of Poitiers archdeacon of Lisieux, who carefully recorded the deeds of the Normans and, after William became King of England, dedicated (*praesentauerunt*) their books to him to gain his favour.[2]

In these accounts there are three datable points. First, WP himself remarks that he was away in Poitiers (*dum Pictavis exularem*) around the time of the siege of Mouliherne, the date of which, though much disputed, must have been somewhere between 1048 and 1051.[3] Second, WP's history extended, according to Orderic, to 1071. And third, WP must have been an archdeacon both before and after 1077, the year in which Bishop Hugh died and Gilbert Maminot was consecrated. In another passage Orderic gives a list of the dignitaries of Lisieux Cathedral at about this same time, naming William of Glanville dean and archdeacon; Richard of Angerville and William of Poitiers, archdeacons; Geoffrey of Triqueville, treasurer; Turgis, precentor and Ralph his son.[4]

[1] OV, ii. p. 258.
[2] OV, ii. p. 78.
[3] WP, p. 22. For the date of the siege of Mouliherne, see p. 75 n. 3 above. Halphen proposed 1048, Guillot 1049, Prentout and Douglas 1051.
[4] OV, iii. pp. 20–1. Geoffrey de Triqueville was the son of William de Triqueville, and while still only a canon of Lisieux was a benefactor of the abbey of Grestain (ex. inf. Dr David R. Bates).

If Orderic is right in saying that WP served as a knight before he became a clerk, we would assume that his military career had been completed before he began his studies at Poitiers, (i.e. before 1048 × 51). At such an early date it is hardly surprising that we cannot trace him, particularly since we do not know his family name; he cannot have been called 'of Poitiers' before he resided there. All that we know of his birthplace, Préaux, is that it contained two abbeys, Saint-Pierre for monks and Saint-Léger for nuns, the one refounded (c. 1034), and the other founded (c. 1040) by Humphrey de Vieilles, the ancestor of the Beaumonts.[1] WP shows himself well-informed about this family, stating that Roger de Beaumont 'son of the illustrious Humphrey', assisted the Duchess Matilda in governing Normandy during her husband's absence for the invasion in which (as WP states twice over) Roger's son, Robert, played a prominent part.[2] It is plausible, therefore, to believe that WP's father could have been a tenant of the Beaumonts; and if his sister was Emma the first abbess of Saint-Léger, it is possible that his family also had assisted in the foundation of that house.[3] But unfortunately we have no solid information.

WP's studies at Poitiers, which must have lasted four or five years at least,[4] included (as we have seen) some date between 1048 and 1051. It may be presumed that he studied at the school of Saint-Hilaire-le-Grand, [5]which had been made famous under the direction

---

[1] For the nunnery of Saint-Léger (now is the commune of Saint-Michel-des-Préaux) and theabbey of Saint-Pierre (now in the commune of Notre-Dame-des-Préaux) see A. Le Prévost, *Mémoires . . . et notes pour servir à l'histoire du département de l'Eure* (3 vols, Evreux, 1862–9), iii. pp. 162–3 and ii. pp. 495–8.

[2] WP, pp. 260, 192.

[3] The statement in *Gallia Christiana*, xi. p. 853, that Emma was WP's sister is no more than an intelligent guess based on Orderic's statement (above, p. 85).

[4] For the length of studies, see A. Cobban, *The Medieval Universities: their development and organization* (London, 1975), p. 208.

[5] There were other schools, at the cathedral and perhaps at the abbey of Saint-Cyprien (*Letters of archbishop Lanfranc*, ed. Margaret Gibson (OMT, 1979), p. 142) but those of Saint-Hilaire were by far the most famous. See Robert Favreau, 'Les Écoles et la culture à Saint-Hiliare-le-Grand de Poitiers, des

of Hildegar (1024–8), the pupil and personal representative of Fulbert of Chartres. We know that Hildegar had connections with Normandy, because two of his letters (*c.* 1022–3) are addressed to Siegfried chaplain of Duke Richard II.[1] We are also told that the abbey of Saint-Hilaire-le-Grand, dedicated on 1 November 1049, had been built largely at the expense of Queen Emma, daughter of Duke Richard I of Normandy and wife successively of Kings Ethelred and Cnut of England.[2] What exactly had formed the connection between Queen Emma and Saint-Hilaire-le-Grand we do not know, but Normandy and Poitou were both enemies of Anjou and therefore likely to be in alliance with each other.

In two passages WP shows that he retained a special interest in Poitou. The first is in his account of the revolt of Guy of Brionne who (as WJ also points out) was the nephew of both Robert Duke of Normandy and William Count of Poitou. WP informs us (which WJ does not) that when he had been defeated in Normandy he went south to the county of Burgundy, where he plagued his brother, William 'tête hardie', for another ten years.[3] The second passage makes a special feature of Aimeri vicomte of Thouars— Thouars being the most important castle on the border between Poitou and Anjou—and states not only that he took part in the conquest of England, but also that it was he who solemnly urged the Conqueror to be crowned King.[4] Neither of these events, if

---

origines au début du XIIe siècle', *Cahiers de civilisation médiévale*, iii (1960), pp. 473–8.

[1] *The Letters and Poems of Fulbert of Chartres*, ed. Frederick Behrends (OMT, 1976), nos 67–8.

[2] '*Istud monasterium magna ex parte construxerat regina Anglorum per manus Gaufredi Coorlandi*', chronicle of Maillezais in *Chroniques des églises d'Anjou*, ed. Paul Marchegay et Emile Mabille (SHF, 1869), pp. 349–433.

[3] WP, p. 14; WJ, pp. 122–4. William 'tête hardie' did not succeed to the county of Burgundy till 1057. This would probably have been about ten years after the siege of Brionne—a possible confirmation of WP's chronology.

[4] WP, pp. 196, 218. For Aimeri, see A. Richard, *Histoire des comtes de Poitou, 778–1204* (2 vols, Paris, 1903), i. p. 298. There may be an attestation by Aimeri (as Aymeri) in the Conqueror's charter granting Steyning to the abbey of Fécamp in 1066. (*Reg.*, i, no. 1.)

events they were, is mentioned by any other source, and it must therefore be concluded that WP had a special interest in Aimeri de Thouars or his family.

We have already pointed out that WP was a man of considerable learning, and it is natural to ask whether he may not have held some official position in Saint-Hilaire-le-Grand or its schools. Lists of treasurers and deans (the Counts of Poitou being titular abbot) have been compiled, and the names of several masters of the schools are known,[1] but we are hampered by our ignorance of the surname which WP may have borne at this date. By itself 'William' is too common a name for the purposes of identification, but there was a William who was *grammaticus* in 1080, and master of the schools in 1090 and 1092. It is tempting to think that this might have been WP because, if he had held his archdeaconry in plurality with these posts, it might be possible to explain why he is so hard to find as a witness of charters in Normandy, and why he did not continue his history to the Conqueror's death. But unfortunately we must reject the identification. Orderic clearly implies that WP returned to Normandy for good, at any rate by the time he became an archdeacon; and the same impression is given by WP's own reference to *dum Pictavis exularem* (1048 × 51). Moreover, the William who was *grammaticus* and master of the schools at Saint-Hilaire-le-Grand had a brother, Thibaud, who had been chancellor to the Duke of Aquitaine in 1068;[2] and though such a chancellor could have been a Norman, it does not seem likely.

If Orderic is right in his statement that WP was 'for many years the king's chaplain', this would presumably have been after his studies at Poitiers (1048 at the earliest) and before he became an archdeacon (1077 at the latest); and since chaplains were normally members of the chancery, one would expect to find WP witnessing ducal or royal charters. But though we have the texts of about 450

---

[1] M. De Longuemar, *Essai historique sur l'église collégiale de Saint Hiliare-le-Grand de Poitiers* (Méms. de la Soc. des antiquaires de l'Ouest, xxiii, 1856), pp. 326–51, and cf. Favreau, art. cit. p. 86 n. 4.

[2] Favreau, p. 476.

of the Conqueror's charters (144 of them before 1066 and the rest after) it is not possible to identify WP in any of them. One might be tempted by 'William the duke's tutor' (*Willelmun magister comitis*), but his only attestations are *c.* 1035–43 and *c.* 1037–45, which would have been before WP's own studies.[1] After the conquest there are said to have been four Williams who served the Conqueror as chaplain, but one of them was probably fictitious since he appears only in forged charters, and another turns out, on closer inspection, to have been no chaplain at all.[2] Of the remaining two, one was William of Beaufai (*Bellofago*) who was promoted bishop of Thetford in 1085, and the other William fitz Suein who was still styling himself *canonicus* in 1082, by which date WP had been an archdeacon for five years at least.[3] If one adds that in the surviving text WP offers no hint that he was a chaplain of the Conqueror, one is bound to wonder whether Orderic could not have been mistaken, though there is an unidentified *Willelmus capellanus* who attested with the Conqueror's whole chancery in a charter of 1068 for St. Martin-le-Grand of London

Orderic was consistent in describing WP as an archdeacon of Lisieux. Otherwise we might have doubted that statement also, since it has proved impossible to trace him in other sources, perhaps because of the sparsity of early cartularies for religious houses in that diocese. But it is surprising to find that when we abandon the search for a royal chaplain or archdeacon and look simply for someone called William of Poitiers, we are rewarded, not just with one reference but two.

---

[1] Marie Fauroux, *Recueuil des actes des Ducs de Normandie de 911 à 1066* (Méms. de la Soc. des antiquaires de Normandie, xxxvi, 1961), nos 100, 103.

[2] *Reg.*, i, p. xxi, where it is noted that William the chaplain occurs only in Durham forgeries. The full text of *Reg.*, i. no. 193 is printed in J. J. Vernier, *Chartes de l'Abbaye de Jumièges* (SHN, 1916), i. p. 107, and shows that William brother of Rainald was almost certainly not a chaplain, though his brother Rainald was.

[3] *Reg.*, i. no. 168, and Lucien Musset, *Les Actes de Guillaume le Conquérant et de la reine Mathilde pour les abbayes caennaises* (Méms. de la Soc. des antiquaires de Normandie, xxxvii, 1967), no. 7, a charter of William fitz Suein, datable

The first comes as an attestation of a charter by Serlo of Lingèvres granting the church of Bucéels to Saint Stephen's abbey in Caen; it is recited in two *pancartes* and can be dated 1079–82.[1] In this case there is nothing to suggest that *Willelmus Pictavensis* was a cleric, let alone an archdeacon. In the second case, however, *Willelmus Pictavensis* must have been both a cleric and a priest, since he figures as a canon of St. Martin's, Dover. In Domesday Book (vol. i, fo. 1ᵛ), it is stated that the prebends of that church, formerly held in common, had been divided among the canons by the Bishop of Bayeux. As a result:

In Sibertesuuald [Sibertswold, Shepherd's Well] tenet Willelmus Pict (vaensis) dimidium solinum et xii acras, et in Addelam [Deal] dimidium solinum xii acras minus, et ibi habet ii villanos et iii bordarios cum i caruca et dimidia. Totum hoc valet lv solidos. TRE iiii libras.

Could this *Willelmus Pictavensis* have been our man? The identification is made attractive by the connection between St. Martin's, Dover, and the English royal chapel, since this would help to justify Orderic's description of WP as a chaplain of the king.[2] It also postulates a connection with Odo of Bayeux, which is made plausible by WP's eulogy of him in Book II, comparable only to the equally fulsome eulogy of Hugh Bishop of Lisieux in Book I. He tells us that Odo was outstanding in both ecclesiastical and secular affairs; that he governed the church of Bayeux wisely and adorned it magnificently; that he was intelligent and eloquent; that his munificence was unequalled in Gaul; that he never took up arms and never wanted to, but was greatly feared by those who did

---

1079–82, is recited (p. 76) in a *pancarte* of 1080–2 which itself has the *signum* of *Willelmi canonici filii Sueini.*

[1] Musset, *Actes . . . caennaises*, nos 7 and 18. Serlo's charter cannot be earlier than 1079 because it refers to abbot Gilbert, nor later than 1082 since that is the latest possible date for the earlier of the two *pancartes* (no. 7).

[2] Domesday Book, i, fo. 1ᵛ notes that one of the pre-conquest canons, Esmellt, was a chaplain of King Edward's. Cf. C. R. Haines, *Dover Priory* (Cambridge, 1930), p. 35; 'Lyons states, but I do not see on what authority, that not only Esmellt, but also Lewin, Edwine, Alwi, Alric, Spirites and Baldwin were chaplains of the King.'

because in cases of necessity 'he gave aid in battle through his most excellent advice'; and finally that he was 'uniquely and constantly loyal' to his half-brother the king.[1]

If we are right in thinking that WP was writing c. 1077, this last statement about Odo's unique and constant loyalty is interesting, because 1077 was the first year of the first rebellion of the Conqueror's eldest son, Robert Curthose. So far as we know, Odo was not implicated in this rebellion, which lasted till 1080, but his subsequent association with Robert was close, and it is likely that his arrest in 1082 did have some connection with Robert's second rebellion (1083–7). Could it be that WP was trying to defend Odo from the king's suspicion? Could it also be that the 'unfavourable circumstances' which (according to Orderic) prevented him from finishing his history were connected with these rebellions? In 1077 Robert's party was particularly strong in the diocese of Lisieux, because it included William de Breteuil, Yves and Aubrey de Grandmesnil, and Roger son of Richard fitz Gilbert de Clare, while on its southern borders were the lands of Ralph de Toeny and Roger de Bellême.[2]

According to Orderic, Odo of Bayeux 'sent promising clerks to Liège and other cities where he knew that philosophic studies flourished, and supported them generously there, so that they might drink long and deeply from the springs of knowledge'.[3] He does not name WP as one of these protégés, but there are indications of a connection between Odo and WP. Odo's father was Herluin de Conteville, and Conteville was only 15km from Préaux, where WP was born. When Herluin founded an abbey at Grestain, some of the first monks were brought from Saint-Pierre-des-Préaux.[4] At a later stage in WP's life, after 1077, his bishop at Lisieux was Gilbert Maminot who, besides being a chaplain and physician of

---

[1] WP, pp. 240–2. Cf. pp. 262–6, 134–6, and 182. For Odo's advice in battle of BT, pp. 67–8, 'Hic Odo episcopus, baculum tenens, confortat pueros.'

[2] C. W. David, *Robert Curthose: Duke of Normandy* (Cambridge, Mass., 1920), p. 22, with refs. to OV, ii. p. 358 and iii. pp. 100–2.

[3] OV, iv. pp. 118–19.

[4] Charles Bréard, *L'Abbaye de Notre-Dame de Grestain* (Paris, 1904).

the king,[1] was a tenant of Odo's in England, holding three estates of him in Kent and two in Buckinghamshire,[2] just as Roger de Beaumont, in whom WP displayed a special interest, was a tenant of Odo's in Buckinghamshire.[3] We might add that the Conteville lands stretched into the diocese of Bayeux and included Tilly-sur-Seulles,[4] which is adjacent to Bucéels where the church was granted to St. Stephen's, Caen, in a charter witnessed (as we have seen) by a 'William of Poitiers'. On the other side of Bucéels was Juaye, a 'peculiar' of the diocese of Lisieux,[5] and 5km to the south there was a Beaumont estate at Saint-Vaast.[6] Taken singly these facts might have been considered coincidences, but there are enough of them to make one suspect that there could be a genuine link between them.

A connection with Odo of Bayeux might also help to explain one of the most puzzling facts about WP's work—that it was apparently a failure. One would have expected that such a fulsome eulogy would, when presented to the Conqueror (as Orderic says it was), have given great pleasure and satisfaction, and that royal and ducal monasteries would have been encouraged to make copies of it. But this does not seem to have been the case. At present we do not know of a single manuscript of the work although—to make the obvious comparison—we know of more than 43 of WJ. It could conceivably be that the style was thought too involved and the Latin too difficult, but other works which were often transcribed were equally difficult, as in the case of Dudo's history of the early dukes,

[1] OV, iii. pp. 18–20.

[2] DB, i. fos. 6ᵛ, 7, 144, 144v.

[3] I am grateful to Dr David Bates for the information that the Roger who in 1086 held nine estates of Odo of Bayeux in Buckinghamshire was Roger de Beaumont, as has been shown by David Crouch in his Ph.D. thesis for the University of Wales.

[4] David R. Bates 'Notes sur l'aristocratie normande', *Annales de Normandie*, 23 (1973), pp. 7–38, esp. p. 23.

[5] H. de Formeville, *Histoire de l'ancien évêché-comté de Lisieux* (2 vols, Lisieux, 1873), p. clxxxiv, cf. pp. x–xi.

[6] In 1133 Robert de Neufbourg, who had inherited part of the Beumont lands in Normandy held two fiefs of the Bishop of Bayeux, at Saint-Vaast and Boulon. *Complete Peerage*, new ed. by Vicary Gibbs *et al.* (13 vols, London, 1910–59), xii, Appendix A, p.5.

of which at least seven manuscripts have survived. Perhaps, then, the reason for the failure was that WP or his patron was in political disgrace. WP does not seem to have received any promotion as a reward for his work, for he was archdeacon of Lisieux already in 1077, and seems to have risen no higher. Orderic's statement that in his old age he gave himself up to silence and prayer and spent more time in the composition of prose and poetry than in discourse suggests rather that he had retired to the obscurity of a religious house. To someone who was too closely associated with the rebellions of Robert Curthose or with Odo of Bayeux, such retirement might have been in the best interests of all. Perhaps that was what Orderic meant when he said that WP was unable to carry his history through to the king's death 'because he was prevented by unfavourable circumstances'.[1]

Unfortunately, none of this can be proven; it must remain speculation. But if the connection with Odo can be established beyond doubt, we may find that we have solved some of the problems of WP's sources. As we have already explained, WP is connected in some way with WJ, except in the account of the conquest of England. At that point the two narratives diverge sharply, WJ taking his own rather uninformative course, while WP expands, following a course similar to, but not identical with, the Bayeux Tapestry. If WP was a protégé of Odo of Bayeux, we would have to assume that the story he told was not so much the 'Norman' story as the 'Bayeux' story at a slightly different stage of development from that to be found in the Tapestry. Perhaps WP was not so much an eye-witness, as the protégé of an eye-witness or participant who was lucky enough to have his story told twice over, once in prose and once in pictorial form.

THE MANUSCRIPTS

Some of the questions posed in this paper might be capable of more definite answers if we could discover a complete text of WP, because it is likely that a dedicatory preface or epilogue would give

[1] See p. 84 above.

more information about his career. What chance have we of finding such a manuscript?

We have already commented that the work seems to have lacked success at the time, with the result that there were few manuscripts of it. Orderic must have seen a copy at Saint-Evroult by *c.* 1114–15 when he began Book III of his *Ecclesiastical History*,[1] but there is nothing to suggest that he knew it when he made his additions to WJ (no earlier than 1113).[2] The MS seen by Orderic could have been the only one in Normandy; Robert de Torigni refers to WP but seems to have derived his knowledge of it at second-hand through Orderic; and Benoît de Sainte-Maure has one or two stories which seem to be derived from WP directly or indirectly.[3] In England also there must have been a manuscript of WP, because the work was known both to William of Malmesbury and the author of the *Liber Eliensis*.[4] One manuscript might have been sufficient for both authors, because in 1075–82 the abbey of Ely was put in charge of a monk of Jumièges called Godfrey, and he subsequently became abbot of Malmesbury (1087/9–1106).[5]

Duchesne's edition of 1619 was based on a MS from the library of Sir Robert Cotton, which could well have been the one from Ely/Malmesbury. Because it cannot be traced in any of the early Cottonian catalogues or lists of loans, its fate has puzzled editors.[6]

---

[1] Chibnall in OV, ii, p. xv.

[2] WJ, p. 151. Orderic's interpolations used to be dated no later than 1109 (Marx, in WJ, p. xxv), but in 'Quelques observations sur les interpolations attribuées à Orderic Vitalis dans les *Gesta Normannorum Ducum* de Guillaume de Jumièges' (*Revue d'histoire des textes*, viii, 1978, pp. 213–22) Elisabeth van Houts has shown that they cannot be earlier than 1113.

[3] See p. 84 n. 1 above, and postscript on p. 100.

[4] See Appendix, p. 98–100.

[5] David Knowles, C. N. L. Brooke, and Vera London, *The Heads of Religious Houses in England and Wales, 940–1216* (Cambridge, 1972), p. 55. For the use of WP by William of Malmesbury and *Liber Eliensis*, see Appendix.

[6] Foreville in WP, pp. l–li. As she points out, 212 of the 958 Cottonian MSS were destroyed in whole or in part in the fire of 1731, but there is no trace of WP in the catalogue made by Sir Henry Savile, in the seventeenth-century catalogue at Trinity College, Cambridge (MS 1243) or in the printed catalogue by Thomas Smith (1696). I have also failed to find it in Cotton's own catalogue

But insufficient attention has been paid to Duchesne's statement that the MS had been borrowed from Cotton's library, not by himself, but by William Camden who, in his turn, had dispatched it across the channel on loan to Nicholas Fabri de Peiresc. Both these men were prolific letter-writers, and their correspondence refers specifically to this loan.[1] In a letter to Camden dated 5 March 1618 Peiresc acknowledges receipt of a transcript of Cotton's WP, but alleges that it was so full of mistakes that it could not be printed. As an alternative, he says: 'Feu Mons. Pithou en avoit un exemplaire tout entier, lequel on m'a promis. . . . Si nous n'avons l'exemplaire de Monsieur Pithou, possible prieray-je Monsieur Cotton de nous envoyer son original.'[2] Evidently the Pithou MS could not be found, because on 29 April 1618 Peiresc wrote to Camden acknowledging receipt of 'l'autographe du fragment de *Guillelmus Pictavensis* bien conditionné'.[3] Though we cannot prove that Peiresc returned it, it is most probable that it was included in the consignment of books which he dispatched back to London in the autumn of 1618,[4] in which case we may presume that it perished in the Cottonian fire of 1731.

Its fate, however, is less important than that of the Pithou MS,

---

of 1621 (British Library, Harley MS 6018) or in the list of MSS lent by Sir Thomas Cotton between 1637 and 1661 (British Library, Cotton MS Appendix xlv. 13) or in the further list of cartularies and loans made in 1638 (British Library, Add. MS 5161). Cf. Kevin Sharpe, *Sir Robert Cotton, 1586–1631: history and politics in Early Modern England* (Oxford, 1979), ch. ii.

[1] For Peiresc, see G. Cahen-Salvador, *Un grand humaniste, Peiresc, 1580–1637* (Paris, 1951), and P. Tamizey de Larroque (ed.), *Lettres de Peiresc aux frères Dupuy* (7 vols, Collection de documents inédits, Paris, 1888–98). For Camden, G. *Camdeni, et illustrorum virorum ad Camdenun epistolae; praemittitur Camdeni Vita*, scriptore T(homa) Smitho (London, 1691), henceforth cited as GC. Cf. Sharpe, pp. 95–8.

[2] *GC*, no. clxxvi (p. 222).

[3] *GC*, no. clxxxv (p. 231).

[4] *GC*, no. ccx (p. 269), cf. pp. 261, 266. The Cotton *Genesis* did not get back to England till April 1622 (no. cclix, p. 326). There had been many complaints about the failure to return that book, but none about WP. Duchesne, whom Peiresc treats as a very subsidiary figure, was able to send his printed volume of *Rerum Normannicarum* to Camden by 15 July 1619 (*GC*, no. ccxxi, p. 282).

since this latter (which could well have been the one used by Orderic Vitalis at Saint-Evroult) was said to have contained the text of WP in its entirety. Pierre Pithou (1539–96), editor of two volumes which became the prototype of Bouquet's *Recueil des historiens des Gaules et de la France*, had a famous library, collected by his father and himself at a time when the monastic libraries of France were being dispersed by the Wars of Religion. Acutely aware of its scholarly value, he made a will with elaborate arrangements to ensure that it was preserved entire, but after his death it was none the less divided and dispersed. What exactly happened is uncertain— as early as 1716 Jean Boivin found two contradictory accounts in circulation[1]—but part found its way to the French royal library, part remained with the family, part was kept in the college founded by Pithou at Troyes,[2] and individual volumes somehow got to the library of the Faculty of Medicine at Montpellier (H137 and H151), the Arsénale in Paris (MSS 483, 2590, 4818), the British Library (Add. MS 11506), and the Burgerbibliothek at Bern (MS 163). Other volumes are believed to be in the private library of the Marquis de Rosambo, a descendant of Pithou's in the female line,[3] and others are doubtless elsewhere.

In these circumstances it might seem unduly optimistic to search for the missing WP, but since the prize would be the full text of the lost portions at the beginning and end, an attempt must surely

---

[1] *Claudi Peleterii Regni Administri vita, Petri Pithoei ejus proavi vita adjuncta accurante Joanne Boivin* (Paris, 1716) is the earliest account. Claude Le Peletier was Pierre Pithou's great-grandson and his share of the library still belongs to his descendant, the Marquis de Rosanbo. See also Louis de Rosanbo, 'Pierre Pithou: Biographie', *Rev. du seizième siècle*, xv (1928), pp. 279–305; and 'Pierre Pithou érudit', ibid. xvi (1929), pp. 301–30.

[2] A catalogue of those still at Troyes was published by Pierre Jean Grosley in *Vie de Pierre Pithou avec quelques mémoires de son père et ses frères* (2 vols, Paris, 1756), ii. pp. 275–86.

[3] The Marquis de Rosanbo is descended from Claude Le Peletier who was Pierre Pithou's greatgrandson. Some Pithou MSS are cited, as being in the Château de Rosanbo, by Louis de Rosanbo, in 'Pierre Pithou: biographie' (*Rev. du seizième siècle*, xv (1928), pp. 279–305) and 'Pierre Pithou érudit' (ibid., xvi (1929), pp. 301–33).

be made. It is unlikely that even the complete text would fill a whole volume, and it is quite possible that it has been bound up with works of a different nature. As Jean Grosley commented, when reporting (1756) on the sad state of Pithou's library at Troyes:

This confusion is the effect of the care and vigilance which the reverend fathers devoted to this precious deposit. One of their superiors, seeing manuscripts mutilated, degraded and without bindings, scattered around the library, had them bound in divers volumes, without regard to their contents, but only to their sizes.[1]

Such heterogeneous volumes, by no means rare in other libraries, are always difficult to catalogue. A hasty cataloguer may miss the end of one work and the beginning of the next; and though the perfect cataloguer will efficiently record the *incipit* and *explicit* of every work, even his pains may be wasted in the case of WP, since without the manuscript we have no idea of what the *incipit* and *explicit* are.

It seems that there are three ways of conducting the search for the lost manuscript. The first is to search in large and imperfectly catalogued libraries where there are known to be manuscripts collected in France at the time of the Wars of Religion, but where it is not to be expected that most librarians had been experts in the history of Normandy. Following this principle I have started my search among the MSS of Queen Christina of Sweden in the Vatican Library at Rome, but without success. The second is to assume that the reason why the full WP has not been discovered is because it is bound up with a very similar work, in the same way as the Valenciennes MS of the *Gesta Stephani* was bound up with the *Gesta Regum* of William of Malmesbury.[2] It has therefore seemed desirable to inspect all known MSS of WJ, the work which would offer the most perfect camouflage for WP. A drawback to this course is that most of the MSS of WJ, being in the Bibliothèque nationale at Paris, would inevitably have been well known to

[1] Grosley, ii. p. 272.
[2] *Gesta Stephani*, ed. K. R. Potter and R. H. C. Davis (Oxford, 1976), p. xiv.

Léopold Delisle who, as the greatest expert on Norman history of this period, could not have failed to recognize WP if he saw it. None the less, since he did not know *all* the MSS there may be some hope in this course, though so far it has proved fruitless. The third, and probably the most promising, method is to hunt down every manuscript which ever belonged to Pithou. Many of them can be identified from the editions which he published.[1] Others can be traced through the history of his family or, since he usually wrote his name in his books, through library catalogues. As a result the number of his known manuscripts is growing. If we can make it grow faster, we may succeed in finding the full text of the *History of William the Conqueror* and then we should be able to discover a great deal more about the life of its author and the reliability of his narrative.

APPENDIX

Reconstruction of the beginning and the end of WP

The end of WP has to be deduced from the use of it made by OV. See Chibnall in OV, ii. pp. xviii–xxi. For the beginning it is necessary to turn to William of Malmesbury's *Gesta Regum* (ed. William Stubbs, 2 vols, RS 1887–9 and henceforth cited as *GR*). In his preface Stubbs (vol. ii, pp. cxi–cxiii) showed that *GR* had used WP as one of his sources. In confirmation of his argument it may be added that *GR* follows WP rather than WJ in placing the revolt of William of Arques after (rather than before) that of Guy of Burgundy; in the additional details he gives about Guy (above, pp. 77, 87); and in stating that Domfront belonged to Anjou rather than Normandy (*GR*, 288, WP 36). *GR* 288 also has the story of William's challenge to Geoffrey of Anjou (WP 38–40). Compare also *GR* 290 and WP 70 (note the use of *Celtigallus*), the acquisition

---

[1] See particularly *Annalium et Historiae Francorum ab anno Christi DCCVIII ad annum DCCCCXC scriptores coaetani xii, nunc primum in lucem editi ex bibliotheca P. Pithoei* (Paris, 1588) and *Historiae Francorum ab anno Christi DCCCC ad annum MCCLXXXV scriptores veteres xi . . . ex bibliotheca P. Pithoei* (Frankfurt, 1596).

of Maine (*GR* 294, WP 86–92), and the deposition of Archbishop Mauger of Rouen (*GR* 327, WP 130–2).

It may also be noted that the *Liber Eliensis* (ed. E. O. Blake, Camden 3rd Series xcii, London, 1962) reproduces almost verbatim (ii. 90) WP's account of the capture and murder of the atheling Alfred (WP 8–10), and in its account of the Hastings campaign uses many of WP's words and phrases, as pointed out by Blake in the footnotes and in his Introduction, p. xxviii.

Using the clues offered by these three works, the following suggestions can be made about the contents of the lost beginning and end of WP.

(i) *Beginning*
 1. William's birth (*GR* 285).
 2. Duke Robert's decision to go on crusade; the nobles' oath to William; Count Gilbert [of Brionne] as William's guardian (*GR* 285).
 3. Duke Robert's death at Nicaea (*GR* 286).
 4. Revolts during William's minority (*ut supra docuimus*, WP 14). Murder of Count Gilbert (*GR* 286).
 5. Marriage of Emma to Ethelred and Canute (*GR* 191, 218–19). This would lead well into the section on England with which the surviving text of WP opens, and would also explain the relatively favourable attitude to Harthacnut (WP 12) as a son of Emma's.

(ii) *End*
 1. Murder of Copsi (*Coxo*) WP 268–70, cf. OV, ii. 206–8.
 2. Loyalty of Ealdred archbishop of York WP 270, cf. OV, ii. 208.
 3. William's return from Normandy. He rallies the waverers (OV, ii. 210).
 4. His capture of Exeter; his great mercy (OV, ii. 212–14).
 5. Coronation of Queen Matilda, Whitsun 1068 (OV, ii. 214).
 6. Revolt of Edwin and Morcar; including William's castle-building, the war-weariness of the Normans and the exhaustion

of the country. (OV, ii. 220 (cf. OV, ii. 236) and *Liber Eliensis*, 185–93.)

7. Swein's invasion; William hears of it in the Forest of Dean. Troubles overcome at York, Montacute, Exeter, Stafford, and Shrewsbury (OV, ii. 226–34; *Liber Eliensis*, 187, 190–1, and *GR* 312).

8. William and the English Church. Council of Winchester; deposition of Stigand; eulogy of Lanfranc; ecclesiastical appointments, including that of Gilbert fitz Osbern, canon and archdeacon of Lisieux, to the bishopric of Evreux (OV, ii. 248–54; *Vita Lanfranci*, chs v, vi.

9. Peace over England—eulogy of the Conqueror's just rule (OV, ii. 256).

10. The arrest of Earl Morcar and the death of the Earl Edwin (OV, ii. 256–8).

POSTSCRIPT

Since this article was written, Dr Elizabeth van Houts has pointed out to me (re p. 94) that the text of WP was also known to Ralph de Diceto, who used it in his *Abbreviationes Chronicorum* (*Radulfi de Diceto . . . opera omnia*, ed. William Stubbs (R.S., 2 vols, 1876), ii. pp. 263–4). She points out that Ralph was a friend of Arnulf Bishop of Lisieux (1141–82) and might have got the MS. of WP from him (cf. G. A. Zinn in *Speculum* lii (1977), 59–60), in which case it could have been the same MS. that Orderic Vitalis had used.

John of Worcester and his contemporaries

MARTIN BRETT

IN 1066 the practice of history in England was almost dead; if it were not for the few monasteries where the Anglo-Saxon annals continued to be kept up, one would have to say that it had ceased altogether. A few learned Flemings, trained in one of the most active centres of hagiography of the time, had been hired or induced to write saints' lives, but this itself illustrates the poverty of native resources.[1]

By the end of the reign of Henry I more history was being written than ever before or often afterwards. History is a general word, and what was being written was very various indeed. At the cathedral at Canterbury, two successive masters of the priory library, Osbern and Eadmer, had devoted themselves to revising and rewriting the lives of the saints, upon whose relics, miracles, and traditions the glory of their church depended. Even more strikingly, Eadmer had turned these skills to contemporary events. His life of St. Anselm fits a long-established pattern, but its companion work, the *Historia Novorum*, is a much more original enterprise. Such a detailed

[1] Among those with whom I have discussed versions of this paper I am particularly indebted to Professor C. N. L. Brooke, Dr V. J. Flint, Dr C. R. Hallpike, and Professor D. Whitelock. I have learnt from them all, though none bears any responsibility for my conclusions. For the careers of Goscelin and Folcard see F. Barlow (ed.), *The Life of King Edward* (NMT, 1962), pp. xliv–lix, 91–111, A. Gransden, *Historical Writing in England c. 550–1307* (London, 1974), pp. 60–6, 107–11. For the Flemish hagiographers see particularly B. de Gaiffier, 'L'Hagiographie dans le marquisat de Flandre et le duché de Basse-Lotharingie au xie siècle', in *Études critiques d'hagiographie et d'iconologie* (Soc. des Bollandistes, Subsidia Hagiographica no. 43, 1967), pp. 415–507.

narrative of great events, illustrated with a mass of documents, had no earlier parallel in England, and very few elsewhere.[1]

At Malmesbury the most learned and talented of all his fellows, William, had written a noble series of works: five books on the deeds of the kings of England, five more on the deeds of the bishops, a revision of the *Liber Pontificalis* to illustrate the relations between England and Rome, a history of the antiquities of Glastonbury, a revised life of Wulfstan of Worcester, and a string of saints' lives and notebooks of ancient and modern history from a variety of sources. In all these a remarkably self-confident stylist is allied to a shrewd and industrious research worker. It is an unrivalled volume of work for a man who was barely forty in 1135.[2]

At Durham between 1104 and 1108 Simeon had produced a history of his church in the form of a series of biographies of its bishops, and possibly a companion volume on the miracles and translations of St. Cuthbert.[3] At Worcester Bishop Wulfstan inspired historical work of many kinds; he gathered the materials for a narrative cartulary of the priory, which Hemming compiled, his life provided a theme for Coleman, his chancellor, and he ordered the monk John to undertake a universal history.[4]

---

[1] For Osbern see the literature cited in Gransden, pp. 127–9; for Eadmer R. W. Southern, *St. Anselm and his Biographer* (Cambridge, 1963).

[2] Study of William's work has been placed on a new footing by the studies of R. M. Thomson, summarized in 'William of Malmesbury as historian and man of letters', *JEH*, xxix (1978), pp. 387–413. See also his 'William of Malmesbury's edition of the *Liber Pontificalis*', *Archivum Historiae Pontificiae*, xvi (1978), pp. 93–112. I am greatly indebted to Dr Thomson at a number of points in this paper, for both information and helpful discussion.

[3] P. Hunter Blair, 'Some observations on the *Historia Regum* attributed to Simeon of Durham', in *Celt and Saxon*, ed. N. Chadwick (Cambridge, 1963), pp. 73–4, H. S. Offler, *The Medieval Historians of Durham* (Durham, 1958), pp. 6–8, Gransden, pp. 115–21.

[4] *Hemingi chartularium ecclesiae Wigorniensis*, ed. T. Hearne (Oxford, 1723), i. pp. 282–6, ii, p. 391; *Vita Wulfstani* ed. R. R. Darlington (Camden 3rd ser., xl, 1928). Orderic's reference (OV, ii. pp. 186–8) is very difficult; he had clearly seen John at work before *c.* 1124 and describes the prefatory tables of the work with some accuracy. His statement that John continued Marianus (d. 1082/3) for about a hundred years, and used extensive continental sources to do so, is

Not only monks wrote history. Henry, hereditary archdeacon of Huntingdon, had completed the first version of his *History of the English* in 1129. Unlike the writers of Malmesbury, Worcester, or Durham, Henry was content to take the bulk of his material from obvious sources. Though he knew that much could be discovered, he preferred to leave such labour to his readers.[1] Hugh the Chanter at York in his *History of the Archbishops* produced a narrative of the primacy dispute closely comparable to that of Eadmer's *Historia Novorum*, a record of legal pleading illustrated by the most material documents. Unlike Eadmer, Hugh cites no source or document earlier than his own lifetime.[2]

This would be a remarkable catalogue, even if it were comprehensive. In fact it represents no more than the tip of a great iceberg of historical activity in the larger sense. Eadmer and William of Malmesbury are only the best known among an army of monks and clerks polishing up the lives of ancient saints at almost every shrine in England. Earlier historians were carefully studied, contemporaries were copied out and annotated almost as soon as written. The earliest laws of the Anglo-Saxons were collected and transcribed, though many of these had long ceased to guide the conduct of the courts.[3] The popularity of historical writing is shown above all in the best seller of his age, Geoffrey of Monmouth, for whom dignified

---

unfounded, as is his apparent belief that Sigebert of Gembloux used some Worcester materials in constructing his chronicle (if, as is generally supposed, he meant Sigebert for Englebert).

[1] On Henry and his sources see F. Liebermann, 'Heinrich von Huntingdon', *Forschungen zur deutschen Geschichte*, xviii (1878), pp. 265–95, Gransden, pp. 193–201, N. F. Partner, *Serious entertainments; the writing of history in twelfth-century England* (Chicago, 1977), pp. 16–48.

[2] Hugh cites only one document in detail from before 1100, a bull of Urban II of 1093/4 (*Hugh the Chantor: the History of the Church of York*, ed. C. Johnson (NMT, 1961), pp. 6–7). The substantial authenticity of this much disputed text is defended in *Councils and Synods*, pt 1 (Oxford, forthcoming).

[3] The most obvious cases are the collections in the *Textus Roffensis* of *c.* 1125 and the *Quadripartitus*, ed. F. Liebermann (Halle, 1892). See also *Leges Henrici Primi*, ed. L. J. Downer (Oxford, 1972), pp. 12–28.

fiction seems to be an end in itself, rather than a means to advance the fortunes of a saint or an estate.[1]

The general background to this strenuous activity has been drawn by Sir Richard Southern.[2] This paper has the limited object of studying the sources used by only one of these writers, John of Worcester, with two aims. The first is to show some ways in which his work is related to that of his contemporaries, and the second is to illustrate from these connections a distinctively monastic community of scholarship in his time.

John has been perhaps the most neglected of the chroniclers of his generation. As a consequence we have no complete or adequate edition of the Worcester chronicle, and as yet no certainty on the part he played in writing it. In what follows I assume that he was responsible for the extant form of all that goes under the name of Florence of Worcester and his continuator. Many of the arguments for this have been deployed elsewhere, and more can be drawn from the manuscript tradition.[3]

The unique interest of John's chronicle lies in this tradition, for alone among his English contemporaries he has left a clear record of the stages by which his work reached its final form. We have

[1] On Geoffrey see Gransden, pp. 201–9; V. I. J. Flint, 'The *Historia Regum Britanniae* of Geoffrey of Monmouth: parody and its purpose. A suggestion', *Speculum*, liv (1979), pp. 447–68, believes that Geoffrey was making very elaborate fun of this historical tradition, though perhaps with some more serious objects.

[2] R. W. Southern, 'Aspects of the European tradition of historical writing: 4. The sense of the past', *TRHS*, 5th ser., xxiii (1973), esp. pp. 246–56.

[3] Most fully set out by Darlington in *Vita Wulfstani*, pp. xi–xviii, and *Anglo-Norman historians* (London, 1947), p. 14. J. R. H. Weaver in *Chron. John*, p. 8n, cited a chronological exercise from Corpus Christi Coll. Oxford MS 157, p. 55, as evidence that the work was in progress in 1103. The possibility clearly exists, but a second exercise on the same leaf for 1106 calls this the first year of the Emperor Charles (Henry V). This suggests a German origin for the exercises. Both occur in a passage which is one of John's later additions to the original manuscript, and is therefore unlikely to preserve an early element in its elaboration. The argument of V. I. J. Flint, 'The date of the chronicle of "Florence" of Worcester', *Rev. bén.*, lxxxvi (1976), pp. 115–19, depends in part on the use of Eadmer, for which see below.

autograph manuscripts of books by Eadmer and William of Malmesbury, but these are either fair copies or reveal alterations more of judgement or style than of substance.[1] John's autograph, which is also the archetype of all the surviving complete copies, is a working text, in which innumerable changes and additions have been made to the original narrative. It reveals a steady accretion of new material, and in its pages we can watch the compiler at work with most unusual clarity.

The manuscript is now Corpus Christi College, Oxford, MS 157. It was written at Worcester in several set hands, but from its earliest pages up to the annal for 1124 a corrector and annotator can be seen, erasing and enlarging the text, and filling the margin with new matter. From 1128 to the end the same hand also wrote the main text. This has been identified with near certainty as the hand of John himself.[2] The manuscript is therefore fundamental, and is usually cited as C.

[1] For two of Eadmer's autographs, Corpus Christi College, Cambridge, MSS 371 and 452, see Southern, *St. Anselm and his Biographer*, pp. 367–74, and his edition of *The Life of St. Anselm* (*NMT*, 1962) pp. ix–xxiv. On William's manuscripts, and particularly the autograph of his *Deeds of the Bishops* in Magdalen College, Oxford, MS Lat. 172, see R. M. Thomson, 'The "scriptorium" of William of Malmesbury', *Medieval scribes, manuscripts and libraries. Essays presented to N. R. Ker*, ed. M. B. Parkes and A. G. Watson (London, 1978), pp. 117–42.

[2] The identification was first made by N. R. Ker in *EHR*, lix (1944), pp. 375–6, and was confirmed and elaborated by E. A. McIntyre, whose thesis 'Early-twelfth-century Worcester Cathedral Priory, with special reference to the manuscripts written there' (Oxford University D.Phil. thesis 1978) is of fundamental importance for understanding the growth and character of the Worcester library after the conquest. The *editio princeps* of the chronicle by W. Howard, *Chronicon ex chronicis . . . Auctore Florentio Wigorniensi monacho* (London, 1592), was based on the incomplete Dublin MS H, described below, contaminated with readings from the Dublin *Chronicula*, but is the only extant edition which includes all the material in its exemplar. The edition by H. Petrie in *Monumenta Historica Britannica* (London, 1848) is based on C, carefully collated with the Lambeth MS (B in his apparatus), but has only the entries concerning England from 450–1000; from 1000–66 it is complete. The standard edition by B. Thorpe (*Flor. Wig.*), though published in 1848–9, is based on Petrie to 1066, and after that on an unstable mixture of C, the Lambeth MS, collated as L, and Howard's edition. Thorpe's inclusion and

Of the four other early copies, two, Trinity College, Dublin, MS 502, from Coventry,[1] and Lambeth Palace MS 42 from Abingdon, clearly depend on C. Much that has been added there in the text and margins by more than one hand is found in the main text of both, and neither contains readings that demand another source. However it seems they derive from C only indirectly through a common ancestor, for they agree in some errors and omissions, and insert marginal notes from C at the same point in their narrative, even where C gives no indication where that should be.[2] Their agreement I call HL. Two factors give HL an importance which mere copies might not seem to deserve. The first is that it often represents an early state of C before later erasure destroyed the original reading.[3] The second is that it enables one to distinguish early alterations to C, which are in HL, from later ones that are not.

---

exclusion of what he thought irrelevant matter has confused innumerable readers ever since. C is the basis of *Chron. John*. The new edition begun by the late Professor R. R. Darlington is being completed by Dr P. McGurk for Oxford Medieval Texts.

[1] The provenance of the book is established by frequent notes against passages of the text dealing with Earl Leofric, called 'huius ecclesie fundator' on fo. 219. These notes are in a later hand, but on fo. 227 a twelfth-century note added under 1070 runs: 'In hoc concilio degradatus est de sede episcopali abbas Leofwinus et reversus est ad abbatiam suam, scilicet Covintr', unde prius assumptus fuerat'. The book presumably reached Coventry before 1200 and might have been written there. See further *Chron. John*, pp. 4–5.

[2] For example, the canons of the Council of London in 1108, a marginal addition at C p. 367, are placed after the death of Gerard of York by H and L (where both omit the accession of Thomas II); the Durham *History of the Kings* enters them after the consecration of Richard of London, Bodl. MS 297 (B) at the same point as the *History*, and Cambridge, Corpus Christi Coll. MS 92 (P), after the death of Richard de Redvers (*Flor. Wig.*, ii. p. 57). These other copies are discussed below.

[3] For instance, under 988/9 (*Flor. Wig.*, i. pp. 148–9) Thorpe reproduces the text of C from 'obiit, cui successit Aethelgarus ...' to 'proturbatis, monachos induxit'. HL here run 'ex hac vita transivit et superne civitatis sedem petivit. Pro quo Athelgarus Seolisigensis episcopus archipresulatum suscepit, unoque anno tribusque mensibus tenuit.' The whole of C here is written over an erasure. Similarly, throughout Cnut's letter (*Flor. Wig.*, i. pp. 185–9) HL rightly speaks of King Rudolf, though C and later copies have been 'corrected' to Robert.

Most notably, it provides a version of the years 1128 to 1131, where both end, which is much shorter than that now found in C. At first sight this presents a problem if C is the archetype. However, in 1128, precisely at the point where the texts diverge, C has been erased and rewritten. There can be little doubt that the text of HL for these years was once found in C, and that HL here represents the original conclusion of John's chronicle.[1]

The two remaining copies are Oxford, Bodleian Library, MS Bodley 297, here cited as B, and Cambridge, Corpus Christi College, MS 92, here cited as P. B was written at Bury St. Edmunds; this is clear from a great number of notices concerning the house which have been added in mid-text as well as in the margins. B is certainly a direct copy of C. The most striking proof is that pp. 31–144 of B coincide exactly with pp. 36–150 of C, the turn over of each leaf occurring at virtually the same word in each book. This was a triumph for the scribe of B but must have been too difficult to maintain. Henceforward the format, though not the content, diverges.[2] Since many of the Bury additions were made *currente calamo* by the main scribe, it seems to follow that C was taken to Bury for copying, a suggestion that is borne out by the appearance in B of extracts from Bede on the visions of Fursey and a thegn of King Coenred of Mercia under 651 and 704, added at the foot of the leaves. At the corresponding point in C rough notes appear in the margin: 'Hoc tempore visio sancti Fursei' and 'tempore

---

[1] More precisely, L ends with the appointment of Serlo of Cirencester at 'abbatis iure preficitur'. H adds notes on the death of Abbots Reginald of Ramsey and William of Gloucester, and of Hervey of Ely and ends. See *Chron. John*, p. 31 and note 4.

[2] The Bury additions were largely printed in *Memorials of St. Edmund's Abbey*, ed. T. Arnold (RS, 1890–6), i. pp. 340–56. B also makes use of the Annals of 'St. Neots' (see below, p. 108 n. 1), Eadmer, and Flodoard's *Annales* to enlarge John's text. For the Bury library see now R. M. Thomson, 'The library of Bury St. Edmunds abbey in the eleventh and twelfth centuries', *Speculum*, xlvii (1972), pp. 617–45, and E. P. McLachlan, 'The scriptorium of Bury St. Edmunds . . .', *Mediaeval Studies*, xl (1978), pp. 328–48. The coincidence of format between C and B was noted by Dr McIntyre (above, p. 105 n. 2).

Kenredi'.[1] The Cambridge manuscript P was later at Peterborough, but was written at Abingdon after 1174. It descends at one or more removes from C after it had been copied at Bury, for the marginal notes on Fursey and Coenred appear rather mindlessly in P's text.[2]

Like HL, B and P have only the text to 1131, without the continuation or the revised version of 1128–31 found in C. However, they incorporate almost all the corrections and alterations now found in C before 1128.[3]

Four stages in the evolution of John's chronicle can therefore be traced in the manuscripts. The first is represented by the original state of C. The second was found in HL, where C has been enlarged and corrected with some care. The third is found in B and P, where the revision and elaboration of the text to 1128 is more or less complete, but the chronicle still only runs to 1131. The fourth is the present state of C, where the passage for 1128–31 has been rewritten and the continuation added. Only this last stage has received an adequate modern edition.[4]

The dating of these stages is more problematic. It is possible that the earlier sections of C were revised before it reached 1131, and that no text ever ran so far without some expansion. However,

---

[1] Compare B pp. 262–8, 276–8, with C pp. 260, 271. B's additions are taken not directly from Bede but from the so-called Annals of St. Neots, edited by W. H. Stevenson in *Asser's Life of King Alfred* (revised edn, Oxford, 1959), pp. 97–145. The Bury provenance he suggested on pp. 98–102 (compare the judgement of T. A. M. Bishop on p. cxli n. 3) is confirmed in the studies of Thomson and McLachlan cited above. Thomson, 642n, would date the MS *c.* 1125.

[2] P.s. ann. 651, 704. P's relation to the other copies is complex, partly because it seems to use the Lambeth MS L as a second exemplar. Its Abingdon provenance is clear from the occurrence of passages from the *Chronicon monasterii de Abingdon* and the Life of St. Ethelwold in the main text. The manuscript had reached Peterborough by the mid-thirteenth century (*Bury*, p. xvii).

[3] Strictly only B has the whole conclusion to the death of Hervey of Ely, since P turns to Henry of Huntingdon after the annal for 1130. The last substantial addition to C before 1128 is the passage from Malmesbury under 1124, *Chron. John*, p. 18n.

[4] *Chron. John* is based on C in its latest state, collated with the Dublin *Chronicula* and H, both of which have some of C's additions as a supplement to the earlier version to 1131.

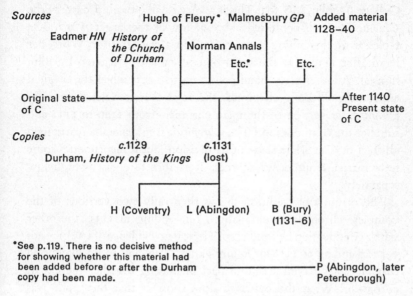

Diagram 1. The outline of the elaboration of John's chronicle

there is evidence that the main annal for 1102 was not written until sometime after 1122; if some of the earliest additions may have been made as early as 1129, it is likely that more had not.[1] The ancestor of HL was clearly written in or after 1131, where it ended, but probably not long after. B may well have been written before 1136,[2] and one has to allow a long enough interval between B and HL for considerable expansion of C. The continuation in C could have been written at any time after the copying of the ancestor of P.

One manuscript stands rather outside this sequence, Trinity

[1] Below, pp. 119-21.
[2] The prefatory tables in all the manuscripts are deceptive guides to date. However on p. 33 Archbishop William (d. 21 Nov. 1136) is the last entry under Canterbury in the main hand, and the only one the length of whose pontificate is not given in years, months, and days. The last pope to be entered according to the original plan was Honorius II (d. 1130). The same hand, or a virtually indistinguishable one, added his successors to Eugenius III (1145-53), but the changed pattern of rubricated letters reveals a break between the entries.

College, Dublin, MS 503. This is a very small 'portable' copy of the *Chronicula*, a self-confessed abbreviation of the larger work. The tables at the beginning were written in a characteristic Worcester hand after 1139, but the main text to 1123 was written by John himself. Another early hand continues to 1125, when the original text breaks off. Long afterwards the work was completed by using a Gloucester version of the main chronicle from 1126 to 1131 and some of the continuation.[1] The *Chronicula* is in general a rearranged abstract of C at a late stage of its revision, but it incorporates some new matter from other sources. It is therefore discussed below separately.

The manuscript tradition shows then only two versions of the complete chronicle in circulation, one ending in 1131, the other with a continuation beyond 1140. There is no evidence of a Worcester version ending at 1118 or at any earlier date, and so no likelihood that Florence played a central part in putting together the extant chronicle.[2] What the evidence does show is that the work was elaborated in well-marked stages, and we are now in a position to examine the character and sequence of the changes that were introduced.

The earliest stage in the construction of the chronicle, found in C before any of its alterations, was comparatively simple in conception. The basis of the work was the chronicle of Marianus the Scot, with a continuation at least as far as 1086. It is generally assumed that the work was introduced to Worcester through Bishop Robert of Hereford, who came from Lorraine, is known to have studied chronology, wrote an abstract of Marianus, and was a close friend of St. Wulfstan, though Hereford remained in close touch with

---

[1] Weaver, describing the manuscript in *Chron. John*, pp. 5–7, recognized the possibility that it might be an autograph. Dr McIntyre (above, p. 105) identified the hand firmly, here and elsewhere.

[2] For the Durham evidence see below. John's words on Florence do not strictly require that Florence ever wrote anything; they imply rather the possession of high technical skill, presumably in the arts of chronography. See *Chron. John*, p. 13.

Germany long after his death.[1] Marianus provided a larger framework of reference than any English historian had used since the days of Bede, a map which extended in time from the Creation to the present and in space from Babylon to the Atlantic. Into this vast design John inserted an English history with two chief components. The first was a set of tables tracing the genealogies of the kings of the Anglo-Saxon kingdoms, with their rise and fall, and a parallel set of successions of bishops, set out to illustrate both their relation to the kingdoms and the process by which the sees were subdivided or united, the whole accompanied by explanatory notes.[2] The second was a narrative of English events, drawn largely from Bede, Asser, and a number of saints' lives, grafted on to a version of the Anglo-Saxon chronicle of complex ancestry.[3]

Two other groups of material cast light directly on his relations with his contemporaries. The first is his use of Eadmer's *Historia Novorum*, which is John's chief source from 1102 to 1121. Between 1109 and 1114 Eadmer wrote a version in four books up to the death of Anselm. No copy of this survives. Later he added two

---

[1] Stevenson in *EHR*, xxii (1907), p. 76; *Vita Wulfstani*, p. xvi n; Gransden p. 145; for later contact see W. Holtzmann, 'Zur Geschichte des Investiturstreites', *Neues Archiv*, i (1933), pp. 246–319, and perhaps above 104 n. 3.

[2] The lay-out of these tables in C is careful but complex. The version printed in *Flor. Wig.*, i. pp. 231–80, is incomplete and confused. For their ancestry see K. Sisam, 'Anglo-Saxon royal genealogies', *Proc. Brit. Acad.*, xxxix (1953), pp. 287–348, and R. I. Page, 'Anglo-Saxon episcopal lists', *Nottingham Mediaeval Studies*, ix (1965), pp. 71–95, x (1966), pp. 2–24, esp. ix. 85–8.

[3] The relation of John's text to the surviving versions of the Anglo-Saxon Chronicle is set out at length in H. Howorth, 'The chronicle of John of Worcester previously assigned to Florence of Worcester', *Archaeological Journal*, lxxiii (1916), pp. 1–170. There is a much better brief account of the relation by D. Whitelock in *English Historical Documents*, i (*500–1042*) (2nd ed., London, 1979), p. 120. The parallels between John and the surviving Peterborough Chronicle, with which he shows no direct acquaintance, are close as far as 1106. After that only the lists of participants in great Canterbury events in 1123 and 1130 seem to demand a common source. This however need not have been a chronicle at all. Since both work within the conventions of the annalist, many of their entries have a family resemblance which is not in itself significant.

books which continued the story of the struggle for the rights of Canterbury up to the death of Archbishop Ralph in October 1122. A largely autograph copy of this version survives, but it is likely that John used a slightly earlier copy of the six-book text.[1] He first quotes from the *Historia* under 1091 in a marginal addition, and continues to annotate his text in this fashion to 1099. Under 1102 for the first time an extract from the *Historia* is in the main text, as are almost all the rest of his quotations to 1121. It follows that the section for 1102 is unlikely to have been written before 1123.[2]

In these years John's contact with Canterbury is also shown by the annal of his chronicle for 1126, where he quotes most of the text of a royal writ granting the archbishop custody of Rochester castle.[3] There is no obvious sign that John's work was known at Canterbury

[1] Brett, 'A note on the *Historia Novorum* of Eadmer', *Scriptorium*, xxxii (1979), pp. 56–8. It is often supposed that William of Malmesbury used the short version of Eadmer in his *Deeds of the Kings*, on a strict interpretation of *GR*, i. p. 2. This may be so, for the collection of primacy documents in *GR*, ii. pp. 347–52, is from a different source than the much fuller series in *GP*, pp. 39–62, which might suggest that William had had access to new materials from Canterbury in the interval. However, the plan of *GP* evidently allows for much more such material than does *GR*, and the conclusion is hard to prove, since the *Deeds of the Kings* treats events after 1109 in so summary a way. Within a matter of months of completing the *Deeds of the Kings* William knew Eadmer's second edition well enough to use and adapt it at length for the *Deeds of the Bishops*. Compare *GP*, pp. 132–3n, with *HN*, pp. 292–3, and *GP*, pp. 63–5, with *HN*, pp. 276–7, a relation first stressed by R. W. Southern, 'The Canterbury Forgeries', *EHR*, lxxiii (1958), p. 213 n. 1.

[2] The use of Eadmer's later books by John is rather peculiar. Between 1114 and 1116 *Flor. Wig.*, ii. p. 67 ll. 18–33, p. 68 ll. 20–4, p. 69 ll. 6–27 (adaptations of *HN*, pp. 225–6, 235–6, 237–8), are all alterations or additions to C. On the other hand *Flor. Wig.*, ii. p. 68 ll. 2–7 and 18–19, and ii. pp. 69–70, on the legation of Anselm (adaptations of *HN*, pp. 229–30, 235, 239), are in the main text, as are all the rest of John's borrowings to 1121. The Durham *History of the Kings* (below, p. 119) has all John's insertions from Eadmer except *Flor. Wig.*, ii. p. 68 ll. 20–4, which was presumably added after the other passages; this suggests that elements of Eadmer were added to the main chronicle in stages over a period of time.

[3] *Chron. John*, p. 23, quoting *Reg.* ii, no. 1475, Appendix no. clxxxviii. There is an almost contemporary copy of the writ in British Library Cotton MS Cleopatra E i, fo. 32ᵛ, which agrees with John and other copies in reading *constabulationem* for the *constabulariam* of the *Regesta* text.

particularly early. On the other hand Eadmer had certainly visited
Worcester, probably more than once, and maintained a correspondence with Prior Nicholas on historical problems at least as early as
1109. As bishop-elect of St. Andrews in 1120/1 Eadmer quarrelled
bitterly with King Alexander of Scotland and with the canons of
York. Nicholas followed the dispute, and supplied Eadmer with a
battery of historical evidence to prove that York had no claim on
him, as well as some excellent advice on his future conduct. A year or
two later the monks of Worcester decided to press the king to allow
them the freedom to elect their own bishop after the death of Bishop
Theulf. In pursuit of this rash scheme, they sought the support of
Archbishop William, William of Winchester, and, less obviously,
Eadmer. His reply was discouraging, but a close bond with Worcester
over many years is well attested. The exploitation of Eadmer's work
by John was part of a much larger pattern of mutual support.[1]

The relation of John's first version to William of Malmesbury is
more complex. Before the second revision of C there is no clear
evidence of borrowing by John from either the *Deeds of the Kings*
or the *Deeds of the Bishops*. However there are a number of passages
where John's text and William's in the *Deeds of the Kings* are
obviously closely related.[2] Deciding the nature of this relation

---

[1] Southern, *St. Anselm and his Biographer*, pp. 279–84, 369. The first letter of
Nicholas on the descent of King Edward the martyr was almost certainly
written before 1109. His account of his sources is striking: 'Haec omnia
antiquitatis auctoritate tam cronicarum quam carminum quae ea tempestate a
doctis patria lingua composita de his noscuntur, caeterarumque scripturarum
testimonio vera esse percepimus' (*Memorials of St. Dunstan* ed. W. Stubbs,
RS, 1874, pp. 423–4). His second letter (*Anglia Sacra*, ed. H. Wharton, ii.
pp. 234–6) can be dated to 1120 and equally displays a wide historical learning.
On the Worcester letters after the death of Bishop Theulf see D. Bethell,
'English Black Monks and episcopal elections in the 1120s', *EHR*, lxxxiv
(1969), esp. pp. 681–4, 694–8.

[2] The connection has been observed very often; see for example W. H.
Stevenson in *Asser's Life of King Alfred*, pp. lx–lxiii, 107–9, Darlington in
Vita Wulfstani, p. xviii n. 2, and D. Whitelock, 'William of Malmesbury on
the works of King Alfred', *Medieval Literature and Civilisation: Studies in
memory of G. N. Garmonsway*, ed. D. A. Pearsall and R. A. Waldron (London,
1969), pp. 78–93.

presents considerable difficulties. It is fairly certain that William's chronicle itself is not John's source, for there are substantial differences in wording between the two texts in their common narrative. While William was relatively exact in transcribing documents, he rehandles his other sources with great freedom; John on the other hand was a very literal compiler who modified his sources as little as grammar and brevity would allow. Since John was still writing his chronicle long after William finished his *Deeds of the Kings*, it is equally unlikely that William was adapting John. As Stubbs saw long ago, both must have used common sources.[1]

Since most of this common material is not known outside the two chronicles it is likely that it was collected by one house or the other. For some material there is no evidence for deciding which,[2] for more it is possible to suggest an origin. The incomplete thirteenth-century copy of the *Deeds of the Kings* at Troyes, first identified by Sir Roger Mynors, differs from all other known versions by the inclusion of two prefatory letters. Addressed to the Empress Matilda and King David of Scotland from the community at Malmesbury, they explain that the work was originally undertaken for Queen Matilda, who died in 1118. The letters were written in 1125/6, when the empress was expected back in England after the death of Henry V, and the accompanying text has been adapted to her sensibilities.[3] However, in other ways it preserves what appears to be a version more 'primitive' than the earliest form known to modern editors. It is distinguished by a few additions and a much

---

[1] *GR*, ii. pp. cxxviii–xxxi.

[2] These include the accounts of St. Wistan (*Flor. Wig.*, i. p. 72, *GR*, i. pp. 263–4), Godwin's gift to Harthacnut (*Flor. Wig.*, i. p. 195, *GR*, i. p. 229), and the raid on Anglesey in 1098 (*Flor. Wig.*, ii. pp. 41–2, *GR*, ii. p. 376). The passages on Anglesey and St. Wistan, though evidently related, must be independent, for each has information not in the other.

[3] The letters are printed by E. Könsgen, 'Zwei unbekannte Briefe zu den *Gesta Regum Anglorum* des Wilhelm von Malmesbury', *Deutsches Archiv*, xxxi (1975), pp. 204–14, from Troyes, Bibl. Mun. MS 294 bis. The alterations made to protect the sensibilities of the childless empress surely include the omission of *GR*, i. p. 117 § 113 on the scandalous carrer of Judith and i. p. 136 § 125 on Ethelfleda's refusal to bear further children.

larger number of omissions. These include the passages on the early
kings of Mercia, East Anglia, and Essex, the list of kings who rowed
King Edgar on the Dee, and a detailed account of the murder of
Walcher of Durham, all of which have close parallels in John.[1] The
letter of Cnut to England, only known in these two chronicles, is
also omitted from the Troyes text, but at the point where it occurs
in the other versions there is a note: 'See the letter at the end of
Book Four, at the letter E'.[2] There is nothing there now. The letter
appears then to be a later addition; and the descents of the early
kings and the details of the murder of Walcher are both read most
naturally as interpolations to an earlier text in the *Deeds of the Kings*.[3]
This does not prove that this matter was drawn from Worcester,
but it is likely, for the descents of the kings are among the earliest
dateable elements in the Worcester chronicle, and can be shown to
have circulated independently of it before 1131 at Bury as well as
Malmesbury.[4] So far it is probable that William enlarged his first

---

[1] The Troyes copy omits *GR*, i. pp. 96–102 § 97–mid § 105, which are
clearly related to *Flor. Wig.*, i. pp. 260–7, *GR*, i. p. 165 § 148 (pt), parallel to
Flor. Wig., i. pp. 142–3, and *GR*, ii. p. 330, all that part of § 271 which is close
to *Flor. Wig.*, ii. pp. 13–16.

[2] Troyes 294 bis, fo. 60, *Flor. Wig.*, i. pp. 185–9, *GR*, i. pp. 221–4; their
versions are collated and discussed in Liebermann, *Gesetze der Angelsachsen*
(Halle, 1903–16), i. pp. 276–7, iii. pp. 189–90.

[3] The Troyes version has no matter in common with John. The additions
in *GR*, ii. pp. 330–1, differ from John only in saying that Leobwin was struck
down by a thousand lances, against John's single axe. This may be no more
than a rhetorical flourish by William. The descents of the kings strike a bald
and incongruous note in William's stylish text, but are wholly characteristic
of the Worcester compiler's work.

[4] See *Asser's Life of King Alfred*, p. 110. In MS C of John, the tables appear
to have been first compiled in 1114/5, for Ernulf of Rochester (el. September
1114, cons. December 1115) is perhaps in the main hand, while Geoffrey of
Hereford (el. October/December 1115) was an early addition. This date has no
visible significance for the composition of the main chronicle, and it is
tolerably clear that the tables were physically distinct from the main manuscript for some time. The other copies do not agree with C (or, in general,
each other) in the sequence of the sections, each of which in C forms a separate
gathering. It is probable that these tables circulated independently of the main
chronicle, and possible that the distinctive work of Florence is to be found
among their pages. The voyage of Edgar on the Dee gives further hints of a

text with materials gathered at Worcester, and later also exploited by John.

The sequence of documents on the investiture crisis of 1111/2, which both William and John include, involves different problems and suggests a different answer. Again there is no question of either borrowing directly from the chronicle of the other, for there are important differences between their versions,[1] but in detail their texts are very closely related. Dr Thomson has recently proved that before 1124 William compiled a papal history which included these documents, and that John had this copied out. At 1111 John began to transcribe the oath of Pope Paschal, but then altered it to read 'extorted the oath which we have described in the Great Chronicle'. A later copy of the same compilation proves that it contained all the texts which John and William share, and in the same textual tradition.[2] Here it seems clear that John was using William's collections.

Worcester provenance. The Troyes version of *GR* has three named kings and an unspecified number of anonymous Welsh kings rowing his ship. *Flor. Wig.*, i. p. 142, and the version in *GR*, i. p. 165, name five Welsh kings, making eight in all. By 1109 Nicholas of Worcester had already written to Eadmer on Edgar's foreign successes: 'octo subregulos in exteris regionibus subditos et sibi servientes haberet' (*Memorials of St. Dunstan*, p. 423). See above, p. 113 n. 1, and W. H. Stevenson, 'The Great Commendation to King Edgar in 973', *EHR*, xiii (1898), pp. 505–7, discussing a passage from Aelfric's Life of St. Swithun, translated by D. Whitelock in *English Historical Documents 500–1042*, 2nd ed., no. 239 (g).

[1] Compare *GR*, ii. pp. 498–504, with *Flor. Wig.*, ii. pp. 60–6. Malmesbury's narrative contains part of the 'official' account which accompanied some copies of the documents. John lacks this but includes the text of the treaty of Ponte Mammolo. See *MGH, Constitutiones et Acta*, ed. L. Weiland, i. pp. 142–5 (nos 91–6) and pp. 571–3, also D. Schäfer, 'Die Quellen für Heinrich V. Romzug', *Historische Aufsätze dem Andenken an Georg Waitz gewidmet* (Hannover, 1886), pp. 144–55, esp. 147–9. For a recent summary with full bibliography U.-R. Blumenthal, 'Opposition to Pope Paschal II: some comments on the Lateran Council of 1112', *Annuarium Historiae Conciliorum*, x (1978), pp. 82–98.

[2] Thomson, *Archivum Historiae Pontificiae*, xvi (1978), pp. 93–112. William's texts have only one marked idiosyncracy, at *GR*, ii. p. 502, ll. 6–7, where 'exceptis . . . consistere' is an addition not found in the other English copies.

A series of converging details, then, suggests that William and John were using from the outset a common stock of material which each adapted to his independent purpose. It is hard to find early evidence of other Worcester borrowing from Malmesbury, but William's interest in Worcester is well known. His translation of Coleman's life of Wulfstan was written after 1124, but the *Deeds of the Bishops* of 1125 shows that he was already familiar with the work.[1] It cannot be as certain that he used other Worcester material, but it is likely that he came to know Asser there; both he and Eadmer would have found a copy of the First Life of Oswald most conveniently there, where the community venerated the saint, where the work was studied, and where the only surviving manuscript was written.[2]

From the outset then John's chronicle was constructed out of materials which were the objects of an active traffic between Canterbury, Malmesbury, and Worcester. Its subsequent revision shows these exchanges widening and intensifying.

The first stage of this expansion, found in the Dublin and Lambeth copies of HL, introduced new information of two main types. The first involved an elaboration of the Norman and Frankish element in the narrative. A copy of the 'Annals of Rouen' in a version close

---

In general William, John, and B. L. Harley 633, the later copy of William's *Liber Pontificalis*, present a version of Weiland's 'C' tradition (on which see further Holtzmann, *Neues Archiv*, l (1933), pp. 283–4). They agree in a number of readings: *GR*, ii. p. 499 (treaty, l. 2), *imperium vel* added; 500 l. 13 *cuncta* for *cetera*; 503 (Council, l. 7) *et abbatibus* omitted after *cardinalibus*, 504, § 429 l. 2 *Semies* for *Sennes*, l. 4 *Capsanus* for *Compsanus* or other readings, l. 11 *Troianus* added, as against all but two of the other collated copies, l. 12 *Siwinus* (*Siguinus* John) for *Bruno*. A striking case occurs at *GR*, ii. p. 503 (Council l. 16), where William reads *preterea* and John (MS C) has a paragraph mark. Both were apparently confused by a tironian *et*, which is the reading of Harley 633. All three texts derive independently from their source, but are more closely related to each other than any is to the other English copies of the texts I have examined.

[1] *Vita Wulfstani*, p. xix.

[2] See Whitelock, above p. 113 n. 2, Southern, *St. Anselm and his Biographer*, pp. 280–4, R. Thomson, 'The reading of William of Malmesbury', *Rev. bén.*, lxxxv (1975), pp. 362–402, esp. 392–4, 402.

to that used at St. Evroult supplied a bare scaffold of Norman chronology.[1] Hugh of Fleury's *Historia Ecclesiastica* of 1110 provided a sequence of more elaborate entries on Frankish history up to the reign of Louis the Pious, and particularly on the translation of St. Benedict to Fleury.[2] The use of Hugh is not in itself remarkable, for the writing of history at Fleury was closely associated with the royal house of England. Hugh dedicated his tract *De regia potestate* to King Henry, the *Historia Ecclesiastica* to his sister, Adela of Blois, and the *Historia Modernorum Regum* of *c.* 1114 to his daughter, the Empress Matilda. Later in his reign, King Henry had another universal history dedicated to him by an anonymous monk of Fleury too.[3] Manuscripts of the *Historia Ecclesiastica* are common in England, and Hugh's purpose was close to that of the English historians, but at present only John and William of Malmesbury are known to have used him so early, and they did so independently.[4]

[1] The Annals of Rouen exist in a multiplicity of forms; see particularly *Orderici Vitalis Historiae Ecclesiasticae Libri Tredecim*, ed. A. Le Prevost (*SHF*, 1838–55), v. pp. 139–73 (a late but complete version), F. Liebermann, *Ungedruckte Anglo-Normannische Geschichtsquellen* (Strassburg, 1879), nos VI–VIII (incomplete editions of English copies), and *Les Annales de l'abbaye Saint-Pierre de Jumièges*, ed. J. Laporte (Paris, 1954), a complete but idiosyncratic version with a valuable introduction. The editions of Thorpe and Petrie omit most of the Norman annals. In the edition of Howard representative entries from them are found s. ann. 416, 490, 588, 677, 876, 898, 917, 942.

[2] The only complete edition of his *Historia Ecclesiastica* is still *Hugonis Floriacencis monachi Benedictini Chronicon*, ed. B. Rottendorf (Münster, 1638) but compare Waitz in *MGH, Scriptores*, ix. pp. 337 ff. In the edition of Howard s. ann. 162, 523, 674, 840 may be compared with Hugh of Fleury, ed. Rottendorf, pp. 74, 133, 153, 180–1, for typical extracts. The interpolation s.a. 555 from a life of St. Austroberta (*Acta SS* Feb. ii. pp. 419–23) is not from Hugh.

[3] A. Vidier, *L'Historiographie à Saint-Benoit-sur-Loire et les miracles de Saint Benoit* (Paris, 1965), pp. 76–85, 111–12; A. Wilmart, 'L'Histoire ecclésiastique composée par Hugues de Fleury et ses destinataires', *Rev. bén.*, l (1938), pp. 293–305; R.-H. Bautier, 'La place de l'abbaye de Fleury-sur-Loire dans l'historiographie française du ixe au xiie siècle', *Études ligériennes d'histoire et d'archéologie mediévales*, ed. R. Louis (Auxerre, 1975), pp. 25–33.

[4] For William's use of Hugh see Thomson in *Rev. bén.*, lxxxv. pp. 387–8, *JEH*, xxix. p. 401, and *Medieval scribes, manuscripts and libraries*, pp. 137–8. Dr Thomson's amended date is to appear in a forthcoming paper. The extracts in Bodleian Lib. MS Arch. Selden B.16 do not coincide with those in John,

The second class of substantial addition made during the early revision contains a number of entries on the history of Lindisfarne/Durham. Some are certainly, and almost all may be, drawn from the *History of the Church of Durham* attributed to Simeon and probably written before 1108.[1] Durham and Worcester had long been in contact, for the monks of Worcester, including Florence and John, were entered in the Durham *Liber Vitae* by 1113, and John already had some detailed knowledge of events at Durham when he first wrote, for his very full account of the death of Bishop Walcher is in the original text and is quite distinct from that of Simeon. Use of the *History* however enlarged John's coverage of the farther north considerably, if not always happily.[2]

His debt was repaid almost at once, for the *History of the Kings*, written at Durham if not by Simeon, uses John as its chief source from 848 to 1119, though it itself continues to 1129. The original character and date of the work are obscured in the only surviving complete manuscript, which contains a revised text. The earlier

---

either in the main chronicle or in the *Chronicula* noticed below, though both use the enlarged version of 1110. William calls his source Haimo, John does not name his. Corpus Christi Coll., Cambridge, MS 265, pp. 443–550, is a Worcester copy of Hugh, which could just have been used by John, with whom it often agrees against Rottendorf's edition. The very common misattribution of the chronicle to Ivo is in a thirteenth-century hand. Of other early copies of Hugh in England one might single out the very fine Cambridge U.L. MS Dd. x. 20, which a late note on fo. 1 claims was given to Chichester cathedral by Bishop Seffrid I (1125–45).

[1] The entries under 635, 651, 664, 676/7, 687, 698, 707, 721, 802, 828, 845, 854, 900, 915, 928, 944, 995, 1020, 1048, and 1070 on Lindisfarne/Durham are all additions in C.

[2] *Liber Vitae Ecclesiae Dunelmensis*, facs. ed. (Surtees Soc., 1923), fo. 22, which is dated by the appearance of Bishop Sampson (1096–1112) and Prior Thomas (d. 1113). For Walcher see *Flor. Wig.*, ii. pp. 13–16, and, for a misplaced interpolation from SD, i. p. 105, which has caused much confusion, *Flor. Wig.*, ii. p. 8, on Bishop Aethelwine. Durham Cathedral Library MS Hunter 100 contains some notes from Bishop Robert's epitome of Marianus that may also indicate early contact with Worcester.

state can be recovered in part from two abbreviations, one to 1121 now best known as an early element in Howden's *Chronica*, the other to 1119. The abbreviations show that the original *History of the Kings* was closer to John's text than the surviving edition is, and that the text to 1119 at least was almost certainly written before 1135.[1] They do not however establish the existence of a form of either John's chronicle or of the *History of the Kings* which ended before 1129. The *History* does not simply copy John to 1119 and then abandon him; the last full quotation comes in that year, but already the *History* was exploiting other sources, and it echoes John into the entry for 1120. The texts diverge slowly.[2] Nor is it easy to

[1] Gransden, pp. 148–51, Offler, *Medieval Historians of Durham*, pp. 9–10, Hunter Blair in *Celt and Saxon*, pp. 67–113, D. Baker, 'Scissors and paste: Corpus Christi, Cambridge, MS 139 again', *Studies in Church History*, xi (1975), pp. 83–123. For early abbreviations see J. M. Todd and H. Offler, 'A medieval chronicle from Scotland', *SHR*, xlvii (1968), pp. 151–9, and the introduction by A. O. and M. O. Anderson to *The Chronicle of Melrose*, facs. ed. (London, 1936), pp. xi–xii. The contribution of Howden's source to reconstructing the original text of the *History of the Kings* is examined in H. Offler, 'Hexham and the *Historia Regum*', *Trans. Archit. and Archaeol. Soc. of Durham and Northumberland*, NS, ii. (1970), pp. 51–62. The abbreviation to 1119 is found in Liège U.L. MS 369C and British Library Cotton MS Caligula A viii, which was used by J. Hodgson Hinde in his edition of the *History of the Kings* (Surtees Soc., 1868). The Liège copy is fully described by B. Mehnan, 'Geoffrey of Monmouth, *Prophecies of Merlin*: new manuscript evidence', *Bulletin of the Board of Celtic Studies*, xxviii (1978), pp. 37–46, who shows that it or its archetype was written before 1135 but after 1124. The arguments from lists of bishops are very hazardous. The relation of these two abbreviations to the full text is clearly shown in two passages ultimately derived from *Flor. Wig.*, ii. pp. 16, 18. Under 1080 SD, ii. p. 211, has the death of Bishop Walcher and his companions 'ob quorum detestandae necis vindictam rex . . .'. Liège abbreviates to 'Walcherus Dun' episcopus a Norhumbrensibus occiditur. Ob quorum detestandae . . .', and Caligula amends *quorum* to *cuius*. Under 1085 Liège abbreviates SD, ii. p. 213, to 'Rex Willelmus tribus suis capellanis, Mauricio scilicet Lundoniensem, Willelmo Tedfordensem dedit presulatum', omitting the promotion of Robert to Chester. Caligula amends *tribus* to *duobus*.

[2] See Darlington in *Vita Wulfstani* pp. xvii–xviii n, though the two texts of the Council of 1125 are certainly independent. John is the *History*'s chief source to 1118; he provides long sections under 1119; the last clear echo of John is under 1120: *Chron. John*, p. 15, 'Rex . . . omnibus prospere et ad velle peractis a Normannia in Angliam redit', SD, ii. p. 258, 'Itaque rex . . . cunctis . . . ad votum prospere peractis . . . in Angliam multo [navigio] revehitur'.

see why the Durham chronicler should have abandoned work originally in 1119 or in 1121; he was clearly writing later than either year, since he quotes from Eadmer's *Historia Novorum* in the form which cannot have been completed before October 1122, and from John who quotes Eadmer.[1]

The Durham version of John's chronicle differs from the other copies in some respects. It is an abbreviation, so that its omissions are not necessarily significant, but it lacks all the additions found only in the later copies and many of those found in the earlier HL.[2] This suggests that its source was a very early state of John's chronicle. The likelihood is increased by the positive differences, for the *History of the Kings* has a set of Norman annals distinct from John's, some entered at different points, and a quite different sequence of entries on Durham wherever John has interpolated sections from Simeon's *History of the Church*. Where he used other Durham sources the *History of the Kings* follows or adapts him.[3] In short, at least two sets of John's earlier additions to his text are not found in the *History of the Kings*.

The simplest explanation of these facts is that the Durham copy of John was made before the additions from the *History of the Church of Durham* had been inserted in C. It is tempting to suppose that Worcester exchanged a copy of John for a copy of Simeon's *History of the Church* in a single transaction sometime before 1135

---

[1] SD, ii. pp. 248–52, follows John's abbreviation of Eadmer, but from then on makes increasing use of Eadmer himself.

[2] Under 1118 the anti-pope is called *Mauricio* in C, followed by all the copies. This was written over an erasure, and the *History* here has *Burdino*. See above, p. 112 n. 2, for an apparently later added note from Eadmer which is found in C and HL but not in the *History*.

[3] Of the Durham entries listed above at p. 119 n. 2 between 854 and 1070 the *History* omits those for 915, 928, 944, and 1070. It has other versions of 854, 899, 995, 1020, and 1048 (under 1043) at SD, ii. pp. 101–2, 121, 136, 156, and 162–4. Of the Norman annals listed above at p. 118 n. 1 the *History* has versions of 876 and 898 at SD, ii. pp. 111, 120, which are close to John's though with small but significant differences in 898. All the rest of John's entries are either omitted or distinct in the *History*.

but after 1122.[1] As at Canterbury and Malmesbury, an exchange of historical materials finds its place among many other connections between the houses.[2]

The first revision of John's chronicle then altered its character, with a new emphasis on the affairs of Normandy and France, and introduced a new set of English sources. The second stage of revision, found in manuscripts B and P, was less complex. Its chief feature was an intensive use of Malmesbury's *Deeds of the Bishops* in marginal notes, corrections, and interlineations. Some of these insertions are not skilfully managed, but they were not wholly mechanical; on a number of occasions John altered the forms of names he found in William to conform to the usage of his earlier tables.[3] The prefatory tables were also revised and extended; John erased the list of popes and replaced it with a much more elaborate one, and added the successions to the kingdom of France and duchy of Normandy to those of the English kingdoms. Other hands added some unreliable notes on the succession to the sees of

---

[1] The dates are provided by the completion of the *Historia Novorum* and the latest possible date for the ancestor of the Liège copy. Obviously these are extremes; since the Durham history ends in 1129 there must be some presumption that the author wrote in that year, though this is beyond demonstration yet. There are some grounds for supposing that the version of John known at Durham was not simply a very early state of C. Under 1088 the *History* has an account of the rising at Worcester and elsewhere which is quite distinct from that in C but closely related to that found partially in John's *Chronicula*, discussed below, and partly in the Worcester conflation of John and Malmesbury's *Deeds of the Bishops* printed by Liebermann in *Ungedruckte Anglo-Normannische Geschichtsquellen*, pp. 15–24, from British Library Cotton MS Vitellius C viii (compare *Vita Wulfstani*, p. xix n). The December storms of 1117 in SD, ii. p. 251, are partially noted in the margin of C p. 371.

[2] There were of course close links between the histories written at Canterbury, Durham, and Malmesbury outside the Worcester connection.

[3] Most of John's additions from *GP* are unprinted, since they are not in Howard's source H, and Thorpe sought to exclude them, not entirely successfully. Compare *Flor. Wig.*, i. pp. 59 (781), 116 n, 193, ii. p. 33, with *GP*, pp. 246, 177, 150, 151. There is an odd case under 675 (*Flor. Wig.*, i. pp. 33–4, *GP*, p. 143), where all the copies include an addition to C which is very close to William and possibly drawn from him. This is not by any means an exhaustive list of passages from *GP* which escaped Thorpe's eye.

Hereford, Lichfield, and Leicester.[1] This second stage of revision was simpler in conception and execution than the first.

The abbreviation of his own work in John's *Chronicula* is clearly close to this second revision, for it has the later tables and uses many passages inserted in C after the copying of HL.[2] However it has several peculiarities of content as well as arrangement. The most obvious are a series of verses, including laments for the deaths of King Edward, King Harold, and Bishop Wulfstan, which reflect the strong ties with the Saxon past Worcester retained long after the Conquest.[3] The *Chronicula* enlarges the Frankish element of its history by making fuller use of Hugh of Fleury, and by using some sources from Rheims and elsewhere which were not exploited at all in the main chronicle.[4] For English events, there appears to be only one substantial new source, apart from the verses, a set of annals which are closely related to the Latin half of the bilingual 'F'

---

[1] For example *Flor. Wig.*, i. pp. 58 n, 61 n, 62 n, 91 nn, 79 nn, 120 n. Few if any of these entries are in John's hand.

[2] In Cnut's letter (above, p. 115) the king of Burgundy is Rudolf with B and P, not the Robert of HL. There are other cases, of which the most striking is the appearance of fos 56ᵛ–7ᵛ of the *Visio Eucherii* attributed to Hincmar of Rheims. This is a marginal addition to C p. 277 and is found in P but not B. It was already known at Bury, for a virtually indistinguishable text of the *Visio* is found in the Annals of 'St. Neots', ed. Stevenson, pp. 126–7 (Trinity Coll., Cambridge, MS R.7.28, pp. 28–9), s.a. 741. For the dissemination of this text see U. Nonn, 'Das Bild Karl Martells in den lateinischen Quellen vornehmlich des 8. und 9. Jahrhunderts', *Frühmittelalterliche Studien*, iv (1970), pp. 111 ff.

[3] Fo. 95ʳ⁻ᵛ where Harold is described as:

Vir hic bellicosus	strenuus, decorus
Alter Machabeus	statura procerus
Et si vellet Deus	rex summus et verus

Fos 102ᵛ–3ᵛ contain the verses on Wulfstan, from which *Chron. John*, p. 6 n quotes four lines.

[4] Hugh of Fleury, ed. Rottendorf, pp. 156–7, 172–3, for example, are used at fos 53 and 57ᵛ–8. The eleventh-century Rheims forgery of a letter of St. Benedict (*MGH, SRM*, iii. p. 349, ed. B. Krusch) is on fo. 47ʳ⁻ᵛ; on fos 58ᵛ–9ᵛ is an account of the synod of Meaux of 858 which is of particular interest. It is a much fuller version of the only other printed record, which was taken by Mabillon from a manuscript of Gembloux in *Vetera Analecta* (Paris, 1675–85), i. pp. 386–7, and *Annales Ordinis S. Benedicti*, iii. p. 198. There are other sources to be identified here yet.

version of the Anglo-Saxon chronicle. F is a Canterbury manuscript, and the source of the *Chronicula* clearly came from Kent, for like F it contains the Kentish council at Bapchild of 694; it was however not F itself, but an independent transmission of the same material.[1] Lastly, the *Chronicula* contains a series of German miracle stories parallel to those entered in the margin of C, but distinct. One is reminded of the stories of this kind with which Malmesbury enlivened his *Deeds of the Kings*, but only one of these is found in the *Chronicula*, and that in a form which is certainly independent.[2] However the entries here and in the margins of the main chronicle show that a stock of such tales was as readily available at Worcester as at Malmesbury. The *Chronicula* is a baffling and unsuccessful work, obscure in purpose and clumsy in execution, yet it is not without value. It shows John making yet further use of Canterbury sources, it shows him well versed in the kind of material William was also exploiting, both in miracles and sober history, it preserves a few annals which are quite different from those used for the main text.[3] In short, it provides another window into the historical workshop at Worcester.

The evolution of the Worcester chronicle can be studied more closely than any other of its time. In the end one may wonder whether all John's effort was worth while. Much of the research

[1] The entries for 616, 633, 640, 648, 685, 688, 697, 785, 793, 806, 1041, 1048 in F. Magoun, '*Annales Domitiani Latini*: an edition', *Mediaeval Studies*, ix (1947), pp. 235–95, are represented in the *Chronicula*, and one or two others may be. Collation of the text of the Council of Bapchild (*Chronicula*, fos 53ᵛ–5ᵛ) with the versions of *Cartularium Saxonicum*, ed. W. de G. Birch (London, 1885–93), i. nos 91–2, seems to show that the Worcester text does not depend on F. It is likely that Lambert of St. Omer also secured a text close to F a few years earlier in compiling his *Liber Floridus* (facs. ed. by A. Derolez, *Lamberti S. Audomari canonici Liber Floridus*, Ghent, 1968, fos 73–5, discussed by R. Derolez, 'British and English history in the *Liber Floridus*', *Liber Floridus Colloquium*, ed. A. Derolez, Ghent, 1973, pp. 59–70).

[2] Compare *GR*, i. pp. 196–206, ii. pp. 230–6, 256–9, with C pp. 325–7 (not reprinted), the legendary account of Hermannus Contractus, and *Chronicula*, fos 79–80 (where the story of the dancers has the date and origin noticed in *GR*, ii. lxxv n, but not in Malmesbury's text), 84–93.

[3] See above, p. 122 n. 1.

was ill-digested. The form in which it was presented was convenient, but it allowed little room for a general view of the causes or purpose of human experience. John could not rival William of Malmesbury as a master of research, or Eadmer as an observer of his own times. Yet such reflections are ungrateful and can easily be exaggerated; for us, as for his contemporaries, John has preserved a mass of precious details of chronology. The modern scholar seeking fixed points for his narrative can still be grateful to John for his resolute if blinkered interest in the dates of men's deaths and the succession to ecclesiastical offices.

Had he never recorded a single event unknown from other sources, the interest of his work would remain considerable, for the Worcester chronicle is set in the middle of a web of extraordinarily complex historical activity, which drew together the chief centres of English Benedictine history. It is in the nature of the annalist's work to build upon the compilations of his predecessors, but the monastic historians at work in England by 1130 were not engaged in a merely mechanical process. Historical research at Durham, Worcester, Malmesbury, and Canterbury was accompanied by a frequent and elaborate exchange of its results as the work progressed. At a much higher level of intellectual activity it recalls the circulation of draft annals among the various compilers of the Anglo-Saxon chronicle before the Conquest. The monks who wrote history under Henry I were not simply responding to a similar challenge with similar responses, they shared the means to a common end. Their purpose was in part to reassert the continuity of experience across the great caesura of the Conquest, in part also to defend ancient title to lands and rights threatened by grasping or ignorant newcomers.[1] Monks were well-placed to remember the past, and had suffered heavily enough from the Conquest, yet neither of these causes affected the monks alone. There were other dangers which threatened the greater Benedictine houses in a more particular way. Their position of unquestioned eminence as the

---

[1] Best shown in Southern in *TRHS*, 5th ser., xxiii. pp. 246–56; illustrated by the intense activity of the post-conquest hagiographers.

pattern of religious excellence was weakened by the growing activity of the bishop and his diocesan agents, seeking to regulate the monks' conduct of their external affairs.[1] Canons and secular clergy challenged their claim to exercise any authority beyond their own cloister walls.[2] New monastic foundations struck more deeply still by contrasting the primitive simplicity of the Rule of St. Benedict with the elaborate customs of life and liturgy by which it was usually surrounded.[3] The monastic vocation was coming under a closer and more hostile scrutiny than ever before.

The justification for each house, and for the greater houses in general, lay in their past. Their saints, their customs, their rights, and their estates were the fruit of long growth in time. Violent political change and a new intellectual self-confidence threatened that tradition, and forced it to become articulate in self-defence. A school of monastic historians was the result.

---

[1] Brett, *English Church under Henry I* (Oxford, 1975), pp. 141–61.

[2] D. Nicholl, *Thurstan, archbishop of York* (York, 1964), pp. 187–91, Bethell, *EHR*, lxxxiv (1969), pp. 673 ff., Brett, *English Church*, pp. 136, 192–3.

[3] OV, iv. pp. 332–4, meets such criticism with a well-conceived historical answer.

The Historical Content of William of Malmesbury's Miracles of the Virgin Mary[1]

PETER CARTER

WHEN Odo, Prior of Christ Church, Canterbury, was visiting the court of Henry II in 1175 on the business of his House, he was horrified to find himself suddenly elected Abbot of Battle by a delegation from that royal foundation. For a long time he vigorously resisted the honour until one day he happened to recall the story of Theophilus and only then did he submit to the election.[2] No medieval witness, whether clerical or lay, would have been surprised to hear of the impact of this Miracle of the Virgin on Odo's reluctance. But perhaps the modern medievalist, no doubt familiar with this most famous of the Mary Legends, is slower to appreciate the significance and sheer size of this corpus of medieval literature. The Bollandist Albert Poncelet was able to number well over 1,800 Miracles of the Virgin, including variants, in 1904, and there have been many more catalogued since.[3] This article is an attempt to

---

[1] My greatest debt is to Richard Southern and Michael Wallace-Hadrill, who taught me the fascination of the Twelfth Century and the Dark Ages. I am also grateful to Hugh Weldon, who helped me to fathom Latin grammar, and to Clare Brant, who typed my text and corrected my English grammar. Finally my old friend and *conscholaris*, Donald Matthew, cast a professional eye over the draft and saved me from several nonsequiturs. All surviving errors are, of course, my own.

[2] J. S. Brewer (ed.), *Chronicon Monasterii de Bello* (London, 1846), p. 154; E. Searle (ed.), *The Chronicle of Battle Abbey* (Oxford, 1980), p. 292.

[3] A. Poncelet, 'Miraculorum B. V. Mariae quae saec. vi–xv latine conscripta sunt index', *AABB*, xxi (1902), 241–360. The most useful bibliography is that by E. F. Wilson, *The 'Stella Maris' of John of Garland* (Cambridge, Mass. 1946), pp. v–ix, 155–210.

make more familiar a tiny fraction of these, those compiled by William of Malmesbury, and to assess the relationship between his work as historian and as hagiographer that is the most obvious question raised by his editorial treatment of the fifty-three stories in his *Miracula Sanctae Mariae Virginis*.[1]

When, in 1923, Coulton protested that the absence of any published edition of William's Treatise was 'to the discredit of English scholarship',[2] he could not have been aware that the lacuna was justified on two counts: the immature state of research on the chronology of twelfth-century compilations of this kind, despite the pioneer work of Adolf Mussafia,[3] and the nature of William's own text, known at that time only in the unsatisfactory Salisbury manuscript.[4] In 1954 I was led to examine, on the strength of a remark by Philibert Ragey in his book on Eadmer, a second manuscript in the Bibliothèque nationale which proved to be one which allowed a proper edition to be contemplated, despite the missing folios and the misbound state of those surviving.[5] Now that this

---

[1] There is rather little here that is not in my unpublished thesis, 'William of Malmesbury's Treatise on the Miracles of the Virgin', submitted at Oxford in 1959 (referred to below as Thesis, i, ii, for the 2 volumes in the Bodleian). But I was prompted to make a fresh attempt at a summary by Rodney Thompson's prolific and impressive articles on Malmesbury's writings and by his publication of some of my findings in his 'The Reading of William of Malmesbury: Addenda et Corrigenda', *Rev. bén.*, 86 (1976), pp. 327–35. Dr Thompson and myself approach William from rather different angles and reach different conclusions: his reassessment of the chronicler's wide knowledge of books has not much tempered my impatience with the way William handles evidence.

[2] G. G. Coulton, *Five Centuries of Religion*, i (Cambridge, 1923), pp. 502–3.

[3] A. Mussafia, 'Studien zu den mittelalterlichen Marienlegenden', *Sitzungsberichte der k. Akademie der Wissenschaften zu Wien (Phil.-Hist. Kl.)*. This major pioneer work appeared in five parts between 1886 and 1898: it was in Vol. CXXIII (1891), pp. 18–28, that he surveyed Malmesbury's Collection from MS Salisbury 97, to which his attention had been drawn by H. L. D. Ward.

[4] MS Salisbury 97, fos 91ᵛ–114ᵛ, early xiii c. This had been listed by B. Botfield, *Notes on the Cathedral Libraries of England* (1849), p. 406, before being included by S. M. Lakin in his *Catalogue of Salisbury Cathedral Manuscripts* (1880).

[5] Paris, BN, MS lat. 2769, fos 55ʳ–84ᵛ, late xii c., from St. Denis. The text is ascribed to Eadmer in a seventeenth-century hand. The ascription of the Prologue to William of Malmesbury was printed in the Corrigenda to Vol. III of the *Cat. des MSS latines de la Bibl. nat.* (1952), p. 404. Fr. Canal, who knew

edition has been published by the Spanish scholar J. M. Canal,[1] using both manuscripts, it is possible to form an opinion of William's competence in the Treatise, temptingly described by Dr Southern in 1958 as 'in many ways the most interesting of his later works'.[2]

The earliest notice of the Collection in post-medieval times already contains an insoluble problem. For Leland, in noticing now lost copies in the libraries of Keynsham and Wells, reported that the latter was in four books:[3] and this can be supported by no surviving evidence. Both the Salisbury and the Paris MSS are divided into two books, but they are very differently arranged and the relationship between these two MSS will require further consideration. In the seventeenth century, the Salisbury MS was studied by Richard James but unfortunately his notice was garbled by Tanner so that Stubbs, in his influential edition of the *Gesta Regum*, followed him in referring to a James MS that never existed.[4] Consequently

---

of this MS from H. Barré, published a full description of it in his edition, cited below, pp. 104–6.

[1] J. M. Canal, 'El Libro de Laudibus et Miraculis Sanctae Mariae de Guillermo de Malmesbury, O.S.B. (†*c.* 1143)', *Claretianum*, viii (Rome, 1968), pp. 71–242 (hereafter referred to as Canal). Fr Canal's edition contains some errors in the text, as indeed does my unpublished edition: he has omitted by oversight a paragraph on *Iustitia* that should follow at p. 112, line 3, and he has had some difficulty with faulty microfilms on pp. 163, 164, and 195. Unfortunately he has included, pp. 209–11, from the Salisbury MS an interpolated Vision of St. Lawrence, which comes from Osbert of Clare (E. W. Williamson, *The Letters of Osbert of Clare*, Oxford, 1929, Ep. 22 (to Cecilia), pp. 93–6), and this has meant that our numbering of the later stories does not coincide. Canal's interest in the Treatise as a work of piety and mine as a work of history also means that our respective commentaries do not have much in common.

[2] R. W. Southern, 'The English Origins of the "Miracles of the Virgin" ' (hereafter cited as Southern, 'Origins'), *MARS*, iv (1958), p. 201.

[3] J. Leland, *De rebus Britannicis Collectanea*, iv (Oxford, 1715), p. 68 for Keynsham; ibid. p. 155 for Wells: 'Gulielmi, cantoris Malmesbiriae, libri 4ᵒʳ de miraculis Divae Mariae'. Leland gives the Incipit: *Multi miracula in Commentarii de Scriptoribus Britannicis* (Oxford, 1709), p. 196.

[4] Oxford, Bodleian, MS James 11, fo. 240, contains notes on 'Priest of One Mass' (Wm. M. No. 29) from *MS Sarisb. bibliotaphii*, i.e. MS 97; T. Tanner. *Bibliotheca Britannico-Hibernica* (London, 1748), p. 360: *MS in bibl. eccl. Sarisb, MS Bodl. James 72 (recte* James 11); *GR,* i. p. cxxiii, n. 7.

Stubbs was persuaded, though with marked reservations, to adopt Hamilton's supposition that William's autograph copy survived in a Cottonian MS which in fact had no resemblance to either William's hand or composition.[1]

Two years after the publication of the *Gesta Regum*, Mussafia published a synopsis of the Salisbury MS but his work remained unknown except to specialists in the field of Mary Legends.[2] He was surprised to discover that this MS presented the stories in a different sequence from what would be expected after studying those later compilations which were clearly derived from William either by selection, abbreviation, or translation. He came to the conclusion that the Salisbury MS must have been subject to a recasting either by the author or by another[3] in order to match the sequence of these later collections and, in ignorance of the Paris MS, he made a very reasonable attempt at calculating the sequence of the lost exemplar. Only in a few small particulars did he err.[4] But it is now possible to assert that the Salisbury MS is a copy of William's draft and that the author himself was responsible for recasting it into the final or 'published' edition, represented, if patchily, by the Paris MS. The evidence for this lies in several small phrases scattered through the Paris MS and elsewhere which only an author would have bothered to insert.[5] It was also Mussafia's

[1] This was MS Cotton Cleopatra C. x, fos. 101–144ᵛ; *GR*, i. pp. xviii–xix; *GP*, p. viii, n. 1.

[2] H. L. D. Ward, *Catalogue of Romances in the Department of MSS in the British Museum*, vol. ii (London, 1893), 586 ff. (Hereafter cited as Ward.)

[3] Mussafia, iv (1891), p. 26. Canal, pp. 100–1, maintains that the Salisbury MS shows a corrupted sequence of the original order and that therefore the Paris sequence is the earlier.

[4] Mussafia placed 'Theophilus' after 'Jerome Bishop of Pavia'; 'Clerk of Chartres' and 'Five *Gaudes*' after 'Prayers of a Friend'; 'Mary Image Confounds Saracens' after 'Mary Image Insulted'. He worked on the principle that the Book II stories in the Salisbury MS must precede Book I stories, in each class, in the final arrangement. But the Paris MS proves, except for the absence of evidence for Wm. M. Nos 50–1, that this was not so.

[5] These are: (i) A new introduction, *Verum quia . . . dignitatis*, to the story 'Jew Lends to Christian' when it is partly recopied in MS Salisbury, fo. 112ᵛ, to fit its revised place after 'Two Brothers at Rome'. (ii) The phrase *de qua prius dixi* (the image in Agia Sophia) in the second text of 'Mary Image

contention that William had from the beginning planned to arrange his stories in a sequence reflecting the worldly hierarchy of the recipients of the Virgin's favour: bishops and abbots followed by monks, clerks, priests, laymen, women, images. But this scheme does not in fact fit the earlier folios of the draft.[1] It was only when he reached the twenty-fifth story, 'Julian the Apostate', that William had clearly made up his mind to introduce such a plan, and it was this which meant that a fundamental rearrangement would ultimately be necessary. The duplication of two stories in the Salisbury MS and the copying out of part of another was not due to the carelessness of a later scribe, but can be explained by the author taking steps to remind himself of the future, revised sequence, for which certain modifications in the text also needed to be made. He decided too that the slight story about a clerk's resistance to female charm, which in the Salisbury MS is given separate status, should go to form an epilogue to 'Love by Black Art'.[2]

Insulted' in MS Salisbury, fo. 113ᵛ—this superceded *de qua post dicemus* in the first text on fo. 101ᵛ. (iii) A new epilogue to 'Jew Lends to Christian'—*Sed haec alias . . . industria Mariae* in the Paris MS, fo. 73ʳ, to introduce the new position of 'Jewish Boy'. This passage could not ever have been a part of the Salisbury sequence, for it refers back to the first words of 'Julian the Apostate' which, in the draft, comes later than 'Jew Lends to Christian'. (iv) A new reference *ut dixi* in 'Clerk of Chartres' in the Paris MS, fo. 77ᵛ. This refers *back* to the story 'Fulbert of Chartres' which in the Salisbury draft is *later* than 'Clerk of Chartres'. (v) A new ending *quam, propter nova narratio, secundi libri novabitur initio* to 'Sudden Death' in MS Cambridge Univ. Mm 6 15, fo. 141ᵛ (not printed by Canal, p. 174), which must be William's own revision since, in the draft, the Prologue to Book II does not follow 'Sudden Death'. (vi) The last words of 'Mary of Egypt' in the Cambridge MS and of 'Wife and Mistress' in MS Balliol 240 may also be by William—these stories are lost from the Paris MS.

[1] The sequence of the first stories and indeed many of the later ones is more obviously dictated by consideration of related places and types of miracle, Thesis, i. pp. 20–1.

[2] The duplicated stories are: 'Stained Corporale', fo. 96ʳ and fo. 108ᵛ, and 'Mary Image Insulted', fo. 101ᵛ and fo. 113ᵛ. The introduction (modified) to 'Jew Lends to Christian' on fo. 101ᵛ is found again on fo. 112ᵛ but the story's length precludes a full transcription. The story of the Clerk, at fo. 97ʳ in the Salisbury MS is later subjoined to 'Love by Black Art' in the Paris MS, fo. 81ᵛ.

After this brief résumé of the manuscripts and their relationship, William's Treatise may be described. The Prologue is nearly an eighth of the whole but is of less interest to the historian than to the theologian. William starts with the premiss that the Virgin epitomizes the Four Cardinal Virtues and their *collatorales* as laid down by Cicero in his *De Inventione*.[1] The application of the Roman barrister's worldly judgements to the Virgin Mary's other-worldly merits seems unconvincing to the modern mind. But, as Canal has pointed out, Fulbert of Chartres had adopted a similar procedure in his sermon on the Virgin's Nativity, and Jotsoaldus in his Life of Odilo had itemized the Cluniac abbot's character in a similar way. Indeed, the identification of *virtutes* with *miracula* goes back at least as far as Gregory's *Moralia*, and Dominic of Evesham's Prologue to his Miracles of the Virgin, which William certainly used, had made the same point, if only in brief.[2] The rest of the Prologue is close to Anselm and his Circle: the arguments of the *Cur Deus Homo* are rehearsed, large parts of Anselm's *Oratio VII* are reproduced verbatim, and Eadmer's *De Excellentia B. Mariae* is influential. The final pages, in which William advocates the truth of the Assumption, make use of Pseudo-Augustine and perhaps Paul the Deacon, as Canal has shown.[3] Beginning with 'Theophilus' William then proceeds to recount the Miracles.

Since the titles given by Mussafia to the Miracles were in German and those by Canal in Spanish, with Latin rubrics of his own devising in the text, it will be convenient to list the contents of William's Collection in its final form. For the titles themselves, which take on a bewildering variety of names in international

[1] *De Inventione* ii, cc. 53–4. For William's extensive knowledge of Cicero, see R. M. Thompson, 'The Reading of William of Malmesbury', *Rev. bén.*, lxxxv (1975), pp. 372–7.

[2] Fulbert's Sermon *Approbate consuetudinis*, PL 141, col. 322 (Canal, p. 112, n. 3); Jotsoaldus, *De Vita et Virtutibus Sancti Odilonis Abbatis*, I, vi (*PL* p. 142, cols 901–2); Gregory, *Moralia in Iob*, XXVIII, ii (*PL* 76, cols 463–6); Dominic of Evesham, Southern, 'Origins', pp. 179–81.

[3] I have listed the main Anselmian references in the synopsis below. For the last two items, Canal, pp. 121, n. 40 and 126, n. 48.

publication, I have relied as far as possible on those used by E. F. Wilson in her elaborate edition of the *Stella Maris*; and for the incipits, on Poncelet's Index in so far as they are to be found there. As for William's sources, something more will need to be said by way of explanation.

SYNOPSIS OF WILLIAM OF MALMESBURY'S VIRTUES AND MIRACLES OF THE VIRGIN MARY

PROLOGUE (The Virtues)

Incip: *Multi miraculi Dei genitricis* (MS Salisbury 97, fo. 91^v)
    Multi Dominae Sanctae Mariae laudes (MS Paris lat. 2769, fo. 55^v)

Explic: *tale constituam referendi principium* (MS Salisbury. 97, fo. 93^v; MS Paris 2769, fo. 60^v)

Main sources: Fulbert of Chartres, *Sermo de Nativitate B.M.V.* (PL 141, col. 322); Cicero, *De Inventione*, II, cc. 53–4; Anselm, *Cur Deus Homo*, I, c. 5 (ed. F. S. Schmitt, ii.p. 52); Eadmer, *De Excellentia B. Mariae*, cc. 4–6, 11 (PL 159, col. 561 ff); Anselm, *Oratio VII* (ed. F. S. Schmitt, iii. pp. 22–3); Pseudo-Augustine, *De Assumptione B.M.V.* (PL 40, cols 1141–8)

MIRACLES

Sequence in MS Salis. 97	Nos in Canal's Editn.	Nos in unpub. thesis	Story titles	Poncelet Index Mir. BVM	Sources of William's Miracle stories
			BOOK I		
(1)	1	1	Theophilus	1634	?DOM 2
(25)	2	2	Julian the Apostate	506	DOM 4
(26)	3	3	Hildefonsus	1720	HM 1 (*GR*, i. 193–4)
(27)	4	4	Toledo	914	TS 1
(28)	5	5	The Jews of Toulouse	1780	★ (*GR*, ii. 455)
(29)	6	6	St. Bon	175	MB 6 BHL 1420 (*GR*, ii. 391)

(30)	7	7	St. Dunstan	150	(*GP*, 3, 30–1) *VD*, 315–17
(31)	8	8	Siege of Chartres	695	*GR*, i. 138
(32)	9	9	Fulbert of Chartres	1221	*GR*, ii. 341 (*GR*, i. 226)
(33)	10	10	Milk: Monk Laid out as Dead	1660 + 1099	TS 11
(34)	11	11	Jerome Bishop of Pavia: *Ibis et tu*	—	HM 13
(34)	11	11ᵃ	Pavia: Theodoric's Daughter	—	*
(34ᵃ)	11	11ᵇ	Pavia: St. Sirus	—	?*
(34ᵇ)	11	11ᶜ	Pavia: St. Augustine	—	(Ferrandus, *Vita Fulgentii*; Bede, *Chron.*)
(34ᶜ)	11	11ᵈ	Pavia: Boethius	—	?*Elogium Boeti*
(2)	12	12	Guy Bishop of Lescar	800	*
(3)	13	13	Elsinus	Cf. 1781	TS 15; *GR*, ii. 312, 317
(4)	14	14	Guimund and Drogo	1648 + 1783	*
(35)	15	15	Devil in Three Beast Shapes	1162	TS 9
(36)	16	16	Drowned Sacristan	398	HM 2
(37)	17	17	Monk of St. Peter's Cologne: *Duo miracula*	—	HM 7 (*GR*, i. 204)
(38)	18	18	Vision of Wettin: *Simile huic*	+1749	Hatto, *Visio Guetini*
(39)	19	19	St. Odo and the Thief-Monk	890	DOM 6 ?TS 10
(40)	20	20	Pilgrim of St. James	397	HM 8
(40ᵃ)	21	20ᵃ	Recapitulation: *Haec profecto*	—	
(41 & 5)	21	21	Stained Corporale	1313	HM 14
(6)	22	22	Prior of St. Saviour's Pavia	1314	HM 12
(7)	23	23	Monk of Eynsham	Cf. 735	*GP*, 314–15
(8)	24	24	Sudden Death: Burgundy	202	MB 2 = Ponc. 1186

BOOK II

(41ᵃ)	—	24ᵃ	Prologue: *Recens narrandi*	—	
(9)	25	25	Clerk of Chartres	668	HM 3
(10)	26	26	Five Gaudes	697	HM 4
(42)	27	27	Clerk of Pisa	1211	HM 16
(43 + 11)	28	28	Love by Black Art	396	MB 5 = Ponc. 1230
(44)	29	29	Priest of One Mass	40	HM 9
(45)	30	30	Prayers of a Friend	505 but not + 36	★
(46)	31	31	Two Brothers at Rome	1183	HM 10 *Dicta Anselmi*
(47 + 24)	32	32	Jew Lends to Christian: Sails to Alexandria	1748	Uncertain
(12)	33	33	Jewish Boy	833	GR, ii. 341–2; DOM 1
(13)	34	34	Bread: Offered to Christ Child	219	?Ponc. 1671
(48)	35	35	Dying Freeliver	1151 + 1779	★
(14)	36	36	Charitable Almsman	393	HM 5
(15)	37	37	Ebbo the Thief	163	HM 6
(16)	38	38	Rustic Church Enlarged: Bury St. Edmunds	736	★
(17)	39	39	Three Knights	1747 + 1074	TS 12
(24ᵃ)	40	—	(*Vision of St. Laurence*)	—	Osbert of Clare, *Letter 22*
(18)	41	40	Mary of Egypt	1536 but not 1620	DOM 11
(19)	42	41	Musa	1030	TS 3
(20)	43	42	Abbess: Confidence Betrayed	605	DOM 12
(21)	44	43	Nun's Penance Uncompleted	1620	MB 3 = Ponc. 1307
(22)	45	44	Childbirth in the Sea	499	DOM 3
(48ᵃ)	46	44ᵃ	Recapitulation: *Multa quidem*	—	

(49)	46	45	Mead	121	VD, 265–6 (TS 14) (GR, i. 142) (GP, 196)
(50)	47	46	Wife and Mistress: *Sunt illa quoque*	1525	MB 4 = Ponc. 1674
(51)	47	47	Murieldis	1524	HM 17
(52)	47	48	Foot Cut Off	1528	TS 2
(52ª)	48	48ª	Recapitulation: *Talibus dicendis*	—	
(53)	48	49	Fire at Mont St. Michel	340	HM 15
(54)	49	50	Mary Image Confounds Saracens	1199	(GR, ii. 248–50)
(55 & 23)	50	51	Mary Image Insulted: Saturday	916	TS 7 + TS 16
(56)	50	52	Constantinople Thrice Saved: *Denique tempore Archadii*	—	(Theodoret, *Hist. Eccl.*) Hugh of Fleury
(57)	51	53	Purification	1195	Hugh of Fleury
(57ª)	—	53ª	First Epilogue: *Plura de talibus*	—	
(57ᵇ)	—	53ᵇ	Final Epilogue: *Sed concede timori* Explic: *ut videam Deum deorum in Sion* (MS Salis. 97, fo. 114ᵛ)	—	

Explanatory Notes:

(1) *MS Salisbury 97*: My numbers show the sequence but are not the numbers found in the MS. These are omitted because, after the numbering of the Prologue chapters, 'Theophilus' is No. xv. The list of contents, fo. 91ʳ, omits xxii and so is out of step.

(2) *MS Paris lat. 2769*: Not given a numbered sequence because of the missing folios. The lacunae run (*a*) from half way through 'Pavia: Boethius' to a point shortly after the opening of the Prologue to Bk II and (*b*) from half way through 'Three Knights' to the end of the Treatise. I have given separate status to all the four Pavian anecdotes on the evidence of this MS.

(3) *Other MSS*: The many other MSS used by Canal and myself are not of much value in establishing the text and are omitted here; they are listed by

Canal, 97–100, in my Thesis, i. 4–6, 99. As for the sequence they provide some evidence that my 51° came to precede my 50°, but like Canal I have retained the Salisbury MS sequence.

(4) *Sources*: HM, TS, and MB are sequences explained in the text. DOM is Dominic of Evesham. *VD* is William's *Vita Dunstani*. Bracketed sources are minor or indirect. An asterisk indicates no known written source.

It has been clearly established by R. W. Southern that the earliest identifiable collection of Mary Legends was put together in England in the early twelfth century by someone who was almost certainly Anselm the Younger, nephew of the Archbishop. This compilation consisted of the sequence called by Mussafia HM together with some uncertain portion of another sequence of 17 stories termed TS. Shortly after this collection was in circulation, Dominic Prior of Evesham, borrowing but a single HM–TS story, that of the Jewish Boy, compiled a shorter collection of 14 stories, called the Elements Series because the first four demonstrate the Virgin's powers over Fire, Air, Water and Earth. Dominic's work no longer survives as a separate work but some unknown compiler used it to form Book I of a conflated text, of which HM and TS go to form Books II and III.[1] It was, however, probably before this took place that William of Malmesbury began his work and although never referring to Dominic by name and only alluding to Anselm by suppressing *his* name, he clearly went through their collections selecting and rewriting in his usual way. In short, he used eight stories from Dominic, all but one from HM (and that omission probably because the story was about a peasant) and all but seven of the full TS series of 17.[2] The only other collection he

[1] Southern, 'Origins', pp. 176–200: I have followed him with only minor quibbles, Thesis, i. pp. 37–41. Dominic's work is also described by J. C. Jennings, 'The Origin of the "Elements Series" of the Miracles of the Virgin', *MARS*, vi (1968), pp. 84–93. The most convenient text of HM–TS (in an early stage) is E. F. Dexter (ed.), *Miracula sanctae virginis Mariae* (Madison, 1927), hereafter cited as Dexter.

[2] Thesis, i. pp. 42–3. It is not clear whether the missing TS stories were deliberately excluded or whether William had only an incomplete TS series to work from. Canal, p. 93, must be mistaken to argue that the HM–TS stories are later than and derived from Dominic and William. As for Anselm

can be shown to have used was the sequence I have termed MB, six stories found usually in rhythmical Latin.[1] This means that only a small fraction of the collect on is original, as far as we can now tell: 'The Jews of Toulouse', 'Guy Bishop of Lescar', 'Guimund and Drogo', 'Rustic Church Enlarged', and 'Mary Image confounds Saracens' all probably come from oral testimony while the stories about Pavian saints (11^a–11^d) and those about Constantinople (52°–53°) are compiled from William's own research. 'Prayers of a Friend' and 'Dying Freeliver' appear to have come from written miracle stories but these have not been traced. In Book II, the Prologue, recapitulations, and epilogues are of course his own inspiration.

After this outline, it is necessary to ask to what use can medievalists who are not specialists in Mary Legends put this Treatise, apart from its value in illustrating the pious literature available to monastic readers and audiences. Miracles of the Virgin, unless they are connected with particular shrines, offer little of value to the social historian investigating for instance the incidence of disease in the medieval community. As William several times remarks, it is the Virgin's distinction to have more concern for the salvation of souls than the cure of bodies.[2] The historian of theology can learn something by observing how certain miracles were used in the Eucharistic controversy, or how others were used in sermons or for

---

of Bury, William suppresses his name in 'Stained Corporale' because 'he is said to be still living' (Canal, p. 171, line 1216). The missing HM story is HM 11 'Rustic who Removed Landmarks'—best explained by William's contention that the Virgin's glory is best shown by favours to men of rank, not to mere peasants.

[1] Thesis i. p. 45 n. 3 lists some of the MSS where these are found. Though not always six in number, they are always in the same order, which is not that of William's Collection: this implies that they are William's source and not vice versa.

[2] Canal, p. 227, lines 1571–92, which refer back to three brief stories which William has just told with extreme brevity and no enthusiasm. They deal with a family quarrel, a case of madness, and the amputation of a leg (Wm. M. Nos 46–8).

advocating particular Marian Festivals.[1] The student of popular songs or plays may glean a little, although not commonly from twelfth-century evidence: William, who was always interested to note these in the *Gesta Regum*, provides two morsels here, for he says that the story of 'Julian the Apostate' was sung in the streets and that the story of 'Ebbo the Thief' was in his time a popular ballad, pre-dating by far but perhaps lying behind the Robin Hood legends whose form is not defined before the later Middle Ages.[2] The iconographers of Medieval Art since the time of Emile Mâle have deciphered many of the more popular Mary Legends found in illuminated manuscripts, stone carving, frescoes, or stained glass, but virtually all of the twelfth-century work has long since been lost.[3] Only the philologists, in fact, have made the miracles of the

---

[1] 'Jewish Boy' was used by Paschasius in the Eucharistic Controversy, *De Corpore et Sanguine Domini*, c. ix (*PL* 120, cols 1298–9), although William relies mainly on his own earlier account in *GR*, ii. pp. 341–2. It is also found in a sermon by Herbert Losinga (E. M. Goulburn and H. Symonds, *The Life, Letters and Sermons of Bishop Herbert de Losinga*, ii, Oxford, 1878, pp. 30–3). There are at least four of William's Miracles (No. 7 St. Dunstan and Nos 50–2) to be found, much abbreviated, in the Exeter Ordinal (J. N. Dalton (ed.), *Ordinale Exoniense*, vol. iii, London, 1926, pp. 341, 346). For Marian Festivals by far the most influential was the story of 'Elsinus' (Wm. M. No. 13), used to promote the Feast of the Conception.

[2] For 'Julian the Apostate' (Wm. M. No. 2) should be noted the reference in William's Commentary on Jeremiah (MS Bodley 868, fo. 105ʳ): 'Iam vero de Iuliani exitu quid attinet dicere, quod pro magnitudine calamitatis *cantitatur* in triviis.' The story of the killing of Swein by the martyr St. Edmund (*GR*, i. 212) is obviously based on this killing of Julian by the martyr St. Mercurius, although to John of Salisbury, *Policraticus*, VIII, p. 21 (ed. C. C. J. Webb, ii. 381–2), the former was proof of the latter, in the absence of confirmation from Orosius! As for 'Ebbo the Thief' (Wm. M. No. 37) as a popular ballad, William asserts: 'Celeberrimae relationis studio apud saeculares maxime frequentatur res gesta de Ebbone fure . . .' (Canal, p. 204, lines 852–3). There are four resemblances to the Robin Hood of later tradition, apart from his name in a phrase like *de Ebbone fure*: his reputation for escaping from traps, his devotion to the Virgin, his sharing of his plunder with the poor, and his final 'retirement' to a convent.

[3] The earliest recorded example in English medieval art is probably the 'pannus lineus cui intexta sunt miracula beatae Mariae', given by Henry of Blois to Winchester Cathedral (Edmund Bishop, *Liturgica Historica*, Oxford, 1918, p. 401).

Virgin their own, because there are convenient Latin analogues with which to compare the earliest known compositions in the romance vernaculars.[1]

By using much the same procedure as the philologists, it is possible to compare William's miracle stories with the sources he used and so understand a little more about his standards of accuracy or his treatment of texts. This is the more valuable because William's handling of these, in particular the Glastonbury traditions, has long aroused controversy. In one sense the conclusions will be disappointing: there will be found hardly any new historical information and much that is mistaken, even when he is dealing with English stories. His redrafting of his own accounts of St. Dunstan's visions is quite alarmingly confused; in retelling the story of Athelstan's visit to Glastonbury, 'Mead', he does not help to clear up the longstanding problem of the mysterious Ethelfleda.[2] 'Rustic Church Enlarged' is a story from Bury that tells us nothing about the Abbey but only how a parish church was rebuilt after a peasant had seen a vision of the Virgin. Only in the anecdote about 'Guimund and Drogo' does William tell us something we did not know already about a figure of some importance—at least at Oxford—the first

[1] The most useful for their publication of Latin text are: C. Neuhaus, *Die lateinischen Vorlagen zu den altfranzösischen Adgar'schen Marienlegenden* (Aschersleben, 1886–7), hereafter cited as Neuhaus, *Die lat. Vorlagen*, and the same scholar's *Die Quellen zu Adgars Marienlegenden* (Aschersleben N.D., c. 1882), hereafter cited as Neuhaus, *Die Quellen*. For William of Malmesbury's influence on vernacular collections, H. Kjellman, *La Deuxième Collection anglo-normande des miracles de la Sainte Vierge et son original latin* (Paris, Uppsala, 1922), hereafter cited as Kjellman, is useful. I have examined his influence on later collections generally in my Thesis, i. pp. 58–80.

[2] 'St. Dunstan' (Wm. M. No. 7), Canal, pp. 143–5, is a conflation of passages culled from his *GP* and from his and Osbern's Lives of Dunstan: the end product, which I have attempted to unravel, Thesis, ii. pp. 348–56, makes nonsense of the visionary tradition. In 'Mead' (Wm. M. No. 45), Canal, pp. 324–6, Ethelfleda is not named, but William continues to identify the recluse of Glastonbury with Athelstan's *nutrex*, which is chronologically impossible (W. Stubbs (ed.), *Memorials of St. Dunstan*, (RS, 1874, p. lxxvii). Southern, 'Origins', p. 195, first pointed out William's historical shortcomings in the Treatise, by showing how he came to mis-date the mission of Elsinus to Denmark (Wm. M. No. 13).

Prior of St. Frideswide's, whose witty words when sailing to Jaffa match the only other story we have of him, of how he came to attract the attention of Henry I by pretending to be illiterate.[1]

The continental stories, on the other hand, form by far the largest component and it will be more appropriate to discuss some of these in detail. Those from France, Burgundy or Germany, perhaps the least interesting, will have to be neglected, and those from Byzantium, which deserve much more attention, reluctantly omitted because of the very complex problems they raise. The stories from Italy will be given some consideration later but those from Spain and neighbouring Aquitaine deserve the first place and give us much the most rewarding insight into William's knowledge of Europe—and its limitations.

For here can be seen most clearly the contrast between the scrupulous historian of the remote past and the contemporary myth-maker. Whereas William's knowledge of Visigothic Spain is impressive, even when inappropriate, the nearer he moves to his own times the more he comes to depend on the insubstantial rumours that were the despair of his greatest editor, Stubbs.[2] Deprived of any real guidance after Isidore of Seville, whose *Chronica Maiora* closed in 615, he could not even be sure of the date of the Saracen conquest of Spain, an event which he was capable of placing almost a century too early or too late.[3] He was also misled by Carolingian sources,

---

[1] 'Guimund and Drogo' (Wm. M. No. 14), Canal, pp. 159–60. Guimund, when the ship was becalmed, suggested that the pilgrims pray to the bilingual St. Mary, because the local saints like St. Nicholas (not *Nihilum*, Canal, p. 160, line 882) only understood Greek! William speaks highly of Guimund in *GP*, p. 316, and had visited St. Frideswide's in person (*GR*, i. p. 213). The only record of Guimund acting as a royal chaplain is in *Reg*. ii, no. 1380 (*c*. 1107–22). For the famous story of how Guimund misread the Rogationtide lesson before Henry I, see S. R. Wigram (ed.), *The Cartulary of the Monastery of St. Frideswide at Oxford*, i (Oxford Hist. Soc., 1895), p. 9. Guimund became prior in 1122, so the miracle dates before that, for William says of the two former royal chaplains *religiosam vitam meditantes*.

[2] R. M. Thompson, 'William of Malmesbury as Historian and Man of Letters', *JEH*, 29 (1978), pp. 398–9, has reached a similar conclusion in his discussion of the evolution of the factual to the credulous in the *De Antiquitate Glastoniensis* and the *Gesta Regum*.

[3] About 500 years before *c*. 1125 (*GR*, ii. pp. 424–5) but 300 years before 1095 (*GR*, ii. p. 395).

notably Alcuin's letter to Colcu, into supposing that Charlemagne's Spanish March extended for three hundred miles and that along the wrong, the *Atlantic*, coast so as to incorporate the whole of Gallicia and Lusitania.[1] This premature restriction of the Saracen frontier to the rivers Guadiana and Ebro, within a century of the Visigothic collapse, would have made it almost impossible for William to understand the very real advances of the Christian kingdoms in his own day. He never refers to the rise of Aragon and Gallicia remains the only Spanish kingdom and Alfonso VI (1065–1109) the only king, of whom he had heard something.[2] This severe limitation of his knowledge of recent Spanish history, revealed by the *Gesta Regum*, was bound to jeopardize his ambition to put the Spanish Miracle Stories in their correct contexts.

The first of these is 'Hildefonsus', the well-known story of how the Virgin Mary appeared to this seventh-century archbishop of Toledo (657–67), displaying a copy of his book on her Virginity; and how he was moved to inaugurate the Feast of her Expectation. She appeared to him a second time to present her devotee with an alb and a throne, but his successor, Siagrius, was struck dead for presuming to enjoy these heavenly gifts. William's source is HM1, which in turn is an elaborated form of the tale first found in the Second Life of Hildefonsus, attributed in some manuscripts to Cixila, archbishop of Toledo (*c.* 774–83).[3]

Faced with an inflated version of a dubious narrative, William was mainly disturbed that the Virgin should have displayed such

[1] Cf. *GR*, i. p. 92, where Alcuin gives the figure of 300 miles and *GR*, i. p. 193, where William equates the Spanish March with these two 'largest provinces in Spain'.

[2] *GR*, ii. p. 337; ii. p. 333: Alfonso's translation of the body of St. Isidore to Toledo, *GR*, i. p. 193, is incorrect—the saint was translated by Ferdinand I to Léon.

[3] Wm. M. No. 3: Canal, pp. 134–5; Thesis, i. pp. 131–3, ii. pp. 323–7. There is a useful summary of this story and its variants in E. F. Wilson, pp. 190–1. It has been frequently studied by Romance scholars because of the variant version, introducing St. Leocadia, found in Gautier de Coinci's French-verse Collection. HM 1 has been printed by Dexter, pp. 15–17. Cixila'a *Vita* is in *PL* 96, cols 43–7.

unusual ferocity when it was his purpose to praise her clemency. But rather than question the story's general reliability, he felt the professional need to substantiate some of the historical details neglected in HM 1, in particular the status of Toledo itself, for he had heard that 'another city has assumed the primatial authority, that is Mérida, distinguished by the relics of the blessed martyr Eulalia'.[1]

This rumour must be based on a misunderstanding since Mérida, the old capital of Lusitania, was of course still in Saracen hands and was to remain so until 1228. But the rights of the old Visigothic see of Mérida had been assigned temporarily to Santiago de Compostela by Cilixtus II in 1120 when it was promoted to archiepiscopal status, although this did not affect the standing of Toledo, which indeed had re-emerged under Bernardo in 1086, after the reconquest of the city by Alfonso VI the previous year, and had been confirmed in its ancient primatial authority by Urban II in 1088.[2] It is true that the twelfth-century disputes between the Spanish prelates both for primatial and metropolitan recognition were very complex and difficult for those to follow who were, as William once put it on another occasion, *trans oceanum Britannicum abditos*,[3] but it is still striking that he believed Toledo to be in eclipse some fifty years after its famous liberation. That he was capable of recording such a misconception can best be explained by his habit of looking at Spain through the eyes of the Visigothic Church: for him the eclipse of Christian Toledo by Saracen Seville is still significant, as his words make plain.[4]

Although the *De Virginitate* by Hildefonsus is mentioned in HM 1, William adds further details of its contents to show his familiarity

[1] Canal, p. 134, lines 233–5.
[2] R. A. Fletcher, *The Episcopate in the Kingdom of Léon in the Twelfth Century* (Oxford, 1978), pp. 23–4, 189–90. It is significant that William does not mention the archiepiscopal status of Compostela in his telling of the story 'Pilgrim of St. James' (Wm. M. No. 20), Canal, p. 170, lines 1166–7.
[3] *GR*, ii. p. 431.
[4] Cf. Canal, p. 134, lines 235–6 with *GR*, i. pp. 193–4, where in both cases he uses the antithesis between Toledo and Seville.

with a work which is often found associated with Miracle Collections. Gotescalus of Le Puy had introduced it to readers outside Spain in 951 and Herman of Tournai, William's contemporary, found it a suitable prologue for his Miracles of the Virgin at Laon, where his patron bishop Bartholomew had hopes of obtaining the heavenly alb from Toledo through the agency of his cousin Alfonso I of Aragon.[1] In his own notice of the *De Virginitate*, William seems to reveal some knowledge of details found in Cixila,[2] but if so, he certainly ignores that author's matter-of-fact explanation of the fate of the presumptuous successor. For Cixila gives his name as Sisebert (690–3), unlike Siagrius a genuine archbishop of Toledo and one whose ejection from his see (or seat) was not engineered by the Virgin's anger but by a decree of the Sixteenth Council of Toledo, for treason against King Egica.[3] Moreover, William prided himself on his knowledge of the Toletan Councils: in place of HM 1's vague reference to the Council which sanctioned the new Feast, he pointed specifically to the first canon of the Ninth Council. Unfortunately there are two errors here: it should be the Tenth Council and this met in 656, in the last year of Eugenius, the predecessor of Hildefonsus, and not after Hildefonsus' death as he asserts. The liturgical explanation that the Council gives, known both to HM 1 and to William, namely that the overshadowing of the Feast of the Annunciation by Easter Week made a new Feast, on

[1] B. de Gaiffier, 'Relations religieuses de l'Espagne avec le Nord de la France: transferts de reliques, viiie–xiie siècle', in *Recherches d'hagiographie latine* (Bruxelles, 1971), pp. 7–29; G. Neimeyer, 'Die Miracula S. Mariae Laudunensis des Abtes Hermann von Tournai, Verfasser und Entstehungszeit', *Deutsches Archiv*, 27 (1971), pp. 135–74.

[2] Canal, pp. 134–5, lines 237–44: the statement that Hildefonsus was Isidore's pupil and that the *De Virginitate* was written *stilo synonymo* (HM 1: *stilo eleganti*) are possible echoes from Cixila. Although William knew the *De Virginitate* (PL 96, cols 53–110), he seems to regard it mainly as a polemic against the Jews.

[3] E. A. Thompson, *The Goths in Spain* (Oxford, 1969), p. 244; J. F. Rivera Recio, *Los Arzobispos de Toledo desde sus origenes hasta fines del siglo xi* (Toledo, 1973), pp. 97–9. B. de Gaiffier has retracted his former view that Cixila is a twelfth-century forgery in 'Les Vies de S. Ildefonse à propos d'attribution discutée', *AABB*, 94 (1976), pp. 235–44, esp. 242 and n. 3.

December 18, desirable, is a perfectly sufficient one and does not require the miraculous accretions, especially those sanctioned by an historian.[1]

The second Spanish story, known as 'Toledo', is taken by William from TS 1. While the Archbishop of Toledo was celebrating Mass on the Feast of the Assumption, the voice of the Virgin was heard accusing the Jews of inflicting new tortures on her Son: when their synagogue had been broken into, a mutilated wax image of Christ was discovered and those Jews who refused conversion were put to death.[2] This episode, devoid of detail as it stands in TS 1, is hard to date: but the thirteenth-century Castilian poet Gonzalo de Berceo believed that it took place on 15 August 1108, a date which must be corrected to 1109 on the grounds that the Assumption in 1108 fell on a Saturday, unsuitable for an archiepiscopal High Mass.[3] But there are other more cogent reasons for choosing the latter year: when Alfonso VI died on 29 June, the inhabitants of Toledo rose against the Jews and massacred many, now that they had lost their protector. Alfonso VII later remitted the fines due to the crown for the Jews murdered after his grandfather's death and their ordeal can be further studied in the Jewish records, especially Judah Halevi's poem *The Diwan*, where he praises Alfonso VI's Jewish physician, Joseph Ferrizuel, for his protection and mourns the murder of Joseph's nephew, Solomon, as a foretaste of what was to come.[4]

Be that as it may, William decided against all probability that the

[1] Canal, p. 136, lines 255–7. The decrees of the Tenth Council of Toledo on the Feast are in J. D. Mansi, *Sacrorum Conciliorum nova et amplissima Collectio* (Florence and Venice, 1759–98), xi. pp. 33–4.

[2] Wm. M. No. 4: Canal, pp. 137–8; Thesis, i. pp. 134–6, ii. pp. 328–33. TS 1 is printed by Dexter, pp. 38–40, by Neuhaus, *Die lat. Vorlagen*, pp. 51–2; *Die Quellen*, pp. 29–32.

[3] Gonzalo de Berceo, *Milagros de nuestra señora*, ed. A. G. Solalinde (Madrid, 1922), No. 18, pp. 101–4; Fidel Fita, 'Cincuenta leyendas por Gil de Zamora', *Boletin de la Real Academia de la Historia*, vii (1885), p. 75; Cf. *Encyclopedia Judaica* (Jerusalem, 1971), 15, col. 1201.

[4] Y. Baer, *A History of the Jews in Christian Spain* (Philadelphia, 1961), i. pp. 50–1, 68–9. *The Diwan of Judah Malevi* is ed. by H. Brody, 4 vols (Berlin, 1894–1930): for the family of Ferrizuel (or Cidellus), vol. ii, Nos 11 and 12.

pogrom belonged to Visigothic history. Once more overlooking the fact that Toledo was long since in Christian hands and ignoring the consideration, which he acknowledges elsewhere, that the Assumption was not widely celebrated even in his own time,[1] he states that the massacre of the Toletan Jews took place under Reccared (586–601). His 'evidence' amounts to nothing more than Gregory I's letter to that king, congratulating him on his refusal to soften the rigour of the laws despite Jewish bribes.[2] He further stresses this misplaced Visigothic context by explaining that King Sisebut (612–21) extended Reccared's repression in the city by demanding the conversion or expulsion of the rest of the Spanish Jews, an episode that he knew from Isidore's *Chronica Maiora*[3] and one which prompts him to deal next with the fate of the descendants of these refugees in Aquitaine.

But before his story of the Jews of Toulouse can be properly assessed, it is necessary to discuss the prologue of 'Toledo', so far neglected, for here he makes what must be the earliest reference to the legend of the Jewish Pope of Narbonne: 'it is constantly reported

---

[1] In the Prologue, Canal, p. 121, lines 263–6. Although the Feast of the Assumption is found in the Mozarabic Rite, it cannot be proved for sixth-century Spain.

[2] Canal, p. 137, lines 304–7. Gregory's letter to Reccared is in *MGH Epistolarum*, t. ii, Pars i (Berlin, 1893), p. 221 ff. Since William's words, 'Ea epistola in Nono Libro Registri invenitur', suggest he had a complete collection of this Pope's letters, it is surprising that he makes so little use of it in his Histories. His *Deflorationes* from Gregory's writings in MS Cambridge U. L. Ii.3.20 are all culled from the Commentaries and Homilies (H. Farmer, 'William of Malmesbury's Commentary on Jeremiah', Appendix iii, *Studia Monastica*, iv (1962), pp. 308–11).

[3] Canal, p. 138, lines 328–30; Isidore, *Chronica Maiora, MGH Auct. Antiq.*, xi (Berlin, 1894), p. 480. William notes the dedication of Isidore's *De Natura Rerum* to Sisebut—his own copy survives in MS Bodleian Auct. F. 3. 14—but he does not seem to know the *Historia Gothorum* where (*MGH*, ibid. p. 291) Isidore expressly criticizes the expulsion. S. Katz, *The Jews in the Visigothic and Frankish Kingdoms of Spain and Gaul* (Cambridge, Mass., 1937) gives the fullest account of the legislation, which may, however, be less severe in impact than Katz implies (R. Collins, 'Julian of Toledo and the Royal Succession in Late Seventh Century Spain', in P. H. Sawyer and I. N. Wood (eds), *Early Medieval Kingship*, Leeds, 1977, p. 33).

that they have at Narbonne a high Pope (*summum papam*), to whom the Jews run from all over the world and who receives there proffered wealth and arbitrates, whenever some issue arises amongst them that calls for a solution'.[1] Although this fantasy is an obvious mirror image of the Papal Curia in its new twelfth-century role, the concept of a 'hidden' Jewish leader can be traced much earlier in polemic and legend. On the one hand Jacob's prophecy of the extinction of the Jewish Kingship with the coming of the Messiah[2] was used as a proof that there could be no such leader; on the other, the continued use by the Jews of the title of *Nasi*, the name given to the president of the Sanhedrin before the Fall of Jerusalem, suggested that it could be otherwise. Since the Hebrew word *Nasi* had partly princely connotations, there was thus room for some sort of Jewish Prester John in the Christian imagination, from the time that the Franks became familiar with the Mediterranean world under Charlemagne.[3]

Here legend played a part when it asserted that Harun el Rashid had sent the Exilarch of the Jews in Persia to the West. When Narbonne had been recovered from the Saracens in 759 by the Franks, it was said that the Jews had assisted them and that this was the reason why Charlemagne permitted a descendant of the House of David to settle in the city. Rabbi Machir ben Judah, whose family is usually called Kalonymus, thus passed on the hereditary title of *Nasi* of Narbonne and acted as the leading local representative of the city's Jews. Although the Carolingian legend that relates these unlikely incidents is a late twelfth- or early thirteenth-century compilation,[4] such reliable Jewish authorities as Benjamin of Tudela

[1] Canal, p. 137, lines 294–8.
[2] Genesis, 49: 10. An early attack on the survival of the Jewish Kingship is in Isidore's *De Fide Catholica*, i, 8, 2 (*PL*, p. 83, col. 464).
[3] S. Katz, Appendix iii, 'The *Nasi* of Narbonne', is the fundamental study.
[4] *Gesta Caroli Magni ad Carcassonam et Narbonam*, c. 14 (ed. Schneegans, *Romanische Bibliothek*, No. 15, Halle, 1898, pp. 176–89), I. Lévi, 'Le Roi juif de Narbonne et le Philomène', *Revue des études juives*, 48 (Jan.–Mar. 1904), pp. 197–207; ibid., 'Encore un mot sur le roi juif de Narbonne', op. cit., 49 (July–Sept. 1904), pp. 147–50. Lévi pointed out that the legend suspiciously resembles the gratitude of Otto II to the Jew Kalonymus after the Battle of Cortone in 982.

and Abraham ibn Daud are familiar with the *Nasi* tradition from *c.* 1160 onwards.[1] It is clear that the Jews of Narbonne, more numerous though they were than in any other Western city, would have welcomed the support of Charlemagne's prestige to retain their precarious privileges under the Count: as early as the pontificate of Stephen III their right to hold and inherit allodial lands had been under attack.[2]

But for the Jews themselves to suggest that the *Nasi* of Narbonne had any authority over them outside the city was fraught with danger. It is from Peter the Venerable's *Liber adversus Judaeorum inveteratam duritiem*, a fair-minded tract despite the title, that such a probability emerges. The abbot of Cluny, in 1143 or a little later, after a long argument for the extinction of the Jewish kingship, makes his Jewish opponents reply that the 'sceptre of Judah' was, on the contrary, still borne by their leaders in exile. Peter retorts: 'Then produce for me a king of the seed of Judah or, if you cannot do that, show me at least a prince. But as for me, I don't accept that king—whom I take to be a joke—whom some of you say you have in the Gallic city of Narbonne and others say at Rouen. For I repeat, I won't acknowledge as a king of the Jews anyone at all, whether in Gaul, in Germany, in Italy or even in the distant parts of the East or Africa or the North or wheresoever Jews may happen to live.'[3]

But the more serious implications of the rumour first reported by William are to be found, within a decade, in the treacherous revelations of Theobald of Cambridge, a convert from Judaism and a monk of Norwich, who in 1144 was apparently claiming that

---

[1] Benjamin of Tudela visited Narbonne *c.* 1165 and Abraham ibn Daud's *Sefer ha-Kabbalah* was completed in 1161 (Lévi, 'Le Roi juif', p. 203).

[2] Pope Stephen's letter to Aribert of Narbonne dates these privileges as far back as Carloman (*PL* 129, col. 857). The Jewish population of the city amounted to about 2,000 in 1143, according to Abraham ibn Daud (*Encyclopedia Judaica*, Vol. 12, col. 828).

[3] Peter the Venerable, *PL* 189, col. 560. This passage was first noticed by I. Loeb, 'Polémistes chrétiens et juifs en France et en Espagne', *Revue des études juives*, 18 (1889), p. 45. For the problem of the date of the polemic, J. Kritzek, *Peter the Venerable and Islam* (Princeton, 1964), p. 25 and n. 77. The reference to a *Nasi* at Rouen has not been satisfactorily explained.

the rabbis and leading Jews of Spain assembled at Narbonne, 'where their royal seed and their pride flourishes exceedingly', not to settle mere Jewish lawsuits but to cast lots to decide which Jewish community in Europe should be responsible for a ritual murder. The death of St. William of Norwich is the beginning of a tragic series of anti-Semitic accusations in which the legend of the Jewish Pope produced its most sinister consequences.[1]

The growing twelfth-century notoriety of the Jews of Narbonne must, however, be related in some way to the crisis in the city itself in and after 1134. In that year the Viscount Aymeric III was killed at the Battle of Fraga, leaving as his heir his sister Ermengarde, who was either unable or unwilling to give the Jewish community the protection assured by her brother. From 1134 to 1143 Narbonne was the scene of a contest between two factions and it was Alphonse-Jordain, Count of Toulouse, who became the champion of the Jewish citizens, but one who was unable to save them from serious harassment and partial dispersal to other towns in Anjou, Poitou and France.[2] By a strange set of circumstances, a Christian disaster at the hands of the Muslims of Spain proved a tragedy for the Jews of Narbonne, whose whole ordeal seems to lie behind the rumours of an international Jewish conspiracy first hinted at by William of Malmesbury.

It is therefore no surprise to find that in introducing his next story, 'The Jews of Toulouse', our author exhibits his most unpleasant anti-Semitic sentiments. Not only is the story itself an attempt to justify the origin of a sadistic ritual, the striking of a Jew every Good Friday, the so-called 'soufflet', but he also claims that it will make his readers laugh. The fact that it has nothing to do with either miracles or the Virgin Mary is bad enough: it is made worse by his claim

---

[1] A. Jessop and M. R. James, *The Life and Miracles of St. William of Norwich* (Cambridge, 1896), pp. 93–4. James was inclined to think that many of the subsequent accusations of ritual murder, in England and France, can be linked in some way with the Norwich case, the earliest known (ibid., pp. lxxv–lxxvii).

[2] G. Saige, *Les Juifs du Languedoc antérieurement au xive siècle* (Paris, 1881); I. Lévi, 'Le Roi juif', p. 204; *Encyclopedia Judaica*, op. cit., col. 828.

that any vengeance for the injuries suffered by the Son redounds to the glory of the Mother.[1] Later compilers of the story were not slow to introduce both a Marian and a miraculous element for which William, who first misapplied the story, must be held partly responsible.

As is his usual practice, he first attempts to place the story in its ecclesiastical and dynastic setting. Toulouse is associated with its patron St. Saturninus, whose spectacular martyrdom while tied to a bull driven over a precipice is culled from Gregory of Tours.[2] As for the incident of the Jewish insult and the Christian revenge, it is placed in the time of 'William the Old Count, the father of Raymond, one of the first to take the road to Jerusalem'. But this is a confusion, found also in his *Gesta Regum*, for the father of Raymond of St. Gilles was Pons, while William III (950–1037), who died at the advanced age of ninety, was in fact his grandfather.[3] In the *Gesta Regum*, William III is given a noble reputation as befits the supposed father of the crusader; in the present story he is depicted as a villain, whose avaricious protection of the Jewish community nearly cost him the fealty of his vassals.

On Feast days, one is asked to believe, the Jews mocked devout worshippers and on one Good Friday one of them picked on a well-born Christian who happened to be doing penance outside the church, and insulted Christ as a magician and Christians as no better

[1] Wm. M. No. 5: Canal, pp. 138–40; Thesis, i. pp. 137–40, ii. pp. 334–41 This story is not found in Miracle Collections earlier than William. The custom has recently been related to the *Altercatio Synagogae et Ecclesiae*, D. A. Bullough, 'Games People Played: Drama and Ritual as Propaganda in Medieval Europe', *TRHS*, 5th series, 24 (1974), pp. 112–13.

[2] Gregory of Tours, *In Gloria Martyrum*, Lib. i (*MGH*, Script. Rer. Mero. i, 2, p. 520).

[3] Canal, p. 138, lines 344–5. Cf. *GR*, ii. pp. 455 and cxxvii. The genealogy of the Counts of Toulouse has been discussed by C. de Vic and J. J. Vaissète, *Histoire générale de Languedoc*, 5 vols (Paris, 1730–45), iii. pp. 276, 340, 364, 385; and by R. R. Bezzola, 'Guillaume IX et les Origines de l'Amour Courtois', *Romania*, LXVI (1940–1), pp. 161–8. Ward, 732, suggested that William IV is meant; Kjellman, pp. liv–lv, that it was either William II or III: but the Count is clearly William III from William's words: tempore Willelmi *antiqui comitis*.

than connoisseurs of dust and ashes. The penitent—'as it becomes a man of rank to show an equal degree of wrath'—struck the blasphemer dead with his fist. The Jewish community then demanded justice, refused a court hearing on the Sabbath, and agreed to appear in court on Easter Monday, meanwhile attempting to bribe the Count to punish the Christian. The Count's vassals, however, refused to tolerate a prosecution and the Count unwillingly agreed to their verdict: a Jew must be given a similar blow on every future Good Friday. And so, *usque ad hanc diem*, a Jew is chosen by lot; his hair is cut off[1] lest it provide a handhold and he is coated with honey by his co-religionists so that the blow may glance aside. But, we are told, the Christians always overcome such subterfuges and there is keen bidding among young noblemen to purchase the right of striking—'or rather braining'—the victim.

That this ritual was practised in the early eleventh century is attested by Adhemar of Chabannes, who mentions that Hugh the chaplain of Aimery de Rochechouart was the Christian 'champion', *c.* 1020, and managed to kill his defenceless target.[2] Whether the custom was older than the reign of William III is not clear but no reliance can be placed on the legend that it was Charlemagne who introduced this punishment on three principle holidays for an alleged betrayal of Toulouse to the Saracens.[3] Whether William is correct in stating that it was still practised in his own time is also uncertain: on the one hand there are records of commutation and on the other the miracle tradition tells of a certain blacksmith whose grim record for fatal blows in yearly encounters was well rewarded by the Count.[4] But this prodigy cannot be dated and the

[1] The shaving of the head is reminiscent of the *decalvatio* or scalping found in Visigothic law, A. K. Ziegler, *Church and State in Visigothic Spain* (Washington, 1930), p. 81 and n. 5.

[2] Adhemar of Chabannes, *Chronicon*, ed. G. Waitz, *MGH, Scriptores*, iv (Hanover, 1841), 139.

[3] *Vita S. Theodardi*, c. 5, ed. G. Catel, *Mémoires de l'histoire de Languedoc* (1633), p. 517 ff.

[4] Bishop Amelius of Toulouse (1106–39) remits a customary payment *pro colafo Iudaeorum*, C. Douais (ed.), *Cartolarium Sancti Saturnini* (Paris, 1887), pp. 200–1. According to the *Encyclopedia Judaica*, Vol. 15, col. 1286, the

miracle tradition becomes increasingly wild until the original giver of the blow himself becomes one-eyed so that a grateful Virgin can restore the missing one to confound identification by his Jewish victim who, in this version, has to stay alive. In the *Cantigas* of Alfonso El Sabio it is a mad dog who disturbs the penitent and it is a gate which is made to fall on two Jews who had laughed.[1] All trace of history has vanished in the telling.

In several other stories in William's Collection, the anti-Semitic flavour may be regarded as more traditional than personal, inseparable from the sources he used, as in 'Jewish Boy', 'Mary Image Insulted', and 'Theophilus'. Yet he is prepared to maintain that to catalogue the efforts of the Virgin Mary to convert her own race would require a major book, despite the violent deaths of Jews in all these stories. This strange claim[2] rests solely on the story 'Jew Lends to Christian', where Abraham of Byzantium's conversion after an encounter with her speaking icon in Hagia Sophia is said to have silenced—not converted—all the Byzantine Jews ever afterwards. Apart from this quite incredible consequence from a single instance, I can point to only one other story where the Virgin's intervention converts a Jew. This is an unpublished miracle concerning a young French Jew called Jacob who travels to Winchester by way of London, Oxford, Gloucester, and Bristol. On the road he is rescued from robbers by St. Mary and is baptised by Robert, Bishop of Bath and Wells (1136–66).[3] In general, there can be no

---

'soufflet' was commuted to a payment of wax and incense in the late eleventh and early twelfth centuries. Kjellman, p. 150, prints the story of the blacksmith, from MS Balliol 240, fo. 156r.

[1] Ward, p. 658, from London, British Library Add. MS 18,929, fo. 82v; *Cántigas de Santa Maria*, ed. W. Mettmann (Coimbra, 1959–64), iii. pp. 89–90: this is Cántiga 286, mentioned by A. I. Bagby, 'The Jews in the Cántigas of Alfonso X, El Sabio', *Speculum*, xlvi (1971), p. 677.

[2] Canal, p. 200, lines 764–6. This is one of the additions made by William to his draft, in this case to link two stories about Jews.

[3] Paris BN, MS lat. 3177 fos 143v–5v; also found in London British Library, Add. MS 15,723, fo. 83, and MS Harley 2250, fo. 87. Jacob is not mentioned among the few named Jewish converts in twelfth-century England, listed by M. Adler, *Jews of Medieval England* (London, 1939), p. 279 n. 4.

doubt that Miracles of the Virgin contributed to the persecution of the Jews, not their conversion.

William's rabid anti-Semitism can hardly be prompted by conditions at Malmesbury, where there was no Jewish community. It was based not on his experience but, like Bede's invective against Arians and Pelagians, it was a bookish fervour, fed by his study of the Prophets and the Classics. This can be seen in his Commentary on the Lamentations of Jeremiah where, for instance, he explains the Jewish disinterest in the concept of eternal life in terms of their too great concern for this world's lucre. Here also he ransacks classical authors for instances of anti-Semitic attitudes in the Ancient World, using Josephus's account of the fall of Jerusalem to Ptolemy I Soter to deride their sabbatinarianism, Lucan's *Pharsalia* to scorn their worship of an 'unknown' deity, Jevenal's *Satires* to mock their practice of circumcision. Not content with these somewhat meagre findings, he goes on to say that even the Saracens, despite their common inheritance, use the term 'Jew' itself as a colloquial term of reproach, according to a trustworthy informant.[1]

The observation that Jews and Saracens share a common stock and religious tradition is one that William makes elsewhere and it has been cited as an example of his scholarly objectivity;[2] but his use of the Saracens as a stick with which to beat the Jews is also an indication of his bias. To him the Saracens were simply worthier enemies of Christendom: they were infidels—even, he was misguided enough to say, idol-worshippers—but they were prepared to fight,

---

[1] Bodleian Library, MS Bodley 868, fos 40va–41ra. The references are to: Josephus, *Antiquities*, xii, 1, although the MS reads *ovidium satabacidem*, a corruption of the latin form of Agartharcides of Cnidos; Lucan, *Pharsalia*, ii. 592–3; Juvenal, *Satires*, xiv. 99. They supplement those listed by R. M. Thompson, 'The Reading of William of Malmesbury', *Rev. bén.* 85 (1975). 371. n. 4 (Juvenal), n. 6 (Lucan) and p. 400 (Josephus).

[2] 'Saracenis etiam sunt opprobrio, quos obliqua gentis linea et sectae respiciunt instituto.' MS Bodley 868, fo. 40va. Cf. R. M. Thompson, 'William of Malmesbury and Some Other Writers on Islam', *Medievalia et Humanistica*, N.S.6 (Cambridge, 1975), pp. 179–80.

although they typically used *non virtus sed virus* to win.[1] That they also humiliated prelates whom they took prisoner is the occasion for William's extreme indignation in the last of his Spanish stories. The account of 'Guy Bishop of Lescar' and his captivity in Saracen hands after the Battle of Fraga in July 1134 has evaded until recently a proper evaluation because of William's imperfect transmission of the name of his see.[2] Yet it is one of his most original contributions in terms of history and provides crucial evidence for the dating of his whole composition. The Battle of Fraga from which Alfonso I of Aragon, after a long siege of the town, extricated himself with the loss of all but a handful of his knights, was one of the most disastrous setbacks in the history of the Reconquista.[3] But it is also one of the most fully described battles in the annals of twelfth-century warfare, thanks to the *Chronica Adefonsi Imperatoris*, the Ecclesiastical History of Orderic Vitalis, and the Arabic narrative

[1] On idol-worshipping cf. *cultor idolorum*, Canal, p. 155, line 758, and *simulacro Mahumet*, *GR*, ii. p. 423; on unsporting warfare, Urban II's speech at Clermont (*GR*, ii. p. 395) reflects the popular view that feigned flight and archery with poisoned arrows demeaned the man-to-man bravery of Western Chivalry.

[2] Wm. M. No. 12: Canal, pp. 152–6, Thesis, i. pp. 158–62, ii. pp. 390–6. Guy's see is given variously as *scarrensem*, *starrensem*, and *sarrensem* in different MSS of this miracle story. Mussafia called him 'Bischof von Scarra' and Ward suggested the word was a corruption of Saragossa and Canal considered Skara (Sweden). The puzzle was first solved by Dr J. R. L. Highfield in 1953: the place-name is derived from Las Escourres and the loss of the article is understandable. Canal's mystification was cleared up in print by B. de Gaiffier, 'À propos de Guido, Évêque de Lescar, et du culte de Ste. Anne', *AABB*, 88 (1970), p. 74. Although the story is found, isolated, in a few other MSS, it is unquestionably by William.

[3] For a general account of Fraga, see M. Défourneaux, *Les Français en Espagne aux xie et xiie siècles* (Paris, 1949), pp. 164–5. For an attempt to mitigate the disaster by making Alfonso I wreak vengeance on the Saracens afterwards, like Charlemagne after Roncesvalles, see F. M. Warren, 'The Battle of Fraga and Larchamp in Orderic Vital', *Modern Philology*, xi (1913–14), pp. 339–46, a reference I owe to Mrs Chibnall's valuable annotations to Orderic. Her date for the Battle, however, is 17 July 1134, that given by the *Chronica* (see following note), although the best editor, Sanchez, p. xxxi, considers this to be a copyist's error and corrects it to 19 July.

of Ibn el-Athir.[1] William's florid account has little value as military history but, set beside the others, many of the reasons for his misunderstandings can be discerned.

In the first place he cannot name the unlucky Spanish king except by his nickname of *parvus*. This can only refer to Alfonso VII of León, who was not in fact present at Fraga but who did lay claim to the Aragonese throne on the news of Alfonso I's death later in the same year. Nor does he know where Fraga is: following, quite correctly, the belief that the king had recently completed an offensive,[2] he wrongly assumes that victories had taken him well to the south, *intra fines ulterioris Hispaniae*, when in fact he had not even crossed the Ebro. His third mistake was to imagine that Fraga itself was in Christian hands, which it was not, and that Guy of Lescar was some sort of castellan trying to convert the infidel inhabitants and protecting the Christian shrines from their hostility. Guy's actual role was rather the safe-keeping of the relics from Sahagún, which were in the camp of the Christian siege force outside the walls.[3] The mention of relics by William's informant must have been responsible for giving him this false concept of the military situation, for shrines to William were always associated with the cities where they had come to rest; that they could still be on the move was outside his English experience.

As for the ensuing disaster, William ascribes this to the uprising

---

[1] *Chronica Adefonsi Imperatoris*, ed. Florez, *España Sagrada*, xxi (Madrid, 1766), pp. 446–8, and ed. Luis Sanchez Belda (Madrid, 1950), pp. 41–7; OV, vi. pp. 408–19; Ibn el-Athir is translated by E. Fagnan, *Annales de Maghreb et de l'Espagne* (Algiers, 1901), pp. 553–5.

[2] Canal, p. 153, line 725: this could refer to the capture of Mequinenza by Alfonso in 1132 or to the earlier successes outside Fraga itself against the Almoravides in 1133.

[3] Guy's presence in the camp is also attested by a judgement of Pedro, Bishop of Barbastro and Roda, dated at Fraga in July 1134. (R. del Arco, 'Referencias a acaecimientos históricos en las datas de documentos aragoneses de los siglos xi y xii', *Estudios de Edad Media de la Corona de Aragón*, iii (1947–8), p. 332. The relics from Sahagún, including Marian items, are listed in the *Chronica* (ed. Sanchez, p. 43): possibly the *archa* or portable shrine has been transformed into the *arces* in William's text.

of the treacherous townspeople rather than to the arrival of Ibn Ganya and his large relief force from the south, which his account fails to mention, together with the panic caused by the simultaneous discovery of the king's absence. What actually happened was that, after a suicidal sortie by the Count of Carrión, the Christian camp was overwhelmed; and the king, on the express orders of the Bishop of Urgel to look to his own safety, fought his way out with a handful of survivors.[1] Only then did the inhabitants of Fraga emerge to loot the camp.

William's narrative now becomes more valuable as he describes Bishop Guy's fate. His first hope had been to escape from the field and return to Lescar by night in the guise of a pilgrim, but he was recognized and taken captive. Our author's indignation at his treatment is strange, for it was not the efforts to make Guy apostasize that enraged him so much as the woman's spindle that he was forced to ply and that chafed his fingers to the very bone and desecrated the hands that dispensed the Holy Sacrament. We know from Ibn el-Athir that only the women of Fraga spared their prisoners so this derisive treatment is likely enough, more credible than the forced circumcision which the *Chronica* insists was his fate.

But William cannot be right to maintain that the Bishop was held captive for a whole year, since he was back at Saragossa before the end of December.[2] His release was brought about by a miracle: the Virgin would not help until he coupled the name of St. Anne with hers in his prayers. When this was done, hostages arrived which enabled Guy to return across the Pyrenees to collect his ransom, a sum unspecified by William but amounting to 3,000 maravedi according to the *Chronica*.

In an epilogue to this long story—most of which is devoted to pious meditations on the signal act of mercy—William untypically

---

[1] Alfonso's plight is graphically recalled by a document expressing his gratitude to those who gained control of his frightened horse, J. M. Lacarra, 'Documentos para el estudio de la reconquista y repoblación del Valle del Ebro', Primera Serie, *Estudios . . . de Aragón*, ii (1946), p. 533 (Núm. 80).

[2] Guy was at Saragossa on 6 December 1134, and on 9 January 1135 (J. M. Lacarra, pp. 528–9 (Núm. 86) and 540 (Núm. 87)).

names his source: 'The story I tell was told about himself by the Lord Guy Bishop of Lescar to a certain archdeacon called Helias, whom he had as his supporter at the Curia of the Lord Pope among the Cardinals and who was his colleague and travelling companion on the journey back from Rome.'[1] Unfortunately, although Guy is known to have acted as legate in 1138 when Innocent II sent him to summon the bishops of Spain and Portugal to the Second Lateran Council that was to meet in April 1139,[2] the natural suggestion that he recounted his story in either of these years to Helias cannot be entertained. For, as Dr Hunt long ago pointed out, Wlliam's Treatise must have been in circulation as early as 1137, for Robert of Cricklade praised it in the course of his *De Connubio Patriarche Iacob*, written at the Augustinian house of Cirencester some twelve miles from Malmesbury. Robert's encomium can be dated by his reflections on the death of Godfrey Abbot of Winchcombe, some twenty folios later, for Godfrey died according to John of Worcester on 6 March 1137.[3] Since Guy could not have left Spain after Fraga until 1135 and since William's Treatise must, in some form, have been available by early 1137, the conclusion seems inescapable that he was composing it in the years 1135-6.

Yet such an early date is not what we would expect from the

---

[1] Canal, p. 156, lines 827-30. His misreading Elias de *Semecripso* (for *semetipso*) has been corrected by B. de Gaiffier (1970), p. 74. Dr R. A. Fletcher has kindly drawn my attention to the same author's 'Guido, Evêque de Lescar († 1141)', in *Recherches d'hagiographie latine* (Bruxelles, 1971), pp. 39-46, but the Bollandist throws no further light on Guy's presence at the Curia in the years 1135-8.

[2] *Historia Compostellana*, sub 1138, *España Sagrada*, xx. pp. 597-8. In a document of the same year issued at Jaca, Guy summons Bernard, Bishop of Coimbra, to attend Lateran II (C. Erdmann, 'Papsturkunden in Portugal', *Abh. der Gesellschaft der Wissenschaften zu Göttingen* (1927), pp. 187-8). That Guy was at Compostela in October 1138 is noted by R. A. Fletcher, p. 209, n. 1.

[3] R. W. Hunt, 'English Learning in the Late Twelfth Century', *TRHS*, 4th series, xix (1936), pp. 31-2, from Oxford Bodleian, MS Laud. Misc. 725, fo. 129vb and (for the death of Godfrey) fo. 152rb. However Dr Hunt's date for the latter, *c.* 1138, has been corrected to March 1137 by R. M. Thompson, 'The Reading of William of Malmesbury', *Rev. bén.*, 85 (1975), p. 393 and n. 5.

opening words of William's Prologue to Book II, which dwells on an illness that had temporarily held up his composition, nor from his final Epilogue, a long prayer to the Virgin written as if by one shortly expecting his death.[1] It is because of this dichotomy between Robert of Cricklade's evidence for a *terminus ante quem* and the impression our author gives that he is making his farewell to the world (it is universally accepted that he died early in 1143), that the identity of Helias and his presence with Guy at the Curia become matters of importance. Unfortunately he remains untraceable.[2] It is perhaps worth noting that William understands them to have returned from Rome, whereas the Papal Curia was at Pisa from November 1133 to March 1137 because of Anacletus II. This is probably a mere slip of the pen rather than a serious objection against the 1135–6 dating, and in any case several of William's stories depend on information gathered from northern Italy, in particular Pavia and Pisa, and these deserve some consideration.

The Pavian 'digression' comes in the form of a long epilogue to the story 'Jerome Bishop of Pavia', whom the Virgin called her 'chancellor'.[3] Ever interested in place-names, William tells how the old name of Ticinus was changed to Pavia (*Papia*) because King Theodoric's daughter had once exclaimed 'Pape!' at her first sight of its impressive walls.[4] He then passes on to tell how St. Sirus, the first apostle of the Pavians, crossed the river Ticino: denied passage

---

[1] Canal, p. 175, lines 1–5 (Prologue to Bk. II) and p. 235, lines 1760–1 (Epilogue). D. H. Farmer, 'William of Malmesbury's Life and Works', *JEH*, xiv (1962), p. 53, suggested that the date of the Treatise was *c.* 1140 as I did myself in 1959.

[2] A possible candidate might be Pedro Helias, Archdeacon of Compostela (and later Archbishop, 1143–9), but Dr Fletcher has pointed out to me that he was Dean by 1128 and is not known to have visited the Curia at the time required. Another man worth considering is Helias, Canon of Roda and author of a Life of St. Raimon-Guillermo, Bishop of Barbastro and Roda (1104–26), written in 1135–43 for canonization purposes; but I do not know if he was ever an archdeacon.

[3] Wm. M. No. 11: Canal, pp. 149–52; Thesis, i. pp. 153–7, ii. pp. 377–89.

[4] I cannot trace this story. In c. xxi of the *De Laudibus Civitatis Ticinensis* (ed. Muratori, *Rer. ital. script.*, xi, Parte i, 1903, p. 50) there are six alternative

by a surly ferryman, he threw down his pallium on the water and propelled himself across on it, using his pastoral staff *quasi remigio*.[1] The third episode describes how the body of St. Augustine was moved to Sardinia to escape the Vandals, how a snake crept out of the tomb, and how King Liutprand purchased the relic and placed it in a crypt in Pavia where, an eyewitness informed our author, a fountain always springs out on the Saint's festival.[2] Finally, we have an account of the martyrdom of Boethius, to whom William ascribed the Trinitarian tracts as well as the *De Consolatione*.[3] It is likely that this collection of anecdotes owes something to a recent visitor to Italy, whether Helias or another.

Concerning the city of Pisa, William makes two interesting historical observations and three incomprehensible errors. In the Prologue to 'Clerk of Pisa', he dwells on the Pisan expeditions in the Mediterranean, already mentioned in the *Gesta Regum*, but adds a new reference to the Mahdia expedition of 1087, when the Pisans 'even took the King of Africa prisoner and held him to ransom', perhaps a pardonable exaggeration for the discomfiture of the emir of Mahdia, Temim ben El-Mo'izz (Thuminus), who though not himself made prisoner, did buy off the Pisans and ransom their

---

explanations of how the city changed its name. The earliest recorded use of 'Pavia' seems to be seventh century (J. M. Wallace-Hadrill, *The Fourth Book of the Chronicle of Fredegar*, London, 1960, p. 59).

[1] I have not found this anecdote in the Vitae of St. Sirus, but I have not consulted Prelini, *S. Siro primo vescovo . . . di Pavia* (Pavia, 1880), i. pp. 178–216. According to legend Sirus was the boy who provided the five loaves and two fishes at the Feeding of the Five Thousand: a later tradition describes a dryshod crossing of the Ticino by St. Odilo (Jotsoaldus, *Vita Odilonis*, PL 142, col. 919).

[2] William cites the Life of Fulgentius (*PL* 65, cols 117–50) for the Vandal persecution in Africa. Liutprand's translation of the body of St. Augustine is taken from Bede's chronicle in the *De Temporum Ratione*, William's own copy of which survives in Oxford, Bodleian, MS Auct. F. 3.14.

[3] Probably from one of the *Elogia Boeti*, sometimes prefixed to the *De Consolatione*, printed in R. Peiper's edition (Leipzig, 1871), pp. xxix–xxxv. But the information that Boethius was buried in the same Church as St. Augustine might well have come from some guide-book: it is S. Pietro *in celo auro* (*De Laudibus*, ed. Muratori, p. 12).

prisoners for a considerable sum.[1] Again, in the prologue to 'Jewish Boy' he observes:

It was in the city of Pisa, which I mentioned earlier and which alone in our own times displays the custom of the ancient Romans with its annually elected magistracy, it was, I repeat, in this city, undefeated in wars abroad, at home well and honestly governed, that my informant, a man of unquestionable good faith, insists that there took place the story that I now relate.

This must be among the earliest references to the consuls of Pisa, or at least their annual election, although whether he is right to call them a revival of the Roman consulate is more questionable. What is curious, however, is the way he insists that this story 'Jewish Boy' takes place at Pisa at all, for all the earlier sources speak of Constantinople until the twelfth century and then, on the authority of Peter of Chiusa, it is said to happen at Bourges.[2] The same erroneous emphasis on Pisa is found in his story 'Bread' which most other accounts place at Speyer.[3] And when we find in the story 'Prior of St. Saviour's Pavia' that Pisa is again regarded as the locale,[4] the reader is bound to wonder whether William of Malmesbury is not

---

[1] Wm. M. No. 27: Canal, pp. 181–3; Thesis, i. pp. 194–6, ii.pp. 478–81. For the Pisan conquest of Corsica and Sardinia, see *GR*, i. p. 92; but the Mahdia Expedition is not found in the *Gesta Regum*. It is described in Geoffrey of Malaterra, *Historia Sicula*, iv. 3 (ed. E. Pontieri, *Rer. ital. script.*, v, pt 1 (Bologna, 1828), pp. 86–7), the *Carmen in Victoriam Pisanorum* (ed. E. du Méril, *Poésies populaires latines du moyen-âge*, Paris, 1847, pp. 239–51) and in Ibn el-Athir, (*Annales due Maghreb et de L'Espagne*, Algiers, 1901, pp. 487–9).

[2] Wm. M. No. 33: Canal, p. 201, lines 767–71. W. Heywood, *A History of Pisa* (Cambridge, 1921), 9–10, gives the earliest references for the Pisan Consuls in the late eleventh century but maintains that they were not yet permanent officials. By his insistence on Pisa here William is deliberately contradicting the Bourges tradition mentioned by his source Dominic and his source 'Anselm of Bury', Southern, 'Origins', p. 192.

[3] Wm. M. No. 34: Canal, p. 202, line 803: *eiusdem urbis*. A possible explanation is that the word *Spiris* (Speyer), with which city this story is usually associated, has been garbled in William's source: the form *Epiris* is known, Ward, p. 623.

[4] Wm. M. No. 22: Canal, p. 172, lines 1233–4. His source, HM 12, in all MSS known to me, gives Pavia not Pisa, notwithstanding Canal's note 77.

guilty of either carelessness or a wilful desire to credit Pisa with miracles beyond her due.

Throughout the Collection, William is under the spell of cities: their fame is in itself the reason given for belief in the truth of the stories connected with them, and their antiquity is proof of the authenticity of their miracles. In the prologue to 'Two Brothers at Rome' and 'Jew lends to Christian' Rome and Constantinople themselves are the guarantees of truth:

Especially since the texts have echoed in our ears from a distant past and because the cities where they happened are the chief ones in Christendom. So on the one hand the high rank of the cities dissolves the cloud of doubt and, on the other, the antiquity of the sources makes good the frailty of memory.[1]

As for Constantinople, 'which for Christians is the second in dignity after Rome', it is virtually the heroine of the last three stories in the Collection, where her famous icons at Blachernae and in Agia Sophia are the equivalent of the saints so often used to 'place' the Western cities. The Virgin's protection of the City is surveyed in three victories won against the Huns, the Saracens, and the Persians; and finally William gives us a useful summary of the reign of Justinian under whom the City was released from the Great Plague and the Feast of the Purification established in gratitude to the Mother of God.[2] Nor does William forget to show his appreciation

---

[1] Wm. M. No. 31: Canal, p. 192, lines 502–6. The story of 'Two Brothers at Rome' is in fact taken by William from HM 10 and the *Dicta Anselmi*, so that his insistence on an ancient text is mere rhetoric, even if he really believes that the events took place under Pope Leo V (Canal, p. 193, lines 510–11) despite a clear reference to Leo IX in the *Dicta* (R. W. Southern and F. S. Schmitt (eds), *The Memorials of St. Anselm*, London, 1969, p. 249).

[2] Wm. M. No. 53: Canal (No. 51), pp. 232–4: 'Justinian and the Feast of the Purification' is partly taken from Hugh of Fleury's *Historia Ecclesiastica*, which he also used for his *Abbrevatio de Gestis Sequentium Imperatorum* in Oxford, Bodleian, MS Arch. Selden B. 16, fos 132ᵛ–138ʳ. The ill-treatment of Popes Silverius and Vigilius is said to have caused the Great Plague (542), which in turn was checked by an icon of the Virgin. The three other Byzantine episodes (Wm. M. No. 52: Canal (No. 50), pp. 231–2) deal with victories over Roilas (Rua) under 'Arcadius' (*recte* Theodosius II in 434), over the Saracens

for what the Greeks had done to influence Marian devotions in the West: 'The enthusiasm of the Greeks has challenged and incited our own people to the love of Our Lady and, as in so many other instances, this exemplary worship has flowed from the Greeks on to Latin soil.'[1]

There were many other cities to attract William's enthusiasm: Canterbury is given an introductory panegyric; Clermont is given its old Latin name of Arvernus, and Sidonius, Gregory of Tours, and the Council of 1095 are recalled to give it lustre; Cologne's ancient name of Agrippina is cited alongside Trajan's new name for it. Chartres, which had no such antiquity, is for William essentially the city made distinguished by Fulbert.[2] Yet despite or perhaps because of this antiquarian zeal, William is equally liable to make unwarranted guesses, as when he claims that the Monk of St. Peter's, Cologne, lived under Louis the Pious[3] or, even more wildly, when he writes that the anonymous and timeless Clerk of Chartres was actually a pupil of Fulbert's and that the even more unidentifiable 'clericus' who sang the Five *Gaudes* was not only a canon of Chartres Cathedral but had even been prompted to this piety by the Clerk's miracle in the same city![4] All this is sheer guesswork,

---

under 'Leo II' (*recte* Leo III in 716–18) and over the Persians under Heraclius (in 627).

[1] Wm. M. No. 51: Canal (No. 50), p. 231, lines 1658–60. Canal reads *latiare* for *Latiale*.

[2] Canterbury (Wm. M. No. 7): Canal, p. 143, lines 469–74, cf. *GP*, p. 3; Clermont (Wm. M. No. 6): Canal, p. 140, lines 397–403, cf. *GR*, ii. p. 391; Cologne (Wm. M. No. 17): Canal, p. 164, lines 999–1001 (for *Tatiano* read *Traiano*), cf. *GR*, i. p. 204; Chartres (Wm. M. No. 9): Canal, p. 146, lines 538–44, cf. *GR*, i. p. 226, ii. p. 341. The duplication of so much information already found in his *Gestae* suggests a certain limitation in his knowledge.

[3] Wm. M. No. 17: Canal, p. 164, lines 995–7. William correctly dates the Vision of Wettin (No. 18) to the reign of Louis the Pious (it occurred in 824), but his dating of No. 17 to the same reign seems due simply to the convenience of a common introduction for these two German stories.

[4] Wm. M. No. 25: Canal, p. 178, lines 71–4; Wm. M. No. 26: Canal, p. 179, lines 124–7. Again, the identification must be a guess, based on Fulbert's Marian devotion.

permissible only on the grounds that what helps to enhance faith must be true.

This curious combination in William of Malmesbury of an historian's dedication and a romancer's freedom to invent—not just conversations and incidents but precise dates and proper names— is the main impression that a modern reader of William's Miracles, armed with a knowledge of his sources, is likely to draw. No doubt it has to be said that we cannot tell the precise state of all his sources, and that Miracles of the Virgin by their very nature nearly always defy chronological certainty and often make even topographical precision very difficult. But the fact remains that William attempted to harness hagiography to history[1] and that he frequently erred in doing so, either because he misjudged the antiquity of his stories or because, as in the cases of Pisa and Chartres, he was too opinionated to accept the verdict of his sources.

To accuse William of fabrication from an excess of pious zeal would be beside the point for most of his mistakes are made from over-confidence as an historian. Naturally he took the usual hagiographical liberties and altered most of the stories to make them, as he thought, more dramatic or more edifying, but he denies that this is deception: 'Far be it for anyone calling himself a Christian even to contemplate the wicked idea that the Mother of Truth may be advocated by lies, however well-expressed . . . there is no need for anyone to fabricate anything or concoct a fallacious story to make her exploits more glorious.' He allows a generous margin for rhetoric when he asserts: 'If indeed any grandeur of language has outrun the true facts, the man who is fair-minded will not therefore judge it any less true.'[2]

The problems of truth are not for William what they are to us:

---

[1] Some scholars have argued, notably C. W. Jones, *Saints' Lives and Chronicles in Early England* (New York, 1947), Ch. IV, that the medieval historian who also wrote hagiography (as did Bede) applied quite different criteria to the different genres: but William certainly did not.

[2] Prologue to Bk. II, Canal, p. 175, lines 12–16; Prologue, Canal, p. 127, lines 26–7.

those that exercise him are not mundane matters of time and place but rather questions of faith about the other world: in what sense can the Virgin still provide milk from her breasts or St. Peter wield his keys as weapons against demons? In what sense can spirits talk without tongues or receive the Sacrament or translate to bodies scars suffered as souls? His answers to these questions are not credulous but sophisticated: how else can spiritual truths be understood unless they are couched in material terms?[1] It is therefore not William's faith that leads him astray, but his trust in books: he simply did not like to admit that he did not know. There is only one passage in the Treatise where he admits to ignorance, over the trifle of whether St. Bon was an earlier or later bishop of Clermont than Sidonius Apollinaris.

William often describes how he sought out books but Dr Thompson has not persuaded me that he puzzled over or was disturbed by conflicting evidence.[2] His older contemporary, Hugh of Fleury, whose historical work he used and who also dedicated his major book to a queen and an empress, provides us with an instance of what can be done by the historian turned hagiographer. Attempting to rewrite the Life of St. Sacerdos—unpromising material—he came across the puzzling name Alticius, a man of rank said to have stood godfather to the obscure bishop of Limoges. Was he to be identified with Ecdicius, the son of the Emperor Avitus and brother-in-law of Sidonius? Was he perhaps given this name for the famine relief which—this he must have got from Gregory of Tours —he organized among the Burgundians? But if so, could St. Sacerdos have really been his contemporary or was he not rather

---

[1] The Virgin's Milk (Wm. M. No. 10): Canal, p. 149, lines 618–23; St. Peter's Keys (Wm. M. No. 17): Canal, p. 165, lines 1044–7; Speech of spirits (Wm. M. No. 17): Canal, p. 165, lines 1034–44; The Sacrament (Wm. M. No. 30): Canal, 192, lines 491–500; Transmission of scars (Wm. M. No. 31): Canal, p. 195, lines 605–14.

[2] R. M. Thompson, 'William of Malmesbury as Historian and Man of Letters', *JEH*, 29 (1978), pp. 393–4, 396–8.

in those days a mere infant?[1] This is not to say that Hugh got all the answers right but he asked the right sort of questions and William too rarely asks them in his Miracles of the Virgin.

No doubt William could have protested that too much research implies an uneasiness of faith: but then, on the other hand, he never allows us to forget that he is an historian, doing what no one had done before to establish these miracles in time and place. He might also have repeated in his own words that he was 'weaving flowers into a garland for the Queen of Heaven' or, with his enthusiastic pen, competing with those 'who build churches in her honour or multiply gems on her shrines'.[2] And what have footnotes to do with garlands, churches, shrines?

[1] I have used for Hugh's questions the Second Edition of his *Historia Ecclesiastica* in Oxford, Bodleian, MS Rawlinson B. 194, fo. 61ʳ, and also a text printed from MS Bordeaux 11, fos 180ʳ–183ᵛ, by C. Couderc, 'Note sur une compilation inédite de Hughes de Sainte-Marie et sa vie de Saint Sacerdos, Évêque de Limoges', *BEC*, liv (1893), pp. 468–74.
[2] Canal, p. 133, line 197; p. 234, lines 1726–7.

History at Bec in the twelfth century

MARGARET GIBSON

LOCAL AFFAIRS

> Let us now praise famous men,
> and our fathers that begat us.   Ecclus. 44:1[1]

IN presenting the lives of the first four abbots of Bec—Herluin, Anselm, William, and Boso—Milo Crispin was writing at the extreme limit of the community's memory: *c.* 1136. He had himself entered Bec in 1094 under Abbot William, when many of the adult monks had known Lanfranc and Herluin personally.[2] Anselm had been succeeded as abbot by two of his own monks: William (1093–1124) and the interlocutor of the *Cur Deus Homo*, Boso (1124–36). These men had known the founders first hand, and they shared their view of life. The opening lines of the *De Veritate* take us straight into the community as it is still best remembered:

> THE PUPIL—Given that we believe that God is truth, and that we say that truth is in many other things, I should like to know if wherever the word 'truth' is used we ought to recognise that it is God ...[3]

An equally valid record of the intellectual outlook of Bec in this early period is the *Dicta Anselmi*, collected for that majority of monks who could understand a parable better than they could construct an argument.[4] But it is the *De Veritate* that conveys the essential

[1] Milo Crispin, *Vitae Abbatum*, praef.: *PL* 150. 695D.

[2] Milo Crispin is 302nd in the profession-list: A. A. Porée, *Histoire de l'Abbaye du Bec* (Évreux, 1901), i. p. 631. For his family see J. Armitage Robinson, *Gilbert Crispin, Abbot of Westminster* (Cambridge, 1911), pp. 13–18.

[3] *De Veritate*, i: *Anselmi Opera*, ed. F. S. Schmitt (Edinburgh, 1946), i. p. 176.

[4] R. W. Southern and F. S. Schmitt, *Memorials of St Anselm* (London, 1969: *Auct. Brit. Med. Æv.* i), pp. 105–95.

vision of Bec: a world that is comprehensible and interesting because it is concerned not with the quirks of individuals but with reason and truth; not with the miscellaneous causes of the passing moment but with the mind of God. Anselm and his contemporaries were completely indifferent to history. They kept no record of events at Bec beyond the severely practical: monastic professions, land-grants and notes of legal and fiscal privilege. They showed no interest in the Norman past nor in world history as a whole—though once more in practical terms Lanfranc was quick to use Bede's *Historia Ecclesiastica* to support the primacy of Canterbury.[1] They were not even concerned with the historical books of the Old Testament, nor with the historical circumstances in which Christianity was anchored: if the *infideles* were to doubt the historicity of the Incarnation, they would be sufficiently answered by a proof of its necessity. Here Anselm and his colleagues were in the main stream of contemporary scholarship, in which abstract analysis and systematic organization were coming to prevail over—indeed threatened to eliminate—history and literature. Conversely the writing and reading of history in Bec, and the acquisition of the relevant books for the library, marks a growing detachment from the professional scholarship of Paris and Poitiers and a break with the intellectual tradition of Herluin, Lanfranc, and Anselm.

Abbot Boso died on Midsummer Day 1136. He had been at death's door for over two years, and indeed had long been so incapacitated by arthritis and chronic blood-poisoning that the routine government of Bec must have devolved on others.[2] The royal charters of the 1130s, for instance, depended on more than the king's goodwill: they imply hard-headed negotiation by the abbot of Bec or his representative.[3] Thus in electing Prior Theobald as Boso's successor the community was confirming the status of a

---

[1] *The Letters of Archbishop Lanfranc*, 4, lines 26–44, ed. V. Clover and M. T. Gibson (Oxford, 1979: *OMT*), pp. 50–3.

[2] *Vita Bosonis: PL* 150. 730C–32C. Theobald had been prior since 1125/6: *Compendium Vitae Theobaldi* (*PL* 150. 733B).

[3] J. H. Round, *Calendar of Documents preserved in France* (London, 1899), i. pp. 125–6: nos 373–5.

man who must to some extent have been the acting abbot. Within three years Theobald in turn had become archbishop of Canterbury. There he was at once the able administrator—as may be seen in the archiepiscopal chancery—and the patron who attracted to his service master Vacarius and John of Salisbury. In Bec he brought the profession-list up to date,[1] and permitted, or encouraged, the first historical essays of Milo Crispin and Robert of Torigny. Again, we may hazard that the extent and variety of the Bec library as recorded in the catalogue of 1164 is due in some degree to Theobald as prior, as abbot and even as archbishop.[2]

The first fruits of the changing climate at Bec were Milo Crispin's *Vitae Abbatum*.[3] The four are conceived as a unit, spanning the century 1034–1136. Gilbert Crispin's *Vita Herluini* and Eadmer's *Vita Anselmi* stood ready to hand; Milo left them unchanged, disparate in style and intention, adding his own lives of William and Boso. These are in no sense a history of the community under William's or Boso's rule: Milo is honouring two local dignitaries and the families to which they belong, and by extension all the other families—some allied with the great, some of very moderate standing—who were patrons of Bec. These men had endowed the community with land and fiscal privilege; their brothers and sons were monks in the house itself or in its scattered priories. Milo's own family was among them, almost as far back as its history could be traced. His grandfather, William Crispin, had given freely to Bec, benefited by the prayers of the monks and received the habit when he came to die (1074). 'His love of Bec', wrote Milo, 'has been left as a kind of legacy to his descendants—from their earliest childhood they have a natural affection for that church, as though they had drunk in its sweetness with their mother's milk. When they call on

---

[1] Porée, i. pp. 629–45; cf. M. T. Gibson, *Lanfranc of Bec* (Oxford, 1978), pp. 201–2.

[2] G. Becker, *Catalogi Bibliothecarum Antiqui* (Bonn, 1885), no. 127; cf. G. Nortier, *Les Bibliothèques médiévales des abbayes bénédictines de Normandie* (Caen, 1966), pp. 57–83.

[3] *PL* 150. 695C–732C. The limiting dates are Boso's death (June 1136) and—arguing *ex silentio*—Theobald's translation (Dec. 1138).

the Virgin, it is always *St. Mary of Bec!*' Equally Bec owed a profound debt to the Crispins—'As a newborn child is taken from the cradle to be nourished, educated and brought to adult life, so our family has sheltered and endowed the church of Bec.'[1] As such men established themselves as the landed oligarchy of twelfth-century Normandy, their ties with Bec grew closer still. They had a common zeal to defend the endowments, a common distrust of the archbishops of Rouen who—justifiably, we may think—wanted their jurisdiction over the abbots of Bec to be formally admitted; all, within and without the monastery, shared Milo's assumption in his prologue to the *Vitae Abbatum*:

Long ago it was customary to set up statues of one's ancestors and to keep a written record of their achievements for the edification of posterity: theirs was the pattern of life to be emulated . . .[2]

Milo's account is founded on the abbot's family. William's father was lord of Montfort-sur-Risle, the first great stronghold on the river north of Bec; his mother was a Beaumont: he was 'related to great men, a candidate of whom the king and the magnates approved'. Boso's parents, though of lesser standing, had given three sons to Bec. Both abbots had endeavoured to maintain the freedom of their monastery without reserve. It did not matter that William's election was—not to put too fine a point on it—'fixed'; what counted was his external independence *vis-à-vis* the duke of Normandy and the archbishop of Rouen. Milo's third constituent is the edifying story. Abbot William's mother prayed to the Virgin and St. Germanus in the castle chapel of Montfort-sur-Risle that she might take her child's sickness on herself; so by the mother's death the child was preserved for the monastic life. Boso appears, in contrast, as showing heroic patience in the extreme of suffering— he could even joke about 'this fleshly prison' in which he lay

---

[1] Milo Crispin, *De nobili genere Crispinorum*: *PL* 150. 741AB.

[2] 'Consuetudo fuit apud ueteres maiorum suorum imagines erigere et praeclara eorum facta memoriae scribendo commendare, ad informationem posterorum: ad exemplum scilicet uirtutis et incitamentum probitatis': *Vitae Abbatum*, praef.: *PL* 150. 695C.

paralysed, bound hand and foot. These were examples that the laity could understand, the more so as the founder himself had been a knight turned monk. Abbot William used to pray at Herluin's tomb in the chapter-house; once Herluin appeared as his companion on an eerie flight over the Bec valley, saying not a word throughout.[1] Herluin remained a power in the community, rather as Dunstan was in Christ Church, Canterbury:[2] a century later he appears on the monastic seal as SANCTVS HERLVINVS PRIMVS ABBAS BECCI.[3] This cult of the founder set a firm limit to Milo Crispin's historical perspective: the *Vitae Abbatum* are only a step away from the local necrology and the local store of unwritten anecdote.

A man of far wider interests and better education, also a monk of Bec, lived in the Bec priory of Conflans-Ste-Honorine on the right bank of the Seine, just west of Paris. He is known only by his autograph manuscript, MS Paris BN lat. 2342, to which he went on adding material over a period of some forty years: sermons and eucharistic proof-texts datable to *c.* 1100; then a collection of 35 miracles of St. Nicholas (*c.* 1099–1129), followed by discussions of monastic profession and the community's legal relations with the secular world; next a lost *summa* of which nothing is known; then a treatise *De libertate beccensis ecclesie* (*c.* 1136) and finally a short collection of the miracles of St. Honorina, the Merovingian virgin martyr whose relics were preserved at Conflans. The texts that concern the history of Bec are the *Miracula S. Nicholai* and the *De libertate beccensis ecclesie*.[4]

---

[1] Ibid., col. 713C–24B (William) and 723D–32C (Boso).

[2] Osbern, *Miracula S. Dunstani*, 18, ed. Stubbs, *Memorials of St Dunstan* (RS, 1874), pp. 143–4.

[3] *Catalogue of Seals in the Department of Manuscripts in the British Museum*, v (London, 1898), nos 18466–7.

[4] A. Wilmart, 'Les Ouvrages d'un moine du Bec: un débat sur la profession monastique au xiie siécle', *Rev. bén.*, xliv (1932), pp. 21–46. The illumination, which was executed in stages as the manuscript was written, is discussed by F. Avril in the exhibition catalogue *Trésors des abbayes normandes* (Rouen, Caen, 1979), no. 169, with plate. The earliest initials can be very little later than 1100, i.e. substantially earlier than Wilmart supposed. The manuscript is now imperfect: see Wilmart's reconstruction, pp. 22–6.

In his collection of recent, and generally local, miracles of St. Nicholas the author was adding to an established corpus of material, rather as Desiderius had collected the more recent miracles of St. Benedict at Monte Cassino.[1] Those of the Nicholas miracles that relate to Bec preserve odd fragments of the early history of the house that are otherwise unrecorded. Gothbertus, the twenty-first monk to be professed, here granted a vision of two apostles and an unnamed saint (doubtless Saint Nicholas), is described as sacrist, one further name in our very imperfect sequence of monastic officials.[2] Again Lanfranc's early acquaintance with Berengar of Tours is related to Lanfranc's scholarly wandering in the late 1030s.[3] But already there is room for doubt: the Conflans author is not necessarily recording independent local tradition; sometimes he is just decorating an originally simple tale. Thus in the *Vita Herluini* Lanfranc arrives at Bec to find Herluin building an oven with his own hands; the *Vita Lanfranci* introduces a brief conversation as the abbot labours; but in the *Miracula S. Nicholai* what is basically the same conversation takes place while Herluin is inside the half-built oven and Lanfranc is peering in. Herluin has to shout up from the depths, 'I receive you in the name of the Lord!'[4] This is mere theatre. The author has studied just enough rhetoric to be able to disclaim any verbal skill whatever. 'In a work of this kind,' he begins, 'I am acutely aware of two conflicting factors: on the one hand, the feebleness of my understanding and the inadequacy of my language and my own status; on the other, my profound devotion to the saint. But although my exposition, however slight, requires that its matter be authenticated and properly understood—and I can do neither—yet with the help of almighty

---

[1] Desiderius, *Dialogi* i–ii: *PL* 149, cols 963C–1002D.

[2] *Miracula S. Nicholai* 5: *Catalogus Codicum Hagiographicorum Latinorum* ... *Bibliotheca Nationali Parisiensi*, ii (1890), p. 408.

[3] *Miracula S. Nicholai*, cap. 7; cf. *PL* 150. 63CD; critical edition by R. B. C. Huygens, 'Textes latins du xie au xiiie siècle', *Stud. Med.* 3, viii (1967), pp. 451–9.

[4] *Miracula S. Nicholai*, cap. 10, pp. 410–11.

God and the merits and prayers of blessed Nicholas himself let me begin some part of the narration.'[1]

In the *De libertate beccensis ecclesie*, which was written some years later, the Conflans author was less concerned with the devices of the schools. This is essentially a legal treatise, directed against the claims of the archbishop of Rouen to a written profession of obedience from the abbot of Bec. As only the first four abbots are discussed, the occasion may have been Theobald's benediction and installation in 1136, when it took Peter the Venerable to persuade Archbishop Hugh to accept a profession 'sine scripto, solo uerbo'.[2] Both Herluin and Anselm had been installed when Rouen was vacant; but William avoided a written profession in 1094 only by Duke Robert's direct intervention at the last moment, and Boso was similarly indebted to Henry I. Bec could not continue to rely on *ad hoc* royal assistance: instead the *De libertate* offers a complete set of precedents for refusing a written profession to the archbishop, and one noteworthy precedent (Boso) for refusing homage to the king. The author agrees in so many details with the *Vitae Abbatum* that he can be assumed to have known Milo Crispin's work: he had only to recast it as polemic. At the same time he is distinctly better informed about secular affairs. Robert of Meulan's brief control of Brionne threatened the freedom of Bec, which lay 'in fisco Brionnensis castri'. When the count did claim jurisdiction, Anselm returned the kind of four-square negative for which he was to be renowned as archbishop—'This is not my abbey: it belongs to the duke of Normandy.'[3] Again at Boso's election the Conflans

---

[1] 'Sed ob duas causas in tali opere ualde coartor, hinc me retrahente exiguitate sensus ac uilitate sermonis personaeque, hinc deuoto amore sancti me impellente. Et quamquam omnis materia dictaminis, licet sit exigua, expetat auctoritatem et expertam scientiam, quod utrumque deest a me *et opere et specie*, quamuis ita sit, tamen fultus auxilio omnipotentis Dei, suffragantibus meritis et orationibus ipsius beatissimi, narrare aliqua incipiam': ibid. 1, p. 406, italicized phrase not translated.

[2] *De libertate beccensis ecclesie*, ed. Mabillon, *Annales Ordinis S. Benedicti*, v (Paris, 1713), pp. 635–40; cf. *PL* 150. 733C (Theobald's profession).

[3] 'Abbatia ista non est mea, sed domini principis Normanniae; quod illi placuerit erit': ibid., p. 636.

author has at once a sound grasp of the king's rights and the inside story (from Notre Dame du Pré) of how these were enforced. Abbot Boso was refusing to do homage to Henry I, on the grounds of a promise made to the pope a quarter of a century earlier; the bishops of Évreux and Lisieux were justly indignant: 'We who are bishops do homage to our lord—but a monk can say he is not doing what everyone else does!' The king replied, 'This case falls within my jurisdiction; the decision is mine.' As he was riding into Rouen, escorted on either side by Archbishop Geoffrey and John of Lisieux, Henry remarked, 'My lord archbishop, you can be sure that this abbot will neither do homage to me nor make you a profession of obedience.' The archbishop pointed out that the profession was his affair, Henry swore at him and the subject was dropped. Then the king sent for Boso; and in private—witnessed only by Archbishop Geoffrey, an unnamed English bishop, and two magnates—he gave him the abbey 'per quandam donationem, sine mentione hominii'. That left the archbishop in a dilemma, which was resolved by a royal directive to bless the abbot 'sine ulla mentione professionis'. When Boso arrived in Rouen cathedral, Geoffrey's words were softer than butter—'My lord abbot, although there is no need for me to put questions to you, as we question and examine others, still for custom's sake I ask you in a word if you wish to be an obedient subject of this holy church of Rouen and those who govern it.' The abbot replied, 'I do'; and the archbishop said, 'Thank God'. After the ceremony the king admonished Boso: 'Be abbot within the monastery according to your monastic vows, and I shall be abbot in its external affairs.'[1] Boso had kept his conscience clear at some cost.

In both the *Miracula* and the *De libertate* the author's commitment to Bec is balanced by a wider knowledge of the outside world than we see in Milo Crispin. These Bec priories along the Seine—Conflans-Ste-Honorine, S. Nicaise, Meulan, and Notre Dame du Pré (La Bonne Nouvelle) at Rouen—surely kept in touch with one

---

[1] Ibid., pp. 638–40.

another, if only in the course of trade up and down the river; thus they were jointly informed about the affairs of Rouen and Paris, whereas Bec had to depend on the intermittent visits of the ducal court to Brionne. Again, the political interests of the priories could not always coincide with those of the mother house. The Conflans author speaks, however briefly, for the growing company of monks who came to Bec for their noviciate and profession, but who spent their lives elsewhere.

PROFESSIONAL HISTORY

What need is there to commit to writing the lives and deaths and various events of mankind, or to record for ever the signs in the sky or the earth or the other elements?

Robert of Torigny answered such critics in traditional style: the deeds of good men inspire us to emulation, the deeds of wicked men are a warning, and portents remind sinners of the wrath of God.[1] But that is not what interests him. Robert was not concerned with the moral value of history, still less with a sequence of ages or a cosmic pattern of salvation. He was engaged in, as he put it, 'chronography', continuing the successive labours of Eusebius, Jerome, Prosper of Aquitaine, and most recently Sigebert of Gembloux.[2] In the prologue to his own *Chronicle* Robert describes the ideal arrangement of a page of Sigebert's text: across the top the names of the eight kingdoms, beneath them the names of the kings, further down still—in the middle of the page—their regnal years and on the outer margin a list of popes, with the year of grace opposite the regnal years.[3] I do not know of any surviving lay-out

[1] L. Delisle, *Chronique de Robert de Torigni* (Rouen, 1872–3: *SHN*), i. p. 92.
[2] 'De chronographia, id est temporum descriptione, in subsequentibus locuturi . . .': Delisle, *Chronique*, i. p. 91.
[3] 'Ponit autem in fronte paginae libri sui primum nomina regnorum diuersorum, uidelicet Romanorum, Persarum, Francorum, Britannorum, Wandalorum, Wisigothorum, Ostrogothorum, Hunorum; postea supponit regnis nomina propria regum; deorsum uero per mediam paginam annos singulorum principum; in margine nomina Romanorum pontificum, et annos Domini respondentes recta fronte annis praedictorum regum': ibid. i. p. 94.

that is quite so elaborate, either of Sigebert's *Chronicle* alone or of Robert's revision; but given a double spread (e.g. fos. 1ᵛ–2ʳ) it would be quite feasible. Number is everything here: Robert belonged to the long and honourable line of historians whose prime interest was in getting the dates right.

His *Chronicle* is in no sense a work of interpretation, either of events or the motives of men; the vivid snapshot, the full-length portrait, even the comprehensive epitaph are never vouchsafed. He was an intelligent man without a trace of romance in his soul.

Robert of Torigny's years at Bec coincided with nearly all the historical writing that the community produced before the fifteenth century. He was professed in 1128, probably as a boy of about 15.[1] He served his historical apprenticeship by revising the *Gesta Normannorum Ducum* of William of Jumièges—in the version already brought up to date by Orderic Vitalis[2]—and by writing a treatise on the new monastic orders, which again owes much to Orderic.[3] But the man who taught him most was Henry of Huntingdon, who stayed at Bec in January 1139 in the entourage of Archbishop Theobald. Henry was an established author, who not only provided Robert with much of the material he needed for the reign of Henry I,[4] but seized with delight on a book that had just reached Bec, Geoffrey of Monmouth's *Historia Regum Britanniae*.[5] Here was data about an entire people, whose past had been inaccessible—'overshadowed and snuffed out'[6]—until the appearance of Geoffrey's work. At last it was possible to bridge the chasms in

---

[1] Porée, i. p. 633.

[2] WJ, pp. 199–334. The original manuscript of Robert's revision is now MS Leiden UnivB. B.P.L.20, fos 2–32ᵛ. See below, p. 183 n. 1.

[3] Delisle, *Chronique*, ii. pp. 184–206; cf. *OV*, iv. pp. 310–41 and p. xiv, with references.

[4] Delisle, *Chronique*, i. pp. 119–96; cf. Henry of Huntingdon, *Historia Anglorum*, vii. pp. 22–43 (ed. T. Arnold (RS, 1879), pp. 233–54).

[5] Delisle, *Chronique*, i. pp. 97–8 and 111; see further note 60. The *Historia Regum Britanniae* was completed after the death of Henry I (Dec. 1135); the dedication to Waleran of Meulan—a patron of Bec—can be dated to 1136/8.

[6] 'Tanta pernities obliuionis mortalium gloriam successu diuturnitatis obumbrat et extinguit': Delisle, *Chronique*, i. p. 97.

Gildas and Bede: to know that Brutus Greenshield was a contemporary of King Solomon and that fifty successive rulers (if not fifty generations) divided King Lear from Julius Caesar. Well might Henry exclaim, 'Can the prowess and valour and magnificence of so many kings be written in books that are unknown to us or even wholly erased from the memory of man?'[1] But in the rapid summary of Geoffrey's *History* that he sent to his colleague Warin Brito Henry's overriding concern was with chronology rather than with noble deeds; and Robert followed him, including the letter to Warin verbatim in his own *Chronicle*.[2] He unhesitatingly assumed, as Henry had done, that the marrow of Geoffrey's work was his genealogies.

Late in the 1130s a monk of Bec, who is otherwise unknown, assembled the *Vita Lanfranci*.[3] I say 'assembled', because such an exceptionally high proportion of his work can be traced to extant written sources; the balance is mostly local anecdote, pre-existing if not previously written down. He began by excerpting Gilbert Crispin's *Vita Herluini*; then, after he had embarked on this task, he acquired the *Gesta Guillelmi Ducis* of William of Poitiers. Stylistically the two are badly matched: William of Poitiers takes far longer to say far less than Gilbert Crispin. But the author of the *Vita Lanfranci* was endeavouring to include all that he could find, written or spoken. In Normandy there was little beyond William of Poitiers, the *Miracula S. Nicholai* and Lanfranc's own treatise on the Eucharist; what made his work possible were the texts from England that had been copied in, or transferred to, the library of Bec. The *Vita Herluini* took him to 1077 (Lanfranc's consecration of the new church at Bec), the *Vita Anselmi* and the *Historia Novorum* supplied some details of Lanfranc's archiepiscopate; but the real

---

[1] 'Tot uero regum praedictorum bella et fortitudines et magnificentiae, nonne haec uel scripta sunt in libris innotissimis, uel penitus a memoria deleta': ibid., i. p. 105.

[2] Ibid., pp. 97–111.

[3] For a more detailed account of the sources and the manuscript tradition see M. T. Gibson, *The 'Vita Lanfranci'* (Toronto, forthcoming). I have abandoned my original view that the author was writing in Canterbury.

treasure trove was Lanfranc's letter-collection, which included the primacy agreement of 1072 and the council of London of 1075: long passages of both are quoted *in extenso*.[1] The author concludes with an anecdote (which had apparently eluded Eadmer) forecasting Anselm's succession as archbishop, and an account of Lanfranc's translation in 1130. By the fifteenth century the *Vita Lanfranci* had been attached to the *Vitae Abbatum*; furthermore a twelfth-century manuscript known to the Maurists and since lost had a marginal note (of uncertain date) attributing the *Vita Lanfranci* to 'Milo Crispin, precentor of Bec'.[2] But the author of the *Vita Lanfranci* is writing in a very different key from Milo Crispin. He has none of Milo's zeal for the patrons of Bec; he is sparing in his attention to the miraculous. Temperamentally he is nearer to the *Vita Herluini*: not only in his moments of direct pastiche—for instance the list of Lanfranc's monks at Caen on the analogy of Herluin's at Bec[3]—but in his implied criticism of contemporary monastic life. When Lanfranc went to Canterbury, Herluin regretted his departure. It is necessary to explain that (unlike today's abbots) Herluin was not jealous of Lanfranc's promotion; he wished to keep him in Normandy only because there too he was indispensable.[4] Lanfranc is presented as an exemplary monk, nothing more. When his remains were exhumed—wrapped in a sheet of lead[5]—one of the Christ Church monks abstracted a piece of his chasuble; all marvelled at the sweet smell. It is not surprising, says the writer austerely,

---

[1] In the Bec library catalogue of *c.* 1164 the relevant items are: no. 73 (*De corpore et sanguine Domini*), no. 100 (*Vita Herluini* and *Vita Anselmi*) and no. 81 (Lanfranc's letter-collection = MS Vatican Reg. lat. 285). See G. Becker, *Catalogi Bibliothecarum Antiquarum* (Bonn, 1885), no. 127.

[2] *PL* 150. 57D–8D.

[3] *PL* 150. 38B–D; cf. J. Armitage Robinson, *Gilbert Crispin, abbot of Westminster* (Cambridge, 1911), p. 103.

[4] *PL* 150. 41CD.

[5] 'Lanfrancus autem archiepiscopus in tabula plumbea ponderosa ualde inuentus est, in qua a die primae sepulturae suae intactis membris, mitratus, spindulatus [sc. wearing his pallium], usque in illum diem jacuerat': Gervase of Canterbury, *Tractatus de combustione et reparatione Cantuariensis ecclesiae*, ed. W. Stubbs, *Gervasii Opera* (RS, 1879), i. p. 25.

that the vestments of a man whose good works have rendered him fragrant in life should be fragrant still after his death.[1] There is no suggestion here that Lanfranc might be proposed for canonization or that he was recognized locally as a saint. Apart from moments of nostalgia for a better monastic past, the author of the *Vita Lanfranci* has no axe to grind; he is concerned only to assemble his material accurately and in good order. But for his inferior latinity, we might identify him with Robert of Torigny himself: certainly he is clear evidence of Robert's historical influence within the community.

In 1149 Prior Roger of Bailleul became abbot of Bec. Robert of Torigny succeeded him as prior, either at once or within a year or so: no exact records survive. By then he had finished the first recension of his *Chronicle*: the earliest version of the preface indicates that his own contribution extended from 1100–50.[2] He seems now to have turned his attention to establishing a full chronicle of the house. In the long and now textually confused *Chronicon Beccense* the basic, retrospective section runs from 1034–1149; thereafter it has been kept up year by year, at least in principle.[3] Some basic chronology was provided by the *Annals of Bec*;[4] the compiler has added verbatim excerpts of other material, that is still extant, notably Robert's own *Chronicle* and the *Vita Lanfranci*.[5] The picture is complicated by

---

[1] *PL* 150. 58B.

[2] Delisle, *Chronique*, i. p. 96 and app. As abbot of Mont S. Michel (1154–86) Robert continued to work on his *Chronicle*. For the Bec recension (with independent material 1157–60) see Delisle, ii. pp. 165–80.

[3] There are two, radically different, texts of the *Chronicon Beccense*: (i) 1034–1468, Luc d'Achery, *Lanfranci Opera: Appendix* (Paris, 1648), pp. 1–28, reprinted *PL* 150. 639D–90D; (ii) 1149–1476, A. A. Porée, *Chronique du Bec* (Rouen, 1883: *SHN*), pp. 13–111. D'Achery used a s. xv paper manuscript now lost; Porée used André Du Chesne's transcript (MS Paris BN lat. 5427) of the Bec historical compendium, MS Vatican Reg. lat. 499.

[4] Again two versions: (i) 851–1154 and (ii) 851–1183. Both are edited by Delisle, 'Les courtes annales du Bec', *Notices et documents publiés pour la Société de l'Histoire de France: 50ᵉ anniversaire* (Paris, 1884), pp. 93–9. The second is also edited by Porée, loc. cit., pp. 1–11.

[5] See for example *PL* 150. 643D–4B (cf. Delisle, *Chronique*, i. pp. 50–1) and the account of Lanfranc's visit to Rome (*PL* 150. 644D–5B), in which the error

passages relating primarily to Notre Dame du Pré and Conflans-Ste-Honorine.[1] But the overall purpose is clear: the construction of an internal chronicle that would replace the *Vitae Abbatum* with a comprehensive history of Bec; the *Vitae Abbatum* are continued only as a series of notes for Theobald (1136–8) and Letard (1139–49).[2] There was no call to maintain Milo Crispin's work on the original scale; indeed it was soon to be rewritten in a new and unnerving manner.

In the 1150s the lives of the first seven abbots, including Roger of Bailleul (1149–79), were rendered into verse by Peter, monk of S. Pierre-sur-Dives.[3] He wrote, he tells us, in response to the insistent demands of Milo Crispin:

> Sepe magis numero fuerim compulsus ad istud
> Domni Milonis / Crispini uoce monentis,
> Omnibus et uotis / nihilominus id satagentis.

The maladroit scansion and Virgilian phraseology continue throughout. Here for instance is Lanfranc's departure from Bec:

> At pater Herluinus / mens ueri conscia cuius,
> Vt se conspexit Lanfranco iam uiduatum ⎫
> Quem successorem gaudebat habere paratum ⎭
> Quoque sue curam / domus ipse refuderat omnem,
> Eligit Anselmum / uita studiisque probatum ⎫
> Lanfrancique loco deliberat ire locatum.[4] ⎭

It need hardly be said that there is not a particle of new information in the whole work. What Peter offered was familiar history in a newly fashionable literary mode. In this respect he was the forerunner of the last of our Bec historians, the poet and rhetorician Stephen of Rouen.

'Leo *octauus*' (644D) derives from the *Vita Lanfranci* (*PL* 150. 36A; cf. 35D–8C for the passage as a whole).

[2] See respectively *PL* 150. 645B–D (Notre Dame du Pré), ibid. 647CD (Conflans) and ibid. 641A–C, 642B–3B, 644B–D (*Miracula S. Nicholai*, caps 3–4, 8, 5).

[3] *PL* 150. 733B–6B.

[4] *Gesta Septem Abbatum Beccensium*: *PL* 181, cols 1709A–18D.

[5] Ibid, 1709B; 1713CD.

THE VISION OF THE PAST

While Vortigern, king of the Britons, was sitting by the pool that had just been drained, two dragons came out, one white and the other red. They met and fought viciously, breathing fire from their nostrils ... As they fought, the king asked Ambrosius Merlin to explain the meaning of this portent. He burst into tears and made prophetic utterance—'Woe unto the Red Dragon, for its end is nigh! The White Dragon, which signifies the Saxons whom you have brought in, will seize its lair. For the Red Dragon signifies the people of Britain, whom the White Dragon shall oppress.'[1]

In prophesying the victory of the White Dragon over the Red, Merlin had left the last part of the tale untold. Ten years later Geoffrey of Monmouth gave him more scope to prophesy that the English in turn would be oppressed by the Normans in their 'two-faced ships' and heavy armour.[2] There was no further talk of dragons, visible as they were on every prow. But it is hard to see how else to interpret the title of Stephen's verse epic, the *Draco Normannicus*.[3] Here the Norman people, emerging from the mists of time with the highest military and genealogical credentials, establish themselves under the rule of Henry I and his descendants in England, Normandy, and Anjou. A third and more powerful dragon, of unspecified complexion, has fought the White Dragon and prevailed.

Stephen 'of Rouen'—he is distinguished by an 'R' in the profession-list *c*. 1143—came of a family that had already sent at least one monk to Bec, Bernard, subsequently abbot of Mont S. Michel.[4] Like Milo Crispin he belonged to the network of patrons

[1] A. Griscom, *The 'Historia Regum Britanniae' of Geoffrey of Monmouth* (London, New York, Toronto, 1929), pp. 384–5.

[2] 'Indeque Neustrenses ligno trans equora uecti, / Vultus ante suos et uultus retro ferentes / Ferratis tunicis et acutis ensibus, Anglos / Acriter inuadent . . .': *Vita Merlini*, lines 654–7, J. J. Parry (Illinois, 1925), p. 70.

[3] R. Howlett, *Chronicles of the Reign of Stephen, Henry II and Richard I* (*RS*, 1885), ii. pp. 595–757; also edited by H. Omont, *Le 'Dragon Normand' et autres poèmes d'Étienne de Rouen* (Rouen, 1884: *SHN*).

[4] Howlett, pp. xii–xvii; see further C. Fierville, 'Étienne de Rouen, moine du Bec, au xiie siècle', *Bull. Soc. Antiq. Norm.*, viii (1875–7), pp. 54–78 421–42, and some illuminating remarks by B. Smalley, *The Becket Conflict and the Schools* (Oxford, 1973), pp. 186–9.

who maintained the prosperity and independence of the house; and it was for them that he wrote. When Waleran of Meulan died in 1166 Stephen at once took up his pen—

> Flos comitum, decus imperii, uis maxima belli,
> Militiae splendor, sensus acutus obit . . .
> Hic de stirpe satus comitum regumque propinquus,
> Quos sensu superat, moribus, ense, throno.
> Hos sequi probitate parum sibi computat esse,
> Vult superare duces, nescit habere parem.[1]

The elegiac couplet came as naturally to Stephen as stringing a noun to a verb: he could keep it going for literally thousands of lines, without undue complexity and without error. He never wrote prose.[2] For the 1160s his style is somewhat old-fashioned: Stephen is a late follower of Hildebert rather than a precursor of Alan of Lille. Sometimes he experimented, less happily, with internal rhyme or two-foot verses or the invention of new metres—a puzzle that had the same fascination as devising a new knot.[3] But his real gift was in extended narrative verse: the best parallel in English is *The Lay of the Last Minstrel*.

The *Draco Normannicus* can be dated exactly to 1169/70.[4] While it is formally addressed to Henry II, it is really a grand pageant of the Normans in history. Stephen had a good library in Bec, both historical and classical: Dudo of St. Quentin, William of Jumièges, Geoffrey of Monmouth, Vegetius, Caesar.[5] But Dudo and William are the staple of his narrative: long passages of the *Draco* are a straight metrical paraphrase of the *De moribus et actis primorum Normanniae Ducum* and the *Gesta Normannorum Ducum*. Beyond the

---

[1] Howlett, pp. 766–7.

[2] The exceptions are Stephen's abridgement of Quintilian (Fierville, p. 54, with reference) and a preface to Isaiah (Omont, pp. 171–2), which requires further study.

[3] Howlett, pp. 772–9; Omont, pp. 189–260; Fierville, pp. 54–78, 436–7.

[4] The limiting dates are the peace of Poissy (Jan. 1169) and the death of Becket (Dec. 1170): Howlett, p. xvi, with references.

[5] For the library of *c.* 1164 see G. Becker, *Catalogi Bibliothecarum Antiquarum* (Bonn, 1885), no. 127.

indici ortū uidebis. Caspiūq: mare unde orirā inueniet:
Licet nō ignorē eē ū nullos. qui et de oceano ingssū ne-
get, nec dubiū : milla qq; austr gnirif repatā mare de
oceano similir influere. S; descripti li mā adtestatioē
ñ debuit. cui sic nob in cognit pseuat.

septemtriouis frigida inhabitabilis

hordeaces in sule

hordeaces in sule

tempata nrā

mare caspium

usta · inhabitabiles

temperata · antipodū

frigida. Australes inhabitabiles

Quod autē nrām habitabilē dixit angusti uerāb; in
latitb; latiorē in eadē de sepcione potiū ad uāe. Illi
qnto longiorē tropicē circ septentonali circo. tanto zona

World map showing the Antipodes: Macrobius, *In Somnium Scipionis*, 2.9.7–8
(MS Lincoln College, Oxford, lat. 27, fo. 160ᵛ: s.xii, English). Actual size.

Normans lay the kings of Britain and the exiled heroes of Troy. Here Geoffrey of Monmouth was to hand, in the same manuscript (still extant) as William of Jumièges:[1] the text that Henry of Huntingdon had admired and Robert of Torigny neglected was to provide the material and the inspiration for some of Stephen's most dramatic lines—a piece of Arthurian apocrypha that goes a long way towards unifying his entire three-decker epic.

In 1167 Henry II was preparing to invade Brittany. So Roland, count of Brittany—not the hero of Roncevaux (and we do need to be told this)—sent a request for help to his own overlord, King Arthur, currently ruling in the Antipodes:

> Traditur Antipodum sibi jus; fatatus, inermis,
> > Belliger assistit, proelia nulla timet.
> Sic hemispherium regit inferius, nitet armis,
> > Altera pars mundi dimidiata sibi.
> Hoc nec Alexandri potuit, nec Caesaris ardor . . .[2]

There can be no doubt that these Antipodes are situated on the external lower half of a sphere, basically as Macrobius had expounded, with an accompanying diagram (see Plate), in his commentary on the *Somnium Scipionis*:

Both (temperate) zones are not assigned to the people of our race; only the upper one, namely I–N, is inhabited by all the races of men that we can know, be they Romans or Greeks or barbarians of whatever nationality. The zone L–F is known only by the inference that, given its comparable climate, it is inhabited in the same way, but by whom we have never been

---

[1] MS Leiden Univ B. B.P.L. 20 was bequeathed to Bec *c.* 1164 by Philip of Harcourt: Becker, no. 86, items 41 (containing William of Jumièges) and 42 (containing Geoffrey of Monmouth). The two items were bound together in Bec: Becker, no. 127, item 117. See Howlett, pp. xviii–xxvi, and J. Lair and L. Delisle, *Matériaux pour l'édition de Guillaume de Jumièges* (Paris, 1910), with a facsimile of B.P.L. 20, fos 1ᵛ–32ᵛ.

[2] 'He is assigned jurisdiction over the Antipodes: the warrior stands there self-sufficient, as fate has decreed; he fears no battles. Thus he rules the lower hemisphere, resplendent in arms; the other half of the world is shared out to him. Neither Alexander's glowing zeal, nor Caesar's, could achieve this . . .': *Draco*, ii. 1165–9 (ed. cit. pp. 703–4).

permitted to know nor shall we be: the torrid zone that lies between prohibits any contact between the two races of men.[1]

No man could cross the torrid zone. Even if Count Roland's letter were to reach the Antipodes, it could not evoke a practical response. But for a man of no great scientific bent the difficulty might be neutralized by another Macrobian text. Proserpina, queen of the classical underworld, is said to rule 'the lower hemisphere of the earth and the Antipodes'.[2] If the Antipodes are at once the lower hemisphere and the underworld, then the poet might turn from one meaning to the other as his narrative required. Certainly Stephen's Arthur is no ghostly visitor from the dead; he is a human warrior, dwelling in the physical Macrobian universe, subject only to a different time-scale. He sends a challenge to Henry II, threatening to invade Cornwall with his legions; they are already on their way. Henry defies him, and only the death of the elderly Empress Matilda allows both sides to withdraw honourably.[3] Now the consensus among both historians and students of courtly literature is to treat such an impossible story as a joke. Stephen was a sophisticated man, writing for a sophisticated audience, as Geoffrey had been a generation earlier; Henry II smiled when he received Arthur's challenge.[4] But we do not suppose that the king smiled when he ordered the monks of Glastonbury to find Arthur's tomb. During the 1180s he paid good money to encourage them; and a hollowed oak coffin was indeed excavated, beneath a stone marked

---

[1] 'Non tamen ambae zonae hominibus nostrae generis indultae sunt, sed sola superior quae est ab I usque ad N incolitur ab omni quale scire possumus hominum genere, Romani Graeciue sint uel barbari cuiusque nationis. Illa uero ab L usque ad F sola ratione intellegitur, quod propter similem temperiem similiter incolatur, sed a quibus neque licuit umquam nobis nec licebit agnoscere; interiecta enim torrida utrique generi commercium ad se denegat commeandi': Macrobius, *In Somnium Scipionis* 2.5.16–17, ed. Willis (Leipzig, 1963: Teubner), p. 112; cf. p. 165.

[2] 'Proserpina ... quam numen terrae inferioris circuli et Antipodum diximus': Macrobius, *Saturnalia* 1.21.3, ed. Willis (Leipzig, 1963: Teubner), p. 116.

[3] *Draco*, ii. 955–1216 (ed. cit. pp. 696–705).

[4] Ibid. ii. 1217–18 (ed. cit. p. 705).

Margaret Gibson

with an appropriately inscribed lead cross.[1] With that discovery, and the solemn translation of the relics, the Arthur legend changed from the advent of a royal warrior rallying the British, whom Henry II in his last years could see as a political threat, to the fable or the literary device of Arthur's return from the dead;[2] but for Stephen of Rouen and his audience *c.* 1170 the older, and more concrete, belief in Arthur could still persist.

Geoffrey of Monmouth offered different things to different readers: hence no doubt his immediate and sustained popularity. For the professional historian he provided chronology and geneaology; for 'the general reader' simple dramas endlessly repeated—campaigns, battles, reduction of kingdoms, noble youths, just kings, heroic matrons, renewed conflict. The stories individually are brief and clear; it is easy to identify with the characters; there are relatively few villains; according to the accepted ground-rules there is astonishingly little dirty play. But taken as a whole the *Historia Regum Britanniae* stretches so far into the past as to be cyclic: the hero conquers the land and founds a kingdom; there is a period of peace and good law, passed over in a sentence; in the next generation everything crumbles, until a new ruler arises and begins again. Aeon after aeon passes so: peoples emerge and flourish and decay. Now whereas Robert of Torigny learned the first of these lessons, Stephen of Rouen learned the second and the third. The *Draco* is packed with raids and skirmishes, sieges, negotiations and treaties, which have the dramatic function of generating further campaigns. It is straight entertainment, written by a monk who was temperamentally closer to the country families of the Risle valley than to Lanfranc and Anselm. But the advent of King Arthur expands his story across the known world into the other hemisphere, and stretches the time-scale back to the half-forgotten eras of British history. The valiant Normans, whether commanded by

[1] Giraldus Cambrensis, *De Principis Instructione*, i, ed. G. F. Warner, *Giraldi Cambrensis Opera* (RS, 1891), viii. pp. 127–8.
[2] See notably K. H. Göller, 'Giraldus Cambrensis und der Tod Arthurs', *Anglia*, xci (1973), pp. 170–93.

Rollo or Henry II, are seen in a long perspective and on a world stage; when Stephen 'cuts' from Henry II to the Norman invasion of France and back again to William the Conqueror he intensifies this impression, surely deliberately.[1] This imaginative apprehension of the past was the great legacy of Geoffrey of Monmouth: to look into the successive layers of time and see the kingdoms and peoples that had once flourished in your own land. In the words of a Northman writing about a century earlier than Stephen of Rouen:

> Boards shall be found of a beauty to wonder at,
> Boards of gold in the grass long after,
> The chess boards they owned in the olden days.[2]

---

[1] *Draco*, i. 482–1303 (ed. cit. pp. 610–42).

[2] §'ar muno eptir undrsamligar / Gullnar tǫflor í grasi finnaz / §aers í árdaga áttar hofðo': *Volospá*, stanza 61 (*Edda*, ed. Neckel and Kuhn, 3 edn, [Heidelberg, 1962], p. 14); translation by P. B. Taylor and W. H. Auden, *The Elder Edda* (London, 1969), p. 152, quoted by kind permission of Faber & Faber and Random House.

St. Anselm and sacred history

GILLIAN EVANS

THE early twelfth-century commentator on Holy Scripture, Rupert of Deutz, saw in the study of history a means of making sense not only of the Bible, but also of Trinitarian theology. In his book *On the Holy Trinity* he set out to show from Scripture, book by book, how the period from the beginning of the world to the fall of Adam might be thought of as the age of the Father, the time from the fall of Adam to the Passion of Christ as the age of the Son; from then to the end of the world he considered to be the age of the Holy Spirit.[1] This interpretation of history, in one form or another, had some currency in the twelfth and thirteenth centuries,[2] but there is about Rupert's account a peculiar insight into the implications of this view. He perceived in the events of sacred and human history a mirror of God himself,[3] an image of the Trinity. It was not an image which other theologians of the day found philosophically helpful, however, partly because it depended for its force on what could only be described as a historical notion of the nature of God.[4] The activities of God, which Rupert refers to as the *opera dei*,[5]

[1] Rupert of Deutz, *De Sancta Trinitate et Operibus Eius*, ed. H. Haacke, *Corpus Christianorum Continuatio Medievalis*, 21 (1971), pp. 122, 111-29. I should like to thank the Revd Prof. H. Chadwick, the late Dr R. W. Hunt, and Miss P. McNulty for their kindness in reading drafts of this paper.

[2] On the development of this interpretation of the *status* of history see M. Reeves, *The Influence of Prophecy in the Later Middle Ages* (Oxford, 1969).

[3] *De Sancta Trinitate*, p. 126.46–50.

[4] See my article 'St. Anselm's Images of Trinity', *Journal of Theological Studies*, 27 (1976), pp. 46–57, on some of the images of the Trinity which were under discussion in the schools.

[5] The *De Sancta Trinitate* deals with the *opera* of God. See its full title.

seemed to many of his contemporaries to be susceptible of a historical treatment in a way that the nature of God was not. The division which they perceived within the subject-matter of theology (to take the word for the moment in its broader modern sense) raised what is perhaps the most important question of theological method which preoccupied them. Rupert is here taking his stand at one end of the spectrum of opinion; he sees no objection to a historical approach even to Trinitarian theology, and he appears to have considered it adequate for his purposes in every area of theological discussion. St. Anselm stands at the other extreme. In the *Cur Deus Homo* he attempted to deal with even overtly historical problems as though they were philosophical problems.

Among the texts which were being read afresh in the schools of the first half of the twelfth century were the *opuscula sacra* of Boethius. In his definition of theology in the *De Trinitate* Boethius lays emphasis upon the immutability of God. The subject-matter of theology, he says, is 'sine motu, abstracta atque separabilis'[1]; it is concerned with what has no motion, what is abstract and separable from any context. These are precisely the qualities which historical matter lacks. As Hugh of St. Victor puts it, when we study history we have to consider 'the person, the business, the time and the place'.[2] Boethius restricts himself to a discussion of the nature of God, and makes of theology a philosophical study, in which the reading of the Bible plays no essential part. He himself found it quite unnecessary to base his reasoning on a Scriptural text. Twelfth-century commentators on his theological works found that the method would carry them so far and no farther: it would enable them to say a great deal about unity and trinity and nothing at all about the

---

[1] Boethius, *De Trinitate*, ii. ed. and tr. H. F. Stewart and E. K. Rand (reprinted London, 1973), p. 8. For twelfth-century commentaries on the *opuscula sacra* see Gilbert of Poitiers, *Commentaries on Boethius*, ed. N. M. Häring (Toronto, 1966) and *Commentaries on Boethius by Thierry of Chartres and his School*, ed. N. M. Häring (Toronto, 1971).

[2] *Didascalicon* vi. 3, ed. C. Buttimer (Washington, 1939), p. 114.1, *PL* 176, col. 799.

changes brought about by incarnation and redemption, or about the sacraments. Boethius' definition of the subject-matter of theology was also, as it turned out, a definition of its method, and of the limitations of that method.

Contemporary interpretation of Romans 1: 19–20 reflects clearly enough the difference which this throws into relief. St. Paul argues that no one has any excuse for not believing in God because God has revealed himself in the created world even to those who have not been instructed in the Christian faith. What he has revealed there, however, is his nature. It seems that we cannot learn about the incarnation and the redemption except through the Bible. There are two ways, Hugh of St. Victor says, in which human beings may learn about God: 'partim scilicet ratione humana, partim revelatione divina',[1] by human reason and by divine revelation. Reasoning based upon observation of the created world can take us as far as an understanding of unity and Trinity. The problems involved here are, up to a point, susceptible of philosophical solutions, or at any rate of philosophical discussion, and so the pagan philosophers have no excuse for their unbelief. But the rest of the subject-matter of the Creeds is not easily to be grasped by reason alone, if it is to be grasped at all. Because the incarnation involves a historical event, we cannot pursue the method of rational enquiry very far into the mystery of the redemption without coming up against our need for some additional revelation—such as the Bible alone provides. We need more facts to work on.

So at least it seemed to those who came after Anselm. He himself made no such concession; he believed that he had extended the scope of rational enquiry into the further area of redemption theology, in the *Cur Deus Homo* and the *De Conceptu Virginali*. When Anselm writes about sacred history he does so as a philosopher, not as a historian. The daring and originality of his attempt becomes plain only when we look at the habits of thought which were forming themselves in the minds of his contemporaries and those who followed him.

[1] *De Sacramentis,* i.3.3, *PL* 176, col. 217.

Unlike those who were writing only a decade or two later, Anselm was not concerned with the question 'what is theology' as a topic for investigation in its own right. He never speaks of *theologia*. When he uses the term *divinitas* he means God, not 'theology'. The only expression he uses which might be regarded as even loosely equivalent to 'theology' is *studium sacrae Scripturae*, the study of Holy Scripture. That is exactly what we should expect to find. He had no occasion to give thought to the problems of methodology which were to be raised soon after, and contemporary scholarship did not present him with the choices which faced thinkers even in Abelard's day. Abelard preferred to concentrate upon issues which allowed the methods of the *artes* to be brought fully into play, that is the theological topics which allow 'rational enquiry'. When he did so, he made a conscious choice not to adopt a historically conceived interpretation of the events described by Scripture. Anselm's preference for a philosophical rather than a historical approach to theological problem-solving reflects no such choice. He was allowed a freedom of movement, methodologically speaking, which Abelard did not enjoy.

Nevertheless, it may be worth asking why Anselm chose not to see the essentially historical problems raised by the historical events of the incarnation in the terms which came so naturally to his contemporaries and to scholars of the next generation. The argument that he was free not to do so is no explanation for his failure to adopt what was, already, the obvious course. The first thing to be said is that he seems to have lacked the historian's taste for the specific, the detailed, even the incidental, except where a small event gave him material for general reflection. When one day he saw a boy playing with a captive bird which he held by a string tied to its leg, he saw in the happening an illustration of the way the Devil plays with the human soul.[1] It came naturally to him to look for a moral truth or a philosophical principle in the events of his own day, rather than for a historical generalization. In *Letter* 190 he makes a brief comment on the events of human history: 'You know

[1] *The Life of St. Anselm by Eadmer*, ed. R. W. Southern (London, 1962), p. 90.

that the events of this world often happen without warning in this way, like storms at sea.'[1] He asks Osmund, bishop of Salisbury, to pray for the king, who is on a dangerous expedition. Osmund is to ask that God may guard the king by a ceaseless protection, 'sua continua protectione', and direct all his actions as may be most pleasing to him. There is nothing remarkable in this; but it echoes two principal concerns of Anselm's: Anselm would have liked nothing better than that the world should be protected from unforeseen changes and that it should run according to the *rectus ordo* which God intended for it. He can think of nothing better to pray for on behalf of the king. Only in the most oblique sense can his remark about the way in which events often happen be taken as a historical generalization. Specific remarks about the happenings in which he was involved or of which he heard are few—except for matters of business which have had to be dealt with by letter. He certainly did not seek out material of historical interest because it might be entertaining or instructive in its own right.

Accordingly, Anselm wrote no chronicles and no accounts of other men's lives, nor of his own. Yet he lived at a time when men of literary talent—including his friend and biographer Eadmer, the 'prop' of his old age[2]—were frequently drawn to the writing of such histories. The absence of any apparent historical inclination in Anselm is not merely a matter of the direction of his working interests as a writer; it has to do with his very cast of mind, which had few, if any, of the qualities characteristic of historians. He had none of Eadmer's frank curiosity about the details of recent events and no desire to discover a great overall pattern in the unfolding of world history. The value of looking at Anselm's contribution to the study of sacred history lies, perhaps paradoxically, in this; it forces us to stretch the sense of the term 'history' to the limit, and to consider afresh the influences which were at work in forming the study

---

[1] *Anselmi Opera Omnia*, ed. F. S. Schmitt (Rome/Edinburgh, 1938–68), 6 vols (=S), S 4.76.7–8.
[2] S 4.104.18, Letter 209.

of history as a branch of the new enlarged theology of Anselm's day and after.

This was a time of conscious reviewing of both historical purposes and historical methods. During Anselm's lifetime and throughout the twelfth century writers often prefaced their accounts with a statement of intent; the didactic and edifying effects of historical study are put forward for consideration; there is a sense of progress and change abroad which is heightened by deliberate comparison of the present state of things with past conditions and attitudes.

But sacred history presents a special case, not least because, as Peter Damian asserts, nothing can be added to it and nothing taken away.[1] It does not permit reassessment and re-evaluation in quite the same way that human history allows. Such *decora materia*[2] requires, as Anselm and others perceived, a special theory of history to accommodate it. Anselm was not alone in treating sacred history as a special case; yet he stands apart as a thinker whose first concern was not to fit the study of sacred history into a grand scheme of universal history, but to examine the problems it raises in their own right, as unique issues of historical philosophy.

Among the topics of theology, it seems that only the events of sacred history allow for the possibility of change. Augustine notes in Book VIII, 6, of the *De Civitate Dei* that even pagan philosophers recognize that God is immutable. The argument from the mutability of created things is extensively used by Aquinas in his two *Summae* and by a number of twelfth-century writers as a means of demonstrating the existence of God. It was common practice for the Jew, in the dialogues between Jew and Christian which became popular at the end of Anselm's life, to point out that Christians appear to accept that God is mutable. For God became man. Anselm's old friend Gilbert Crispin is the author of one of these dialogues, written or enlarged perhaps as a result of conversations with him at the time of his election to the see of Canterbury. Anselm himself

---

[1] *Dominus Vobiscum*, iv, PL 145, col. 234.
[2] S 2.49.21.

found food for thought in their talks which may have added something to his thinking in the *Cur Deus Homo*.[1] In this work Anselm has hit upon the one area of theology in which the fact of historical change has to be reconciled with the axiomatic changelessness of God. It is because this is a philosophical problem as well as a historical one that we must speak of Anselm's handling of sacred history as in some sense an exercise in philosophical history.

On a broader front, Anselm of Havelberg, a student at Laon in the second or third decade of the twelfth century, describes in his *Dialogus* the major changes he perceives in the course of history from Creation to the end of the world. Each change is attested by some upsetting of the natural order, some *terrae motus* occasioned by the greatness of the event: 'propter ipsarum rerum magnitudinem'.[2] The first, heralded by thunder and lightning, witnesses the change from the worship of idols to the time of the Law; the second, marked by a great earthquake and the opening of tombs, demonstrates the change from Law to Gospel. The last huge natural disaster will come at the end of the world.[3] These changes, *transpositiones* or *mutationes*, are graphically described, but a more abstract conception underlies Anselm of Havelberg's words. The essential characteristic of history is that it involves change.

But to medieval eyes, change is not a desirable thing. There is no changeableness in God: 'nulla in deo quidem mutabilitas'.[4] And so history looks forward to a condition of stillness and stability, in which, at the end of time, there will be no change. Anselm of Havelberg promises that 'after the tribulations of the Church ... there will be silence of divine contemplation, the year of jubilee will begin, the octave of infinite blessedness will be celebrated'.[5] The progression of the ages tends always towards the time when there

---

[1] See R. W. Southern, 'St. Anselm and Gilbert Crispin, Abbot of Westminster', *Mediaeval and Renaissance Studies*, 3 (1954), pp. 78–99.

[2] Anselm de Havelberg, *Dialogus*, ed. G. Salet (Paris, 1966), p. 58.

[3] Ibid.

[4] Thierry of Chartres, ed. cit. p. 75.27, p. 163.12.

[5] Anselm de Havelberg, p. 114.

will be no change.[1] It is necessary to point out that the present state of things is not in any way a reflection of imperfection in God himself, but only an indication of man's fallen state:

> But this variety is not caused by changeableness in the unchanging God, who is always the same and whose years do not fail, but by the weakness of the human race and the changes brought about by time from generation to generation.[2]

Thus the state of affairs at any point in history is undesirable, and history may be regarded as edifying only in a strictly limited sense. The events of the past present awful warnings or hint at rewards to come, but the reading of history will not do for a man's soul what the study of the eternal verities will do.

Anselm's own views about the role of change are never apparent in the *Monologion* or the *Proslogion*, where he meditates[3] upon the unchanging nature of God. It is only when he comes to discuss the events of sacred history, the fall of Satan,[4] the fall of man, atonement and redemption,[5] that he considers the operation of forces of change or *motus*. He states at the beginning of the *Cur Deus Homo* that, although he cannot deal with them adequately in the space available to him, he considers that some discussion of the three principal forces of change is indispensable to the treatment of the topic in hand:

> I see another reason why it will be almost, or entirely, impossible for us to deal with this matter fully here, for a knowledge of 'power', 'necessity' and 'will' and of certain other matters, is required, and they bear such a relation to one another that none of them can be fully discussed without reference to the others.[6]

These three 'forces' reappear repeatedly in the course of Anselm's consideration of theological problems which have to do with specific events of sacred history. They provide him with indispensable principles of division, since each has a different bearing upon

---

[1] Ibid. p. 116.
[2] Ibid.
[3] S 1.7.3, S 1.93.2.
[4] In the *De Casu Diaboli*.
[5] In the *Cur Deus Homo* and the *De Conceptu Virginali*.
[6] S 2.49.7–10.

man and upon God. God's will, for example, is always right, and so God cannot sin; but man's will errs when it does not conform with the will of God, and so man can sin. God's power is unlimited, and so he can accomplish wonders beyond the scope of man. No necessity is capable of compelling or constraining God, but he may choose to accept the direction in which necessity drives mankind and allow it to work upon himself. By such means Anselm is able to show that God is a special case and that he is able to intervene in the course of history, not by altering the universal laws of cause and effect, motion and change, but by inhabiting those laws in his own Person.

All this involves a good deal of verbal sleight of hand, not least in the *De Concordia* where Anselm sets out to demonstrate that there is nothing irreconcilable in the operation of God's fore-knowledge, predestination, and grace and of man's individual free will. Here, we are not dealing with named events of history so much as with the general principles which may be detected at work in men's lives in every generation. He generalizes from the observations he has made about historical cause and effect in which God is directly involved (in his work of atonement) in order to postulate the existence of much the same laws in the working out of ordinary events. He has, in other words, hit upon a principle of historical analysis as central to the medieval view as that of 'change': he makes no allowance for alteration or modification of the rules under changing circumstances, because he has no sense of period. There can be no room in a philosophy of history based upon the events of sacred history for any sensitivity to differences in the particular flavour of one age or another. All events must be governed by the forces of change which God himself appears to have harnessed in order to redeem the world.

This presupposes, in its turn, a further underlying assumption. The forces of change are not inanimate, but intimately associated with living, sentient beings. Will and power are not, in this respect, quite like the force of gravity, although, like a physical force, they act upon the world. Necessity works upon sentient beings as upon

inanimate objects. The eclectic scholar Honorius Augustodunensis
(an admirer of Anselm) has a good deal to say in his *Clavis Physicae*
about the *motus* of the universe, and he draws upon an enormously
wider reading than that of Anselm himself.[1] He borrows from
'Maximus' the view that *motus* is a natural power, a *virtus naturalis*,
which hastens towards its proper end; it is an *operatio activa*.[2] There
are *motus animae*[3] and a *vitalis motus*[4] which bind body and soul
together during life. Without benefit of Honorius' extensive collection of authorities, Anselm has come to the same view of the
force of change as both a pure force and something normally set in
motion by or acting upon a sentient being.

Entirely in keeping with this concept of change is Honorius'
assertion that every *passio* moves towards its proper end where all
passion is spent: 'cuius finis est impassibilitas'.[5] If change is in itself
undesirable, made necessary now only by man's fallen condition,
and to be altogether absent in the life to come, then motion and
change must be seen as issuing ultimately in stillness. Anselm himself was clearly most comfortable, both personally and philosophically, in the contemplation of that longed-for state of stillness.
The *Monologion* concludes with a passage on the misery of those
who do not love the Highest Being,[6] for in the life to come they
will feel an inconsolable need: 'inconsolabilem indigentiam'.[7] They
will not, in other words, enjoy that sensation of utter contentment
which consists in being free of the pull of any *motus* of desire. This
state Anselm describes at the end of the *Proslogion*, where he explains
that every want will be quite specifically supplied.[8]

---

[1] Honorius Augustodunensis, *Clavis Physicae*, ed. P. Lucentini (Rome, 1974-)
Temi e testi, 21. Lucentini identifies a number of Honorius' sources in his foot-
notes. On Honorius himself, see R. W. Southern *St. Anselm and his Biographer*
(Cambridge, 1963), pp. 209–17, and also below, pp. 212–38.

[2] *Clavis*, p. 45.2–6 (65).

[3] Ibid. p. 69.4 (96).

[4] Ibid. p. 216.2 (269) and p. 217.10.

[5] Ibid. p. 45.2 (65).

[6] S 1.81–2, chapter lxxi.

[7] S 1.82.3.

[8] S 1.118–22, chapters xxv–xxvi.

The experience of history is therefore an experience of longing. Anselm of Havelberg mentions the yearning of the souls of the saints who wait under the altar of God for the end of the world, crying, 'How long, O Lord, how long?'[1] Hermann of Tournai says that the patriarchs longed for the coming of the incarnation.[2] Throughout history those caught up in the sequence of change and subject to the forces of change wait with some impatience (paradoxically enough) for a further change which will bring about the state of permanent stillness they long for.

It is a contemporary assumption, and one shared by Anselm himself, that the order of procedure in historical events is irreversible. Change, like time, runs only one way and what has happened cannot be made, retrospectively, to have happened any differently. As far as ordinary history goes, that is straightforward enough. But God is beyond time, and it is a little surprising to find no substantial twelfth-century advocacy for the view that he could have caused the fall of Adam not to be, at some point after it had taken place. On the contrary, the subject-matter of the *theologica hypothetica*, the 'hypothetical theology' which is a favourite topic of such later twelfth-century theologians as Simon of Tournai and Alan of Lille, raises a number of questions in connection with created spirits, both man and angel, which presuppose the irreversibility of the changes brought about by the fall of Satan and the fall of Adam. One common debating point is whether man was created to supply the gaps left in the number of citizens designed for the city of heaven, when Satan and his followers fell.[3] Anselm perceives several helpful parallels between the sin of the angels and its aftermath and the sin of Adam and its consequences. He makes some crucial distinctions: the good angels were confirmed in their goodness, while redeemed

---

[1] Anselm de Havelberg, p. 108, cf. S 1.99.15.

[2] *PL* 180, col. 24.

[3] The question is raised in the Sentences which have survived from the school of Laon. See O. Lottin, *Psychologie et morale aux xiie et xiiie siècles*, v (Gembloux, 1959), p. 125. St. Bernard also mentions it in one of his liturgical sermons. *S. Bernardi Opera Omnia*, ed. J. Leclercq and H. Rochais, v (Rome, 1968), p. 294–8, for Michaelmas, I; cf. *Cur Deus Homo*, i. 16–18, S 2.74–84.

men are still able to sin.[1] The evil angels could not be redeemed like the sons of Adam because they did not all derive from the same stock, and their sin could not therefore be wiped out by any one being who stood for them all collectively.[2] But on the question of the irreversibility of Satan's deed and the chronological sequence of the changes it brought about, Anselm takes a view every bit as historically conceived as the view he has of Adam's sin and its consequences.

Just as God's special relation to, and control of, will, power, and necessity set him apart and make it possible for him to alter the direction of forces of change, so God is able, because he stands outside time, to enter time and therefore history at crucial moments and intervene in the affairs of created beings 'As long as (*quamdiu*) man does not repay what he has stolen, he remains in a state of sin.'[3] *Quamdiu* implies that a state of affairs exists in time and that that state of affairs may be changed by some act within time. Anselm's interest in eternity is stated much more openly than this. In large measure he owes his grasp of the subject to Augustine,[4] but it is also something which normally came under consideration early on in the study of dialectic, since the problem of time is raised by Aristotle in connection with continuous and discrete quantity.[5] A dialectician who may have lived more or less contemporaneously with Anselm even mentions the idea that time may constitute a dimension.[6] The background to Anselm's notion of time and eternity was philosophical rather than historical, and his own curiosity was engaged by such philosophical issues as the questions whether there can be more than one eternity,[7] how it is that God has

---

[1] S 2.276.8, *De Concordia*, iii, 9.

[2] *Cur Deus Homo*, ii, 21, S 2.132.

[3] S 2.68.21–2.

[4] Augustine discusses the notion of time extensively in the *Confessions*, especially Book ix.

[5] For Boethius' remarks on this material, see *PL* 64, pp. 201–16.

[6] Garlandus Compotista, *Dialectica*, ed. L. M. de Rijk (Assen, 1959), p. 26.16.

[7] S 2.33.25, *De Incarnatione Verbi*, xv.

no beginning or end,[1] how he is not in time or in place but all times and places are in him,[2] what we mean by 'beginning' and 'end'.

In his *City of God* Augustine had put forward a large-scale interpretation of history in which he showed the unfolding of God's purpose throughout its sequence. This could be done with particular forcefulness for the events of sacred history, where the working out of God's plan throughout the Old Testament could be seen to have borne fruit in the incarnation. Richard of St. Victor follows in the same tradition, when he attempts to reason forward to the future in his *De Judiciaria Potestate in Finali et Universali Iudicio*. He suggests that there will be three groups at the Last Judgement: those who are to judge and those who are to be judged. Of those who are to be judged, some will be saved and some will be damned.[3] He also looks at the modes of knowing which are to be enjoyed in the life to come, and how they will differ from those available to men at present, in the fullness of their realization of what is known.[4] Anselm is not much concerned with the Last Judgement, although he does give some thought to the number of inhabitants who are to dwell in the Heavenly City.[5] But he shares with Augustine and many of his fellows a conviction that God's purpose is being worked out in everything which happens, that, in this special sense, 'omnia cooperantur in bonum'.[6] In the *Cur Deus Homo* he speaks of the 'propositum dei', the plan of God: ('Deum constat proposuisse')[7] that the places in the heavenly city left by the fallen angels in the heavenly city were to be filled by good men made perfect. Both the natural irreversibility of time and the plan of God give the sequence of history a single direction of change, in which there is something very like linearity. Hermann of Tournai speaks of the

---

[1] S 1.32.6–33.23, *Monologion*, xviii.

[2] S 1.115.6–15, *Proslogion*, xix.

[3] Richard of St. Victor, *Opuscules théologiques*, ed. J. Ribaillier, *Textes philosophiques du moyen age*, xv (Paris, 1967), p. 144.

[4] Ibid. p. 145.

[5] S 2.74–84, *Cur Deus Homo*, i. pp. 16–18.

[6] Romans 8: 28.

[7] S 2.74.12, *Cur Deus Homo*, i. 16.

'linea generationis humanae',[1] the line of human generations, in his account of the incarnation. Anselm, too, has a similar notion.[2] Just as the forces of change are living forces, set in motion by sentient beings, so the time-line of history is, in some sense, a human chain. God's purposes are at work not merely upon a state of affairs, but upon the men who are caught up in its changing conditions.

This view of the matter does not prevent Anselm from engaging in some very unhistorical activities. His tendency is to look not generation by generation at the working-out of the effects of Adam's sin throughout the Old Testament—as many of his contemporaries were doing when they wrote about sacred history— but at the direct effect of Adam's sin upon any single generation. For such purposes the stage-by-stage progression through intervening generations is immaterial, so long as we assume, as Anselm clearly does, that there is no progressive diminishing of the taint of sin.[3] Anselm telescopes the events of history, and proposes that the working of cause and effect must operate directly even though a chain of intermediate causes and effects has been omitted. He can do so only because he is dealing with a particular problem of sacred history. It is not a method he could have transferred to the writing of conventional history.

This brings us to one of the significant differences between Anselm the 'sacred historian' and the vast majority of his contemporaries. He prefers a thematic approach, while they favour, almost to a man, the use of a narrative scheme. Eadmer found that he had set himself an unusually difficult structural problem in attempting to write a *Life* to set beside his account of the events of Anselm's archiepiscopate in the *Historia Novorum*.[4] He resolved it by presenting two parallel narratives; the earlier work, he says, takes the form of a self-contained narrative.[5] It will therefore stand on its own, but

[1] *PL* 180.17.

[2] *De Conceptu Virginali*, chapters xxiv–xxvi.

[3] Ibid., and cf. *Memorials of St. Anselm* ed. R. W. Southern and F. S. Schmitt (London, 1969), p. 52, *De Humanibus Moribus*, chapter 38.

[4] Eadmer, *Historia Novorum in Angliae*, ed. M. Rule (RS, 1884).

[5] *The Life of St. Anselm by Eadmer*, ed. R. W. Southern (London, 1962), p. 2.

no reader should find difficulty in reading the two works as a pair; indeed Anselm himself, their common subject, is not to be fully understood by anyone who has not taken the trouble to read both. Two generations later, John of Salisbury, also the author of a largely eye-witness account of events of his own day,[1] falls into the common contemporary habit of trying to place his work in the sequence of history from Old Testament times. He adopts the rather more unusual procedure of reviewing the historians of sacred history, beginning with the authors of the books of the Bible and continuing with the Fathers, until he reaches the historians of his own time.[2] But his approach too is essentially a narrative one. Eadmer uses the word, *disponere*, of his own organizing of his material,[3] and John of Salisbury, too, is very conscious of the need to think out a policy before he begins to compose his history.[4] Neither seems seriously to have considered the possibility of adopting a 'thematic' approach, even though both have entirely new material to treat, and neither is limited by the existence of a previous account which has to be accommodated in his own version.

That is not to suggest that the use of a narrative form disposes of problems of selection. Eadmer tells us that he has chosen to reject unnecessary detail, so that his account in the *Historia Novorum* is brief: 'succincte excepta'.[5] But such a scheme does avoid those problems which Anselm himself discusses so happily and naturally when he writes about sacred history: Anselm selects a philosophical and theological issue and brings to bear such events of sacred history as have a direct connection with the solutions he wants to propose. Otloh of St. Emmeram had attempted something of a similar kind in his *Dialogus de Tribus Quaestionibus*. He shows how by the sin of man the whole human race perished,[6] how God's justice is apparent

---

[1] John of Salisbury, *Historia Pontificalis*, ed. M. Chibnall (London, 1956), p. 4.
[2] Ibid. pp. 1–2.
[3] *The Life of St. Anselm*, p. 2.
[4] *Historia Pontificalis*, pp. 1–4.
[5] *The Life of St. Anselm*, p. 1.
[6] PL 146, col. 73, chapter 11.

in the condemnation of the fallen angels,[1] how variously the principle
of necessity may be seen to apply to incarnation, Passion, resurrection, to the vicissitudes of human life ('necesse est ut veniant
scandala').[2] The theologians of the School of Laon in Anselm's day
and immediately afterwards were also in the habit of taking distinct
topics from their study of biblical history. They speak of the profit-
ableness of the fall of man and of the angels: 'De utilitate casus
hominis et angelorum.' No man or angel would have been good if
none of his kind had been evil.[3] There is some speculation as to the
point in sacred history where the angels were created; one sentence
points out that if the angels were created immediately before the
creation of the world ('statim ante mundum') it is difficult to see
'where' they were until the world was created.[4] Another sentence
asks how God could have made all things at once, although Genesis
speaks of the work occupying several days.[5]

In some of the theological writings of the 'school' of Peter
Abelard, a similar topical approach is adopted towards the events of
sacred history. Remedies against sin are listed, for example, beginning with circumcision, and continuing with the Law, the prophets,
and the remedies which are available *sub gratia*.[6] A series of reasons
for the incarnation is put forward.[7] None of these topical approaches
quite matches Anselm's, chiefly because each of these authors is
first concerned to fit the whole scheme of sacred history into the
patterns of interpretation he proposes. Anselm's thematic approach
is not that of a pattern-maker. He rarely if ever looks for parallel
examples. A single instance generally serves the purposes of his
argument.

---

[1] *PL* 146, col. 66, chapter 4.
[2] *PL* 146, cols 82–3, chapter 18.
[3] O. Lottin, *Psychologie et morale aux xii*e *e xiii*e *siècles*, v (Gembloux 1959),
p. 37, no. 40.
[4] Ibid. p. 83, no. 99.
[5] Ibid. p. 84, no. 101.
[6] A. Landgraf, *Écrits théologiques de l'école d'Abelard: Spicilegium Sacrum
Lovaniense*, 14 (1934), pp. 130–54.
[7] Ibid. p. 158.

Nor does Anselm normally employ his selected passages of sacred history as moral examples. This particular use of the Scriptural *exemplum* was to become more common in succeeding centuries.[1] Anselm's practice, however, in such remnants of his pastoral writings and his conversation and sermons as do survive, is to take as the basis for his analogy some homely incident or some familiar contemporary arrangement of things. The boy he once saw snaring a bird reminded him on several subsequent occasions of the Devil trapping a human soul, and he used it as an analogy more than once.[2] Analogies between kings' and emperors' relations with their subjects and God's relations with man often seem to have suggested themselves to him.[3] Anselm's thematic approach to the writing of sacred history itself was not of this moralizing kind, and in this respect, too, he stands apart from tradition.

One conclusion seems inescapable; Anselm's interest in the possibilities of applying a special historical method to the resolution of certain theological and philosophical problems was generated by the peculiar difficulties with which a few specific issues presented him. His historical work is largely limited to the treatises of his middle years, and, above all, to the *Cur Deus Homo*. It was not to provide him with fresh insights in the resolution of other problems, or to lead him to write works of an altogether different kind in the future. As is the case with so much of Anselm's learning, he has demonstrated in the works which come after the *Cur Deus Homo* group[4] that he can discard a procedure when it is no longer helpful to him as readily as he adopts it when it first seems to him to be potentially helpful.

[1] A bibliography of recent work is included in B. Smalley, 'Oxford University Sermons 1290–3', *Mediaeval Learning and Literature: Essays Presented to R. W. Hunt*, ed. J. J. Alexander and M. T. Gibson (Oxford, 1976), pp. 307–27, and see B. Smalley, *'Exempla' in the Commentaries of Stephen Langton* (Aberdeen, 1933).

[2] *The Life of St. Anselm*, p. 90–1, cf. *Memorials*, pp. 11 for a list of analogies used more than once by Anselm.

[3] *Memorials* pp. 56, 64, 66, 70.

[4] That is, the *Meditation on Human Redemption*, the *De Conceptu Virginali*, and the *Cur Deus Homo* itself.

But Anselm is by no means as negative in his approach to historical matters as this would seem to suggest. He did not share the interest of his contemporaries in historical writing, certainly—except perhaps as a reader—and he did not choose to introduce historical considerations into more than a few of his works where they were especially helpful. That is wholly characteristic of his instinctive grasp of what is germane to any matter. Yet at the beginning of the *Cur Deus Homo* he proposes a historically breath-taking procedure. He says that he will attempt to demonstrate that even if Christ had never become man, and nothing at all were known of the events which followed the incarnation, it would be possible to reconstruct the sequence of those events by considering the circumstances which made the incarnation necessary.[1] However firmly convinced medieval writers might be that God's plan for the world was unfolding in every event of history, it seems unlikely that any of them would have gone so far as to suggest that the necessity for each event could be shown by reason alone. This procedure could only reasonably be applied to the events of sacred history, and perhaps most fittingly of all to the atonement, as Anselm is quick to perceive. He does not try to extend the method so as to apply it to other events. When he refers to the principle he has adopted later in the *Cur Deus Homo* he substantially repeats what he has already said: 'Let us therefore posit that the incarnation of God and what we say of him as a man never took place.'[2] He has adumbrated a historical procedure of considerable philosophical interest, which fits the special case of sacred history uniquely well.

Secondly, in the *Cur Deus Homo*, he proposes the setting-out of fixed experimental conditions within which the sequence of events can be seen to unfold automatically.

Let it be agreed between us that man was made for blessedness, which he cannot have in this life, nor attain it unless his sins are forgiven; that no man can pass through this life without sin, and that amongst other things faith is necessary to eternal salvation.[3]

[1] S 2.42.12. [2] S 2.67.12–3. [3] S 2.67.13–6.

Once these conditions are agreed, Anselm can set to work upon his demonstration, beginning with the notion that the first necessity is the remission of sin, without which man cannot attain the state of blessedness for which God created him. It might be argued that Anselm is not here suggesting anything very close to a modern scientific method. His experimental procedures take a severely restricted form. The system of rules he sets out is a closed system, because every conclusion is in view from the beginning. Indeed, had Anselm not in fact known how the story of the incarnation was to unfold, it is doubtful whether he could have fulfilled his bold promise as adequately as he does. Nevertheless, in its conception, the scheme is novel because it contains something which approaches an experimental theory of history. The fact that its application must, like the *remoto Christo* principle, be restricted to the events of sacred history in no way detracts from the freshness of Anselm's historical invention here.

Anselm was always most at home with problems which involved no unpredictable element. He preferred to find the materials on which he worked few enough in their essentials to allow him to perceive all their possibilities of interrelation at the very beginning. These are not the instincts of a historian. Eadmer, too, found the novelties of his day a source of discomfort, but they captured his interest. He speaks of the 'insolitas rerum mutationes'.[1] Yet he, unlike Anselm, was not able to limit the scope of his discussions to matters which were not only in the past, but which had been described in a form which made it impossible that anything might be added to the record of the events themselves. Scripture could be interpreted, and it was ever more fully and inventively interpreted in Anselm's day. But no one could add to the words of the Bible, in the way that someone with an additional story to tell could add to Eadmer's collection of material for the writing of his history. Anselm's ready acceptance of the 'finished' quality of his material is an important element in his view of its possibilities of historical interpretation.

[1] *The Life of St. Anselm*, p. 1.

No less important is the directness of God's personal involvement in the events of the redemption. God had to enter into history as man and be in some measure affected by it. Yet it is a cardinal principle of Anselm's thought that God is *impassibilis* and cannot suffer or be affected by anything outside himself. Anselm thus saw his own task in recounting the events of the atonement as involving an explanation of God's movement into history. This he tried to do in such a way that he showed God conferring something of his own changelessness upon those events and making them inevitable.[1] For this reason, Anselm, unlike the historian of human affairs, enjoys an unquestioning confidence in the inevitability of what happened. He is able to discover a necessary sequence in the events with which he has to deal.

This involves him early on in the explicit discussion of necessity. It was clearly necessary, from mankind's point of view, that redemption should be brought about. God himself is to be supposed to have determined that he would not abandon man to his fate, that nothing should frustrate his purpose of making man blessed.[2] But God cannot, by the ground rules of Anselm's theology, be reckoned to have been under any necessity in so doing. Every act of God must be regarded as a free act, carried out in accordance with his own divine will.[3] Some reference has already been made to Otloh of St. Emmeram's broad-ranging concept of a necessity which embraces not only the necessity of the atonement, but also that of the brightness of the sun, the heat of fire, the care of the sick and of the poor, and even of persecutions and temptations.[4] Anselm's discussions of necessity involve a more closely defined philosophical concept, which he has got more or less directly from Boëthius.[5] Neither writer can be said to be concerned with a specifically 'historical necessity' of cause and effect in events. The novelty of Anselm's view lies in his readiness to apply philosophical principles

---

[1] S 1.106.3–14, *Proslogion*, viii.   [2] S 2.52.8–11.
[3] S 2.59–68, *Cur Deus Homo*, i. 8–9.
[4] *PL* 146, cols 82–3.
[5] D. P. Henry, *The Logic of St. Anselm* (Oxford, 1967), pp. 172–80.

of necessity to the essentially historical problem of the reason for the atonement. He looks, not for a specifically historical necessity, but for the ways in which the forces of necessity at large may be said to operate in a historical context.

The ideas about necessity with which Anselm is principally concerned in the *Cur Deus Homo*[1] cannot be entirely separated from the notion of fittingness which has caused a good deal of controversy among modern scholars.[2] Anselm assumes that all his readers will accept the force of an explanation which appears to rest upon considerations of *convenientia* or *decentia*, providing that that fittingness is recognizable to each of them personally. Indeed, the tone of Anselm's appeal to reason throughout the treatise is of very much this character.[3] But whereas the hard necessity of a consequence would seem in general to result from some single cause,[4] what is appropriate or fitting more often seems so because it rests easily within a whole complex of circumstances.[5] Anselm has, perhaps inadvertently, overlooked a distinction which conventional historians might make between events whose direct causes can be traced, and happenings which are made to seem probable by the character of their surrounding circumstances. Yet once again, the special nature of the sacred history with which Anselm deals makes the distinction redundant for his own purposes. He envisages the *convenientia* or *decentia* of his explanations as possessing every bit as much force of conviction as the 'necessity' of Christ's incarnation, within the terms of reference of sacred history.

[1] He has more to say about necessity elsewhere, particularly in the *De Concordia*.

[2] See M. Charlesworth, *St. Anselm's Proslogion* (Oxford, 1965), Introduction, and J. Hopkins, *A Companion to the Study of St. Anselm* (Minneapolis, 1972), pp. 48–51.

[3] Gillian Evans, 'The Nature of St. Anselm's Appeal to Reason in the *Cur Deus Homo*', in *Studia Theologica*, 31 (1977), pp. 33–50.

[4] Cause and effect, like necessity, was a topic of considerable contemporary interest among students of dialectic.

[5] This, at any rate, is the drift of Anselm's argument in the *Cur Deus Homo* where he has to contend with something more complex than a chain of cause and effect.

If Anselm shared little else with contemporary historians, he did have in common with them a respect for the niceties of style. He opens his *Cur Deus Homo* with a number of preliminary reflections, among them some thoughts on the importance of writing in a style which befits the beauty of his subject-matter. It is by no means uncommon for contemporary historians of less elevated matters to introduce their work with some reference to the style in which they have chosen to write. Eadmer himself modestly calls his writing in the *Historia Novorum* plain and lacking in art.[1] Whether or not this is false modesty is immaterial. Eadmer, like almost every author of his time, could not compose any work for publication without consciously setting out to cast it in an appropriate style. There is ample precedent for this practice both in the theory of the *artes*,[2] and among the examples provided by Scripture and the Fathers.[3] It is within exactly this tradition that Anselm writes in the *Cur Deus Homo*:

> Therefore I am afraid that, just as I am in the habit of finding myself offended by an ugly picture, when I see the Lord himself portrayed by a crude likeness, so I may offend others if I presume to write of such wonderful matters in a careless and unadorned manner.[4]

Anselm's delicacy of feeling on the matter is perfectly in keeping with contemporary views, although in his case it seems likely that it needed very little development. He is able to state his position with a characteristic freshness because he has experienced a real aesthetic discomfort when he sees crude pictorial representations of things which possess great spiritual beauty for him. He sees the writing of sacred history, like the painting of sacred pictures, as a work of art.

But in almost every other respect, Anselm's innovations of historical method have limited possibilities of application to the study of history in general, because they have been framed to suit

[1] *The Life of St. Anselm*, p. 1.
[2] *Rhetorica ad Herennium*, ed. H. Caplan (London, 1954), p. 253, IV. viii. 11.
[3] Augustine's, *De Doctrina Christiana*, Book iv is of prime importance here.
[4] S 1.49.19–22.

the purposes of a theologian who is making use of sacred history in philosophical demonstration. They are none the less important for that if only because they make it plain that a mind of exceptional reach and penetration could think about the writing of sacred history in a wholly original manner in an age when the foundations of historical study were being comprehensively relaid. They raise a further possibility, too. Sir Richard Southern points out in the first of his Presidential Addresses to the Royal Historical Society that in Aristotle's view 'the works of the historian cannot have the universal truth which is the hallmark of great art'; this, it seems, is inevitable, 'since the material of history lacks universality'.[1] Aristotle's quarrel with history is that historical events do not involve matters of common human experience as poetical incidents do. They do not speak directly to every man. But in the subject-matter of incarnation and redemption he might perhaps have found material which did possess a certain universality because its implications touch every man's life directly. And perhaps in Anselm's handling of the subject he might have found great art. Peter Damian calls this *incomparabilis materia*; Aristotle certainly knew of nothing comparable with it in the field of history. Anselm cannot be said to have met Aristotle's stricture exactly, since he is writing philosophical history and not poetical history. But a concern for the expression of universal truth in a form conceived from the first as art marks the *Cur Deus Homo* from its beginning. Anselm refers to his subject-matter as *decora materia* precisely because, as he says, he is anxious to do it justice in the beauty of his writing. He makes of the treatment of the historical events of the atonement something remarkably close to Aristotle's notion of a great work of art. No other kind of historical subject-matter would have permitted or even encouraged him to make the attempt. Perhaps we should not be surprised that his achievement proved inimitable and that, increasingly, philosophical and historical theology went their separate ways.

[1] R. W. Southern, 'Aspects of the European Tradition of Historical Writing. 1. The Classical Tradition from Einhard to Geoffrey of Monmouth', *TRHS*, 5th series, 20 (1970), pp. 175-6.

World history in the early twelfth century; the 'Imago Mundi' of Honorius Augustodunensis

VALERIE FLINT

I

THE *Imago Mundi* of Honorius Augustodunensis was, in the twelfth century, enormously popular. Twenty surviving twelfth-century manuscripts of the whole text are known to me now; a further nineteen of parts and fragments may be added to that number.[1] The whole was issued, I think, in 1110, and was revised by its author three times, in 1123, 1133, and 1139 respectively.[2] The work was written in South Germany, most probably at St. Emmeramm's in Regensburg, and the most important of the surviving manuscripts come from the areas of South Germany and Austria.[3] An early

[1] A provisional list of the surviving twelfth-century manuscripts of the *Imago Mundi*, both complete and incomplete texts, is set out in the appendix to V. I. J. Flint, 'The place and purpose of the works of Honorius Augustodunensis', *Rev. bén.*, 87 (1977), pp. 123–4. The present paper was completed with the help of the Humanities Research Centre, A.N.U., Canberra, and the Research Committee of the University of Auckland. I am grateful to both, and, once again, to the care and advice of my colleague, Philip Rousseau.

[2] Here I differ from Wilmanns, *MGH, Scriptores*, x. pp. 127–8. A part of the material which has led me to the conclusion that the work was written in 1110 and reissued in only three recensions ascribable to Honorius himself will be set out below. I hope to set out the rest more fully in my forthcoming edition. Wilmanns printed that section of Book III which dealt with the sixth age and had items of German interest. The whole text of the *Imago Mundi* was last printed in *PL* 172, cols 115–88. All detailed references will be to the chapters and pages of this edition.

[3] The suspicion that it was written in Regensburg comes from the specific entry (of a kind which is rare) in the section dealing with Bavaria (Book I, xxiv) 'in qua est civitas Ratispona'. It is supported in general by the distribution of the surviving twelfth-century manuscripts.

form of the text, however, circulated in England, where Honorius may also have spent an early part of his career.[1]

The plan was not unambitious; the work covers space and time and the history of man. It was meant, furthermore, to be consulted easily and to save its readers time and effort. This fact its author drives home.[2] He insists too that he saves his readers time in order to direct them to truth; a truth that is firmly traditional and equally firmly Christian.[3] Ease of consultation implies, indeed requires, the sacrifice of questioning, of novelty, and, above all, of non-Christian criticism. This once accepted, the rewards appear to be great. The information supplied is most carefully compiled and most easy to assimilate in detail; and one may be sure that it will not lead one into deep and difficult waters.

The treatise is composed of three books. It is subdivided, in the best manuscripts, into some three hundred carefully headed chapters. Book I deals with the constitution and geography of the known world, with some confident glimpses into the unknown, then the composition and disposition of the further elements of water, air, and fire. The planets, zodiac, and constellations claim attention next. The geography, beginning with the four rivers of paradise, is underlaid by biblical geography. The discussion of the elements owes much to the work of biblical scholars—Isidore, Bede, and Rabanus. Book II describes the time of the world and of the heavens with its liturgical and secular measurements. It adds practical advice on the computus and guides to the major ecclesiastical feasts. The same three scholars, with Helpericus, are here in evidence again. Book III is a world history, and it is with this that we shall be chiefly here

---

[1] V. I. J. Flint, 'The career of Honorius Augustodunensis', *Rev. bén.*, 82 (1972), pp. 75–80.

[2] The short passage dilating upon Honorius's labours, beginning 'Rogo te lector' and printed by Migne (*PL* 172, col. 197) as a preface to the *De Luminaribus* is in fact attached, in fifteen of the thirty-nine surviving twelfth-century manuscripts I have mentioned, to the *Imago Mundi*.

[3] The first prefatory letter begins with tributes to the sevenfold spirit and the Trinity. The second ends with a tribute to tradition. 'Nihil autem in eo pono, nisi quod majorum commendat traditio.' *PL* 172, col. 120.

concerned. It was an integral part of the treatise from the beginning.[1] It recounts, in the briefest outline, the pre-history and history of the human race. It begins with the fall of the angels, and proceeds with the creation and the fall of man. It extends the story through the kingdoms of antiquity and the Old Testament, to the Roman Empire, then the German, the direct successor to the Roman.

Book III is constructed in accordance with a highly traditional Christian plan, the plan, that is, of the six ages of the world, and it uses sources upon which, within a structure of this kind, one would expect Honorius to draw. Genesis, Numbers, Orosius, Eusebius-Jerome, Isidore, Cassiodorus, Bede, the *Historia Miscella*, Frutolf of Michelsberg provide in their chronicles almost all the material Honorius needs for his account of the first five ages. For the sixth he supplements this by drawing upon Hermannus Contractus, both the *Chronicon* and the *Compendium Bernoldi*, and perhaps upon an early text of the *Chronicon Wirziburgense*.

The annexation of an historical section to a geographical and computistical treatise seems to have no surprises to offer. The composition of Easter Tables involved, after all, so often the addition of historical information in the convenient spaces provided. Examples of this are legion. The *Annales Majores* of St. Emmeramm's are themselves to be found in a ninth-century codex containing computistical information, and a more famous Munich computistical collection, also from St. Emmeramm's, contains (ff. 1–7) a short chronicle and the *Annales Minores* of the abbey.[2] Special stimuli towards the compiling of histories of the deeds of men as an extension

---

[1] I have found the whole or parts of Books I and II without any part of Book III in only four of the thirty-nine twelfth-century texts I have examined that is, in MSS BL, London, Royal 12 C xix, Pierpont Morgan Library, New York, 107, BN, Paris, Lat. 11130, Bibl. Vat., Rome, Lat. 1890.

[2] Bayerische Staatsbibliothek, Munich, clm. 14456 and 210. Famous English examples of such a combination in manuscripts of the eleventh and twelfth centuries are to be found in MS St. John's College, Oxford, 17, in MSS BL, London, Cotton Caligula A xv, Cotton Nero C v, Harley 3667, 3859, in MSS St. John's College, Cambridge, 22, Trinity College, Cambridge, 884, 1369. For a discussion of the first and of some other examples see C. Hart, 'The Ramsey Computus', *EHR*, 85 (1970), pp. 29–44.

of exegesis of the Bible were to the fore, furthermore, just when Honorius was writing. The great master Anselm of Laon (d. 1117) gave particular attention to the book of Genesis[1] and Hugh of St. Victor singled out the literal/historical interpretation both of the historical books of the Bible and of the others, for special emphasis in his *Didascalicon*.[2] These attentions were accompanied by an enormous increase in that type of historical writing which took the form, on the model of Orosius, of a world chronicle *ab initio peccati hominis*. This form was especially prevalent in Germany[3] and Honorius contributed to it in his own *Summa Totius*, a treatise which begins with a disquisition on the books of Holy Scripture and proceeds with the history of man from the fall. Wilmanns rightly thought that Book III of the *Imago Mundi* was in part an epitome of this. An interesting outcrop of historical writing of this kind was to be found in the West of England, in that version of the *Universal Chronicle* of Marianus Scotus of Mainz which Robert bishop of Hereford (1079–95) had imported and which John of Worcester extended. Marianus constructed his history within a revised computistical framework. One of the most important manuscripts of the *Imago Mundi*, furthermore, MS Corpus Christi College, Cambridge, 66, both shows asssociations with Hereford and connects the author of the text with Mainz.[4] We seem to have in all

---

[1] Many of the *sentences* attributed to him have reference to this book, for example, those printed by Lottin; O. Lottin, *Psychologie et morale aux xiie et xiiie siècles*, v (Louvain, 1959), pp. 30, 36–41, 44–5.

[2] C. H. Buttimer (ed.), *Hugonis de Sancto Victore Didascalicon de Studio Legendi* (Washington, 1939), VI, iii.

[3] M. Manitius, *Geschichte der Lateinischen Literatur des Mittelalters*, iii (Munich, 1931), p. 320. An admirable study of the history of the world chronicle is provided in A. von den Brincken, *Studien zur Lateinischen Weltchronistik bis in das Zeitalter Ottos von Freising* (Dusseldorf, 1957).

[4] The Mappa Mundi which prefaces the text of the *Imago Mundi* in Corpus 66 has long been known to be related to the Hereford Map. W. L. Bevan and H. W. Phillott, *Medieval Geography. An Essay in Illustration of the Hereford Mappa Mundi* (London, 1874), pp. xxxvi–xxxix. The relevant passage reads as follows: 'Iste Henricus qui hunc librum edidit fuit canonicus ecclesiae sancte marie civitatis Magontie, in qua ecclesia sunt canonici seculares bis quater quaterdeni.' Henricus was perhaps Honorius's real name; V. I. J. Flint, 'The Career of Honorius', pp. 63–75.

this an apotheosis of that tradition within which the historical section of the *Imago Mundi* was formed.

We know, finally, that the computus was, in the twelfth century, considered essential equipment for a priest.[1] It is possible that the historical notes which went with it so often were intended to serve as a *philacterium* for a longer story; one suitably edifying for an audience.[2] Honorius was deeply concerned for the office and the efficacy of the priest. The addition of a history to a computus and a Christian geography makes excellent sense within the context we may reconstruct for the *Imago Mundi*, and one of the functions of Book III may have been as a *recapitulatio*, most probably of the *Summa Totius*, for the use of the priest in the movement for ecclesiastical reform.

Book III appears, then, a somewhat unremarkable piece of work. The project was a grand one, but it had been tried before. The realization of it was meticulous; but meticulousness of detail and simplicity of expression are characteristics of all of Honorius's works. It was not the most ambitious of historical enterprises, even of those of Honorius, and it was a part of a tradition we can readily describe. One may well ask, then, by what right it claims attention here. The rights, I would contend, are very many, and their discussion forms the substance of this paper. Book III was not the largest effort of Honorius at history, but it was by far the most popular.[3] There may be something to be learnt from this. The text of the *Imago Mundi*, Book III as well, appears quite unexceptional; the context of Book III completely suitable. There is very much more to be learnt, I

[1] Gratian numbers a computus among the books without which a priest is scarcely worthy of the name. E. Friedberg, *Decretum Magistri Gratiani* (Leipsig, 1879), Prima Pars, Dist. xxxviii, c. 5, pp. 141–2.

[2] Bede says of his own chronological recapitulation that it was written 'ob memoriam conservandam'. B. Colgrave and R. A. B. Mynors (ed.), *Bede's Ecclesiastical History of the English People* (Oxford, 1969), v, 24, p. 560. The close relationship between this *recapitulatio* and Easter Annals is discussed by C. W. Jones, *Saints Lives and Chronicles* (Ithaca, 1947), pp. 31–8.

[3] Only one twelfth-century copy of the *Summa Totius* survives, MS Österreichische Nationalbibliothek, Vienna, 382, and this is incomplete.

think, than this. There is certainly more to be learnt about the text, to which we will turn in the next section. There may then be more to be seen in the context, to which we will turn in sections 3 and 4. Book III, I will contend, fits into the whole so snugly now because our knowledge of the whole is incomplete. There are gaps in our present understanding of this context, and there are traps in that simplicity so characteristic of Honorius's work. The place of Book III of the *Imago Mundi* may emerge as almost the opposite of that which I have so far described for it. Far from being a mere historical annex, and to be dismissed as such, it may be treated as a source for the illumination of our understanding of a whole genre of medieval historical writing. This is a large claim to make; but it may prompt further enquiry, not least by myself.

2

The changes between the original text of the *Imago Mundi* and the three recensions which cover the period 1110 to 1139 are marked by, among other things, internal variants to the text. The variants are distributed throughout the books but fall by subject into the following simple categories. There are variants dealing with alternative computistical methods, variants giving information about wells to which certain extraordinary characteristics are attached, variants telling of remarkable stones and metals and animals, variant mythical stories about the constellations, variants dealing with weather forecasting and the horizon, and, in the historical section, variants dealing with the deaths of emperors. The original text was gradually expanded by the addition of information concerned exclusively with these matters. A few examples of these pre-occupations may be given.[1] To Book I xiii the recension of 1123 adds the following sentence:

India quoque magnetem lapidem gignit, qui ferum rapit, adamantem etiam, qui non nisi hircino sanguine frangi poterit.

---

[1] I omit, for reasons of space, the computistical variants, the weather signs, and II xxv De Orizonte (added in 1133).

To I xiv this:

Persida lapidem pyrrhitem mittit, qui manum prementis urit, et sinelitem cuius candor cum luna crescit et deficit.

To I xix this:

in hac equae a vento concipiunt sed foetus non amplius triennio vivunt.

To I xxvii this:

Arcadia arbeston lapidem mittit, qui semel accensus extingui non potest. In Epiro est fons in quo faces accessae extinguuntur, et interum extinctae accenduntur . . .

To I cxxvi it adds to the sentence on Anticanis:

qui canis Orionis fertur, et ob insigne meritum inter sidera locatur.

In I xxxiii, to the section on the Garamantes we have added:

Apud quos est fons tam frigidus diebus ut non bibatur, tam frigidus noctibus ut non tangatur.[1]

The same recension varies the information given in the original text about the signs of the zodiac Cancer and Scorpio and about the star Delphinus. The original text of I xcv (as opposed to that which Migne prints and the 1123 recension adopts), for example, reads, for its first sentence:

Quartum est cancer, qui maximum a neptuno hominibus inmissus a perseo interemptus, ob insigne inter sidera est translatus.

Of I xcix:

Octavum est scorpius, qui maximus Orionem percussit dum bestias terrae occidit, et ob terrae gratiam astra meruit.

Of I cxix:

Cui coniungitur Delfinus, qui arionem chicaristam de piratis eripuit.[2]

---

[1] I take the text of this recension from one of the best manuscripts containing it, that is MS BL, London, Cotton Cleopatra B iv.

[2] For these variants I rely on one of the best copies of the original text, MS Corpus Christi College, Cambridge, 66.

The variant passages are carried into the successive recensions. One variant which distinguishes two later copies of that which I take to be the earliest form of the text (MS Corpus Christi College, Cambridge, 66 and MS BL, London, Royal 13 A xxi) concerns the signs of the zodiac. Seven of these, in the Royal manuscript, are given a consciously Christian and, in some cases, a consciously natural explanation. They begin on folio 20 of the text, immediately after I xcviii, and read:

Primum signum est aries, eo quod Abraham optulit arietem pro Ysaac filio sui. Vel quia aries habet longa cornua de capite procedentia, ita sol in illo mense extendit radios suos. Vel sicut sol vadit ad dextrum maris ionium, ita aries iacet super latus dextrum in marcio, ut dicit Beda.

Secundun signum est taurus, eo quod Iacob sicut taurus luctavit cum angelo usque mane dum benediceret ipsum.

Tercius est gemini, eo quod Adam et Eva de uno corpore facti sunt.

Quartum est Cancrus, pro eo quod Iacob cancerius sum librum pensavit.

Quintum est leo, pro eo quod Daniel in lacu leonum fuit.

Sextum est virgo, pro eo quod tempus illud est sterile sicut virgo intacta.

Septimum est libra, eo quod Iudas Scarioth pretium sanguinis accepit. Vel quod in illo mensium est equinoctium.

After the seven intrusions the text continues with I xcix.

A still later recension, dateable tentatively to 1133, maintains the interest in stones and wells and stars, adds computistical material and adds material of a far more grisly kind. In the short accounts of reigns of Roman emperors, given in Book III, there appears, sometimes above the written text, sometimes incorporated within it, specific information about the ways in which the emperors met their ends. Excellent examples of this type of addition are to be found in MS Stiftsbibliothek Zwettl, 172. Thus, for example, to the record of the reign of Antoninus Pius it adds the information 'morbo obiit' and 'similiter id est morbo' to that of Marcus Antoninus Verus. Again, to the records of Constantius, Constantine and Constans are added respectively the legends, 'dolore periit', 'occiditur a fratre Constante', and 'hic in Hispania occiditur'. Similarly, to the entries for Constantius and Galerius Maximus we have added 'In Anglia moritur' and 'seipsum interfecit'.[1] This attention to the deaths of emperors is to be found in the *Summa Totius* too.[2]

A close examination of the manuscripts has revealed one other feature which, whilst not distinguishing the recensions, is none the less striking enough to be worthy of note. The chapter on the planet Saturn (I lxxvi) is the object of a great deal of attention. The sentence 'In cuius exortu post triginta annos qui imaginem de aere fuderit, loqui ut hominem probabit', is very frequently displaced.

We may, of course, attribute many of these additions and attentions to the discovery of new material[3] or to the chance vagaries of scribes. There is more to be said, however, than this. For one thing, much of the added information is readily to be found in the *De Civitate Dei* of St. Augustine,[4] a text Honorius knew well in 1100 and one upon which he can hardly therefore be supposed to have fallen accidentally in 1123. Secondly, and far more importantly, the material is linked by nature. We are in a world of calculation by the sun and by the moon, a world which looks to the stars and, with

[1] *PL* 172, col. 181. There is much more interpolated information of this kind.

[2] In the one surviving twelfth-century manuscript of this such information is often inserted, once again, between the lines as though it had been added. The insertions here, however, are less startling, for this manuscript contains much marginal information which would reward close examination.

[3] In MS Österreichische Nationalbibliothek, Vienna, 1180 (late twelfth century), there is (fo. 188) a treatise *De Septem Lapidibus* which contains together all the material on stones Honorius scatters through his own. I have not found a source for the Christian interpretation of the zodiac but parts of it are clearly related to the *Livre des Créatures* of Philip of Thaon. T. Wright (ed.), *Popular Treatises on Science written during the Middle Ages* (London, 1841), pp. 35–6. In its emphasis on Jacob, too, it may reflect that astrological preoccupation with the twins, Esau and Jacob, which characterized the late twelfth century. M.-Th. d'Alverny, 'Astrologues et théologiens au xiiᵉ siècle', in *Mélanges offerts a M.-D. Chenu* (Paris, 1967), pp. 38–41. The Royal copy is of the early thirteenth century.

[4] *De Civitate Dei*, XXI, v.

careful reference to their demonic origins, amends its star myths.[1] This world expects exceptional qualities to be attached to springs and wells and stones and animals, and is prepared to ascribe, though perhaps with some misgivings, qualities to the planet Saturn which bear a remarkable resemblance to pre-Christian stories of a kind one may find, for example, in the *Asclepius*.[2] It is concerned, lastly, about fate; especially about the fates of pagan rulers. We have, in the *Imago Mundi*, in short, a geography, cosmology, and history consciously Christian, and yet one which through its various recensions betrays a consistent interest in material from a quite different world. The material is related to the world of primitive magic[3] and astrology.[4]

3

The historical section of the *Imago Mundi*, then, is an integral part of a treatise which displays, throughout its recensions, one consistent concern. This concern is for the repeated inclusion of material whose unifying characteristic is its relevance to the worlds of astrology and magic. In the light of this concern we may think again about the function in the treatise of Book III, and again about the various contexts within which historical writing in the Middle Ages may have been produced. It may be that there is a connection

[1] The condemnation is to be found in I cxxxvii, after Honorius has drawn on Hyginus's *Fabulae* and *Astronomicon* for these myths.

[2] A. D. Nock and A.-J. Festugière (ed.), *Corpus Hermeticum*, ii *Asclepius* (Paris, 1946), chapters viii and xiii, pp. 326, 347–9.

[3] The *Indiculus Superstitionum*, for example, *MGH*, *Leges*, I. i. 19–20, condemns superstitions associated with stones and wells, and auguries from beasts including, interestingly enough, horses. The making of gifts to stones and wells was a preoccupation of early Christian penitentials in the Germanic world; J. Raith, *Die Altenglische Version des Halitgarischen Bussbuches* (Hamburg, 1933) p. 29.

[4] The capacity of adamant to attract iron is often cited in astrological works. It is, for example, one of the instances used by Alkindi to illustrate his own astrological beliefs. Planets, signs of the zodiac, and stars with their representations form a preoccupation of the *Liber Introductorius* of Albumasar in its Latin translation. M.-Th. d'Alverny and F. Hudry, 'Alkindi. De Radiis', *Archives d'histoire doctrinale et littéraire du moyen âge*, 41 (1974), pp. 142, 144.

not merely between Book III and the magical preoccupations of the *Imago Mundi* itself but between the writing of world history and that half attractive, half feared magical dimension of thought and action by which Christian society in the West was at times both served and beset. To examine this possibility we may look a little more closely at the constitution of this dimension and the quality of the attention it received.

It is hard to know how widely in the early Middle Ages the magical arts were practised, and it is hard to know how well the science of astrology was understood. Certain assertions may, however, be made with comparative safety. Astrology the science could never be separated far from that science of astronomy by which the computus was supported;[1] nor, on the other hand, was it at all easy to divorce it from that magic the Christian liturgy must in part reject. The problem was compounded by the fact that, for certain sorts of magic, Christianity had a use. It had a use, for example, for that magic which inspired a fear of demons, for that divination which could put dreams to Christian moral purposes, and for that kind of supernatural intervention which, called miraculous, could be ascribed to prayer and grace.[2] The wholesale censure, then, which would embrace both astrology the science and the soothsaying, oracles, divination, incantation, wonders, and all the paraphernalia of augury by birds and beasts, objects and dreams, it so often brought

[1] A. Van de Vyver, 'Les plus anciennes traductions latines médiévales (x–xi siècles) de traités d'astronomie et d'astrologie', *Osiris*, i (1936), pp. 655–91, shews how closely linked astronomical and astrological translations were to computistical collections.

[2] In a seminal article to which I am deeply indebted M.-Th. d'Alverny drew attention to the relationship manifest in a late twelfth-century French manuscript between magical incantation and Christian prayer. M.-Th. d'Alverny, 'Récréations monastiques. Les couteaux a manche d'ivoire', in *Recueil de travaux offert a M. Clovis Brunel* (Paris, 1955), pp. 11–12. The line between grace and erotic magic was very hard to draw, see, for example, the remarks on Ficino in F. Yates, *Giordano Bruno and the Hermetic Tradition* (London, 1964), p. 127. The need for careful distinction in the cause of preserving belief in Christian miracles was felt by Augustine, *De Civitate Dei*, x. 9, but in practice the distinction was, even to him, a very fine one.

in its train[1] could not be maintained. Patristic condemnation weighed upon it[2] but astrology and its magical accompaniments remained an object of attention in the early Middle Ages, and conspicuously so in the areas with which we are here concerned. In one of the chief feasts of the liturgy, even, the feast of the Epiphany, there was provided a recurrent occasion for reactions of a complicated kind. There was room for the condemnation of alarming magical and astrological practices,[3] but also for more sober reflection upon the respectably supernatural. Thus, behind the somewhat theatrical repetition of fiercely hostile views,[4] there remained a deeper current of receptive thought. Here astronomy, astrology, and some even of their more dubious adjuncts could be received[5]

---

[1] A. Bouché-Leclercq, *Histoire de la divination dans l'antiquité*, i (Paris, 1879), pp. 92–104.

[2] Some further helpful references to these condemnations are to be found in H. Bober, 'The zodiacal miniature of the Très Riches Heures of the Duke of Berry—its sources and meaning', *Journal of the Warburg and Courtauld Institute*, ii (1948), pp. 4–5.

[3] Thus Gregory the Great uses a sermon on the Feast of the Epiphany to attack astrologers; *Homiliae in Evangelium. In Die Epiphania*, PL 76, cols 1110–12.

[4] Caspari found in a ninth-century Einsiedeln manuscript the heading 'et qui fatum malum aut bonum in hominibus esse credunt, transgressores et pagani sunt'. This and other condemnations of astrology and astral magic in Latin sources in the early Middle Ages may be found in F. Boll, C. Bezold, W. Gundel, *Sternglaube und Sterndeutung* (Leipsig, Berlin, 1931), pp. 173–87.

[5] Besides the Latin *Asclepius*, astrological material was transmitted through the *Astronomicon* of Manilius and the *Mathesis* of Firmicus Maternus. It came to the north-west, too, through translations (A. Van de Vyver, 'Les plus anciennes . . .') and was by some eagerly sought. R. Latouche (ed.), *Richer: Histoire de France*, ii (Paris, 1937), iii. 43, 50–3, pp. 50–1, 58–63. E. Svenberg, *Lunaria et Zodiologica Latina* (Gothenberg, 1963), adds to the sources mentioned above by editing nine texts of lunar and zodiacal prognostications taken from manuscripts of the ninth to the twelfth centuries, and refers to another three manuscripts from these centuries with such texts. As early as 1916 Cumont drew attention to two ninth-century manuscripts, one then at Dresden (MS 193), and one at Paris (BN, Nouv. Acq. lat. 1614), and to a further tenth-century one from Notre Dame (BN, Lat. 17868), which showed a clear interest in astrology; F. Cumont, 'Astrologica', *Revue archéologique*, 3 (1916), 11–16. In 1941 M. L. W. Laistner drew together valuable references to the reception of astrological material in the West in the early Middle Ages;

and even welcomed.[1] It is within this deeper current that, if I am right, the *Imago Mundi* as a whole is to be placed.

As in general with deep currents, so in particular with this one, the overwhelming need was, on the part of the thoughtful, for understanding tempered by care. This need was recognized early, and led to definition and distinction. Thus Isidore, Bede, Hermannus Contractus[2] (to name only a few, and those few well known to Honorius) allowed the claims of astrology to the attention of certain Christians, by insisting on a division. Some parts, the *naturales* could be pursued. Others, the *superstitiosas*, were to be rejected. The pursuit remained 'natural' provided that no attempt was made to determine through it human destinies and mores. Such an attempt plunged one into the superstitious,[3] for human destinies and mores

M. L. W. Laistner, 'The Western church and astrology during the early middle ages', *Harvard Theological Review*, 34 (1941), pp. 251–75, reprinted in his *The Intellectual Heritage of the Early Middle Ages* (New York, 1957), pp. 57–82.

[1] A form of astrological medicine was often employed to help in the practice of blood-letting. Practitioners allowed themselves to be guided towards and away from certain days in certain months, and relevant information was often provided in computistical collections. The Ramsey Computus (MS St. John's College, Oxford, 17) contains much information of this kind; for example on fos. 4, 16–21ᵛ. See also E. Wickersheimer, 'Figures Medico—Astrologiques des ixᵉ, xᵉ et xiᵉ siècles', *Janus* (*Archives internationales pour l'histoire de la medecine*), 19 (1914), pp. 157–77. 'Egyptian Days', days especially unlucky not only for blood-letting but for numerous other activities as well, are often listed in early manuscripts; see, for example, the list in L. Thorndike, *A History of Magic and Experimental Science*, i (New York and London, 1923), pp. 695–6. Valuable references to such concerns in early English manuscripts are to be found in H. Henel, 'Altenglischer Mönchsaberglaube', *Englischer Studien*, 69 (1934/5), pp. 329–49.

[2] Hermannus Contractus wrote works on the astrolabe. J. Drecker, 'Hermannus Contractus über das Astrolab', *Isis*, 16 (1931), pp. 200–19.

[3] W. M. Lindsay (ed.), *Isidori Hispalensis Episcopi Etymologiarum Sive Originum Libri XX* (Oxford, 1911), III, xxvii. In his *De Natura Rerum* he allows influence over man and under providence to the moon and to comets; xix. 2, xxvi. 13, *PL* 83, cols 992, 1000. Bede condemns astrologers in his *De Temporum Ratione*, iii; C. W. Jones (ed.), *Bedae Opera De Temporibus* (Cambridge, Mass., 1943), pp. 183–4. In his own *De Natura Rerum*, xxiv, however, he accepts Isidore's position on the influence of comets, and in his *Expositio in Actus Apostolorum*, i, he allows lot casting under apostolic conditions; *PL* 90,

had to remain firmly within the scope of divine creation and the hope of divine providence and grace. To maintain this complex distinction a deal of common ambiguous ground between astronomy and astrology on the one hand, and astrology and magic on the other, had, for the Christian scholar, continually to be traversed, reviewed, demarcated, and the perspectives and purposes of the knowledge so acquired continually adjusted. The essence of the exercise lay in the devising of a means of acceding to that which was good and of service without danger of contamination by that which was harmful. This exercise, for its success, required great subtlety and intricate checks and balances.

It is hard, too, to know the place of magic and astrology in the twelfth century; but again some few things may be said with certainty. We do know that some of the magical arts which were practised were feared and condemned.[1] We know too that the complex distinction between the respectable 'natural' and the unrespectable 'superstitious' was repeated and sustained.[2] A third fact

---

cols 243–4, *PL* 92, col. 945. The distinction between 'natural' and 'superstitious' may to some extent correspond with our distinction between the scientific and the non-scientific. But, in default of contemporary remark, one may not assume this.

[1] Gratian showed great concern about the place in Christianity of magic and divination, and quoted a deal of Augustine and Jerome and a number of conciliar decrees condemning both. E. Friedberg, ed. cit., Part II, Causa xxvi, Questiones i–v, vii (13–18), pp. 1020–36, 1044–6. In England, the Council of London 1125 included the canon: 'Sortilogos, ariolos et auguria quaeque sectantes eisque consentientes, excommunicari precipimus, perpetuaque notamus infamia'. *Chron. John*, 21. And see the *Policraticus* of John of Salisbury, l. 12; C. C. J. Webb (ed.), *Policraticus Sive De Nugiis Curialium et Vestigiis Philosophorum Libri* viii, 1 (Oxford, 1909), p. 50; William of Malmesbury on Gerbert and the witch of Berkeley; *GR*, i (RS, 1887), pp. 193–203, 253–5, and Marbod of Rennes, *Liber Decem Capitulorum*, *PL* 171, cols 1704–5.

[2] In his *Didascalicon* ii. 10, written before 1130, Hugh of St. Victor again divided the respectable 'natural' part of astrology from the 'superstitious'. As he revised his *Didascalicon* Hugh added a further condemnation of magic and the corruption of morals divination brings with it, C. H. Buttimer, ed. cit., VI, xv. Notable among the others are William of Conches, *De Philosophia Mundi*, II, v, *PL* 172, col. 59 (wrongly attributed to Honorius), and Abelard, *Expositio in Hexaemeron*, V. Cousin (ed.), *Opera Hactenus Seorsim Edita*, i (Paris, 1849), pp. 647–51.

is, at first sight, more surprising, though for these purposes, as I think, revealing. Some magical and astrological interests were maintained[1] and others were pursued in the Christian West with a vigour which has no previous parallel. Early and important evidence of the maintenance and pursuit of this further knowledge comes from Bavaria and from England; from, in short, those very areas with which the *Imago Mundi* shows some clear early connection. Later and striking evidence comes from the period 1123–39 within which, if I am right, the text was revised. The early Bavarian evidence is indicative.[2] The later, and partly English, evidence is of a more concentrated kind than is generally made clear. This fact deserves to be stressed.

The corpus of knowledge about astronomy, astrology, and divination received an enormous reinforcement in the late eleventh and early twelfth centuries. To put the matter a little more strongly, it is, in truth, remarkable how large a proportion of the energies of the most distinguished scholars and of the most famous translators of this period was devoted to astronomical, to astrological, and to magical material. Devotion of this gravity raised the status of the subject and was, most probably, designed to do so. More remarkable still, for the purpose of this discussion, is the fact that some of the

[1] Five of the best manuscripts of the Latin *Asclepius* are twelfth-century ones. A. D. Nock and A.-J. Festugière, *Corpus Hermeticum*, ii *Asclepius* (Paris, 1946), pp. 259–60. Knowledge of Firmicus Maternus seems, too, to have undergone a revival. Marbod of Rennes finds him worthy of attack; *Liber Decem Capitulorum*, PL 171, col. 1704; Bernard Silvestris, of imitation; B. Stock, *Myth and Science in the Twelfth Century, a Study of Bernard Silvester* (Princeton, 1972), pp. 82–6. He is known, too, to William of Malmesbury, see below, p. 236, n. 1.

[2] St. Emmeramm's Regensburg had an important eleventh-century copy of some of the writings of Hermannus Contractus on the astrolabe, now MS, Bay. Staatsbibl., Munich, clm. 14836. St. Peter's, Salzburg, has a twelfth-century copy; MS Stiftsbibliothek St. Peter's Salzburg, a V 7. Clm. 560, seemingly a Bavarian manuscript, contains an eleventh-century copy of the *Mathesis* of Firmicus Maternus, Books I and II, and MS Bay. Staatsbibl., Munich, clm. 22307, an eleventh-century manuscript from Windberg, has the Letter of Petosiris. A. Van de Vyver, art. cit., pp. 674–6. For Lorraine and England see M. C. Welborn, 'Lotharingia as a centre of Arabic and scientific influence in the eleventh century', *Isis*, 16 (1931), pp. 188–99.

best of the evidence for the influx of this material into Europe comes from the West of England, not far in time and place from Robert of Hereford's importation of the computistical method and world chronicle of Marianus Scotus. In England, for instance, Walcher, prior of Malvern from *c*. 1091, paraphrased the *De Dracone* of Petrus Alphonsus, and, between 1108 and 1112 and then again before 1120, produced two astronomical treatises. The astronomical work of Petrus Alphonsus himself was well enough known in England by 1120 to influence Walcher's second treatise.[1] Passages in Petrus's *Disciplina Clericalis* (1, 9) are, if we are to take them seriously, of especial interest, for he seems to admit divination and even necromancy to the company of the liberal arts.[2] Peter also wrote a *Letter to the Peripatetics* in which he was especially concerned to defend the science of astronomy.[3] Adelard of Bath, working seemingly a little later than Peter, translated in 1126 the tables of Al Khwarismi (a compilation especially useful in the casting of horoscopes), and translated also the *Liber Prestigiorum* of Thabit ben Qurra and the *Isagoge Minor* of Albumasar. In his *De Eodem et Diverso* (written before 1115, just possibly in England) Adelard claims for celestial bodies power over the sublunary world, and, for men learned in astronomy, powers of prediction.[4] Though he

---

[1] For Walcher and Petrus Alphonsus see C. H. Haskins, 'The introduction of Arabic science into England', in *Studies in the History of Medieval Science* (Harvard U.P., 1924), pp. 113–18. References to the two treatises and to the paraphrase of the *De Dracone* are to be found together with another by Walcher in MS Bodleian Library, Oxford, Auct. F.1.9, fos 86–99. They precede the *Khorasmian Tables* of Adelard of Bath. This manuscript comes from Worcester and also contains a copy of Robert of Hereford's revision of Marianus.

[2] L. Thorndike, op. cit., ii. pp. 72–3.

[3] This letter is to be found in a single manuscript of the late twelfth century, MS BL, London, Arundel 270, fos 40ᵛ–44ᵛ. This treatise contains references to astrological medicine, suited perhaps to Petrus in his capacity as doctor to Henry I; Thorndike, op. cit., pp. 70–1. It contains, fos 23ᵛ–33ᵛ, a copy of the historical section of the *Imago Mundi*. See below.

[4] H. Willner, 'Des Adelard von Bath de Eodem et Diverso', *Beiträge zur Geschichte der Philosophie des Mittelalters*, 4 (1903), pp. 31–2.

travelled widely Adelard was certainly in the West of England in 1130, and perhaps made his translation of the tables of Al Khwarismi there.[1] Both Walcher and Adelard were familiar with the use of the astrolabe, and the latter wrote a treatise on it also.[2] The chronicler John of Worcester knew of Adelard's version of the Khorasmian Tables.[3]

This interest in 'scientific' astrology became especially intense in the third and fourth decades of the twelfth century. Compilations and translations very largely astrological and divinatory occupied the energies of John of Spain, Plato of Tivoli, Robert of Chester, Herman of Carinthia, Hugh of Santalla. Some of the more striking of their works may be named and on occasion dated.[4] The abridgement of Ptolemy's great astrological treatise the *Quadripartitum*, an abridgement known as the *Centiloquium* or *Fructus*, was translated possibly as early as 1136 by John of Spain, and then again by Hugh

---

[1] One early manuscript of a version of these, MS Corpus Christi College, Oxford, 283, a twelfth-century manuscript from St. Augustine's, Canterbury, has bound with it some material by Petrus Alphonsus. In this (fo. 142ᵛ) Petrus is described as the 'translator' of Adelard's work. This may mean that Adelard used Petrus as an interpreter; Haskins, 'The introduction of Arabic Science', p. 118.

[2] The astrolabe, together with other early medieval astronomical instruments, seems primarily to have been used for calculation, especially for astrological purposes. E. Poulle, 'Les instruments astronomiques de l'occident latin aux xiᵉ et xiiᵉ siècles', *Cahiers de civilisation médiévale*, 15 (1972), p. 40. For Adelard see C. H. Haskins, 'Adelard of Bath', in *Studies*, pp. 20–42. If Adelard was indeed the author of a *Mappe Clavicula*, he was also interested in alchemy. Adelard was employed for a time in the exchequer of Henry I. In that he employed such men as Petrus and Adelard in such important practical positions Henry I may himself have been more sympathetic towards astrology than we have supposed.

[3] J. H. R. Weaver, ed. cit., p. 53.

[4] For these see Haskins, *Studies*, pp. 9–14, 43–66, 67–81. See also Francis Carmody's caveats on some of the attributions; F. J. Carmody, *Arabic Astronomical and Astrological Sciences in Latin Translation. A Critical Bibliography* (Berkeley, Los Angeles, 1956), p. 5. This is a helpful compilation but erratic in its description of manuscripts. I use for convenience here the latinized forms of names to be found in this.

of Santalla.[1] The whole *Quadripartitum* was translated by Plato of Tivoli in 1138, in a version which was widely popular, and Plato may have been the translator of yet another version of Ptolemy's hundred aphorisms on astrology. The majority of the other translations by John of Spain was astrological,[2] including the rudiments of the science (*De scientia astrorum*) by Alfraganus (translated 1135–7), the *Liber Introductorius*, to the mystery of judgements by the stars, by Alcabitius, and the *Introductorius*, containing a detailed defence of astrology, by Albumasar. Many of the astrological works of Messehalla were transmitted to the West by John. Then, in 1142, John compiled his own *Epitome Totius Astrologiae*. To the two translations by Plato of Tivoli already mentioned may be added the *De Motu Stellarum* of Albategni (1134–8), the *Capitula Stellarum* of Almansor and the *De Nativitatibus* of Albohali (both seemingly in 1136),[3] and Robert of Chester's contribution to the growing astrological and quasi-magical corpus included the *De Iudiciis Astrorum* of Alkindi, and treatises on alchemy and the astrolabe. Robert's friend, Herman of Carinthia, with whom he was in 1141 involved in the translation of the Koran for Peter the Venerable, added a

---

[1] Hugh was asked for his translation by Bishop Michael of Tarazone (1119–51) especially to provide a guide through the growing forest of astrological material. Between these years Hugh produced at least five other related translations including the *De Motibus Planetarum* (a commentary on Alfraganus) and a *De Nativitatibus*, possibly of Messehalla. A version of the *Compendium Aureum* on gems, magic, and alchemy, ascribed to Hugh, is to be found in the twelfth-century MS BN, Paris, 13951, fos 1–31.

[2] A fuller list than that provided by Haskins of John's translations from the Arabic is to be found in M. Steinschneider, 'Die Europäischen Übersetzungen aus dem Arabischen bis Mitte des 17 Jahrhunderts. A. Schriften bekannter Übersetzer', *Situngsberichte der Kaiserliche Academie der Wissenschaften in Wien, Philosophisch-historische Klasse*, 149 (1904), no. 68.

[3] For other undateable astrological works by Plato, for example the *De Revolutionibus Nativitatum* of Alkasan, see Steinschneider, 'Die Europäischen', no. 98. He may also have translated a geomancy, to be found now in a very late copy from Polling, MS Bay. Staatsbibl. Munich, clm. 11998. Attention is drawn to the learned nature of Plato's work on geomancy and that of some of his near contemporaries by T. Charmasson, 'Les premiers traités latins de geomancy', *Cahiers de civilisation médiévale*, 21 (1978), 121–136.

translation of the *Fatidica* or *Prognostica de Revolutionibus* of Saul ben Bischr (1138), another translation of the *Introductorius* of Albumasar (*c.* 1140) and perhaps one of his *De Occultis*, and a translation of Ptolemy's *Planisphere* in 1143. Herman's own *De Essentiis* (1143) contains a deal of astrological information. The effect of these translations on the West was not, perhaps, immediately widespread; but the concern which led to their being commissioned was undeniable. The energy with which the 'natural' aspects of astrology and divination were pursued suggests that the danger from the darker side of these arts may have been a lot more pressing than we have been inclined so far to suspect.

I have said that the response such interests demanded of thoughtful Christians was a complex one. The material required both concession and containment; the variants to Book I and II of the *Imago Mundi* provide again, I think, some indication of the quality of the response these concerns received. One striking feature of the variants is the orthodox source of some of them; the *De Civitate Dei* of Augustine. Now this text was itself designed both to concede to its own source and to contain those implications in it which were threatening to Christians.[1] Another characteristic shown by the variants, and this characteristic extends to other sections of the treatise, is Honorius's tendency to stop short at the possibly 'superstitious'.[2] He is even wary of concessions made by Isidore.[3] There

---

[1] For two of the stones Augustine mentioned, for example, adamant and pyrrhites, he drew upon the *Natural History* of Pliny, xxxvii. 61 and 144. Pliny, however, ascribed to the former power to drive fear from the mind of man, and to the latter the power (attested by the Magi) of subduing human violence. Augustine omits both these remarks. Some limited commentary on the constellations, too, was permitted by Gregory the Great, *Moralia in Job*, IX, ix, *PL* 75, cols 865–9.

[2] Honorius's treatment of the planets is an obvious example of this tendency. He ascribes to them colours (I lxxviii) in the manner of Bede's *De Natura Rerum* xv, *PL* 90, cols 230–1, but, with the exception of the curious passage on Saturn I have mentioned, no part in the government of human affairs. This is in marked contrast to, for instance, the *De Essentiis* of Herman of Carinthia, Thorndike, op. cit., ii. p. 42. It is also in contrast to the *De Philosophia Mundi* of William of Conches, II, xvii–xix, *PL* 172, cols 62–3, although Honorius makes use in other parts of William's source for these passages, Macrobius.

seems to be in this a clear consciousness of that common ambiguous ground of which I spoke; a realization of the need to pay attention to, but show reserve about, that material upon which the 'natural' and the 'superstitious' may make common cause. The secret of safety lay in knowing when to venture upon the natural, and when to draw back and fend away the clearly superstitious by a christianized semblance of it. Yet even when such distinctions had been made, and even when the status of the subject had been so raised, some underlying problems of emphasis, attitude, and perspective may still remain. Even when the respectable aspects of astronomy, astrology, and magic were known and so controlled, and even when their superstitious concomitants had been so conjured away as to make it all seem quite innocuous, there could be something about the whole which still would threaten Christian morality. To abandon subjects to which such serious attention had been so consciously devoted was clearly beyond question: a further control had to be found. This brings us, lastly, to Book III. We may look again at the function of historical writing, both within the *Imago Mundi* and outside it.

4

A fundamental source of opposition between magic and astrology, and the Christian view of man, lay in the attitudes of each to free

---

J. Willis (ed.), *Ambrosii Theodosii Macrobii Commentarii in Somnium Scipionis*, i (Teubner-Leipzig, 1970), 18–20, pp. 76–7. This belief in the harmful qualities of, for example, Saturn and Mars, and the contrasting benevolence of Jupiter, was almost a commonplace when Honorius wrote. It is to be found, in the Pseudo-Clementine *Recognitions*, which were well known (Laistner, 'The Western Church', pp. 78–80), and also in the *Liber Alchandreus*. Honorius's reserve is perhaps all the more marked in that we have a surviving important eleventh-century text of this; MS Bay. Staatsbibl., clm. 560, apparently from Bavaria (this same codex also contains a copy of Firmicus Maternus).

[3] In Book I, lxviii, Honorius describes the planets as *erraticae* because of their wandering courses, a description drawn from Isidore's *Etymologies*, III, lxiii. In his *De Natura Rerum*, however, Isidore described the planets as *errantia* because they induced men to err; xxiii. 3, *PL* 83, col. 996. Although he used this work Honorius again stopped short at this addition. In I cxxxvii, and unlike Isidore again, Honorius allows only that comets *portend* events.

will.[1] Magic and astronomy, even at their most respectable, would still submit the will of man to the power of the stars, and the future to the future of the horoscope and determinings of particular acts and objects. The Christian would submit it ultimately only to hope in the providence of God, to that power of choice which allowed man to reject this, to that grace which would restore to man the means of responding once again in time. One way of demonstrating the Christian perspective, its attitude to providence and its emphasis on hope, became very early clear to Christian apologists. It lay in the writing of world history. The demonstration of God's fore-knowledge, his part in creation and in its subsequent passage under the direction of man through time, was a formidable weapon against a narrow fatalism, and was recognized as such.[2] The Bible, especially the historical books, and treatises on providence and free will themselves were, of course, valuable assistants in the cause. The writing of history, especially of history from the fall, gave a further strength. If astrology and magic were ways of foretelling the future in such a way as to uphold its submission to the stars and dreams and particular natural objects, the writing of Christian history was a way of recounting the past in such a way as to hope to submit that future to the control of Christian man.

This particular means of combating magic and those aspects even of the science of astrology which threatened Christian morality

[1] One of the clearest expositions of this opposition is to be found in the *Homiliae in Hexaemeron* of St. Basil, VI, 5–7, *PG* 29, pp. 127–34. Many expressions of it are to be found, of course, in the works of St. Augustine, for example *De Genesi ad Litteram*, II, xvii, *PL* 34, cols 278–9. Thorndike points to the acknowledgement in the *Questiones Naturales* of Adelard of Bath of a possible conflict between independent scientific observation and the expression of orthodox beliefs about the nature of God and the divine will. Op. cit., ii.28.

[2] *De Civitate Dei*, V, i–xi. C. Zangemeister (ed.), *Pauli Orosii Historiarum adversum Paganos Libri VII* (Teubner, Leipsig, 1889), Preface, pp. 6–7. In the *De Doctrina Christiana*, II, xxviii, Augustine opposes books of history to 'libri . . . haruspicum'. J. Martin (ed.), *Sancti Aurelii Augustini De Doctrina Christiana* (Corpus Christianorum, Turnholt, 1962), II, xxviii. pp. 44, 63. Cassiodorus advances a similar view in his *Institutes*, in the chapter 'De Historicis Christianis'. R. A. B. Mynors (ed.), *Cassiodori Senatoris Institutiones* (Oxford, 1937), I, xvii. p. 55.

was recognized, if I am right, early in the Middle Ages.[1] It may not be mere coincidence that those scholars, of whose accommodating attitudes to astrology I have spoken, wrote histories and chronicles *ab initio peccati hominis* on the model of Orosius, and included in them miracles, Christian dreams and prophecies, and promptings to Christian ethical behaviour.[2] This particular aspect of this enquiry, unhappily, may not be followed here. My purpose in this last section is to make claims simply for Book III. The claims I would make are these. The first four decades of the twelfth century were, I have tried to show, again preoccupied to a striking degree with the problems of magic and astrology, and with the need for Christian morality to triumph. Book III of the *Imago Mundi* was related to these needs in the same way as the non-historical sections of the text were related to them, and as earlier historical writing was related to such preoccupations. Book III, that is, like the non-historical material, tried to concede an interest in the strange and supernatural, and then, in company with the earlier historical treatises, many of which it used, to contain its more dangerous effects within a Christian perspective. This process is reflected in the contents of the early codices which contain the text. Lastly, we may assign to Book III the role of guide. It may be that other twelfth-century historical treatises were, in part at least, compiled to

---

[1] Ælfric, for example, condemns the taking of auguries from horses in that same part of his sermon on auguries in which he speaks of the goodness of God's creation in seven days, and refers too to the power against the superstitions he had mentioned of free will and the command 'Declina a malo et fac bonum'. W. W. Skeat, *Aelfric's Lives of the Saints*, EETS, 82 (London, 1885), pp. 370–5, 379–83. I owe these references to Dr Audrey Meaney.

[2] The *Chronicles* both of Isidore and of Bede follow, in the *De Natura Rerum* and the *De Temporum Ratione* respectively, chapters on the Christian Easter, PL 84, cols 86–107, PL 90, cols 516–79, as if to demonstrate the association between the redemption and Christian history and responsibility. That the connection between early Christian historical writing and ethical purpose was a deep one has long been observed; C. W. Jones, 'Bede as early medieval historian', *Medievalia et humanistica*, 4 (1946), pp. 31–2. See also some illuminating passages in R. W. Hanning, *The Vision of History in Early Britain* (New York, 1966), pp. 75 ff.

countermand that fatalism which the most respectable interest in astrology might involve. We may take these claims in order.

Five of the number of manuscripts of the *Imago Mundi* I have already mentioned have in them interpolations to Book III. These illustrate the first claim I would make; that of the effort to concede and contain. Four have a short addition at the very beginning, after the birth of Cain and Abel:

Occiso autem a Caym Abel, Adam centum annos duxit in luctu et merore, et deinceps conjugali thoro uti noluit. Post hoc divino iussu ammonetur a sancto angelo, ut denuo uxorali fruatur contubernio, quatinus maledictio Caym excludatur benedictione nascentis. Post hec genuit filium nomine Seth.[1]

The curse of Cain is overthrown through the intervention of a divinely directed angel. One manuscript has six far longer interpolations of which I can here only recount the contents. Four of the interpolations, all from Book VIII of Cassian's *Collations* ('De principatibus seu potestatibus'), are, again, about moral choice assisted by divine and angelic intervention, and about the power of man to triumph over evil.[2] The last of the four refers directly to the danger presented to this power by indulgence in the magical arts.[3] I have not been able to find a source for two of the interpolations but they are preoccupied again with this same subject. One is given over to a discussion of the sentence 'In principio fecit deus celum et terram'. The principles of God's control over creation are re-asserted. The power given both to angels and men is stressed, and so

[1] MS BL, Cotton Cleopatra B iv, fo. 22ᵛ. The other three manuscripts are MSS Paris, BN, 15009, and Bibliothèque Mazarine, 708; London, BL, Add. MS 38665.

[2] MS Bay. Staatsbibl., Munich, clm. 22225, fos 150ᵛ–152ᵛ, 152ᵛ–153, 154–6, 157ᵛ–158, *Collatio* VIII, vi–xii, xvii, xxiii–xxv, xxii–xxiii, PL 49, cols 730–4, 750, 761–70, 758–60. *Collatio* VIII is, of all Cassian's *Collations*, the one most preoccupied with magic arts. It is singular that it is from this that the extracts are made.

[3] 'Hanc ergo scientiam ... aereos daemones venerarentur et colerent'. PL 49, col. 758. This reference to the successive vulnerability of the seed of Seth connects well with the interpolation common to the previous four manuscripts, and may perhaps reflect contemporary discussion.

is the fall of both, the resulting vulnerability of man to sin and to the devil, and the effects in the struggle of redeeming grace. The second interpolation is a tissue of biblical legends. There are wonder stories about the burial of Adam, the hill of Calvary, the wood of the tree of paradise, and the signs foretelling the day of judgement. Portents, high places, and wood are prominent; but again man is lifted above the determined by his capacity to respond to angelic and divine intervention manifested in a profoundly, but to the compiler respectably, supernatural way.[1] In all these interpolations, in fact, the emphasis is placed upon Christian responsibility and susceptibility, their direction through time and protection against ill by divine intervention.

This effort to show interest in, but to contain the effects of, the magical and fatalistic is echoed by the contents of many of the collections with which the *Imago Mundi* was early bound. The very best text of the 1139 recension, for example,[2] is bound with traditional and Christian wonder stories (the seven wonders of the world, the seven miracles associated with the birth of Christ), visions, charms, cures, the *Liber Proverbiorum* of Otloh of St. Emmeramm's, the Bestiary, and extracts which in part bear directly upon the reception of superstitious belief.[3] In other words, that need for wonder and for signs of supernatural intervention which could so easily choose a doubtful path was fed, as it was in the *Imago*

[1] Fos 153–4, inc. 'In principio fecit deus celum et terram', fos 156–7 inc. 'Secundum dicta dominica terra es et in terram ibis. Erat autem adam xxx cubitorum altitudinis.'

[2] MS Bay, Staatsbibl., Munich, clm. 536, from Prül.

[3] For instance fo. 62ᵛ contains the following entry upon lucky and unlucky days. 'Tres dies sunt et noctes in quibus si virilis fuerit genitus sine dubio corpus eius integrum manet usque in diem iudicii. Hoc est in vi et in iii idus et in iii kalendas februarii et est mirabile misterium. Quot in anno sunt dies, tot uniuscuisque membra mulieris, id est ccclxvi, et tot elemosinis peccata hominum sunt redemenda. Tres dies maledicti dicuntur. Non in his tribus diebus sanguinem minuas, aut de ansere manduces, vel potionem sumas. Hoc est viiii kalendae aprilis, die lune, intrante augusto, die lune, exeunte decembre, die lune. Hi tres dies maledicti dicuntur.' Honorius, in the *Imago Mundi* II cix, re-echoed that belief in the Egyptian Days which was early accepted as respectable.

Mundi itself, by material to confine it within accepted boundaries. Similar items are to be found bound with other important early manuscripts.[1] Two very slightly later codices (of the late twelfth or early thirteenth centuries) fulfil this need in a different but related way. They bind parts of Book III, and, in the second case, Book III alone, with astrological and magical texts defensibly 'natural'. MS Preussische Staatsbibliothek, Berlin, lat. 956, has, with parts of the *Imago Mundi*, the translation of Alfraganus's *De Aggregationibus Scientia Stellarum* by Gerard of Cremona, a treatise on alchemy, three lapidaries, and one of the fullest available accounts of astrological practice and of the materials astrology required, the *Liber Introductorius* of Alcabitius, translated by John of Spain.[2] The second codex, BL, London, Arundel 270, which has Book III alone, binds with it a treatise 'De Utilitatibus Astrolabii' and the only copy we have of the *Letter to the Peripatetics* of Petrus Alphonsus.[3] In these two codices we have, actually in the same collection as parts of the *Imago Mundi*, rare copies of 'scientific' and acceptable works upon astrology and magic of precisely the sort to which, in its own way, Book III as well was related.

We may turn lastly to the role of Book III as a guide. It may be that more Christian writers than we have so far suspected turned to history with both the attraction and the threats of magic and astrology very much in mind. This idea may not be explored far here; but there are signs to which we may point. Long ago Thorndike drew attention to the consciously christianized cosmology and astrology of the chronicle of Raoul Glaber.[4] The early twelfth-century evidence is, so far, less striking. But it is there. William of Malmesbury was, for example, one of the most distinguished of Honorius's

[1] For example MSS Bay. Staatsbibl., Munich, clm. 14348 and 14731, both from St. Emmeramm's Regensburg, contain the same extracts. The first manuscript has the Bestiary too.

[2] A very full description of this codex is given in V. Rose, *Die Handschriften—Verzeichnisse der Königlichen Bibliothek zu Berlin*, II, iii (Berlin, 1905).

[3] Thorndike, op. cit., ii. pp. 70–2.

[4] Ibid. i. 674–6. More recently M.-Th. d'Alverny has drawn attention to the fact that Helinard of Froidmont attacked astrologers in his *Chronicle*. M.-Th. d'Alverny, 'Astrologues', pp. 39–49.

contemporaries in the writing of history. William wrote within easy reach in time and space of that area of England in which the revival of interest in astronomy and astrology was so vigorous, and he was himself involved in it.[1] His ambiguous attitude to the subjects is a striking aspect of his historical writing. He both condemned and reverenced them.[2] We may have in William's interest in history, in conscious succession to Bede, that same desire to distinguish, accommodate, and, above all, to contain. I have mentioned the *Didascalicon* of Hugh of St. Victor, its firm condemnation of the superstitious and of harmful magic, but its defence, in Book II, 10, of the 'natural' aspects of astrology. In this same chapter Hugh again defined and condemned the superstitious by its incompatibility with man's free choice. Hugh's attitude to, and illustration of, the guidance of free choice has been proved, most convincingly, to be an historical one.[3] A third person, well worthy of attention in this context, is Otto bishop of Freising (1137–58). Otto, once a pupil of Hugh, devoted his own life to the writing of

[1] MS Bodleian Library, Oxford, Auct. F. 3. 14, a computistical, astronomical, and astrological collection, was probably drawn up for him. N. R. Ker, 'William of Malmesbury's Handwriting', *EHR*, 59 (1944), p. 374.

[2] William made much of Gerbert's nefarious reputation for dabbling in the occult, and told with some disapprobation of how Archbishop Gerard of York was suspected of reading Firmicus Maternus in secret. He spoke of the results of Robert of Hereford's successful divination from the stars, however, with respect and, in the *Historia Novella*, showed deference to prognostications from the stars and sun and weather. *GR*, i. pp. 193–203; *GP*, p. 259, n. 6; K. R. Potter (ed.), *The Historia Novella by William of Malmesbury* (NMT, 1955), pp. 43, 50.

[3] R. W. Southern, 'Aspects of the European Tradition of Historical Writing: 2. Hugh of St. Victor and the idea of Historical Development', *TRHS*, 5th series, 21 (1971), p. 164. Hugh, like William, was interested in, and knowledgeable about, astronomy and astrology. He knew the *Asclepius* and the Pseudo-Hermetic *Liber Hermetis Mercurii Triplicis de VII Rerum Principiis*; J. Taylor, *The Didascalicon of Hugh St. Victor* (New York, 1961), p. 20. MS BN, Paris, lat. 14754, an early twelfth-century codex of astronomical texts from St. Victor, may also have been his own: A. Van de Vyver, 'Les plus anciennes', p. 685. It seems, too, that he wrote a world chronicle; R. Baron, 'La Chronique de Hugues de St. Victor', *Studia Gratiana*, xii (1967), 167–79. This is bound with a copy of the *Imago Mundi* in MS BN, Paris, lat. 15009.

history. In his own *Chronicle* (written between 1143 and 1146/7) he consciously set himself within the tradition of Augustine and Orosius[1] and subscribed with an equal vigour to their view of the associations between history, the guidance of divine providence, and Christian morality.[2] We may even detect signs in Otto's work of that 'naturalizing' of myth and wonder which, I have suggested, was so conspicuous a part of the recensions of the *Imago Mundi*.[3] Finally, it is a commonplace to observe that medieval chroniclers were alive to the influence in human affairs of comets and aerial phenomena. Less commonly observed is the possibility that this too had a context. Comets and aerial phenomena of this kind lay on the common ground between the natural and the superstitious in astrology. We may have, in the admission of their influence, not evidence of the credulous superstitions to which medieval writers of history were prey, but evidence instead of a far from credulous concern for that proper accommodation of astrological knowledge in which historical writing played so important a part.[4]

I have looked, in this discussion, at only one of the many possible motives for the medieval writing of history. I have looked at history as a counterpoise in a balance of very great delicacy; and I have

[1] Transl. C. C. Mierow, *The Two Cities* (Columbia University Press, 1928, reprint 1966), p. 95.

[2] Ibid. pp. 94, 402–3. This same purpose is evident in the very first sentence of his *Gesta Frederici*; F.-J. Schmale (ed.), *Ottonis Episcopi Frisingensis et Rahewini Gesta Frederici seu rectius Chronica* (Darmstadt, 1965), p. 114.

[3] Otto's tendency to find, where possible, 'natural' or 'historical' interpretations for Greek myths was noticed by Mierow in his introduction to *The Two Cities*, p. 56. Interestingly, the feast to which Otto paid the most marked attention in his historical writing was the feast of the Epiphany. L. Arbusow, *Liturgie und Geschichtsschreibung im Mittelalter* (Bonn, 1951), pp. 20–1.

[4] Weaver, for instance, sums up the work of John of Worcester; 'Where he deviates from his task as an annalist, it is that he may record an edifying vision or miracle, the last hours of a fellow monk or some remarkable natural phenomenon.' J. R. H. Weaver, ed. cit., p. 11. John's interest in comets, aerial phenomena, and the demonstration of the just judgement of God in history is very striking. He too, of course, knew of the contemporary interest in astrology and mentions that of Adelard of Bath; ibid. p. 53.

suggested that some kinds of medieval historical writing, especially the world chronicle, may have been undertaken less for themselves than as responses to a particular demand. This demand was generated in its turn by a particular kind of enquiry; enquiry legitimate, even desirable; but enquiry of a type which, if left to itself, could constitute a threat to the basis of Christian society. This type of enquiry I have defined as broadly magical and astrological. It gained especial currency in the first four decades of the twelfth century. In the form of a distinction between the 'natural' and the 'superstitious' it carried from the first some counterpoise within it; but at a time of increased interest, Christian society may, I have argued, be expected to feel the need of more constraints upon it. These constraints historical writing could, in certain forms, supply. Through the preoccupations of the early twelfth-century recensions of the *Imago Mundi*, and the involvement in them of its historical book, Book III, I have tried to suggest that in the twelfth century the world chronicle did supply these needs and was designed to do so. Here there is an irony. Though astrology was early encouraged by that same concern for the computus which fostered the beginnings of Christian history, the first made, with time, an enemy of the second. This irony the *Imago Mundi* encapsulates too.

In laying so much stress upon world history as a counterpoise, I do not mean to suggest that this was the only, or even, perhaps, the chief part that it had to play. I mean still less to imply that history was the most forceful opponent of astrology and magic the Christian world could devise. But as the disparity in object between the world chronicle and that determinism which denies a place to human choice is at all times so very striking, so too, at certain periods, is the concurrent appearance of the two so different types of interest. This concurrence deserves some thought. We may have, in the world chronicle, work of a far more complex order, and signs of threats to Christianity far more frightening, than we have previously suspected.

The chronicle of Romuald of Salerno

D. J. A. MATTHEW

I

THE chronicle of Romuald of Salerno is the first attempt made in Italy since antiquity to write a universal history. It is also the only one of several histories written in Norman Italy which puts the Normans into some kind of historical perspective. The Norman kings of Sicily appear there as the most recent of the great rulers of the world, the beginnings of whose lust after dominion is traced back to Ninus of Assyria, and forward to the year AD 1178. As far as we know, this was the only specific source of information about the whole human past, available in South Italy in the twelfth century.

The ascription of authorship to Romuald II, archbishop of Salerno (1153–81), a leading prelate of the Norman kingdom with political ambitions, has gratuitously enhanced its significance. There is contemporary evidence for Romuald as a physician, but not as historian. His authorship of the chronicle rests on an interpretation of one sentence near the end of the chronicle. Romuald, with Roger count of Andria, had represented the king of Sicily at the peace negotiations between Alexander III and Frederick I at Venice in 1177. After noting that they reported back to the king at Palermo in November, the chronicle then says:

Haec autem omnia quae praediximus ita gesta fuisse nulli dubitationis vel incredulitatis scrupulum moveant quia Romualdus secundus Salernitanus archiepiscopus qui vidit et interfuit scripsit haec et sciatis quia verum est testimonium ejus.[1]

---

[1] *Romualdi Salernitani Chronicon*, ed. C. A. Garufi (*Rerum Italicarum Scriptores*, t.vii, pt i (1909–35), pp. 293–4). Garufi's edition was criticized by C. Erdmann,

Haec omnia in this context certainly refers to the negotiations at which the archbishop was present. They may even be the concluding words of his written report, reproduced here by the compiler of the chronicle, since it would not be thought necessary to expunge such personal references when borrowing from sources. The words themselves, even as they stand, imply that what the archbishop had not seen or been present at he made no claims to speak of with authority, and might therefore be construed to *exclude* his authorship of the whole chronicle, though admittedly they could be used to stretch the period of validation to his own lifetime. Even giving these words their widest possible meaning would still leave open the question of who was responsible for the whole work, however, and granted that they cannot account for the three-quarters of the work about the history of the world before he was born, it seems more likely that they refer specifically to the Venice negotiations alone.

Hitherto there has been no discussion of the problems involved in considering the simple facts about this chronicle since the archbishop's authorship of the whole has not been doubted. On reflection, however, it is far from being self-evident that a diplomat, having written his report, should wish to write a universal history or even arrange for his report to be tacked on to such a work. Twelfth-century writers of contemporary history who thought it desirable to link their original compositions to earlier history were normally content to take over an existing chronicle for this purpose, as Robert of Torigny added to Sigebert of Gembloux's chronicle. For a chronicler to write a universal history from the beginning of the world simply because he had something to report of his own times would in itself be remarkable enough to rouse comment. Yet in this case it has been accepted as a matter of course.

Neues Archiv (1930), 48, pp. 510–12, no. 646, Garufi's rejoinder (p. xxxvii) was both pathetic and ineffectual. Painstaking and enthusiastic, he provided enough evidence to make critical study of the text possible, without himself realizing what was required for the kind of text he was editing. W. Arndt based his edition (*MGH, Scriptores*, xix, pp. 387–461, Berlin, 1866) on the Paris manuscript but his text is not complete.

Since the chronicle gives no overt information about its manner of composition, and no compiler, continuator, or final editor provided preface or dedication to explain his purpose or acknowledge his debts, only close analysis of the text can help to explain it. This immediately reveals that down to the early twelfth century most of its sources can be accounted for, though from 839 the text has independent value because some of them are now no longer extant separately. Only for the period 1126 to 1178 does the chronicle have real claim to be treated as an original composition, though even this part could have been compiled like the rest from other men's works, since until it reaches the Venice negotiations it gives no impression of being written from first-hand experience. The present study tries to account for the whole compilation: first by showing how the remote past was written about in twelfth-century Italy; second how the contemporary part of the history was composed.

There are three medieval manuscripts of the chronicle. The oldest and best is Vatican Latin 3973. Until the early seventeenth century, it was in Salerno cathedral, where it is assumed to have been for over four hundred years. It is a well-written fair copy, probably faithful to its exemplar, but on inspection turns out in places to be so muddled and inaccurate that it is impossible to believe in it as an author's or editor's final draft.[1] Both the other two manuscripts (Paris, BN MS Lat. 4933, thirteenth century, and Rome San Pietro E 22, fourteenth century)[2] show that the Vatican text was

[1] This manuscript is described by H. Hoffmann in his article 'Hugo Falcandus und Romuald von Salerno, *Deutsches Archiv*, 23 (1967), pp. 116–70. Hoffman believes in Romuald's authorship of the whole chronicle and ventures to characterize his original historical outlook. As he does not correctly identify all the chronicle's sources, he is, however, mistaken in thinking that Romuald was himself responsible for certain phrases, though it may of course still be significant that 'Romuald' uses certain words written by others. See n. 3, p. 245.

[2] These manuscripts both break off in 1177 but since they include material obviously added later it is assumed here that they represent a later version of the text. The manuscript tradition of the chronicle is rather more complicated than appears at first sight and reveals that there must have once been many copies of the text each in its own variant version.

later revised to include excerpts from several newly skimmed works, some pieces from Lupus Protospatarius, notices of events relating to south Italy and Antioch, especially for the years 1127–9, and a long highly improbable story about Roger II's eunuch Philip, who was condemned to the stake by the pious king for being a crypto-Muslim.[1] This is not corroborated elsewhere, and smacks more of the thirteenth than the twelfth century. These extracts, not originally part of the Vatican text, were, however, copied into its margins from San Pietro E 22, probably at the same time as one missing quire and one missing folded folio of the Vatican manuscript were made good from the same source. This was when the manuscript was brought to Rome and first studied in the early seventeenth century. These insertions have no twelfth-century authority, but for the rest the Vatican manuscript is taken as reliable evidence of the state of the chronicle's text in Salerno shortly after 1178, the last date given in it. The later manuscripts do prove, however, that revisions continued to be made to the chronicle after the Vatican manuscript was written. Since inspection of the Vatican manuscript rouses suspicion that its text too had been revised a number of times to allow for the incorporation of fresh extracts from other sources into a basic core, the process of accretion might have continued for

---

[1] The chronicle gives entries for the years 1070 and 1075 on Guiscard's capture of Bari, Palermo, and Salerno which come from the small Norman chronicle. Extra notices of the capture of these places under the years 1070 and 1076 interpolated from Lupus add only confusion. Similarly the chronicle records Guiscard's storming of Capua in July 1083 and then his campaign against rebellious Cannae in Apulia while an interpolated notice from Lupus under 1083 records the 'Lombard' invasion of Italy and Guiscard's siege of Cannae in May with its capture in July. The additions prove that the revisor was more interested in adding what looked like new material from a newly acquired source, than he was in trying to correct or reconcile discrepant evidence. See n. 1, p. 258. The interpolation of the episode of the eunuch Philip is fully discussed by Garufi, p. 234 n. 2, with references. The heretic-burning king is a thirteenth-century figure. This dramatic proof of Roger's orthodoxy is quite superfluous in a chronicle that never doubts his conventional piety. The story makes better sense if it is read as an example to impress later Sicilian kings like Frederick II or Manfred, whose orthodoxy was often doubted.

as long as a century. In these circumstances it is difficult to think of pinning down one author or final editor. The chronicle of Romuald of Salerno is a compilation with a complicated history of its own.

The manuscript begins, not with the chronicle, but with a good early copy of the *Mirabilia Urbis Romae*, a work composed in Rome *c.* 1140.[1] Immediately after the end of the *Mirabilia* at the foot of fo. 14ᵛ the scribe wrote the heading *De aetatibus* and in the same quire at the top of fo. 15ʳ began the chronicle with words lifted from Bede's *Chronica Minora*.[2] Bede's name does not appear in the text here, but since it was not uncommon for his chronicle to be copied anonymously under the title 'De aetatibus' the scribe presumably believed that the chronicle was as anonymous as the *Mirabilia*. Nor was it inappropriate to follow the first—a work on the marvels of the world city Rome, with the second—a history of the whole world, in which Rome figured prominently.[3]

Though the chronicle appears to begin as no more than a copy of

---

[1] *Codice Topografico delle Citta di Roma*, ed. R. Valentini and G. Zucchett (Fonti per la Storia d'Italia, iii, Rome, 1946), pp. 17–65.

[2] The division of the history of the world into Six Ages was made by Julianus Africanus in the early third century AD and its use in histories was made popular by Bede. The title *De aetatibus* was often used for Bede's *Chronica Minora*. Bede, *De sex aetatibus mundi*, ed. T. Mommsen (*MGH, Auctores Antiquissimi*, xiii). *Chronica Minora* (1898).

[3] It would be satisfactory to establish textual links between the *Mirabilia* and the chronicle that follows. The *Mirabilia*, chapter 11, gives the Orosian story that Octavian declined to be treated as a god, which is also found in thei chronicle; the note that the Emperor Phocas's grant of the temple of Cybele to Pope Boniface, in chapter 16, is referred to in different terms in the chronicle; the place where a fount of oil ran in the time of the Emperor Augustus, mentioned in chapter 31, is also found in the chronicle. They are not very convincing proof of links between the two works. A more positive link is the long passage in the chronicle on St. Peter's appointment of Clement as his successor which though based in part on Bonizo of Sutri is actually identical with the passage found in the papal chronicle of Benedetto of St. Peter's, Rome. This forms part of his Polyptic, a work composed *c.* 1140 for Guido di Castello, cardinal priest of St. Mark (later Pope Celestine II). This work also contained the *Mirabilia*. P. Fabre and L. Duchesne, *Le Liber Censum de l'église Romaine* (Paris, 1910), ii. p. 165. There is some slight evidence that the chronicle of Romuald went out of its way to notice cardinals of St. Mark. It is worth noticing that Alexander III himself had been cardinal there before 1159.

Bede's *Chronica Minora* it almost immediately tries to improve on the original by putting in extra numerical calculations, made by adding up the years of the patriarchs. The sums are not always correct, and are obviously not an improvement on Bede's text, but they show a symptomatic confidence that the editor believed he could do better than his sources. Bede continues to provide him with a framework for the chronicle down to the early eighth century (fo. 168vo): of the 600 odd chapters of Mommsen's edition he finds some use for 95 per cent. In due course, however, ever more extracts from other historians, the Bible, and Jerome's biblical commentaries are fitted into the text. For post-Christian history the chronicle draws on Orosius[1] and Paul the Deacon.[2] These are

[1] *Paulus Orosius: Historiarum Adversum Paganos*, ed. Zangemeister (Teubner, 1889).

[2] Eutropius, *Breviarium ab urbe condita cum versionibus graecis et Pauli Landolfique additamentis*, H. Droysen (ed.) (*MGH*, Berlin, 1879). The compiler used a text similar to that found in Vatican MS lat. 3339. There are only a few passages which could have been derived from Landulf's additions: seven groups of notables under various Roman emperors (33 names in all), some lines on Julius Caesar, and two sentences on the Emperor Hadrian. This information is, however, just as likely to have come from an interpolated copy of Paul's *Historia Romana* as directly from Landulf, whose work was not well known. Though Paul the Deacon is personally twice referred to in the chronicle, there is no acknowledgement that both the *Historia Romana* and the *Historia Langobardorum* (ed. G. Waitz and L. Bethmann, *MGH, Scriptores Rerum Langobardarum et Italicarum*, Hannover, 1878) had been pillaged. For the latter, a text resembling that of the twelfth-century manuscript from Benevento now in Parma (see ed. cit. p. 30) was probably used. Since Paul takes the history of the Lombards no further than King Liutprand, and the chronicle knows a little of the last four Lombard kings, such entries presumably came from a continuation of Paul, like that of Monte Cassino, and also from the *Liber Pontificalis*. Garufi believed that Romuald used the *Chronicon Salernitanum* (ed. V. Westerbergh, Stockholm, 1956). But the story given there (pp. 11–13) about Charlemagne's attempt to coax Paul away from his loyalty to the Lombard royal house is much more melodramatic than that in the chronicle and it is difficult to see why it should have been so bowdlerized had it been known. The few other resemblances between the two texts depend rather on their common resort to Paul and the Beneventan annals. The phrase 'astussimus et ferox', used in the *Chronicon Salernitanum* to describe King Aistolf, is found also in the small Norman chronicle, where it describes the Norman Count William, *Bras de Fer* (U. Schwarz, *Amalfi im Frühen Mittelalter*, Tübingen,

supplemented with information about the popes, taken from at
least three new sources—a papal catalogue,[1] Bonizo of Sutri,[2] and
the *Liber Pontificalis*—and about the Franks for whom the *Historia
Francorum* of Aimoin of Fleury and his continuator is used.[3] The
compiler often quotes these sources *in extenso*, but even paraphrased

1978). So it may have been a cliché. For these questions see also D. Bianchi,
'L'epitafio di Ilderico e la leggenda di Paolo Diacono', *Archivio storico lombardo*,
ser. 8, vol. 5 (1956), pp. 55–115.

[1] The chronicler used a papal catalogue similar to that found in a copy of
Anselm of Lucca's Decretals (Vatican MS lat. 6381) and printed by E. A.
Schelstrate, *Antiquitas Ecclesiae* (1692), i. pp. 644–50. There were other catalogues of this type available in southern Italy. The model came from Farfa,
see note 2, p. 247.

[2] Bonizo, bishop of Sutri (1078–82) and of Piacenza (1082–90), wrote
something about popes in his *Liber ad Amicum* (1085–6), ed. E. Dümmler,
Libelli de Lite I, 571–620 (Hannover, 1891), and a summary of papal history
in book iv of his *Liber de Vita Christiana* (c. 1090), ed. E. Perels (Berlin, 1930).
The compiler made slavish use of this text, correcting very few of its many
errors. When Bonizo's interest in the papacy trailed away the compiler was
forced back to the *Liber Pontificalis* (ed. L. Duchesne, Paris, 1886–1957). The
compiler used a text that went no further than 772. Most of the entries give
only the pope's nationality, paternity, length of reign, decrees, and place of
burial, and, from the seventh century, a brief eulogy of his Christian virtues.
More positive evidence of the use of the *Liber Pontificalis* comes in the accounts
of Silvester I and Leo I for their relations with the emperors; for pontificates
that began with disputes about elections: Liberius, Boniface I, Symmachus,
Boniface II, Conon, Sergius I; for popes who cleared themselves publicly of
false accusations—Damasus and Sistus III—and other cases illustrating papal
relations with the east: Simplicius, Felix III, Silverius, Boniface III, and
Boniface IV: all historical precedents still of interest in the twelfth century.

[3] Aimoinus of Fleury, *Libri Quinque de Gestis Francorum*, ed. J. Du Breul
(Paris, 1602). This edition, taken from BN, MS lat. 12711, is described by J. F.
Lemarignier, 'La Continuation d'Aimoin et le manuscrit latin 12711 de la
Bibliothèque nationale', in *BEC*, 113 (1955), pp. 25–36. See also K. F. Werner,
'Die literarischen Vorbilder des Aimoin von Fleury und die Entstehung seiner
Gesta Francorum', *Medium Aevum Vivum Festschrift für Walther Bulst* (Heidelberg,
1960), pp. 69–103. Aimoin's history was written at Fleury for Abbot Abbo
(d. 1004). The narrative reached no further than 654. In the mid-eleventh
century it was continued to c. 840 and later (1082/1103) further notes on
Frankish history down to 1015 were added at St. Germain des Prés, though
material from Sens was incorporated in it. This was the version used in this
compilation; a further continuation of Aimoin was made in mid-twelfth
century at St. Germain. The compiler however knows nothing of Frankish

they are usually easy to recognize and obscurities in the text may often be resolved by reference to them. Key words necessary for the sense have somehow fallen out of the copies; some words have been misread; some passages are too much abbreviated to make sense.[1] These sources make it impossible for the compilation to have been made before the very late eleventh century at the earliest.

The compiler continued to use the Frankish history and Bonizo on the popes for the years after 839 but, from that year, it is difficult to account for the bulk of the text by reference to its sources because by the ninth century the compiler's prevailing interest caused him

history after 1015 except the royal succession, which could have been taken from other sources. The Aimoin continuator made use of Paul the Deacon's Lombard History so on occasions it is difficult to know whether the compiler is using Paul directly or indirectly through Aimoin. He certainly used both together. When they differed, as over the death of the Emperor Phocas, he chose Aimoin's story. The importance of showing the chronicle's use of Aimoin may be indicated by reference to Hoffmann's interpretation of a parenthesis, relating to Pope Gregory I, which he supposed to be made by Romuald. It is in fact lifted from Aimoin, Hoffmann, p. 147. The notice on Gregory I is a complicated blend of Aimoin, Bonizo, Bede, and Paul. Apart from the way they are combined there is nothing original about it.

[1] On fo. 134[vo], when giving the divisions of Clovis's kingdom amongst his four sons, Metz is omitted as Thierry's portion, and Garufi does not seem to have understood the significance of this (p. 110). The word is found in Aimoin. Similarly on fo. 136vo, with less obscure results, the chronicler has omitted certain words from Aimoin to explain why King Guntram made an offering to the shrine of St. Marcel at Chalon-s-Saône (ed. cit. p. 112). Since he leaves out Bede's chapter 298 on the height of the Colossus, the sense of chapter 336 which he does include remains obscure (ed. cit. p. 61). He misreads Paul's 'facta pacem in annum unum magnam pecuniam' and writes on fo. 148 'facta pace vim magnam pecunie', p. 121, which is meaningless; he misreads the *Liber Pontificalis* on Stephen III and writes 'irrita' where 'iterata' is correct and meaningful (p. 149); likewise he misreads Aimoin on Leo III and has him on fo. 186 proceeding 'ad Laetaniam' instead of 'ad aedem b. Laurentii' (p. 154); worse still on fo. 197[vo] he says that King Lothair made peace with King Otto in 963 'consilio Ugonis ducis' (p. 166) where Aimoin says that this was done 'contra voluntatem Hugonis'. Little matter if the compiler confuses Otto I and Otto II. He also completely changes the sense of the eulogy of Count William in the small Norman chronicle by writing 'inconstans' for 'constans' (see Schwarz, p. 210). Excessive abbreviation appears to have induced error in his use of Bede on Falasar (fo. 33[vo], p. 19) and Sinerdes (fo. 44[vo], p. 27).

to focus on south Italian affairs and he used historical materials which have not always survived independently. To a considerable degree he was forced to rely on defective catalogues of rulers. For the papacy, at least, this meant some little improvement on Bonizo,[1] even if the catalogue available was one of those listing the imaginary Pope Donus II and two popes John XIV.[2] He also had some information about the imperial succession at Constantinople; however incomplete and inaccurate, this probably reflects a genuine revival of interest in the Greek empire once the Carolingian presence counted for nothing in south Italy.[3] Spasmodic details about the Frankish kings involve astonishing errors; about the Germans

[1] Bonizo jumps from Zacharias (d. 752) to Hadrian I (772–95) and has no popes at all from Formosus (891–6) to John XV (985–96). The chronicler supplies the missing names and unlike Bonizo even manages to distinguish Boniface III (607) from Boniface IV (608–15).

[2] The Casino catalogue was printed by O. Holder-Egger in *Neues Archiv*, xxvi (1901) pp. 548–55. It is dependent on La Cava catalogue (printed by J. Vignoli, *Liber Pontificalis*, Rome, 1724, Catalogue II), which was shown by I. Giorgi to be in fact part of a Farfa manuscript of the Liber Pontificalis. I. Giorgi, 'Appunti intorni ad alcuni manoscritti del liber Pontificalis', *Archivio della Società romana di storia patria*, xx (1897), pp. 266–73. He describes the manuscript (Vatican lat. 3764) and remarks on the decoration of the initial of St. Jerome's letter to Pope Damasus at the beginning. Such a decoration might have encouraged reference to the lives as Jerome's work. The *Chronicon Volturnense* (ed. V. Federici, Fonti per la Storia d'Italia, i, Rome, 1925), pp. 70–100, also has a catalogue of popes. The compilation makes a number of mistakes about the lengths of papal reigns, but some of these mistakes could have been taken over from the papal catalogues; it is not clear why their dates were preferred to those of the *Liber Pontificalis* itself, if the latter were used at all; anyway, the version of the *Liber Pontificalis* available was very defective. P. Fedele, 'Richerche per la storia di Roma e del papato nel secolo x', *Archivio della Società romana di storia patria*, xxxiii (1910), pp. 227–9.

[3] After mentioning Leo III (717–41) the chronicle names no emperors until Constantine VI (780–97); and again omits those between Leo V (813–20) and Michael III (842–67). There are other inaccuracies for the rulers of the Macedonian dynasty like dividing Constantine VII (913–59) into two and assigning the first a reign of six years, and the second a reign from 939. Romanus II (959–63) is called 'Basil' and Basil II and Constantine VIII are described as sons of John Tzimisces. The double entry on Alexius Comnenus whose death occurs twice, in 1108 and in 1118, must be explained as a result of clumsy revision.

his information is if anything worse.[1] But even for southern Italy the chronicle is not notably accurate. There is no precise date for the setting up of the independent principality of Salerno—which is said to have occurred *tempore* Pope Sergius II (844–7). Of the princes there he gives only a few names and a few unconvincing dates.[2] Though he records the translation of the body of St. Matthew from Paestum to Salerno in 954, he says nothing about the consequent elevation of the see to an archbishopric (probably in 983), though a similar privilege for Capua is recorded. He becomes a little more informative after Guiscard's capture of Salerno in 1076, and notices the foundation of the Norman cathedral, but names no archbishop until 1137 and of the city makes only the banal remark that it was 'civitatem medicinae utique artis diu famosam atque praecipuam'.

Apart from the various catalogues of rulers at his disposal, the compiler probably had a set, or sets, of local annals containing entries

---

[1] He invents children for Charlemagne by Desiderius's daughter. He writes Burgundy instead of Bavaria as the portion of Louis the German. He muddles Louis son of Carloman with Louis son of Charles the Bald; Charles the Fat is confused with Charles the Simple. Louis IV is dead by 922 and his son Lothair reigns from 922 to 976. He thinks Otto I (?) was made king at the instance of Duke Hugh the Great, that he was emperor from 963 to 981, that Otto II reigned only two years (981–3). Other, later errors he took from Bonizo.

[2] Neglect of Salerno means that there is no mention of any legendary foundation. It is also odd that those who granted it privileges like Henry II (1022) and the popes Sergius IV, Clement II, Leo IX, Stephen IX, Gregory VII, Urban II, and Paschal II (not to mention Anacletus II) were not treated more graciously. The first pope to grant privileges to the cathedral according to this chronicle was Alexander III. As it is known that Romuald II was responsible for securing confirmations of early privileges from the local princes, Gisulf I (933–77) and Gisulf II (1053–76) in 1171 and 1178 (L. Pennachini, *Pergamene Salernitane*, Salerno, 1941, and A. Balducci *Rassegna Storica Salernitana*, anno XII, 1951), it is odd, if this part were written at Salerno, that neither prince is treated in the chronicle as a benefactor of Salerno. The only rulers of the principality of Salerno named are Sichenulf, Guaimar, Gisulf I, Giovanni II, Guaimar IV, and Gisulf II. The dates are very shaky and Guaimar I is combined with Guaimar II and Giovanni II with Guaimar III.

about the tenth-century invasions chiefly of places in Apulia by Muslims, Slavs, and Hungarians, some scattered information about Benevento (987, 1001, 1088, 1102, 1115),[1] and some fairly densely recorded information about earthquakes, volcanic eruptions, famines, eclipses, comets, and stars. Earlier notices about such events derived from his authorities prove that this was no new interest; its greater prominence at this stage is only due to the sparseness of other material. It suggests that the records used had given even more attention to the history of natural calamities than to human affairs. Only for the eleventh century, recounting Norman exploits, did he have access to an identifiable source of some interest—the so-called small Norman chronicle.[2] This is for the most part used *in extenso*, for the compiler has little to interpolate, but he is capable here, as elsewhere, of breaking off in mid-chapter to switch to another source, or to make interpolations of his own. (There are no signs that he had read any of the *gestae Normannorum* valued by modern historians.)

There are two notable features of the section of the chronicle for the years 839–1126. Formally, it is arranged on a strictly annalistic basis; in subject matter, there is an obvious concentration of interest on south Italy. Both points deserve further elaboration.

[1] See O. Bertolini, 'Gli Annales Beneventani', in *Bolletino dell'Istituto Storico Italiano per il Medio-evo*, 42 (1923).

[2] U. Schwarz, ed. Chronicon Amalfitanum in *Amalfi im Frühen Mittelalter* (Tübingen, 1978). Chapters 23–41 (pp. 204–21) are an interpolation, probably a verbatim copy of the small Norman chronicle for the years 999–1081 (*sic*). H. Hoffmann, in *Quellen und Forschungen aus Italien, Arch. und Bibl.* 49 (1969) pp. 95–144, argues for a date *c.* 1100 for this Norman chronicle. Schwartz himself prefers a date after 1139 on the grounds that the history of the Norman princes of Capua, written *c.* 1139 and given in the Amalfi chronicle chapter 29, was an integral part of the Norman chronicle. His arguments for this are not convincing. 'Romuald' knows nothing of the battle at Aquino between Prince Richard and Duke Godfrey, and on Schwarz's own argument this ought to mean that the passage was not originally in the small Norman chronicle. It is notable that in the passage on the sons of Tancred of Hauteville, reference is made to William of S. Nicandro's son, Robert count of the Principality (d. 1099), but not to any sons of Count Roger of Sicily—which would be a strange omission for a text written in or after the time of Roger II. A date *c.* 1100 seems much more likely for this work.

Given the nature of the sources for this part, the compiler may have been naturally led to rearrange his material on a strictly chronological basis, but from the threshold of the eleventh century it looks as though a special effort was made to marshal the materials by numbers so that down to 1127 the record advances year by year, leaving almost no year unaccounted for. What is more, the date references were reinforced by correctly giving the years of the Byzantine indiction (where the new year began in September). The small Norman chronicle, which supplied many dates, does not give them in the same methodical way, so the emphasis on dates is at this point due to the compiler. His intentions are the more remarkable because in his exemplar of the Norman chronicle the dates had not always been fully written out. Far from being daunted by this, he simply left the dates incomplete and they were not always correctly filled in later.[1]

The second point relates to the prominence of south Italy. This surely indicates the place of the compilation's origin. It seems sensible therefore to wonder whether the compiler had not consistently tried where possible to give details of local interest, even if the earlier sources at his disposal had not helped much. Perhaps the earlier mention of Pacuvius, tragedian of Brindisi, Ennius, poet of Taranto, Pythagoras, philosopher of Crotone, amongst the ancient worthies listed by his sources were reproduced in the chronicle for reasons of local interest. It certainly seems likely that the Bedan order of the different *patriae* of Latin speakers was deliberately rearranged to name Apulia first and include the Samnites Bede had forgotten.

[1] Schwarz (p. 139 n. 119) shows that the incomplete dates of the Vatican manuscript discussed by Hoffmann (in article cited in n. 1, p. 241) have parallels in Vatican MS Ottoboniano lat. 2940 fos 16ʳ–18ᵛᵒ. Though this is of the fourteenth century, it gives a text of the 'Romuald' chronicle for 976–1070 which must from its form be taken from a manuscript older than the Vat. MS latin 3973. Gaps in the dates of such an early text suggest that they were left incomplete in the small Norman chronicle itself and this may explain why from 1062 it becomes an almost invariable rule that the date was written in the Vat. MS lat. 3973 in two separate stages: the original source of the information did not give the full date. Hoffman explains this differently and argues from this evidence that the manuscript was written in Romuald's lifetime.

More specifically still the compiler must have added Ecana (=Troia) and Ortona (=Ordona) to the list of places invaded by the Lombards according to Paul the Deacon. Who would do this without having a connection with one or other of those towns?

In the matter of the saints mentioned, there are also helpful clues. Saint Barbato of Benevento may have been known from the available manuscript of Paul the Deacon. In the case of St. Nicholas of Myra, his popularity in twelfth-century Apulia may suffice. The reference to the (legendary) martyrdom of the prophet Isaiah could have been prompted by his cult at Brindisi. But again it is Troia that attracts attention; there are as many as five saints specifically mentioned in connection with that episcopal city: Bishop Eleutherius, whose martyrdom under Hadrian is the earliest recorded for a saint of only local importance; Bishop Mark, martyred under Diocletian, Bishop Secundinus, Pope Pontianus and Anastasius confessor, whose bodies together with that of Eleutherius were translated to Troia in 1105.[1]

The importance of the Troia saints gives additional significance to the other notices of the place, which figures more prominently than any other of southern Italy in the eleventh-century annals. A few notices occur even in the early part of the chronicle, but they are particularly notable from 1018, when it is said to have been re-founded on the orders of the Greek emperors.[2] It is last mentioned

---

[1] The 'Romuald' chronicle gives the translation under the year 1106; the Troia chronicle says specifically July 1105. *Chronica Trojani fragmentum*, ed. A. A. Pellicia, *Raccolta di varie croniche* (Naples, 1782), v. 129–40. Pope Pontianus (230–5) was martyred in Sardinia and his body restored to Rome by one of his successors, Anterus or Fabian; Anastasius confessor may have been identified by the chronicler with *Anastasius Persa monachus* on whom he quoted Bede's account, including the burial of his relics in a Roman monastery. The chronicler states that the bodies were brought to Troia from Rome though the account of the translation printed by A. Poncelet ('La Translation des SS Eleuthère, Pontien et Anastase', *AABB*, 1910, Vol. 29, 409–26) claims that the bodies were moved from Tivera in the diocese of Velletri (the bishop of Velletri is twice mentioned in the chronicle). See also P. Franchi de' Cavalieri, 'Il testo originale della legenda di S. Eleuterio', *Studi e testi*, vi (Rome, 1901), pp. 137–46.

[2] In the chronicle this is given under the year 1013. No explanation for the

in 1140 when King Roger received its submission. Some of these notices are found in the small Norman chronicle, but not all. They did not come from the Troia chronicle as it has come down to us. That chronicle at least indicates the existence of an historical interest in that city in the twelfth century. This might have been stimulated by the several bishops of foreign extraction amongst whom are listed Normans and other Frenchmen, as well as Gerard of Piacenza (Bonizo of Sutri's see). The translation of the bodies of the saints in 1105 inspired the writing of an account that has survived separately and we know that about the same time, in Durham, the translation of St. Cuthbert had implications for the writing of history. The revival of the ancient town of Troia; its claim to have initiated good relations with Guiscard well before his occupation of Salerno; the special links which were established with the papacy and which led to the separation of the see from the province of Benevento;[1] all these could have prompted an interest at Troia in history. Had suitable annals been written in Troia it would not be remarkable if a later writer from another place had used them to eke out his narrative. But a chronicler who deliberately inserted into the Bedan account of Hadrian the notice about Eleutherius's martyrdom could only have done so out of special devotion to that saint. And the most likely place for him to do so would be in Troia itself, probably at a time when the translation of 1105 was still fresh in men's minds. Since Troia is barely mentioned again in the chronicle and Salerno became the place most frequently mentioned in it from the 1120s, there is little doubt that whatever claims may be made for a Troian

---

name Troia is given. Is it possible that this name inspired at least some special interest in Troy, in Homer, and in Dares, the fabulous historian of Troy? Even before the Trojan war the chronicle records that Troy was outstanding for its chariots in the days of Trous its first ruler—a statement not derived from any well-known source (fo. 26vo, p. 13), so there were other versions of early Trojan history available in Norman Italy than what we have.

[1] The annals for 1061 and 1071 stress Guiscard's relations with the city; those for 1093, 1106, 1120 the interest of the papacy.

origin, they can only apply to the historical, and not to the contemporary, part of it. Is this sufficient justification for dividing the chronicle into two? There seem to be five supporting arguments.

(i) The final section of the work differs from the preceding part in that the sustained effort at annalistic presentation is abandoned. After the death of Honorius II in 1130, no date at all is recorded till 1143; thereafter, with a couple of exceptions, the only dates given are those of the death of princes and popes.[1] It is difficult to believe that the same mind was responsible for organizing the materials of both parts.

(ii) The chronicle's interest from this time forward in the affairs of Salerno and the kings of Sicily (in particular their relations with the Roman church) makes it strange that so little attention is given in the earlier part, either to Salerno or to Sicily. Opportunities to stress the importance of the princes of Salerno to the Norman successes of the eleventh century are passed over. The chronicle is interested in the kings of Sicily as successors to the dukes of Apulia, and not to their Sicilian inheritance as such. If this fits the interests of Salerno, it is none the less clear that the earlier part is focused more on Apulia proper than on the Campagna. For example, though Duke Roger Borsa is described as being in the west at the sieges of Capua (1097) and Benevento (1102) and as a benefactor of Salerno cathedral, his activities in the east involve smaller places like Canosa, Monte Sant'Angelo, and Lucera, which is understandable if the record of his movements was derived from an Apulian source.

(iii) The sources used in the early part of the work, particularly the extensive use of Bonizo of Sutri, and the second, but not the third, Aimoin continuation strongly suggest scholarship of the early

---

[1] Between 1062 and 1126 (64 years) there are 44 dates given in the chronicle; between 1126 and 1178 (52 years) there are only 16. Of these 16, seven are dates of the deaths of popes and two kings of Sicily. Even so the scribe hesitated about 6 of these 16 dates and wrote two of them incorrectly. The chronicle could still get events in the wrong order—giving Roger II's settlement with Innocent II (1139) as completed before the deaths of Lothair and Louis VI (1137).

rather than the late twelfth century. Could a compiler in the Salerno of Alexander III's time have had such meagre sources of information about the popes as this chronicle implies? Would no better source of Frankish history be found, than an old-fashioned edition of Aimoin? Would a Salernitan historian have owed so little to the learning of Monte Cassino? A compilation based on the few sources shown here to have provided the bulk of the early part is more easily understood if it were made at an earlier period, in a more provincial centre.

(iv) Though no sharp division between the historical and the contemporary parts can be shown, this is because the continuator's purpose obliged him to revise, and probably, to complete, the notices relating to Duke William of Apulia, Roger II's cousin and predecessor as ruler of Salerno. The chronicle takes great pains to stress that Roger's succession was approved and prepared by William. William's frequent and punctilious performance of homage to successive popes (1115, 1118, 1120, 1125) is emphasized in a chronicle that goes on to show how eager Roger II and his successors were to do likewise. The continuator may have based his case for Roger on the precedents for William he found in the Troian part, but it is more likely that he presumed to 'improve' the precedents. The words of the papal grants to William appear for example to be given verbatim, as though documents were quoted; these words indicate that the history of this ceremony went back to 1080.[1]

---

[1] He takes from others his interest in investiture *per vexillum*. His notice on Leo III and Charlemagne (fo. 185ᵛ, p. 154), comes from Aimoin. Bonizo (*Liber ad Amicum*, ed. cit. p. 583) refers to Conrad II asking the pope for a *vexillum*, by which is meant authority to act on the pope's behalf. The chronicle, to show how the pope made Otto I emperor, says that Otto received 'totius Italiae vexillum' at his coronation, and swore to keep faith with the Roman church. The treaty of Melfi in 1059 is not mentioned in the chronicle. According to the chronicle Robert Guiscard began his career at the invitation of the citizens of Troia, took Reggio di Calabria, and became duke of all the Normans. He was then recognized by Nicholas II, became his liegeman, swore fealty, and was invested 'per vexillum de honore ducatus sui'. The small Norman chronicle which was used in the chronicle is much less explicit than this though the words 'per vexillum' certainly appear in it.

However, the chronicle gives precedents earlier still, for Guiscard is said to have become the liegeman of Nicholas II in 1061 and of Alexander II in 1062. This information may in substance come from the small Norman chronicle, but its text was amended to include the words 'ligius' and 'de honore ducatus sui'. These discrepancies about the record for these important ceremonies raise the problem as to when the amendments were made: was it before, or after, they were added to this chronicle? Since there are good grounds for thinking that the homage entries for William were made with Roger II's reign in mind, it seems likely that the precedents of 1061, 1062, 1080, and 1090 may have been 'improved' for the same purpose, though probably on two separate occasions. At all events, it is only in the light of the dutiful obedience of William to the popes and of the willingness of the popes to take his homage, that the chronicle's later views about Roger II's rights become intelligible. If the continuator wished to get the relevant record of the earlier years in the chronicle correct it would explain why he could not simply draw a line at the end of the previous work and start a new page.

(v) Finally, it is at this stage useful to recall that the thirteenth-century manuscript now in Paris (but not the San Pietro manuscript it otherwise resembles) bears a note in the middle of the entry for the year 1125 (or, to be more precise, between its report of Honorius II investing Duke William with his duchy and its account of Duke William's mildness to his barons) 'Ab hoc loco adjunctum est huic chronice per Romoaldum/secundum Salernatanum archiepisco-pum'.[1] This sentence forms part of the text, but has been underlined in red, possibly by the original rubricator, and seems to be the oldest authority for claiming the archbishop as (part-) author of the whole

---

[1] BN, MS lat. 4933 fo. 153 recto and verso. Dr Maurice Keen kindly checked this reading for me. From this point in the text there are two notable changes in style, first the narrative becomes more dense, and second the frequency of giving dates declines. Since the passage on Duke William goes straight on from this point to discuss the preparation for Roger's succession and William's death it was probably composed, like the rest of this part, much later.

chronicle. Since in its present position it breaks into the sense, it was probably copied into the text from a marginal entry in the exemplar. The authority of such a marginal annotation is not great. It is not corroborated by either of the other manuscripts. Its precision does not even inspire confidence. But it at least shows that as early as the thirteenth century there was a tradition that Romuald composed the latter part of the chronicle. For all we know that tradition arose from the appearance of the Paris manuscript's exemplar. The comment may represent a reader's inference from the words that occur after the Venice negotiations; it could be a note by someone who actually knew. Quite apart from its value as the oldest comment we have about the authorship of the chronicle, it strengthens the argument for believing that the chronicle is composed of a historical and a contemporary part.

Concluding therefore that the historical part was composed at Troia *c.* 1126, it remains to consider what explanation for it can be offered. A writer who proceeds with as much insouciant determination as shown here must be credited with some idea of what he was trying to do, even if he had not much natural talent for historical scholarship. His work provided a summary of information about the rulers of the world from the beginning, about the prophets, priests, and men of culture in their respective times, and some account of the vicissitudes of the relationship between the Roman church and the secular power. He takes a sympathetic view of the Roman church's claims to independence, but does not conceal the real power of the secular authorities and their value for churchmen.[1] He has several marvellous stories and some consistent attention to

---

[1] The chronicle demonstrates that popes cleared themselves on oath and were not judged by others (Marcellinus, Damasus, Sistus III); yet it also shows Boniface III getting from Phocas a ruling on Rome's superiority to Constantinople. It shows emperors authorizing church councils (Nicaea, Chalcedon), suppressing schismatic bishops at the behest of Pope Pelagius I, normally consenting in early times to papal elections (Silverius, Gregory I, Pelagius II, Conon), and even settling election disputes (Boniface I, Symmachus). Justinian II did honour to Pope Constantine. All these were important precedents still worth quoting in the twelfth century.

celestial phenomena, earthquakes, famines, and the like, set down, apparently, as implicit comment on human history. He preserves stories of saints from his sources and goes out of his way to include others they did not. On the whole, however, the tone of the chronicle is not particularly clerical or pietistic and it seems more likely that the compiler had a secular readership in mind. He notes the inventors of prisons and tortures as well as those of astrology, the harp (Apollo), the lyre (Mercury);[1] he seems to give special attention to the original law-givers of the past, Cadmus, Foroneus, Numa, Justinian, and the Lombard kings.[2] Some of this information comes from his standard sources, but since some does not, he was prepared to go out of his way to find it.

This chronicle had not much to commend it to a clerical readership; it had no literary graces, was laboured in composition, and imperfectly executed. It was all the same an impressive achievement to excerpt from various sources a résumé of the history of the world that would include the Normans of south Italy. It belongs to the Lombard-Frankish world and reflects its concern for relations with the papacy. In the context of the early twelfth century, it was understandable that a chronicle giving all the proper precedents would have value, for against the theoretical claims of churchmen, secular rulers and their advisors could only answer by quoting history. Duke William, who was married in 1115, was a suitable recipient for this work, since the young duke, unlike his father, had succeeded to the title too young to have learnt much already from parental experience or instruction. For him, or his expected heir, such a

---

[1] Similar entries are found in Ado of Vienne's *De aetatibus*, a source which could have even suggested dates for this fabulous material, though the stories themselves, as familiar fictions, do not need to be traced to a source (see G. H. Bode, *Scriptores Rerum Mythicarum Latini tres Romae nuper reperti*, Celle, 1834, for the story of Hercules (i. pp. 21, 58); Mercury (p. 89); Apollo (90); giants (p. 92); Sibylla (p. 105). Paul names Tarquin Superbus as the inventor of tortures.

[2] Foroneus appears to be an afterthought since he is mentioned after his son. The interest in royal (and papal) law-making is continuous and noteworthy. Even King Ratchis, is noted for his additions to the laws of the Lombards.

chronicle as this would have been a means to political education. Although this is mere speculation, it shows that it is not impossible to explain the origins of the work in plausible terms. Assuming therefore some such purpose, it is convenient now to consider the manner of composing the historical or 'Troian' part, before taking the contemporary or 'Salernitan' part into account.

2

The historical part of the chronicle was compiled by excerpting from a few, fairly obvious sources of information. It is reasonable to suppose that the compiler did his best to organize the extracts in chronological order and hard to see why the same scholar would deliberately duplicate material, which could only confuse the dating of events or muddle the record. Yet the text does precisely this. Though it is easy to understand that the original compiler would wish to include as much information about the past as he could cull from his sources, and to fill gaps in his information, how are we to explain why the same man should record no less than three different dates for Homer (from Orosius, Isidore, and Paul the Deacon) varying from about the year 2790 to the year 3064 since Creation by Bede's reckoning? While it is just possible that he overlooked the fact that he had already given Homer's dates from Orosius and subsequently copied out Paul's notice inadvertently, the careful insertion of the date from Isidore must surely be the work of a later editor, or a marginal correction gathered into the text by a plodding scribe. A similar example is the double notice of St. Anthony of the desert who appears first before AD 252, where the chronicle's source is not clear, and second in a precise notice of his death aged 105 before 363 taken from Bede.[1]

---

[1] Persons mentioned twice include Demosthenes, Pantenus, and St. Severinus. The doubling for Paul the Deacon (fos 176, 182vo, pp. 145, 151) and Silvester II (fos 198^r and 198^v, 200vo, pp. 170, 172) show that two different sources were drawn upon, probably at different times, and not even brought into the text at the same point (unlike the double entries on the Caesars discussed below). Cf. n. 1, p. 242.

The impression that the text was revised by the incorporation of fresh material is accentuated by another curious feature of the text, namely the attribution (but only between folios 22^v and 112^v) of certain passages to his 'authorities': Orosius, Jerome, and Bede. Admittedly the compiler appears to be somewhat generous in admitting his debts, but since he is also capable of taking some names, like those of Josephus and Eusebius, from his sources (as though he recognized the advantages of scattering references as freely and as painlessly as possible) they cannot be regarded as proofs of real scholarship. In general allusions to the sources are brief and unparticular; not footnotes to specific extracts. What explanations may be offered for the cases of Orosius, Jerome, and Bede? They each raise different problems and need to be considered in turn.

The case of Jerome seems to be the most straightforward. He is cited more than twenty times, chiefly from his commentary on Daniel. Extracts, mostly of between 100–300 words apiece, provide supplementary information relating to the history of the Jewish and neighbouring kingdoms and must have been inserted into the narrative at a late stage, since the information is never combined with the Bedan-Orosian-Pauline agglomeration, may duplicate material in it and is often inserted slightly out of its proper place. If the Troian compiler himself was responsible for deciding to add these words from Jerome, it must have been after the basic task of assembling his text had been done. But they need not be the work of the original compiler at all.

There is also another difficulty about the use of Jerome's name in the text. Three passages relating to papal history are labelled as being from Jerome; they are in fact from the late eleventh-century work of Bonizo on the popes. Based in (small) measure on the *Liber Pontificalis*, Bonizo's work might just have been mistaken for that source and there are at least thirteenth-century comments showing that the earliest papal lives were attributed to Jerome himself.[1] Other

---

[1] O. Bertolini, 'Il Liber Pontificalis' in *La Storiografia Altomedievale* (Settimane di studio, xvii (1), 1970, Spoleto), pp. 387–455, especially p. 398 n. 55 and p. 400 n. 68.

notices about the popes in the chronicle are never ascribed to Jerome however, so that only an ignorant and inconsistent reader could have provided such original marginal comments. And such a reader was not necessarily also responsible for the correct labelling of passages relating to the Old Testament. The simple case of Jerome is sufficient to show that attributions of authorship are not all correct, that some appear to derive from attempts to indicate an interpolation, and that no one person, compiler, or reader is likely to have been responsible for all of them.

The case of Orosius also raises difficulties. He is first introduced when the compiler turns aside from merely depending on Bede, to take a new author as his guide, and admits it rather conscientiously for many folios. After a time, however, this use of Orosius becomes habitual and the chronicle becomes so intricately woven out of Bede, Orosius, and Paul's Roman history that the practice of giving references is abandoned. Orosius nevertheless continues to provide information and words for long after this, so despite the number of times he is cited openly(31), the acknowledgement is far from being exhaustive. Some seven of these occasions are to indicate a mere matter of date, sometimes when authorities differ. One of these citations turns out to be a whole phrase from Paul's *Historia Romana*. The possible confusion between Orosius and Paul is shown again when, quoting from Paul, Orosius is claimed as the source. Other Orosian passages may have a few elements from him, but be substantially composed of extracts from Bede and Paul together. Some Orosian passages are so short that the footnote appears excessively conscientious; some are only summaries of biblical information. A few longer passages are in fact made up from several different sentences from Orosius, not consecutive in his text, but strung together by the compiler. The fullest passages claimed as Orosian concern the great generals, Alexander the Great and his uncle, and the six Caesars: Julius, Augustus, Tiberius, Claudius, Caligula, and Nero.

The chronicler's motive for indicating on occasion that Orosius was his source is obscure. The simplest explanation is that a later annotator provided most of them as marginal comment. However, it is also possible that the longer Orosian extracts were slipped into the text at a later stage, either by the Troian compiler, or by someone else, and that they were then deliberately labelled because of this. Take as an instance, the passages on Tiberius and Caligula. Bede provides the chronological framework. Christ's crucifixion is dated to Tiberius's 18th year; there follows the stoning of Stephen and the despatch of Herod Agrippa to Rome in chains: *Hactenus Beda*. Then indicating a change to Orosius it begins, under the *17th* year of Tiberius when Christ was crucified, to tell how Pilate's report of the great earthquake at the time of the crucifixion was received in Rome and how Tiberius tried to persuade the Senate to recognize Christ as God. No attempt is made to conflate the two accounts or to provide a single date for them. When the long passage from Orosius comes to an end, the text immediately reverts without warning to the *Historia Romana* and to Bede for the account of Caligula. After copying without acknowledgement from them, it once again turns to Orosius, gives an Orosian date A.U.C. and some new stories and then, partly summarizing, duplicates Orosius's story of Pilate's suicide and Caligula's incest which had already been given in their Pauline and Bedan form. There is nothing surprising about the duplication, since Bede used Orosius and Orosius used Eutropius—Paul's source. But it seems unlikely that the same compiler would carefully extract his material from two common sources, put it together, and then himself deliberately go back to a third source and repeat the same stories—even if *en passant* he added a few more details as well. This is more plausibly explained as the work of a later revisor.

This brings us finally to the case of Bede. The compiler had begun to use him without acknowledging Bede's authorship of his basic source, so that when Bede is later specifically mentioned some ten times between folios 64^v and 112^v he looks like a strange new authority, introduced for the first time. In one case Bede's name is so misplaced as to appear immediately before an extract from the Roman history, a mistake again best explained as due to a scribe incorporating a marginal note from the exemplar into his text at the wrong point. In three cases however Bede is specially mentioned because his date differs from that of other authorities: his testimony is thus contrasted with theirs. This possibly explains why other passages are marked as Bedan. If some of the Orosian passages were introduced after the main text had been prepared, the compiler or a later reader then indicated what parts of the work depended on which sources.

There is therefore reason to believe that the Vatican manuscript represents a text that had been several times revised. The original text of the chronicle may have been simply composed by weaving together strands taken from a few authors but without acknowledgement. The text thus assembled was then in various places summarily improved, as likely as not by an editor. The most elaborate instance of such a revision is the way the Lombards and Franks are introduced together into a narrative that had been mainly dependent on Bede, Paul's Roman history, and papal material. Paul combines in one chapter the death of Theodoric (525) and the change of emperor at Constantinople (527); the compiler chooses to separate them with matter of his own. There are, first, two sentences on the death of Pope Felix IV (526–30) and one on St. Benedict and then, between the names of Justin and Justinian, summaries of early Lombard and Frankish history. This long aside involves a return to the fourth century and extends to include the story of the vision of King Guthrum (who died in 593). It is so shapeless chronologically that a few asides have been included (from marginal notes?) to date episodes in it by reference to saints and popes. It then reverts to the succession of Boniface II (530–2) and John II Mercurius (533–5) before taking up the last sentence of Paul's chapter which brings him to Justinian. Considering what is to come, it was certainly necessary to prepare for the entry of both the Lombards and the Franks, but it cannot be claimed that the task has been well done. The most likely explanation is that a folded folio of new material roughly inserted in a manuscript perhaps intended for use in revising the text was incorporated into the narrative by another scribe without paying proper attention to finding the right place for it.

The 'original' compiler must however himself certainly be held responsible for some errors. Take as an example his text for the second half of the seventh century where he combines passages from Paul's Lombard history, the papal sources, and Aimoin, clearly aiming to keep them all going contemporaneously as far as possible. After giving the death of the Roman Emperor Constans II (668) he names the papal succession—Vitalian (657–72), and Agatho (678–81)—then that of the Lombard kings—Grimoald (661–71) and Perctarit (672–89)—before going back to retrieve King Dagobert whose death in 639 interested him for the marvellous story of how his soul was rescued by his patron saints over Vulcano island (off Sicily).[1] His manner of work is in a way systematic, but chronologically confusing, so that it is not surprising, if when he reverts to the story of the Roman emperors, he blunders, stupidly writing 658 instead of 668 for the accession of Constantine IV. Leaving aside Bede's useful reminder that Constantine reigned seventeen years, he goes straight on to copy out Bede's entry on a Saracen invasion of Sicily after the death of Constans (668) but ascribes it instead to Constantine's 17th year (685). This is not merely a consequence of using Bede carelessly; it owes something also to a hasty glance at Paul's entry for 685 noting a Saracen raid on Carthage (not Sicily).

Mere carelessness cannot explain the compilation's characteristics, for the compiler's own manner of treating the sources created difficulties. He might, for example, change the sequence of events in his sources, as when copying Paul's story on the hoard of coins found by Tiberius II, he decided to insert at that point the description of the imperial coins given to Frankish envoys at Constantinople, which in Paul came in the following chapter. His motive for bringing together these two passages on the imperial coins is plain enough. Unfortunately, by breaking up Paul's narrative he makes it seem, when he returns to Tiberius's victory over the Persians, as though

---

[1] The eruption of this island in the second century BC is recorded in Paul's *Historia Romana* and in the chronicle (fo. 56ᵛᵒ, p. 37).

the expedition was one by King Chilpert. Some of his rearrangements have no possible justification. Paul tells a story of how Charles Martel made a pact with King Liutprand to get Lombard help against the Muslims (which is also found in Aimoin) but in this compilation the sequence is broken and the pact is weakly explained as Charles's means of being in a position to beg Liutprand not to cause trouble for the Roman church. These examples also serve to show that though the chronicler uses other men's words, he makes them serve purposes of his own.[1]

This indifference to proper historical sequence also affects the relationship between cause and effect. Dependent on Bede as his main historical guide, he can quote Bedan chapters in a non-Bedan order, so that chronologically they are misplaced. He cares far more for the little nuggets of fact than in getting them into the right order. If this attitude was common in twelfth-century south Italy it would explain how easily marginalia could have been added without sufficiently clear indications of their proper place in the text; the compiler's manner of interrupting his sources to insert extraneous material reveals the same insensitivity. Where Orosius follows his account of Arianism with the horrible earthquake which was the divine sign of disapproval, the compiler separates them by extracts from Bede and the account of popes Liberius and Felix, so that the earthquake becomes a commentary on Felix's martyrdom. The account of Alaric's sack of Rome in 410 oscillates between Orosius and Paul's *Historia Romana* (itself making use of Orosius), and fastens attention on Pope Innocent in safety at Ravenna, so that when Bedan material is then introduced the pope appears to dedicate the church of SS Protasius and Gervase in Ravenna rather than in Rome.

Carelessness is thus not the only explanation for the compiler's peculiarities; more to blame is his persistent desire to rearrange his

[1] One interesting example of an actual gloss is provided by his translation of Aimoin's 'generalem populi sui conventum' into 'conventum vavassorum suorum more solito' for the account of the assembly called by Charlemagne to judge Tassilo of Bavaria (fo. 184vo, p. 152).

sources. This can very occasionally be defended as when, at the end of his account of Charlemagne, he compiles a character study by extracting a few sentences from several of Einhard's chapters, deliberately putting Christian piety before care of pilgrims and the description of his personal appearance, temperance, and eloquence because this must have seemed to him a more satisfactory order of merit; Hugh of Fleury did much the same. But it is not possible to excuse many of his changes.[1]

There is another certainty about the compilation: its treatment of dates and numbers. The numerous mistakes of the manuscripts in this regard cannot all be blamed on the scribes, though it would remain significant that in the milieux where the text circulated the obvious mistakes in it were never rectified by the scribes, even if all the manuscripts could be traced back to one faulty exemplar. For pre-Christian history, following Bede, large, clear marginal indications of the years since Creation were provided. Unfortunately these signposts of chronological sanity cannot be depended on.[2] The scribes faithfully copied the numbers they read, without presuming to correct manifest errors. With the era of the incarnation, the problem of finding a sure guide to dating should have become easier: it was no new problem in the twelfth century. Yet the compiler does not standardize his dating system and without compunction combines the dating styles of his sources, like the Orosian A.U.C. and the regnal years of the Frankish histories. As he is constantly gliding from one source to another, the opportunities for error and confusion are endless. The problems of putting together contemporary events from different parts of Christendom often defeat him. It is clear too that he occasionally revelled in the chance to give the various computations of the year according to different authorities, as though their sonority added force rather

---

[1] He rearranges the account of how the (false) Emperor Michael approached Guiscard from the small Norman chronicle so that the material is assigned to its correct years.

[2] Twenty-one of Bede's dates BC are wrongly given in the text; 10 of them BC and all of them AD are omitted.

than bombast to his work. All this is parade of scholarship, for it shows no understanding of the purpose and value of precision with dates.[1]

Apart from the light this throws on the scholarly ambience of the chronicle's transmission, it also reflects ill on the basic intelligence of those involved. This is most glaringly exposed in the passage which states that Count Roger (Roger II's father) died in 1101, in the fifty-first year of his age and the forty-first year of his rule as count. If a matter of local history could be so absurdly put down, it will come as no surprise to learn that the Emperor Henry who died in 1106 is said to have become king in 1039 (which is to treat Henry III and Henry IV as one person). Here errors of date lead to confusion of persons, and there are regrettably other examples of this, affecting not only northern rulers, but princes of Salerno too. All this reveals an attitude to numbers that makes them a means of rhetorical punctuation, rather than a guide to precise order. Similarly, the compiler aspires to impress by the use of numbers in his reports on the size of battle casualties. Unfortunately, his carelessness sometimes spoils the effects intended, for the great numbers of the sources are given as smaller than they should be.[2] Perhaps the compiler did not always understand what numbers the Latin letters stood for.

This weakness with numbers is in strong contrast none the less with the marked concern of the eleventh-century annals to assert precise and accurate dating. This section seems anomalous. Only a

---

[1] A complicated pattern of dates was however also used by Bede and Paul. The chronicler's indifference to accuracy is illustrated by two equivalent dates he gives on fos. 78ᵛ, 79 (p. 55) where he states first that AD 88 = A.U.C. 846 and then that AD 99 = A.U.C. 851.

[2] The Bible (2 Chr. 13 : 17) records that King Abijah slew 500,000 men of Jeroboam's army; the chronicle gives this as MD (fo. 30ᵛᵒ, p. 16). He also gets wrong Dares's numbers of Greeks and Trojans killed: 362,000 Greeks: 166,000 Trojans before capture: 266,000 after; Dares gives 886,000 Greeks and 676,000 Trojans altogether: *Dares Phrygius, De excidio Troiae Historia*, ed. F. Meister (Leipzig, 1873), p. 52. Of the numbers killed at Poitiers in 732, Paul says 375,000 Saracens and 1,500 French fell; the chronicle, following him has 360,000 and 1,150 (fo. 169ᵛᵒ, p. 140). He also gives, gruesomely, the number of Julius Caesar's victims: 1,192,000 (fo. 62ᵛᵒ, p. 41).

desperate explanation, such as this being the work of a 'sub-editor' with a more developed sense of the importance dates could have in a chronicle, seems possible. Whatever the truth may be, the unevenness of treatment over dates and numbers reinforces the argument for supposing that more than one guiding hand was responsible for the chronicle.

3

Turning at last to the Salerno part of the chronicle, not the least of the problems to be discussed, is how the Troia chronicle could have come to be used as the basis for the Salerno continuation. For want of other evidence, it is necessary, however, as before, to begin by analysing the text of the contemporary section to see what it is about. As already stated, it is not shaped annalistically and on reflection looks like a narrative composed in the late 1170s to cover Norman-papal history since the 1120s. The high point of the chronicle is reached in 1177, when King William II was acknowledged before all the world at Venice as the pope's chief ally. With such a glorious end in view, a chronicler could well have set out to compose a coherent account that traced the history from Roger II's early difficulties in getting recognition in south Italy and dare to record the bleak period in mid-century when the papacy was hostile to the kings. If the story was told once the conclusion was known, its selectivity is more easily accounted for. Thus Roger II's attempts to perform homage to Pope Innocent II are the main theme of the chronicle's account of the 1130s and when they were finally successful it loses momentum. Clearly aware of the dubious status of Anacletus II, the chronicle represents Roger as being respectful to him, but non-commital; there is nothing about his part in the foundation of Roger's kingship. For a Salerno writer with Innocentian loyalties, it must also be significant that the name of Archbishop Romuald I (1121–37), a cardinal loyal to Innocent II, is never mentioned, nor is there any notice of Innocent's attempt to appoint his successor as late as 1137, a move which Roger frustrated. So though the events of these years were certainly written up after

[267]

Roger's reconciliation with Innocent (1139) it was probably long after. The account of Roger's reign is disconcertingly selective and episodic. It does not even give the impression of having been written as one piece just after Roger's death. The explanation for this uneven quality seems to be its preoccupation with the problem of papal relations. Putting Roger's campaigns against the Muslims of North Africa first, it alludes to the unsuccessful second Crusade, and Louis VII's visit to Roger on his return, followed by the French king's visit to Pope Eugenius III; it does not record any reconciliation between Eugenius and Roger brought about by Louis.[1] After some desperate moral reflections on God's reasons for punishing Roger, in case he became too proud of his other achievements, it notices Eugenius's death and the papal succession before reverting to the king. Then it enlarges generally on his merits: his beautiful palaces in Palermo and its environs, the use Roger made of them according to the seasons, his advisers, his construction of Cefalù, his efforts to convert Jews and Muslims to Christianity, and his other gifts to churches. These generalized remarks without chronological structure are an elaborate panegyric of a great Christian ruler whose bad relations with the pope disturb the chronicler; they are a plea on his behalf against a Roman church that must be badly advised. They may reflect the feelings of Roger's contemporaries, but in their present form they cannot possibly have been written in his reign.

In some ways the chronicle is even less satisfactory when dealing with the reign of William I. It is surprisingly uncertain about when the king began to reign, calculating it in one place from July 1150, in another from April 1151. It knows something of the Beneventan campaign of 1156, but does not elaborate on the terms of the treaty at which Archbishop Romuald II was himself an envoy. Then it notices the rebellion against Maio, and Romuald's part in securing the king's release at Palermo in 1161. William's later hostility to Salerno threatened it with misfortune, and only the intervention of its patron, St. Matthew, frustrated the king's intentions: the chronicle

---

[1] As Garufi believed: see ed. cit. p. 230, n. 4.

is discreet but manifestly lacks enthusiasm for William I. Romuald is, however, described as being called to the king's bedside as physician in his final illness, though he arrived too late to save him. All this reads like the work of someone from Salerno cathedral.

Once the chronicle reaches the reign of William II, it proceeds with more assurance, though it is still far from giving an impression of being composed year by year. There is for example a summary of the case of Becket, probably written after his canonization in 1173.[1] Another famous archbishop, Conrad of Mainz, is also noted. His departure from Germany to join Alexander III at Sens is recorded in 1165, but it is difficult to believe that this fact alone would have secured it a place in the chronicle, even if Romuald had received him at Salerno when Alexander III visited the city in 1165. His historical importance for the chronicle is better explained by his conduct in 1177, when he showed a commendable readiness at Venice to sacrifice his own rights for the sake of general peace.

Taking these various clues together, it looks as though a writer from Salerno decided to set down the events of the reigns of Roger II and the two Williams in 1177. Though the work naturally stressed the archbishop of Salerno's personal services to both William I and William II as well as his respect for Alexander III, it was not particularly interested in domestic affairs. Of foreign rulers it notices Manuel I of Constantinople, who is prominent because of the proposal of a Sicilian marriage alliance, the collapse of which is attributed to the emperor. This insult to the king of Sicily is considered so offensive that the emperor's defeat at Myriokephalon in 1176 at the hands of the enemies of the faith is described as divine punishment for his treachery. Was this remark intended to salve William II's injured pride? The much greater attention given to the western emperor, Frederick I, explains his part in the affairs of the schism, of northern Italy, and ultimately at Venice in 1177, all of which

[1] In May 1179, at the suggestion of Alexander III, Romuald II granted to the hospital of Jerusalem the church of St. Thomas martyr founded at Montoro by Count Robert of Caserta. A. Balducci, *Rassegna Storica Salernitana*, xii (1951), pp. 152–73. 'L'archivio della curia arcivescovile di Salerno'.

could have formed the preliminary part of the archbishop's diplomatic report; certainly the interest shown in the grievances of the Lombard communes, particularly of Cremona and Alessandria, would indicate the source of the chronicle's or of the archbishop's information.

The account of the Venice negotiations occupies nearly one tenth of the chronicle's total space and is its most valuable contribution to historical knowledge. As the report of an eyewitness however, it has the limitations as well as the advantages of first-hand reporting. What the archbishop had not seen, was not interested in, or did not think important simply got left out. The archbishop thought public ceremonies, clever speeches, passionate loyalty to his king mattered more than trying to penetrate the motives of pope or emperor and in the end he rather gave a vivid account of the kind of thing that was said and the way business was negotiated than a clear statement of the final terms agreed. He was clearly pleased to emphasize the importance of the king of Sicily's role, without explaining it; to modern eyes his own words suggest that the Sicilian envoys played little more than a formal role throughout. He does not appear to have been in anyone's confidence or to have had a very clear idea of what he was doing there. He is certainly pleased to create the impression that he did a great deal. This makes it very difficult to believe that the archbishop could have written about other great events he took part in with so little personal detail or sense of occasion.

The unambiguous declaration that the account of the Venice negotiations is taken from the written, eyewitness, and true account of Archbishop Romuald confirms at least that the last part of the chronicle, like the earlier part, is to that extent still a compilation.[1] It resembles the earlier part in several other ways. Its matter is woven together out of several identifiable strands of interest, the pope, the east and west emperors, the king of Sicily, and the Lombard communes; its preoccupation is still the relationship

[1] The reports of Roger II's campaigns in the 1130s are very likely derived from some existing written record.

between the papacy and the great rulers of the day and its outlook
indicates a conservative position of respect for the legitimate rights
of such rulers as pay proper courtesies to popes. It continues the
tradition of offering panegyrics of rulers at their death, and noting
the serious natural disasters and celestial phenomena. On such
grounds as these it is possible to argue that the author of the last
part had so absorbed the procedures and interests of the 'Troian'
chronicle that he could extend it effectively. The conventional view
is that the same compiler was responsible for the historical and the
contemporary sections, but given the extent to which the text
itself betrays signs of successive revisions, it seems simpler to allow
for a Troian stage in its development, before the work was transferred to Salerno for its late twelfth-century continuation.

It is not difficult to believe that the editors at both stages were
interested in the proper relationship between the rulers of Apulia
(or kings of Sicily) and the papacy, and their views on such matters
probably reflected those of the great prelates of the Norman realm.
Both Romuald of Salerno and Bishop William III of Troia (with
others) represented King William I at the Beneventan negotiations
with the papal envoys, who included Cardinal Roland of St. Mark,
in June 1156.[1] The business of defining the royal position *vis-à-vis*
the pope certainly involved the quotation of historical precedents.
We do not know from which sources the negotiators derived their
historical information, but it cannot be doubted that had Bishop
William brought the Troian chronicle with him to prompt his
memory, it would have been very useful. Nor is it impossible that
from the many informal discussions that assuredly took place,
Romuald, or someone in his entourage from Salerno, could have
decided a copy of such a history worth acquiring. At the time there
may have been no thought of revising or continuing it. We do not
know enough to be precise. But we do know that the great men
involved at Benevento had motive and occasion to discuss the past

---

[1] *Regesta Pontificum Romanorum*, ed. P. F. Kehr (Italia Pontificia, vol. viii,
Berlin, 1935), p. 48 n. 185.

and to assess its potential use for the political interests of the Norman kingdom.

The chronicle of 'Romuald' that resulted is in both its past and present parts secular in tone. Imitating the authorities used throughout the rest of the work, the compilers had added conventional obituary notices to the accounts of the Norman rulers of southern Italy from Count Drogo onwards, and it is difficult to resist the conclusion that a work of this kind was intended for the Norman rulers of Italy who had so obviously taken up the burdens of secular government described in the chronicle. And maybe the final edition was prepared with the idea of making a suitable present to the newly wed William II, of a reference work on rulers of the past for his anticipated heir; no other work known to us could have provided more or better information for such a purpose.

What lessons were to be learned from it? The last lesson of the work was that the king of Sicily, after years of being in the wilderness, had been recognized by the pope in the full view of the world as his principal ally. The chronicle is much concerned to demonstrate right relations between the secular and the priestly power. It is full of examples to be used as models or warnings. It is sympathetic towards the church's claim to independence and the pope's immunity from secular judgement. Its interest in the history of disputed papal elections stretches from the problems of the succession to Peter down to the schism of 1159 which was only settled in 1177 at Venice. To put things in perspective it might seem necessary to tell much of the history of the world, and certainly take the history of the Roman church back to St. Peter. But in the end the chronicle shows no sympathy with the pretensions of Gregory VII who is described as the first pope to assume the administration of the *regnum* for himself *ut rex*.[1] Rulers are advised to be respectful of the pope. Duke William of Apulia had held the pope's stirrup at Troia; the Emperor Frederick did the same for Alexander III. But

---

[1] This remarkable statement on Gregory VII has a slight parallel in his words on Leo IX, for which the original Vatican manuscript reading has been lost. It must be noted, however, that these ideas and phrases are taken

the chronicle shows too that in times past the emperors had settled papal disputes (even the Arian Theodoric had given a ruling about papal elections) so Bonizo of Sutri's diatribes about Henry III are omitted. When the chronicle reports that Justinian obtained the consecration of a new patriarch by Pope Agapitus I, it modified the *ex praecepto augusti* of the *Liber Pontificalis* into *ex rogatu*, perhaps in the light of its own information that the pope had found Justinian to be a heretic. But it is not often so careful. And once the schismatic Frederick I was reconciled to Alexander III, the chronicle seems to imply that he recovered his rights to respect from his rebellious Lombard cities.

Given the nature of the Sicilian kingdom it is important to notice that from Salerno at least, the Muslims appear only as enemies to be defeated and evicted from the lands they had improperly expropriated. Of the Greeks only grudging mention is made after the sixth century. A world history composed in the Norman Italy of modern imagination might have been expected to be more cosmopolitan. In fact it is thoroughly Latin. The early part was derived from the scholarly achievements of an earlier era, and not until the final section, the Venice negotiations, are there any signs of the literary power and emotional range shown in the eighth-century models, Bede, Paul, and the author of the *Liber Pontificalis*. For the intervening period of nearly four centuries the chronicle itself exemplifies the disarray of historians. Its final message was that the Norman kings had by 1177 taken their proper place in history as rulers of European importance. This drove home the point that they were either ready to learn, or needed to learn, from this

---

from the small Norman chronicle: and their adoption here must involve a self-conscious attempt to refute Bonizo of Sutri, who defends the use of the sword by the pope, and can only explain Leo's defeat as the inscrutable will of God. (Liber ad Amicum p. 589.) Here the chronicler is in the happy position of seeing defeat as punishment for a pope who did not rely strictly on teaching and example. The chronicle presents Alexander III, meek in the face of adversity and ultimately victorious, as a more admirable pope than his famous eleventh-century predecessors.

review of great historical rulers something of royal duty, like that of law-giving in the tradition of the Romans and Lombards, and what punishments awaited those who were unfaithful in marriage, usurpers of priestly rights, abusers of riches, idolatrous, heretical, or merely greedy and proud.[1] Of spectacular other-worldly events, it is notable that the different fates of the kings Theodoric and Dagobert over the volcanic gates to hell off Sicily itself are the most spectacular.

It has no literary merits to commend it to the educated. At no stage, not even in the fair copy written for Salerno, did anyone try to impose a final shape on this history, smoothe away its anomalies, or tidy up its chronology. Admittedly the enterprise was carried through to the present despite the considerable labour involved. No very extended historical research was undertaken, and few books would have been necessary to provide all the materials for the compilation.[2] There is no denying that the compilation has character, but its purpose remains inexplicit. Its clumsiness may be pleaded in part extenuation of this. Yet the scale of the enterprise may also be an excuse: it would not be the least World History beaten by the complexity of the subject.

---

[1] Numerous are the examples of kings with a weakness for women: David, Solomon, the Emperor Gallienus, Chilperic the Frank, Rodoald the Lombard. Idolatrous rulers include Josaphat and Valerian; Lothar, Anastasius Philip, and Leo III were heretics; Ozias usurped priestly rights; Constans II was greedy; Josiah and Mascelzer were proud and abused their riches. Valens persecuted monks, and Thierry of the Franks had St. Desiderius stoned to death. Most rulers could be shown up as examples for good or ill.

[2] It should be noted that the Monte Cassino manuscript now in the Laurenziana LXV 35, contains Orosius, Paul, the Frankish history (=Aimoin?), Einhard, and a papal catalogue. Likewise Vat. MS latin 1984 contains Eutropius, Paul, and other works, with extracts from the *Liber Pontificalis* on Zacharias, Stephen II, Stephen III, and Leo III written in the 1120s on blank spaces. The chronicler would not in fact have needed many manuscripts to assemble all the material he needed. It is even possible that a few details apparently derived from Gregory the Great's Dialogues were cited from memory, like the two or three references to Isidore.

Confession as a historical source in the thirteenth century

A. MURRAY

I. INTRODUCTION

The church consists of souls, millions of them. This fact creates a problem today in the subject we choose to call church history, above all for that peculiarly 'churchy' period the Middle Ages. The problem is that souls, especially among the popular millions, are precisely what we know next to nothing about.

The aim of this paper is to signpost a path to the heart of this problem. The paper will be in two parts, after this introduction. For the problem itself is double. Our own modern ignorance, after all, stems chiefly from the failure of medieval sources to enlighten it; that failure itself needs explaining; and one element, at least, in any explanation must be the surmise that the authors of the sources, the literary higher clergy, were themselves partially ignorant. Educated men, usually of high-class birth, they did not automatically know all the intimate case-histories, religious and moral, of the illiterate millions round them. The degree of their ignorance can be debated. Some slight degree of it is certain. And in the second main part of this paper we shall detect some of these literary clergy learning: by the same path as ourselves, if with different motives and different results.

The two intertwined problems, the modern and the medieval, are historical. Their subject is 'intimate case-histories'. Both, consequently, are (or were) relieved by a historical procedure. It is an old one. The first historical utterance ever made by a human being, if a debated account is to be trusted, was Adam's reply to God: 'the woman . . . gave me fruit . . . and I did eat'. That reply summed up the history of the human race up to its time, so it counts as general history. But it was more ostensibly forbear to one very particularized type of history. It was one man's review of his own past, provoked by a private question from authority, and interpreted morally. And for most of church history that procedure came to have its own name: confession.[1]

Historians and theologians have discussed confession from many angles. Here it will be discussed from only one: as a means of historical discovery. For discovery it was; it opened up a new world:

> I am not now investigating the tracts of the heavens, or measuring the distances of the stars. I am investigating myself, my memory, my mind. Its wide plains and innumerable caverns are full beyond compute of countless things of all kinds. My mind has the freedom of them all: I can probe deep into them and never find an end.[2]

Cortez on the Pacific shore was no more deeply awestruck than the author of that rhapsody, Saint Augustine. Augustine's famous confessions might not be the private, oral kind later called sacramental. But they served a similar purpose, and his words—well known to medieval writers on confession—well describe the novelty and extent of the world that procedure opened up.

And it was a historical world, the medium of its exploration,

---

[1] No less so when it was—as in Adam's case—a *bad* confession: cf. Archbishop Federigo Visconti of Pisa [† 1277]: Florence, MS Laur. Plut. 33 *sin.* 1, fo. 91rb [=Sermon 61, in the MS numbering]: 'oportet ut peccator se accuset non alium . . . talis fuit confessio Ade. Quando dominus redarguit ipsum ne de ligno scientie boni et mali commederet, dixit "mulier quam dedisti michi . . . dedit michi et commedi" [Gen. 3: 12]. Non dixit "domine male feci". Immo accusat mulierem. Et forte plus peccavit Adam in accusando illam quam in transgrediendo mandatum.' On the MS: A. Murray, 'Archbishop, Mendicants and Laity in Thirteenth-Century Pisa', in K. Elm (ed.), *Bettelorden und Stadt* (*Ordensstudien* 2; Duncker and Humblot, West Berlin, 1981).

[2] Augustine of Hippo, *Confessions*, X, cc. 16 and 17 (condensed and elided). Cf. cc. 8–30 *passim*; XI, c. 18, etc. I have used, with some freedom, the translation by R. S. Pine-Coffin (Harmondsworth, 1961). As 'discovery': C. S. Lewis, *The Allegory of Love* (Oxford, 1936), pp. 65–6.

memory. A confessor's manual from the period we shall be concerned with, the thirteenth century, describes as follows how confession should be undertaken. No one who has engaged in historical research can miss the analogy. Past deeds, the author insists, should not be recalled pêle-mêle, but in order:

He who wishes to confess fully should subject the whole treasury of his memory to careful scrutiny, extracting from it his past acts, and passing them all in review before his mind's eye. The review should be thorough, orderly, and conducted chronologically: that is, considering first what one did in the first year one can remember, then in the second, and so on. As far as possible the review should distinguish acts also according to the successive seasons of the respective years. For it is a great help in remembering facts, to sort them into due chronological order.[1]

The chief witness, memory, may need coaxing:

It is in the nature of memory that if it reflects merely on the time we did something, it often fails to recall it. But it may be able to recall the same act by association with the faculty or instrument by which it was done; or again from the type of act itself, or the place. Our self-scrutiny should therefore carefully run through all these, and any other circumstances likely to arouse memory. Thus it should recollect as far as possible where we have been, in case our memory can fill in, from the image of a place where we have done it, an act it cannot recall just from the season. It should turn also to the inner faculties of the soul, so that by searching it may find what it missed by mere reflection.[2]

---

[1] MS Bodleian 52, fo. 153ʳ [square brackets enclose preferred variants from MS Bodl. 830, fo. 169ᵛᵇ]: 'Debet itaque qui plene vult confiteri cogitacione sua perscrutari totum thesaurum memorie sue ut de illo eruat omnia facta sua omnium temporum preteritorum et coram oculis intelligentie sue statuat ut hec fiant plene et ordinabiliter secundum ordinem [temporum preteritorum], primo scilicet primi anni unde recolit facta perscrutans, secundo secundi et ita deinceps, et in singulis annis per singulorum quantum potest distinctas separatim partes vigili perscrutatione incedat. Non enim parvum est iuvamentum ad facta memoranda ordinatim per temporum seriem distinguens perscrutatio.' On this treatise see p. 305 n.1 below.

[2] MS Bodl. 52, fo. 155ʳ [Bodl. 830, fo. 170ᵛᵇ]: 'quia sic se habet nostra reminiscentia quod plerumque id quod egimus in aliquo tempore non recordatur ex eiusdem temporis apprehensione, et fortasse eundem actum revocabit in recor-/[fo. 155ᵛ] dationem vel ex apprehensa virtute operante vel ex apprehenso instrumento cum quo operatum est vel ex genere ipsius actus

When the witness fails recourse may be had to inference:
[We should further include] those acts of ours we cannot recall, but which we learn from the reliable testimony of others, as Augustine did in his *Confessions* [1:7], when he deduced from watching other children what he himself had done as a child, which called for correction and confession.[1]

Like much in scholasticism this prescription has a pedantic, impracticable air. But here again typical of its school, it was elaborately thought out, and an ideal: and such an ideal, as its influence spread and penetrated, could not but stimulate its own peculiar kind of historical research, and hence of historical discovery.

The process of discovery will be charted here, as I have indicated, through two studies. They will illustrate the function of confession as historical source respectively as it serves us, and as it served the literary clergy who wrote our sources. The subject of each study is a sample of its class, picked from a number of candidates. Neither is exhausted. I may be charged with treating disparate subjects partially instead of one thoroughly. But the juxtaposition of these strange and emaciated bedfellows will in fact serve a purpose that could not have been served without: it will render obvious the answer to at least one old and stubborn question.

Before launching on the first of these studies I should give two preliminary explanations about their historical context. One explanation concerns the general shape of the history of confession, in the central Middle Ages. The thesis in this paper assumes one particular

---

vel ex loco in quo gestum debet nostra perscrutatio vigilanter discurrere [per] haec omnia et signa sunt alia ex quibus potest commoneri et expergisci nostra memoria. Recogitet igitur quantum potest nostra perscrutatio etiam loca in quibus fuimus, si forte ex loci in quo quid gessimus ymaginatione occupat memoria quod non potuit recordari ex tempore. Convertat se etiam perscrutatio ad vires anime interiores, ut perscrutando inveniat quid delinquit in apprehendendo.'

[1] MS Bod. 52, fo. 153ʳ [Bodl. 830, fo. 170ʳᵃ]: 'set etiam facta que possumus racionando arguere et ex aliorum credibili relatione/[fo. 153ᵛ] intelligere licet a nostra exciderint memoria nos ea fecisse. Hoc enim facit Augustinus in libro confessionum suarum, ex simili videlicet quod videt in aliis pueris arguens quidem ipse puer corrigendum et confitendum egerit.'

view of that shape. It is a view on which scholars still split for and against: none the less sharply for the great dearth of evidence from before 1200, and all the *more* sharply because the ghosts of Reformation polemic still haunt the subject.[1] The view is that the practice of confession, outside monasteries, and other than as immediate preparation for death, was nothing like universal before the thirteenth century; and that it gradually approached universality as a result of a reforming impetus begun at the very end of the twelfth century in the University of Paris. The impetus—according to this view—was both expressed and augmented by the twenty-first decree of the Fourth Lateran Council in 1215, *Omnis utriusque sexus*, which enjoined annual confession on all adult Christians.

There is no proving this view in a short space.[2] But a few reasons for entertaining it can be set down briefly. They start with the explosive growth in ground-level evidence of lay confession after about 1200. That growth does not by itself establish an equivalent growth in lay confession; far from it. But the character of some of the evidence helps to do so. For instance, *exempla*: these moral stories, often from real life, were an old genre and allow comparison before and after 1200. References to sacramental confession abound in them after 1200, as we shall see; but they are remarkably sparse before. A second consideration is the spate of confessors' manuals which began about 1200, with Alan of Lille's *Liber Poenitentialis*

---

[1] B. Poschmann, *Penance and the Anointing of the Sick* (Freiburg, London, 1964), is the best short theological history. Documents in Latin are printed by O. D. Watkins, *A History of Penance*, 2 vols (London, 1920); and selected documents on the origins of confession, translated into French with a perceptive commentary, by C. Vogel, *Le Pécheur et la pénitence au moyen âge* (Paris, 1969). The school of historians from whom I dissent nevertheless includes the first two of these authors (Watkins, pp. 735–6; Poschmann, p. 140). For another, and references to the main advocates on both sides: F. Broomfield, ed., Thomas of Chobham, *Summa confessorum* (Louvain, Paris, 1968), xli. An excellent treatment of the subject in the late middle ages is J. Toussaert, *Le Sentiment Religieux en Flandre à la fin du moyen âge* (Paris, 1963), pp. 106–22.

[2] I shall make the attempt however in a forthcoming article, where fuller references will be offered for the contentions in the following two paragraphs.

(1191/1203),[1] and would grow to a flood in the next three centuries. It was as if priests, bewildered by a duty newly exacted from them, were crying out for instruction. Looking *into* the evidence, thirdly, we see the priests had reason. For it shows that despite hearty efforts by thirteenth-century reformers, scandalous shortcomings survived in the priests' conduct of confession, not to mention lay attendance at it. That leads us to suspect confession was not universal before. A fourth, more elusive indicator comes from the theology of penance. In the first half of the thirteenth century the theologians' definition of what precisely brought about the penitent's reconciliation with God, shifted from a more *sub*jective to a more *ob*jective criterion. (In technical terms: it shifted from pure contritionism to one modified by the assignment of an efficacious role to absolution.)[2] This shift would nicely correspond to a growing degree of 'mass production'. It was as if subjective contrition alone was too shaky a guarantee of salvation when offered to illiterates: they might well not know what contrition was, and hence whether they were saved or not.

Fifth, and finally, binding these features together, is the long-term pattern in pastoral practice from 1215 to the Reformation. In the field of confession as in others pastoral authorities harked back to the Council of 1215 as a point of departure. Again, in this field as in others the reform movement was largely shaped by mendicants, whose orders grew, multiplied, and intermittently reformed themselves, to form a clergy within the clergy: a pastoral élite especially influential in towns. Largely through their activity the practice of confession appears to have spread and developed steadily over the three centuries in question. By 1500 it had become so efficient, so well-fortified with literature and theology, and so nearly universal, that, far from being scandalously inadequate, it threatened to exceed the other way and become a tyranny. Hence the early sixteenth century saw for the first time widespread *radical* criticism of the sacrament; and this criticism in turn bore fruit in a doctrine designed

---

[1] J. Longère (ed.), 2 vols (Louvain, Lille, 1965); date: i. pp. 213–16.
[2] Poschmann, pp. 157–93.

specifically to replace confession and its accoutrements: justification by faith.[1]

Those are the historical horizons of the thesis in this paper. My second preliminary explanation concerns confessional secrecy. Since our subject is confession as conduit of information its secrecy must appear an insuperable obstacle. From the earliest times of which record of ecclesiastical confession survives, and right through the history of the institution, the penitent's words were meant to be strictly secret.[2] The purist argument for secrecy would be that these words were spoken to God, and to the priest only as God's representative. *Qua* man he should be as if he had not heard them. There was a more practical argument, in evidence from the ninth century. It was that a penitent would not confess fully if he feared his confidences might be revealed. The term 'Seal of Confession', which appeared in the second half of the twelfth century, simply gave a new and fitting name to this old rule.[3]

The Seal of Confession apparently puts a seal also on the hopes anyone, medieval or modern, might have of learning anything useful from confession and hence on the very idea of this paper. As for modern learners this pessimistic outlook has been so general among historians as to frighten them into silence. A specialist on thirteenth-century confession voices the general pessimism thus: 'Le secret de la confession [he writes] a été bien gardé, même pour l'historien, qui ne peut guère sortir de la banalité pour en parler.'[4]

Now there are a number of *non*-banal things to be said about

---

[1] Literature and theology: T. N. Tentler, *Sin and Confession on the Eve of the Reformation* (Princeton, 1977). Tyranny: S. E. Ozment, *The Reformation in the Cities* (New Haven, London, 1975), pp. 17, 26–32, 50–6, 67–8, 72–6, 100, 153–60.

[2] L. Honoré, *Le Secret de la confession* (Bruges, 1924), pp. 25–31, 125; Poschmann, pp. 91–2.

[3] Purist: Robert Pullen, *Sent.* VI, c. 51 [*PL* 186, col. 898B]. Cf. Honoré, pp. 42, 61–2. Practical: Honoré, pp. 37, 41, 62–4, 95–7. *Signaculum-sigillum*: Honoré, p. 45.

[4] C. Carozzi, 'Le Ministère de la confession chez les Prêcheurs de la province de Provence', *Cahiers de Fanjeaux*, 8 (Toulouse, 1973), 321–54; p. 326.

that very opinion. The first is that it makes a massive assumption about the rectitude of medieval priests. Did they then never, *ever* break the Seal? The assumption that they never did has been surprisingly common. Cardinal Suarez in the sixteenth century took the assumption as so sound as to use it as evidence against protestants of the divine origin of confession.[1] Evidence on this particular of confession is of course as elusive as on others. Nevertheless, the ubiquity of medieval priestly abuse in better-documented areas might have been expected to discourage such conclusions. And in fact that great hunter of priestly abuses, H. C. Lea, records signs of this one in his *History of Auricular Confession* (1896; i. 450–7). Even for the thirteenth century, with its relatively thin evidence, careful enquiry makes it clear that the *proditor confessionum* was a well-known type of sacerdotal delinquent.[2]

The illegal betrayal of confessions is not, however, why those historians are wrong who say they can learn nothing from medieval confessions. Why it is not, is that parish-pump indiscretion, whatever pain and damage it might cause locally, was unlikely to reach written record. The priests who wrote the records were usually keepers of the rules. They often actually wrote in order to defend them. So to find if there are cracks in the Seal we have to look at the rules. And if we do, we see that despite all the dire penalties threatened over the ages against the slightest breach, the Seal was not in fact totally watertight. For one thing, a long series of *causes*

---

[1] Honoré, 124. Fr. Honoré's chapter on Violations is itself largely devoted to the explaining-away of alleged cases.

[2] St. Bonaventura, *Quare fratres minores praedicent et confessiones audiant*, in *Opera omnia*, viii (Quaracchi, 1898), 375–85; §15 (p. 379L) and §19 (p. 381L). St. Antony of Padua, *Sermones dominicales*, ed. Fr. Locatelli (Padua, 1895–1903), execrates blabbers of confessional secrets 'irrisorie vel applausorie' (p. 45b), and ends 'Cavete, o confessores, o sacerdotes' (p. 46a). A Montaillou heretic said he avoided confession because priests 'postea ... facient suam delusionem de vobis, trufabunt inter se de vestris peccatis'; J. Duvernoy, *Le Registre d'Inquisition de Jacques Fournier* (Toulouse, 1965), ii, p. 229; E. Le Roy Ladurie, *Montaillou* (Paris, 1975), p. 504. A living example: Caesarius of Heisterbach, *Dialogus miraculorum*, ed. J. Strange, 2 vols (Cologne, 1851), Bk III, c. 42 (vol. i. p. 162).

célèbres, from the early Middle Ages until our own century, has invited casuists, usually under political or legal pressure, to *find* cracks in the Seal: along the lines of 'it all depends on what you mean by'—a breach, the Seal, or confession.[1] Then again, even without casuistry, and throughout the later Middle Ages, village amateurs at canon law could often surmise, from whom a person confessed to or what penance he or she performed, what had been said in confession. (The manuals kept trying to stop this hole, which shows it persisted: for instance in the matter of the all-too-well-known penances for adultery.)[2] Yet a third crack opened up in the matter of what someone had *not* confessed. In the thirteenth century the highest authorities thought nothing of quizzing the confessor of a supposedly holy person, especially just after the latter's death, to make sure he or she really *was* holy, and could be prayed to or for accordingly.[3] Last but not least, a priest's obligation to keep the Seal intact could be challenged by other duties, sanctioned by equally dire penalties to those sanctioning the Seal: notably in the case of heresy. Even those theologians strictest about the Seal could

[1] Honoré, pp. 65–97, 124–30; P. Winckworth, *The Seal of the Confessional and the Law of Evidence* (SPCK Pamphlet, London, 1952).

[2] Honoré, pp. 34–5, 129; Tentler (as on p. 281 n. 1), pp. 309–11, 330 n. 35; Lea, *Hist. of Auric. Conf.*, p. 456.

[3] Visconti (as on p. 276 n. 1), Sermon 67, fo. 102rb: of a dead priest 'reconciliavit se et humiliter et devote per cordis contritionem . . . sicut enim perhibet testimonium confessoris eius et precipue iste Prior noster sancti Petri, signa magne contritionis fuerunt in eo sicut perpendere potui per eius confessionem . . . et frequenter confessus est humiliter.' Likewise in Sermon 65, for a dead archbishop, fo. 98va: 'in caritate decessit sicut vehementer presumimus, propter eius laudabilem vitam transactam et testimonium confessoris sui'. And in Sermon 68, for the late prior of the Pisa Dominicans, fo. 104ra: 'licet forte aliquando ceciderit per vicium vel per peccatum, quia tamen surrexit per virtutem, per contritionem, confessionem et satisfaccionem sicut per ipsius confesso[ris] testimonium perhibet . . .' A similar use in Sermon 72, fo. 108ra; Sermon 75, fo. 109ra; and perhaps Sermon 86, for 122vb: for the blessed Ubaldesca 'que sicut pro certo didicimus virgo fuit'. Cf. *Vitae* of St. William of St. Brieuc [†1234], in *AASS*, July VII (1731), 122CD; and St. William of Bourges [†1209], ibid., Jan. I (1643), 636B; as also Thomas of Chantimpré (as on p. 288 n.1), II 23 §5; 30 §48; and perhaps 25 §6.

admit that the priest who knew of heresy through confession should give some vague, general hint to a bishop to look to his diocese. The historical value of this loophole to a modern historian can be considerable. To give only one example: it was a few words whispered to a friar in confession, in the autumn of 1301, that ended by bringing the Inquisition, and centuries later Professor E. Le Roy Ladurie and his readers, not to mention television cameras and tourists, tumbling down on the Pyrenean hamlet of Montaillou.[1]

Even for keepers of rules, then, there were pinhole cracks in the Seal of Confession. The historian is well-advised to keep an eye open for these. But there is another crack for which he does not even have to keep his eyes wide open: the crack itself gapes. This time it all depended on what you meant by secrecy. Could a priest reveal what he had heard if he gave no names, and if he gave no hint which would enable names to be discovered? These questions, like the others, allowed divergences of view. Councils in the twelfth and early thirteenth centuries sometimes said the Seal should be kept 'generaliter vel specialiter'.[2] That *generaliter* suggests a priest could not reveal things even anonymously. Practical pastors however upheld a laxer rule. It was clearly stated by one of them in 1223–4: 'The confessor [he wrote] can betray the sins of those who confess to him in many cases, so long as identities are not revealed.' (He went on to give an exception even to that condition.)[3] Of course even the rule thus stated could be bent this way and that. What precisely is a revelation of identity? (Is 'a certain woman in Cambrai, some years ago' such a revelation?)[4] Rigorists and laxists

---

[1] Heresy: Honoré, pp. 55, 58. Montaillou: Le Roy Ladurie (as on p. 282 n. 2): For the date of this episode see Duvernoy, i. pp. 323–4 (but Duvernoy's n. 148 is in my view misconceived). Another historians' landslide originating in confession is described by J.-C. Schmitt, *Le Saint Lévrier: Guinefort guérisseur d'enfants depuis le xiii⁰ siècle* (Paris, 1979); cf. Étienne de Bourbon, *Anecdotes historiques*, ed. A. Lecoy de la Marche (Paris, 1877), p. 325.

[2] Honoré, pp. 48, 51; cf. p. 58; Carozzi (as on p. 281 n. 4), p. 345.

[3] Caesarius (as in n. 15), Bk III, c. 31 (i. pp. 148–9).

[4] A case from Thomas of Chantimpré (p. 288 below), II 30 §3, on which he is reprimanded by his Counter-Reformation editor (*Annotationes*, p. 91).

would still have much to argue about. But from the historian's viewpoint, as we shall see, the cat is out of the bag—none the less out for being an anonymous cat.

That is the first reason why those historians are wrong who have despaired of learning anything from confessions. There were holes in the rules. There is a second reason, applying particularly to the century with which this paper is concerned. It concerns, not the rules of confession, but its institutional background. Thirteenth-century penitents were supposed in the first instance to confess to their parish priests. But it is clear that where permitted they often preferred to confess to friars. Not only were friars usually better-educated and better-disciplined. They were not part of the parish: so a penitent could bare his heart with less embarrassment. This fact, the extra-parochiality of friars, is the obverse of the reason such confessors are useful to us. For instead of the parish the friar had an organization of his own: an international order. The order threw him together, often very closely, with a big, mobile professional brotherhood. The brotherhood served among other things as a transcontinental information exchange. When walking in pairs on the road, or meeting at general chapters, friars had plenty of time to talk. We know that they did talk from their reminiscences—which the Dominican order in particular, furthermore, had the historical sense to record.[1] The conversation of such sworn brothers was as within a family, where rules of confidentiality were different from those outside. This is illustrated in a Cistercian source from 1223–4, Caesarius of Heisterbach. (Cistercians just then must be included in the above remarks, as in many respects foreshadowing the Dominican friars.) Caesarius records an indiscretion uttered in confession by a high-ranking laywoman. Caesarius had his story from a second Cistercian who had it from a third, who had heard the original confession. In taking the liberty he did with the Seal of Confession, this third

[1] See Humbert de Romans' prologue to Gerard of Frachet, *Vitas fratrum O.P.*, B. M. Reichert (ed.), *Monumenta o.P. historica*, i (Rome, 1897), p. 4; Thomas of Chantimpré was one who obeyed, dedicating the result to Humbert (*Prologus*, p. 2). For some of the talk, see pp. 289–90 below.

Cistercian, the confessor, had protested that he would not have breathed a word on the subject *if he had not been in the order*.[1] In sum: friars and their aliases, popular as confessors partly because attached to an order, were placed by this attachment in a brotherhood which multiplied the didactic effect of anything they learned in confession.

So much the more instructive for us. So much the more instructive for them.

II. THE CONFESSOR TEACHES: THOMAS OF CHANTIMPRÉ, O.P.
(*c*. 1201–1270/80)

One reason why the parish indiscretions of *proditores confessionum* had no chance of getting into the record was that medieval church literature was in principle inimical to anecdote. It would have been the obvious receptacle for such tales. But luckily for us, modern cultural features sometimes slipped into the medieval church in discreet disguise; and the anecdote is one of these. It was not writers as such who admitted it, but preachers. Unlike pure writers, preachers had their audiences in front of their very eyes. They could *see* that too much abstraction sent the common run of mankind to sleep. A story woke them up. To awaken their audiences some preachers told just any story, respectable or otherwise. But again, these were the less serious, and so also the less literary. The serious, literary preachers had to reconcile common taste with lofty principle. They did so by telling stories to suit the former *if* they illustrated the latter; or if they pretended to—for the pretence could at times be thin. Thus, anyway, was born the *exemplum*: the illustrative moral tale, culled from tradition, hearsay, or one's own experience.[2] The thirteenth century was its golden age. As preaching techniques developed during the century this one followed the trend of the others into becoming institutionalized. Older preachers helped younger by compiling collections of *exempla*, often marshalled

---

[1] Caesarius, Bk III, c. 43 (i. pp. 162–3); Humbert (as on p. 285), p. 5 ('Nolumus . . . quod extra Ordinem . . .').

[2] J.-Th. Welter, *L'Exemplum dans la littérature religieuse et didactique du moyen âge* (Paris, Toulouse, 1927), esp. pp. 68–71.

under the lofty principles they were meant to illustrate: like 'The Seven Gifts of the Holy Spirit'. It is in this dubious clerical collar that we find our thirteenth-century anecdote hiding. So it is here too, every clue suggests, that the historian must go if he wishes to eavesdrop on those private confessions, made seven hundred years ago.

At least four big, thirteenth-century *exempla* collections offer suitable keyholes. One of the twelve books of the so-called *Dialogus miraculorum*, written in 1223-4 by the Cistercian preacher mentioned a moment ago, Caesarius of Heisterbach, is wholly devoted to confession. It gives many real-life instances (not necessarily 'miracles' at all: there is another false clerical collar there). More instances can be found in *exempla* scattered through the vernacular sermons given between 1227 and 1240 by Jacques de Vitry, who 'so moved France [according to a late contemporary] by the use of *exempla* that memory cannot recall anyone's doing the like before or since'.[1] A third such compilation, made between 1250 and 1261, is that *De septem donis Spiritus sancti*, by the Lyons Dominican Stephen of Bourbon—who smuggles out to his reader under that theological title a whole treasury of his experiences as travelling preacher and confessor.[2] But the collection I have chosen is one less well-known than these. Why it is less well-known, is largely that has not been printed since the early seventeenth century. But that neglect in turn probably reflects in part its offences against the proprieties and rationalism of the intervening centuries. And those offences are bound up with the work's main virtue for us now: that of such collections, it is conspicuously the richest in spoils for would-be confessional eavesdroppers.

I refer to Thomas of Chantimpré's *Bonum universale de apibus*:

---

[1] Welter, 118. T. F. Crane (ed.), *The Exempla . . . of Jacques de Vitry* (London, 1890); see nos 220 (pp. 91-2), 284 (pp. 190-200), 301 (p. 126). Cf. R. B. C. Huygens (ed.), *Lettres de Jacques de Vitry* (Leiden, 1960), *Epist.* II (p. 97, lines 196-201).

[2] As on p. 284 n. 1. Of confessor: a few instances on pp. 270, 34, 369, 387, 445; cf. 162 f., 324, 387, 392, etc.

(*The Common Good* [*expounded*] *in Relation to Bees*).[1] Thomas of Chantimpré was what we would call a Belgian. By the boundaries of his own day he was a Brabantine, born near Brussels about 1201. At five he was sent to be schooled for the priesthood in Liège, where among other experiences he heard the preaching of that virtuoso of the *exemplum*, Jacques de Vitry. At sixteen or so Thomas became an Augustinian canon at Chantimpré near Cambrai (an independent bishopric then, not quite in France), and stayed for fifteen years. But in 1232 he was attracted by the new Dominican order, and joined its convent in Louvain. He remained a busy Dominican pastor for the next forty or so years until his death, which occurred between 1270 and 1280. He was an equally busy Dominican scholar. He studied under Albert in Cologne, and knew Aquinas in Paris. Between 1235 and 1250 he wrote his first work, the scientific *De natura rerum*. The book included a chapter 'On Bees'. This served as basis for a second book, begun in 1256 and finished probably about 1260, with later touching-up. Using an old analogy between bees and men, Thomas took each separate sentence from the chapter (for instance, 'Bees all live in one house'), moralized it, and added a series of *exempla* to illustrate the moral. The result was *Bonum universale de apibus*. It was dedicated to the Dominican minister-general, Humbert de Romans.

---

[1] Georgius Colvenerius (ed.), *Thomas Cantimpratanus, Bonum universale de apibus* (Douai, 1627). On the superiority of this edition over the earlier two by Colvenerius, as also on the extreme rarity of all three, see A. Kaufman, *Thomas von Chantimpré* (Görresgesellschaft, Cologne, 1899), p. 15. The first of the two 'books' into which the work is divided concerns the clergy, the second the laity. Nearly all my references will consequently be to Book II. So I shall include the book-number only in the exceptional case of its being 'I', or where there is risk of confusion. References calling for greater precision will be augmented in parentheses with the page-number of the 1627 edition. (The pagination of the 1605 edition, the only other one I have closely examined, differs by one page or less.) For instance: '30 §41 (346)' means 'Book II, chapter 30, sub-chapter 41; the words referred to are on p. 346 of the 1627 edition'. Biography: Kaufman, pp. 8–15. Pastoral milieu: S. Axters, 'Dominikaansche Zielzorg in de Nederlanden der dertiende Eeuw', *Ons Geestelijk Erf*, 13 (Tielt, Antwerp, 1939), pp. 149–84.

Dominican pastors like Thomas both preached and heard confessions. But they did not necessarily do so in equal quantity. Thomas only once mentions preaching among his own activities, and even then it is paired with confession.[1] On the other hand he very often mentions his hearing of confessions. 'I have for thirty years', he tells us, 'acted in various regions on behalf of bishops, in the hearing of confessions' (30 §48 (354)). Elsewhere he says he heard confessions in the diocese of Cambrai for 'many' years, on the bishop's behalf (30 §3 (188–9)). One anecdote opens with his sitting in a church in Brabant one Good Friday hearing confessions (55 §2 (532)). There are many more such allusions. Some relate to the source of a story. No fewer than ten of Thomas's stories certainly, and another seven probably, come directly from what he has been told in confession.[2] He also generalizes from his confessional experience: 'I call God to witness', he exclaims in one place, 'that I have heard very many women in confession who have . . .'; or again, 'I have often verified this, by learning in confession that many men . . .' (30 §54 (358); 30 §11 (325)). Confession, then, as distinct from preaching, was Thomas's chief pastoral preoccupation. It fits with this that preaching is mentioned in *De apibus* altogether less than thirty times, while confession is mentioned more than twice as often.

It is unlikely that the same bias touched all Thomas's friends and acquaintances. Many of these nevertheless had confessional experience, and what *is* likely is that Thomas's own preoccupations affected his conversation with them and what he learned from them. His circle of friends who were priests was in the first place big and varied. It included a dean of Douai, canons of Soissons and Lille, a chaplain to Cistercians, a learned cardinal, and naturally several canons of Chantimpré and friars—to say nothing of casual

---

[1] 53 §32; as against references to others' preaching at I 3 §4; I 4 §6; II 1 §§4–8, §15, §20; II 34 §§4, 5; 42 §4; 44 §2; 49 §2, §4, §23; 53 §4; and many more oblique allusions.

[2] Certain: 25 §§8, 9; 30 §§3, 4; 55 §2; 57 §§14, 25. Probable: I 10 §3(40); II 29 §20; 30 §§9, 27, 51; 50 §§5, 6. Further possible cases at 30 §§32, 55; 57 §50.

priestly acquaintances with whom he chatted. Some of these friendships were old and close: 'he was very dear to me', Thomas will say,
or 'I have known him since youth'; and so on.[1] With anyone whom
Thomas recognized as a colleague his conversation would be
relaxed and often lengthy. 'I was coming down the Rhine once,' he
will recall, 'from Trier to Cologne, with some German Friars
Preacher, and heard many memorable things. One, told to me by
one of the friars, was . . .'; or 'a certain Friar Preacher who had
travelled as pilgrim in many lands and over many seas, told me . . .'
(49 §17 (453); 53 §30 (509–10)). This freedom of conversation, plus
Thomas's own special interest in confession, might perhaps lead us
to expect that he heard and remembered things his priest-friends
repeated from confessions. We know that he did. A bishop of
Lausanne, for instance, staying in Paris, told Thomas 'and many
others, that he had heard a certain clerk confess that . . .' (30 §6
(322)). About half a dozen of Thomas's anecdotes appear to come
directly from such revelations.[2] That these are far from exhausting
what he heard from confessions to other priests is suggested by such
a remark as (after Thomas has put forward a view about certain
women): 'How true this is, those know best who hear the confessions of that type of woman' (30 §49 (354)).

Thomas was both a confessor, then, and a friend of confessors.
It should further be remembered that both Thomas and his friends
were, *qua* confessors, active also on what may be called the periphery
of sacramental confession: beside sickbeds and deathbeds, for
instance, or helping in personal crises and disputes. This would
extend still further their exposure to the confidences of the laity.
And of all sorts of laity: in Thomas's case the sorts stretched from
a wealthy knight like Philip of Montmirail, patron of Cistercians
and Beguines, whose court was a veritable international news-agency
for news of religious interest (38 §2 (392)), down to the 'totally

---

[1] 57 §58 (583);49 §2(442). Cf. 40 §2 (400) etc: I have noted twelve examples
of such phrases.
[2] Certainly: 30 §§6, 38; Probable: 29 §21; 30 §§10, 29; 42 §2. Thomas
heard the story 'privately' in I 24 §2.

uneducated layman' whom Thomas designates as the source of another of his anecdotes (26 §8 (262)). Nor were the laity only men. Thomas in the course of duty met plenty of pious, and some impious, women; and these, like the others, can be expressly identified as sources of stories in *De apibus*.

Thomas functioned, then, at the centre of a world of confessors. This fact affected the character of his book both in general and in particular. In general, it is what gave the book its principal quality: the quality of being down-to-earth. The constant hearing of confession, even more than constant preaching, focused a priest's mind on hard moral fact as distinct from tradition and convention. In a literary priest it also reversed the common literary tendency then for interest to float upwards towards kings and bishops, away from the *hoi polloi*. It is true that *De apibus* excels most such collections in supernatural elements. But in the pastoral sphere it is what Thomas's own *De natura rerum* was in the philosophical. It treats of common, palpable things as they actually are; and is in this sense 'naturalistic'.

The down-to-earth quality of *De apibus* is itself brought down to earth by a numerical analysis of Thomas's 352 *exempla*. My own analysis, too bulky to reproduce, is summarized in Graphs 1 and 2.[1] The first collective distinction of Thomas's *exempla*, shown in Graph 1(*a*), is their relative contemporaneity. A similar distinction touches their sources: they contain a low proportion of literary stock-in-trade, duplicated from earlier literature; and a high proportion of accounts from the author's own experience, or that of his colleagues and immediate predecessors (1(*b*)). This closeness to experience is shown in the stories' geographical distribution: most are set in places Thomas knew and lived in (1(*c*)).

Turning from sources to content, and from Graph 1 to Graph 2,

---

[1] In making the analysis I have naturally met difficulties in categorizing the elements in the *exempla*. On doubtful boundaries I have sought to arbitrate on a basis of 'fair play'. Aggregates, as distinct from individual items, can I hope therefore claim a reasonable objectivity. The 352 *exempla* have been abstracted from a total of 648 sub-chapters, the remaining 296 consisting of argument, quotation, or link-passages.

a similar down-to-earth quality is seen in the breakdown of the stories' characters. While clergy and religious preponderate (Graph 2(*a*)), a conspicuous majority in this category is made up of the author's peers and acquaintances, mainly friars engaged on similar pastoral work to his own (2(*b*)). Laity meanwhile form a large minority. The make-up of this laity is equally significant. While the biggest single group in it is the noble and knightly class, traditional favourites for narrators (and as it happens the class to which Thomas himself was born; (57 §28 (560)), this upper class is not, now, in overall majority. It is overtopped by a coalition of the middle and lower classes, both urban and rural poor being well represented

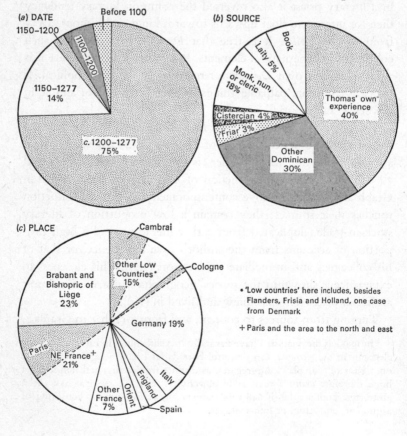

Diagram 2.

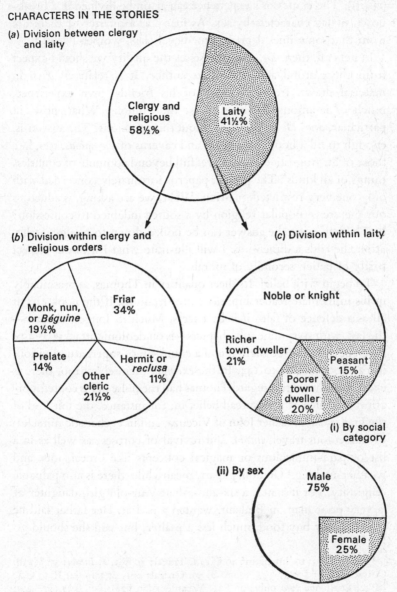

CHARACTERS IN THE STORIES

(a) Division between clergy and laity

Clergy and religious 58½%

Laity 41½%

(b) Division within clergy and religious orders

Friar 34%

Monk, nun, or *Béguine* 19½%

Prelate 14%

Hermit or *reclusa* 11%

Other cleric 21½%

(c) Division within laity

Noble or knight

Richer town dweller 21%

Peasant 15%

Poorer town dweller 20%

(i) By social category

(ii) By sex

Male 75%

Female 25%

Diagram 3.

(2(*c*[i])). The confessor's experience can again be divined in a break-down of lay characters by sex. As many as a quarter of them are from that sometimes depressed medieval class, women (2(*c*[ii])).

In general, then, *De apibus* possesses the quality we should expect from the pastoral activities of its author. It is relatively rich in material drawn from Thomas's or his friends' own experience, much of it among ordinary souls: the millions. What, now, in particular, does *De apibus* tell us about these millions? The answer is, enough to fill a book. The plains and caverns of *De apibus*, too, like those of St. Augustine's mind, are 'full beyond compute of countless things of all kinds'. The present paper is fortunately concerned with only one very restricted question. What, we are asking, is added to our picture of popular religion by a source indebted to confession? In Thomas's case the answer can be boiled down to one generaliz-ation: he adds a dimension. I will illustrate what I mean in respect firstly of belief, secondly of morals.

To begin with belief. Its sheer quantity in Thomas, as presumably in his immediate readership, need not detain us. If the book errs at all as a defence of faith it is by excess. Much its longest chapter— the last, with sixty-nine sub-chapters—is on demonic attacks ('Wasps hate bees and pursue them'), and a count-up of supernatural visions in the book comes to 144. In the *exempla* themselves, too, there is every sign that in this regard Thomas had the pulse of his contempor-aries: evidence of widespread belief in, for instance, the miracles of the Franciscan preacher John of Vicenza, and in eucharistic miracles; in miraculous travel, *incubi*, and revival of corpses; as well as in a list of para-miraculous or magical concepts like ordeal, lots, and weather-making.[1] Credulity apart, meanwhile, there is also palpable religiosity. For instance, a six-and-a-half-year-old girl, daughter of 'a very poor man' in Brabant, wanted a psalter. Her father said he could hardly buy food, much less a psalter, but said she should go

---

[1] John: 1 §§3–10. Eucharist: 40 §§1, 2. *Travel*: 40 §§3, 4. *Incubi*: 57 §§13ff. Corpses: cf. 43 §7; 57 §§8, 17, 20–2, 59. Ordeal: only at I 16 §2; II 29 §22; 36 §2. Lots: one case only: 29 §23. Weather: (29 §28); (57 §2); (57 §27); 57 §29.

to the Sunday-school teacher who taught rich men's daughters. The girl did so, and the daughters' rich mothers, seeing her piety, bought her a psalter and much later helped set her up as a 'recluse' (I 23 §3 (90–1)). A similar infant prodigy was a five-year-old of a village near Ostend who so admired the Franciscans that he begged his parents to let him adopt their habit and practices. He corrected his bibulous father and overdressed mother as occasion arose, preached publicly, and behaved in every way like a friar until he died—at the age of eight (28 §§2–7). Adult piety is represented as dramatically. An example is that of a knight's daughter who, after numerous misfortunes, took service as children's nurse with a Jewish family, and by patient example converted her mistress to Christianity (29 §21 (301)).

This is all mainstream *exemplum* material. The rehearsal of it could go on. But it is not primarily all this faith*ful*ness of the supposed age of faith that adds to our knowledge of it. There are almost as many stories—perhaps more: the cautionary tale is the *exemplum par excellence*—of *ir*religion and *dis*belief. *De apibus* has circumstantial references, well-known to scholars, to 'heretics', and one (also well-known) to an outright, blasphemous sceptic.[1] Again, two stories (one set in a distant country, the other in an unlocalized tavern) start with men mocking 'the fables of clergy' (53 §30 (511); 56 §2 (536)). Moving from outspoken to implicit dissent, one story figures a seaman 'without fear of God or pity for man' (29, §27 (308)), while in connection with yet another Thomas says the habitually lustful live 'without fear of God' (30 §41 (346). Thomas may also have comparable irreligion in mind when he refers at one point to 'perverse laity' who 'hate the clergy' (4 §2), and in a comment on a biblical prophecy, to the 'many faithful' who never think about things to come, only about things present.[2] As to religious observance, there is a handful of references to individuals who scorn to go

---

[1] Simon of Tournai (49 §5). The same story in Giraldus Cambrensis, *Gemma eccles.*, i. 51, in *Opera*, II (Rolls Series 1862), 149–50. Heretics: I 5 §2; II 1 §3; 47 §3; 57 §§23, 68.

[2] 43 §1 (414). Thomas himself was nevertheless touched by only the faintest vestige of the contemporary craze for prophecy: as at I 11 §2 (42) (tyranny

to Mass, and a larger one to those who do the same by confession—in the context, in both cases, of anecdotes with appropriate morals.[1] Finally, we see signs of both casual heterodoxies and plain ignorance. Thomas has at various times heard people query this or that church doctrine: the value of crusading indulgences; whether saints can really be happy in Heaven if they know their relations are in Hell; and a bundle of doctrines concerning observance or ethics, on which as confessor he has found people (as he puts it) 'ignorant'. And alluding to a probably more deep-seated ignorance, Thomas twice speaks of the wild and rude state of the populations of some deeply rural areas: the Moselle wine-growing area in particular.[2]

None of these sorts of faithlessness, however, any more than those sorts of faith, constitutes the 'dimension' I am seeking to characterize as Thomas's special contribution to our picture of his church. The dimension lies rather in the range of differences and in the tensions between the two extremes. Thomas portrays belief as both variable and beset by difficulties. Its variability is strikingly shown in an experience of his own. In 1254 a eucharistic miracle was reported at Douai. It was a type of miracle fairly widely reported in the Middle Ages, especially after just these years, when the doctrine of transubstantiation was most fully elaborated. At Douai the consecrated Host appeared to onlookers as 'an extremely beautiful boy'. Thomas went to see. As the Host was exposed to a view a cry went through the crowd: 'there he is! [i.e. the boy]'. Thomas saw nothing; or rather, he saw only the white bread of the Host; and he stood in amazement, wondering why he alone was blind to the miracle. Then, he says, came a change. He did see something. But it was not a boy. He saw Christ as at his death, with a crown of thorns, and blood on his face. Thomas knelt, and when

---

will end when Christ rules); II 3 §15 (Antichrist: the only mention). In 1256 storms herald the End for some Germans, 57 §2; cf. I 19 §6 (69). The Mendicant Quarrel as the biggest crisis yet: 10 §29.

[1] Mass: 32 §3 (368); 51 §4; probably at 42 §2. Confession: 30 §40; 42 §2; 50 §2; 51 §4 (470); cf. 56 §6; 57 §12; 77 §61.

[2] 25 §12 (253): 'agrestes moribus' (on the Moselle); cf. I 1 §4: 'rudem ... populum' (near Troyes).

he rose the vision had changed again. Thorns and blood had gone. Describing in detail what he saw Thomas says that within the same hour others claimed to have seen quite different things: Christ on the cross; Christ in judgement; Christ as a boy.[1]

Variety in the subjective experience of eucharistic miracles is witnessed by other authors. But this testimony to it is exceptionally explicit. The same goes for another of Thomas's affirmations about the supernatural. This time his knowledge apparently derives, not from one episode, but from his years of conversation with various classes of people on their own religious experiences. Thomas's subject is 'spiritual demons' (he is commenting on St. Paul's 'spiritual wickedness in high places'). Spiritual demons are distinct, Thomas says, from the demons who assume bodily appearance. And the spiritual sort are worse: much more persistent, and so subtle that they can ruin even someone who has attained perfection. Most tell-tale of all, Thomas suggests that the corporeal sort trouble mainly the uneducated. There follows a case-history, heard in confession, of a noble girl attacked by the spiritual kind of demon.[2]

The case-history tells of the girl's agonies of temptation and struggle. Struggle: more even than mere variety it is this element which constitutes Thomas's special 'dimension' as a historical source. Some of the struggle concerns belief. The best-drawn case is of a young man of Bruges. He too should probably be assigned to that élite which attracted spiritual demons. For he was *en route* between the two states of layman and priest. After a good secular education he had joined the Dominicans as a novice and begun to study theology. But 'his mind, being not yet illumined, nor prepared by prayer, was stunned by the light, and his unenlarged soul was

---

[1] 40 §4 (400–1). In general: P. Browe, *Die eucharistischen Wunder des Mittelalters* (Breslau, 1938).

[2] 57 §24 (555): '. . . Illi enim simplices et idiotas decipiunt: per istorum vero nequissima et astutissima tentamenta, et iam homines perfectissimi cadunt.' Cf. 30 §5: some saw, some did not see, a 'black sow'; for 'certum . . . est, quorumdam oculos minus esse habiles demonum phantasmata cernere . . .' At 57 §27 (558) it is again the hearts specifically of the 'simple' which are baffled by aery demonic 'demonstrations'.

buffeted hither and thither by the wind of inconstancy'. Were Christians wrong, and Jews or pagans right?, he wondered. His doubts nearly drove him from the order. In the event he was saved, and persevered to become an exemplary friar and even himself a theology lecturer (10 §19 (172)).

This doubter had a special problem, in the transition from one status and age to another. We can guess from several of Thomas's allusions—as we know for sure from other sources—that his was not an uncommon problem for medieval novices.[1] But analogous agonies were not confined to them. One of Thomas's relatively few references to preaching impugns intellectuals who 'perturb' listeners by raising unnecessarily difficult questions in sermons (48 §1). A few people could be perturbed even without this stimulus. To their number should be assigned an uneducated fourteen-year-old boy who once, while Thomas was hearing confessions, fell weeping at his feet crying 'Help me, help me! Something terrible happened to me today!' He had been terrified by a vision. The boy's agony went on even after Thomas's absolution. A week later the boy's mother asked Thomas to come to him on his sickbed, where the boy related another horrifying experience, in which his soul seemed to be cast into Hell 'like a lump of cold ice into flames'. 'Note, reader,' Thomas interjects, half-consciously authenticating this betrayal of the very words of a confession, 'the wonderful metaphor used—as Christ is my witness—by such a boy.' The boy died soon afterwards, after Thomas and the parish priest had induced in him a calmer state of mind (55 §2 (533)). Another kind of spiritual struggle, possibly involving a species of religious doubt, can be surmised in the half-dozen or more cases of or allusions to 'despair', of the sort leading to suicide or the contemplation of suicide.[2]

If variety and tension are present in Thomas's references to faith among his contemporaries, they are so equally in references to their

---

[1] I §19 (120); 57 §48 (575–6). Cf. *Vitas fratrum* (as on p. 285 n. 1), 202–5, 208–9, and more generally G. G. Coulton, *Ten Medieval Studies* (Cambridge, 1930), 195.

[2] 51 §9 (476); 29 §21; 30 §47; 49 §§8, 11; 29 §38 (316); 49 §18 (454–5).

morals. A confessor's reminiscences will throw light especially on the field of morals most prone to secrecy: love and sex. Thomas has more than most contemporary narrators to say on these subjects—and may as I suggested have lost the honour of a nineteenth-century edition for this reason. Whether confession, with its secrecy and later its confessional box, has caused an overconcentration by Catholic theology on sexual morals, and whether, with or without that, it has influenced Catholic sexual ethics and vice versa, are questions this paper cannot explore.[1] We are studying confession only as a conduit of information. And in this particular there is no question: it *was* such a conduit, both for the confessor and for us. Thomas himself twice admits ignorance of people's sexual conduct, outside his knowledge as confessor: in respect of the extent of clerical concubinage, and of the regularity of other religious orders than his own. But where he or his friends *were* confessors, he knows. When he takes up a stance—for instance in affirming the continence of Dominicans, or the prevalence of this or that sexual vice—he does so expressly on the basis of confessional knowledge.[2]

As with belief and unbelief, so in this field of morality Thomas reveals, against a plentiful background of morality, much that is *im*moral. Cautionary tales illustrate the perils of *luxuria*, in forms ranging from the most scandalous down to that of mere lewd behaviour.[3] There are allusions to people whose addiction to lust has become incurable; to cases of clerical incelibacy; and to prostitution.[4] Incest comes in more as a conceptual *nec plus ultra* than as

---

[1] But see J. Bossy, 'The Social History of Confession in the Age of Reformation', *TRHS*, 5th ser., 25 (1975), pp. 21–38, esp. 30–1; and Tentler (as on p. 281 n. 1), pp. 134–232, see esp. 223–32.

[2] Ignorance: I 20 §9 (78); II 30 §48 (354): 'credo . . unum esse inter ordines istum . . . sicut ipse expertus sum, qui a triginta annis in diversis regionibus vices Episcoporum, confessiones audiens, exequebar'. Cf. below, pp. 301 and 304.

[3] Scandals, e.g. 30 §§19, 20. Lewd songs: 49 §§21, 22; games: 49 §23; 57 §4.

[4] Incurable: 30 §41. Clerks: 3 §§19, 20, and *passim*. Prostitution: 30 §§38, 39 (the only mention).

a practice.[1] But practices are alluded to which Thomas regards as
equal or worse. Most such allusions are in a chapter called 'The sin
against nature'. The austerity of Thomas's patristic education was
sharpened, as he lashed the assortment of sexual vices in this chapter,
by an Aristotelian's respect for nature. (Or rather, what he saw as
nature: his observations can be clearly tendentious, as for instance
in the epigraph to this very chapter: 'Bees do not promiscuously lie
with each other.') Thomas's hostility to the unnatural is thus the
obverse of a respect for the natural. Such a respect is implied in his
outburst, in the middle of an attack on unnatural sex: 'as if they did
not get enough pleasure from licit coitus with their wives!' (30 §55.)
The chapter on the Sin against Nature is, after that on demons, the
second longest in *De apibus* (with fifty-six sub-chapters). This should
perhaps not be taken too seriously as a guide to current mores. Not
only does Thomas spend much of the chapter wandering off the
subject. As bishop's representative he would have heard more than
his share of 'reserved' cases, which included vices under this heading.
Their presence in his book may also reflect the urban and scholarly
milieux in which Thomas moved. Other contemporary sources
suggest that these milieux were more prone to such vices than the
countryside.[2]

But in morals, as in belief, it is not the bad any more than the good
which constitutes Thomas's special 'dimension'. It is again the
tension between them. The nearer we get to confession as source of
one of Thomas's stories not only the more vivid the story becomes;
the stronger also grows the element of tension. Many of the case-
histories Thomas heard in confession involved, for instance, what
we would call unhappy love affairs. A handsome youth in Brabant

---

[1] A case: 29 §21 (the infanticide mother plans suicide). As bugbear: 30 §54
(358); and probably 51 §7 (473).

[2] Le Roy Ladurie (as on p. 282 n. 2), 209–15; A. Murray, 'Religion among
the Poor in Thirteenth-Century France', *Traditio*, 30 (1974), 316 n. 180. The
only cases of sodomy in a strict sense assigned by Thomas to a place are three
in the University of Paris (I 19 §6 (69); II 30 §8) and one in or near Cambrai
(II 30 §9). See p. 296 n. 2 above for Thomas's inexperience of private lives in
outlying countryside.

came to Thomas in agonies of conscience because a girl had pined
to death for love of him (30 §27 (334–5)). A well-born girl wept as
she told in confession how she yearned for a certain young man, and
found all but impossible Thomas's advice to stop seeing him (57
§25 (556)). Other women would relate to Thomas the course of
'temptations' long past. One had suffered for no less than sixteen
years until a vision cured her.[1] From another in the same predica-
ment Thomas as confessor eventually wrung the admission that the
temptations were the woman's own fault: she had once, long ago,
consented to her sexual imaginings.[2] Thomas knew of comparable
cases through his confessor-friends: of a noble German lady, whose
drastic attempt to elude the importunity of adulterers ended by her
placing herself humbly under her confessor's direction; of a converted prostitute, and her former adventures; and of a carpenter's
wife in Rheims, who withstood a rich man's enticements to leave
her husband.[3]

Tension in the love-lives of ordinary, marrying people became
tenser still when extended to those who sought to rise above, and
those who fell below, the norm. Novices, the same who sometimes
suffered doubts, were among the former. One Dominican castrated
himself to defeat temptation (54 §8). Young Beguines were warned
that their aspirations to lifelong virginity made them exceptionally
vulnerable to the indiscretions of well-meaning youths (30 §50
(355), etc.). At the other end of the scale were Sinners against Nature.
The note of struggle is here at its most dramatic. Thomas stresses
the deadweight of habit in this regard. Many, he says, have failed
to escape from unnatural vice after repeated attempts. One sodomite,
brought to Thomas by the parish priest, persuaded the confessor to
endorse his adjuration 'if I ever do it again may God strike me
down!' Thomas regrets having agreed: for the man did it again, and

---

[1] 25 §9: 'ut mihi ipsa cum lacrymis revelavit; cf. §8: 'mihi sicut confessori';
and 51 §12.
[2] 57 §14: 'ab ea violenter extorsi'; cf. §13: 'in confessione pluries audivimus'.
[3] 30 §29 (335–7); 30 §38: 'illi, qui hoc mihi retulit, sequenti die confessa . . .';
30 §37 (342).

died horribly (30 §9). Another recidivist sodomite, originally corrupted as a youth by a Paris don, dies still victim to the vice, after a long struggle. His dying cry—and Thomas's moral—is 'Woe to the man who first seduced me!' (30 §8.)

For today's historian, then, Thomas of Chantimpré's *exempla* offer a glimpse into a few souls, poor as well as rich, from among those millions. The glimpse reveals more features instructive to a historian than there is time to identify now. But if one stands out as characterizing Thomas's book, it is that it presents his religious environment as a Jacob's ladder: with extremes of up and down, and vigorous movement between them. In faith sometimes, in morals often, Thomas's characters are such that they could not themselves have said if they were good or bad Christians, or even at times Christians at all. Most conspicuously in those he tells of most intimately, they were struggling.

It is natural that a confessor's picture should highlight this feature. A confessor's job was not primarily to learn, or even merely to absolve. Part of his function was to *cause* a struggle: to cleave the penitent's heart in two, urging him to throw away the worse part. So of course struggles make their mark in a confessor's record.

But the confessor's participation in a penitent's struggle had another consequence than the mere recording of the latter's problems for our sake. The problems affected him. Abundant thirteenth-century testimony from confessors leaves no doubt that good ones found their struggles very hard labour.[1] Among many

---

[1] 10 §7 (161-2). Archbishop Visconti spoke similarly of the confessor's 'battle' in Sermon 56 (date 1257), quoted in the article mentioned on p. 276 n. 1. Compare the instructions of Robert Grosseteste *De confessione II* (as on p. 305 n. 1), MS Oxford, Bodl. 801, fol. 192ᵛ [variants from MS Oxford, St. John's Coll. 190, fo. 145ᵛᵇ]: 'Diligenter ergo cum de hiis omnibus fuerit penitens examinatus ut veram habeat attricionem de omnibus que se iam fecisse confitetur hortandum est et hoc per humani corporis et materie vilitatem per peccatorum enormitatem per vite fragilitatem ut per labores, dolores, languores et ad ultimum per mortis instabilitatem sive certitudinem et per penas infernales et per glorias essenciales. Postremo per ipsam domini nostri passionem que si pro [pio] affectu et ardore caritatis discernitur mens audientis proculdubio/[fo. 193ʳ] etsi lapidea esset disgregabitur [disgelabitur]

results of that is that the confessors learned. Every student of history knows that there is nothing like hard labour for embedding knowledge in one's head. It did so for confessors. They learned in the first place many little things, of which they remembered some, of these repeated some, and of these recorded some—to produce that fragment of a fragment of a fragment which has come down to us in Thomas's stories. But they also, with all that labour, learned things not so little: things which, if they stare from the page of *De apibus* less obviously than the nightmares and love affairs, can be read there between the lines and probably lodged more deeply in the author's mind.

One of these deeper lessons forms the subject of my concluding observation about *De apibus*. The last story I repeated from it ends with a sinner's crying 'Woe to the man who first seduced me!' Thomas endorses the moral; and his doing so has a moral also for us. Thomas's lifelong concern with private lives within restricted regions gave his ethical views themselves what I may call a historical element. Because he and his friends knew some of their penitents over a long period they knew the beginning and end of their stories. Our author himself had a strong sense of dates and of lengths of time of up to about a century before he wrote: he tells how a centenarian cousin recalled her own young days (49 §6 (446)); how his father remembered fighting under Coeur-de-Lion (57 §28 (560)); and within his own life he will often identify moments and periods of 'twenty', 'thirty', or 'forty' years (ago), and place incidents by their date.[1] The same mental time-range carried over into his experience of others' lives. Two women had suffered their temptations for

nimirum cum in ipsius dominice passionis hora lapides scinderentur et monumenta aperirentur.' Cf. Tentler (as on p. 281 n. 1), pp. 102–3, 126; and for some live examples, besides many in *De apibus*, Jacques de Vitry, *Epist.* (as on p. 287 n. 1), II. 90.270–6; also 88. 216–8; *Idem, Exempla* (as in the same note), No. 63 (p. 25); and Stephen of Bourbon (as on p. 284 n. 1), pp. 162–3.

[1] Some periods: 30 §45 (349): 'annis iam fere quadraginta elapsis'; 11 §1 (188–9): 'triginta annis, et eo amplius'; 30 §48 (354) (see p. 299 n. 2). Some dates: I 29 §5 (Year 1238): I 17 §5 (Year 1242); I 20 §8 (78) (Year 1248); II 25 §5; 51 §12.

'many years' (57 §14 (547); 57 §25 (556)); a canon of Lille, for his disobedience, suffered for 'twenty-five years' (I 22 §2 (86)). This long-term acquaintance with biographies had among other effects that of enriching Thomas's psychological judgements. To have remained chaste all your life, he warns, is no guarantee that you will not fall in old age: he tells of a parish priest who lost his chastity at the age of sixty (30 §47). Again, youths corrupted by sodomy, who have not reformed by the age of thirty-three (the age of the Lord of Nature when he redeemed mankind), will not normally reform afterwards: as Thomas knows who has (he says) 'heard men of eighty and a hundred confessing this sin' (30 §11). In yet another instance Thomas teaches that without regular prayer even the best man will gradually fall: taking as example a man he knew who was 'almost an angel', but because he scorned to go to Mass or say other prayers, gradually fell into every kind of lust and crime (32 §3 (368)). Others he has seen go in the other direction. Intelligent youths, even if not conspicuously devout, will often reform if chosen as bishop; and he gives a case (I 2 §§2 and 3). It was this long observation of human vagaries that gave Thomas such reverence for those who had both begun virtuously and kept it up: a regard evinced both in *De apibus* itself and in separate hagio-biographies Thomas wrote of no fewer than five contemporaries.[1]

In the characteristic moral miracle-story someone commits a sin and is at once struck down for it. In measure as Thomas moralized on the basis of the long stretch of people's lives he moved away from this genre. There remain of course in his book an abundance of thunderbolts and other supernatural visitations. But behind the punishment *ex machina* there are distinct signs of an experiential ethic showing through (from time to time it even expressly competes with the miraculous):[2] an ethic, that is to say, which makes sin and

---

[1] I 10 §3; II 23 §5. Cf. 53 §23; 50 §§4–8; 25 §6. Thomas also wrote hagio-biographies of John of Chantimpré, Christina 'Mirabilis', Margaret of Ypres, Mary of Oignies, and Liutgard of Aywières; cf. Kaufman, pp. 37–43.

[2] 30 §21; two die in unlawful coitus: was it a miracle or a heart attack? 'Respondeo, quod miraculose et naturaliter fieri potuit . . .'

virtue matters not only for will, but also for practical wisdom, learned from life.

If one confessor learned this from the experience of *his* life may not others, less literary than he, have learned it too? And if each learned it individually, and if they habitually shared their experiences, may they not in some sense have learned it collectively? This is again mere hypothesis; and vague enough at that. But if we decamp now across the sea north-west from Louvain there may be a way of meeting both shortcomings.

III. THE CONFESSOR LEARNS: ROBERT GROSSETESTE, BISHOP OF LINCOLN, 1235–1253

Robert Grosseteste was bishop of Lincoln from 1235 to his death in 1253. In England the Lateran Council of 1215 had been followed up by provincial councils, and Grosseteste's appointment both arose from and added to a momentum towards 'reform'. We are in this paper considering the most intimate aspect of the reform. So did Grosseteste. He wrote at least half a dozen treatises on confession; and they betray first-hand knowledge.[1] Unlike a mere friar like

---

[1] S. Harrison Thomson, *The Works of Robert Grosseteste* (Cambridge, 1940), pp. 125–6 (Nos 79–83) and 155 (Nos 114–15). I have used in this section three of the Latin treatises:

De confessione I	MS Bodleian 52, fos 151ᵃ–160ᵇ
	MS Bodleian 830, fos 168ᵈ–174ᵇ
De confessione II	MS Bodleian 801, fos 173ᵃ–193ᵃ
	Oxford, MS St. John's College 190, fos 131ʳ–146ᵛ (this MS is not listed by Harrison Thomson)
De modo confitendi	MS Bodleian 828, fos. 211ᵃ–215ᵇ

My impression that these treatises betray first-hand knowledge is based, quite apart from any deductions from Grosseteste's status as priest, especially on those passages which speak of penitents in the indicative. For instance (Bodl. 801, fo. 180ᵛ; St. John's 190, fo. 136ʳᵇ): 'quidam dicunt se non posse abstinere a malo reputando se omnino in hac vita esse confirmatos in malo'; (Bodl. 801, fo. 190ᵛ; St. Johns 190, fo. 144ʳᵃ): Querendum ut si vicium pro virtute reputatur sicut dicunt quidam habundanciam temporalium esse virtutem'; (Bodl. 830, fo. 172ᵛᵃ; Bodl. 52, fo. 159ʳ): 'volens confiteri necesse habet predicto ordine vel competentiori si sciat et possit se ipsum perscrutari ut statuat se contra faciem suam'; and others too numerous to itemize.

Thomas of Chantimpré, however, Grosseteste as bishop had not merely to hear confessions, but to organize their hearing by others. Here as in other fields he found his parish clergy inadequate. This was largely why he wrote treatises on confession. But more was needed than treatises. He must have help. 'My diocese is bigger and has a more teeming population [than others]', he wrote characteristically in 1237. 'So I need both more and more skilled help.'[1]

The skilled help Grosseteste had in mind was that of friars. Other reforming bishops were looking the same way. Grosseteste made a practice of having two Franciscans and two Dominicans by him always, in relays supplied by the orders' English provinces. Their value is witnessed by the urgency of his appeals when any were missing or late in coming. What gave them their value? It was partly, to be sure, their function of preaching, which was central to the reform, and which so many parish clergy found too difficult. But there was a second function, as important as preaching. In Lincoln as in Louvain the friars heard confessions. Grosseteste's appeal of 1237, just quoted, specifies the help he needs as 'in the preaching of God's word and in the hearing of confessions and the imposing of penances'. Again, lauding the Franciscan order to the pope in 1238 he would write: 'if only your Holiness could see how devoutly and humbly people come to hear the word of life from them, to confess their sins and be instructed in the rules of the good life; and how clergy and religious gain by their good example'.[2] Confession, in short, was one of the two principal functions of Grosseteste's auxiliaries.

As we have seen, more confession meant more knowledge, by confessors, of people's inner lives: their case-histories. In the context of the moral struggle in which confessor and penitent participated, this meant in turn closer acquaintance above all with their specifically moral dilemmas. Bishops and their advisors, to whom by canon

---

[1] *Epistolae*, ed. H. R. Luard (RS, 1861); *Epist.* 40 (p. 132) and—almost identical—*Epist.* 41 (p. 134).

[2] *Epist.* 58 (p. 180). A comparable position is described in my paper on mendicants in Pisa (as on p. 276, n. 1).

law priests had to refer hard cases, were only too well aware of this. A younger contemporary of both Grosseteste and Thomas of Chantimpré, the Franciscan minister-general Bonaventura, saw as one feature of the ecclesiastical crisis through which he was living, with its inadequate parish clergy, 'the perplexity of cases which arise'. 'We see both more-and-more new sins discovered [he wrote], and the daily emergence of more complicated cases.' Friars should be brought in on the hearing of confessions because 'the additional sins and difficulty of cases are now too much for the parish priests'.[1] Bishop Grosseteste himself confirms this testimony. His appeal for the friars' help in 1237 ends his list of needs with: 'and also more prudent advice in the proper and more edifying determination, according to the true meaning of Scripture, of the various new issues that arise day after day'.

These new issues were far from merely academic. They were the very problems portrayed in Thomas of Chantimpré's *exempla*: human problems of love, doubt, despair, and so on. They insisted on practicable solutions. And here was the difficulty. Friars might be better informed than secular clergy. But even friars did not know everything. Thomas himself was in fact typical: he often, in *De apibus*, qualifies an opinion given in summing up a story with an admission of ignorance like 'saving a better opinion'.[2] He and his colleagues had studied in Paris with the best theologians. But even there, after generations of study, not all moral dilemmas had ready-made answers. The science of Christian ethics, in other words, had limitations.

The limitations arose from the whole course of cultural development since 1100.[3] The century and a half since then had witnessed an

---

[1] *Quare fratres . . . confessiones audiant* (as on p. 282 n. 2), §9, p. 377L; §13, p. 378R; *Additamentum*, §13, p. 385R.

[2] 40 §7 (405); 49 §7 (448); 53 §2 (488); 57 §14 (547); 57 §22 (553). In the last instance, on posthumous bodily appearances, Thomas relates 'interrogavi super hoc supradictum magistrum Albertum [=Magnum], sed ille dissimilavit, et noluit aliquid definire'; thus proving, if proof were needed, that confessors 'in the field' could put their questions to scholastics.

[3] My main authorities for the following paragraph are R. A. Gauthier, *Magnanimité* (Paris, 1951), pp. 119–61, and K. Heitmann, *Fortuna und Virtus:*

evangelical movement, of which the rise of the friars was itself a culminating expression. There was a paradox in this movement. It put a new stress on personal ethics in the name of a Gospel which is not, in the ordinary practice of life, an explicit and unequivocal guide to the subject—what with its unjust stewards, prodigal sons, commendations of usurers, and so on. The early Fathers had helped out on some doubtful questions. But they themselves had learned much of their ethics from pre-Christian writers. And one aspect of the twelfth-century 'renaissance' was that scholars in this subject turned more directly to the same classics. They turned most notably to Cicero and Seneca, whose Stoicism harmonized not only with the asceticism of the Fathers, but also, if more distantly, with the rigour of those early penitential canons which guided the confessors.

Now Stoicism has always invited one criticism. Its austerity is unrealistic. Perhaps it is so for anyone. It is certainly so for the great mass of people. This is where the confessors came in. For the spread of confession after about 1200 exposed this flaw. From the very first the *Summae confessorum*, mouthpiece of the new generation of confessors, worked on the principle that 'human nature used to be stronger once', when those harsh penances were invented; that the confessor must therefore not apply old laws rigidly, but use his judgement—like a doctor who must cure, not kill.[1] Judgement: it was precisely this faculty, bombarded daily with individual problems, which thirsted for a more realistic, solid guide to ethics than the schoolmen had so far provided.

---

eine Studie zu Petrarchas Lebensweisheit (Cologne, 1958), pp. 98–120; cf. A. Murray, *Reason and Society in the Middle Ages* (Oxford, 1978), p. 133 (and 447–8, nn. 86–9). On the evangelical movement: M.-D. Chenu, *La Théologie au douzième siècle* (Paris, 1966), pp. 225–57; and H. Grundmann, *Religiöse Bewegungen im Mittelalter* (Hildesheim, 1961, 2nd edn), pp. 13–69.

[1] Alanus de Insulis, *Liber poenitentialis* (as on pp. 279–80), *Liber* II, *c.* xiii (ii. 54–5); Grosseteste, *De modo confitendi* (as on p. 305 n. 1), fo. 212^r: 'Et quia in diebus istis multi inveniuntur qui tam graves penitencias sustinere non possunt, oportet sacerdotem humane infirmitati condescendere et ipsas penitencias temperare ut vel leviores vel breviores fiant ita ut tollerari possint.' Other references in Tentler (as on p. 281 n. 1), 17 and n. 16.

But Bishop Grosseteste, besides being a confessor, *was* a school-man. So was Bonaventura. So in varying degrees of eminence were others daily involved in the hearing of confessions. Could they not themselves do the providing? This question takes us to a third city, geographically far from both Louvain and Lincoln: Lyons, domin-ating the Rhône valley, and itself dominated in matters of religious reform, in the middle years of the century, by its Dominican con-vent. In Lyons as elsewhere Dominicans were much involved in confessions. They had their own 'Thomas of Chantimpré' in the person of Stephen of Bourbon, whose *De septem donis Spiritus sancti* was, like *De apibus*, largely a collection of his own and his friends' reminiscences, including those from confession. In his early days in the Lyons convent Stephen had had as colleague Humbert de Romans, later the very minister-general to whom Thomas would dedicate *De apibus*. The convent had other literary claims. One contemporary of Stephen and Humbert was Hugh of St. Cher, formerly in turn pupil and master in the Dominican school in Paris—the school begun by Grosseteste's later friend and Dominican coadjutor in Lincoln, John of St. Giles. Hugh of St. Cher would go on, after his Lyons days, to edit the compilation of the most thorough biblical commentary of the Middle Ages.[1] The most important of all these Lyons writers, however, from the viewpoint of confessors, was the man who in 1261 became prior of the Lyons convent: Guillaume Peyraut. He was in some ways typical of his colleagues: when the Franciscan Salimbene came across Peyraut in Vienne, Peyraut was busy there 'preaching and hearing confessions'.[2] What was special about Peyraut was that he did something to meet the shortage of solid ethical manuals. His *Summae virtutum ac viciorum*, composed in Lyons between 1236 and 1249, would become the most widely read such manual—indeed one of the most widely read books—of the late Middle Ages.[3]

---

[1] B. Smalley, *The Study of the Bible in the Middle Ages* (Nôtre Dame, 1965), pp. 270–4 and *passim*.

[2] Salimbene de Adam, *Cronica*, ed. G. Scalia (Bari, 1966), 344.27–9.

[3] A. Dondaine, 'Guillaume Peyraut: Vie et Oeuvres', *Archivum fratrum praedicatorum*, 18 (Rome, 1948), pp. 162–236; see esp. pp. 193–7.

Peyraut's two *Summae* formed a handy compendium of scholastic ethics up to his time. But they had a flaw. They included the limitations. For all the success of his book, and its importance in literary history, Peyraut himself was little more than an eclectic with a big library. The breach of the limitations called for a greater mind, and perhaps a smaller library—libraries being sometimes an encumbrance when new departures are called for. And when the breach did come, as it was about to do as Peyraut wrote, it came through minds at once stronger scholastically than his, and operating far from the old scholastic centres where the big libraries were. This takes us back to Lincoln.

Thomas of Chantimpré tells of a Lyons Dominican who was English, and who returned on a visit to England taking his prior. The episode must be dated just before 1225. It serves to remind us that Lyons and Lincoln were not so far apart in terms of human intercourse as they were in mere miles.[1] In the generation that followed the two cities would in fact be drawn closer together than at any other time in the Middle Ages. Politically, the marriages of the four daughters of the otherwise childless count of Provence were already beginning to cement a vast, Francophone axis from Scotland to Sicily, soon to replace the discredited German Empire, and held together by a route that went through both Lincoln and Lyons. Ecclesiastically, Innocent IV, chased from Italy by Frederick II, would settle in Lyons between 1244 and 1251, making it the centre of the church, anticipating Avignon. Innocent held a general council while in Lyons, in 1244–5. Northern bishops attended, and momentous friendships between north and south were formed. One was between Grosseteste, who took with him his Franciscan friend Adam Marsh, and a certain Provençal Franciscan.

The name of this Franciscan was Hugh of Digne. Very few firm facts are known of him.[2] But the firmest of them is that the two

---

[1] 57 §28 (558). Date: before the death of Henry of Cologne (†1225).

[2] They are mostly contained in A. Sisto, *Figure del primo francescanesimo in Provenza: Ugo e Douceline di Digne* (Florence, 1971). The main narrative passages are in Salimbene, *Cronica*, pp. 324–68, and Joinville, *Histoire de S. Louis*, ed. N. de Wailly (Paris, 1868), cc. 11 (p. 20) and 132 (pp. 235–7). The

most successful potentates of the age, Louis IX and Innocent IV, held Hugh in awesome respect. Why we know so little else is that Hugh's genius—no lesser word is permitted by the rare testimonies about him—was mainly oral; and that this apparently suited the small towns of Provence, whose most charismatic preacher he was, and where he founded and guided various penitential communities. The book-learning of the Lyons Dominicans would have been less appropriate. Hugh knew plenty of Dominicans, of course. But it suggests a certain difference in his own approach that he thought the order inclined to learned pomposity.[1] He had certainly been a scholar himself, and in some respects remained one. (His admirer Salimbene of Parma used the phrase of him, as he did in separate passages also of Grosseteste and Adam Marsh, 'unus de maioribus clericis de mundo'.[2]) But by the time Grosseteste met him Hugh was both less and more than a scholar. He was less because Franciscans, in that region at least, were allowed only a minimum of books. The few writings of Hugh himself are comments on St. Francis's rule, and on poverty in particular. They are strict comments, and books are no exception to the strictness: a Franciscan may not have any but those which directly serve his pastoral function.[3] Why Hugh was at the same time more than a scholar is because of this very function. He was a pastor, *par excellence*. He was apparently more a preacher than a confessor. But he probably combined the

---

meeting at Lyons must be surmised from Salimbene, 335.26–7 and 324.31, and our knowledge that Grosseteste was in Lyons from late 1244 to late 1245 for the council, and again in 1250. Hugh's part in the foundation of the *Fratres de poenitentia Jesu Christi* is described by K. Elm, 'Ausbreitung, Wirksamkeit und Ende der provençalischen Sackbrüder in Deutschland und den Niederlanden', *Francia*, 1 (1972; Munich, 1973), pp. 257–324; pp. 284, 295–6, 297, 321.

[1] Salimbene, 364.17.

[2] 324.17; 335.27–8 and 335.31; 365.23–4.

[3] *Disputatio inter zelatorem paupertatis et inimicum domesticum eius* (text in Sisto, p. 364): 'usus ... rerum quam dixisti [=libri ecclesiastici, etc. ... que pertinent ad officium predicationis] non solum est tibi licitus, sed etiam necessarius ... Sed superfluus usus, sive sit ... que pertinent ad sapientiale studium ... professoribus paupertatis illicitus est.' Cf. also pp. 351–2.

two tasks like many in his order. And even as preacher he shared confessors' problems, not least that of 'the perplexity of cases which arise': i.e. an urgent interest in ethics. For St. Francis himself had said that the main subject-matter for sermons was to be 'vices and virtues', and Hugh knew it.[1] These vices and virtues return us to the meeting of Hugh with Grosseteste. Looking back from the 1280s Salimbene would describe Grosseteste and Adam Marsh (with the Franciscan John of Parma and Archbishop John II of Vienne) as two of Hugh's four most intimate friends (335.25–34). Intimate friends will talk of something of common interest. So at their meeting Hugh, Robert and Adam must have discussed such a subject. Since according to Salimbene all three had international pre-eminence as scholars it was probably something learned. Probably? Almost certainly: for we have strong clues as to what it was.

Historians of philosophy must excuse this journey through the undergrowth of church history. For we have emerged, rediscovering *en route* what I believe to be the lost medieval road, at a spot very familiar to them. Robert Grosseteste is well known to have translated Aristotle's *Nicomachean Ethics*.[2] Modern students of this translation, the first complete translation from Greek of all ten books (only three had been generally known before), have agreed about two things. The first is that it introduced, with remarkable speed, a

[1] St. Francis of Assisi, *Secunda regula*, c. 9; *Opera omnia*, ed. J. J. Van der Burg (Bologna, Bonn, 1899), p. 79. Hugh of Digne, *Expositio super regulam fratrum minorum*, c. 9 (text in Sisto, p. 295): '*De vitiis et virtutibus* quia in huiusmodi homines sunt maxime instruendi, nec sunt subtilitatibus vel curiositatibus detinendis' (*Curiositas* is used here in the usual sense).

[2] On the following: D. A. Callus, 'Robert Grosseteste as Scholar', in *Robert Grosseteste: Scholar and Bishop* (Oxford, 1955), pp. 1–69, esp. 62–6; J. Dunbabin, 'Robert Grosseteste as translator, transmitter and commentator: the "Nicomachean Ethics"', *Traditio*, 28 (1972), pp. 460–72; bibliography, pp. 461–2. The philosophical context: F. Van Steenberghen, *Aristotle in the West* (Louvain, 1955), esp. pp. 68, 92–4, 98, 104–8, 125, 136–7, 163; and more fully in *Idem*, *La Philosophie au xiiie siècle* (Louvain, Paris, 1966), esp. pp. 140–4, 162–3, 343–5.

fundamental and lasting shift in Christian ethics: a shift first detectable in lectures given on Grosseteste's version in 1250 by Albert of Cologne (the course of whose life and thought it changed); and subsequently in Albert's pupil Aquinas.[1] The second point of agreement is the unfathomable mysteriousness of Grosseteste's motive in making the translation at all. Why, it has been asked, if he was going to translate the work, should he have waited until he was an exceptionally busy bishop, rather than broach the task in the more tranquil Oxford years, when he wrote other works related to Greek philosophy? The contemporary Roger Bacon said it was because Grosseteste could only now, in the 1240s, get help from Greek speakers and Greek texts from southern Italy. That certainly fits with the picture of a north–south axis drawn just now. But Bacon's explanation has never taken historians far. Even the great Sir Maurice Powicke could offer nothing better than: 'it would be a pleasant task for a bishop in the evenings, when the day's work was done, and he sat among his friends in the manor house at Buckden Fingest.'[2]

The foregoing study of confessors and their needs has surely given us a better answer. Grosseteste's translation was not done *after* his day's work. It was *part* of his day's work; and was undertaken as a contribution to the day's work of many other pastors. The probability of this construction is raised to virtual certainty by the role in it of that Provençal Franciscan, Hugh of Digne. For the first dateable, overt reference to Grosseteste's translation is to a copy made

---

[1] Van Steenberghen, *Philosophie*, p. 278; Dunbabin, p. 464. The shift: O. Lottin, *Psychologie et morale aux xiie et xiiie siècles* (Louvain, Gembloux, 1942–60), iii. pp. 539–75, on the growing 'intellectualism' in ethics in Albert and Aquinas, with a general remark on Aristotle's influence in this particular on p. 276; and the same story on the virtue of prudence on pp. 257–80, with identification of Aristotle as prime mover on p. 276. A simultaneous shift in the concept of 'magnanimity' is charted by R. A. Gauthier, *Magnanimité* (Paris, 1951), pp. 295–302 (the place of Grosseteste's translation), pp. 307–10 (the change in Albert after his lectures on Grosseteste's text).

[2] 'Robert Grosseteste and the Nicomachean Ethics', *Proc. Brit. Acad.*, 16 (1930), pp. 85–104; 104–5. The unfathomable mysteriousness: Dunbabin, 462.

for the use (*ad opus*) of this very man.[1] The author of the reference is Adam Marsh. He goes on to tell Grosseteste, his correspondent, how the (bulky) work can be got from Lincoln to Provence (by being left with the London Franciscans, where a Provençal doctor in Queen Eleanour's service will pick it up). Hugh cannot of course have originated the idea of the Lincoln translation. For work on it began in the early 1240s, before Hugh met Grosseteste and Adam Marsh in late 1244. But there can be little doubt that the work was a subject of their talk. And it is Hugh's interest, an interest strong enough to justify a considerable feat of furniture removal, that tells us definitively about the motive for the translation. For at the end of the furniture removal was a man who, whatever his personal tastes may or may not have been, was only *permitted* to use books strictly for a pastoral purpose.

When this fact has been digested it will be useful to wash it down with a reconsideration of Grosseteste's literary output as bishop. In his episcopal period the works he chose for translation, other than the *Ethics*, were not philosophical. They were theological and pastoral. The first main one was Damascenus, whose compendium of theology was widely seen in the West as Greek equivalent to Peter Lombard, and of which Grosseteste revised an earlier Latin version made for the Cistercian Pope Eugenius III.[2] The second was Pseudo-Denys, keystone of mystical theology. There were others of similar ambiance. The *Ethics* came after and crowned this work.

If it seems strange thus to join Grosseteste's *Ethics* with the work of confessors and preachers, it is because the one name 'Aristotle' has lent a deceptive unity to the movement for translating that

---

[1] Adam of Marsh, *Epistolae*, ed. J. S. Brewer, *Monumenta franciscana*, Epist. 25 (p. 112), clearly alluding to the same object as *Epist.* 26 (p. 114), which gives the destination. 'De Berions' is now generally agreed to represent Hugh of Digne's *alias* 'de Bariola' (Salimbene, 324.15). It was his mother's name (Sisto, 6).

[2] Callus (as on p. 312, n. 2), 46–54; J. de Ghellinck, *Le Mouvement théologique du xiie siècle* (Bruges, 1948), pp. 374–412, esp. 410–2. Pseudo-Denys: Callus, pp. 56–61.

philosopher. The movement had in fact two distinct and even opposing currents, currents which respectively harmonized with the two
church–political currents of the age. One current of translation
started in the 1220s and flowed mainly from the Sicilian–Neapolitan
realm of the king of anti-clericals Frederick II, especially through
the pen of his astrological protégé Michael Scot.[1] This current
brought books north to the so-called 'Arts' faculties of Padua, Paris,
and finally Oxford. Conceptually it reached its extremity when
the Oxford schoolman Grosseteste became bishop in Lincoln. There,
in the still unsophisticated north, the current turned. Moved now
by the needs of a bishop supervising the cure of souls, not merely
those of a philosopher, the current flowed back down the north–
south axis, touching both Cologne and Provence in 1250 with the
arrival there of the Latin *Ethics*. The reaction would be completed
in the 1260s, with the baptism (by total immersion) of Aristotle, at
the hands of the Neapolitan Aquinas working in Paris. Simultaneously a Guelf Naples replaced a Ghibelline, under Beatrice of
Provence's husband Charles of Anjou.

The pattern of currents and cross-currents was of course subtler
than I have drawn it. For one thing Toledo should come into it. But
if it does, and is given the same scrutiny as other parts of the pattern,
Toledo only confirms the latter's dual character. The 'reverse-flow'
of translation in Toledo is represented by Hermann 'the German'.
Hermann is usually mentioned as if twin to Michael Scot. Both
translated Aristotle in Toledo. But the resemblance ends there.
Their choice of works, their careers and their patronage, were
different. Michael chose physical works. Hermann chose works on
morals or language. His main work was on Arabic commentaries
and paraphrases on the *Nicomachean Ethics*, which he did at roughly
the same time as Grosseteste's translation, in those now significantly
familiar years 1240–4. He went on in 1250 to translate the *Rhetoric*:
as if the symmetry of confession and preaching in contemporary

---

[1] Van Steenberghen, *Aristotle*, pp. 89–94, and *Philosophie*, 110–17, for the
basic data on translation, underlying this paragraph.

pastoral reform were reproduced in the selection of these two works. In 1256 he turned to the *Poetics*. Hermann's career is obscure. But what little is known of it, and of the quarter from which it was promoted, sets him off equally sharply against the Ghibelline astrologer Michael. In 1266 Hermann was made bishop of Astorga (which he remained until he died in 1272). The leading English authority on the Spanish church at the time, Dr Linehan, says Hermann's learning 'had no particular relevance to the episcopal calling'.[1] Some reason to doubt this has already been seen. And an even greater authority thought otherwise. This was the patron who made Hermann bishop. He was not any anti-clerical German king, this patron, but a French canon lawyer who was in these very years busy driving the last of those German kings from Italy: Pope Clement IV. Clement's letter of appointment to Hermann is unequivocal. The pope knew his man: Hermann is 'multo tempore nobis noto'; the pope mentions Hermann's long years of study, and recalls a time long before when he and Hermann had studied and lodged together in Paris. As for the deliberateness of Clement's choice: it ran in the face not only of the Astorgan chapter, but of Hermann's own reluctance. Hermann had pleaded age, inexperience of anything but study, and a canonical impediment as son of a priest. The pope replied he was not thinking of individual interests but those of the church, and ordered Hermann to accept.[2] Nor would the appointment of an up-to-date expert on moral theology have been inappropriate in Astorga. Not long before, in 1246, the most prodigious pastoral career of medieval north-western Spain had ended with the death of the Dominican saint, Peter Gonzales. Even if Gonzales was not Astorgan born and bred, as one old tradition said, we can surmise pretty certainly that the city had known his influence. And the principal hallmark of that influence, by general

---

[1] P. Linehan, *The Spanish Church and the Papacy in the Thirteenth Century* (Cambridge, 1971), p. 236.

[2] E. Martène and U. Durand, *Thesaurus novus anecdotorum*, ii (Paris, 1717), col. 431, *Epist.* 415.

agreement, had been the saint's indefatigability in one field above all: the hearing of confessions.[1]

To return once more to Lincoln: the bombardment of confessors by moral dilemmas, arising from the case-histories of ordinary lay-folk, has been suggested here as the main stimulus for Grosseteste's translation of Aristotle's *Ethics*. It remains to see what effect the new Aristotle may have had on these confessors. The search must begin with Grosseteste himself. The most illustrative of his treatises on confession in this particular, as also the longest, is that called by his bibliographer, *De confessione II*.[2] The treatise rarely quotes authors at all. It cannot be dated more nearly than to Grosseteste's episcopate. So there is no telling if it came before or after work began on the *Ethics*. But Grosseteste was personally an Aristotelian before the date his project saw the light. He almost certainly knew, besides the standard Books I-III, Latin and Greek fragments of other books of the *Ethics* even before he got a full Greek text of it.[3] So while we may not expect dateable footprints of Aristotle in *De confessione II*, it is reasonable to look for his spirit.

And we find it. It is specifically present in the book's systematic moderation. The Aristotelian 'Mean' (Latin: *Modus*) had long been common coin for moralists, in and out of confessional literature.[4] But Grosseteste's scheme of virtues and vices in this treatise is shaped by the idea of the Mean, to a degree uncommon at his date. His virtues, that is, have two vices attached, in excess and deficiency. Such a scheme inevitably determines the book's temper. An illustration of the temper is in Grosseteste's treatment of pious excess. It is

---

[1] [H]enrique Florez, *España sagrada*, 23 (Madrid, 1757), esp. §7 (pp. 249–50); cf. §13 (p. 256); and for the date and authority of this Le Tuy legend, p. 137. Gonzalez is made an Astorgan in the *Life* by the sixteenth-century Portuguese Dominican Sempayo, to which the Bollandists lent their authority in *AASS*, April II (1675), col. 391E.

[2] See p. 305 n. 1 above.

[3] Dunbabin, p. 463.

[4] e.g. in the eleventh-century *De vera et falsa poenitentia*, §21 [*PL* 40, cols 1120A].

a vice. Grosseteste eccentrically calls the vice 'curiosity', and makes it an excess of the virtue of 'occupation', as *accidia* is its deficiency.

> Curiosity [writes Grosseteste] is an immoderate exercise of good works. St. Paul condemns it in saying 'let your service be reasonable' [Rom. 12: 1]. Some people torture themselves by staying up at night, or by constant prayer, or they mortify themselves physically with endless weeping, hard beds, or other unbearable austerities, to such a degree that they either fade away altogether or make themselves very ill. Others, unsatisfied with the most paltry diet or the harshest flagellation, think up all sorts of self-torture, which easily precipitate them into sin or physical injury: people who kill themselves by self-mutilation, for instance, or gird and bind themselves with iron fetters, and other things not fit to be spoken of.

The indiscretions are rarely found in women; but sometimes amongst youngsters, 'of whom one may legitimately doubt if they will persevere in the indiscreet penances they have assumed'.[1] This last phrase betrays the source of Grosseteste's moderation: experience.

---

[1] MS Bodleian 801, fo. 185ᵛ [variants from MS Oxford, St. John's College 190, fo. 140ʳᵃ]: 'Curiositas est immoderatum bonorum operum exercicium. Contra quam dicit Apostolus rationabile sit obsequium vestrum. Sunt autem quidam qui in nocturnis vigiliis se tantum cruciant alii qui tam assiduis oracionibus insistunt, alii continuis fletibus alii duris cubilibus et ceteris laboribus intollerabilibus corpus mortificant, quibus aut omnino deficiunt aut [in] infirmitates magnas corruunt. Et sunt alii qui nec tenuissimis dietis nec asperis disciplinis contenti/[fo. 186ʳ] sunt set quedam genera nova indiscrete cruciandi cogitant in quibus de facili ruunt in peccatum vel in corporale *periculum velut qui communiter se extingunt mutilacione et qui se [*peccatum vel in mutilacionem membrorum qui] vinculis ferreis cingunt et stringunt et cetera que dicenda non sunt. In paucis tamen mulieribus talis indiscretio invenitur, [nisi] tamen ypocrisis est, et ideo non multum indiget inquisicione nisi in mulieribus coniugatis que [quandoque] sponsis invitis ieiunia immoderata assumunt observandas et hic male quia mulier non est potens sui set vir. Huiusmodi enim indiscretas penitentias assumunt quidam inconstantes in puericia, de quibus dubitandum est ne in fine deficiant.' *Occupatio* (or *labor*) was a newcomer to the scheme of virtues when Grosseteste was bishop. See S. Wenzel, *The Sin of Sloth: 'Acedia' in Medieval Thought and Literature* (Chapel Hill, N. Carolina, 1967), pp. 91 and 231-2 n. 95 (mentioning this treatise); also 249 n. 40; and (for the attitude) Murray, 'Religion among the Poor' (as on p. 300 n. 2), p. 313. The standard work on schemes of vice, and to some extent virtue, is still M. W. Bloomfield, *The Seven Deadly Sins* ([East Lansing], 1952).

Other examples of the same moderate and experiential ethic could be given. *Extenuacio* (excessive abstinence) is one: it gets closely similar treatment to *curiositas*.[1] Another concerns sex. Grosseteste was as austere as anyone else on 'illicit' sex, especially—in this like his fellow-Aristotelian Thomas of Chantimpré—when 'unnatural'. (Though even here the confessor's bark can be worse than his bite.)[2] But Grosseteste's austerity is not against all sex. On the contrary, his negative views can be seen as designed to *protect* sex, when it is licit (i.e. married and natural); most notably in that he makes a sin of 'insensibility' in conjugal sex, a deficiency which tempts the partner into illicit paths.[3]

This is once more an experiential ethic, as well as a moderate one. These qualities do not prove a specific influence on Grosseteste's treatise by the *Nicomachean Ethics*. What they do is show why Aristotle was congenial to this author. The mind that wrote the treatise was ripe for whatever Aristotelian influence it had not yet undergone. The consequence of this for later confessors who came definitely *after* Grosseteste's translation will be clear from a study of their manuals. The manuals, mostly by Dominicans and Franciscans, have been

[1] MS Bodl. 801, fo. 188r; MS St. John's Coll. 190, fo. 142ra. The passage similarly ends 'revocandi sunt penitentes quia pauci tales perseverant'.

[2] Cf. *De modo confitendi*, MS Bodl. 828, fo. 213v: 'Qui polluit se manu sua propria sodomiticam operatur turpitudinem, et gravius peccat quam si fornicationem vel adulterium naturaliter cum muliere commiteret. Et tamen ne aliquis qui ad hoc se facilem et pronum sentit fuisse in desperationem precipitetur, solet pro hoc peccato levior vel adeo levius penitencia iniungi sicut pro simplici fornicacione vel adulterio.' I quote the two sentences as bark and bite respectively.

[3] *De confessione II*, MS Bodl. 801, fo. 190r [variants from MS St. John's Coll. 190, fo. 143va]: 'Restat de insensibilitate querendum, que appetitum purgandi mortificatus et sensibiles concupiscentias insensibiliter sustinet nec affectat. Hoc peccato delinquunt coniugati ut quando alter alteri debitum reddere [negaverit. Huiusmodi negacio aliquando est] causa effusionis seminis, aliquando causa fornicationis vel adulterii, similiter et aliorum quod patuit in eva. Et fit quandoque causa ire quandoque causa vilitatis coeundi, quandoque causa contemptus mulierum. Similiter et mulier vel quia aliquem plus amat vel quia nequam est debitum similiter prohibet, vel ne dolorem partus senciat vel ne paupertate gravetur vel ne laboret nutriendo, vel quia tediosum/[fo. 143vb] est quod facere non tenetur.'

subject to a thorough study by T. N. Tentler. The following passage from the study relates Aristotle, for instance, to a change in confessors' views on the now familiar confessors' subject of sex.

It became a commonplace of moral theology to call sinless uses of sexuality not merely 'licit' as Raymond of Peñaforte [1233/8] had done, but even *meritorious*. For the history of theology the critical era for this development is, once again, the thirteenth century, when Aristotelians like Albert the Great and Peter of Tarantasia [Dominican archbishop of Lyons, who died as Pope Innocent V in 1274] find the exercise of conjugal rights with the proper motives and informed by the love of God not merely excusable but honourable.

Instances are given from various widely read manuals, from *c.* 1280 onwards.[1] What this summary does not say, and what we can now add, is that Aristotle did not impinge on confessors' ethics as it were from the outside. It was they who invited him in. The same is probably true of the generally moderate influence Tentler finds in the manuals, especially the more widely copied ones. He finds a 'humane tendency ... which occasionally appears in their liking for some opinion of Duns Scotus [Franciscan, † 1308] or Albert the Great, as well as in their general preference for theology over canon law' (theology being more receptive than canon law to Aristotelian influence).[2] The idea of the Mean is common in Tentler's manuals, especially in the central issue of rigorism against laxism: confessors are urged to avoid the inducing on one hand of despair by severity, and on the other of presumption by laxity.[3]

Our findings have a common drift. They suggest that what confessors learned in confession inclined them towards the moderating influence of Aristotelian ethics. Their manuals show signs that it did. So, finally, do their essays in scriptural commentary. Miss

---

[1] 224–5. The date of John of Freiburg's manual, the earliest instance quoted in the new tradition, is commonly given as 1280–98. See also Tentler, pp. 180–4, 272.

[2] 36. Instances of this tendency, especially pronounced in the more successful manuals (*Sylvestrina, Angelica, Astesana,* Gerson, etc.), see pp. 50 n. 36; 272; 332–40 *passim.*

[3] Tentler, pp. 128, 131, 261.

Smalley's *English Friars and Antiquity in the Early Fourteenth Century*[1] portrays a series of 'classicizing' friars, English forerunners of the Italian Renaissance. The movement, she says, was begun by a Franciscan called Walter of Wimborne, who became theology lector in Cambridge *c.* 1263–5, after apparently varied Franciscan experience elsewhere (p. 50). It was he who inspired the others. And what was his own inspiration? In a commentary Walter gives his idea of Heaven, and that for which he prays. The image he chooses is that of listening among the blessed to a reading from the heavenly throne. The book: can we guess? It is Aristotle's *Nicomachean Ethics*.[2] So swiftly had Grosseteste's translation won apotheosis. It is appropriate that Walter's favourite book stood at the very core of the interests of his successors. The Oxford Franciscan Burley translated it yet again, and gave the result to Richard de Bury, bishop of Durham. The *Philobiblion* attributed to this book-lover, according to Miss Smalley, breathes the very spirit of Aristotle; and 'not the dry Aristotle of the text books, but the living gentleman scholar, the anti-puritan' (p. 72). The book's Aristotelian character means all the more here in that it was probably not all written by Bishop Richard himself, but partly also by a friend, Robert Holcot. Holcot was a Dominican, and one known to have been especially experienced in hearing confessions: he may even have died in that capacity during the Black Death. Holcot also wrote biblical commentaries showing acquaintance with the *Ethics*. The commentaries show too that 'humane tendency' we have associated with the Aristotelians. 'The theme of hope for repentant sinners constantly informs his pages,' writes Miss Smalley: 'only long intercourse with Holcot will make the reader aware of his consistency in this direction.'[3]

---

[1] Blackwell, Oxford, 1960.

[2] Ibid. pp. 50–1: 'quibus doctor angelorum/legit librum ethicorum/ in sublimi cathedra'.

[3] 191. *N.E.* (Bk VII) cited in a biblical commentary, pp. 200–1; passage on Christ as sitting in every church ready to confer grace on penitents 'ut ad confessionem accedant', p. 332; life and death, pp. 135–6. Cf. B. Smalley, 'Robert Holcot, O.P.', *Archivum fratrum praedicatorum*, 26 (1956), pp. 5–97, esp. 7–9 (life and death), 89–97 (character).

'Le secret de la confession a été bien gardé.' But a little of this secret has, I hope, now been tapped. It is only a little. As St. Augustine said, the subject is endless. Confession has only been treated here as a source of instruction: as it comes through to us, rich in detail; and as it latently affected a whole generation of contemporary confessors—in both cases acquainting the learners with the moral realities of lives otherwise obscure. There was of course another category of learner: the penitent himself, whose reconstruction of his own past was meant to show him himself as he really was, in pre-emptive anticipation of the Last Judgement. Another paper could be written about him. For that was history too. Perhaps it is even what all history is. It is certainly what history will be. After all, if Adam was the first historian the last will be the Recording Angel, doing much the same thing better.

English chroniclers and the affairs of Scotland, 1286–1296 ([1])

LIONEL STONES

THERE need be no doubt that Edward I was determined to create, in his royal archives, a full official record of his main dealings with the Scots during all the years of his reign after the death of the Maid of Norway in 1290. The full extent of such texts is truly prodigious, and one may suspect that Edward here went too far, and obscured his tale by excess of detail. These *pièces justificatives* have received much study, especially in recent years,[2] but far less attention has been given to the passage of information on Scottish matters (whether by official means or otherwise) to the eyes and ears of English chroniclers of the period. The present paper is an attempt to deal with some of the problems of this particular piece of source-criticism. The chronicle texts of the 1290s are no easy field of study, and we shall depend very much here on Dr Antonia Gransden's admirable pioneer work entitled *Historical Writing in England, c. 550–c. 1307* (1974). Dr Gransden observes that English chronicles dwindle in number in the last decade of the thirteenth century. One ends in 1291, two more in 1293, one in 1295, two in 1297, and one

[1] I would like to thank several friends who kindly read the typescript of this paper, and supplied suggestions and corrections. Mention should be made of the paper by Dr R. A. Griffiths which was not published in time for any account of it to be taken here ('Edward I, Scotland and the chronicles of English Religious houses', in *Journ. Soc. Archivists*, vi (1979), 191–9).

[2] F. Palgrave, *Documents and Records Illustrating the History of Scotland* (1837, hereafter Palgrave, *Documents*); E. L. G. Stones and Grant G. Simpson, *Edward I and the Throne of Scotland* (2 vols, 1978, hereafter 'Stones and Simpson').

in 1298. She remarks that the end of Edward's conflicts with the church and the barons, and his lack of conclusive success in Scotland, seem to have reduced the enthusiasm of chroniclers for writing at all.[1] We may draw some consolation from the fact which, in a sense, follows from this, that a large amount of English chronicle-writing on Scottish matters (as on other things) towards the close of the century is fairly close to the events themselves, as the native Scottish chronicles, in the form that we have them, certainly are not.[2] Thus a study of reports in English chronicles of Scottish events may be expected to show something of the extent of contemporary English knowledge, and, if we are fortunate, may reveal something of its sources. We confine ourselves to the years 1286–96, years of special importance, which also have in themselves a considerable dramatic unity.

The fluctuations in the amount of space given to Scotland by English chroniclers at different points in our ten years are extreme. From 1286 until early in 1291 there is very little: surprisingly little if we reckon that those years include the violent death of King Alexander III, the minority and death of the Maid of Norway, and the long and complex negotiations for her marriage to Edward of Carnarvon. The long drama of the Great Cause in 1291 and 1292 is reported more fully, though (in view of the size of the undertaking, and the large number of people who took part in it), with disappointing thinness. Unhappily, too, most chroniclers quite misunderstood the nature of the assembly, describing the case as an arbitration, rather than a trial in Edward's court, and by so doing they have sadly misled posterity.[3] The reign of King John of Scotland, which follows, receives very little attention until its last year, 1296. Once Edward has begun his march north to settle accounts with John, however, there is excitement in the chronicles, and for part of 1296 Scottish affairs come near to filling the whole

---

[1] Gransden, p. 443.

[2] Bruce Webster, *Scotland from the Eleventh Century to 1603* (Sources of History Series, pp. 17, 42–57).

[3] See Stones and Simpson, i. p. 1, n. 2, and i. pp. 207–8.

canvas. With the Scots defeated, and their king deposed and exiled, information again becomes scanty. Never again in Edward's reign, however great his activity in Scotland, is there as much news as there was in 1296. This, however, takes us beyond our chronological limits. A matter of special importance, within our decade 1286–96, is the trough of obscurity, lying deep between the succession of Balliol to the Scottish throne in 1292, and the outbreak of Edward's war against Scotland in 1296. This is the crucial period when trouble is brewing between the two kings, but in which we are so unaccountably ill-informed by official records, and need help from chronicles which they do not supply.

Our starting point, the death of King Alexander III in 1286, despite its importance in the eyes of posterity, could hardly be handled more quietly by the English chronicles. The typical narrative gives a bare statement of Alexander's death, with no mention of its violent manner.[1] though Trevet adds that he fell heavily from his horse and Guisborough, with the caution 'ut dicitur', says further that he broke his neck.[2] We may find it not easy to recognize that for contemporary English chroniclers there was no call for foreboding in the death of the king of Scots at that particular moment, even though he left no heir of mature years. The Lanercost chronicler, indeed, does give a sombre tale of Alexander's last journey through night and storm, imbuing it with a strongly critical note of disapproval of Alexander's life.[3] But whatever historical value there may be in his details (and his obvious dislike of Alexander may have led him to darken the colours of his story) the narrative was not composed in England, but somewhere in Scotland, perhaps at

[1] So *Bury*, p. 86, *Dunstable*, p. 323, *Flores*, p. 74, *Worcester*, p. 492. *Oseney*, p. 305 comments very briefly. *Cotton*, Hagnaby, and *London* altogether ignore the event.

[2] *Trevet*, p. 316. *Guisborough*, p. 233.

[3] *Lanercost*, pp. 115–17. Some of the circumstantial details of Alexander's death given in modern narratives are not easy to find anywhere in the original sources. In particular, there seems no authority for the common story that he fell down a cliff.

Haddington, and copied later into the Lanercost chronicle.[1] It is not evidence for the knowledge of the event current, at the time, in Northern England, though it does, of course, show one way in which English writers might gain knowledge of Scottish affairs.[2]

Within a mere eight weeks of Alexander's death and, we may suppose, only some six weeks after he had first heard of it, Edward set out on a long-prepared and long-drawn-out visit to France and Northern Spain.[3] He was abroad for more than three years, and though he must certainly have kept in touch with the Scottish regency while abroad, neither records nor chronicles tell us very much of his negotiations. After his return in 1289, busy though he was in dealing with the outcry against his ministers for their alleged misdeeds when he was abroad,[4] he speedily brought matters to a head, and as early as November 1289 concluded the Treaty of Salisbury, followed in March 1290 by the Treaty of Birgham.[5] Of these agreements for bringing Margaret, the heiress of Scotland, from Norway, and marrying her to the young Edward, the chronicles tell us virtually nothing, but there is no call for wonder here, when the interests of three countries, Scotland, England, and Norway were all concerned,[6] and the whole situation was so

---

[1] Gransden, pp. 494–501.

[2] Accounts (of much later date) by Scottish chroniclers will be found in *Johannis de Fordun Chronica Gentis Scotorum* (ed. W. F. Skene, Edinburgh, 2 vols, 1871), i. p. 309, and in *Johannis de Fordun Scotichronicon* (ed. W. Goodall, Edinburgh, 2 vols, 1759), ii. p. 128. They are both brief, the former exceedingly so.

[3] J. P. Trabut-Cussac, 'Itinéraire d'Edouard Ier en France, 1286–89', in *BIHR*, xxv (1952), pp. 160–203.

[4] F. M. Powicke, *The Thirteenth Century, 1216–1307* (1962), pp. 361 ff.

[5] Ibid., pp. 598–600; *Scotland from the Earliest Times to 1603* by W. Croft Dickinson, 3rd edn by A. A. M. Duncan (1977), pp. 141–4. The name Birgham is the modern form of the medieval 'Brigham', given by Powicke, and by the original documents.

[6] The background is admirably given in Ranald Nicholson, 'Franco-Scottish and Franco-Norwegian Treaties of 1295' (*SHR*, xxxviii (1959), pp. 114–32).

delicate that great discretion and confidentiality were necessary. Bartholomew Cotton, who wrote in Norwich, and always had an ear for news from the ports of East Anglia, gleaned the news that a beautifully equipped vessel (*pulcherrima*) had left Yarmouth in 1290 to fetch the Maid of Norway; he does not mention (or more likely did not know) that that particular mission was unsuccessful.[1] Even the normally well-informed Dunstable annalist knew the bare fact of intended marriage, and no more.[2] Some meagre scraps of information trickled through to Guisborough, Rishanger, and Trevet,[3] but none of these profess to have knowledge of the terms of the treaties. The *Scalacronica* of Sir Thomas Gray does have a brief and misleading summary of them; he, however, was writing after the middle of the following century.[4] Few people in England at the time can have known much of the agreements which might have united the two kingdoms centuries before 1603.

Because the death of Margaret, in October 1290, took place in Orkney (then part of the Norwegian kingdom), we might expect the English chroniclers to know very little about it; nevertheless it is curious that neither they nor, apparently, any other sources give a really precise date.[5] In England it was soon quite overshadowed, as a piece of news, by the death of Eleanor of Castile a month or so later. Yet we know from unquestionable record evidence that

---

[1] *Cotton*, p. 174. For the very elaborate list of stores laden in this ship see J. Stevenson, *Documents Illustrative of History of Scotland* (2 vols, 1870), i. pp. 186–92. Cf. J. Bain, *Calendar of Docts. Relating to Scotland*, ii (1884), no. 464. These various records concerning missions to Norway deserve closer examination.

[2] *Dunstable*, p. 359. On this chronicle see C. R. Cheney, 'Notes on the Making of the Dunstable Annals', in *Essays Presented to Bertie Wilkinson*, ed. Sandquist and Powicke (Toronto, 1969), pp. 79–98.

[3] *Guisborough*, p. 233; *Rishanger* (whom we cite thus *passim*, but without prejudice to the question of authorship), p. 119; and the same words in *Trevet*, p. 316.

[4] *Scalacronica*, p. 110.

[5] A. H. Dunbar, *Scottish Kings* (2nd edn, 1906), pp. 106–7.

Edward had decided before her death to intervene in Scotland,[1] and it is to the credit of Trevet that he knew this, and realized that Eleanor's death and funeral had delayed Edward's action.[2] When at last Edward emerged from isolation in his mourning for Eleanor, and showed clear signs of moving to Scotland, quite a chorus of English chroniclers takes up the story, but there are some strange gaps in their reporting. We find singularly little interest in the movements to and from Scotland of the crowd of notables whose presence was required for the Great Cause (competitors, auditors, magnates, officials, lawyers, and the like), nor in the arrangements for providing urgently for the needs of this small army of people who were to be stationed for so long on the banks of Tweed. Cotton of Norwich, however, is again on the watch, and he records the arrival at Yarmouth of the competitor Florence, count of Holland, giving in addition the only reference in any source to the presence also of Florence's friend the count of Cleves, and curiously noting that the two men brought horses with them, as if such provision were unusual.[3] It is this same writer, we may note here, who records that on every Monday, Wednesday, and Friday during the Great Cause, King Edward gave a penny to every poor man who was present, a detail which we cannot confirm from official sources because of the loss of the household accounts of the period.[4] The unpublished Hagnaby chronicle in the Cottonian collection, to which we shall have to make more important reference later on, notes that Edward ordered grain to be gathered in Lincolnshire and sent to Scotland for the needs of his court.[5] This is certainly justified by record evidence, but the records tell of similar requisitions in

---

[1] Stones and Simpson, i. p. 6, n. 5.

[2] *Trevet*, p. 317.

[3] *Cotton*, p. 180; Stones and Simpson, ii. p. 398.

[4] *Cotton*, p. 429 (a passage found in one MS only, but the details in the whole section seem remarkably accurate).

[5] British Library, MS Cotton Vesp. B xi, fo. 33: 'Jussit eciam [sc. Edwardus] frumentum congregari per totam Lindeseiam, et usque ad Scociam ubicumque inventum fuerit, tam de ecclesiasticis personis quam de secularibus, et sibi et suis in sustentacionem apportari.'

many other counties,[1] and concerning these the other chronicles are silent.

One would have expected many of the chronicles to report under 1291 that they had received royal letters asking for historical precedents to be supplied to Edward for his claim to be overlord of Scotland. Scores of monasteries received such letters, and a large number of them replied, but none of them copied the letter into their chronicle, and only Rishanger specifically mentions it.[2] It is less strange, though regrettable, that no chronicle gives the text, or even mentions the existence, of royal letters convening the great assembly or parliament which met at Norham for the Great Cause in May 1291;[3] less strange because that essential but elusive summons seems not to have survived anywhere. But if it is true, as we shall see later, that monks were summoned to Norham to give evidence, how curious it is that no chronicle even says that its own house was asked to send a monk, let alone giving the letter which made the demand.

Little though the chroniclers knew of the preliminaries to the Great Cause, they learned, in various ways, a fair amount about the assembly itself, even though they quite misunderstood its exact legal nature. Some things they did learn by official means, for Edward supplied copies of two brief texts to a wide range of religious houses in England. We shall have to ask why these were distributed and apparently no others, some of the latter seeming to us far more important for history and precedent. Second, some much longer texts came, it seems unofficially, into the hands of the abbey of St. Albans. Third, a few monasteries became interested enough to carry out researches of their own into the history of

---

[1] Stones and Simpson, i. p. 198.

[2] Rishanger, p. 123. Rishanger, however, suggests, apparently with no warrant, that Edward's enquiry extended to Wales and Scotland as well as England. On that point see Stones and Simpson, i. p. 147. Worcester cathedral priory mentions a general search in chronicles, but says nothing of its own part, nor of receiving a letter from Edward on the matter, though its actual reply to him survives (Worcester, p. 504; Palgrave, *Documents*, pp. 129–34).

[3] Stones and Simpson, i. pp. 102–3.

English claims over Scotland, and inserted the results into their chronicles. In the course of this work it seems possible that some monastic writers were able to gain a sight of a few official texts produced by Edward's clerks for the Great Cause. Lastly there is an indefinable element of eyewitness knowledge in the chronicles, harking back, presumably, to the reports of monks present at the hearings, or of magnates, clerks and others who took part.

(i) In July 1291, during the first long adjournment of the case, the English government sent out copies of the submission of the competitors for the Scottish throne to Edward's jurisdiction, and of their consent to his having seisin of Scotland during the hearing (the term 'Award of Norham' has traditionally been applied to one or both of these texts).[1] The copies went to a large number of English religious houses, and to some (perhaps, if we knew the full story, to all) of the secular cathedrals,[2] with the order to put the texts on record. As a result a large number of chronicles inserted them in full, even including, in many cases, the whole of the royal order itself. Sometimes they wove them into some sort of description of the Great Cause, but more often they inserted them with such wooden abruptness that in the worst examples the reader can make no sense of their place in the narrative.[3] Indeed if official texts were ever to be circulated, it seemingly showed a striking lack of imagination to do so in this manner, giving no explanation of their place in the long legal process to which they belonged, but expecting the unfortunate monks to make sense of them. But we must beware of interpreting Edward's intentions by ideas foreign both to his time and to his character. What precisely was his motive? Presumably not to ensure the mere survival of the competitors' submission, of

---

[1] Ibid. ii. p. 120.

[2] We know of York Minster, where, since there was no chronicle, the texts were read aloud in chapter, and copied into the Dean and Chapter register; of Wells cathedral, where they were noted in the *Liber Albus*; and of St. Paul's London (Stones and Simpson, ii. p. 6, 120n; Hist. MSS Commission, *Calendar* of MSS of Dean and Chapter of Wells (1907–14), i. p. 313; *Flores*, p. 75n).

[3] e.g. *Dunstable*, p. 368.

which he was careful to have duplicated exemplars in the royal archives,[1] and which would be included in the central notarial record of the whole case, for which arrangements were already in hand. Nor simply to distribute all over England the news of the submissions, for they could have been made public more effectively by simpler means. His reasons may have been mere annoyance that his recent request for historical precedents had produced so little from the chronicles that was of any use to him, and determination to force into them the very first Great Cause texts that might be useful in future. This would be in keeping with what we know of his character.[2] It may seem strange that nothing more (so far as we can tell) was sent out to monasteries after this early stage of the case. Might one not have expected Edward to supplement the Award of Norham, which dealt only with a procedural emergency, by distributing some of the far more decisive texts which were available from the final stages of the case? In particular one may think of the unconditional declaration of homage by King John for the realm of Scotland in December 1292?[3] Here, indeed, was the kind of text for which Edward's clerks had searched in vain early in 1291. One wonders whether a distribution of this text was made late in 1292 or early in 1293, of which all trace has now been lost? It is very unlikely.[4] Apart from all other considerations, one may note that though many chronicles report the actual act of homage, none of them save Rishanger, Trevet, and the versifier Langtoft give the very words used, and none of these three suggests that the words

[1] On these duplicates see Stones and Simpson, ii. pp. 69, 75.

[2] The impulsive side of Edward deserves closer study, for it might affect his conduct in great matters, as well as in such bizarre episodes as his assault on a squire with a stick on the wedding-day of the king's daughter Margaret, in 1290 (PRO, C 47/4/5, fo. 47ᵛ), and the similar oddities noted in Hilda Johnstone, *Edward of Carnarvon, 1284–1307* (1946), pp. 123–4.

[3] Ibid. ii. pp. 260–3.

[4] If a letter circulating it to monasteries had been issued other than by the chancery we might have no traces, but only if all original exemplars had vanished, and no chronicle copied the text. The distribution of 1291 was under the exchequer seal (Stones and Simpson, ii. p. 120).

came by official means.[1] On the whole it seems certain that the distribution in July 1291 stands alone, and that the opportunities for later circulation of more decisive documents were not taken. It may be that the mere administrative effort in 1291, when many extra clerks had to be hired in order to make the large number of copies needed,[2] had proved too great. But we suspect rather that the first impulse, which had launched Edward into the very dramatic gesture of sending out the Award of Norham, had died within him as the Great Cause moved to its end.

(ii) Little need be said about the fortunate survival at St. Albans of a supremely important group of texts now known as *Annales Regni Scotie*, for an analysis of them is available elsewhere.[3] As they stand in the manuscript, they are a confused mingling of a draft notarial instrument recording the first stage of the Great Cause, with a mass of non-notarial reports of the subsequent part of the case. The confusion goes far beyond what would be possible with a coherent mass of texts sent out officially. Evidently St. Albans had come by an entirely unarranged collection of working papers, prepared by a clerk, or clerks, who had been present at the case, the notary John of Caen certainly having some hand in them. St. Albans also had possession of other Great Cause texts, for in another part of the same Rishanger volume which contains *Annales Regni Scotie* we find a summary in Latin of the reply which the Scots gave (in French) to Edward's demand for acknowledgement of his overlordship[4] (a document not found at all, be it noted, in the *Annales*). Compared to this 'scoop' by St. Albans, no other chronicle has much to show, except for Walter of Guisborough, who in some manner came by a version of the opening speech in the case given by Justice Roger Brabazon.[5] He gives it, however, in a form en-

---

[1] *Rishanger*, pp. 135–6, *Trevet*, pp. 324–5, *Langtoft*, pp. 192–4, the words being given in prose inserted in the verse text.
[2] Stones and Simpson, ii. p. 120.
[3] Ibid. i. pp. 61–5; and printed also in *Rishanger*, ii. pp. 10–258.
[4] *Rishanger*, pp. 124–5, with which cf. Stones and Simpson, ii. pp. 30–1.
[5] Stones and Simpson, ii. pp. 17–19.

tangled with a strange pedantic addition which he ascribes to the Dominican scholar William Hotham.

(iii) The evidence in print for the historical researches carried out at monasteries privately (though beyond doubt stimulated by the royal enquiries), is to be seen in the surveys given by Rishanger, Henry of Knighton, and the chronicler of Oseney, the second and third of these being presumably taken from the first.[1] Beyond these one must note that at least one manuscript of Guisborough seems originally to have included a longer text which is now lost.[2] A number of unpublished monastic manuscripts contain similar materials. A point of special interest here is the evidence that some monastic writers had seen a text of the official historical survey prepared by Edward's clerks.[3] How this may have happened is uncertain, but it seems unlikely to be evidence of an official circulation to monasteries by the government.

(iv) As for accounts by eye-witnesses, the careful summary of much of the Great Cause in the *Bury Chronicle*[4] does have an air of personal experience, but we must remember that there is no mention in the records of the presence of an English monk or monks, and no chronicle allusion to their presence except at the outset of the case, when they came to furnish evidence on precedents for the English claim to overlordship.[5] This, of course, does not rule out the receipt at Bury of a report from someone, for example a royal clerk, who had been present.[6] On the whole, however, the monastic reports do not have the kind of personal eye-witness flavour which we find, for example, in Guisborough's description of the inauguration of John Balliol as king of Scots at Scone, soon after the end of the case.[7] In that narrative we have the best extant account of the Scottish royal inauguration, with the setting of the king on

---

[1] *Rishanger*, pp. 123–4; *Knighton*, pp. 287–9; *Oseney*, pp. 337–8.
[2] Stones and Simpson, i. p. 160.
[3] Ibid. i. pp. 158–9.
[4] *Bury*, pp. 98–103, 114–15.
[5] Stones and Simpson, i. pp. 147–8.
[6] It is surely improbable that such a narrative was based solely on a sight of the official notarial records!
[7] *Guisborough*, pp. 238–9.

the traditional chair during mass, and of his remaining seated there (*lapidatus*, in allusion to the famous stone) for the rest of the rite, save during the elevation of the host. Despite doubts about the accuracy of the description of the stone, which was perhaps concealed by drapery and vestments, the narrative there has a pictorial quality not to be found in any chronicle account of the Great Cause, despite the wonderful spectacle that the Cause must have offered.

Throughout the years 1293 and 1294, and for much of 1295, the English chroniclers have little interest in Scotland. This is due, no doubt, in part to excitements in Wales and growing troubles with France, but even more to lack of communication with Scotland as soon as Balliol was left in charge of the kingdom as King John. The silence is at last broken in the middle of 1295, when a number of English chroniclers give the strange tale of King John being placed under the control of a council of twelve magnates (four bishops, four earls, and four barons). The only Scottish evidence of this, in a much later account, is placed under 1296,[1] but it seems likely that the episode is connected with the Scottish parliament which met at Stirling in July 1295.[2] The most important early authorities for it are Guisborough, Rishanger, and the so-called 'Annales Anglie et Scotie'.[3] The origin of their information is entirely unknown. In October 1295 the famous Franco-Scottish treaty was ratified at Paris. The text seems to have been discovered by Edward's clerks soon after the invasion of Scotland in 1296, and in the years to come great publicity was given to it by the government in England, as the culminating proof of Scottish duplicity, until it won pride of place in the Great Roll of Andrew de Tange.[4] One might have imagined that Edward would have sent it to the chroniclers, but in

[1] *Fordun*, ed. Skene (as above, p. 326, n. 2), pp. 327–8. It seems worth while to emphasize that the contemporary evidence for this event is all English, and scarcely impartial.

[2] Dickinson, ed. Duncan, p. 151; Powicke, *Thirteenth Century*, p. 612. The statement of some chroniclers that the parliament met at Scone seems to be an error.

[3] *Guisborough*, p. 264; *Rishanger*, p. 152; 'Annales Anglie et Scotie' in *Rishanger*, pp. 372–3.

[4] Stones and Simpson, ii. p. 286 and n.

fact it is given only by Guisborough, and copied from him by Knighton, though Rishanger at St. Albans had evidently seen a copy too.[1]

Edward marched into Scotland in March 1296, and from that point information flowed back to English chroniclers in abundance. There is a curious twilight period, however, immediately before his arrival in Scotland. Certain events of that period, in Scotland, were recorded in English chronicles. In view of the obvious lack of means for conveying immediate knowledge of them to England, we may think it likely that they did not become known in England until the English invaders heard of them; but we cannot be entirely sure. Whence did Guisborough hear that Pope Celestine V had absolved King John from his fealty and homage to Edward, a story to which Langtoft adds that John agreed to hold Scotland as a papal fief?[2] The tale has no other support, but it is not entirely impossible, and it might have come as a rumour from the papal court, if not from Scotland. Guisborough seems to say that some English merchants who escaped from a Scottish attack at Berwick came to Edward with news, and it is not impossible that other fugitives also gave accounts of this, and of other events, which reached the priory of Guisborough.[3] Then by some means knowledge was gained of the treachery of the Englishman Robert Roos, at Wark, a man allegedly induced by a Scotswoman, quite in the manner of later border literature, to intervene on the side of her countrymen. Of this queer affair Guisborough gives the fullest tale.[4] It may have come to him, by some means, from one of the few English soldiers who (he says) made their escape from Robert's trap. He gives elaborate details, among them the sign and countersign. His informant strikes one as more literate than the rank and file, and perhaps he may have been the *millenarius miles* ('battalion commander') whom Guisborough mentions?

[1] *Guisborough*, pp. 265–9; *Knighton*, pp. 292–8; *Rishanger*, p. 151.
[2] *Guisborough*, p. 270; *Langtoft*, p. 222. Celestine V was pope only for the second half of 1294.
[3] *Guisborough*, loc. cit.
[4] Ibid. pp. 271–2.

What we have termed the twilight stage in the chronicles gives place, by the end of March 1296, to a brief period, lasting only until Edward's departure from Scotland on 22 August, of remarkable daylight. To pursue the sources whence chroniclers drew this knowledge is an irresistible attraction, but the results are rather inconclusive; they might be less so if we had modern editions of more than two of the essential chronicles, that is, the Bury chronicle and Guisborough. To start with there are two official documents given in a small group of chronicles: King John's formal 'defiance', bearing no date, but known to have been handed to Edward at Berwick on 5 April 1296,[1] and his renunciation of the throne in July.[2] We know for certain that Edward ordered an official record of the former: the notarial copy made by John of Caen survives,[3] and we have mention of yet another notarial text, certified further by the seals of four English bishops.[4] Guisborough says that Edward ordered it to be enrolled in chancery. Perhaps this is only a confusion with the notarial texts. But did Edward also have copies sent to monasteries? The defiance is given only by Cotton, Guisborough, Knighton, Rishanger, and Trevet, and of these Knighton is certainly not independent. It appears also in the register of the bishop of Carlisle.[5] Nowhere is it accompanied by any royal command for its preservation. The case is similar with the other official document. Guisborough gives it in the original French, and there are Latin translations, probably made from his French text, in Rishanger and

---

[1] *Anglo-Scottish Relations, 1174–1328: Some Selected Documents*, ed. E. L. G. Stones, 23; *Cotton*, pp. 308–9; *Guisborough*, pp. 275–6; *Knighton*, pp. 300–1; *Rishanger*, pp. 158–9; *Trevet*, pp. 344–5.

[2] Stones, *Documents*, no. 24 (given at Kincardine, 2 July 1296); *Guisborough*, pp. 280–1 (10 July); *Knighton*, pp. 308–9 (no date); *Rishanger*, pp. 161–2 (10 July); *Trevet*, pp. 348–9 (10 July).

[3] Stones, *Documents*, no. 23.

[4] F. Palgrave, *Antient Kalendars and Inventories of the Exchequer* (1836), iii. p. 108.

[5] *Register of John de Halton* (Canterbury and York Society, 1913), i. p. 68, given, like the chronicle versions, without date, whence it would seem that no date may have been given in the original text of the 'defiance'.

Trevet. This relatively meagre publicity seems unlikely to be the whole result of an official distribution, even though to us the texts might both seem well worthy of perpetual preservation in chronicles.[1] Perhaps the government was too busy to think of the matter, or felt too secure in its position to have need of everlasting public justification. If so, that feeling of security did not last for long, but the circumstances of 1296 were undoubtedly favourable to false optimism in England.

The chroniclers' main knowledge of the English triumphs of that year must have been reports by individuals who followed Edward on his campaign. More Englishmen must have crossed the border in 1296 than ever before. There had never been an incursion which allowed them to see so much, and for so long. It is at this time (if we may begin with the literary efforts of the majority) that we begin to possess those soldiers' songs which are the medieval equivalent of the ballad of the Siegfried Line.[2] For an example we venture to adapt freely an authentic fragment whose barrack-room flavour might vanish in a scholarly translation from Middle English:

> For those Scots,
> I rate 'em as sots,
> What a sorry shower!
> Whose utter lack
> In the attack,
> Lost 'em at Dunbar . . .[3]

We shall never know how these crude ditties came to be written down, but whatever the means was, they came into the hands of the chronicler Langtoft, who fortunately quotes long sections of them. We need not despise them as material for history, because they show how Englishmen in 1296 could think, talk, and sing about

---

[1] We do not discuss here the origin of the Scottish submissions in *Guisborough*, pp. 281–4, and *Trevet*, pp. 350–1, but with so small a distribution, it seems unlikely to have been official.

[2] On the songs see R. M. Wilson, *Lost Literature of Medieval England* (1952), pp. 206–14.

[3] Original in Wilson p. 210; Langtoft, p. 252.

Berwick and Dunbar as their descendants were to do, centuries later, about Jubbulpore, Ypres, and Armentières.

If the common soldiers were thus celebrating their *annus mirabilis*, their social betters had their own more sober ways of doing so, but their medium was prose, which is harder to detect when woven into a chronicle. Only one document composed as a private record during the campaign seems to have survived complete, and without being merged in a chronicle text. It is the remarkable 'war-diary', as we should now say, called 'Itinerary of King Edward in Scotland in the year 1296', which survives in its original French form in at least three manuscripts, and in an English translation of much later date.[1] It covers the king's daily movements from 28 March 1296, when he crossed the Tweed, until 22 August, when he left Scotland. Its author is unknown, but he must have been with the royal headquarters throughout the campaign. This text seems to be unique, and to owe its preservation to the interest which it aroused in later medieval times. It did not, however, come into the hands of any chroniclers. None the less it helps us to understand the origins of the 'news-letters' which have left clear traces in Edwardian chronicle writing. The kind of man who wrote the itinerary (well-informed, literate, anxious to place on record his own recollections of great events not for the future reader of chronicles, but for his friends) was the kind of man who would write letters from Scotland about the battles and sieges that he had seen. Suspicions have already been aroused, in recent publications, concerning the presence of material from news-letters in the unprinted chronicles of Hailes[2] and Hagnaby[3] where they deal with the events of 1296. With the kind agreement of Dr Michael Prestwich, to whom the suggestion

---

[1] French original printed in several works, but best in Thomas Thomson's *Instrumenta Publica* (Bannatyne Club, Edinburgh, 1834), pp. 177–80; English version (with introduction by Nicolas) in *Archaeologia* xxi (1827), pp. 478–98.

[2] E. L. G. Stones and Margaret N. Blount, 'The Surrender of King John of Scotland to Edward I in 1296' (*BIHR*, xlviii (1975), pp. 94–106).

[3] M. C. Prestwich, 'The English Campaign in Scotland in 1296 and the Surrender of John Balliol: Some Supporting Evidence', (*BIHR*, xlix (1976), pp. 135–8).

concerning the Hagnaby chronicle is due, we print the relevant section of that text at the end of this paper.

News-letters survive in such numbers from the Hundred Years War that there is some danger of thinking them to be almost an invention of that period.[1] In fact they go back at least as far as the early twelfth century,[2] but we may find it easier to specify the undoubted marks or 'notes' of the species by reference to the mid-fourteenth century, when many survive unabbreviated and undisguised by inclusion in a chronicle. Such marks are the details of battle casualties, the expression of sorrow for the slain, and of satisfaction, or gratitude, for a small death-roll on one's own side. Knowledge is often shown of details not likely to be remembered except by an eye-witness; frequent reference is made to 'rex noster', 'gens noster', or 'nostri', and phrases such as 'thanks be to God' are common.[3] A reader who knows a number of intact letters of this sort may feel fairly sure of his instincts for detecting fossil fragments buried in a chronicle narrative, even in the earlier period when there are few undoubted letters for comparison.

One must admit that the textual problems in 1296 are complex, since different chroniclers may either be using different parts of one letter, or separate letters, and in any case the campaign of that year has several episodes which are distinct, but may be confused in the chronicles. The capture of Berwick on 30 March is overlapped by the Scottish raids on Carlisle, Corbridge, and Hexham late in March and early in April. The fighting at Dunbar lasts from 23 to 27 April, and is followed by the pursuit of the Scots, the capture of Edinburgh castle, and (in July) by the submission of Balliol. For the capture of Berwick, our longest narrative is found in Guisborough.[4] It begins

[1] No full list of these is known to have been printed, but see Stones and Blount, p. 103. The notes to *Anonimalle Chronicle*, ed. V. H. Galbraith (1927), are an admirable starting-point for investigation, e.g. pp. 160, 162, 164, 171.

[2] For example, the two letters describing the battle of Tinchebrai (1106), one printed by H. W. C. Davis in *EHR*, xxiv (1909) pp. 728–32, and the other in *HN*, p. 184.

[3] Even as early as the letter printed by Davis, cited in the previous note, one may see many of these features, including a 'deo gratias'.

[4] *Guisborough*, pp. 274–5.

with the creation of new knights by Edward outside the town, a scene observed by the crews of 24 English warships outside the harbour, who were thereby misled into making a premature entry, and were attacked, with the loss of 28 men. The smoke from their burning ships was seen in Edward's camp, and he sounded the trumpets for attack on the town. The Scots were taken by surprise, and did not seriously resist. Thirty Flemings bravely defended the 'Red Hall' until the hour of Vespers, only then to be burned in the ruins. The brother of the earl of Cornwall[1] was killed by a missile through his visor. Of the enemy there were slain more than 8,000. The castle surrendered, on terms, with 200 men: the women of the burgh were allowed to go in peace to their kindred. The king stayed for fifteen days in Berwick, and made there a new ditch 80 feet wide and 40 feet deep.

These details, which we summarize from Guisborough, are very circumstantial, and not only do we find figures of casualties, but the words 'noster' and 'nostri' are not infrequent. The figure of fifteen days is too small for Edward's stay at Berwick (he was there for about four weeks[2]) but in general the narrative is very accurate. The escape of the sailors in one ship belonging to Durham priory is said to be 'miraculous', a formula essentially not far different from the conventional 'thanks be to God'. It is conceivable that the source of the whole story may be a letter sent back to Durham priory by, perhaps, a clerk who was on board the Durham ship.

Several other sources for the capture of Berwick show signs of depending in some degree on written accounts by eye-witnesses.[3] The Hagnaby narrative, printed below, duly exclaims 'prohdolor' in giving the list of casualties (surely much exaggerated in giving 11,660 Scots, Flemings, and Poitevins, and differing from Guisborough in the number of sailors slain). The Worcester annalist

---

[1] On this brother see below, p. 346 n. 4

[2] See contemporary itinerary of Edward I in *Instrumenta Publica* (as above), pp. 177–8.

[3] The writer of *Lanercost* (p. 173), says that he saw the bodies of the slain, but his circumstances were exceptional (above, pp. 325–6).

has only one sentence, but his mention of the defence lasting 'until Vespers' suggests, perhaps, that he had seen a text similar to Guisborough's source.[1] The Dunstable chronicler, though here much shorter than Guisborough, and having no verbal resemblances, has a comment most unlikely to be his own invention, but one which would occur very naturally is a letter written very soon after the event: 'quantas divitias, quos thesauros in villis et in castro rex invenerit, nemo novit'.[2] He makes a curious mistake by placing the capture of Berwick on 1 March instead of 30 March. He may therefore have had before him a text like that used by Sir Thomas Gray, in his *Scalacronica*.[3] Gray's account begins by describing Edward's arrival at Berwick, and continues 'et le primer jour qe il enveint . . . un nief de sez vitaillers . . . secchist sur terre Descoce'. Dunstable may have misunderstood this 'the first day' as meaning 'the first day of the month'. Indeed there is a good deal in Gray's account to suggest that it was founded upon a contemporary letter different from that apparently used by both Guisborough and Hagnaby, and it is unfortunate that Gray's text, at any rate as printed, seems very corrupt.

As one might expect, the chronicle accounts of the raids by the Scots do not show signs of resting on news-letters, for the terrified inhabitants and fugitive soldiers are not likely to have had either time or inclination for writing. In general one might say that it is victors who write home, not vanquished. But when the English captured Dunbar castle, and won a complete triumph over the Scots nearby, there was ample material and motive for writing. The Hagnaby narrative is certainly based on a letter; it is not clear whether the letter is a continuation of that used for the capture of Berwick, or a new one, but the detail is now given much more fully than before. Typical signs of its character are the words 'we came to Dunbar'; 'hostages were handed over to us at Vespers on Thursday';

---

[1] *Worcester*, p. 526.
[2] *Dunstable*, p. 403.
[3] *Scalacronica*, p. 122.

'when we hastened to battle the Scots, thanks be to God, turned tail, but we chased them'; 'the same day we returned to Dunbar'; and 'in the castle we found the earls of Ross and of Atholl . . . and 22 Scottish knights'. Here we certainly need have no doubts. In other chronicles the epistolary style is more diluted, yet it emerges at some points with but little overlay. In the annals of Worcester this passage occurs:

'And in the battle [sc. of Dunbar] they [sc. the Scots] left dead on the field Ingram de Balliol, the bishop of Aberdeen, and Patrick Graham, with many nobles, and three thousand foot-soldiers; but none of our troops fell, and the only wounded were two knights'.[1]

It does not alter the verdict on the nature of this passage when we find that the names of both the bishop of Aberdeen and Ingram de Balliol are mistakes, presumably made by the English letter-writer in the uncertainty of the period when the dead were being identified.[2] The Furness chronicle was also misled into making the bishop of Aberdeen die on the field.[3] It seems probable that for Ingram and the bishop we should read Robert de Keith and Thomas Sinclair,[4] and that the mistakes are testimony to the early composition of the original source. Guisborough has a long narrative, containing the formulae 'ut altissimo placuit', and 'insequebantur nostri cedentes et trucidantes', and giving the distance of the pursuit, 'quasi spacio vij. leucarum vel viij. usque ad forestam de Selkyrke'.[5] Trevet, who often follows Guisborough very closely, must here have had some independent access to the same or a similar original

---

[1] *Worcester*, p. 527.

[2] Henry Cheyne was bishop of Aberdeen from 1282 until 1328. Note that the Hagnaby extract below (p. 348) mentions him as a prisoner after this date. Ingram de Balliol seems, in fact, to have survived until not long before February 1299 (Bain, *Calendar of Docts*, ii. no. 1060).

[3] *Furness*, p. 581 (continuation of William of Newburgh).

[4] cf. *Flores*, pp. 97–8. We venture to emend the 'Robert de Ketinge' of this chronicle into the much more likely 'Keith'. The Hagnaby extract below (p. 346) has 'Kethors'.

[5] *Guisborough*, pp. 277–9.

source, because he mentions John of Inchmartin, Alexander of Moray, and Edmund Comyn as Scottish prisoners, but they do not appear in Guisborough.[1]

There is some detail in several chronicles about the siege and capture of Edinburgh castle in June 1296. The Bury chronicle explodes with enthusiasm at the bombardment by siege engines: 'Ecce nunc loca feriantur concava, nunc subter[r]anea. Eya, cuncta regi nostro applaudenter subministrant elementa.'[2]

Despite the word 'noster', this kind of writing is far too artificial to have been condensed from a news-letter. Happily we have some apparent letter-material for the story of the final pursuit of Balliol across the Forth, and his surrender, not only in the Hagnaby narrative, of which we have already made use above, but also in the unpublished Hailes chronicle.[3] The Hailes account includes two texts which, on first discovery, appeared to be verbatim copies of official texts, one a note of Edward's original terms of peace with Balliol, the other a record of the last few days of negotiation between the two men.[4] Further investigation made it seem more likely that the two texts came to Hailes as part of some kind of news-letter. No sooner were the texts published than Dr Michael Prestwich was able to show that the Hagnaby chronicle gave a condensed version of the same documents, though adding an important point concerning the part played in the negotiations by the bishop of Durham.[5] It is somewhat chastening to realize that so important an addition to our knowledge can be found in two neglected chronicles, both in the Cottonian collection. At present we can hardly say for

---

[1] *Trevet*, p. 346.

[2] *Bury*, p. 132. *Guisborough*, p. 279, mentions siege-engines, but with no rhetoric.

[3] Above, p. 338.

[4] Stones and Blount, pp. 104–5.

[5] Prestwich also suggests that the writer of his newsletter may have been a knight called John de Pothenovere. It is, indeed, to persons of that class that we may look as authors of many such letters.

certain whether the two chronicles were both using the same letter. The abridgement in Hagnaby may not be the work of the chronicler, but a result of his citing a shorter account from a different original source.[1]

Our subject, the passage of information about Scottish affairs to English chroniclers, was chosen as a contribution to the general theme of this volume because relatively so much was known of the origin of the English official records concerning Scotland, that it seemed high time to attempt some study, over a short period, of the private enterprises of monastic reporters. (For reporters they may be called, if we think of them as the medieval equivalent of political journalists, in contrast to King Edward's notaries, who wrote the equivalent of White-papers and Blue-books.) We may now feel that such a study of chronicles does raise important questions. Evidently we should try to find out more of the extent to which our chroniclers were drawing on common sources which are now lost. In this matter a minute comparative textual analysis of the Edwardian chronicles, with special attention to those still unpublished, or available only in obsolete editions, might have valuable results. In general, we have seen how casual was the access of chroniclers to news, how very dependent on chance. And we have certainly cut away support from the rather hazy assumption that chance ruled less in Edward I's day than at other times. If there ever was ground for believing that Edward had some 'special relation' with his chroniclers, apart from merely asking them to help him with information, or that he systematically supplied them with 'press-releases', we can now be fairly sure that his impulse so to do was, like some of his other actions, an urge which had a short life within him. Though perfectly characteristic of the man, it was an isolated act on his part which sent out in 1291 the submissions of the competitors for Scotland to scores of monasteries, and even to some

---

[1] Conceivably *Guisborough*, pp. 279–80, may be based on another letter. The passage describes the pursuit and surrender of Balliol. Though a single 'rex noster' is certainly not decisive, the passage as a whole has the tone of a rather drastic summary of a letter.

doubtless astonished secular cathedrals, with the imperious command *quod faciatis in cronicis vestris ad perpetuam rei geste memoriam annotari.*

APPENDIX: 1296 IN THE HAGNABY CHRONICLE

Hagnaby was a Premonstratensian house in eastern Lincolnshire, four miles south-west of Spilsby; the site has given its name to the present Hagnaby Abbey farm. The chronicle seems to have been seen by Leland, or some unknown contemporary of his, who described what he saw as 'Cronica regum Anglie ab anno domini millesimo usque ad annum ejusdem millesimum cccxijmum.'[1] The text which survives, however, in MS Cotton Vespasian B xi, fos 1–61ᵛ, covers the years from Harold Godwinsson to 1307. As far as the year 1252 it seems to be based on the Annals of Waverley, but thereafter it seems to be original, and from about 1293 it grows in fulness, and contains texts of documents. One good example is the letter about the battle of Maes Madog, noted by Dr Michael Prestwich in his *War, Politics, and Finance under Edward I* (1972), p. 108 (referring to Hagnaby chronicle, fo. 37). In general see Antonia Gransden, *Historical Writing in England, c. 550–c. 1307*, p. 406, note.

The extract given below begins on fo. 40ᵛ.

Scocia[2] Item hoc anno post Epiphaniam [*6 Jan. 1296*] mandavit rex Anglie literatorie universis comitibus, baronibus, militibus, et eciam de novo creatis [?] Anglie, ut essent parati cum armis in principio Martis, et aput Novum Castrum.[3] Prima die Veneris Marcii [*2 March 1296*] exivit rex videre exercitum suum, in quo erant capitanei episcopus Duramie, comes mariscal, comes Warannie, comes Warwich', comes Herefordie, comes de Hulvester, et dominus Johannes filius Thome, et justiciarius Ybernie,[4] cum equis ferro tunicatis lxᵃ, et peditum vj., M., Morgan[5] Wallie cum xxxᵃ equis

---

[1] See *EHR*, liv (1939), p. 93. Leland probably misread the date Mcccvij at the head of fo. 61ᵛ as Mcccxij; an easy mistake. In fact there are two jottings at the end of the text, one dated 1435, the other of the sixteenth century. The second concerns books given to Arthur Wadington, see N. R. Ker, *Medieval Libraries of Great Britain* (2nd edn, 1964), p. 94.

[2] *Scocia* is written in margin.

[3] The correct date of the writs of summons to Newcastle is 16 December 1295, not January 1296, but 1 March is correct as the date of assembly (*Parliamentary Writs*, ed. Palgrave, i (1827), pp. 275–7.

[4] The justice of Ireland was John Wogan. This list of the *capitanei* does not seem to be found elsewhere.

[5] The word 'Morgan' is preceded by a paragraph-mark, perhaps in error for 'et'.

ferro tunicatis, et xvj. M. peditum.[1] Et inde profectus est rex versus castellum domini Roberti de Ros, scilicet Weirck [*Wark*]. Ibi fuerunt in die Pasce [*25 March 1296*], deinde feria tercia [*27 March*][2] transivit vadam super Tuede, et hospitabatur apud sancti [*sic*] moniales de Cal[d]estrem et Heckles [*Eccles*].[3] Feria vj [*30 March*] pervenit ad civitatem de Berwick in ebdomada Pasce, et ipsam in manu forti et brachio extento expugnavit, et per graciam dei sibi subdidit. Dominus Willelmus de Duglas, miles in armis strenuus, quem premisit rex Scocie cum v. milibus Scotorum ad munimen civitatis, et Ricardus Frisel, vicecomes Scocie et custos castelli de Berwick, isti reddiderunt regi Anglie castellum salvis sibi vita et bona [*sic*]. Set prohdolor, in capcione civitatis occisi sunt de Flandria et Pictavia et Scocia in numero xj. M[1]dclx, ex Anglia xvj, miles quidam, scilicet dominus Ricardus, frater comitis de Cornewal,[4] et quindecim naute. Rex vero fecit moram ibidem usque ad festum sancti Georgii.[5]

Et sciendum quod die sancti Georgii martyris venit exercitus Scocie ad Dunbarre et obsedit castellum quod redditum fuit eisdem in crastino per manum fratris comitis Patricii, sed nos eadem die venimus ad Dunbarre cum M[1]. equis armatis et vj M. peditum, et obsedimus castellum undique, et tradite sunt nobis obsides die Jovis ad vesperam [*26 April*]. Et inane miserunt dominum Robertum de Kethors[6] de castello ad exercitum regis Scocie, qui

[1] No accounts survive for this campaign to make a check of the numbers of troops possible (cf. Prestwich, p. 51), but the total of the figures of 6,000 and 16,000 foot given here may be compared with the 30,000 'hommes de pie' given in the Itinerary (*Instrumenta Publica*, p. 177).

[2] Cf. 'le merquedy de Pasque sur le xxviij jour de Mars passa le roy E. la rivire de Twede' (*Instrumenta Publica*, 177).

[3] Coldstream and Eccles, both communities of Cistercian nuns, were strangely unsuitable billets for Edward's troops, and it is not surprising that great damage was done to Coldstream (Bain, *Calendar*, ii. no. 733).

[4] Commentators on the printed chronicles have shown lack of curiosity about this Richard, but Sir James Ramsay characteristically attempted an identification where others had not even tried: 'Richard of Almaine, younger son of the late king of the Romans by his second wife, Senche of Provence' (J. H. Ramsay, *Dawn of the Constitution* [1908], p. 426). But no such son is otherwise known. The most likely thing is that this Richard was a bastard son of the king of the Romans, cf. *DNB*, xvi. 1060. See also N. Denholm-Young, *Richard of Cornwall* (1947), 112 n.

[5] In the Itinerary Edward hears the news of the Scottish siege of Dunbar while at Berwick on 23 April, but remains where he is until the night of Friday 27 (*Instrumenta Publica*, pp. 177–8).

[6] Kethors: on the probable emendation to 'Keith', see above, p. 342. *Flores* (pp. 97, 286) asserts that in this year he had been knighted by the king of France.

erat apud Hadingtone, ut premuniret se de exercitu nostro ne constri[n]geret-
[ur]¹ et scire voluntatem regis quali modo reddere posset castellum sine
occisione hominum. Sed die Veneris [*27 April*] proxima, adduxit secum
fraudulenter totum exercitum regis Scocie, scilicet vj. C. armatorum et
xlij. M. peditum, et nos fuimus M. armatorum et sex M. [fo. 41] peditum.
Et cum ad bellum properassemus, Scoti tergaverterunt, dei gracia, fugientes,
set nos viriliter insequentes iter vj leucarum, sed non sine [?] magno dampno
Scotorum et occisione, quia ibi occisus fuit dominus Patricius de Grame,
miles in armis strenuus,² et dominus Thomas de Sencler, miles factus ibidem,
et quatuor alii milites capti, et multi equites mortui in bello, et peditum
quorum non scitur numerus, nos eadem die ad Dunbarre regressi sumus.
Sabbato sequenti [*28 April*] venerunt rex Anglie et episcopus de Durame et
comes de Sauvey³ et Othes de Grancounz⁴ cum signifer', et redditum fuit
regi castellum ad ejus voluntatem. Et invenimus in eodem comites de Rosse
et de Asceles, et comitem de Menevet⁵ [*sic*], et dominum Johannem de
Comin, et fratrem domini Willelmi de Sencler, Ricardum Seward cum
signiferis et xxxij milites de nobiliore genere Scocie, cum sequela armiger-
orum et ccc peditum, qui se reddiderunt ad regis voluntatem.⁶ Et sciendum
quod die sabbati post Ascensionem [*5 May*] redditum fuit regi castellum de
Rokesburg' per dominum Jacobum, senescallum Scocie, qui se optulit regi
cum xxvij equis ferro tunicatis.⁷ Deinde profectus est apud Edinburgh, et
cepit castellum, et sic insecutus est regem Scocie usque ad sanctum Andream,⁸
deinde ad sanctum Johannem [*Perth*], et post pervenit apud Moneros

¹ MS *constrigerent*.

² Graham is described by the Bury chronicle (p. 131) as 'qui flos milicie
dicebatur', and by Guisborough (p. 278) as 'inter sapienciores regni illius quasi
primus, et inter potenciores nobilissimus'. The Itinerary (p. 178) calls him
'grand seigneur'.

³ Amadeus, count of Savoy. His presence in England in 1296 is very sparsely
recorded; for his previous visit see A. J. Taylor, 'Count Amadeus of Savoy's
Visit to England in 1292' (*Archaeologia*, cvi. 124–32).

⁴ Sir Otto de Grandison.

⁵ *rectius* 'Meneteth' (Menteith).

⁶ Record evidence for the number and the names of those captured in the
castle is given in Bain, *Calendar*, ii. no. 742. It totals well over 100.

⁷ According to the Itinerary (p. 178), Edward did not reach Roxburgh
until Monday 7 May, and spent the night at the Franciscan convent, moving
to the castle next day. In the next passage the Hagnaby writer passes very
lightly over the full month between this point and Edward's siege of Edinburgh
castle: *deinde* is hardly appropriate (cf. Itinerary, loc. cit.).

⁸ The Itinerary does not record Edward's presence at St. Andrews.

[*Montrose*] juxta mare Scocie, ibi prestolabatur adventum regis Scocie. Venit[1] igitur prefatus rex Scocie apud Moneros per consilium episcopi Duramie et comitis de Warenne, ad regem Anglie die Dominica proxima post translationem beati Thome martiris [*8 July*], et tradidit se voluntati regis Anglie, et concessit eidem et heredibus suis totum regnum Scocie, sine aliquo retenemento vel clamio de se et heredibus suis in perpetuum. Pro hac vero donacione, concessione, et quieta clamacione concessit eidem rex Anglie et heredibus suis hereditarie unum comitatum in Anglia in perpetuum. Ceteri vero qui cum ipso venerunt, scilicet Johannes Comin de Badenagh et comes de Bouhan et comes de Mar, episcopus de Abredene et dominus Alexander Bailof [*Balliol*], de hiis omnibus ordinavit rex ut exularentur ad tempus. Rex itaque convenit consilium apud Berwik in festo nativitatis beate Marie [*8 September*],[2] et sic reversus est in Angliam circa festum omnium sanctorum [*1 November*][3] et tenuit consilium apud sanctum Eadmundum[4] ubi peciit a clero auxilium, et sic communiter omnes contradixerunt auctoritatem domini pape. A populo peciit xij*mam*, et optinuit.

---

[1] This following passage, as far as 'ut exularentur ad tempus', was printed by Dr Prestwich, *BIHR*, xlix. 137–8.

[2] If the reference is to Edward's parliament at Berwick, the date should be 22 August; see *SHR*, xxv (1928), pp. 309–10. Conceivably the Hagnaby writer may have confused the nativity of St. Mary with the Assumption (15 August).

[3] A misdating. Edward crossed the border into England on 16 September (*Instrumenta Publica*, p. 180). There is probably confusion with the date of the parliament at Bury, mentioned immediately afterwards. It was summoned for 3 November.

[4] Cf. *Bury*, pp. 134–5.

History and action in the sermons of a medieval archbishop

THE BISHOP OF CHICHESTER (E. W. KEMP)

ON Thursday 2 January 1315, the body of Piers Gaveston, which had lain unburied in the house of the Dominicans at Oxford since he was killed on 19 June 1312, received solemn burial in the king's chapel at Langley. The burial was attended by the king, the archbishop of Canterbury Walter Reynolds, and a great gathering of magnates, lay and clerical.[1] About that time the Chancellor of the University, M. Henry de Harkeley, preached at Oxford a remarkable sermon about Thomas Becket, possibly on the previous Sunday 29 December, which was the feast of the martyr. One of the surviving manuscripts of the sermon connects the two events.[2]

The sermon is remarkable for its length and complexity and its wealth of historical allusions, contrasting markedly with the Becket sermons by Thomas Brinton.[3] Its text is taken from Lamentations

---

[1] *Chronicles of Edward I and Edward II*, ed. W. Stubbs, (RS, 1883), ii. p. 209. BL Cotton MS Cleopatra D III, fo. 56ᵛ (Hales Abbey Chronicle).

[2] Lambeth Palace Library MS 61, fos 143–147ᵛ. The heading reads: 'Magister Henricus de Hercley predicavit hunc sermonem sollempniter in universitate Oxon eo anno quo Petrus de Gavyston fuit translatus apud Langele.' This attribution is repeated at the end of the sermon. M. R. James, in his catalogue of the Lambeth Palace Library MSS, suggests that this part of the MS may have originally belonged to BL Royal MS 14 C. xii, which now contains only a text of Higden's *Polychronicon*, but a seventeenth-century table of contents shows it to have contained a work listed as 'Hen. de Hercley concio Th. Beckett.' I have used the spelling of Harkley's name adopted by *BRUO*.

[3] *The sermons of Thomas Brinton, Bishop of Rochester (1373–1389)*, ed. M. A. Devlin, Camden Society 3rd series, lxxxv, lxxxvi (London, 1954).

5: 16, *cecidit corona capitis nostri*, assumed by the preacher to come from Jeremiah's lament at the death of good King Josiah (2 Chronicles 35). It is divided into two main parts of unequal length, the *Thematis introducio* and the *Thematis exposicio*.

In the first of these the preacher is equated with Jeremiah and St. Thomas with Josiah. Five conditions for a sacrifice are said to have been fulfilled by the saint, and the fifth of these, the cause of the sacrifice, draws forth a number of historical allusions. It is argued that he who observes the evangelical counsels as well as the precepts is more perfect than he who observes the precepts alone. Some people are said to maintain that martyrs for the faith excelled Thomas who was only a martyr for the freedom of the Church, but this is not so for it is as great, or greater, to die for what is not strictly necessary as for what is necessary. To die for the precepts is necessary but to die for the counsels is voluntary. Thomas could have given way to the king, but he chose to die rather than lose the merit of supererogation.

William of Newburgh is then criticized for having said that Thomas had a zeal for the law but not according to knowledge and that no good came from his opposition to the king, only the increase of the king's anger.[1] Biblical allusions are given, and Gregory the Great's willingness, in letters to St. Augustine, to tolerate what was not contrary to the Christian faith. However, this, the preacher argues, would not hold good for Gregory was telling Augustine to go gently in weaning the newly converted Christians away from their pagan ways, whereas Henry II had been born and brought up as a Christian and Thomas's opposition and death caused him to stop doing what was wrong. Further, the cause of Thomas's martyrdom is confirmed by Anselm's argument for the sanctity of St. Alphege against Lanfranc's objections, for if Alphege was willing to die for a small matter he would certainly have been willing to die rather than deny Christ. So also John the Baptist who

---

[1] *Chronicles of the reigns of Stephen, Henry II and Richard I*, ed. R. Howlett RS, 1884), i. p. 142, 143.

was not asked to deny Christ but died for the truth when he rebuked Herod for taking his brother's wife.

This leads Harkeley to say that he had read in a life of Thomas at Oseney that when one of the knights, Richard Brito, struck Thomas he said, 'Take this for love of my Lord William, the King's brother.' Thomas had opposed the marriage of William with the widowed Countess Warenne on grounds of consanguinity.[1] John the Baptist forbade adultery which is always illicit, but Thomas forbade what could have been made licit by dispensation, so the cause of martyrdom in him was greater than in John.

The introduction concludes with the assertion that if we look at the evils which have come from the cutting of the *corona* of Thomas we shall say 'Woe to us for we have sinned'. This leads to the exposition which deals with the ignominy of the persecutors and the glory of the martyr. Three classes of men, it is said, persecuted Thomas, kings, bishops, and knights and all three were punished. Harkeley passes shortly over the bishops and concentrates on the kings and the knights.

In the time of Henry II the power and dominion of the kingdom of England was at its greatest, as Henry acquired the duchy of Aquitaine, the kingdom of Ireland, and the principal lordship of Scotland, King William doing homage to him. Because of St. Thomas this dominion had been broken and diminished by the middle of John's reign. The judgement of God visits the sins of the fathers on the children in the third and fourth generations because often the father repents but they are imitators of his crimes. So Henry repented and was punished as William of Newburgh describes, but John imitated his father's crimes. And if we reckon rightly we are now in the fourth generation in the direct line, for five persons make four generations. (This seems to mean Henry II, John, Henry III, Edward I, and Edward II, omitting Richard I.) We are now in the fourth generation and the fifth person and we

[1] This story is found in Fitzstephen's Life of Becket. *Materials for the History of Thomas Becket*, ed. J. C. Robertson and J. B. Sheppard (RS, 1875–85), iii. p. 142.

may fear that the final punishment for the sins of Henry II is reserved until now. This should be said to inculcate fear and persuade people to do good and put away sin. Therefore let those, or he who is in the fourth generation from Henry (presumably Edward II), take care that he be not an imitator of the father's crimes and then without doubt the sins of the father will not be punished in him.

Two possible objections to this are considered and answered. First that it is not necessary to dissuade modern man as no one today would think of committing such a crime: to which it is replied that even if no one today would kill a priest in church yet many do the things which Thomas opposed. Look at the Constitutions of Clarendon which Thomas resisted. The deed of the father is fulfilled today.

The second objection is that there is no ground for thinking that what happened under John had anything to do with Thomas. To this Harkeley replies that it is written in the Chronicles of the French that when King Philip, son of Louis VII who sheltered Thomas in exile, won the battle of Bouvines and defeated the Emperor Otto, John's nephew, on the same day as another French army defeated John himself in Poitou, the Germans cried out in their flight 'Heu, heu, male comparavimus mortem sancti Thome Cantuariensis' and attributed their whole confusion to the vengeance of Thomas. Further, John imitated his father's crime by his treatment of Stephen Langton and lost the crown of England, making England and Ireland tributary to the pope and bringing his successors into perpetual servitude. When John did homage for the kingdom of England the papal legate, Nicholas, bishop of Tusculum, tore the crown from his head as a sign of subjection, and afterwards replaced it.

Harkeley adds that the misfortune which came on realm and people because of Thomas's death were foretold by the Abbot Joachim, and a somewhat obscure prophecy is then linked with the story of the murder of Zacharias as recounted in 2 Chronicles 24, with its New Testament reference in Matthew 23: 35 and from this latter passage the mention of 'righteous Abel' is equated with St. Alban, first martyr of our island who, like Thomas, was killed for protecting a clerk, as Bede tells.

On passing to the knights much is made of what John the Baptist said to the soldiers as recorded in Luke 3, and John is said to have instituted the knightly order. The four knights who killed Thomas served the knightly religion badly, and so do the knights of today. What wonder, therefore, if our knights suffered confusion and ignominy on St. John the Baptist's day, and that at the hands of a people held for nothing, namely the Scots (a reference to the battle of Bannockburn, 24 June 1314). This was in accordance with a prophecy recorded by Archdeacon Henry at the beginning of Book VI of his Chronicle. The same holy man said that in future ages the caprices of men would be reflected in a great variety of clothing and there is now a greater variety among us than our fathers saw to the third and fourth generations.[1]

The second part of the exposition consists of the four words of the text taken one by one. On *cecidit* there is a specimen of word play to show that Thomas suffered in all six grammatical cases. *Nominative*: because of his stand for justice. He was made ignominious where he had before been most renowned. Not only courtiers and kings but also clergy and prelates imputed to him not justice, constancy, and virtue, but pride, rage, and arrogance. *Genitive*: the king afflicted his relations, but Thomas stood fast. *Dative*: the king would not allow anything to be given him. Because of threatening letters from the king to the Cistercian abbot and chapter he was removed from Pontigny and anyone who gave him anything was held a public enemy. *Accusative*: because at Northampton he was accused of many things. *Vocative*: not only kings but the bishops his suffragans insulted him publicly. Gilbert Foliot of London said 'You always were a fool' and Hilary of Chichester called him a perjurer and later, before the pope, called him impious. *Ablative*: temporal

[1] *Henrici archidiaconi Huntendunensis historia Anglorum*, ed. T. Arnold, (RS, 1879), i. pp. 173–4.

help was removed from him for he was deprived of his goods, but also spiritual help for people were forbidden to pray for him. At length his life was taken and he fell in death.

On *corona* it is said that Thomas obtained the victory by a great struggle and therefore was crowned with the palm—so that he is, as it were, wholly Mars. All his memorable acts happened on the day of Mars—Tuesday. He left Northampton on Tuesday and went abroad. He returned to England on Tuesday. He was killed on Tuesday.[1] Harkeley says that he has read in a life of Thomas at York that he was born on St. Thomas's day five days before Christmas and died on the fifth day after Christmas. Christ was in the midst. Thomas the Apostle went east to India. Thomas of Canterbury went west to England, but the English, though Christian, were much more cruel to Thomas than the Indians, though infidels, were to the Apostle.

On *capitis* it is pointed out that Thomas was head of the province and was raised first through humility. Pope Alexander III was able to judge this when Thomas resigned his office into his hands, recognizing that his appointment had not been canonical and the pope, seeing him poor and humble, restored him completely.[2] It is noted that Thomas by what he did enlarged the liberty of the Roman Church more than any before him. His entry into the archbishopric was the same as other great and holy men before him such as Anselm and Lanfranc for it was the custom for the kings to give bishoprics to whom they wished. Thomas by resigning his see to the pope abrogated this custom. Harkeley thinks that if such a custom still existed it would not be so easy to abolish it, for it is still not possible to remove the collation to parish churches from the hands of laymen. When King John was accused by the papal legates of having usurped the liberty of the Roman Church by conferring bishoprics he alleged the custom of his forefathers, English and

---

[1] Cf. *Radulfi de Diceto decani Lundoniensis opera historica*, ed. W. Stubbs (RS, 1876), i. p. 344.

[2] *Chronicles of the reigns of Stephen . . .*, i. p. 140. This story is recounted by William of Newburgh.

Norman, and quoted the example of Wulfstan of Worcester, appointed by Edward the Confessor, whom William the Conqueror tried to remove because of his lack of French but subsequently left in peace. The same William deposed Stigand and appointed Lanfranc, and similarly his father had appointed Thomas to Canterbury. To that the legate Pandulph replied that the custom had been abolished by Thomas when he resigned all that he had into the hands of the pope and from that time the Roman Church was made *domina et magistra* of all others of this realm.

Finally, *nostri* is taken to signify pastoral protection. Thomas was our head, says Harkeley. Augustine planted, Thomas watered with his blood, but God gave the increase. Thomas is specially the head of the clerks, no saint was such a protector of clerks. It was a principal cause of his passion that he opposed the king who wished to decree that clerks taken in crime should be subject to the secular courts in life and limb. He delivered clerks from the wolves whereas his fellow bishops who opposed him would have left them to the wolves as Abbot Joachim prophesied. He fed the sheep with solid food. Little ones are given milk to drink, but clerks and priests and specially bishops are leaders and warriors and need solid food. Lastly Thomas cared for the infirmities of his subjects after the example of Christ as recorded in Hebrews 4.

This summary of Harkeley's sermon has omitted most of the purely biblical and theological argumentation in order to concentrate on the mass of historical detail contained in it and the references made to various historical works. Perhaps only a university sermon would have been of such length and had these features.

It is precisely these distinguishing marks which make the other known text of the sermon stand out in the collection in which it appears. Hereford Cathedral MS, P.V. 12, written in the fourteenth century, contains the treatise of Hugh of St. Victor *De claustro animae* and a collection of thirty-one sermons none of them attributed to any individual. Harkeley's sermon is number 28 in the collection and occupies folios 99ᵛ to 107ᵛ. It is followed by a much shorter sermon on the Translation of St. Thomas occupying folios 107ᵛ to 110ᵛ. This is in three sections following the words of the text *Fide Enoch translatus est* (Hebrews 11) where the name Enoch is understood to mean 'walking with God'. The historical references are fewer, and only one Life is referred to which appears to be that by William of Canterbury.[1] The story of the knight Richard Brito and Thomas's rebuke to William the king's brother is repeated much as it is found in Harkeley's sermon, but otherwise there is little to link the two.

The first sermon in the collection is on the Holy Spirit, the second on the dedication of a church, and the third on the reconciliation of a church. Then follow six sermons for visitations, a sermon preached among religious, three sermons on ordination and one at a funeral. Sermon fifteen is for the safety of the king and is followed by four on particular seasons of the Christian year. Sermon twenty is delivered to judges and advocates, and twenty-one in a congregation of prelates and clergy. Sermon twenty-two asks for prayers for the preacher in tribulations and persecutions and then come five seasonal sermons. The two Becket sermons come next and are followed by two sermons preached in a congregation of prelates and clergy.

This collection was noticed by W. D. Macray who published some extracts in Volume VIII of the *English Historical Review* in 1893.[2] He concluded that the period of the sermons was the reign of Edward III, that the sermon asking for prayers pointed to the authorship of Archbishop John Stratford, that consequently the whole collection was connected with him and that the Becket sermons belonged to the time of his conflict with Edward III in 1340–1.

It is also referred to by Dr Owst who gives an extensive summary

---

[1] Fo. 109ᵛ appears to refer to the incident of the woman of Stamford or Stafford recounted by William of Canterbury, *Materials*, i. p. 6. The book and the chapter correspond but it is less easy to identify the further reference at the top of fo. 109ᵛ.

[2] Pp. 85–91.

of Harkeley's sermon and makes a brief reference to the Translation sermon without suggesting an attribution of either. Of Harkeley's sermon Owst writes:

For its length as well as for its industry, this sermon is certainly a most remarkable specimen of the art. But it is remarkable for a further reason. For in it we behold the English pulpit as the mouthpiece of a new national spirit, even where clearly an audience of clergy is concerned, all too suspicious to their lay fellow countrymen. St Thomas, troubler of his King, is yet lauded here as the special head and protector of the clergy of *England*. His title is stoutly defended against all comers. That same spirit of national pride and national ambition, so quickly nettled at foreign interference with the sacred lands and liberties of England, is to be seen again in the sermons of Archbishop Fitzralph and Bishop Thomas Brinton.[1]

Macray's attribution of the Hereford collection to Archbishop Stratford was adopted by G. T. Lapsley in his important article on the Crisis of 1341[2] and by Miss McKisack in the *Oxford History of England*,[3] both of whom suggest that the longer of the two Becket sermons is that preached by Stratford at Canterbury on 29 December 1340, in spite of the fact that the text stated to have been used by the archbishop is a different one.[4] The discovery of the sermon in the Lambeth MS, however, makes that identification impossible and reopens the question of the authorship of the Hereford collection. The Harkeley sermon stands out by its length, complexity, and organization and is markedly different from the other thirty sermons. It is reasonable to set it aside for the moment and consider whether there are reasons for connecting any other of the sermons with Stratford.

[1] G. R. Owst, *Literature and Pulpit in Medieval England* (Oxford, 1961), p. 131.

[2] G. T. Lapsley, 'Archbishop Stratford and the Parliamentary Crisis of 1341', *EHR*, xxx (1915), pp. 6–18, 193–215. Reprinted in *Crown, Community, and Parliament in the later Middle Ages. Studies in English Constitutional History By Gaillard T. Lapsley*, ed. H. M. Cam and G. Barraclough (Oxford, 1951).

[3] M. McKisack, *The Fourteenth Century (1307–1399)* (Oxford, 1959), p. 169 n. 4.

[4] H. Wharton, *Anglia Sacra* (London, 1691), i. 21.

Macray himself seems to have been prompted to make the identification first by sermon 22 which is headed: *Ad impetrandum subsidium oracionum in tribulacionibus et persecucionibus* and is on the text from the Epistle to the Romans (15: 30) *Iuvetis me in oracionibus vestris ad dominum.* Two things are immediately clear in this sermon, namely that it was addressed to monks and that the preacher was a person in a pastoral office of some responsibility. The sermon is arranged in three parts following the divisions of the text. The first section concerns the need for help which can be in material things, in body and in soul. The first two of these are briefly dismissed as irrelevant to the present case. The third, spiritual help, receives more extensive treatment. One reason, it is said, why tribulations are sent by God is that the sufferer may be purged and turned to better things that he may destroy and confound those who afflict him. This, the preacher says, is the need in which he is placed: 'I seek your help. It could be said of me as in Deuteronomy 32 *He forsook the God who made him.* God puts away sin when men repent. Whatever I was before this time I now repent. Please help my penitence that I may come to the divine mercy by patiently enduring tribulation.' The second section concerns the nature of the help which is by prayer. Again the hearers are addressed in the second person plural. The reflections on the high calling of the monastic life and the importance of the prayer of monks in the Church, with which this part of the sermon is interspersed, indicate that the hearers were themselves monks. The third section concerns the power of the one who wills—namely God. The preacher says that he is not asking for prayer for temporal benefits, and certainly not like the mother of Zebedee's children that he should sit with kings and princes. Rather it is that he should be delivered from the faithless men who say 'Let us oppress the just because he is against our works.' The preacher hopes that truth will prevail and recalls the Lord's saying that the truth will set us free. The sermon concludes with the words: 'Similiter iuvetis me in oracionibus vestris ut pastoris officium quod ante hec tempora male dereliqui iuxta illud Zacharie[1] iiii, O pastor

---

[1] The correct reference is Zechariah 11: 17.

et ydolum et ali prout grex quia non est eis pastor: illud valeam sic assumere et exercere; quod sit ad honorem dei et salvacione animarum.'[1]

Birchington's Life of Stratford says that in his sermon in Canterbury cathedral on 29 December 1340, the archbishop 'per gradus S. Thomam multipliciter commendavit' and at the end blamed himself for having from the start of his archiepiscopate occupied himself in the secular affairs of the king and kingdom and having oppressed the clergy and community by procuring taxes for the king's needs. He recited in English his neglect of the Divine Offices and his secular occupations in general and in tears sought pardon from those standing round. He declared that in future he would protect the liberties of the Church and churchmen in parliament and give himself wholly to the performance of his pastoral office setting aside all secular occupations.[2] All that can be said at the moment is that these sentiments would fit very well with the contents of the Hereford sermon just summarized and that among the prelates of the fourteenth century there is no other very obvious candidate.

Macray also noted particularly sermon 15 headed *Pro salute Regis*. This is a sermon asking for prayers for the king on an expedition against the Scots. The preacher says that the king has not only expended money and temporal possessions but also exposed to danger himself, his brother, and his friends and acquaintances. There is also reference to the severity of the winter, to bad harvests, and a time of great scarcity and mortality. Macray rightly points to Edward III's expedition of 1336, a year when such conditions prevailed, and when the king was in Scotland with his brother, John of Eltham, who died at Perth in September and was buried by Archbishop Stratford in Westminster Abbey in January 1337.[3]

Macray seems to have overlooked, however, the significance of the three sermons entitled *In congregacione prelatorum et cleri*. The

[1] Fo. 92ᵛ.
[2] Wharton, loc. cit.
[3] Macray, p. 87; *Chronicles of Edward I and Edward II*, i. p. 365.

first of these, sermon 21, contains phrases which make it clear that the preacher was a bishop,[1] and, like some other sermons in the collection, has a number of references to parts of the *Corpus Juris Canonici*. The preacher exhorts his hearers in their deliberations to be mindful of the impoverishment of the country by war and of the harm done to ecclesiastical liberty, all of which are now past but the causes of which must be considered if future evils are to be avoided. In sermon 30 there are similar phrases which make clear that the preacher was one of the bishops,[2] but there is also a phrase of which the most natural interpretation would be that it was spoken by the archbishop himself: 'Quilibet enim huc vocatus auctoritate metropolitica dicere potest idem 1 Reg. 111. *Ecce ego assum quia vocasti me.* Parati sumus cetus negocium pro quo venistis, deo inspirante et assistente, ad debitum et ecclesie honorificum finem deducere.'[3] It does not seem that any other bishop could have spoken to the assembly of the business 'for which *you* have come'.

There are other passages in this sermon which suggest that if this is the archbishop speaking then it is most probably John Stratford. I have written elsewhere of the significance of the form of citation sent out by him in July 1341, summoning a provincial council to meet at St. Paul's on 19 October, and of the citation a year later for the provincial council of 14 October 1342. I have drawn attention to his very careful observance of the prescriptions of the canon law concerning such councils and to the marked difference between these assemblies and those of his first six years.[4] Early in the sermon is a passage which sets out the different kinds of councils and who may summon them, with references to appropriate sections of the *Decretum Gratiani*. It concludes with the sentence: 'Cantuariensis vero Metropolitanus est et Primus et apostolice sedis legatus et

---

[1] Fo. 89ᵛ: 'ordinem episcopalem sumus professi; similitudine dignitatis quia omnes episcopi, operis quia omnes sumus dispensatores sacrorum ecclesie et misteriorum dei'.

[2] Fo. 112: 'religione quia ordinem episcopalem sumus professi'.

[3] Fo. 113.

[4] E. W. Kemp, *Counsel and Consent*, the Bampton Lectures for 1960 (London, 1961), pp. 103–4.

iccirco de eo dubium non est nec hactenus fuit qui provinciale concilum poterit convocare.'[1] A similar sentence comes near the beginning of sermon 31. While there is evidence of archbishops of Canterbury claiming and exercising legatine powers at earlier times, Dr I. J. Churchill writes that 'the words "apostolice sedis legatus" have not so far been found in any document giving the formal style of the archbishops till the time of Simon Meopham (1328–33)'[2] and gives the date of the first example she has found as 1332. Meopham did hold a provincial council in January 1329 but the title *apostolice sedis legatus* was not used in the citation.[3] It would seem, then, that Stratford is the earliest archbishop likely to have preached these sermons. As I have shown elsewhere, no archbishop after him distinguished so clearly between the taxing assembly, convocation, and the canonical provincial council.[4] There are, therefore, good grounds for believing that sermons 30 and 31 are by Archbishop Stratford, and it would be natural to conclude that they were preached at the opening of the provincial councils of 1341 and 1342. If sermon 21 is also by him it may belong to his third provincial council of October 1347.[5]

A few other passages in sermons 30 and 31 may support this attribution. An attack on the vices of the contemporary clergy and in particular the luxurious dress of some of them[6] could be linked with chapter 2 of the third set of Constitutions associated with Stratford.[7] A passage attacking prelates who in time of difficulty care more about wool than about the sheep[8] reminds us of the prominence of taxes on and in wool in the controversies of this

[1] Fo. 111ᵛ.

[2] I. J. Churchill, *Canterbury Administration* (London, 1933), i. p. 157.

[3] *The Register of John de Grandisson, Bishop of Exeter (A.D. 1327–1369)*, ed. F. C. Hingeston-Randolph (London, 1894), p. 446.

[4] Kemp, pp. 106–11.

[5] *The Register of John de Trillek, Bishop of Hereford (A.D. 1344–1361)*, ed. J. H. Parry (Hereford, 1910), pp. 306–7.

[6] Fo. 112ᵛ.

[7] D. Wilkins, *Concilia Magnae Britanniae et Hiberniae* (London, 1737), ii. p. 703.

[8] Fo. 114ᵛ.

time. More significant is the last section of sermon 30.[1] This sermon is on the text *Vocate cetum congregate senes* (Joel 1). The preacher gives a number of scriptural references to support the argument that in both Church and State counsellors should be chosen from among prudent and wise men of mature age. The story of Rehoboam spurning the advice of the old men and following that of young men to the destruction of his kingdom is quoted. The point is made at some length. It is reasonable to connect it with the comment made by Adam Murimuth on Edward III's dismissal of his ministers in December 1340 and appointment of new officials, 'consilio juvenum utebatur, spreto consilio seniorum'.[2] Still more may this link be made with Stratford's letter to the king on 1 January 1341, in which he attacks Edward's changes of counsellors and quotes the story of Rehoboam.[3]

The other sermons in the collection are consistent with being a group of utterances composed for use on various pontifical occasions. The earlier ones are full of references to the canon law, and several sermons have passages about lay interference with ecclesiastical places and persons, the dignity or misbehaviour of the clergy. It is a pity that Stratford's registrar at Winchester did not keep a note of the texts used by him for sermons at Visitations, such as are found in the register of his successor there, Orleton. The only sermon in the collection on a text known to have been used by Stratford is the Ash Wednesday sermon, 23, on the passage from the second chapter of Joel *Nunc ergo convertimini ad me in toto corde vestro*. Birchington's Life of Stratford records that he preached in Canterbury cathedral on this text on Ash Wednesday, 21 February 1341, at the end of which he said that certain royal letters directed against him had been sent to the Prior and Chapter and asked that they should be read. This having been done he replied protesting his innocence.[4] The beginning of this sermon is similar to that of a sermon of the celebrated

---

[1] Fo. 113ᵛ.

[2] *Adae de Murimuth continuatio chronicarum. Robertus de Avesbury, De Gestis mirabilibus Regis Edwardi Tertii*, ed. E. M. Thompson (RS, 1889), p. 118.

[3] Ibid. pp. 324–7.

[4] Wharton, i. p. 23.

preacher John of Lausanne.[1] The two run closely parallel for the first twenty-six lines of the Hereford text and then diverge. I have also noted similar links between sermons 7, 9, 11, 17, and 19 and sermons of John of Lausanne.[2] Like many a later orator, the preacher of these sermons seems often to have found his initial inspiration in other men's works.

We have therefore in this Hereford manuscript a sermon collection which has a strong association with Archbishop John Stratford. As already remarked, the Harkeley sermon stands out as something different from all the rest. How does it come to be there? Stratford's career is summarized by Dr Emden.[3] He was a D.C.L. of Oxford by 1312 and composed a Repetitio on the canon *Commissa* in the *Sext* of Boniface VIII which is referred to by the canonist John de Acton[4] who writes of Stratford as *doctorem meum*. This testimony to Stratford's standing as a canonist is of importance in relation to the canon law which appears in the sermons and in his official acts. Apart from a connection as legal counsel to the Cathedral Priory at Worcester, his native diocese, Stratford's career outside Oxford is not recorded earlier than 1317 in which year he was first summoned to give legal advice in council and parliament. He was ordained sub-deacon that same year although he had begun to collect benefices, beginning with the rectory of Kempsey in the Worcester diocese in 1316. It seems likely therefore that Stratford was still at Oxford at the beginning of 1315 and could have heard Harkeley's sermon and obtained a copy of it. Whether this was the beginning of his interest in Thomas Becket is impossible to say. We know, however, that it had developed sufficiently by 1331 for him in association with his younger brother, Robert, to found in that year a chantry of St. Thomas the Martyr for five

---

[1] Paris, BN, MS lat. 3552, fos 52ᵛ–54ᵛ.

[2] Ibid. MS lat. 18181, fo. 317 (sermon 7); fo. 316 (sermon 9); fo. 318ᵛ (sermon 11); fo. 66ᵛ (sermon 17); MS lat. 18183, fo. 14ᵛ (sermon 19). On John of Lausanne see *Recherches de Théologie ancienne et médiévale*, xxvii (1960), pp. 72–132.

[3] *BRUO*, iii. pp. 1796–8.

[4] Ibid. i. pp. 11–12.

priests in the south aisle of Holy Trinity Church, Stratford-on-Avon, his birth-place. Shortly afterwards he bought the advowson of the church from the bishop of Worcester.[1] This shows clearly that he had a devotion to Becket long before the crisis of 1341. If, as now seems probable, he kept among his collection of sermons a copy of this detailed, elaborate, and politically explosive panegyric of Harkeley's, it is understandable that faced with the attacks of the king and his brash advisers, he should have assumed at Canterbury the role of a new Becket.

There is further reason to think that more than play-acting and skilful political manoeuvring were involved. As Dr Lapsley, Miss McKisack, and others have indicated, there are signs that during the two years before 1341 the archbishop was becoming uneasy about the war with France and the heavy demands that it was making on clergy and laity in England.[2] His profession of penitence and a change of heart should not be lightly dismissed. Although he was formally reconciled to the king in May 1341 and gradually taken back into favour as a counsellor, he did not again hold office. The last seven years of his life were taken up with a substantial programme of ecclesiastical reform. The three provincial councils and the constitutions associated with them have already been mentioned.[3] To these should be added the important set of statutes and ordinances for the Court of Arches which he issued in 1342.[4] The two sets of his household accounts which probably belong to December 1341 and March 1343 give valuable glimpses of his domestic life in this period, of those magnates and officials of the diocese and province who shared his table from time to time, of the contacts that he

---

[1] Ibid. iii. p. 1798; *MS Register of Simon Montacute, Bishop of Worcester*, i, fos 50–61.

[2] Kemp, pp. 102–3. Lapsley's classical essay cited above, p. 357 n. 2 must now be read in the light of G. L. Harriss, *King, Parliament and Public Finance in Mediaeval England to 1369* (Oxford, 1975), chap. x–xiii.

[3] Cf. C. R. Cheney, 'Legislation of the Medieval Church', *EHR*, 1 (1935), pp. 415–17.

[4] Wilkins, pp. 681–95.

maintained with Stratford.[1] Although the loss of his Canterbury register leaves a sad gap in our knowledge, yet in other respects we have a greater variety of evidence for him than for most medieval prelates. In this range of material the Hereford sermon collection occupies an important place, a meeting point of history and current events.

[1] Westminster Abbey Muniments 9222 and 9223.

Andrew Horn: law and history in fourteenth-century England

JEREMY CATTO

NOT many Englishmen 'have understood the past and could view it as a whole'.[1] Least of all, perhaps, was an historical imagination thought necessary for intellectuals about 1300, the heyday of professional expertise in the theological schools and the lawcourts: among such chroniclers as there were in the England of that generation, Andrew Horn was perhaps the only man in some measure to possess it. His modest place in English history does not depend upon it: his work as a compiler of custumals of the City of London, and as an expert annotator of legal records has been recognized by modern students of London history, but his achievement has been seen only on a municipal scale.[2] The purpose of this paper is to consider his historical work in its broadest sense, including his collections of documents as well as the *Annales Londonienses* which he almost certainly compiled; for taken as a whole, it has a number of features which were unusual in the established tradition of historiography. The *Annales Londonienses* in their present form are a chronicle compiled largely from the Westminster *Flores Historiarum*, but the genre of the monastic chronicle was for the first time transferred to a larger and less coherent community, the city of London. Moreover,

[1] R. W. Southern, 'Bede', in *Mediaeval Humanism* (Oxford, 1970), p. 7.
[2] First of all by H. T. Riley, in his edition of *Liber Custumarum*, in *Munimenta Gildhallae Londoniensis*, ed. Riley (RS, 1859–62), ix–xi, xcvi–xcvii. See also M. Weinbaum, *London unter Eduard I und Eduard II* (Stuttgart, 1933), i. pp. 34–6; M. Williams, *Mediaeval London* (London, 1963), p. 78.

Horn's several surviving compilations of laws and ordinances,[1] *Liber Horn*, Corpus Christi College Cambridge, MSS 70 and 258, and *Liber Legum Antiquorum Regum*, are closely related to his historical activity, and the *Annales* were probably once part of these compilations, sharing with the documents the same practical purpose: as Edward I was aware, rights and precedents could be established by searching the chronicles as well as from documentary sources. Through these compilations, the mind of the chronicler can be observed more clearly in Horn's case than in those of his predecessors or contemporaries. Horn's collections show that he had read the *Trésor* of Brunetto Latini, and there are indications that its political ideas were relevant to his view of Edward II's reign. His Florentine contemporaries, Dino Compagni, Dante and Giovanni Villani, would see a larger significance in the events of their time; Andrew Horn, confined in the traditional genres of compilation and chronicle, is far less explicit. Yet taken as a whole his historical work suggests that at least he had a distinctive view of English history, and related the past to the political world of his own time.

Unlike his chronicler predecessor Arnold FitzThedmar, Horn was not a member of a long established city family who saw the affairs of London and England from the perspective of his own kindred. He was one of the fishmongers who became prominent in the city about 1300, and, as chamberlain of the city from 1320 to his death in 1328, he belonged to the administrative or judicial rather than the aldermanic world of London. The name of Horn is too common to permit speculation on his kinsmen: nothing connects him with John Horn the sheriff of a generation earlier. Two brothers, a fishmonger Simon, and William, the rector of Rotherhithe, are mentioned in his will, as are a nephew and niece, William Doget

---

[1] The present *Liber Custumarum* in the Corporation of London Records Office (here referred to as CLRO) and its text as printed by Riley are cited here as *Lib. Cust.*; but the original books of which it, with other MSS, are made up (on which see references, p. 376 n. 2 below), *Liber Legum Antiquorum Regum* and the medieval *Liber Custumarum*, are referred to as *LLAR* and *LC*. I am grateful to the staff of the Corporation's Records Office for their kindness during my work on the records in their care.

and Christina.[1] He must have been mature by 1307 when he was warden of the fishmongers, and according to the *Annales Londonienses* a son was born to him in 1305 and died a few weeks later.[2] 'Fishmonger of Bridge Street, London', in 1311, he appears as liable to a modest 5s. contribution to Bridge Ward's share of the London subsidy of 1319, and as a witness of a number of Bridge House deeds from 1321 to 1327.[3] The accumulation of the texts of statutes and city ordinances, made largely from Guildhall sources between 1311 and 1319, which now constitute *Liber Horn*, implies an active interest in the law, and it is probable that Horn had some position in the legal world of the Guildhall before he became chamberlain. He was installed on 13 January 1320, and until his death his name is frequently mentioned in an official capacity in the London letter books. The chamberlain, as the permanent financial and judicial officer of the Guildhall, had a cardinal role in the city's growing administration. A number of accounts, including two of Horn's, illustrate his financial charge, but the sums at his disposal were not great and his power was limited by the auditors established in 1311. Probably the business of the chamberlain's court always took up the larger share of his attention; and, together with the recorder, it was his business to defend the city's privileges, the 'customs and liberties in the rolls and books of the Chamber'. If the chamberlain was not a professional lawyer, he must by Horn's time be familiar with the formidable body of royal edict and civic ordinance which governed

---

[1] *Calendar of Wills Proved and Enrolled in the Court of Hustings, 1258–1688*, ed. R. R. Sharpe (London, 188–90), i. pp. 344–5. On the fishmongers, see Williams, *Mediaeval London*, pp. 189–90.

[2] *Calendar of Letter Books of the City of London*, ed. R. R. Sharpe (London, 1899–1912), Letter Book A, 157–8. The letter books are cited here as LBA, LBB, etc.: originals by folio, calendars by page; *Annales Londonienses*, ed. W. Stubbs in *Chronicles of the Reigns of Edward I and Edward II* (RS, 1882–3), i. p. 137.

[3] CLRO, *Liber Horn*, fo. 206; *Two Early London Subsidy Rolls*, ed. E. Ekwall, Skrifter utgivna av Kungl. humanistska vetenskapssamfundet i Lund xlviii (Lund, 1951), 1319 Roll, Bridge Ward no. 47; CLRO, Bridge House Deeds, C. 63, 65; D. 13, 64, 66, 71.

his official acts.[1] Horn's account of the Eyre of 1321, which put his legal ingenuity to the test, is an attempt to put some of this expertise down in permanent form. The record of the proceedings shows Horn acting in close concert with the mayor, Hamo de Chigwell (another fishmonger, to whom Horn possibly owed his promotion), who had come to office in 1319 and resumed it in 1321, holding it with only brief intervals until 1328. Chigwell's mayoralty replaced the authoritarian professionalism of the city official, John Wengrave, who had combined the offices of mayor, recorder, and coroner, and his first achievement had been the constitution conceded by Edward II in 1319, which forbade such practices in the interest of regular and even-handed government. That he nevertheless remained in control for a decade was due to the difficult position of London with its Lancastrian sympathies in the years of Despenser rule.[2] Chigwell collaborated with their regime, preserving himself only with difficulty; and some echoes of his ambiguous rule can perhaps be detected in Horn's precepts on the mayoralty adapted from the *Trésor*. It is likely that Horn's views were in accord with those of Chigwell: the relation between the Crown and established liberties was the underlying theme of his legal collections. The vindication of their careful policy came after the fall of Edward II, with the charter of 1327 whose terms, according to the *Annales Paulini*, he explained to a mass meeting.[3] His unrivalled knowledge of London's customs was amply justified in this confirmation of the city's autonomy.

The lasting monument of Horn's erudition was the series of books which he left to the Guildhall by his will:

Item lego camere Gildaule London[ie] unum magnum librum de gestis anglorum in quo continentur multa utilia, et unum alium librum de veteribus [word omitted] anglorum cum libro vocato Bretoun et cum libro

---

[1] LBE, 25, 216–17; Williams, *Mediaeval London*, pp. 91, 94–5.

[2] Williams, *Mediaeval London*, pp. 285–305; Natalie Fryde, *The Tyranny and Fall of Edward II* (Cambridge, 1979), pp. 169–75.

[3] *Annales Paulini*, ed. Stubbs, *Chronicles of Edward I and II*, p. 325; Williams, *Mediaeval London*, p. 299.

vocato speculum Justic', et alium librum compositum per Henricum de Huntingdon[ia]. Item alium librum de statutis Anglorum cum multis libertatibus et aliis tangentibus civitatem.[1]

Except for the volume of Henry of Huntingdon, all these books can be identified with extant manuscripts, so that a tentative list of Horn's books may be drawn up.

(1) CORPORATION OF LONDON RECORDS OFFICE, MS LIBER HORN

This primary source of much of the documentary evidence for London history has been partially analysed by Ker and Weinbaum.[2] Its contents and medieval name identify it as the fourth in Horn's will, the attribution resting upon the colophon (fo. 206):

Iste liber restat Andree Horn piscenario London' de Breggestrete in quo continentur Carta et alie consuetudines predicte Ciuitatis. Et carta libertatis Anglie et Statuta per Henricum Regem et per Edwardum Regem filium predicti Regis Henrici edita. Quem fieri fecit Anno domini mcccxi Et Anno Regni Regis Edwardi filii Regis Edwardi vto.

The contents of the volume's 376 folios are a comprehensive collection of the statutes of Henry III and Edward I, accompanied by a series of legal treatises of the thirteenth century; a continuation consisting mainly of the Ordinances of 1311 and selections from Britton, largely on procedure; Edward I's charter for London in 1299, followed by a large and miscellaneous collection of London customs, ordinances of the city, and the guilds, writs, and letters relating to London, extracts from rolls of the Eyre and other documents; a small collection of royal charters for London; and at the beginning and end of the two main divisions, accumulations of further documents. Yet in this apparent jumble of material it is possible to discern an overall scheme which the gradual assemblage of material tends to obscure. The colophon of 1311, now placed in the middle

---

[1] CLRO, Hustings Roll 57, no. 16.

[2] N. R. Ker, *Mediaeval Manuscripts in British Libraries* (Oxford, 1969 sqq.), i. pp. 27–34; Weinbaum, *London unter Eduard I und Eduard II*, ii. pp. 91–101.

of the volume, shows that the original plan was a modest statement of London practice introductory to a conventional, if unusually exhaustive, collection of statutes.[1] Written by a small number of professional hands, the text is corrected and annotated, particularly with authentications by reference to the source, by a hand which is presumably Horn's. The first section, the London ordinances, was then enlarged to nearly eight times its original size with further documents, some of which were recent cases in the London courts or new royal letters. The first of these new documents is a case heard on 25 April 1313; the latest, a copy of the Ipswich franchises of 6 May 1318.[2] The writing, though changing frequently, is no longer as professional, and some or all of it may be examples on different occasions of Horn's own hand. The documents were derived from the past or current muniments of the city: the rolls in the possession of the Common Clerk, and the first five letter-books. Horn, therefore, had access before he was chamberlain to administrative records still in use, some of which he went through systematically.[3] The common law section grew more modestly with the addition of the Ordinances of 1311 and the notes from Britton, and by 1319 the volume had been reorganized and given a new table of contents.[4] This is a volume clearly intended for practical use. Only a few additional leaves, with extracts from *Leges Anglorum*, hint at the larger conceptions in his mind.

(2) CORPUS CHRISTI COLLEGE, CAMBRIDGE, MSS 70 AND 258

These two manuscripts, originally one, in two places have Horn's device *Horn mihi cognomen Andreas est mihi nomen;*[5] and the contents

---

[1] *Liber Horn*, fos 206–26; 16–176.

[2] *Liber Horn*, fos 226ᵛ–369ᵛ; cf. fos 226ᵛ, 336–339ᵛ.

[3] *Liber Horn*, fos 309ᵛ–339ᵛ, extracts in the original order from LBC, vols lvᵛ–ciiᵛ; LBD, fos xcviiᵛ–cclxiv; LBE, fos iᵛ–lxxii.

[4] The second table, fos 8ᵛ–9 and 14ᵛ.

[5] Corpus Christi College, Cambridge, MS 70, fo. 51; MS 258, fo. 1. The original manuscript of which these two are part is referred to here as the Corpus manuscript.

exactly fit the description of the second book in his will. The three works it contains, *Leges Anglorum*, the *Mirror of Justices*, and *Britton*, were written by three hands, one of which was responsible for the text of most of the laws and all of the *Mirror*, and bears some resemblance to the scripts in *Liber Horn*; it may be his own. The texts were carefully corrected, and that of the *Leges Anglorum* also bears historical annotations in a hand strongly reminiscent of the notes in *Liber Horn*. The Laws are supplemented by a number of charters of Henry III and a description of Edward I in the style of the original text; and almost the last item is a list of the statutes of Edward I with additional documents which precisely fits *Liber Horn* as it presumably was in 1313–14, when the Corpus MS was compiled. It was still in use in 1321, as a marginal annotation, citing a case before the Justices in Eyre in 1321 on the ownership of the Thames was inserted in or after that year; the case was marked by one of Horn's personal appearances in the proceedings.[1] His discovery of the *Leges Anglorum* was an important episode in his understanding of English history, and influenced all his subsequent compilations; and the additions are clearly a somewhat botched attempt at a continuation. It was abandoned: after a bare list of statutes in *Liber Horn*, a brief note adumbrates a future attempt to bring the Laws up to date.[2] Maitland suggested rather fancifully that Horn was himself, as a young man, the author of the *Mirror of Justices*, a work evidently written about 1290. His only argument was the incorporation of Horn's device as the last line of the verses prefixed to the text; but a glance at the manuscript shows that it was not intended to be a part of the verse.[3] Moreover, in a note in Corpus MS 70, Horn called the *Mirror* and *Britton* 'books not sealed by the King albeit much pleaded in the time of Edward I and Edward II', language clearly

---

[1] Corpus MS 70, fos 93ᵛ–94ʳ; *Lib. Cust.* pp. 407–9.

[2] Corpus MS 70, fo. 96: 'quia intendo ex libro isto et aliis magnum codicem componere quia utile duxi posteris praesentia temporum nostrorum exprimere'.

[3] Corpus MS 258, fo. 1. See *The Mirror of Justices*, ed. W. J. Whitaker with introduction by F. W. Maitland (Selden Soc., 1893), xlvii–li.

not that of an author on his own book.[1] However, the text survives only in this copy, which together with the resurrected text of the early thirteenth-century *Leges Anglorum* renders the Corpus manuscript a significant item in the legal literature of the fourteenth century.

(3) ANNALES LONDONIENSES

The third work attributable to Horn is the set of annals termed by Stubbs, its editor, *Annales Londonienses*.[2] The text, which survives only in an eighteenth-century transcript, derives from a Cotton manuscript, Otho B iii, now almost wholly destroyed by fire. The remaining fragments seemed to Stubbs to have been written in the second quarter of the fourteenth century, too late to be part of a book written by or for Horn, but there are cogent reasons nevertheless for attributing their composition or compilation to him, as Stubbs cautiously suggested. First, there is the notice, under 1305, referring to the birth and death of Horn's son. In the same year, the birth of two children of William le Cupere is mentioned; but William, as an inhabitant of Bridge Ward, was almost certainly a neighbour and, if he was William de Horne, coupere, admitted to the franchise in 1311, perhaps also a relation of Andrew Horn.[3] Secondly, the annals contain three documents, ordinances of Edward II on prices and extravagance, which are among the additions to *Liber Horn*, and are given in the same form addressed to the London sheriffs.[4] Thirdly, there is a quotation from the *Annales* on the circumstances of the seizure of the city's liberties in 1285, in the *Liber Albus*, the Custumal compiled in 1419, which cites them as in *Chronicis Maioris Libri Horne*.[5] This makes it likely that the exemplar

---

[1] Corpus MS 70, fo. 95ᵛ. 'Et non sunt libri sigillati per regem attamen taliter placitabantur temporibus regum Edwardi filii regis Henrici et Edwardi filii regis Edwardi.'

[2] Stubbs (ed.), *Chronicles of Edward I and II*, i. pp. 1–251.

[3] *Annales Londonienses*, p. 134; Ekwall, *Two Early London Subsidy Rolls*, 1319 Roll, Bridge Ward no. 59; LBD, 76.

[4] *Annales Londonienses*, pp. 232–3, 237–9; *Liber Horn*, fos 347–349.

[5] *Liber Albus*, ed. Riley in *Munimenta Gildhallae*, i. p. 16.

of the *Annales* was the first of the volumes mentioned in Horn's will. On these grounds the traditional attribution seems beyond reasonable doubt.

The *Annales* are, however, made up from more than one element. At the core of the work is the history of the first few years of King Edward II, the critical events of which culminated, for the author, in the king's dramatic appeal to the Londoners in 1312. His reign is introduced with prophecies from Geoffrey of Monmouth and the Book of Daniel: the ram of the Castle of Love, who will darken the whole island with his cloudy breath, and whom Merlin compared to Alexander of Macedon, 'will strenuously take and seize Scotland, Norway, Denmark, France, and all the lands which Arthur, most victorious of knights, acquired by the sword'.[1] This vision of Edward II as a second Alexander could not have been penned in 1307, for Horn's unfriendly description of Piers Gaveston and account of the crisis of the Ordinances are treated as integral parts of the story and not as the dénouement of disappointed hopes. Far from appropriate after Bannockburn, such a prophecy was perhaps imaginable in the aftermath of Gaveston's death and the apparent reconciliation of parties in 1312–13; and it is likely that the annals from 1307 to 1312 are the original part of the work, written as a contemporary record of the triumph of lawful and customary government over the spirit of party, both in England as a whole and in London. Then or later, annals from an unknown date (before 1195) to 1307, based upon the Westminster *Flores Historiarum* but in their later stages incorporating many details from Horn's judicial and administrative knowledge, must have been prefixed to the history of Edward II. When Horn added to his sources, his concern with the pleas of the Crown and the sheriff's jurisdiction is apparent: under 1209, for instance, recording that pleas before itinerant justices were held in the Tower, he noted that before Henry FitzAylwin the city had no mayor, but sheriffs 'qui habuerunt potestatem et libertatem ad determinandum placita coronae'.[2] The

---

[1] *Annales Londonienses*, p. 151.
[2] Ibid. p. 14.

annals were continued with brief entries and documents (some of them also in *Liber Horn*) down to 1317; a reference to the plague of 1315 lasting 'about three years continuously' shows that they were compiled in 1318 or later.[1] Finally, the *Annales* seem to have been incorporated into the *Greater Liber Horn* from which the surviving text derives.

(4) LIBER LEGUM REGUM ANTIQUORUM

The earlier of the two custumals written in the early fourteenth century and still in part in the Guildhall's possession has perhaps the best claim to be the *Greater Liber Horn*. The history of its dismemberment has been traced by Ker, on whose reconstruction of the manuscript any further conclusions must rest.[2] The two custumals fell into the hands of Sir Robert Cotton, who divided them into more than twenty different fragments, reassembled them into three piles, returned one to the Guildhall (the modern *Liber Custumarum*), kept another (British Library MS Cotton Claudius D ii), and gave the third to Sir Francis Tate (Oriel College, Oxford MS 46). Fortunately fifteenth-century tables of contents of both manuscripts survive.[3] The earlier of the two was known in the fifteenth and sixteenth centuries as *Liber Regum Antiquorum* or *Liber Legum Regum Antiquorum (LLAR.)*[4] It was certainly intended as a formal record, carefully written and elegantly initialled, and prepared to an overall plan: it contains an enlarged text of the *Leges Anglorum*, the London compilation of about 1200 incorporating the laws and charters of English kings from Ine to Henry II; a collection of charters of kings from William I onwards, though mainly of Henry III; a further collection of London ordinances down to 1312, with a small

---

[1] Ibid. p. 236.

[2] N. R. Ker, 'Liber Custumarum and other manuscripts formerly at the Guildhall', *Guildhall Miscellany*, iii (1954), pp. 37–45, cf. 39–42; *Mediaeval Manuscripts in British Libraries*, i. pp. 20–2; Riley, *Lib. Cust.* ix–xxiv.

[3] Ker, 'Liber Custumarum', pp. 42–5; *Lib. Cust.* pp. 488–90.

[4] Ker, 'Liber Custumarum', p. 42; LBD, 317–18 (fifteenth-century list of books belonging to the Guildhall).

miscellaneous appendix (down to 1316); the statutes of Henry III and Edward I with some law tracts, the Ordinances of 1311 and related documents; a file of London documents of 1312–16; the regulations of the London companions of the *Feste de Pui*, a fraternity of foreign merchants; a list of mayors, sheriffs, king's chamberlains, and coroners of London from 1276 to 1321; and a fragmentary register of writs. A curious section containing Henry of Huntingdon's description of Britain, FitzStephen's description of London, and the extracts from the *Trésor*, forms a separate quire inserted into the text of the *Leges Anglorum*.

Can this book be the 'magnum codicem ... quem utile duxi posteris presentia temporum nostrorum exprimere', adumbrated by Horn in the Corpus manuscript, which would contain a new body of Edwardian statutes? The combination of history and law in the projected volume could be identified with the contents of the 'magnum librum de gestis anglorum in quo continentur multa utilia', described in his will; and its historical element, quoted by John Carpenter in his *Liber Albus*, seem to be the annals once part of the *Greater Liber Horn*. On the other hand, though the *Leges Anglorum* could be construed as a history of England down to the age of Richard I, *LLAR* as reconstructed by Ker could hardly be *magnum librum de gestis anglorum*; even less does it expound *presentia temporum nostrorum*. There is some evidence, however, that *LLAR* as defined by the fifteenth-century table of contents does not completely represent the volume in its fourteenth-century state. The presence of some quires bodily removed from the original volume and added to *Liber Albus* (where they form fos 16–39) was noted by Riley.[1] These leaves were not foliated before their removal to *Liber Albus*, nor do they appear in the list of contents of *LLAR*. Their extraction must have involved some dismemberment of the original volume. They consist of a number of brief tracts, lists and digests useful as precedents for the civic response to a judicial Eyre, and, though none of the texts may be Horn's own composition, the inclusion of his extracts from the Eyre Roll of 1244, which are in

[1] *Liber Albus*, pp. 51–127; *Lib. Cust.* xiii, n. 3.

Liber Horn, suggests that they were collected by Horn himself. If these pages were removed in 1419 it may be surmised that the original of *Annales Londonienses*, down to that point in the *Greater Liber Horn* was also removed, and subsequently lost. Besides the material on the Eyre, the inclusion of the *Leges Anglorum*, known to have been copied by Horn in the Corpus manuscript, testifies to his hand in the volume, as does the list of city officers from 1276 to 1321, which is evidently a revised and extended copy of the list incorporated in the returns of the city to the justices, and included in Horn's narrative of the Eyre. The revision, which refers to the accounts of the king's chamberlains in order to correct their dates of office, is characteristic of Horn.[1] The specific purpose of the original list of officers somewhat vitiates Riley's argument that *LLAR* must have been made in 1321, but it cannot have been compiled much later without attracting the inclusion of additional officers in the list. On these grounds, the tentative conclusion may be drawn that the original *LLAR*, a large volume incorporating an English chronicle, a collection of ancient laws, and charters, statutes, and London ordinances of current application, is likely to have been the volume bequeathed by Andrew Horn.

(5) MODUS ET ORDO NOVUS PLACITORUM APUD TURRIM LONDONIARUM

This text, a narrative of the London Eyre of 1321, is found in the second and later of the two custumals dismembered by Cotton, the original *Liber Custumarum* (*LC*), the quires of which are now dispersed in the same manuscripts as *LLAR*.[2] The form of the volume as indexed in the fifteenth-century table of contents seems in this case the original. The latest document included in the original hand is a charter dated 16 June 1324; the earliest addition is Edward III's charter for Southwark (6 March 1327) in a contemporary hand.[3] *LC* must have been made, therefore, between 1324 and

[1] *Lib. Cust.* pp. 239–46, revising ibid. pp. 291–5.
[2] Ker, 'Liber Custumarum', pp. 38–9; *Mediaeval Manuscripts of Great Britain*, i. pp. 21–2.
[3] *Lib. Cust.* pp. 275–8, 435–6.

1327. It was a somewhat miscellaneous collection of statutes, charters, and London ordinances, most of which are derived from *LLAR*, the earlier London custumal *Liber Ordinationum*, or *Liber Horn*, where instructions for copying the documents selected for *LC* were written in the margin. These sources indicate that despite its functional appearance it was compiled in the Guildhall, presumably to be used as a reference book, during Horn's chamberlainship, reflecting his interests and using his books; if it were already the property of the city it would, as is the case, be ignored in his will. Its original features are a list of the old and new pleas of the Crown (*Lib. Cust.*, fos 136ᵛ–138) and the narrative of the Eyre itself (fos 224ᵛ–263ᵛ). Sources for the former were doubtless available in the Guildhall, and there are internal indications of Horn's authorship of the latter. It is made up of selections from the official roll of proceedings, where the business bore upon the interests or privileges of the city, and strung together by a skeletal narrative.[1] Occasional legal notes show that the compiler, at least in his own opinion, was more familiar with the proper procedure than the justices themselves: on a writ which laid down the citizens' right to essoin, he commented that 'it was not perpetrated according to the ancient custom of the city, since few understood the ancient mode of pleading at the Eyre';[2] and in a note on purprestures two London cases are alleged to illustrate the power of the mayor and aldermen to rule whether a nuisance was caused.[3] These notes are consonant with Horn's interests, and his own part in the proceedings appears in the lengthy section on the complaint of certain fishmongers against the prohibition of retailing, in which Horn and Chigwell were defendants. Part of it derives from the official roll, but a rider recorded an argument of 'Hamo and Andrew' which was not enrolled, citing the excessive profit of the blackleg fishmongers.[4] Horn was the only

---

[1] *Lib. Cust.* pp. 285–432. The original rolls are PRO, Just. Itin. 1/546 and 1/547A. See *The Eyre of London*, 14 Edward II, AD 1321, ed. H. M. Cam (Selden Soc., 1968–9).

[2] *Lib. Cust.* p. 288.

[3] Ibid. pp. 366–7.

[4] Ibid. p. 406.

witness with both the opportunity and the motive to remember this detail, and his authorship of the narrative seems likely.

(6) SUMMA LEGUM PER ANDREAM HORNE

The list of manuscripts of Westminster Abbey drawn up for Bernard's *Catalogi Manuscriptorum Angliae et Hiberniae* includes this entry: the manuscript was presumably burnt in 1694. As it is not mentioned in the 1672 catalogue, its sojourn there must have been brief. Its title recalls the verses prefixed to the *Mirror of Justices*, of which it may have been a modern copy.[1]

(7) MARGINAL ANNOTATIONS TO MANUSCRIPTS, BOOKS, AND DOCUMENTS

(*a*) *British Library Cotton MS Titus A xxvii*

As Liebermann noted, the section of this early thirteenth-century manuscript containing the *Leges Anglorum* was collated by Horn with the text in the Corpus manuscript, and a short passage from Cnut's second code omitted in the latter was copied into the margin.[2] The *Leges Anglorum* in this manuscript are annotated in a hand which may well be Horn's, and a brief list of legal points raised has been made on fo. 175^v. Many of the notes are simply old English legal terms repeated in the margin; others suggest antiquarian interests (*nota nomen uxoris regis henrici*; Henry I: fo. 157), or mark a reference to natural law (fo. 153).

(*b*) *Corporation of London Records Office*, Liber Ordinationum

This compilation of statutes and London ordinances was made soon after 1300 and was completed between 1311 and 1316. Some of the materials were evidently taken from rolls of early Eyres found in the Tower by Hugh Waltham, the Common Clerk, who may therefore have been the compiler. Marginal notes in Horn's hand have been detected on an early set of legal points from the Eyre roll

---

[1] M. R. James, *The Manuscripts of Westminster Abbey* (Cambridge, 1909), 56, no. 208.

[2] F. Liebermann, *Über die Leges Anglorum Saeculo XIII Ineunte Londoniis Collectae* (Halle, 1894), p. 2.

of 1244; but the notes merely refer to Horn's own more comprehensive collection now part of *Liber Albus*.[1]

(c) *British Library Additional Charter 3153*

This is the London copy of the roll of the London Eyre of 1276. Among these annotations are some notes of precedents from the proceedings; and these notes are indexed at the end. Both have been attributed tentatively to Horn, and the hand is not unlike his.[2]

At first sight Horn's corpus of work is not particularly original. It consists, or rather consisted when the manuscripts were complete, of three compilations and part of a fourth: *Liber Horn*, the Corpus manuscript, *LLAR* with the *Annales Londonienses*, and the narrative of the Eyre in *LC*. The vast majority of the documents which constitute them were statutes, ordinances, and records of suits drawn up by other hands than his. He was responsible for the selection in *Liber Horn* of the extracts from Britton and from the Eyre Roll of 1244; in *LLAR*, for the short treatise on the mayor based on the *Trésor*, and for the *Annales Londonienses*. There is no reason to ascribe the *Mirror of Justices* to him, as has been shown. His responsibility for the collection of instructions and precedents for the holding of the London Eyre, which were later transferred from *LLAR* to *Liber Albus*, should probably be shared with Hugh Waltham: the *Liber Horn* copy of the second of these items, a list of the questions of the Eyre extracted from the lost rolls of 1221 and 1226, bears the marginal note 'et dominus Hugo hoc ibidem habuit ad turrim et verum est' (fo. 303ᵛ). Since both this and the first item, 'Modus et Ordo qualiter Barones et Universitas Civium Londoniarum se debeant habere et gerere erga Regem et Justitiarios suos', are first found in *Liber Ordinationum*, it seems that Waltham was responsible both for the materials on the Eyre and possibly for the whole of the

---

[1] *Liber Ordinationum*, fos 207–222; *The London Eyre of 1244*, ed. H. M. Chew and M. Weinbaum (London Record Soc., vi, London, 1970), xi–xv.

[2] *The London Eyre of 1276*, ed. M. Weinbaum (London Record Soc., xii, London, 1976), xi–xii.

compilation.[1] Horn's contribution was his own more expert legal extracts from the Eyre roll of 1244 and his collection of precedents from ancient and recent pleas of the crown.[2]

Nevertheless the compilations mark a significant intellectual progress. *Liber Horn* is a lawbook of material gathered for the guidance of city courts, combining statutes and case law with civic custom. It is one of the most comprehensive collections of statutes, having to draw upon, in the Guildhall, what was probably the richest secular archive, after the Exchequer, in England. The editors of the *Statutes of the Realm* knew of some of the lesser Edwardian statutes, such as *De sacramento ministorum regis in Itinere*, *Super vicecomites et clericos suos*, *De Gaveletto*, or *De Finibus et Attornatis*, only from Horn's copies, which may indeed be unique. Only on the flyleaf did Horn indulge the antiquarian whim of comparing the Old English text of William I's London charter with its Middle English rendering.[3] Otherwise, every document might have a use in the court of the mayor, the chamberlain, or the sheriffs. The Corpus manuscript, compiled as *Liber Horn* was accumulating, was the result of Horn's discovery of two texts of *Leges Anglorum*. He continued its pattern of short historical paragraphs introducing collections of laws down to the reign of Edward I, though he included no more than the titles of the Edwardian statutes; and he also included the *Mirror of Justices*, a work which harked back to the biblical language of Alfred's laws. However remote the ordinances of Aethelstan and Cnut might be from the world of the Westminster Bench and the city courts of Edward II's reign, the stately procession of laws from Ine to Edward I, many of them couched in the language of Deuteronomy, justified historically the body of thirteenth-century statute which the courts applied. Since the Corpus manuscript did not completely

[382]

join ancient to modern law, Horn included a note to state his intention of making a third compilation, presumably *LLAR*. This is a lawbook of a more formal kind; the *Leges Anglorum* probably came at the beginning, followed by charters of liberties, ordinances of London, a much more select group of thirteenth-century statutes, and, in an order which cannot now be established, the *Annales Londonienses* and the extracts from the *Trésor*. The manuscript is a solemn and public statement of the belief that London's and England's liberties were not the creation of Magna Carta but ascended to remote antiquity and had their roots in the Mosaic law. It is a perspective on the English past which Horn shared with Stubbs himself, who edited his annals and was uniquely familiar with the material in his collections.

Why should a practical man with business in the city courts turn to history? There is some evidence of sheer antiquarian curiosity in Horn's collections, reminiscent of William of Malmesbury, and hardly to be found again until the time of John Rous and William Worcester. The annotations in the Corpus manuscript show his interest in the origins of the Angles and Saxons in lower Saxony; in the significance of the thegn; in the proper use of the old English letters *wen* and *thorn*; in the hide (citing Bede); in the ordeal as a permissible procedure (citing Bernard of Pavia); in margraves, landgraves, and other ranks of German society.[1] Further historical information was noted in the margins of the Titus *Leges Anglorum* and *Liber Horn*.[2] But it is clear that these interests grew out of his careful search for precedents; and he had access to the municipal archives which opened the door to London's and England's past. Procedure in court instilled a habit of absolute verbal precision, as a case might be invalidated by an inaccurate *conte*.[3] Particularly characteristic of *Liber Horn* are the frequent notes, probably in his

[1] MS Corpus 70, fos 1, 1ᵛ, 2, 2ᵛ, 16, 33. The note on *thorn* and *wen* is also in *Liber Horn*, fos 205ᵛ, 362.

[2] *Liber Horn*, fo. 7.

[3] See T. F. T. Plucknett, *Early English Legal Literature* (Cambridge, 1958), p. 85.

own hand, certifying the accuracy of the text: 'examinatur per ceram', or 'sigillatum in cera in Gildaula Lond'. Many of the documents were authenticated by reference to their source: 'istud breve est in Gildaula Lond'in secunda cista in tega cum litera T. sigillata cum magno sigillo domini R.' or 'hic invenies in magno libro Gildaule cum litera a prope in fine'.[1] In an age of professional justice, the written record was easily the best warrant of title, as the author of the *Mirror of Justices* confessed,[2] and Horn merely took further than his contemporaries the authentication of his legal references. It was more original to include among them, in the *Annales Londonienses*, an historical narrative which incorporated numerous precedents for the civic authorities; but narrative was nothing new to the fourteenth-century pleader, or *narrator* whose role has been compared to that of the romancer or singer of tales.[3] The immediate ancestor of the prose of *Annales Londonienses* is the record of legal processes, frequently found in the London letter books and sometimes in Horn's collections, like the record, part narrative and part documentation, of a case in the Exchequer about a house in Milk Street.[4] Its analogue is Horn's own account of the Eyre of 1321, and the *Annales* themselves were briefly continued in 1330 with a memorandum of an important case.[5] A closer model, though with a different provenance, was the monastic chronicle with its long-established practice of incorporating documents. In the reign of Edward I, the chronicle of contemporary events was evidently a genre kept alive by the sense of senior officials of great monastic houses—sacrists, sub-priors, occasionally perhaps even abbots—that it was their duty to record both local and national affairs.[6] The public expectation that monastic chronicles should be

[1] *Liber Horn*, fos 346, 247.

[2] *Mirror of Justices*, p. 152.

[3] M. T. Clanchy, 'Remembering the Past and the Good Old Law', *History*, lv (1970), pp. 165–76, cf. 175; *From Memory to Written Record* (London, 1979), pp. 221–2.

[4] *Liber Horn*, fos 350–354ᵛ; *Lib. Cust.* pp. 135–47.

[5] *Annales Londonienses*, pp. 241–51.

[6] Antonia Gransden, *Historical Writing in England, c. 550–c. 1307* (London, 1974), p. 439.

the repositories of the national memory was underlined in 1291, when Edward I summarily commanded religious houses to search their histories and records for evidence of his claim to Scotland.[1] With this modest ambition, the monastic chroniclers of the end of the thirteenth century were at best, like the author of the West-minster *Flores*, the Guisborough chronicler, Bartholomew Cotton at Norwich, or William Rishanger at St. Albans, competent archivists and annalists, not given to forthright opinions. As a work built upon the Westminster chronicle and dedicated to the impartial accumulation of precedents, the *Annales Londonienses* were a natural adaptation of the genre to record the often identical concerns of a London secular lawyer.

The *Annales*, nevertheless, mark a new departure in English historiography. The monastic chronicle was a form of historical writing which since the time of Matthew Paris had palpably ceased to excite the enthusiasm of either its authors or its readers; if the events of the 1290s sent a last ripple of interest through the mona-steries, most of their annalists had laid down their pens by 1307.[2] Livelier and more opinionated narratives, from men involved in the burgeoning business of the Crown and nobility, were beginning to take their place. Thomas Wykes was perhaps the harbinger of the new mode; and friars such as Richard of Durham and his Franciscan continuator (whose lost works lend verve to the Lanercost chronicle) must have composed their chronicles from genuine interest and concern in the political scene. The *Vita Edwardi Secundi*, another spontaneous and even passionate piece of contemporary history, has been credibly ascribed to the civil lawyer John Walwayn, D.C.L.[3] The *Annales Londonienses* are another example, in spite of the author's wholly divergent legal training, of the relation between knowledge of the law and historical writing. In their extant form

---

[1] E. L. G. Stones and Grant G. Simpson, *Edward I and the Throne of Scotland* (Oxford, 1978), i. pp. 137–48.

[2] Gransden, *Historical Writing*, p. 443.

[3] *Chronicon de Lanercost, 1201–1346*, ed. J. Stevenson (Edinburgh, 1839); *Vita Edwardi Secundi*, ed. N. Denholm-Young (London, 1957).

disguised as a chronicle in the monastic tradition, their core, as has been suggested, is likely to be a similarly spontaneous account of the first dramatic years of Edward II. A third account covering the years 1321–31 and now incorporated in the *Annales Paulini* is likely to have been composed by a notary familiar with the Guildhall.[1] The contemporary historians of Edward II's reign, therefore, had on the whole a very different experience from the historians of the previous generation: they had some professional standing, either as notaries or in the learned or customary laws, or in theology (like Richard of Durham, his Franciscan continuator, and Nicholas Trevet, O.P.), and consequently they had more varied and mobile careers than the monastic chroniclers. In this they foreshadowed the more original historians of Edward III's reign. Only in the last quarter of the century, when monks were beginning to acquire the training now necessary for secular business, did they regain the initiative in historiography.

A second feature of Horn's historical work, however, is not exactly paralleled by contemporary writers: his resurrection of the *Leges Anglorum*. Using as exemplars the Rylands (or a very similar text) and the Titus manuscripts, he gave it pride of place in the Corpus compilation and in *LLAR*, and included an extract in *Liber Horn*.[2] The *Leges* were a text compiled in London in the reign of John, on the basis of the *Quadripartitus* and the pseudonymous *Leges Edwardi Confessoris*: all three are instances of the continuing interest of the Old English laws in a period of rapidly developing legal institutions.[3] The sense of continuity in the laws of England appears again, about 1290, in the *Mirror of Justices*; the author, regarding as defective the law as applied by modern judges, appealed to fundamental law, 'riules donees par nos seinz predecessors

---

[1] *Annales Paulini*, ed. Stubbs, pp. 291–356; see H. G. Richardson, 'The Annales Paulini', *Speculum*, xxiii (1948), pp. 630–40.

[2] John Rylands Library, Manchester, MS lat. 155; see F. Liebermann, 'A contemporary MS of the "Leges Anglorum Londoniis Collectae" ', *EHR*, xxviii (1913), pp. 732–45.

[3] Liebermann, *Die Gesetze der Angelsachsen* (Halle, 1898–1916), iii. pp. 308–10, 339–42.

en seinte scripture', and to the sound practice of King Alfred.[1]
Horn rescued both the *Mirror* and *Leges Anglorum* from oblivion.
Something of his reading of the *Leges* can perhaps be seen in the
passage included in *Liber Horn*: the beginning of the laws of Edward
the Confessor, which recounts the Conqueror's consultation of the
'English nobility, their wise men and learned in the laws' and
confirmation of the 'laws of liberty and peace' of the Church and
the other fundamental rights of the Anglo-Saxon past.[2] The
customs of London, in this perspective, were but the expression of
the underlying law of the land, distorted as it may be by the
practice of modern justices; and knowledge of customary law was
as relevant in 1321, in the proper response to the Eyre, as it had been
in 1067. In an age when forms of procedure overwhelmingly
dominated English legal literature at the expense of juridical
principle, Horn's publication of the *Leges Anglorum* was a notable
challenge to Geoffrey de Scrope and his like.

English history set a standard for the governors of London: but
in at least one important respect, precepts of classical ethics, as
distilled by the thirteenth-century moralists, particularized it. The
most curious of Horn's extracts are the passages from the *Trésor* of
Brunetto Latini on the conduct of a podestà in an Italian city,
edited for the guidance of a mayor of London. They appear, with
Henry of Huntingdon's description of England and FitzStephen's
of London, in a single quire of *LLAR*, placed incongruously (and
no doubt not until the fifteenth century) in the middle of *Leges
Anglorum*.[3] No references to the *Trésor* are made in the text, and in
the contents the extracts are distinguished by the titles 'doctrina
eligendi gubernatoris, de forma eligendi maioris', and 'qualiter
maior se habebit'. A strong indication that Horn as chamberlain
made the extracts as given in the interpolation to the effect that the
mayor on leaving office should not omit to ask the chamberlain
and other important citizens to deliver all undetermined pleas to

---

[1] *Mirror of Justices*, pp. 2, 8, 166–71.
[2] *Liber Horn*, fo. 275ʳᵛ; Liebermann, *Gesetze*, i. pp. 627–33.
[3] CLRO, *Liber Custumarum*, fos 1–11; *Lib. Cust.*, pp. 1–25.

right judgement.[1] The *Trésor* was an encyclopedia of practical knowledge: its author presented his scheme of knowledge leading up to the science of politics, on which other branches of knowledge were to depend. His work, as Carmody has shown, is a compilation of sources, some of which remain unidentified, and it is clear that in the section on politics he owed less to Aristotle's *Ethics*, though they are cited, than to a native Italian tradition of moral-political writing. By far the most important source is the *Liber de Regimine Civitatum* of John of Viterbo, a book of advice of Ghibelline inspiration for the *podestàs* of Italian cities, based in its turn of the writings of Innocent III and a selection of classical moralists.[2] Brunetto's purpose in his third book, from which these extracts are taken, was to provide a mirror both for princes and for communities. He envisaged a city electing a *podestà* from outside its walls for a limited time, and after some generalities about the necessity of lordship and the qualities necessary in *signori*, he proposed in some detail how a new lord should be elected, how he should respond to an invitation to govern a city, the general principles on which he should rule, how he should receive and send ambassadors, and how he should discharge his judicial duties. This is followed by a section on the moral qualities of good rulers, which includes a disquisition on whether it is better to be feared than loved. Finally, after a brief excursus on how a lord should make war, Brunetto ended by laying down how he should leave office and how the commune should proceed to a new election. Book III of the *Trésor* ranged, therefore, from a moral discourse to an *Ars Dictaminis*, including a number of model letters.

Horn took some trouble to adapt this material. Only a small proportion of Book III is represented in the extracts. Horn omitted the first chapter (III, 73), and began with the chapter on the basis of lordship in justice, reverence, and love, which he left unchanged, except to substitute *mayor* or *governor* for Brunetto's *Sire*. His

[1] *Lib. Cust.*, p. 20.
[2] *Li Livres dou Trésor*, ed. F. J. Carmody (Berkeley, California, 1948), xxxi–xxxii.

second chapter is virtually Brunetto's III, 75, on the qualities to look for in a prospective ruler, though he omitted Latini's insistence that the ruler shall be over 25, presumably because there was no such rule in London. However, Horn detached the last paragraph of the chapter and raised it into a separate chapter, 'on the discords and struggles which arise in towns through the neglect of guardians'. Brunetto rather casually regretted the spirit of faction in Italian towns and the prevalence of force in elections. Horn, giving the passage more emphasis, put the blame not on force but on wealth, retinue, and intrigue, reflecting perhaps the conditions of fourteenth-century London and England.[1] At this point Brunetto went on to discuss the method of election, with a model letter from a commune to a new lord, and then launched into his disquisition on how a lord should behave. Horn rejected this, no doubt as not applicable, and turned instead to the last chapters of the *Trésor*, where Brunetto discussed the preparations for electing the next lord. He followed the *Trésor* in laying down that the electors should consult 'prudhommes' who knew the procedure, but he underlined the role of these 'prudhommes' by adding that the election should be made with their advice. Perhaps he was thinking here not of the aldermen, who were the electors anyway, nor of the paid officials, who might advise on procedure but not on the choice of man, but of his own inter-mediate position as chamberlain. There is another significant addition here. Latini advised the outgoing lord not to accept re-election if it were offered. Horn, following the spirit of the charter of 1319, repeated this; but qualified it with the words 'if he can honestly escape from it'.[2] The repeated re-elections of Hamo de Chigwell had doubtless modified the brave resolutions of 1319.

Brunetto then laid down how the outgoing lord should hand over his office to the commune, and how he should address the citizens. Horn followed this text, adding that the mayor should not omit to hand over all unfinished pleas before his court to the chamberlain for determination. This may refer to the delays of

---

[1] *Trésor*, iii. p. 75; *Lib. Cust.* p. 19.
[2] *Trésor*, iii. p. 102; *Lib. Cust.* p. 20.

business in the mayor's court which the charter had tried to eliminate.[1] In the *Trésor*, this was virtually the end, but Horn then went
back to III, 97, where Brunetto had explained the general principles
by which a lord should conduct himself, and reproduced the
passage more or less verbatim. Finally, he jumped back again by one
chapter to Latini's discussion of the difference between rulers who
wished to be loved and those who wished to be feared. Horn's
selection of this seems to refer more naturally to national politics
than to civic, in the arbitrary last years of Edward II's reign; and
this impression is confirmed by the last four paragraphs of Brunetto's
chapter which Horn elevated into a separate section, and entitled it
'the difference between a King and a Tyrant'. This section strikingly
begins 'Platon dist . . .'; in fact, Horn has cut in half the *Trésor*'s
citation of John of Viterbo, who was himself in the middle of a
quotation from Seneca *De Clementia*; and it was Seneca who quoted
Plato. The violence done to the text shows how Horn seized on a
rather casual phrase of Latini on the difference between kings and
tyrants.[2] It was a difference already touched on in the preamble to
the Ordinances of 1311, which he had incorporated into the *Annales
Londonienses* and *Liber Horn*. And on this defiant note, the extracts
conclude.

The general principle of their editor is clear: where he altered or
omitted passages, it was to establish a detailed, practical procedure.
The precepts which he took over from Brunetto, therefore, must
have been intended to be taken seriously as a guide to practice. The
inclusion in this context of Brunetto's remarks on political morality
and the distinction between king and tyrant confirm the impression
that Horn's assertion of the privileges of London was but one
element in a larger political view. Universal principles should guide
the city's choice of ruler, and as his interest in the Old English laws
suggests, *Libertas Londoniensis* was but a surviving fragment of a
primaeval natural order of freedom and justice. In the eyes of Horn
this was no nostalgic dream but a solid, if submerged, base for the

[1] *Lib. Cust.* p. 269.
[2] *Liber Custumarum*, fo. 8ᵛ; *Lib. Cust.* p. 24.

practicalities of modern government. Underpinning the *minima iudicia cuiuscumque municipii*, a great contemporary had seen the universality of Roman law;[1] it was odder, but not entirely irrational, to find a similar bedrock in the earliest stratum of the native legal tradition. For nostalgia about the Anglo-Saxon past, there were many precedents;[2] but the combination in *LLAR* of pre-Conquest antiquity with modern political wisdom, contemporary history, and current law, made it a school for statesmen, if only Guildhall statesmen, with broad responsibilities. Whether Horn's successors made anything of it is another matter.

---

[1] Dante, *Monarchia*, i. p. 14.
[2] Southern, 'England's First Entry into Europe', in *Mediaeval Humanism*, p. 154.

Chivalry, heralds, and history

MAURICE KEEN

'THEY sought by eloquence to teach men virtue and to stimulate them to right conduct.'[1] So writes Professor Wilcox of the historians of the early Italian renaissance, among whom Bruni's name is perhaps the most famous, who brought a new perspective to the writing of history, fashioned by their studies in classical literature. In context, the word eloquence has special overtones, reminding us of the debt of the Renaissance writers to the rhetorical techniques of antiquity. If, however, we forget about these overtones for a moment, what Professor Wilcox has said would be just about equally true of the chivalrous historians of the later Middle Ages, of whom Froissart was the doyen. Their didactic intention was similar, and explicit: I sit down to record a history, says Froissart, 'so that the honourable enterprises, noble adventures, and deeds of arms performed in the wars between England and France may be properly related . . . to the end that brave men, taking example from them, may be encouraged in their well doing.'[2] The object was not lost upon those to whom he addressed himself. 'Read Froissart', urged Caxton in the epilogue to his Ordre of Chyvalry in which he upbraids English knighthood for its laxity, '. . . and also behold that victorious and noble King Henry Vth, and the captains under him . . . whose names shine gloriously by their virtuous and noble acts'.[3] To stimulate men to virtue and right conduct was indeed

[1] D. J. Wilcox, The Development of Florentine Humanist Historiography in the Fifteenth Century (Cambridge, Mass., 1969), p. 29.

[2] J. Froissart,, Œuvres, ed. K. de Lettenhove, ii (Brussels, 1867), p. 4.

[3] W. Caxton, The Book of the Ordre of Chyvalry, ed. A. T. P. Byles (EETS, 1926), p. 123.

quite as characteristically the business of the chivalrous chronicler as it was of the Renaissance historian.

There were, of course, differences of emphasis, and very important ones, in their respective conceptions of virtue and right conduct. But as Huizinga has reminded us, even here we should not exaggerate the distance separating the two worlds. 'The thirst for honour and glory proper to the men of the Renaissance is essentially the same as the chivalrous ambition of earlier times...', he writes. 'The passionate desire to find himself praised by contemporaries or by posterity was the source of virtue with the courtly knight of the twelfth century and the rude captain of the fourteenth, no less than with the *beaux-esprits* of the *quattrocento*.'[1] Huizinga here was writing of those men whom history was supposed to inspire, not of historians, and he was a little less generous when he came to treat of the historians of chivalry. Founded in the 'traditional fiction' of chivalry, history as they conceived it becomes, in his view, simply 'a summary of feats of arms and of ceremonies'.[2] This conclusion seems rather surprising, if we think about it. If the aspirations of the men of the 'chivalrous' later Middle Ages foreshadowed those of the Renaissance, should we not expect the historical literature which nurtured their aspirations to amount correspondingly to something a little more than this, to foreshadow, in some related degree, the sophistication of the historical literature which nurtured the aspirations of the early Renaissance? The object of this paper will be to try to explore a little further what sort of historiography could be founded on the 'traditional fiction' of chivalry, the degree of sophistication of which it proved itself capable, and the values which it promoted.

Huizinga's use of the word 'fiction' itself poses a problem that must be faced at the outset of our enquiry. Just how sharp a line are we entitled to draw, in the particular context in question, between history and fiction? The quest for the origins of the 'traditional fiction' of chivalry will take us back to stories which, in a literary

[1] J. Huizinga, *The Waning of the Middle Ages* (London, 1924), p. 59.
[2] Ibid. p. 59.

form, first achieved popularity in the twelfth century, that is to say to the *chansons de geste* and to the early romances of Troy, of Alexander, and of Arthur's court. We nowadays discuss these works as fictions, but their authors assumed at least some substructure of truth underlying them, and seldom made any effort to distinguish the fact from the fantasies that were blended in their poems. There is, it is true, a formal difference between a *chanson de geste* and a verse history, the former being written in decasyllabic verse with an assonant weave, the latter in rhyme, sometimes octosyllabic, sometimes decasyllabic, sometimes Alexandrine. The distinction however does not seem to be relevant to the question of whether the content of the verse is factual or fictional. Chrétien's verse is more like that of the histories than that of the *chansons*, and both Wace and Benoît de Sainte-Maure moved easily from factual to fictional matter (using the word fictional in a modern sense) without feeling any need to alter their manner of versification. They did not feel the need to do so because they did not see any very significant difference between the sort of matter that was dealt with in the *Roman de Brut* on the one hand and the *Roman de Rou* or the *Chroniques des ducs de Normandie* on the other.

Those who listened to *chansons* and histories do not seem to have worried very much about the distinction between them either. Those who did worry seem moreover to have been, as a rule, more concerned on account of the didactically false consequences of allowing fancy too free a hand than on account of its fictitious quality. Be careful of reading too much of the stories of Arthur, great as was his worldly valour, Philippe de Mézières warned the youthful Charles VI of France: his history is too full of *bourdes*. But read, he says, 'of the great deeds of the Christian emperors . . . and especially of the great battles and marvellous deeds of your great predecessor, the blessed Charlemagne . . . and read often the fair and true history of the valour of Duke Godfrey of Bouillon, and of his noble and holy chivalry'.[1] That 'fair and true history' of Duke

[1] P. de Mézières, *Le Songe du Vieil Pèlerin*, ed. G. W. Coopland (Cambridge, 1969) 2, p. 222.

Godfrey, in Philippe de Mézière's fourteenth century, meant the cycle of the *Chevalier au Cygne*, the latest of the great heroic cycles, and the only one whose development, from its historical origins into full blown myth, can be traced in detail.[1] The oldest part of the cycle, the *Chanson d' Antioche* (put together before *c.* 1130), has a reasonable title to be called an historical work, since the narrative which its minstrel author cast into poetic form for a secular audience tallies well with what we learn from the most reputable chronicles of the first crusade. The author of the *Chanson de Jerusalem* however, who wrote not much later and carried the story forward to the capture of Jerusalem and the battle of Ascalon, clearly did not have a reputable chronicle before him when he was composing his marvellous stories of Godfrey's confrontations with the Moslem prince and hero Cornumarant. The *Roman des chétifs*, telling of the survivors of the crusade of Walter the Penniless who after extraordinary wanderings miraculously rejoined the crusaders before the capture of the Holy City, has even less basis in fact.[2] The

[1] The *Chanson d'Antioche* has been edited by P. Paris (2 vols, Paris, 1848): the *Chanson de Jerusalem* and the *Chevalier au cygne* by C. Hippeau (Paris, 1868 and 1874–7). None of these editions is wholly satisfactory. On the crusade cycle generally, see H. Pigeonneau, *Le Cycle de la croisade* (St. Cloud, 1877), the first full study of its development; and S. Duparc-Quioc, *Le Cycle de la croisade* (Paris, 1955), an important monograph, incorporating the results of intervening research; her findings are considered in a review article by C. Cahen, 'Le Premier Cycle de la croisade', *Le Moyen Âge*, 63 (1957), pp. 311–28.

[2] The historical criticism of the poems which are incorporated into the crusade cycle is complicated. The original version of the *Chanson d' Antioche* by Richard le Pèlerin is lost, and what we have is the revamped version put together by Greindor de Douai about 1200. Something can be learnt of the degree to which the original has been altered by comparing Greindor's text with the surviving fragment of Grégoire Bachada's Provençal *Chanson d' Antioche*, published by P. Meyer in *Archives de l'Orient Latin*, ii (1884), pp. 467–509, since Bachada used Richard le Pélérin as a source. Bachada in turn was used by the thirteenth-century Spanish author of *La Gran Conquista de Ultramar*, and so more again can be learnt about Richard's poem by comparing Greindor's version with this text: See G. Paris, 'La Chanson d'Antioche provençale et la *Gran Conquista de Ultramar*', *Romania* 17 (1888), pp. 513–42; 19 (1890) pp. 562 ff.; and S. Duparc-Quioc, 'La Composition de la *Chanson d'Antioch*', *Romania*, 83 (1962), p. 1 ff., 210 ff. Opinion remains divided as to whether Richard le Pèlerin was an eyewitness of events, or put his account

stories of Godfrey's youth and descent which were finally woven in as the beginning of the cycle take us clear out of the world of history into that of legend—to the fairy story of the Swan Knight better known as the story of Lohengrin. There *is* history in the *Chevalier au Cygne*, but there is a lot else besides.[1] Nevertheless, and chiefly because it was an edifying story, it was the kind of work which Philippe de Mézières could recommend as prescribed historical reading, 'fair and true'.

Alongside this story de Mézières singles out specifically for favourable mention the history of Charlemagne, whose deeds, with those of his paladins, formed the matter of the most famous poems among the epic cycles. About their influence on writers of history there can be no question. The debt to the *chansons de geste* of Geoffrey Villehardouin, who may surely be claimed as the first acknowledged master of historical writing in the chivalrous mode, is generally acknowledged.[2] The debt is however even clearer, and much more explicit, in the work of the numerous vernacular historians who wrote in verse between the early twelfth and the late fourteenth centuries, and is only less acclaimed, probably, because they are less often read. The story of Charlemagne in these works becomes virtually the stock historical foil to the history of the

---

together from the chronicles (principally from Robert the Monk): S. Duparc-Quioc and A. Hatem, *Les Poèmes épiques des croisades* (Paris, 1932), argue the former case; Pigeonneau and Gaston Paris, both cited above, for the latter. Greindor de Douai also reworked the *Chanson de Jerusalem*, and linked the two poems into one whole with some skill: for historical criticism see Duparc-Quioc in *Position des thèses*. *École des chartes* (1937) pp. 137–43; and ibid.,' La Famille de Coucy et la composition de la *Chanson de Jerusalem*', *Romania*, 64 (1938), pp. 245–52. On the historical element in the *Roman des chétifs* see Cahen, 'Le Premier Cycle'.

[1] See G. Paris's review of H. A. Todd's edition of *La Naissance du Chevalier au cygne* (Baltimore, 1889) in *Romania*, 19 (1890), pp. 314–40: and E. Roy, 'Les Poèmes Francaises relatifs a la première croisade: le poème de 1356 et ses sources', *Romania*, 55 (1929), pp. 411–68.

[2] See J. M. A. Beer, *Villehardouin: Epic Historian* (Geneva, 1968), chap 3.

more recent past. Things were not like this in the days of Charlemagne and Agolant—or indeed when Antioch was taken—writes
Ambroise, lamenting the quarrels of the French and the English on
the Third Crusade. In those times all worked together honourably
to the one end, regardless of race, and so well that

> Que hom i peust essample prendre
> Non pas li uns l'autre entreprendre.[1]

It is clear from other things that he says in verses close to this that
Ambroise was thoroughly grounded in the poems of the Carolingian
cycles,[2] and in this he was not singular. On Jordan Fantosme, as
R. Bezzola has shown, their influence is deeply impressed.[3] The
author of the Provençal *Chanson* of the Albigensian crusade knew
the story of Charlemagne's seven-year siege of Montessor, and of
Raoul de Cambrai's harrying of the church of Origny, and the
whole poem is full of references to the emperor, to Roland, and to
Oliver.[4] At the very beginning of the poem he tells us that he will
make his song after the manner and in the measure of the *Chanson
d'Antioche* (not Richard the Pilgrim's French poem, it would seem,
but the Provençal version of it).[5] Some authors seem indeed to go
out of their way to display the width of their reading in chivalrous
fiction, as for instance Ambroise does in one passage: as also and
later does Cuvelier, the fourteenth-century minstrel biographer of
Bertrand du Guesclin, in the splendid speech that he puts into the
mouth of the Black Prince as, bound for the Spanish war, he bids
farewell to his wife Joan of Kent:

---

[1] Ambroise, *L'Estoire de la Guerre Sainte*, ed. G. Paris (Paris, 1897), ll.
8517–18.

[2] Ibid. ll. 8480–96: and compare ll. 1388, 4179–92, 4665–6.

[3] R. Bezzola, *Les Origines et la formation de la littérature courtoise en occident*, 3,
pt 1 (Paris, 1963), pp. 198–206.

[4] *La Chanson de la croisade contre les Albigeois*, ed. P. Meyer, ii (Paris, 1879),
pp. 28, 30, 90, 114, 352. I have quoted the modern French translation, as my
knowledge of Provençal is inadequate.

[5] Ibid. ii. pp. 2–3. Only a fragment of the Provençal poem on Antioch
survives: see above p. 396 n. 2.

> Qui veult avoir le non des bon et des vaillans,
> Il doit aler souvent a la pluie et au champs,
> Et estre en la bataille, ainsi que fist Rolans,
> Et li bers Olivier, et Ogier li poissans,
> Les iiii fils Aymon, Charlemains li grans,
> Li Ducs Lion de Bourges, et Guion de Cournans,
> Perceval le Galois, Lancelot et Tristans,
> Alixandre et Artus, Godefroi li sachans;
> De coi cilz menestrelz font ces nobles rommans.[1]

For this sort of author, the pseudo-history of the *chansons* and romances was the most familiar and at the same time the most instructive history that was known, after that given in the Bible: and in many of their works it was a history to which they appealed for examples more often than they did to Holy Writ.

It must be stressed how often these references to past history in the verse chronicles are not there just for decoration, but to emphasize the author's edifying intent. A great host of references could be put together to show how comparisons with the traditional heroes are used to pin point the chivalrous qualities and standing of more recent warriors—as Ambroise uses them, for instance, to celebrate the *prouesse* of Geoffrey de Lusignan in the fighting before Acre, where he did so well that

> Que puis Rodland et Olivier
> Ne fud tel los de chevalier.[2]

But the tally would be too long for recital. It is worth noting, though, how the same comparisons can also be used by the minstrel chroniclers to point up the failings even of their heroes. To Peter de Langtoft Edward I was, after Arthur, the flower of chivalry. But he did not always live up to the standard, for he could be mean:

> En gestes aunciens trovoums nous escrit
> Quel rays et quels realms ly rays Arthur conquist,
> Et coment sun purchace largement partyst . . .
> Li rays Sir Eduuard ad done trop petyt.[3]

---

[1] Cuvelier, *Chronique de Bertrand du Guesclin*, ed. E. Charrière, i. (Paris, 1839), ll. 10711–19.

[2] Ambroise, ll. 4665–6.

[3] *Chronique de Pierre de Langtoft*, ed. T. Wright (RS, 1868), ii. p. 296.

The teaching of virtue by example, which is the object in these passages, is indeed a principal object throughout chronicles of this kind. The references to past heroes put more recent deeds and enterprises into perspective, showing what was important about them, what was worthy of being remembered. In that sense the chivalrous histories teach the same *sort* of lessons (though not of course quite the same lesson) as does the history of the Renaissance writers, and their authors paid a similar attention to eloquence, though it is eloquence of a different kind. That is what is significant about the explicit statement of the Provençal author of the *Chanson de la croisade* quoted earlier, that he is taking the *Chanson d'Antioche* as his model: he is aware of seeking a manner and a poetic measure apposite to the story he proposes, and to the values that it will emphasize.

The virtues that these verse histories teach define themselves with clarity. They are the quintessentially chivalrous virtues, for which Gervase Mathew and others have taught us to look in chivalrous literature, from the twelfth to the fourteenth century; prowess, generosity, wisdom, loyalty, courtesy, *franchise* or *debonaireté*. [1] Roger of Comminges was *preux* and wise, accomplished in *largesse* and in all good qualities: that is the picture of the good Knight from the song of the Albigensìan crusade. [2] As they stood by the body of Jacques d'Avesnes, Ambroise tells us

> Li un regretoit sa proesce,
> L'autre retraiot sa largesce. [3]

The key words and virtues are the same as those in the lament for the young King Henry in the *Histoire de Guillaume le Maréchal*:

> He Dex! que fera or largesse,
> E chevalerie e proesce,
> Qui dedenz lui soloient meindre. [4]

Bon, loiaux, and *hardiz* are the words of highest praise for a knight from Cuvelier's hero, *Bertrand li cortois. Cortois* is another keyword,

---

[1] G. Mathew, *The Court of Richard II* (London, 1968), chap. xiii.
[2] *Chanson de la croisade contre les Albigeois*, ii. p. 295.
[3] Ambroise, ll. 6721–2.
[4] *L'Histoire de Guillaume le Maréchal*, ed. P. Meyer, i (Paris, 1891), ll. 6941–3.

for courtesy and *franchise* among equals are the foils to daring and recklessness in battle in the ideal warrior:

Au fait des armes fiers et estouz
En ostel douz et debonnaires

as the *Song of Caerlaverock* has it.[1] Its praise here of John Hastings underscores precisely qualities of knighthood that the Lady of the Lake in the prose romance explicitly stresses as complementary to one another in her famous advice to her foster child Lancelot.[2] Loyalty is another principal value singled out as essential to true chivalry. Honour, overall, is the key note of the aristocratic scale of values which the minstrel chroniclers single out from history's record, just as a place of honour on the roll of those remembered as *preudhommes* is accepted as the legitimate aspiration for all knighthood—a place, that is to say, alongside the heroes of what we call legend. Both with regard to what they seek to record and with regard to what they seek to impart in the way of values, chivalrous history and chivalrous literature stand, in the verse histories, in a mutually interpenetrative relation.

The chivalrous chroniclers of the later Middle Ages were not for the most part minstrels, like their forerunners with whom we have so far been dealing: and for the most part they wrote in prose. Here history keeps pace with the pattern of the development of letters: the triumph of prose as the medium for vernacular romance is one of the most exciting passages in the literary history of the end of the twelfth and the beginning of the thirteenth century. As to the author of romance so to the vernacular historian prose, in the later period, opened new ranges of flexibility and also of precision in the use of language, and some were clearly quite aware of this. Master John, who translated the Latin chronicle of Pseudo-Turpin for Rainald of Dammartin in 1205, was quite clear about the advantage of prose

---

[1] *The Siege of Carlaverock*, ed. N. H. Nicolas (London, 1828), p. 54.
[2] H. O. Sommer, *The Vulgate version of the Arthurian Romances*, iii (Washington, 1910), pp. 115–16.

over verse as a medium for historical writing, and says so.[1] Jean le
Bel makes the same point still more explicitly in the Prologue to his
chronicle. The passage is interesting, because he puts the point into
an historiographical context. The trouble with verse histories, he
says, is that they tend to exaggerate (*bourdes* again), and he sees that
this is partly the result of the stresses to which a factual record is
exposed by the demands of metre and rhyme. The consequence is
that they too often attribute to individuals about whom they are
writing achievements which are *oultrageuses* and incredible, which in
turn will in the long run serve to demean the hard-won reputations
of their heroes, not to enhance them. Strict accuracy is the only way
in which a writer of history can do justice properly to the high deeds
and enterprises of arms done in the wars between England and
France about which he proposes to write.[2] Jean le Bel's object
remains the same as that of the verse historians, to instil the principles
of nobility of conduct by recorded example; and his framework of
values is the same as theirs, inherited from them. But his historical
sophistication is greater: as a writer of prose history he has become
more aware of his obligation to his subject—to Clio as the muse of
history.

Jean le Bel makes another interesting point in his prologue. From
his record of their knightly deeds, he tells us, we shall be able to
distinguish those who were entitled to be called *prœus*, and those
who can be called *souverains prœus*—introducing a distinction
between the two.[3] The treatment of the chivalric virtues will
become in consequence of this added delicacy of standard more
elaborate and intricate. In fact a greater elaboration—a more ornate
approach—is typical of the later chivalrous chronicles, both in verse
and prose. In this mood Froissart tells the story of how Edward III

---

[1] *The Old French Johannes Translation of the Pseudo-Turpin Chronicle*, ed.
R. N. Walpole (California, 1976), p. 130.

[2] *Chronique de Jean le Bel*, ed. J. Viard and E. Déprez (Paris, 1904), i. pp. 1–2.

[3] Ibid. p. 3: and compare G. de Charny, *Le Livre de chevalerie*, in J. Froissart,
Œuvres, ed. K. de Lettenhove, i, pt 3 (Brussels, 1873), p. 504: 'Encore en y a
d'autres que souverainement l'en doit plus tenir a preux . . .'

awarded to Eustace de Ribemont 'le pris de la bataille deseure tous aultres' after their fight outside Calais, and of the chaplet of pearls that the king gave him to wear for a year in witness of it.[1] Barbour can record of Sir Giles d'Argentine that he was known for the *third* best knight of Christendom.[2] The influence of romance and especially of Arthurian story, with its careful record of who it was that won the sovereign prize for prowess at this or that tournament or battle, is no doubt at work here, though it is by no means the sole influence. The whole mythology of chivalry was becoming more intricate by the fourteenth century, and provided richer veins of literary and didactic allusion than before. It is for instance in the early fourteenth century that we first hear of the *neuf preux*—the nine worthies of chivalry:[3] and later, in consequence, we begin to hear of contemporary heroes being hailed as the tenth *preux*, as Du Guesclin and Robert the Bruce were.[4] Three of the original nine worthies are heroes already very familiar: Arthur, Charlemagne, and Godfrey de Bouillon. Beside these and the biblical three— Joshua, David, and Judas Maccabeus—there now stand three pagan heroes, Hector, Alexander, and Caesar. More and more, in the later fourteenth and in the fifteenth centuries, we find the chivalrous historians turning to classical history for examples and parallels that will illuminate the significance of more recent achievement. A much wider range of erudition is coming to be expected of the chivalrous historian.

In the context of a school of historical writing where the historian is bidden to keep his eye open to award the prize for prowess, one particular development from the contemporary interest in the age of

[1] *Œuvres*, xvii. p. 269.

[2] J. Barbour, *The Bruce*, ed. W. W. Skeat, i, (EETS, 1870), p. 318 (Book XIII, l. 321).

[3] On the Nine Worthies see R. L. Wyss, 'Die neun Helden', *Zeitschrift für Schweizerische Archäologie und Kunstgeschichte*, xvii (1957), pp. 73–106; and K. J. Höltgen, 'Die Nine Worthies', *Anglia*, 77 (1959), pp. 279–309.

[4] Cuvelier, l. 9875 (du Guesclin); and 'Ane ballet of the Nine Nobles', in *The Parlement of the Thre Ages*, ed. I. Gollancz (Roxburghe Club, London, 1897), p. 134 (Robert the Bruce).

Arthur deserves special mention. A series of references in the Arthurian Vulgate cycle describe Arthur ordering that the adventures of particular knights should be recorded in writing, on the basis of their own sworn statements. It was widely thought that it was from these written records of Arthur's own day that Walter Map had put together the history of Arthur. In one variant version of *Merlin* this process of recording is actually explicitly connected with the judgement of prowess: '(le chevalier jura .. que) si tost coume il s'en partira de court qu il dira voir au revenir de toutes les choses qui li seront avenues... ou soit s'ounour ou soit sa honte. Et par chou porra on connoistre la proueche de chascun.'[1] Now the Round Table was, in the later Middle Ages, taken to be the model for a number of the secular orders of chivalry which were then being founded, notably for the Order of the Garter, which was the first of them to achieve widespread fame.[2] The statutes of a number of these orders (though not those of the Garter) lay down that a record shall be kept in which there shall be entered the deeds and adventures of the companions of the Order. The companions of the Order of the Star were supposed to keep such a record, and the same was the case with the order of the Toison d'Or, and with René of Anjou's Order

---

[1] *Merlin*, ed. G. Paris and J. Ulrich, ii (Paris, 1886), p. 98.

[2] The date of the foundation of the Order of the Garter is impossible to pin down; the first recorded chapter was that held on St. George's Day 1350, see *Chronicon Galfridi Le Baker*, ed. E. M. Thompson (Oxford, 1889), pp. 108–9. Both Edward III and the Black Prince were displaying Garter insignia before that, however: see G. Beltz, *Memorials of the Order of the Garter* (London, 1841), Appendix I. The Garter emblem itself has no Arthurian echoes, and though Adam Murimuth (*Continuatio Chronicarum*, ed. E. M. Thompson, RS, 1889, p. 232), Froissart (*Œuvres*, iv. pp. 203–6), and Sir T. Gray (if Leland's notes are a trustworthy guide: *Scalacronica*, ed. J. Stevenson, Edinburgh, 1838, p. 300) suggest that it was modelled on the Round Table, they have all clearly conflated the stories of the foundation and of the Round Table celebrations held at Windsor in 1344. The Arthurian Round Table was however generally assumed to be the model for the Order: see the wording of Jean Werchin's letter to Henry IV, challenging the Garter knights to joust: 'et aussay ay entendu que aucun[s] roys du dit royaume en recompansant la dite ordre [de la Table Ronde] ont establi celle qui s'appelle la Jarretiere' (*BL*, Add. MS 21370, fo. 1).

Maurice Keen

of the Croissant.[1] Unfortunately, the records in question have not survived, and in the case of the Star at least may well have never been put together. Lost too is the record book of Louis of Naples' Order of the Knot, which we know existed from Boccaccio's jibe at Nicolo Acciaivoli: 'he wrote in French of the deeds of the knights of the Holy Spirit [an alternative title of the order], in the style in which certain others in the past wrote of the Round Table. What laughable and entirely false matters were set down, he himself knows.'[2] What a tragedy that no trace of this fascinating book can now be found!

However, if we have no surviving book of the adventures of any of the great princely orders of chivalry, we do at least know a good deal about one group of men who must have had something to do with their making, the heralds; we should remember that several of the chief heralds took their titles from their sovereigns' orders, as did Garter and Toison d'Or Kings of Arms.[3] Indeed, about the nearest thing we still have to a formal book of adventures is Wrythe's Garter Book, a record compiled late in the fifteenth century by John Wrythe, Garter, of the arms of all the Garter Knights, with brief biographical notices of the chivalrous acts and character of a number

---

[1] *Chronique de Jean le Bel*, ii. p. 205 (Star): *Chronique de Jean Le Févre*, ed. F. Morand, ii. (Paris, 1881), pp. 249, 250 (Toison d'Or): and BN, MS Fr. 25204 fos. 7ᵛᵒ, 16 ᵛᵒ (Croissant).

[2] F. Corazini, *Le lettere edite e inedite di Messer Giovanni Boccaccio* (Florence, 1877), p. 161: and see D'A. J. Boulton, 'The Origin and Development of the Curial Orders of Chivalry' (Oxford University D.Phil. thesis, 1975), pp. 190–1. It is to be hoped that this very interesting study will be published: I have found Dr Boulton's views most illuminating.

[3] In the case of Toison d'Or and the Croissant, the responsibility of the Kings of Arms for furnishing information which would be enregistered is statutorily defined, see *Chronique de Jean Le Févre*, ii. p. 250, and BN, MS Fr. 25024, fo. 16ᵛᵒ. That Croissant at least commenced his task is clear from the record of Louis de Beauveau's Senatorship of the Order (22 Sept. 1451 to vespers, 22 Sept. 1452), since we are told it was concluded 'par l'advis et deliberation de tou les dessusdits [those present at Chapter] que le Roy des Armes les [i.e. les aventures et louenges] meltra par escript bien loyaument et veritablement ainsy que ja il a commence' (BN, MS Clairembault 1241, p. 920). I owe this reference to the kindness of Dr M. Vale.

[405]

of them. A couple of entries may give some impression of the flavour of these notices.

Sir John Astley a manly man and often did armes on horseback and on foot. In the streete of St Anthony of Paris In the prescence of King Charles VIIth he ran his adversarie thorough the hede and after ther was a Spaniard called Sir Francoys le Arragonais that had desired thorow the realme of France to doe armes at outrance and for lak of Knyghthode of that roylme he came into Englande and this Sir John delivered and wan him in Smithfield. After be fortune of were tan prisonnier into France: paid his rauncon wherefore he contynued after in poverte. Died in London, buried at White freres in Fletstret. [Fo. 16].

Sir Edward Wodeville a noble and a coragious knight and without reproche he warred against the Sarrasins in Garnardo. Slain at the rencontre of St Aulbin in Bretaigne in the right of the (? duchess) of Bretagne where he lieth also buried. A noble joustour a gentil a free and a liberal knight . . . [Fo. 28vo].[1]

Here are, as it were, the bare bones of chivalrous history, awaiting the eloquence of the chronicler to blow life into them. Interestingly there is an Arthurian analogue to this magnificent armorial record. A fifteenth-century armorial of the arms of the Knights of the Round Table survives in a number of MSS versions, and in some of these brief biographical details, put together from the romances, are entered under the arms of each knight.[2] It is clearly at least possible

[1] BL, Add. MS 37340, fos 16, 28vo. This MS is a facsimile copy of the original (in the possession of the Duke of Buccleuch), made for Dugdale: See A. R. Wagner, *Catalogue of English Medieval Rolls of Arms* (Oxford, 1950), pp. xxv, 122–4.

[2] The names of the knights, with their shields, are published by E. Sandoz, 'Tourneys in the Arthurian Tradition', *Speculum*, 19 (1944), pp. 389–420. He also publishes the treatise on the form of the tourney in the time of King Uterpendragon and the form of oath of the knights of the Round Table. These appear together with the Round Table armorial and the biographies of the knights in a number of fifteenth-century MSS. (I have examined BN, MS Fr. 12497, and Lille, Bib. Municipale MS 329; both virtually identical, it seems, with Sandoz's text.) The collection is dedicated to the *Prince de Vienne* (probably Gaston de Viane, son of Gaston IV of Foix) and was probably put together by or for Jacques d'Armagnac, Duc de Nemours (ob. 1477). The illuminations of his splendid copy of the prose *Lancelot* (BN, MS Fr. 112) reproduce with precision the blazon of the Armorial. On MS 112 and Jacques

that an Arthurian roll of arms similar to one of these was the inspiration behind Wrythe's book. But such a relationship is not necessary to explain its composition. It had in Wrythe's time been long the acknowledged business of heralds 'to inquire in the day of battle who has shown prouesse and courage, in act or in council, and to record the names of the dead and the wounded, and whether they were in the van or the rear . . . that there may be honour to whom honour is due'.[1]

In Wrythe's time the heralds' interest in legendary matter was of long standing too. In some of the very earliest rolls of arms we find the arms of legendary heroes, as Roland, Arthur, and Gawain, and later those of the *neuf preux*, recorded together with those of contemporary aristocrats.[2] Such was the interaction of legendary and historical records of prowess that we do not need to look for a specific model from the fictional realm to explain a text that is historical.

We have, in any case, one example of a herald's ability as a registrar of the historical record of prowess (though it is not connected with any order of chivalry), from a period well before that of John Wrythe. The matter which Claes Haenen, the famous herald Gelre, put into his *Lobdichten*, a series of short poems celebrating the deeds of a selected group of knights of the mid-fourteenth century, was very similar to that which Wrythe put into his little notice of Edward Woodeville, though it is more detailed and cast into a

---

de Nemours see further C. E. Pickford, *L'Évolution du roman Arthurien en prose vers la fin du moyen âge d'après le MS 112* (Paris, 1966).

[1] BL, Stowe MS 668 fo. 79vo; and compare Froissart, *Œuvres*, ii. p. 11: 'Afin que . . . li biau fait d'armes . . . soient notablement registré . . . me voel ensonnyer de les mettre en prose . . . selonch la vraie information que je ay eu des vaillans hommes . . . et ausi par auquns rois d'armes nommé hiraus et lors marescaux qui par droit sont et doient estre juste inquisiteur et raporteur de tels besongnes.'

[2] The Herald's Roll (late thirteenth century) gives the arms of Roland, Prester John, Bevis of Hampton, and other fictional characters: see N. Denholm Young, *History and Heraldry* (Oxford, 1965), p. 52. R. L. Wyss, *cit. sup.* pp. 98–102, gives a list of rolls and armorials that blason the arms of the Nine Worthies.

polished literary form. His notice of Rutgher Raets, a vassal of Cologne, is a good example of his style, and an interesting one, since Gelre admitted that he had never met him, and had put together his account from enquiry. Raets was first armed at Cassell, he says, fighting the Frisians, but local wars did not satisfy his chivalrous spirit: 'avonture vast gesocht'. He went on pilgrimage to the Holy Sepulchre and to St. Catherine's monastery: he was at Crécy, and saw service for the French in Gascony. At the taking of La Mothe his banner was to the fore:

> Do he zich ondernam.
>
> Des had he eer ind gewin:
>
> Siin wimpel was ten eersten in.[1]

He was at Poitiers, and was taken prisoner there; and he fought repeatedly against the pagans in Prussia:

> Haet gewandelt ind geroden
>
> Twe und dertich winter in Prusen.[2]

He died in 1369. He was forty-three years in arms, and all his life he was devoted, says Gelre, to three 'ladies': Humility (*acht*), Goodwill (*gouste*), and Virtue (*doghet*). Gelre's subjects were historical, but his manner of telling of them cast over their lives the aura of romance. His notice, for instance, of another of his heroes, Adam de Moppertingen, is introduced by the story of how he heard in a wood a maiden lamenting the 'Knight of Lady Honour', whose body is now given over to worms. It was she who gave him the name of one who could be compared to a Roland.[3] The literary influence on the historical outlook of a herald, and so on those a herald might serve, is here abundantly clear: so is his anxiety to do justice to virtue through eloquence.

In some late medieval texts the heralds are referred to as doctors of knighthood or *clercs des armes*, a kind of secular priesthood of

---

[1] *Wappenboek ou Armorial ... par Gelre Héraut d'Armes*, ed. V. Bouton (Paris, 1881), i. p. 45.
[2] Ibid. p. 46.
[3] Ibid. p. 90.

chivalry.[1] A glance at the list of books bequeathed by Thomas Benolt, Clarenceux, in 1534 will give an impression of the range of real erudition in which late medieval heraldic science was grounded (it is incidentally clear that a good number of the books were inherited from his predecessors).[2] He had Froissart in four volumes; the History of the fall of Troy; a book of Galahad; a book of the *Neuf Preux*; Geoffrey de Charny's book of Chivalry; a French translation of the Old Testament, and a French translation of Valerius Maximus; Vegetius *De Re Militari;* the canonist Bonet's *Arbre de Batailles*; and several learned treatises on heraldry, including that of Bartolus. These are just a few items from a long list: they testify eloquently to the development, in the later Middle Ages, of a specialized and predominantly secular erudition connected with chivalry. With this list before us, the range of chivalrous erudition displayed by the prose chronicles and their elaborately classified treatment of chivalrous acts and events is unsurprising. The same heralds who were the 'doctors' of this learning were indeed among their most valued informants. Froissart, it is clear, obtained a good deal of information from heralds and regarded them as expert witness.[3] We know that Lefèvre de St. Remy, Toison d'Or King of Arms, furnished particular information to Chastellain for his chronicle.[4] Heralds were the natural men to look to for reliable information as to who had shown prowess in which battle, about the arms they bore and their significance, and about the occasions on which additions had been made to them for particular reasons. Their books and their memories had become the repositories of a great store of knowledge about the lore of chivalry, which could be put at the disposal alike of the historian, the aspirant author of romance,

---

[1] See for example the author's 'excusacion', at the end of Gille's tract on blazon 'Certes je ne suis clerc darmes ne nourris en ceste science' (BN, MS Fr. 1280, fo. 138ᵛᵒ–139).

[2] A. R. Wagner, *Heralds and Heraldry in the Middle Ages* (2nd edition, Oxford, 1956), Appx. F, p. 150 ff.

[3] Froissart, *Œuvres*, ii. pp. 2, 7, 11.

[4] *Chronique de Jean Le Févre*, ii. pp. xxxviii, lx.

and the master of ceremonies charged with the staging of some chivalrous spectacle for a princely banquet or a *pas d' armes*.

It is not in the least surprising to find in the later Middle Ages a number of heralds themselves turning historian, as did Chandos Herald, the biographer of the Black Prince; Gilles le Bouvier, Berry Herald; Lefèvre de St. Remy; and Claes Haenen himself, who put together a substantial chronicle of the Counts and Dukes of Holland.[1] Here we are dealing with a heraldic activity which springs from long established traditions that take us back into the age of the verse chronicles discussed earlier. References to heralds, from the later twelfth century on, make a very close association between them and the minstrels, whose song was so often of knightly heroes of both the distant and the more recent past. In England in Edward I's time, and indeed after it, the household clerks actually lumped heralds and minstrels together when recording payments to them, under the single heading *ministralli*.[2] And the *Song of Caerlaverock* shows us a minstrel herald in the act of performing both roles simultaneously, that of the expert in blason and the chivalrous verse historian. In the first part of his poem he lists the captains of the host, showing at the same time how versed he was in chivalrous history, throwing out references to Arthur and Merlin, to Robert de Tony's claim to connection with the Swan Knight, and to the great Marshal's deeds in the East.[3] In the second part he describes the siege of Caerlaverock in the manner we should expect of him as a *raconteur*, telling us who gave and who received the sternest blows and of the brave acts of the men who strove to be first over the wall.[4] His poem lacks the more consciously erudite manner of the famous chronicles of the

---

[1] Chandos Herald, *Life of the Black Prince*, ed. M. K. Pope and E. C. Lodge (Oxford, 1910): Berry Herald, *Le Recouvrement de Normendie*, ed. J. Stephenson (RS, 1863): *Chronique de Jean Le Févre*, ed. F. Morand (Paris, 1876–81). Gelre's chronicle, beautifully illuminated with the armorial bearings of the counts and their connections and as far as I know unpublished, is Brussels BR, MS 17914.

[2] Denholm Young, pp. 54–60: A. Wagner, *Heralds and Heraldry*, pp. 27–31.

[3] *The siege of Carlaverock*, pp. 26, 42, 54, 369–70.

[4] Ibid. pp. 74–86.

later fourteenth century: he is working, as has been said, within established traditions that link him rather with the earlier verse historians. The *Song of Caerlaverock* foreshadows, however, more clearly than most earlier works, that link between heraldic science and history which was to have such a powerful influence on historians in the next generation and succeeding ones.

Peter de Langtoft, whose chronicle is near enough contemporaneous with the *Song of Caerlaverock*, wrote of Edward I's banquet for the knighting of his eldest son—the Feast of the Swans—that he had heard of nothing like it as a feast of *noblesce*, unless it was the story of King Arthur's court at Caerleon.[1] In its pageantry, purpose, and spirit this Swan feast of 1306 anticipated such occasions as the more famous Burgundian feast of the Pheasant in 1454 and the royal feast at Paris in 1378 when the capture of Jerusalem was elaborately staged as an *entremés*.[2] The concern of later chivalrous chronicles to record the detail of such spectacles and the ornate staging of jousts and *pas d' armes*, all three matters of particular interest to the heralds and much discussed in their books, is one of the principal grounds on which they have been charged with superficiality in their approach to the historian's task. But their interest in such matters is hardly surprising—it is an accurate reflection of the attitude of an age in which chivalry had become a subject of erudition in its own right—and they were not undiscerning observers of ceremony. Late medieval knights did not confuse the risks to be run and the glory to be achieved in the lists with those of real war: Geoffrey de Charny (whose book the herald Thomas Benolt possessed) was indeed emphatic that they were to be valued differently.[3] The chroniclers did not confuse them either, and nor indeed did the literary authors: Malory quite clearly distinguishes

[1] *Chronique de Pierre de Langtoft,* ii. p. 368.
[2] See *Flores Historiarum,* ed. H. R. Luard (RS, 1890), iii. pp. 131–2 (Swan Feast): *Chronique de Mathieu d'Escouchy,* ed. G. Du Fresne de Beaucourt (Paris, 1863), ii. pp. 116–237 (Feast of the Pheasant); and *Chronique des regnes de Jean II et Charles V,* ed. R. Delachenal (Paris, 1916), ii. pp. 235–42 (Feast of 1378).
[3] G. de Charny, *Livre de chevalerie,* pp. 464–72.

Lancelot's elaborately staged *pas d' armes* in his twelfth Book from what he regarded as real adventures.[1] Chroniclers and romantic authors did, it is true, see mock war and true war and the prizes won in them as connected rather than contrasted matter. But that is only their way of reminding us that late medieval chivalrous spectacle and late medieval chivalrous history paid tribute to the same values and used the same historical models to point up their significance. If the age and its authors are in consequence to be charged with superficiality, what must be examined are the values that ceremony and history alike sought to teach and uphold. Values should not be regarded as hollow simply because they are celebrated with ceremony.

'Simplified', 'shallow', 'perhaps rather adolescent', these are the sort of adjectives that have been applied both to chivalrous cere-mony and to the chivalrous conception of history. The early verse chronicles are perhaps rather simplistic sometimes, and no doubt there is a touch of adolescence in that cult of youth which Duby has identified in chivalrous writing of the late twelfth and early thir-teenth centuries.[2] And it cannot be denied that the chivalrous conception of history failed to embrace the wide range of social and economic factors—though in this regard the Renaissance concept of history did not really do much better. Civic humanism did, it is true, recognize a wider scope for virtuous activity in the service of the public weal than was allowed for by the chivalrous idea of virtue, with its narrower emphasis on martial endeavour. Admitting the mercantile patrician into the circle of those who may achieve virtue is not, however, the same as understanding the range of economic factors in history. And the chivalrous historians did have their own ways of classifying and evaluating events and actions, which were based on a far from inconsiderable historical erudition—

---

[1] See L. D. Benson, *Malory's Morte Darthur* (Cambridge, Mass., 1976), pp. 183–5, 195–201.
[2] G. Duby, 'Au XIIᵉ siècle: les "Jeunes" dans la société aristocratique', *Annales*, 19 (1964), pp. 835–46.

of its own kind admittedly, yet not for that reason to be treated as lacking in seriousness. We should surely beware of treating as unserious a school of history so consistently concerned with virtue, and the manner of striving after it, as was theirs. Jean le Bel's standards are not our standards: he is for instance, explicitly, less interested in who won a battle than he is in who distinguished himself in it.[1] But who are we to call that shallow? It is a reflection of a real interest in human endeavour and the value to be set on it.

Certainly the values of Jean le Bel and Froissart and their fellows are aristocratic, and here there is some contrast with the Renaissance, whose attitude is perhaps better described as patrician. But they are not *just* aristocratic: merit, in their system of values, is the overriding consideration. 'Honour is worth more than gold or silver without any comparison' Ramon Lull had written in his much read book of the *Ordre of Chyvalry*, and the historians reflect that view accurately.[2] It was the general view of knights. One of three things awaits the man at arms, wrote Jean de Bueil, the fifteenth-century French captain and memorialist: you may be killed, you may conquer lands and wealth by *prouesse et notable gouvernement*, or you may live poor and honoured 'et que chascun parlera de vous et des vostres, dont il sera renommee apres vous, comme il a este de messire Bertran de Clayquin, Messire Gadiffer de la Salle et autres bons chevalliers qui sont mors povres'.[3] In other words, you may earn by virtue a place in history. Jean de Bueil's book shows already the imprint of the quickening interest in antiquity of the late Middle Ages and their wider knowledge of its history, but his secular and individualistic ideas about honour and nobility, here indicated, do not need explanation in terms of those developments. Lancelot, in the early thirteenth-century prose romance, was already speaking

---

[1] *Chronique de Jean le Bel*, i. p. 3.

[2] *The Book of the Ordre of Chyvalry*, p. 50.

[3] *Le Jouvencel*, ed. L. Lecestre and C. Favre (Paris, 1887), i. p. 43. Gadifier de la Salle was one of the conquerors of the Canary Islands: for a review of his career see *Le Canarien*, ed. G. Serra and A. Cioranescu (Tenerife, 1959), i. pp. 163 ff.

eloquently of the virtue of nobility (*gentillesse*), which is achieved by individual effort and should be prized on that account:

ne sai ge par quel raison li un ont plus que li autre
de gentillece se l'an ne la conquiert par proesce
autresin com l'an fait les terres et les onors. Mais
tant sachiez vos bien de voir que se grant cuer
faisoient les gentis hommes, ge cuideroie encores estre
des plus gentils.[1]

Jean de Bueil and Lancelot alike talk in terms of a predominantly secular system of honour and values, which already in the thirteenth century was prising history loose from a purely providential framework, and which laid its emphasis on the individual achievement of virtue. That system of values which they both propose provided a way of looking at things equally relevant to the knight, to the author of romance, and to the historian. I hope I have said enough to show that I not only believe that Huizinga was right when he said that chivalrous notions anticipated the Renaissance cult of virtue, but that, furthermore, the chivalrous historians had developed a way of looking at their own age in relation to the past that was worthy of that anticipation.[2]

[1] See E. Kennedy, 'Social and Political Ideas in the French Prose *Lancelot*', *Medium Aevum*, 26 (1957), pp. 90–106, especially pp. 103–4: and see H. O. Sommer, iii. p. 89.

[2] I must acknowledge a debt of great gratitude of Miss Juliet Bateson, whose assistance with the proofs of this chapter eliminated a large number of my errors.

John Blacman : Biographer of Henry VI

ROGER LOVATT

THE inadequacy of the chronicle sources for the history of England during much of the fifteenth century has long been stressed. In his inaugural study of the subject C. L. Kingsford acknowledged the 'general poverty' of historical writing in the period and remarked that the central years of Henry VI's reign were in this respect particularly ill-served.[1] Kingsford's assessment has often been repeated and it is therefore surprising that historians of the period have in general dealt so superficially with the account of Henry VI that was compiled by his own chaplain, John Blacman. This work, known as the *Collectarium Mansuetudinum et Bonorum Morum Regis Henrici VI*, does not apparently survive in manuscript form but it has been accessible since it was published by Robert Copland between about 1514 and 1523, and during the next two centuries it became known in some guise to a number of writers and scholars, including the compilers of Holinshed's *Chronicle* and John Speed, Archbishop Ussher, and Archbishop Sancroft.[2]

[1] C. L. Kingsford, *English Historical Literature in the Fifteenth Century* (Oxford, 1913), pp. 3, 10.

[2] Copland's edition has commonly been attributed to c. 1510 but on no very clear grounds. Copland does not seem to have begun to print under his own name until about 1514 and a copy of the edition at Ushaw College bears a note of ownership dated 1523. Copland's work has in general been neglected and it is not possible to date the edition more precisely from internal, typographical evidence. See F. C. Francis, *Robert Copland, Sixteenth Century Printer and Translator* (Glasgow, 1961), pp. 26–7. A. I. Doyle, 'Books Belonging to R. Johnson', *Notes and Queries*, cxcvii (1952), pp. 293–4. Copland's edition was reprinted by Thomas Hearne in *Duo Rerum Anglicarum Scriptores Veteres* (Oxford, 1732). The standard edition is now *Henry the Sixth. A Reprint of*

It was in fact Archbishop Sancroft who paved the way for the subsequent denigration of Blacman's work by asserting, in an annotation to his own copy, that the biography was originally compiled by Blacman at the request of Henry VII while the king was negotiating with the papacy for the canonization of his uncle.[1] It is not clear how Sancroft came to make this assumption. Despite its note of confidence it was probably no more than a hypothesis arising from Sancroft's knowledge of the fact that the canonization process had been initiated. Nevertheless the view has taken root that Blacman's account of the king was in some way written to order as part of the canonization dossier and historians have therefore dismissed the biography as a mere *pièce d'occasion*, a work of semi-official propaganda. Hence Kingsford himself referred to the work as a 'panegyric', very probably written after 1485 with the canonization in mind; and even more damningly, K. B. McFarlane—perhaps swayed by the fact that Blacman misunderstood the negotiations between Henry VI and the executors of Cardinal Beaufort—condemned him roundly as an 'unreliable hagiographer'.[2]

Such judgements arise from a number of misconceptions. In reality Blacman's biography was written before Henry VII came to the throne. Far from being officially prompted it was composed against the background of a hostile regime. It is true that Blacman, writing after the king's death, looked back on him with respect and

---

John Blacman's Memoir, ed. and trans. M. R. James (Cambridge, 1919), referred to henceforth as *Henry the Sixth*; see pp. xi, 45–6.

[1] *Henry the Sixth*, p. xi. Sancroft's copy of the *Collectarium* is now in the Bodleian Library.

[2] Kingsford, p. 149. K. B. McFarlane, 'At the Deathbed of Cardinal Beaufort', in *Studies in Medieval History Presented to F. M. Powicke*, ed. R. W. Hunt, W. A. Pantin, R. W. Southern (Oxford, 1948), p. 422. In his account of Henry VI in the *DNB* T. F. Tout also appeared to associate the production of Blacman's biography with the launching of the canonization process, and a similar supposition is made in a recent survey of Henry VI's government: B. P. Wolffe, 'The Personal Rule of Henry VI', in *Fifteenth-Century England, 1399–1509*, ed. S. B. Chrimes, C. D. Ross, R. A. Griffiths (Manchester, 1972), pp. 37–8.

affection and that his account dwells on Henry's virtues and his devotional life, all to the virtual exclusion of public affairs. Similarly Blacman was doubtless writing in order to encourage the almost clandestine cult of Henry VI which had developed spontaneously after his death. At the same time it is also the case that he was exceptionally well-informed about his subject. He had served as the king's own chaplain and had enjoyed familiar, personal contact with him. He had been one of the earliest fellows of Henry's beloved foundation at Eton. He knew many of the king's closest associates and was able to draw on their recollections in compiling his biography. Furthermore Blacman was himself a man of some academic distinction, the owner of a large library and remarkably well-read in modern devotional literature. His is far from an unbiased account of the king but it is also something much more intimate and revealing than mere official hagiography. Bearing in mind the precept of Blacman's eighteenth-century editor, Thomas Hearne, that contemporary accounts of Henry VI 'are very barren ... which therefore makes any Thing of that Age about him to be much valued', one might feel that this fragmentary insight into the mind of the king merits at least a moment of precise attention.[1]

John Blacman was a west-countryman, born in the diocese of Bath and Wells in either 1408 or 1409.[2] He must have begun his studies at Oxford by about 1432, and in 1436 he was elected a bachelor fellow of Merton College where he remained until 1443. Blacman's intellectual activities at Oxford seem to have been rather more than usually wide-ranging. By 1439 he had completed the arts course and had moved on to the higher faculty of theology in which he eventually took the bachelor's degree. Such an academic

---

[1] T. Hearne, *Remarks and Collections*, x, ed. H. E. Salter (Oxford Hist. Soc. lxvii, 1915), pp. 442–3.

[2] This is to interpret literally the remark made by Blacman in 1474 (O.S.) that he had seen sixty-six winters; Bodleian Library, MS Laud misc. 154, fo. 2ᵛ. For an outline of Blacman's career, see *BRUC*, pp. 670–1. A slightly fuller, but less accurate, account is given by the same author in *BRUO*, i. pp. 194–5.

progress was entirely conventional. What is slightly more un-expected, in view of his theological interests, is to find that Blacman subsequently qualified for appointment as a notary public. The training of notaries in medieval England is still an obscure matter but it would seem most likely that Blacman acquired the necessary grounding in basic legal principles and in notarial practice while he was still at Oxford. In England, unlike Italy, no formal training was provided for the notarial profession but it is well known that the teaching of various business skills—the drafting of documents, the keeping of accounts, and a knowledge of elementary legal proced-ures—was firmly established in Oxford by the first half of the fifteenth century, and Blacman's notarial qualifications could conveniently have been acquired through these unofficial means.[1] There are, in fact, some signs that Blacman possessed administrative talents which came to be recognized before he left Oxford. In 1438–9 he acted as one of the two Keepers of the Ancient University Chest and a little later he served as subwarden of his own college. Blacman seems subsequently to have retained an affection for Merton. Some five years after his departure from the college he contributed towards the cost of building its new bell tower, and it may well be more than coincidence that his library contained a copy of the astronomical tables compiled by William Rede, one of the most notable of the Merton scientists of the previous century.[2] Certainly Blacman was directly indebted to the college. At some time during his residence he borrowed a number of books from the college library which he subsequently pledged to a Merton loan chest and which had not been redeemed at the time of his death,

[1] C. R. Cheney, *Notaries Public in England in the Thirteenth and Fourteenth Centuries* (Oxford, 1972), ch. 6. A recent account of the informal, business training available at Oxford is in A. B. Cobban, *The Medieval Universities* (London, 1975), pp. 223–5.

[2] *Oxford City Documents, Financial and Judicial, 1268–1665*, ed. J. E. Thorold Rogers (Oxford Hist. Soc., xviii, 1891), p. 314. The complete list of Blac-man's books is in Bodleian Library, MS Laud misc. 154, flyleaf and fos 1ʳ–2ᵛ; no. 21 includes a 'canon tabularum Rede'. For a fuller account of his library, see below pp. 442–3.

and, on a more fundamental level, it is possible to see that friendships and connections formed while he was at Merton survived well into his later life.[1]

It was probably one such connection which lay behind Blacman's departure from Merton in 1443 and his appointment as a fellow of Eton. The first fellows of Eton were nominated by Henry VI in his foundation charter of October 1440 and, although the college's subsequent statutes vested in the provost and fellows the right of election to their own number, it seems likely that for a few years after the initial foundation the fellows continued in practice to be directly appointed by the founder. However, the first provost of Eton, Henry Sever, had the strongest of links with Merton.[2] He had been admitted to the college in 1419 as founder's kin and he had already been a fellow for some fifteen years when Blacman joined the fellowship. Subsequently Sever returned to Merton as its warden, and was a munificent benefactor both to the college's library and also to its estates. What is more, Sever was close to Henry VI. He had been chaplain to the king in 1437. He was undoubtedly selected personally by Henry VI as the first provost of his new foundation, a post that the king would have regarded as of the highest importance, and later Sever was to serve for several years as the king's almoner. It is hard to avoid the conclusion that Blacman was initially brought to the king's attention by Sever, and that he owed his appointment at Eton to these Merton associations.

Blacman remained at Eton for a decade. The statutes of the college imposed residence on the ten fellows and within this small, and noticeably homogeneous, community he was in familiar surroundings. Virtually all of the earliest fellows were, like Blacman, Oxford

---

[1] *Registrum Annalium Collegii Mertonensis, 1483–1521,* ed. H. E. Salter (Oxford Hist. Soc., lxxvi, 1923), pp. 178, 185. Salter seems to have misunderstood the pledging arrangements; see F. M. Powicke, *The Medieval Books of Merton College* (Oxford, 1931), pp. 115, 118. One of the books was a copy of Gregory's *Moralia,* another was a glossed *Luke and John.*

[2] For Sever's career, see *BRUO,* iii. pp. 1672–3. Sever resigned as provost in 1442, and his role in the foundation of Eton has commonly been overlooked in favour of his famous successor, William Waynflete.

graduates with degrees in theology. The prevailing tone of the group was distinctive—learned, orthodox, and conservative—and there are clear signs that Blacman involved himself fully in their communal life.[1] For some eight years he served as precentor, a post which was filled by annual election amongst the fellows, and he also acted as the college's notary. At one stage he apparently planned to make a benefaction to the college library, and he seems to have taken a particular interest in the progress of the new buildings at Eton.[2] But the real importance of Blacman's residence at Eton is that it provided the opportunity for him to become acquainted with the founder, Henry VI.

Henry's personal involvement in his foundation at Eton is apparent at every turn. In the management of the affairs of the college he showed an application to business and a sense of purpose—almost an obsessive concern—which was in sharp contrast with the

[1] I am indebted to Mr Patrick Strong, archivist of Eton College, for information about Blacman's activities there. The previous careers of many of his contemporaries at Eton followed a distinctively similar pattern of Oxford fellowships and degrees in theology. A large number of them can also be shown to have owned books, usually of a markedly conservative flavour, which they subsequently bequeathed to various Oxford colleges and to Eton itself. See, for example, Thomas Barker, John Boner, Thomas Harlow, Robert Hesyll, John Mawnsell, and William Westbury in *BRUO*, *s.n.* The early collegiate library at Eton was noticeably of a similar, traditionlist character. M. R. James, 'Chapel Inventories', *Etoniana*, xxv–xxviii (1920–1), pp. 442–7. The only two fellows whose interests seem to fall partly outside this pattern were John Mabulthorpe, who owned an unusual collection of books ranging from the mystical theology of the Pseudo-Dionysius to modern anti-Wycliffite writings (see, for example, Eton College MS 47 and Lincoln College, Oxford, MS 101), and William Wey, the enthusiastic pilgrim who visited Jerusalem twice and also had links with the Bridgettine community at Syon. *BRUO*, ii. pp. 1198–9, and iii. pp. 2028–9.

[2] The Eton statutes included a provision that there must be a resident notary public and Blacman fulfilled this function in 1453–4. See the earliest Eton College lease book, fos 62–66ᵛ. The arms of Eton were added at various points to one of Blacman's MSS, now Eton College MS 213, and it seems reasonable to assume that he intended the book to be a gift to Eton, although the volume was in fact given to the Witham Charterhouse. The same MS contains a remarkably accurate drawing, which may well be in Blacman's own hand, of Windsor Castle and of the temporary chapel erected at Eton in c. 1447.

attitude which he often assumed towards more public business. The college was placed alongside the king's castle at Windsor, his own birthplace, so that he could supervise its growth and participate in its life.[1] Henry laid the foundation stone of the new church in person and took a direct interest in the most minute details of the subsequent building programme. When papal support for the college was being sought, the king was reported as making daily enquiries about the progress of the Eton negotiations at the curia.[2] Eventually Henry secured a series of papal bulls that granted a remarkable range of ecclesiastical privileges to the college, including quite exceptional indulgences to penitents visiting its church. The series of statutes and the lavish endowments granted by the king demonstrate a watchfulness over the college that might almost be characterized as meddlesome. Indeed so closely was the college associated with Henry himself that Edward IV, on his accession, sought initially to have the foundation suppressed. It was a natural consequence of this concern for its affairs that the king should also have shown a close interest in the various members of his new foundation. The king had personally nominated the first fellows and Blacman himself recorded the care taken by Henry to select the best 'living stones' for his foundation, that is, 'boys excellently equipped with virtue and knowledge, and priests to bear rule over the rest as teachers'.[3] When the king met any of his Eton scholars in Windsor Castle he was in the habit of giving them money, exhorting them to follow virtuous ways and, in particular, advising them to avoid the corruptions of the royal court.[4] In these circumstances it was inevitable that Blacman, as a fellow of the college, should come into contact with the king, but the evidence is clear that these contacts were more than merely casual or occasional. Some fifteen years

---

[1] For what follows, see Sir. H. C. Maxwell Lyte, *A History of Eton College*, 4th edn (London, 1911), pp. 1–60.

[2] *Official Correspondence of Thomas Bekynton*, ed. G. Williams (RS, 1872), i. p. 175.

[3] *Henry the Sixth*, p. 12.

[4] Ibid. p. 12.

later, someone who knew Blacman well recorded that he had been the king's chaplain, or *minister*, while he was at Eton.[1] It is not certain whether this statement was meant to suggest that he had been formally appointed to such a post. It is perhaps more likely to mean that Blacman was closely involved in the king's religious life and was acting in some sense as his spiritual advisor. Certainly, in his account of the king, Blacman recorded how he celebrated mass before Henry VI, apparently in private. At another point he described an incident when he was alone with the king at Eltham Palace reading devotional literature and discussing spiritual matters; and a similarly intimate meeting with the king took place on another occasion at Windsor Castle.[2] Furthermore, although Blacman's biography is not arranged in any strict chronological sequence, he was particularly well-informed about the activities of the king and about life at court during the years around 1450, precisely the period when he was in continuous residence at Eton. The genesis of Blacman's account of Henry VI must then be sought at this time when, for a decade, he was a member of a small community which occupied a central place in the king's concerns, was personally involved in the king's spiritual life, and was accustomed to familiar, private contact with him.

In December 1452 Blacman was appointed warden of King's Hall at Cambridge. This appointment did not necessarily entail residence and, in fact, he continued to spend periods at Eton until at least the beginning of 1454, but after this date his connections with the college appear to lapse and it seems likely that thenceforward a larger part of his time was occupied at Cambridge.[3] Since its foundation by Edward II, initially as an offshoot of the chapel royal,

[1] Ibid. p. 60. This account of Blacman was written by a monk of Witham Charterhouse, perhaps c. 1465–70, and is otherwise accurate in the information that it gives. See Bodleian Library, MS Laud misc. 152, fo. 1ʳ. The text is not entirely legible.

[2] *Henry the Sixth*, pp. 13, 15, 16.

[3] As a notary Blacman attested instruments in the Eton Lease Book in May and November 1453 and, finally, on 31 January 1454. By February 1454 he had apparently been succeeded by another notary.

King's Hall had been remarkable for its association with the king
and the royal court, and Blacman's immediate predecessors as
warden had all, like him, been drawn from Henry's personal
entourage. One had been secretary to the king, another was dean of
the Chapel Royal, and a third had been one of the king's chaplains.[1]
However, from 1446 onwards Henry VI had implemented a scheme
to transform the status of the Hall, removing it from direct dependence on the king and placing it under the jurisdiction of his two new
colleges of Eton and King's. Between 1446 and 1448 the crown's
right to appoint the warden and scholars of the Hall was transferred
to the provosts of Eton and King's, and the two provosts were given
powers to visit the Hall, reform its statutes, expel recalcitrant fellows,
and impose an oath of obedience—almost of dependence—on the
warden. The effect of these reforms was to unite King's Hall with
Eton and King's College as 'a third, though subordinate, member of
the family of sister colleges', and Blacman appears to have been the
first warden to assume office under the new arrangements, having
been appointed by William Westbury, provost of Eton, and Robert
Wodelarke, provost of King's. This subordination of the Hall may
have been partly a result of the various disorders which had afflicted
its internal life during the previous years, but it also seems that the
king envisaged using the Hall to absorb a growing number of Eton
scholars who could not all be found scholarships at King's. For a few
years the Hall was to be administratively entwined with the other
two foundations, almost an extension of Eton and an inferior
alternative, as it were, to King's. A substantial number of Eton
scholars became members of King's Hall and, from this point of
view, Blacman's wardenship might be seen as a natural culmination
to his years as a fellow of Eton.[2]

Little trace of Blacman's activities in Cambridge has survived

[1] Richard Caudray, Robert Ayscogh, and Nicholas Close; see *BRUC*,
pp. 27, 126–7, 142.
[2] A. B. Cobban, *The King's Hall within the University of Cambridge in the
Later Middle Ages* (Cambridge, 1969), pp. 184–6, 188–93. I am indebted to
Dr Cobban for answering my enquiries concerning Blacman's period as
warden of King's Hall.

although there is evidence that he would have found the affairs of King's Hall in a state of some disarray. The statutes had apparently not been observed and the finances of the college were in an unhealthy condition. The king himself had visited the Hall in 1448–9, and again in the very year when Blacman became warden, and must have been aware of these problems. It may even be that the appointment of Blacman—a man known to be in the king's confidence—was itself part of the programme for reforming and disciplining the life of the community. However, although he seems to have been responsible for the introduction of some form of probationary period for new members of the Hall, there is no sign that he made any fundamental changes in the life of the college.[1]

One reason for this may lie in the fact that in January 1456, while still warden, Blacman became head of another collegiate foundation on his appointment as dean of the College of the Holy Trinity at Westbury upon Trym, near Bristol. This post, like that of the wardenship of King's Hall, did not necessitate residence but it should not be regarded simply as the type of sinecure characteristically held in plurality by the *sublimes et litterati*. During the years immediately before 1456 Bishop Carpenter of Worcester had initiated an extensive refoundation of the ancient, but virtually moribund, church of Westbury.[2] The college was being rebuilt and enlarged on a lavish scale and, only some six months before Blacman assumed office, Bishop Carpenter had issued new statutes which had the effect of removing from the dean the day-to-day responsibility for running the college and entrusting it to a new officer, the sub-dean, while simultaneously reducing the value of the prebends in order to finance a development of the foundation in other directions. As this scheme came to fruition the college rapidly expanded to include a group of priest-fellows and choristers, a schoolmaster, almshouses

---

[1] Ibid. pp. 184–6, 191–2.

[2] For Westbury College, see H. J. Wilkins, *Westbury College from 1194 to 1544* (Bristol, 1917), esp. pp. 139–208, *V.C.H.*, *Gloucs.*, ii. p. 108, and R. M. Haines, 'Aspects of the Episcopate of John Carpenter, Bishop of Worcester 1444–1476', *J. E. H.*, xix (1968), pp. 11–40, esp. 35–6.

for six men and six women, and a chantry to be served by six aged priests. Bishop Carpenter's direct personal involvement in this development is noticeable at every point. He was himself probably born in Westbury, he made extensive benefactions to the college, visited it frequently, appointed his closest friends and officials to benefices on the foundation, styled himself patron and founder of the community and was finally buried in a specially constructed chapel in Westbury church.[1]

Against this background Blacman's appointment as dean assumes an added significance. The refoundation of Westbury was Bishop Carpenter's major enterprise as diocesan and Blacman became dean at a crucial stage in the college's evolution, soon after the promulgation of the reforming statutes. His immediate successors as dean were, firstly, Henry Sampson, the distinguished provost of Oriel College and a lifelong friend of Carpenter who was ultimately to be one of the bishop's executors, and, secondly, William Cannynges, greatest of all Bristol merchants who retired from business life and entered the priesthood in 1468. In Bishop Carpenter's eyes the selection of Blacman could not have been a matter of indifference and the origins of the appointment are almost certainly to be found in the environment of Eton. Like Blacman, Carpenter had been close to Henry VI, a royal clerk and chaplain to the king throughout the 1430s. In particular he had been directly involved in the foundation of Eton and was actually consecrated bishop in the church of Eton in 1444.[2] By this time Blacman was already a fellow. He must have been acquainted with Carpenter and, for a short time in 1452-3, he was also to hold a living in the bishop's diocese.[3] Furthermore, the precise form that Westbury came to assume, the combination of a college of priests with an

[1] Wilkins, pp. 146-56, 162-3. Haines, p. 35.

[2] *BRUO*, i. pp. 360-1. Maxwell Lyte, pp. 13, 30.

[3] In January 1452 Blacman became rector of Sapperton, Gloucs., on the presentation of Robert de Lisle but he had vacated the living by September 1453. There is no evidence that Blacman ever resided at Sapperton. *BRUC*, pp. 670-1, *VCH Gloucs.*, xi. pp. 87-99.

almshouse and an educational function, was notably reminiscent of the arrangements at Eton itself. Carpenter was familiar with Eton and, if he had it in mind as a model when developing Westbury, it would be entirely natural for him to appoint as the first dean of the reformed college a man who had himself spent a decade at Eton during its formative years. Equally striking in this connection is the fact that the first sub-dean of Westbury to take office under the new statutes, the official who was appointed by Blacman, as dean, to be immediately responsible for the proposed transformation in the life of the college, was Thomas Stephens, another Oxford theologian, who within a year was himself to move on to become a fellow of Eton.[1]

Until he was about fifty years old Eton formed the mainspring of Blacman's adult life. At Eton he became familiar with the king. The wardenship of King's Hall was almost a natural progression from Eton, and similar associations would seem to lie behind his links with Bishop Carpenter and his appointment at Westbury. But at this point Blacman's life radically changed direction. In July 1457 he resigned as warden and by about the end of 1458 he had ceased to be dean of Westbury. Soon afterwards, perhaps immediately, he entered the Carthusian order, the most austere and distinguished body of religious in fifteenth-century England. The precise chronology of his career in the order is not entirely clear. At one stage he was certainly a member of the London Charterhouse and it seems most likely that he first entered this community. There survives a spiritual commonplace book which was compiled by Blacman, apparently at about this time, and which provides an intensely revealing insight into his frame of mind as he abandoned his preferments and opted for the 'caves of the Carthusian desert'.[2]

---

[1] *BRUO*, iii. pp. 1772–3.

[2] BL, MS Sloane 2515; Blacman's opening meditation is on fos 3^r–5^r. For this MS, see, A. Gray, 'A Carthusian *Carta Visitationis* of the Fifteenth Century', *BIHR*, xl (1967), pp. 91–101. Father Gray's study is largely concerned with the unique visitation report which forms the binding leaves of the book but he does make some comments on the body of the MS.

The book is imbued with a world weariness, an obsession with mortality and with preparations for death, whose origins can only be guessed at. Perhaps the resolution of the disorders at King's Hall or his involvement with the expansion of Westbury had generated such feelings. The book opens with an emotional and convoluted meditation by Blacman around the theme of Susanna's reproach to the Elders, *si hoc egero mors mihi est*. Blacman applied these words to his own entry into religion, contrasting a temporal with an eternal death, associating temporal death with his membership of the Carthusian community but trusting that such temporal death would be the means to eternal life. Then, as a remedy for his fear of physical mortality Blacman recommended a fervent study of the remaining contents of his book. These consist of a *florilegium* of short tracts on the art of dying, many of them works which are known to have enjoyed a wide popularity in fifteenth-century England.[1]

Blacman's reflections at the beginning of his book are more concerned with his spiritual condition than with his earthly state, and his references to his own position in the London Charterhouse are at times obscure. It is clear that he had been accepted as a member of the community and the implication seems plain that he had only recently renounced the external world. Again, although the London Charterhouse contained residents of varying status, Blacman's words suggest—and they receive some independent corroboration—that he was testing his vocation as a monk, possibly that he was undergoing the obligatory probationary period of at least a year, and that he was contemplating the taking of his final vows.[2] However, for whatever reason, Blacman seems not to have

[1] BL, MS Sloane 2515, fos 5ᵛ–56ʳ. The remainder of the MS seems originally to have been a separate compilation, although it is written in Blacman's hand; certainly, from fo. 58 onwards, the theme of the collection changes.

[2] Blacman speaks of 'our' prior and uses distinctively Carthusian phraseology concerning, for example, his wish to enter the *societas* of the community. His words also indicate that he had been allocated a particular cell. At the same time, his tone suggests that in some sense he had still to make the irrevocable decision to enter the order, a position which would indicate that he was at the time under some form of probation. Some fifty years later, in Copland's

persisted in his vocation at London and subsequently he reappears at the Charterhouse of Witham, in Somerset, not as a monk but as a *clericus redditus*.[1] The *clerici redditi* occupied an anomalous position in the order and were eventually suppressed, but during this period the General Chapter had come to permit the presence of two or three in every Charterhouse. These *redditi* were professed, clad, and tonsured like the monks and sat with them in choir and chapter, but they retained possession of their property and were free on adequate grounds to leave the order at any time.

The exact date of Blacman's move to Witham is not known. He was certainly a member of the house in 1474 and must have joined the community several years previously, perhaps shortly after 1460.[2] In any case his decision to move is readily explained. Witham cannot have been far away from Blacman's birthplace

edition of the *Collectarium*, Blacman was described unequivocally as having been a monk of the London Charterhouse, but external observers were often not fully aware of the precise gradations of Carthusian status. As part of his introductory reflections to the Sloane MS Blacman provides texts of the twenty-four Latin verses which were apparently inscribed over the doors of the cells in the London Charterhouse. See MS Sloane 2515, fo. 3ʳ, and Gray, p. 93 and n.

[1] In the account of Blacman written by a monk of Witham he is described unambiguously, and precisely, as a *redditus* of the house. Bodleian Library, MS Laud misc. 152, fo. 1ʳ.

[2] When Blacman dated his third book list, in 1474, he was a member of the house and the nature of the lists indicates that he had then been resident at Witham and acquiring books over a period of several years. See below p. 442 and n. It has sometimes been argued that Blacman first entered the Witham Charterhouse and only later moved to London. The evidence is not totally conclusive but the plain meaning of Blacman's remarks in his commonplace book seems to show that his first direct contact with the order took place in London. There is also quite considerable circumstantial evidence to the same effect. The brief account of Blacman given in Copland's edition of the *Collectarium* indicates, at least negatively, the primacy of London, and Blacman's gift of his books to Witham suggests some sense of settled commitment to that house. In general it was common for monks to move from London to one of the West Country Charterhouses, to such an extent that the General Chapter legislated against the practice, but much less usual for such movement to be in the opposite direction. E. M. Thompson, *The Carthusian Order in England* (London, 1930), p. 303.

and many of the other members of the community also came from the West Country. Blacman knew something of the prior, John Pestor, for by an odd coincidence the two men had been ordained on the same day at Wells some twenty years previously.[1] The Witham monks also had unexpected links with Henry VI and his court. The king himself had been a benefactor and in 1459, probably just before Blacman's arrival, he had been granted the privileges of confraternity.[2] The king's former secretary, Thomas Bekynton, the 'second founder' of Eton, was then bishop of Bath and Wells and had financed the building of a new dormitory at Witham.[3] Blacman's own attachment to the community was strong and Carthusian spirituality had a profound effect on his own devotional life as exemplified in his reading. He gave Witham his large library as well as some vestments and was apparently respected by other members of the house. It is therefore the more surprising that he seems subsequently to have taken advantage of his status as a *redditus* and to have died outside the order. The exact date of his death is not known but he is recorded as having been buried on 23 January 1485.[4]

---

[1] *The Register of John Stafford, Bishop of Bath and Wells, 1425–1443*, ii, ed. T. S. Holmes (Somerset Record Soc., xxxii, 1916), pp. 394–5. Other monks of Witham whose names appear during this period in the ordination lists of the bishops of Bath and Wells include Hugh Boscawen, John Taunton, and Nicholas Exeter.

[2] E. M. Thompson, *A History of the Somerset Carthusians* (London, 1895), pp. 102–5. The original grant of confraternity is now amongst the documents in the Henderson Bequest in the Fitzwilliam Museum, Cambridge.

[3] W. Worcestre, *Itineraries*, ed. J. H. Harvey (Oxford, 1969), p. 296.

[4] The dating of Blacman's death presents a slight puzzle. His name does not appear in the full lists of Carthusian obits which is a clear sign that he died outside the order. Sir Wasey Sterry, in his account of the fellows of Eton (*Etoniana*, lvi, 1934, p. 94), stated categorically that Blacman was buried on 23 January 1485. No source for this information was given, or has been discovered, but there is no reason for regarding the statement as dubious. In general Sterry was accurate and his precise specification of the date of burial, rather than the date of death, carries conviction. Also, it is certain that Blacman was sixty-six in 1474 and so would have reached the age of about seventy-seven in 1485.

It is important to establish the details of Blacman's life. Many historical writers of the fifteenth century are shadowy figures and Blacman's credentials as a biographer are to some extent established by the pattern of his career. Henry VI reached the age of twenty-one in 1442, the year before Blacman moved to Eton; then, in 1461, only a year or so after Blacman withdrew into the Carthusian order, Henry began the long sequence of exile, hiding, and imprisonment which culminated in his murder in the Tower. Across these two decades of Henry's active life on the throne it is possible to identify a complex web of links between Blacman and the king, strongest during the ten years at Eton but also apparent at King's Hall, then almost a daughter house of Eton and closely under the eye of the king. Similarly, Blacman's patrons were men in the king's innermost circle. They included Henry Sever, royal chaplain and first provost of Eton; Robert Wodelarke, the man mainly responsible for bringing the foundation of King's to fruition, who nominated Blacman to King's Hall; and finally Bishop Carpenter, royal clerk and chaplain. At the London Charterhouse there were more than formal ties between the monks and the king, and even in the remoteness of Witham the king shared in the daily suffrages of the house.[1]

This is the network of royal associations which lies behind Blacman's biography, a network which the biography, in turn, reflects and amplifies. In the *Collectarium* Blacman frequently mentioned his sources. Sometimes he stated that he had himself witnessed an incident. Often he referred to the authority of various anonymous intimates of the king, 'men worthy of credit who were formerly attendant on him' or 'some in his confidence to whom he was wont to reveal his secrets'.[2] Elsewhere he was more specific and his informants can be identified as the king's closest associates.

---

[1] The London Charterhouse owned two books which had belonged to Henry VI and in the *ex libris* inscription on one of the MSS the king is referred to as 'sanctissimus . . . rex'; see Bodleian Library, MS Bodley 277 (an English Bible) and King's College, Cambridge, MS 4 (a *Vitae Patrum*).

[2] *Henry the Sixth*, pp. 4, 20.

Evidence as to the purity of the king's life was provided by Bishop Ayscough who had been Henry's confessor for ten years. Sir Richard Tunstall, Henry's devoted chamberlain who accompanied the king during his wanderings in the north of England and eventually defended him physically against his pursuers, bore witness to the king's love of spiritual reading. A description of the king's mentality while in hiding appears to be based on the testimony of two clerks, John Bedon and Thomas Mannyng, who had also shared Henry's desolate exile in the north, were amongst the last handful of his servants to remain loyal, and were ultimately captured with the king in July 1465. Earlier Mannyng had served for five years as the king's secretary. Similarly, Blacman's account of Henry's frame of mind during his imprisonment in the Tower is apparently based on the recollections of the chaplain who was then attending him, probably the faithful William Kymberley.[1]

The character of his sources was of a piece with Blacman's own life, dependent upon the king and participating in his central interests. In the same way, the *Collectarium* is not the work of a detached, self-conscious historical writer. It is both a sketch of Henry VI and also an expression of the king's own sentiments. It is prejudiced but revealing in its prejudices, artlessly frank in its picture of the king's defects as a ruler but redefining his public defects as private virtues. It is sometimes erroneous but also entirely independent as a witness. It is, as it were, a natural product of Blacman's own experiences, a series of almost informal reminiscences, reflecting his own interests and his own partial, idealized perception of the king. But the *Collectarium* was also an unofficial work in another sense. As it stands, it dates from some years after the death of Henry VI in May 1471. However, it must have been completed by January 1485 and it seems clear that it was in fact compiled before August 1484 when

---

[1] Ibid. pp. 4, 15, 19, 21. For Bedon and Mannyng, see *BRUO*, *i.* p. 147 and *ii.* pp. 216–17. The most detailed account of Henry's pursuit and capture is in C. L. Scofield, *The Life and Reign of Edward the Fourth* (London, 1923), *i.* pp. 381–4. For William Kymberley, who initially attended Henry in 1465–66 without any payment, see *Issues of the Exchequer*, ed. F. Devon (London, 1837), p. 490.

Henry's body was moved to Windsor from its original burial place at Chertsey Abbey. It might plausibly be attributed to about 1480, possibly after Blacman had left the Witham Charterhouse.[1] It is a product of the years when the cult of the king developed spontaneously, well before the canonization cause was taken up by Henry VII or the canons of Windsor acquired a vested interest in establishing his claims to sanctity. Within a few years of Henry's death accounts were circulating of miracles being performed at his tomb, his name was popularly invoked as that of a saint, poems were written in his honour, pilgrimages were made to his burial place, and, as early as 1476, a chantry was established at York Minster for two chaplains to pray for Henry's soul. All of this took place in the face of strong official discouragement.[2] In 1479 the archbishop of York forbade the public veneration of a statue of Henry VI in the

[1] Blacman refers to the 'long series' of miracles at the king's tomb, which implies a date after c. 1475. Even without the external evidence of Blacman's death in January 1485 there are convincing internal grounds for a date before 1485, particularly the studiedly elliptical references to dynastic issues, the vagueness of the account of the manner of Henry's death, and the clear implication that his body was still at Chertsey. What is more, compared with the Windsor *Miracula*, Blacman is strikingly unconcerned with the miraculous and must have been writing before the launching of any formal canonization process. *Henry the Sixth*, pp. 3, 19, 45–6.

[2] *Henrici VI Angliae Regis Miracula Postuma*, ed. P. Grosjean (Brussels, 1935). These *Miracula* have in general been accepted too uncritically as a source for the early development of the cult. They refer largely to the period after 1484, when Henry's body was at Windsor and when the canons had a strong vested interest in, and governmental support for, establishing the king's claims to sanctity. The *Miracula* were compiled at the instigation of the Windsor canons; they contain surprisingly little evidence about the cult between 1471–83 and at times show an overt concern, manifested elsewhere by the canons, to discredit the monks of Chertsey. However, see pp. 176*–7*, 240*—1*, *Miracula*, nos. 40, 47, and 74. Also, *The Great Chronicle of London*, ed. A. H. Thomas and I. D. Thornley (London, 1938), p. 220; H. Harrod, 'Extracts from Early Wills in the Norwich Registries', *Norfolk Archaeology*, iv (1885), p. 338; and *The Fabric Rolls of York Minster* (Surtees Soc., xxxv, 1858), ed. J. Raine, p. 301. A recent account, which also concentrates on the 'official' cult after 1485 is J. W. McKenna, 'Piety and Propaganda: The Cult of King Henry VI', in *Chaucer and Middle English Studies in Honour of R. H. Robbins*, ed. B. Rowland (London, 1974), pp. 72–88.

Minster as an insult to Edward IV. A year later the king made known his own displeasure at the increasing number of pilgrims to Chertsey, and the translation of Henry's body to Windsor by Richard III in 1484 was undoubtedly an attempt to exercise some control over the spread of the cult. Certainly the monks of Chertsey seem to have demonstrated an undignified enthusiasm to be rid of their embarrassing royal charge.[1]

The politically almost subversive character of the work, combined with the informality of Blacman's manner, also go some way to explain the disordered textual state of the *Collectarium*. It cannot be claimed that the work is a model of lucidity. At its best Blacman's style is elaborate and convoluted, even ungrammatical; but Copland's edition also contains a large number of errors, many of them clearly the work of an incompetent editor, others arising from his defective exemplar. More fundamental are the structural inconsistencies. The *Collectarium* is a series of reflections on the life of the king. It has no very clear plan and, although it begins with Henry's birth and ends with his imprisonment and death, it does not in general follow any chronological sequence. In fact there are strong indications that the work was originally compiled over a period of time rather than as a unified whole. The last section, for example, which is largely concerned with the king's experiences while in hiding and later in the Tower, bears all the hallmarks of an afterthought. It repeats material which has appeared earlier in the work, and it follows an account of the king's death and his translation to an eternal kingdom which, both in content and manner, has the unmistakeable appearance of a conclusion.[2] Furthermore, although Blacman clearly stated that he was writing after the king's death, he unaccountably referred to individuals who are known to have been dead by May 1471 as though they were still alive,

---

[1] *Miracula*, ed. Grosjean, pp. 157*-8*, 182*, 112. *Acts of Court of the Mercers' Company*, ed. L. Lyell and F. D. Watney (Cambridge, 1936), p. 139.

[2] *Henry the Sixth*, pp. 13 and 20 (the empty pyx), and pp. 14 and 20 (the vision at the Eucharist). The last section of the penultimate chapter opens 'Quid plura?'; see p. 18.

indicating perhaps that he had collected material concerning the king from various sources and at different times but did not subsequently edit the information in any consistent fashion.[1] This impression is reinforced by the fact that Blacman showed himself to be especially well-informed about two widely separate periods in the king's life. He recounted many incidents which took place during the years 1443–53 while he was at Eton, such as the king's negotiations with the executors of Cardinal Beaufort, his visit to Bath, Waynflete's elevation to Winchester, and the last-minute pardon granted to some of the supporters of Humfrey, duke of Gloucester.[2] He also had access to detailed information about the period 1465–71 when the king was a fugitive in the north and was later imprisoned in the Tower. Conversely he had almost nothing to say about the intervening decade. If Blacman did acquire his information at very different times, over an extended period, this would add weight to the supposition that the composition of the *Collectarium* was in some way a prolonged, and even disorganized, process.

Despite its obvious defects of structure the work does have a certain straightforward value as a chronicle in the sense that it is a unique source for some, albeit miscellaneous, information about the king. For example, Blacman shed a little light on the obscure subject of the upbringing of the king's half-brothers, Edmund and Jasper Tudor, and Henry's concern to have them properly educated.[3] Quite incidentally he also recorded how Henry was responsible for altering the traditional form of the State Crown and devising a new

[1] This is particularly apparent in the references to Edward, prince of Wales, and to Thomas Mannyng who died in 1469. Ibid. pp. 7, 21.

[2] Ibid. pp. 8, 10, 11, 17. M. E. Christie, *Henry VI* (London, 1922), pp. 383–4. *Calendar of Patent Rolls, 1446–52*, p. 68, and also K. H. Vickers, *Humphrey, Duke of Gloucester* (London, 1907), pp. 303–5. It is noticeable that the pardon is associated with an Eton indulgence.

[3] *Henry the Sixth*, p. 9. All of the extant information, such as it is, about the early lives of the two brothers has been assembled by R. S. Thomas, 'The Political Career, Estates and "Connection" of Jasper Tudor, Earl of Pembroke and Duke of Bedford' (University of Wales, Swansea, Ph.D. thesis, 1971), esp. pp. 26–7, 32.

pattern which was to survive virtually unchanged until the seventeenth century.[1] Similarly the *Collectarium* provides a circumstantial account of Henry's maltreatment in the Tower, including an apparent attempt at murder, which runs contrary to Yorkist propaganda.[2] In the same vein it can be shown that Blacman made mistakes in detail. But the importance of the *Collectarium* lies not in such matters but in the general picture that it gives of the character of Henry VI. Blacman has customarily been dismissed as a hagiographer because of his exclusive concern with the king's virtues. It would be more accurate to argue that he gave an almost comprehensive picture of the king's defects as a ruler, but that he chose to interpret such public inadequacy as private rectitude.

Modern accounts of Henry VI have taken sharply opposing views of his role in government. On one side he is regarded as almost a cypher, neglectful of business, too frequently absent from the royal council, almost reclusive in his habits, and all too readily influenced by those about him. On the other he is credited with considerable personal responsibility for the actions of his government. It is argued in particular that he pursued a policy of peace with France at any price, oblivious of advice and with a reckless disregard for the consequences in terms of governmental paralysis and public disorder. In a word, the king 'allowed no one . . . any real initiative, and nothing much could be done without him'.[3] Blacman's

---

[1] *Henry the Sixth*, p. 6. The significance of this passage has escaped modern historians of the regalia, although it is well known that the design of the State Crown changed between c. 1380 and c. 1532. M. Holmes, 'The Crowns of England', *Archaeologia*, lxxxvi (1937), pp. 73–90, and H. D. W. Sitwell, *The Crown Jewels and Other Regalia in the Tower of London* (London, 1953), pp. 28–34.

[2] *Henry the Sixth*, pp. 17–18. For supporting evidence, concerning Henry's condition on his release, see John Warkworth, *A Chronicle of the First Thirteen Years of the Reign of Edward the Fourth*, ed. J. O. Halliwell (Camden Soc., 1839), p. 11, and G. Chastellain, *Œuvres*, ed. Kervyn de Lettenhove (Brussels, 1863–6), v. p. 490. Cf. the 'Croyland' version in *Rerum Anglicarum Scriptores Veterum*, ed. W. Fulman (Oxford, 1684), p. 539.

[3] B. P. Wolffe, 'The Personal Rule of Henry VI', p. 36. The opposite view is well represented by R. L. Storey, *The End of the House of Lancaster* (London, 1966), pp. 29–42.

account of the king goes some way towards resolving these contradictions by delineating the odd mixture of indifference, enthusiasm, and censorious meddlesomeness which constituted Henry's attitude towards public affairs. In one of his most vivid passages Blacman recalled an episode he had witnessed at Eltham when the king was disturbed during his devotions and complained that he was so interrupted by public business that he could scarcely snatch a moment for spiritual refreshment. A similar event also occurred at Windsor, but such incidents are merely illustrative details in the general picture drawn by Blacman of a king who was at best apathetic, and often even hostile, towards many of the public roles of monarchy, such as accessibility, good lordship, and external display.[1] Reluctant to participate in hunting or banquets, Blacman's king is remote and self-absorbed, not conversing easily with his entourage or readily sharing their mundane concerns. It is a detached otherworldliness which, as Blacman himself hinted, could readily lapse into the withdrawal and mental prostration which were the main symptoms of Henry's periods of insanity. Blacman identified these traits accurately but interpreted them in terms of the king's devotional fervour. Henry did not indulge 'in vain talk or chatter . . . and indeed he used but very brief speech', he was 'more given to God and to devout prayer than to handling worldly and temporal things, or practising vain sports or pursuits: these he despised as trifling'.[2] And Blacman precisely described Henry's bouts of insanity, when he was 'for the time not conscious of himself or of those about him, as if he were a man in a trance', but glossed such occasions as spiritual rapture with the king 'on the verge of heaven, having his conversation in heaven'.[3] The same spirit of devout resignation appears at its most moving in Blacman's account of Henry's reaction to his long captivity, which he endured 'with no broken spirit but with a calm mind, making light of all temporal things if he might but gain Christ'.[4] At the same time this

---

[1] *Henry the Sixth*, pp. 15–16. [2] Ibid. pp. 5, 15.
[3] Ibid. p. 16. [4] Ibid. p. 11.

detachment could rapidly be transformed into energy and enthusiasm where Henry was persuaded of the righteousness of a cause. In Blacman's eyes the obvious example of such a transformation was provided by the foundation of Eton where he described the king as supervising every detail, taking a close interest in the choice of teachers, and even involving himself in the spiritual lives of individual pupils. In another context exactly the same moral commitment might well be directed towards the cause of peace with France.

However, it is also clear that this moral enthusiasm could manifest itself on a more personal level in a form of vigorous censoriousness whose likely political effects even Blacman's glosses cannot disguise. Here, more than anywhere else, Blacman portrays a king at odds with the *mores* of his court. The king was 'a diligent exhorter and adviser, counselling the young . . . and admonishing men of mature age'.[1] It was perhaps no more than conventional piety for the king to write letters to his clergy 'full of heavenly mysteries and most salutary advice', to forbid hawks and weapons to be brought into church, or to be shocked by the fashion for bared breasts which became popular amongst the women of the court during the 1430s.[2] But it was less usual for the king to instruct his aristocracy to pray more frequently, to spy upon the behaviour of his courtiers, and to rebuke his own chamberlain for setting an evil example to his servants by swearing.[3] Blacman recorded these incidents as aspects of the king's devotion and of his concern for the spiritual well-being of others. In his treatment of the king's qualities of charity and mercy he was equally frank, and equally oblivious to the political implications of his subject. Nevertheless, in the light of modern studies of the reign his words assume a significance which is obscured by their apparent artlessness. In recent years criticism of Henry's administration has often concentrated on two particular issues, the indiscriminate largesse of the king, especially with regard to the crown lands, and the failure of the government fully to

[1] Ibid. p. 5.
[2] Ibid. pp. 6–7, 8.
[3] Ibid. pp. 7, 8, 16.

enforce the rigours of the law. Blacman was eloquent on both counts. Henry was 'most wary and alert against that pest of avarice' and 'enriched very many others with great gifts'; he was 'bountiful in his gifts to the confusion of avarice', particularly—as Blacman precisely noted—to the members of the royal household.[1] Equally Blacman emphasized the king's mercifulness. He did not wish that 'any person, however injurious to him, should ever be punished'. He was 'exceeding gracious and merciful' and subsequently even forgave those who had attacked him while he was in the Tower. In their own language such words fairly accurately hint at the recent discovery that Henry's government was issuing general pardons at the rate of well over three thousand a year during the very period when Blacman was a fellow of Eton.[2] Private charity and private mercy can be redefined, perhaps rightly, as governmental irresponsibility but Blacman's words cannot be dismissed as meaningless pieties. He deployed the manner and the language of the hagiographer but at the same time detailed many of the king's major defects as a ruler. Blacman's statements require a particularly exact attention and nowhere is this more the case than with regard to his general picture of Henry VI which, far from being one of bland sanctity, is both precise and pregnant with meaning.

In Blacman's eyes Henry's external life was at all points one of simple, austere puritanism. He was 'a second Job, a man simple and upright without any crook of craft or untruth'. This was true of his appearance. He rejected 'all curious fashion of clothing' and normally dressed entirely in black, wearing the long gown with a rolled hood of the ordinary townsman, with a full coat reaching below his knees and round-toed shoes like a farmer's. On formal occasions when he wore his crown he would put on a hair shirt beneath his robes.[3] The king's clothing exemplified his social and moral

---

[1] Ibid. pp. 9–10. Compare B. P. Wolffe, *The Royal Demesne in English History* (London, 1971), pp. 97–112.

[2] *Henry the Sixth*, pp. 16–18. Cf. Storey, *The End of the House of Lancaster*, pp. 210–16, and J. Bellamy, *Crime and Public Order in England in the Later Middle Ages* (London, 1973), pp. 191–8.

[3] *Henry the Sixth*, pp. 4, 14.

attitudes. He despised all forms of sport as frivolous and is recorded as having developed a particular distaste for hunting, not caring 'to see the creature, when taken, cruelly defiled with slaughter'.[1] Henry was notably uncompromising in his social life, disliking feasts, never talking much, not joining in gossip and harsh in his disapproval of any profane language, confining himself to the simple oath 'forsooth and forsooth'.[2] The king was chaste before his marriage, faithful to his wife despite their long periods apart, and rigorous in his condemnation of immorality in others. He insisted on reverent behaviour in church, forbidding chatter or the conduct of secular business. But this forthright tone was not incompatible with a natural modesty and humility. The king was of a retiring disposition, detesting cruelty, and readily forgiving injury. He was totally indifferent to worldly possessions and charitable to all in need.

As his former chaplain Blacman naturally also concentrated his attention on the king's devotional life and here there is an even greater immediacy to his words. Henry was more than punctilious in all external religious observances. He used 'wholly to devote the high days and Sundays to hearing the divine office and to devout prayer'. He would be present at the beginning of the office and did not weary 'even though it were continued until after noonday'.[3] But his spiritual life also had a number of markedly individual features. He was in the habit of participating actively in the Mass, making the responses, reading to himself the Mass prayers, epistles, and gospels, and even acting as a server. All of this was an aspect of his general devotion to the Eucharist, and particularly to the Real Presence. When riding past a church he would normally bare his head in honour of the pyx and he claimed at times to see Jesus in human form in the hands of the celebrant at the elevation. Henry also manifested a particular veneration for the suffering humanity of

---

[1] Ibid. pp. 5, 18. Blacman's words are not entirely accurate in the sense that Henry is known to have hunted on various occasions.
[2] Ibid. pp. 15–16.
[3] Ibid. pp. 6, 15

Jesus. He was a devotee of the cult of the Holy Cross and of its more specific and recent variant, the cult of the Five Wounds. On this account he reshaped his crown, in order to include a row of crosses, and he had a representation of the Five Wounds set at his table before meals.[1] Furthermore Henry combined in a distinctive fashion the contemplative and visionary temperament with a more practical and scriptural piety. Compared with some later biographies the *Collectarium* lays little stress on the miraculous but Blacman did refer to a number of visions experienced by the king. Recurrently, on St. Edward's Day, he had a vision of the Assumption of the Virgin Mary accompanied by Christ in Majesty and during his period in hiding Henry enjoyed a premonition of his eventual capture and imprisonment by means of a revelation from St. Dunstan and St. Anselm. By contrast the educational foundations at Eton and Cambridge were equally seen by the king as central manifestations of his piety, established—as their foundation documents stress repeatedly—to the glory of God and of the Blessed Virgin Mary, provided with magnificent chapels, and statutorily committed to an elaborate liturgical ritual. Similarly Henry emphasized that the teachers in both colleges might even be deficient in their knowledge of the secular arts rather than ignorant of the scriptures. He was here recalling a central element in his own spirituality for, as Blacman himself witnessed, the king was regularly occupied in reading the bible.[2]

The resonances of this account of Henry's religious life are unmistakeable. In Blacman's eyes Henry was a model of that form of lay piety which has come to be seen as characteristic of later medieval England. One aspect of it was a fervent, puritanical moralism which pervades contemporary sermons and which Henry possessed in abundance. Indeed in his hostility to swearing and his regular bible reading he had some affinity with the most extreme

---

[1] Ibid. pp. 6, 13, 14, 20. See R. W. Pfaff, *New Liturgical Feasts in Later Medieval England* (Oxford, 1970), pp. 84–91.
[2] *Henry the Sixth*, pp. 12, 20–1.

exponents of such a piety, the Lollards.[1] More accurately, Henry is explicitly described by Blacman as following a regimen which was almost monastic.[2] The simple clothing, the disregard for possessions amounting to a spiritual poverty, the rigorous chastity outside marriage, and the regular and prolonged participation in the divine office are all sharply reminiscent of an ideal of monasticism, without formal rule or enclosure, whose widespread hold over the imagination of the time can be seen from the béguinages to the household of Sir Thomas More. This same lay piety was also distinguished by a note of individualism, of spiritual self-improvement, even a flavour of anti-clericalism which Blacman equally clearly discerned in the king's spirituality. In one context it is apparent in Henry's concern for education as a means of evangelization. It also expressed itself in his confident private piety, nourished on reading the bible for himself, active participation in the Mass, and on the experience of an immediate personal contact with God which even emboldened the king to write letters of spiritual advice to his own bishops. But this same piety had another face, emotional and visionary, while also obsessed with the concrete and the physical, the sufferings of the Crucifixion, the pains of Hell, the unique intercessory virtue of the Real Presence in the sacrifice of the Mass. It was a piety which had its spokesman in Richard Rolle and its most excitable practitioner in Margery Kempe. It found its popular echo in a vigorous iconography of carving and wall-painting and in the multiplication of Masses for the dead emanating from chantry after chantry. Again, these traits are equally apparent in Henry's religious life, in his visions and voices, his devotion to the Cross and the Wounds, and in a veneration for the Real Presence which was intensified to the point of visualization.

---

[1] It is worth noting that Henry possessed a copy of the Wycliffite Bible, now Bodleian Library, MS Bodley 277. This lay piety has often been characterized but see especially K. B. McFarlane, *Lancastrian Kings and Lollard Knights* (Oxford, 1972), pp. 224–6.

[2] *Henry the Sixth*, pp. 4, 13. The simile is repeated by Blacman in different contexts and is clearly more than a commonplace.

These themes in Blacman's essay have only to be brought together for their meaning to emerge. However, his openness to such a piety and his recognition of its distinctiveness derived not just from his contact with the king but from his own spiritual background. Here, more than anywhere, the rapport between Blacman's own experience and his account of the king is fundamental. Between 1463 and about 1474, while he was a member of the Carthusian order, Blacman assembled the most remarkable private library of devotional literature which is known to have existed in fifteenth-century England. Forty-two out of this collection of forty-four books seem to have been given to the Witham Charterhouse in 1474, and the other two probably soon followed, but Blacman almost certainly remained in the community for some years afterwards and the books provided the spiritual and intellectual context from which his sketch of the king emerged. Perhaps surprisingly the library included no works in English and, with the exception of Rolle's *Incendium Amoris*, none of the writings of the English Mystics. Otherwise it was a strikingly wide-ranging collection containing books representative of many different schools of spirituality and texts written as recently as about 1461.[1] The

[1] This account is concerned entirely with Blacman's 'second' library, listed in his own hand in Bodleian Library MS Laud misc. 154, fo. 2, headed 'perquisita postea' and numbered by him separately from his earlier collection. His 'first' library, which was probably acquired largely before he entered the Carthusian order, contained twenty-four volumes, which are listed twice over on Laud misc. 154, flyleaf and fo. 1. The first list, which gives most of the contents of each volume, is written in an unidentified hand; the second list, which gives only one work in each volume but adds the second folio *incipit*, is in the hand of the 'Witham Librarian' who 'accessioned' these volumes by inscribing on them a note to the effect that they belonged to Witham and were Blacman's gift (see Bodleian Library, MSS Bodley 801, fo. 1ʳ; Digby 104, fo. 21ʳ, and Laud misc. 152, fo. 1ʳ). In both lists the title of the twenty-fourth volume has been added by Blacman himself. Both of these lists of the 'first' library must date from after 29 August 1463 as they include a MS which was completed then (Laud misc. 152, fo. 286ᵛ). The relationship between the two libraries is not clear-cut, but it would seem that Blacman gave his first collection of books, largely acquired outside the order, to Witham probably soon after 1463 and not long after his arrival there. The 'second' library, which is of a quite different character, appears to have been

library ranged from the *Vitae Patrum* to an epistle of Pope Pius II but it was especially strong in works from the later period. It included the two most popular major devotional texts produced in later medieval Europe, Suso's *Horologium* and the *Imitatio Christi*, works which were in fact comparatively unfamiliar in England, as well as the *Revelations* of the two most influential female visionaries of the period, St. Bridget of Sweden and St. Catherine of Siena. Blacman was familiar with béguine *Vitae*, with the Franciscan piety of David of Augsburg's *Formula Novitiorum*, and with the Rhineland school in the form of Henry Suso and the *De Adhaerendo Deo*. By means of a recent compilation known as the *Donatus Devotionis* he had access to excerpts from Ruysbroeck's *Spiritual Marriage* and the *devotio moderna* was represented by Thomas Kempis. Alongside these major texts his library also included a number of works by lesser authors and a large group of apparently anonymous devotional anthologies. Blacman studied these books with care. One of them was annotated by him in such a way as to show that he was in the habit of comparing the treatment of particular devotional themes in his various books. Equally, although he could scarcely have written all of the volumes himself, it is nevertheless striking that the only two extant manuscripts from this collection are both in his own hand.[1]

The *Collectarium* is the work of a man who had known the king well, who had participated in his enterprises and shared his devotions. At the time when he finished the work Blacman had spent perhaps twenty years in the most austere and esteemed of religious orders. No other English contemporary can be shown to have had

---

assembled through Carthusian sources while he was at Witham and was given to the house largely, if not completely, in 1474 (Laud misc. 154, fo. 2ᵛ). The lists are printed in conflated, and inaccurate, form in Thompson, *Carthusian Order*, pp. 317–22. A full account of Blacman's libraries by the present author is now near completion. I am indebted to Dr A. I. Doyle for information about Blacman's MSS.

[1] Lambeth Palace MS 436, see fo. 52ʳ, and St. John's College, Oxford, MS 182. This latter volume of béguine lives is catalogued misleadingly as *Fragment' collect'* in Blacman's library list.

such an extensive knowledge of recent devotional literature. The *Collectarium* must be placed firmly in this context. When Blacman mentioned Henry's veneration for the Five Wounds it would have been immediately recalled in this milieu that the Five Wounds were the badge of the Bridgettine community at Syon, by far the most distinguished monastery to be founded in fifteenth-century England. When he spoke of the king as an 'imitator' of Christ he was not using commonplaces but deploying a term of art.[1] The work may, in a sense, be hagiography but hagiography from such a source requires not dismissal but an even more patient analysis than many other forms of chronicle evidence. With all its defects of partiality and gullibility, and they are many, the *Collectarium* must be seen as an important insight into the mentality of Henry VI and as a mirror to the piety of its age.

[1] *Henry the Sixth*, p. 18.

The German town chroniclers

F. R. H. DU BOULAY

A STRIKING contrast exists between England and Germany in the number and variety of their urban vernacular chronicles of the late Middle Ages. In England town chronicles mostly come from London but even these are in the aggregate not copious. Both in London and the provinces anonymity of authorship was usual, and historians may feel fortunate to know even the names of an Andrew Horn, a Robert Bale, William Gregory, or Robert Fabyan. Germans, on the other hand, wrote variegated notes and narratives, sometimes voluminously, in their High and Low vernaculars from the fourteenth century onwards and, although the largest cities were naturally the most vocal, smaller places too produced pieces of interest. The systematic edition of this material was undertaken in 1862 by the Historical Commission of the Bavarian Academy of Sciences, and after the publication of 38 volumes its work still continues.[1] Many big cities still have no chronicle printed by this Commission and there must be other towns as small as Landshut, Mühldorf, or Neuss, already represented in the series, which have yet to yield their narratives: a single example would be Göttingen which had already in 1387 produced its first German-language historical record in the form of a feud book.[2] The Swiss towns,

---

[1] *Die Chroniken der deutschen Städte vom 14. bis in 16. Jahrhundert* [hereafter *CDS*], hrsg. durch die Historische Kommission bei der Bayerischen Akademie der Wissenschaften (Leipzig u.a., 1862–). So far texts have appeared from Augsburg, Bremen, Brunswick, Cologne, Dortmund, Duisburg, Landshut, Lübeck, Magdeburg, Mainz, Mühldorf (Bavaria), Neuss, Nuremberg, Regensburg, Soest, and Strassburg.

[2] Hans Patze (hrsg.), *Der deutsche Territorialstaat*, II (Vorträge und Forschungen xiv, Sigmaringen, 1971), p. 21 n. 42.

properly part of Germany till the 1490s, have attracted the detailed attention they well deserve.

The German town chroniclers might be clerical or lay and a few of them were members of religious orders, but with rare exceptions they were scribes and administrators who held public office. Some were anonymous, and Cristianus Wierstraat chose to put his name to a rhymed story of the siege of Neuss in 1474–5 by means of an acrostic,[1] but in town after town their names are either openly announced or easily discoverable. It would be possible to present them here biographically but massed detail of that kind is not very illuminating and it is more interesting to enquire into the purposes for which they wrote. An analysis like this is bound to be somewhat artificial because town chroniclers often had mixed motives. But if their motives are considered in an orderly way these writers may be rescued from the charges sometimes preferred that they were mere annalistic doodlers using office hours, quite parochial in outlook, or even barely educated.[2] They differed amongst themselves. Some were brief and business-like and others rambled, some set out to entertain and instruct, others to preserve in written form ceremonies required by a town's dignity, wrongs suffered, victories gained, or the doing of kinsmen whose very existence provided the framework of society. But an appreciable number have geographically wide vision and some the habits of accuracy and of historical proof.

In later medieval Germany town administrators were thick on the ground. An example may be taken in south-western Germany, comprising Swabia, western Franconia, and Switzerland, where by the end of the fifteenth century 140 towns are known to have had

---

[1] *CDS*, xx. p. 481.
[2] e.g. '. . . the barely educated literate townsman' (Donald Matthew, *The Medieval European Community* (1977), p. 73). On the blinkered vision of German town chroniclers see the interesting but rather exaggerated interpretation of Heinrich Schmidt, *Die deutschen Städtechroniken als Spiegel des bürgerlichen Selbstverständnisses im Spätmittelalter* (Göttingen, 1958), esp. pp. 84 ff., based on three chronicles from Augsburg, Nuremberg, and Lübeck respectively.

town scribes.[1] The largest towns are usually the first to show evidence of having these officials: and in Augsburg, Basel, Böblingen, Ehingen, Ellwangen, Esslingen, and Freiburg-im-Breisgau there are notices from the thirteenth century which allude variously to certain townsmen as *notarius, scriptor, scriba, rector puerorum,* or *notarius civium.* By 1500 there can have been no place larger than a village which did not have its trained writer. By then the post of *Stadtschreiber* had prestige and the office-holder might be the patron of schoolmasters, not a schoolmaster himself. Whether or not it was well-paid is as always a matter of opinion and of whether the comparisons are made upward or downward. A town scribe in Augsburg got £26 a year in 1362 together with fees for writing letters for other people.[2] In fifteenth-century Frankfurt-am-Main his salary was round about 80 florins a year together with 15 florins clothing money, some other fees, journey expenses, and accommodation, but out of this he had to pay a junior (*Jungschreiber*).[3] In fifteenth-century Lucerne chancery officials were sometimes part-time: Schilling was active in the wine-trade and Schradin kept an inn. There was a tendency for the senior post, town clerk perhaps it should be called, to run in families, like that of Neidhardt of Ulm, a landed family whose members served as town clerks there for a century while at the same time it supplied important clerical offices elsewhere in south Germany, like canonries at Constance and Augsburg. Sometimes the town clerk was appointed from outside the city. In Nördlingen there is an unbroken series from 1407 to 1513 of the heads of chancery who came from elsewhere in the region, probably on account of a rule intended to secure a man neutral in civic disputes.[4] Elsewhere, however, an outsider might be appointed by reason of his marriage to the daughter of a civic

---

[1] Gerhart Burger, *Die südwestdeutschen Stadtschreiber im Mittelalter* (Böblingen, 1960).

[2] Ibid. p. 128.

[3] M. J. Elsas, *Umriss einer Geschichte der Preise und Löhne in Deutschland,* ii (Leiden, 1936), p. 619.

[4] Burger, pp. 300–3.

magnate, like Bartholomew Neidhardt of Ulm who was given the chancellorship of Nuremberg after he had married Barbara Ammann. At Ulm the town clerk apparently had to be handsome ('von auffallend hübscher Gestalt').[1]

Late medieval Germany abounds in town officials and chroniclers who were immigrants from other towns or who spent much time in travel, sometimes to distant places. Burkhard Zink of Augsburg had been a wandering scholar and then a travelling merchant to Italy and the Mediterranean. Sigmund Meisterlin, historian of Augsburg and Nuremberg, was a restless monk who travelled even to France where 'he dwelt far from home'.[2] Switzerland is particularly rich in instances. Hans Fründ, chronicler of Zürich, had been born in Lucerne, was *Landschreiber* in Schwyz and *Stadtschreiber* of Rapperswil. He not only wrote about the Toggenburg succession war (1436–50) but was able to boast, 'I was there and fought, like any good Swiss'. Fricker of Bern had a doctorate in law from Pavia, Diebold Schilling of Bern and his younger brother of Lucerne were both born in Solothurn and both fought in Swiss armies, of which they were proud. The family of chroniclers called Russ had come from northern Italy, and Russ the younger died as a common soldier in the service of Uri, having served as envoy in Vienna and Budapest. These and numerous others were ambassadors, soldiers, travelling scholars, and councillors as well as historians of Swiss towns in the later fifteenth century. They were not uneducated men, nor study-bound writers.[3]

In the pages which follow seven distinct motives have been put forward as reasons for the work of the German town chroniclers. Any one town, or indeed any one chronicler, may well have

---

[1] Ibid. pp. 74, 53.

[2] *CDS*, iii p. 313.

[3] Jean-Pierre Bodmer, *Chroniken und Chronisten im Spätmittelalter* (Monographien zur Schweizer Geschichte, Bd. 10, Bern, 1976); Fritz Ernst, 'Die Schweizer Chronisten: ein biographischer Versuch', in *Neue Zürcher Zeitung*, 3 January 1954 (Samstag/Sonntagausgabe, Nr. 12(1), p. 6). I am grateful to my former pupil, Mrs Sarah Metzger-Court, for her trouble in obtaining a photocopy of this article for me.

produced narrative writing for more than a single reason, and there may have been other purposes too. But the most important appear to be these: to furnish memorials of a leading family; to record the ceremonial reception of kings; to keep reports on feuds and wars in which the town engaged against external enemies; to chronicle internal rebellions; to gratify the private wish of the chronicler in recording whatever he wished about his town's history; to write a chronicle for the literate town public on the chronicler's own initiative; and to write a town chronicle or history for money or reward on the overt commission of the town.

It is not surprising that memorials of family history, addressed to members of the family living and to come, should be among the earliest of burgher writings, for they celebrate the most fundamental social grouping of the medieval world. The beginnings of historiography in the German language, especially in Nuremberg, have this familial character and were not intended as town histories at all. Ulman Stromer, member of the famous Nuremberg family of that name, began his 'Little Book of my family and of adventures' (Püchel von meim geslechet und von abentewr) in 1360 and continued it till 1407 when he died at the age of 78.[1] He wrote down what he had heard and experienced and was able to go back to the family ancestor (Stammvater), the knight Gerhard von Reichenbach who at the beginning of the thirteenth century possessed the castle of Kammerstein near Schwabach. A son of this man, called Conrad, married a Nuremberg girl of the Waldstromer family which did not yet possess citizenship but provided imperial foresters in the neighbourhood of Nuremberg. By this and his subsequent two marriages Conrad was said to have had 33 children, a fecundity which helps to explain both the long existence of many German

[1] CDS, i. For something of the Stromer family which produced this first autobiography of a German burgher and the first business history too, possibly influenced by the recent autobiography of Charles IV which the Nuremberg council had paid £3½ to have translated into German, see Lore Sporhan-Krempel and Wolfgang von Stromer, 'Das Handelshaus der Stromer von Nürnberg und die Geschichte der ersten deutschen Papiermühle', in Vierteljahrschrift für Sozial- und Wirtschaftsgeschichte, 47 (1960), pp. 81–104.

town dynasties and the size of audience for memoirs such as these. The 'Little Book' is a collection of genealogical information about the Stromer and other related patrician families (*Geschlechter*), to which variegated notes were added in a formless way on such matters as mercantile weights and values. The book is extremely reticient on political matters, doubtless because the author was cautious. For instance, it contains not a hint that King Rupert had stayed with the writer in 1403 at Dinkelsbühl.

Nuremberg is probably the city richest in these family memorials. There is the *Memorialbuch* of Endres Tucher and his family which relates to the years 1386 to 1454.[1] The author like so many young men of Nuremberg had been sent to Venice where he had learned mercantile skills and in due course he returned and married the daughter of Konrad Paumgartner, another Nuremberg business man who left family notes. Tucher's book is the journal of a prosperous and alert burgher who tells of his own experiences and those of his uncle Berthold. These were the sort of men who knew royal families personally, embellished the great Nuremberg churches like St. Lorenz and St. Sebald, and trembled at the Hussite threat. Hans Haller, another of the sort, published his *Geschlechtsbuch* in 1490 and, after the example of Stromer, noted all the 'worshipful people' living in his time. Such family memoranda merge easily into civic annals, like the Nuremberg Yearbooks which were continued through the fifteenth century by Heinrich Deichsler, beer brewer, out of bits of other people's work, archival reports, and his own observations.[2]

The blurred boundary between a family book and one written for a social circle or even as an official assignment for the town itself is shown in different ways both in Hector Mühlich's chronicle of Augsburg (1348–1487)[3] and the Dortmund chronicle of Johann Kerkhörde (1405–65).[4] Mühlich was no self-made man but the

---

[1] *CDS*, ii, x, xi.
[2] For the Nuremberg Yearbooks, see Heinrich Schmidt.
[3] *CDS*, xxii.
[4] *CDS*, xx.

sprig of a rich Augsburg family, evidently of noble origin, and called 'enlarger of society' (*Mehrer der Gesellschaft*) by reason of his marriage to a girl from another of Augsburg's oldest families. The use of the word *Mehrer* in this context makes an interesting parallel with the Golden Bull's description of Charles IV in 1356 as *Mehrer* of the empire, at a moment when he had already contracted three advantageous marriages. Mühlich of Augsburg began his own chronicle with Charles IV's reign, and composed in his pages a rich man's picture of the mercantile world as he had experienced it, supplying detail about distant countries but remaining silent on town politics save for some snarling at the Augsburg rabble and the arrogant cathedral clergy. His second marriage was to Jakob Fugger's sister Anna, and the wedding-register of the Augsburg *Herrentrinkstube* shows the family as a long flourishing one.[1] Mühlich was a *Mehrer* indeed.

Kerkhörde of Dortmund, on the other hand, was a more modest man from a modest town, the only imperial city of Westphalia, and one neglected by emperors till Charles IV. Kerkhörde's authorship is known because someone noted his name in the margin,[2] but he tells us a good deal of himself in the course of his historical writing, how he came from a nearby village, acquired town property and a pension, fought in the Soest feud of 1446–8, was imprisoned at Iserlohn, but came later as a man of the people to represent the gilds on the town council. In 1451 another Dortmund man wrote, 'this year the lords of Dortmund let their archives be thoroughly searched and a chronicle prepared by Johann Kerkhörde, councillor'.[3] Yet Kerkhörde said it was just for himself and his family that he was writing, and indeed the text refers constantly to his kin, and then only by their Christian names as he complains crossly about the town's treatment of him and his. So the lack of clear distinction between family man and town chronicler may be shown as much

---

[1] *CDS*, xxii, p. xv.
[2] *CDS*, xx, p. 4.
[3] Ibid. pp. 9–10.

in a writer's petulance as in his geniality and satisfaction with fortune.

A second major preoccupation of town chroniclers was with the formal reception of king and emperor. This is again a rather specially Nuremberg motif, so far as the published records go, since the town took pains to record the ceremonial for future reference both when Sigismund was received in 1414 and Frederick III in 1440.[1] Of the first there are two manuscript and one printed version, and the second, kept in the civic chancery, also recounts a series of negotiations by the council for the confirmation of privileges. Behind all the elaborate ceremonial can be glimpsed the intense desire of townsmen to please and to be favoured. Of course this is neither remarkable in itself nor peculiar to Nuremberg. In Augsburg Peter Egen was deeply gratified that Frederick III stayed with him and permitted him afterwards to change his name to von Argon.[2] In Bern the chronicler Justinger cynically observed how you get what you pay for, after Sigismund's successful visit there in 1414 had been sweetened by the provision of beautiful women for the emperor and his train.[3] Town recordings of royal visits merely underline their consciousness of how much the king might do for them.

Much more common in the experience of German town writers than the arrival of royalty was, unfortunately, the need to keep war reports and feud books. This constitutes a third activity of the town historian, and one which distinguishes him from his English counterpart. The requirement to document military matters touches on the very nature of German urbanization and the skills in writing which accompanied it. Because the king's power was localized and fitful, towns suffered more continuously than in England from the attacks of outsiders, whether great princes or minor nobility based in their castles. Many chroniclers give their readers some sense of the countryside's danger, like Zink of Augsburg to whom the forest

---

[1] *CDS*, iii. pp. 337 ff., 349 ff.
[2] *CDS*, iv. p. 338.
[3] Bodmer, p. 12.

was a place full of ghosts and huge swine and castles were thought of as barred by thorn hedges, and for whom Mainz's conquest in 1462 by its own archbishop after street-fighting was a portent of disaster for his own city. 'Dear men of Augsburg, man the gates with pious people, for you have many wicked neighbours who gladly wish you dead.'[1]

But if town warfare was a constant ingredient of the chronicles, the specific war diary was often itself a kind of specialized chronicle. Nuremberg again furnishes good early examples. 'The Campaign of Lichtenburg'[2] of 1444 is the narrative of a single event. The lords of Waldenfels in their castles of Wartenfels and Lichtenburg near the Thuringian frontier used to set upon merchants' transport on the road between Nuremberg and Leipzig. The last straw was when Fritz von Waldenfels took some Nuremberg townsmen prisoner in November 1443 without any preliminary declaration of war. Goaded beyond endurance, Nuremberg mustered allies from Rothenburg and Windsheim, appointed war captains, and counter-attacked in the Bayreuth Oberland by capturing the castle of Wartenfels and the township of Lichtenburg. Lichtenburg castle itself escaped capture because of snowfall, failure of the besiegers' gunpowder, and quarrelling among the towns' gunners, and in the end the margrave of Brandenburg was called in as arbitrator. All this was recorded for Nuremberg's archives by an anonymous official who wrote soberly, in the third person.

In 1449-50 another war report was occasioned by a savage campaign between Nuremberg and the margrave of Brandenburg himself.[3] Whoever drafted the original minute, the city archives named Erhard Schürstab as its editor, and his account was accompanied by documents of procurement and of ransoms owed and owing and was intended at least partly to improve military performance in the future. One version came down in the Schürstab family

---

[1] Schmidt, pp. 38, 32.

[2] *CDS*, ii (*Der Zug nach Lichtenburg*), esp. p. 60.

[3] *CDS*, ii. pp. 95 ff. (*Krieg gegen den Markgrafen Albrecht v. Brandenburg: Kriegsbericht und Ordnungen, zusammengebracht von Erhard Schürstab.*)

archives, and another was given to the city council, an arrangement which shows yet again how closely bound up together were the memorials of official families and the efforts of cities fighting for their lives.

Brunswick had a feud book which went back to the fourteenth century (1377–88) in annalistic form, itself apparently continued from lost waxen tablets,[1] though the town council felt no need till the very end of the fifteenth century to recall the past in a proper chronicle. The earlier impulse was not to glorify the past or present but primarily to note down all the injuries done to the men of Brunswick. As time went on these acts of urban paranoia were increasingly replaced by information concerning castles pledged to the town, which is to say records of success rather than failure. But Brunswick never became safe from private war in the medieval period. A separate document noted the great feud of 1492–3 against the Welf dukes with their princely allies supported by armed peasants and loot-hungry *Landsknechte* and mercenaries. All this was described by a deeply outraged town compiler.[2] The type is common.

Feud books were kept by many towns, including Cologne, Neuss, Soest, and Lüneburg.[3] Reports on the Soest feud against Cologne were written by the town secretary, Bartholomäus van der Lake, who came from an old town family. He had been a notary attached to Cologne diocesan court at Arnsberg and was a married graduate in minor orders. He had to use the greatest discretion in conducting negotiations on behalf of Soest with the chapter of Cologne and the family of the archbishop, Dietrich von Mörs, as well as with the royal Chamber before which Soest was cited by the archbishop. Eventually van der Lake was rewarded for his hard and delicate work by the duke of Cleves, ally of Soest, who made him Official to the bishop of Soest with the right of succession in this post to his sons. (It is of some interest that a lay prince possessed the right to

---

[1] *CDS*, vi. pp. 12–17.
[2] *CDS*, xxv.
[3] *CDS*, xii, xx, xxi, xxxvi.

such an ecclesiastical appointment.) These examples illustrate the deep involvement between town writers, their families and men of power in the neighbourhood, and the impossibility of using such evidence to prove any regular kind of ideological grouping. Towns might have to fight lesser nobility and great princes, but equally they might find themselves at odds with each other or thrown into alliance with landed magnates. Feud books and war reports are simply the records of alarms and excursions which happened by historical chance in a world where royal power provided insufficient cohesion. The greater the threat the more nearly the documentary reports approach the generality of political ideas, as in the wide-spread German town attitudes of fear and hatred towards Charles the Bold, clearly noted in Lübeck but also celebrated in prose from Switzerland and rhyme from Neuss,[1] or in the abiding Swiss detestation of the Habsburgs and the perpetuation of the William Tell legend in the White Book of Sarnen,[2] put together by Hans the *Landschreiber* of Obwalden.

The fourth category are those chroniclers whose purpose was to write about their town's internal conflicts. Conscious political motive has been much more tenaciously studied in these civic rebellions than in the towns' external relations. In particular, good use has been made of the text of chronicle and allied sources from three German cities which experienced severe internal revolts: Lübeck (1403–8), Mainz (1444–6), and Cologne (1396–1400).[3] In all of them, and in the numerous other towns too which experienced rebellions during this era, a fundamental desire of the rebels was to break the monopoly of a patriciate composed of certain leading families whose members formed the ruling councils. The details are not relevant here but the attitude of the chroniclers and the use

---

[1] Schmidt, ch. 2 (3); Bodmer, ch. 1; *CDS*, xx. p. 481.

[2] Bodmer, pp. 23 ff.

[3] Reinhard Barth, *Argumentation und Selbstverständnis der Bürgeropposition in städtischen Auseinandersetzungen des Spätmittelalters* (Kollective Einstellungen und sozialer Wandel in Mittelalter, hrsg. von Rolf Sprandel, Bd. 3, Böhlau: Cologne, Vienna, 1974).

made of their writings are an important aspect of urban historiography, for it is evident that one of the major reasons for chronicle writing at this period was to justify the attitudes of one side or the other, and usually of the urban upper class.

The Lübeck writers took the patrician side firmly. Rather exceptionally, the chroniclers at this time were friars,[1] but for all that they felt themselves to be at one with the ruling patriciate and wrote with the superciliousness of men who possessed the monopoly of political information and good sense. It was true enough that townsmen not engaged in long-distance trade were less likely to be able to write and to have access to records. The council, as Dr Reinhard Barth has pointed out, was the very centre of the town's 'writing society' (*Schriftlichkeit*),[2] and the chroniclers were usually members of the same social circle as the councillors. In Lübeck the rebels of 1403–8 had not been on the council before and were regarded as necessarily and completely ignorant of the city's best interests. The Lübeck writers in fact go beyond the other sources in their use of insult and accusation. The council's actual letters, where these have been reported, were phrased with a patrician suavity: 'we don't mind what stupid people say, but are distressed to be accused of untrue things . . .'; 'we are all sworn to act honourably . . .'; 'this will distress all decent people . . .'. But the chroniclers spoke of rebels with harsher voices, calling them devils in human form and enemies of religion, ignorant, stupid and fomenters of dissension.[3]

Mainz was another city in which the chronicler steadily adopted the patrician attitude against internal dissentients. The revolt of 1444–6 is treated in the 'Chronicle of Ancient Matters' (*Chronik von*

---

[1] CDS, xxvi, xxviii (the Franciscan Detmar and the Dominican Hermann Korner).

[2] Barth, p. 14.

[3] Pp. 350–1 and nn. with annotated references (e.g.: ' "unbeschedenheit", "dumkonicheit", "schedderlik twedracht", "vrevelheit" und ein Werk von "grymmicheit und torne" nennt die Lübecker Chronistik die Vorgänge von 1403–08.')

alten Dingen der Stadt Mainz),[1] the very title of which betrays its attitude of conservatism. In the conflict between the patricians (*Geschlechter*) and the commonalty (*Gemeinde*) the former were the 'honourable friends of the city' or 'the ancients'. The chronicler had access to the archives and had some historical skill in allowing the documents to speak for themselves. Through these an unusually vivid scene can be glimpsed of the councillors sitting in their dining club, calling each other 'brother' and their president, Henne Knauff, 'the abbot'. Even the more offensive words about them used by the commonalty are allowed to stand, such as 'lounge lizard' (if that be a permissible translation of *Zimmerkrose*). In the chronicler's own narrative, however, he displays the practised courtesy of the patrician as against the brusque rudeness of the opposition. Patricians tended to identify themselves with 'the honour and need of the city', while rebels spoke more easily of the misdeeds of the patricians in spending money on buildings, giving credit to uncreditworthy people, holding expensive banquets in the town-hall, or granting town scribes inadmissible extra pay. To the patrician or the chronicler who wrote for him it was painful to think how much it cost to have the goodwill of the archbishops of Mainz and Cologne and of the king of the Romans for the confirmation of the city's privileges. To the gildsmen it was 'amazing how long the elders have been allowed such privileges' and how much they all ate and drank.

Interestingly, the tone in the Cologne chronicle is different, for the surviving documents in the largest of German cities tended rather to side with the rebels. *Die weverslaicht* is a little rhymed chronicle about the rebellion of the gilds in 1369–71 and its swift suppression by the patricians. This particular writer was a partisan of the city nobility who disliked what he had seen of town rebels in Flanders, but he wrote calmly and saw faults on both sides. The rebellion of 1396–1400, however, found a documented narrative much more partial to the weavers and their allies in *Dat nuwe boich*. The title of 'new book' was in deliberate distinction from the 'book of the city of Cologne' of the thirteenth century, Cologne's oldest German

[1] *CDS*, xviii, esp. pp. 315–20.

chronicle, written in rhyme by the town scribe, master Gotfrid Hagen. The 'new book' was by Gerlach van Hauwe, also a clerical notary, educated in Cologne, but an opportunist who switched to the stronger faction of the merchants and craftsmen when they seized power in summer 1396.[1] In Cologne the disturbances were more bloodthirsty than in many German towns and events were reflected in the chronicle with extremist phrases. But here, as in Lübeck and Mainz, the chroniclers show patricians and oppositions normally employing the same kinds of basic argument. Everyone agreed that the antiquity of law and custom was good. Patricians, however, argued that this is what they represented, while the opposition from below claimed to have been forcibly robbed of its share. In Lübeck the opposition was not historically clear-sighted enough to point out the family and professional interconnections among the members of the town oligarchy, but they shouted for participation. In Mainz and Cologne it was much the same. The chroniclers in fact show the two sides in city conflicts each appealing to history yet without any exact historical sense of how power had come to be concentrated in certain hands. Each claimed, with a strength of conviction unequalled in England, that the past conferred an eternal validity on the city's rights, but each thought his own party represented the whole city, not a mere section, and hence the city's welfare.

In these three great towns the emphasis of chronicle writing was particularly on internal social conflict, but that was hardly the general rule, and there remains a galaxy of towns where the chronicler, in a fuller, completer sense, flourished. The remaining three categories of writer to be discussed here share one major characteristic, namely, that they produced chronicles which were attempts at a more wide-ranging history of their towns rather than specialized accounts of families, ceremonies, or conflicts, and the distinctions which are here drawn between them may seem needless-ly artificial. None the less, the attitudes of these town histories seem different in important ways, according to whether they were writing

[1] *CDS*, xii.

primarily for themselves or for a public, and according to whether they were writing on private initiative or by an open commission for pay or reward. Several town chroniclers give little evidence of writing for anyone's satisfaction but their own. One such was Erhard Wahraus of Augsburg, whose chronicle runs from 1126 to 1445.[1] His family probably came from Eichstätt. In 1409 Wahraus first appears as a young citizen and gildsman, and he can be traced over the years, growing in wealth and importance and becoming the creditor of various noblemen in the neighbourhood. His chronicle was cobbled together carelessly from old sources for his own interest; some contemporary matters are ignored, others are treated with brief or sweeping judgments, such as the remark that in 1442 King Frederick III came to Augsburg 'and he was duke of Austria and did not rule well'.[2]

A more detailed and personal volume was the memorial book of Hans Porner of Brunswick, covering the years 1417 to 1426.[3] Porner's family was neither old nor rich and he was elected to the town council in 1398 simply on account of his meticulous efficiency. He was a shop-keeper and then a money-changer, 'a merchant through and through', his editor calls him, a householder who loved order and wanted to owe no one anything, tirelessly calculating and everlastingly wanting a clear overall view of his business. When he wrote his *Gedenkbuch* he was a widower without children who lived with a young male cousin and had a circle of good friends. Like so many of the time he often expressed fear for his salvation and went on two pilgrimages, both to Rome and one continuing on to Jerusalem. He also went on business to Constantinople on one occasion. A town book kept by him is full of details about the town's financial and material affairs, and he began a separate book of all the properties Brunswick had in pledge. But the memorial book was peculiarly his own and contained notes about

---

[1] *CDS*, iv, esp. p. 203 ff.
[2] 'was ain hörtzog von Östenreich, er regiert nit wol' (ibid. p. 237).
[3] *CDS*, vi. pp. 218–81.

his private property even though it refers in passing to certain official matters which had fallen within his own competence. There are notes on the city's past, especially wars and shortages, but it is upheld by a firm and joyous belief that God was good and things were done best in Brunswick.

In Lüneburg, Hinrik Lange wrote a little chronicle in 1455 to 1456 of a more or less autobiographical nature.[1] He was an official in the saltworks, a councillor for many years, and a great worker for town charities and churches. His chronicle was a labour of domestic leisure and a 'reckoning' of his life-work's progress. Like a great German after him, he wrote what he thought had actually happened: '. . . hebbe ik geschreven, alse dat gescheen is', and not what was in men's minds 'which only God knows'.

A last example of the town chronicle as a private venture is the Duisburg narrative of Johann Wassenberch which runs from 1474 to 1517. The autograph, on paper, survived in private ownership in Münster till it was printed for the first time in 1895.[2] Wassenberch was only 20 when he began it. His father was a tin-founder with a workshop near the town-hall and Johann was made a clerk and given an education. He entered the order of Knights Hospitaller in his home town and evidently studied the Cologne chronicle written by a cleric and later printed by Koelhoff. Wassenberch seems to have written his own chronicle simply because he wanted to and not under obedience, but the narrative gained much through his Order's wide geographical connections. The fate of his own town was foremost in his mind, yet at the same time all kinds of document came his way, like *Flugblätter* or like Amerigo Vespucci's letter on his voyages written to his friend Lorenzo di Pierfrancisco de Medici, which Wassenberch noted was too long to copy in. This again reminds us that a place did not have to be very big to hear about distant events, and a small-town writer might have anything but a small-town mind. Like Lange, though, Wassenberch qualified his

---

[1] *CDS*, xxxvi. His editor wrote in 1931 that Lange's factuality and reflectiveness makes his work a pearl of Middle Low German.
[2] *CDS*, xxiv.

careful and exact text with reflections on God's total knowledge, both of men's thoughts and of the significance of events and wonders: 'wat der beteinkenis is ende werden sall [of the comet of 1506] is gade bekant, den gein dinck en is verborgen'.[1]

Naturally, a more important place is occupied by chroniclers who wrote deliberately for public consumption, and here it is inevitable we start from Strassburg. This was the cultural capital of the upper Rhine region with a historiography going back to the tenth century and a wide-ranging influence throughout the medieval period.[2] The first chronicler to write in German was the priest Friedrich Closener, who ended his story in 1362 and used the copious Latin material he found for a German-reading audience. His own family had been episcopal *ministeriales*, and his father was a citizen. Closener himself had a minor prebend in the cathedral and busied himself with a history of the bishops. Ultimately, this turned into a chronicle of the city, much concerned with campaigns, plagues, fires, and local quarrels. What is of more general interest is that, like many of his fellow-citizens, he was favourable to the Wittelsbachs in general and Ludwig of Bavaria in particular, approved of Marsiglio's *Defensor Pacis* and held the idea that the pope should have no wordly power. His chronicle is one of the oldest to be written in German and a first attempt to write the history of a German city as such. Although a cleric, Closener felt himself above all to be a burgher of his city, consciously German and hostile to nobles and Jews. His importance is all the greater because he was encouraged to write for those who could only read German by the great Jakob Twinger or Königshofen, who himself soon proceeded to copy this task.

The famous book by Twinger was called a chronicle 'of emperors, popes and many other things', written in both Latin and German forms, and improved upon until his death in 1420. He wrote explicitly for educated laymen (*die klugen Laien*) who were, he remarked, just as fond of reading about such things as learned priests, and he alludes to the lack of books in German. His own book turned

[1] Ibid. p. 208.
[2] *CDS*, viii.

into a world chronicle, narrowing down to local history and ending with an alphabetical index of historical events with their dates. Although Twinger was a priest like Closener, an archivist, and a curator of various foundations, he was also both a patrician and a popularizer. He treated his materials freely, abbreviating what he thought boring and embroidering even Scripture. He worked tales of the Trojan wars and of Alexander the Great into his narrative and was in fact a good story-teller, read as real history by literate merchants who were doubtless misled by his inaccuracies. To us this matters less than his attitudes to questions of his own time. Like Closener he was more favourable to the emperor than to the pope. He noted faithfully enough the papal view that emperors were mere trustees of their realm, but his own opinion was that Charlemagne was in reality chosen by the Romans and simply crowned by the pope at their behest. The clergy derived their worldly status from emperors and kings—a common enough view by then in both England and France—and Marsiglio of Padua and his patron the Emperor Ludwig had got their ideas right. More than this, Twinger shows a decided German feeling by arguing that Charlemagne and the Franks were German rather than French, so that France had sprung from German stock and not the other way round. What had given the Roman Empire to German kings was their devoutness or *Frumekeit*; '. . . and so the Emperor Charles IV and Wenzel possessed the empire and were kings in Bohemia, and yet they were of German stock . . .'[1]

The impulse to address a German civic audience was also strong in Augsburg, in the work of Hector Mühlich (already referred to more appropriately as a family book) and in that of Burkhard Zink whose chronicle was written between 1450 and 1468.[2] Zink used an existing, anonymous chronicle for the period before his own lifetime, but from 1416 onwards he tells of his own past annalistically

---

[1] *CDS*, viii. p. 422 ('. . . also Keyser Karle der vierde und Wenzelaus sin sun das rich besossen und künige worent zu Behem, und doch worent von dütschem geslehte . . .').
[2] *CDS*, v. and Schmidt, part 2 (1).

though writing, as he chose to explain, as a historian (*Geschicht*). Another Augsburg writer who aimed deliberately at being a historian was Clemens Sender, monk of SS Ulrich and Afra in his native city, the abbey from which so many learned men came. Sender's classical education did not prevent him writing a barbarous Latin, so it was fortunate he decided also to write a German chronicle. It ends in 1536 and was dedicated to Jerome Fugger. He admired that financial family greatly and praised its members exuberantly for their business skills, their charity, and the piety which led them to treasure the old religion. Sender's work was set down as a diary from written and oral sources, strongly anti-Lutheran but without fabrications so that it is a good source for the conflicts of the Reformation in Augsburg.[1]

Lübeck was another first-rank city for whose public a chronicle was written. The Council Chronicle (*Ratschronik*) was continued on from that of Detmar, the Franciscan reading-master, by a succession of town scribes: Johann Hertze, Johann Wunstorp, and Dietrich Brandes who ended his section in 1482.[2] These men were all clerics of some sort and all from an intensely mercantile background. Their political viewpoints seem in odd contrast with those of the Strassburg writers, for the south Germans were noticeably more secular or anyhow anti-papalist than those from the north. The Lübeck writers, especially Hertze, expressed a belief in the pope's unlimited authority and explained that it was the duty of the German princes to protect the faith of the church under this 'supreme judge on earth'. Admittedly, he was full of reproaches for indulgence swindles, but so too was he complete in his condemnation for anyone, even the archbishop of Cologne, who had anything to do with the unspeakable Bohemian heretics. For him the real hope of the world lay not in the Teutonic Knights but in King Vladislav of Poland under the Apostolic See. In other words, the Lübeck town chronicler reflects closely and not unintelligently, even if subconsciously, his city's

---

[1] CDS, xxiii; also *Allgemeine Deutsche Biographie*, vol. 34 (1892). There is a sketch of Sender amongst Fugger familiars by Holbein the Younger.
[2] CDS, xxx, and Schmidt, Section 2 (3).

interests, which were hostile to all kinds of plundering and blood-shed but deeply anxious to achieve a universal Christian world order. Such an order was not consonant with princely cupidity nor with the financial demands of legates but was furthered by the co-operation of the Prussian cities, by the building of fortifications and by good Christian leaders. Hertze, Wundstorp, and Brandes have in these points a single voice, just as they had similar experiences in notarial training acquired in eastern Germany and families who traded in the Baltic region.

Two little Bavarian towns produced chronicles written for the benefit of their burghers and illustrate the same genre in quieter surroundings.[1] The Mühldorf Annals (1313–1428) come from an independent township in a fruitful countryside dominated by a well-to-do nobility. The text gives a strong sense of the intermingling between town and countryside. Town councillors were armigerous. Some citizens came from outside the town boundaries yet owed military service to the town itself and not to any seignorial representative. The device on the town's seal was a mill wheel. The chronicle was written by Nicholas Grill, councillor and affluent merchant, whose seal displayed a grasshopper, or *Grille*. He lived in a house next a barn on the corner of St. Peter's Lane and died there after 56 years of contented marriage. 'There is a legend about the origins of this province . . .', he began his Annals of Old Bavaria, and went on to recount the old tale of Prince Barbarus who came from Armenia after the Flood, adding his own notes on local happenings and the special bravery and patriotism of the men of Mühldorf. A similar placidity is suggested by the Council Chronicle of Landshut, 55 km away, which covers the years 1439 to 1504 and was written in a relatively tranquil time under the three 'rich' dukes of Lower Bavaria. It is fundamentally a Council register carried on year by year by the town scribe, Paul Murnauer (d. 1464), and then his son Alexander (d. 1488). The final portion was written by Hans Vetter, an immigrant official from the Upper Palatinate who married Magdalena, daughter of the mayor of Landshut.

[1] *CDS*, xv.

These are sleepy, provincial matters. In the seventh and final category of town chronicler must be placed the men who are known to have received overt commissions to write a town history, and the three best examples of these are drawn from widely different areas of the German-speaking territories: Magdeburg, Bern, and Nuremberg.

About 1350 the town scribe of Magdeburg addressed his masters, the city's elders (*Schöffen*), with the words he placed at the opening of his chronicle: 'To love and honour God and my good lords the *Schöffen* of the town of Magdeburg I have read over many chronicles and thereafter in accordance with the will of these lords have made this book . . .'[1] Although he brings himself freely into his chronicle, it is only by archival evidence and not by any announcement in the chronicle that we know his name, which was Hinrik van Lammespringe. He had had some difficulty in getting his post as town clerk, which went with the chantry altar of Holy Cross in St. Peter's, but good fortune has preserved for historians the personality and work of a man who affords so vivid a glimpse of fourteenth-century political life. Until 1372, when he died, one of van Lammespringe's tasks was to represent the town in a dispute with Duke Rudolf II of Saxony. It was part of the continuing conflict between late fourteenth-century German towns and the German princes who resented their political self-consciousness. Van Lammespringe went on one mission in 1359 before the Emperor Charles IV in Mainz. A citizen of Magdeburg who was with them spoke and the emperor said he could not understand, so van Lammespringe took up the speech in Latin, and the emperor answered in the same tongue. After a few moments the emperor switched to German and ordered van Lammespringe and his colleague also to talk in German which he said he well understood. From this incident it seems to follow that Charles IV did not regard Low German as German at all. The duke of Saxony who was standing by tried to persuade the emperor not to give judgment for the city, and Charles answered that what the princes advised him in

---

[1] *CDS*, vii, p. xii n. 1.

his court was more important than any law, by which he appears to have meant the Saxon law, given to Magdeburg. In van Lammespringe's words, 'then spoke the emperor and said he could hold to no law but what the princes found in his court, and that should abide...'[1] On another embassy for Magdeburg to the emperor at Prague, van Lammespringe showed himself a courageous and imperturbable defender of his city's interests. This time it was a question of who should be burgrave, and again it showed the difficulty of getting royal protection when some local prince was against a city. Another dispute still was with the archbishop and cathedral clergy over a building on some land which the town claimed as its own. After van Lammespringe's day the *Schöppenchronik* (as it later became known) was continued by other town scribes or officials, all of whom were learned and business-like men. The section from 1411 to 1421 was probably by Engelbrecht Wusterwitz who originated in Brandenburg. This man was sent as Magdeburg's envoy to the royal court in Regensburg and on a round trip to Hungary, Silesia, and Bohemia. Later he returned as a clerk to Brandenburg where he wrote something of that province's history.

The Swiss chroniclers present a much more complex network of interrelationships but they exemplify both singly and collectively the pride taken in their towns, particularly Bern, Zürich, and Lucerne, by the city councils and the wish to perpetuate their fame in commissioned chronicles. In 1420 the council and burghers of Bern decided to have a chronicle of the city from the beginnings up till their own time. This was just after it had conquered the Aargau. As its writer the former town scribe, Konrad Justinger, was chosen.[2] He had learned about both administration and historiography from

---

[1] For these stories, ibid. p. xv ff. and 228: '... des sprak de keiser he kerde sik an nein recht, wenn wat sine vorsten in seinem hove vunden, dat scholde bliven...'

[2] Bodmer, ch. 2. Schilling later portrayed Justinger receiving his commission, and the picture of the writer sitting at his desk and receiving the city councillors is in Bern's Burgerbibliothek, MS h.h.I.16, 41.

Twinger in Strassburg, and in 1415 or thereabouts had on his own account written a chronicle of Bern, perhaps as a continuation of Twinger's work. His new and official chronicle began at the time of Barbarossa and gave the origins of Bern in historical not legendary form by referring to the Zähringer foundation. Justinger uses the first person singular and explains he is writing a memorial to supply what human memory cannot, not from 'old books and chronicles' but from archives in the town's chests and the instruction of old and trustworthy people. He believed men could learn from history about the providential hand of God and about how to avoid foolish behaviour. He remarked, for instance, that the battle of Nicopolis (1396) had been lost to the Turks because the French knights had disregarded Sigismund's advice to avoid preliminary skirmishing.

Later on, when Bern had become practically a state in itself and the Swiss were a byword in Europe for their military resistance to Charles the Bold, the city council under its chairman Adrian von Bubenberg again ordered a town chronicle 'from the beginning to the present day' and gave the task to Diebold Schilling. This man (encountered at the beginning of the present paper) had worked in the Lauber *atelier* in Hagenau, Alsace, at the craft of writing and illustrating books. By 1460 he was a town official in Bern. The story of his chronicle is a complex and obscure one which cannot be followed here. At all events, this official town chronicle was ready by Christmas 1483, in three volumes in Schilling's hand, 'illustrated by me with 600 costly figures'. It was written partly on the basis of Justinger's work together with much reporting of events in which Schilling himself had taken part, but the text was heavily censored by the town authorities who required him to play up the arrogance of the Burgundian enemy and the patriotism of the Swiss. The French connection was to be minimized. Schilling was somewhat scandalized over the Swiss scramble for Burgundian booty, but the censor allowed his remarks on this matter to go through as no individuals were named, and the writer was thus able to carry out one of his moralistic aims in showing the shady side of victories when the winners are corrupted indiscriminately with looted wealth. For all that, Schilling wrote as a Swiss patriot and not as just a Bernese one. In 1487, the year after Schilling's death, another writer (Fricker) was given the task of editing Schilling's description of the battle of Murten for formal reading to the council and the community each year on the anniversary, as though it were a sort of secular gospel.

If the Swiss examples of chronicles written on commission are the most copious, proudly patriotic and solemn, the most elaborate is the Nuremberg chronicle of Sigmund Meisterlin.[1] He was like Clemens Sender a Benedictine monk of SS Ulrich and Afra in Augsburg, where he had been trained up since the age of 15 under a succession of learned abbots. In Augsburg he used the excellent cathedral library and often encountered savants from Italy. In 1456 he wrote a Latin chronicle for Augsburg and turned it into German at the instance of a leading citizen 'for the common use' ('zu ainem gemainem nutz').[2] Then Meisterlin left his abbey and appears in 1476 as preacher in Würzburg cathedral, and in 1481 as a parish priest in the same diocese. In 1488 he got paid for writing a chronicle of Nuremberg and gave the receipt under his private seal ('under meinem secret'). In order to fulfil the contract he had been given by Nuremberg council he had travelled widely in Bavaria, Franconia, and Swabia, looking in monasteries for materials. He had also been in the Tyrol, the Rhineland, Alsace, and France. Much of his travelling was paid for by Nuremberg where he was well known to leading citizens and notable people like the world chronicler Hartman Schedel. In the work itself Meisterlin shows certain affinities with Twinger of Strassburg. He wrote spaciously about the old days, compressing as he approaches his own time. He too revered the Roman past and saw in classical antiquity the true foundation of German cities. At the same time he wrote for the laity a *Volksbuch*, in which instruction and entertainment should mingle, piety with local lore, allusions for the learned with coats of arms for the proud-of-family, and explanations of tribal and urban origins to

[1] *CDS*, iii.
[2] *CDS*, iv.

[468]

gratify a new public curious about its past but not literate in any humanistic sense. Interestingly too, Meisterlin displayed a distinct German patriotism, in his case in relation to Bohemia, just as Twinger and Closener were showing themselves sensibly German in relation to both France and papacy. Meisterlin's phrases[1] are not very acute or startling but they betray a mood that was to be long in vanishing:

Bohemia is a land which belongs to *Germania*, that is, to the German nation [zu teutscher nation]: on its east is Moravia and Silesia, to the north Saxony, on the west the Voigtland, Nordgau and Bavaria, and to the south again the Bavarians who live by the Danube, and Austria. And so that kingdom is surrounded by Germans; [but] the people of that [Bohemian] land are great drinkers and eaters and are always in need of something new ... unstable and thievish, and they say they came in ancient times from among the Slavs ...

This is thin stuff when so much might have been made, either in amazement or as awful warning, of recollections of Hus and Tabor, Zizka, Prokop, and the rest. But then Meisterlin for all his mercenary industry does not come through as a very intelligent chronicler. His self-conceit is lightened for the observer only because it is ludicrous. Nuremberg which paid him was full of people against whom he complained. He did not like criticisms and he did not like paying his taxes: the voice almost breaks as he refers to his classical books sold to pay what he owed. Yet he admits he had been paid a considerable sum, 'because he was a very skilled historian'. This made him valuable, and he proclaimed that he had a duty in writing this 'great work which has cost me time and trouble enough ... Would that I had worked for my soul's salvation as industriously as for this chronicle'.[2] In a letter to Schedel he explained: 'I know I have put in some matters which will not please everyone, but this kind of thing is necessary in histories, nor ever is it done otherwise ... *habet enim historiographus et leges suas.*'

---

[1] *CDS*, iii, Bk. 3, ch. 26.
[2] *CDS*, iii. pp. 11, 311.

Greek historians on the Turks: the case of the first Byzantine-Ottoman marriage

ANTHONY BRYER

SIR RICHARD SOUTHERN divided Western medieval scholarly views of Islam into an 'Age of Ignorance', the twelfth century of 'Reason and Hope', and a cold-blooded 'Moment of Vision' in the decade 1450–60.[1] The same sequence can be discerned among Byzantine intellectuals too, but their vision was enlarged by experience of Westerners (whose behaviour they could not help comparing with that of Muslims),[2] and limited by the fact that they had to live not so much with Islam, as with Muslims. Symbiosis did not necessarily make Byzantines more aware of the nature of Islam than were Westerners. Indeed it deprived them of the focus of distance. Some later Byzantines, faced with the facts of Turkish conquest and Western superiority, did not evade the question of why their God-protected Empire was in palpable decline.[3] But none of the four Westerners who shared Sir Richard's 'Moment of Vision' in 1450–60 were faced with the realities of the problem that the anti-Unionist Patriarch Gennadios Scholarios was left to explain to his faithful after 1453. In fact he did not waste much time in speculating on the

---

[1] R. W. Southern, *Western Views of Islam in the Middle Ages* (Cambridge, Mass., 1962).

[2] The contrast between the Norman rampage in Thessalonike in 1185 and Saladin's relatively well-ordered conquest of Jerusalem two years later did not escape Niketas Choniates, *Historia*, ed. van Dieten (Berlin, 1975), pp. 297–306, 575–7. See also S. Vryonis Jr, 'Byzantine attitudes towards Islam during the late Middle Ages', *Greek Roman and Byzantine Studies*, 12 (1971), pp. 263–86.

[3] I. Ševčenko, 'The Decline of Byzantium seen through the eyes of its intellectuals', *DOP*, 15 (1961), pp. 167–86.

waywardness of Fortune, and few, if any, Byzantines had enjoyed the luxury of formal debate with Islam since before 1430.[1] For Gennadios, the question of marriage was more pressing, and the application of the principle of 'Economy' to relax canon law to protect what he could of Byzantine family structure which the Turk had long broken and assimilated in Anatolia, but which the Ottoman conquest of Constantinople came by Fortune just in time to attempt to salvage in the Balkans.[2]

So Byzantines' very intimacy with Muslims, especially Turks, translates Sir Richard's three stages into, first, a honeymoon; second a marriage; and third, not divorce, but the almost simultaneous realization that there had been no marriage at all. These stages overlapped, all three in 1346.

The first stage belongs to the heroic age of Byzantine-Muslim courtship celebrated in epic poetry which stretched into the fifteenth century. The Armenian David of Sassoun and the Byzantine Digenis were both 'twyborn' heroes, effective brothers of their Muslim antagonists. In the ballads and romances of the *ghazi* Sayyid Battal, the *Melikdanishmendnâme* and Dede Korkut, Orthodox and Muslims fight and inter-marry like clean-limbed heroes, who are not the sort of people who are much bothered by religious or cultural obstacles. The Türkmen Danishmendids were not above tacking an Armenian genealogy on to their own (a useful claim to rule in that dynastically minded land), while their own epic boasts of alliance with the Byzantine Gabras family.[3] In Sir Richard's 'Century of Reason and

---

[1] See Manuel II Paléologue, *Entretiens avec un Musulman*, ed. T. Khoury (Paris, 1966); and J. D. G. Waardenburg, 'The two lights perceived: Medieval Islam and Christianity', *Nederlands Theologisch Tijdschrift*, 31 (1978), p. 276.

[2] Ch. G. Patrineles, *Ho Theodoros Agallianos tautizomenos pros ton Theophanen medeias kai hoi anekdotoi Logoi tou* (Athens, 1966), 68–71; S. Vryonis Jr, 'The conditions and cultural significance of the Ottoman conquest in the Balkans', *IIe Congrès international des études du sud-est européen* (Athens, 1970), pp. 1–10; and the same's 'Religious change and continuity in the Balkans and Anatolia from the fourteenth through the sixteenth century', in *Islam and cultural change in the Middle Ages* (Wiesbaden, 1975), pp. 127–40.

[3] Irène Mélikoff, *La geste de Melik Danismend*, i (Paris, 1960), *passim*; P. Wittek, *The rise of the Ottoman Empire* (London, 1963), p. 20. Among growing

Hope' when in Anatolia some marriages pass from epic and romance into reality, there at first seemed no good reason why it should not be hoped that both Seljuks and Türkmens should be baptised into the Empire, as had the Slavs in the past. Of nine known members of the Gabras family in that century, between 1098 and 1192, one was canonized, four (including the saint) served the Byzantines as dukes and generals, three served both Byzantines and Seljuks in the same capacities, and two served the Seljuks only (the last, perhaps inheritor of St. Theodore Gabras's estates, as a *vizir*).[1] A Gabras was naturally involved when in the 1140s the daughter of the Seljuk *Sultan* Masud married the Byzantine John Komnenos to become (according to a later Byzantine memorialist) grandparents of Osman and great-grandparents of Orhan, the first Ottoman ruler to marry a Byzantine princess.[2]

It is this marriage, between the *ghazi emir* Orhan and Theodora Kantakouzene in 1346, which I want to examine in the chronicles. It symbolizes a turning-point in Byzantine-Turkish relations and illuminates all other imperial alliances. It tells less of the fate of countless lesser Christian, Muslim, and *mixobarbarian* Anatolians when they found that it was too late to speculate on whether Islam was St. John of Damascus's 101st heresy, or even the authenticity of the Gospel of Barnabas, for they were now wedlocked.[3]

---

literature on Dede Korkut, the most recent English translation is *The book of Dede Korkut*, trans. F. Sümer, A. E. Uysal, and W. S. Walker (Austin and London, 1972); and the most recent study is Kh. Korogly, *Oguzskiy geoicheskiy epos* (Moscow, 1976).

[1] A. Bryer, 'A Byzantine family: the Gabrades, *c.* 979–*c.* 1653', *University of Birmingham Historical Journal*, 12 (1970), pp. 175–81; C. Cahen, *Pre-Ottoman Turkey* (London, 1968), p. 210.

[2] G. Sphrantzes, *Memorii 1401–77*, ed. V. Grecu (Bucharest, 1966), pp. 208–12; Wittek, *Rise*, p. 9; Bryer, *UBHJ*, 12 (1970), p. 177.

[3] Nikephoros Gregoras, *Byzantina Historia*, ed. L. Schopen, III (Bonn, 1855), p. 509 (on the *mixobarbarians* of Bithynia) and 555 (on Constantinopolitans with Latin heads and 'Persian'—i.e. Turkish—bodies); Doukas, *Istoria Turco-Bizantina 1341–1462*, ed. V. Grecu (Bucarest, 1958), p. 61 (on *mixobarbarians* of Constantinople); S. Vryonis Jr, *The decline of medieval Hellenism in Asia Minor and the process of Islamization from the eleventh through the fifteenth century* (Berkeley, Los Angeles, and London, 1971), pp. 176, 182, 228–9, 440, 446;

The background is the contest between the Byzantine usurper and former regent, John VI Kantakouzenos (1341–55), in Thrace, and the legitimate Emperor John V Palaiologos (1341–91) and his mother, Anna of Savoy, who, with their chief minister Alexios Apokaukos, were holed up in Constantinople. All Byzantine rulers were competing for the support of a nest of four west Anatolian emirates which had emerged on the marches of the old Seljuk state now that the Mongol *Ilhans* of Iran had lost control of it. The two leading emirates were of Ottoman Bithynia (which had the advantage of being nearest Constantinople) under the *ghazi emir* Orhan (1324–62), and of Aydin (which had the advantage of controlling the port of Smyrna) under the *ghazi emir* Umur (1334–48). Kantakouzenos, and Palaiologos and his mother, were seeking Turkish support as much against each other as against the Serbian ruler Stefan IV Dushan (1331–55).

The evidence

Kantakouzenos wrote his great *apologia* for his rule before about 1369, when he was the monk Joasaph. In it he states that he betrothed one daughter to the Despot Nikephoros II of Epiros in 1342, when he noted that he had two others. He first met Umur of Aydin in 1335, the year after the *emir* had taken Smyrna and had embarked on a piratical career in the Aegean. Umur came over to Thrace to assist Kantakouzenos in 1342, 1343, and 1344; they were comrades in arms.[1]

Enveri composed his *Düsturnâme* in about 1465. It is of substantial historical value, although he was not shy of interpolating his own

---

H. I. Cotsonis, 'Aus der Endzeit von Byzanz: Burkludsche Mustafa, ein Martyrer für koexistenz zwischen Islam and Christentum', *Byz. Zeits.*, 50 (1957), pp. 397–404; P. Charanis, 'Internal strife in Byzantium during the fourteenth century', *Byzantion*, 15 (1941), 230 (on religious syncretism); John of Damascus, *PG* 94, cols 764–73. A *ghazi* is a dedicated warrior for Islam.

[1] John Kantakouzenos, *Historiarum libri IV*, ed. L. Schopen, i (Bonn, 1828), pp. 476–95; ii (Bonn, 1831), pp. 195, 336–48, 390–403, 529–34; D. M. Nicol, *The Byzantine family of Kantakouzenos (Cantacuzenus) ca. 1100–1460* (Washington, D.C., 1968), pp. 42, 45, 53, 55, 59, 60, 66, 100.

experiences into his poetic account.[1] Book 18 comprises the *gesta* of Umur, a very perfect *ghazi*. Lemerle dates an encounter between Umur and one of Kantakouzenos's daughters in Didymoteichos (between Selymbria and Adrianople) to 1344, his last campaign with him.[2] Enveri versifies what seems to be two versions of the same incident. In the first the *tekfur* Kantakouzenos feasts Umur in his palace. The *tekfur*'s three daughters are displayed: they are as beautiful as *huris*. One, simply entitled the *Despoina*,[3] is even more beautiful than the others. But Umur, *shah* of the *ghazis*, would not look upon them. The *tekfur* says: 'O Lord of the World, I am your poor slave,

---

[1] *Le destān d'Umŭr pacha*, ed. and trans. Irène Mélikoff-Sayar (Paris, 1954), to be read in conjunction with the commentary by P. Lemerle, *L'Émirat d'Aydin, Byzance et l'Occident* (Paris, 1957). As Lemerle, *Aydin*, pp. 139–41, points out, Enveri's account of Umur's improbable raid on Kilia in the Black Sea, supposedly of 1341, in *Destān,,* ll. 1209–1306, appears to be based on Enveri's experience of following Mehmed II on his attack on Kilia in 1462, when it was in the hands of the *voivode* Vlad III Dracul (1456–76), called the Impaler. But Lemerle's explanation that Enveri's story, of how the Turks terrified local prisoners by pretending to be cannibals, might be a reference to Vlad's infamy is unconvincing: Vlad impaled his victims; he is known to have roasted only one and never to have eaten them; see N. Stoicescu, *Vlad Tepes* (Bucarest, 1978), pp. 68–95; Doukas, ed. Grecu, 431. On the other hand, S. Vryonis Jr, 'Evidence on human sacrifice among the early Ottoman Turks', *Journal of Asian History*, 5 (1971), pp. 140–6, offers evidence of the survival of (among others) the custom of offering human sacrifice for the distinguished dead among Turks until the fifteenth century, when there seems to be a case of cannibalism in Anatolia under the *ilhans* in 1277; see A. Bryer, 'The fate of George Komnenos, ruler of Trebizond (1266–1280)', *Byz Zeits.* 66 (1973), p. 346 n. 68 (where for 'beaten' read 'eaten'). According to George Pachymeres, *De Michaele et Andronico Palaeologis*, ed. I. Bekker, i (Bonn, 1835), p. 134, Anatolian Greeks believed that nomads practised cannibalism and in the context of their other cultural survivals, the fear that the Turks also practised cannibalism may have been real enough, if actually unfounded, in 1341 or 1462, among the inhabitants of Kilia. I am most grateful to Mr M. E. Martin for discussion.

[2] Lemerle, *Aydin*, pp. 175–9.

[3] A *tekfur* is usually a Christian, and so subordinate, ruler. *Despoina* is usually a title, 'lady', the equivalent of *hatun*, rather than a personal name. Princesses of Trebizond who married Türkmens took the composite title of *despoina-hat* (*un*).

you are my *han*. My goods, myself, my son, my daughter: everything I have is yours. Take one of my three daughters.' Umur blushes and retreats to his tent, where an evil voice urges him to take the girl. He replies: 'Is he right to give a daughter to his brother? The *tekfur* is my brother; his daughter is my daughter. In our faith that cannot be done.'[1]

Enveri then describes a second encounter (or version), heading it 'The purity of the *pasha*'. The lovely *Despoina* goes on a secret hunt 'in the forest of faith'. Clothed in robes encrusted with pearls, rubies, and other jewels, she unveils herself before Umur, protesting her love for him and begs the *ghazi* to take her. Umur asks her name. The *Despoina* asks him to accept her first. Umur refuses; such an alliance is *haram* in his faith. The *Despoina* pleads. The *emir* sends her away. Glancing back through her tears she sees Umur covering his eyes: a *ghazi*'s duty, day and night, is to wage holy war and resist worldly desires.[2]

On 28 October of that year, 1344, Umur lost Smyrna to the Latins who kept it until Timur's invasion of 1402. His emirate was now largely landlocked and he was of no further strategic use either to Kantakouzenos, or to Anna of Savoy who was already negotiating with the Ottoman *emir* Orhan, who thus became the most useful (or dangerous) Byzantine neighbour, for he was now the *emir* with most room for manoeuvre. So early in 1345 Kantakouzenos was in the process of changing sides from Umur to Orhan. He subsequently defended himself at painful length against the charge of having invited the Ottomans into Europe.[3] It is quite true that he was not the first to introduce the Turks, but Kantakouzenos's decisions of 1345–6 did much to decide which Turks would eventually take Constantinople. His decisions were the more painful because while Orhan was a relatively unknown quantity, it is evident that Kantakouzenos and Umur had been warm friends. Writing before 1360, Nikephoros Gregoras emphasized

---

[1] *Destān*, ll. 1739–74.
[2] *Destān*, ll. 1775–1820. *Haram* (opposite to *halal*) is that which is forbidden.
[3] Kantakouzenos, ii. pp. 502–24.

how close the emperor had been to the *emir*, a barbarian who had behaved almost like a Hellene. The two were like Orestes and Pylades, and Kantakouzenos grieved when the Latins killed Umur in 1348. But Gregoras also makes clear the lively and vehement passion which Orhan had developed for Theodora (whom he calls Maria) Kantakouzene, a tradition developed by Doukas, a century later.[1]

Doukas was what would later be described as a 'Levantine'. He was the sort of Greek whom Latins chose to represent their interests at the Ottoman court. He was a Uniate by confession, but his rhetorical lament on the Fall of Constantinople reveals him to have been deeply Byzantine by instinct. His chronicle breaks off in mid-sentence as he witnessed the Ottoman conquest of Genoese Lesbos in 1462. His grandfather, Michael Doukas, had been among two hundred opponents of Alexios Apokaukos, Anna of Savoy's minister and former protégé of Kantakouzenos, who had been rounded up in Constantinople in summer 1345. The captives assassinated their captor when he came to inspect their prison, but only six, including Michael, escaped execution. It is significant that Michael Doukas did not join Kantakouzenos thereafter. He had had enough, and the emirate of Aydin offered a kind of solution. Here Umur's brother Isa

installed him in Ephesus. Doukas adopted his foreign residence for his homeland, and esteemed and honoured the foreigner and barbarian as one crowned by God, recalling to mind the wicked deeds of the Romans. My grandfather foresaw that shortly all the lands from Thrace to the Danube would fall into the hands of the Turks who would soon become absolute masters just as it happened not long before in Phrygia and Asia and in the provinces beyond.[2]

Doukas maintained that it was Kantakouzenos who unexpectedly

---

[1] Gregoras, ii (Bonn, 1830), pp. 648–9, 762–3, 835; Doukas, ed. Grecu, pp. 58–61. Laonikos Chalkokondyles, *Historiarum libri decem*, ed. I. Bekker (Bonn, 1843), p. 24, is neutral.

[2] Doukas, ed. Grecu, 47; trans. H. J. Magoulias, *Decline and fall of Byzantium to the Ottoman Turks by Doukas* (Detroit, 1975), p. 65; D. I. Polemis, *The Doukai. A contribution to Byzantine prosopography* (London, 1968), p. 196.

made Orhan the offer of a marriage contract for Theodora, with lavish dowry, in January 1346. Understandably enough Kantakouzenos's story is that it was Orhan who first sent an embassy to ask for his daughter's hand. But Kantakouzenos goes on to say that before he agreed to Orhan's proposal he sent a legation to Umur (a *symmachos* whose moderation and loyalty he respected) to ask for his approval, and by implication permission, for the marriage.[1] This should have been in late 1345 or early 1346, depending upon whether one accepts Doukas's or Kantakouzenos's version of who made the first move. But Kantakouzenos's story makes it highly probable that it was the *Despoina* Theodora who was the princess whom Enveri made Umur meet in 1344.

On 16 April 1346 Stefan IV Dushan had himself crowned emperor at Skoplje. On 21 May 1346 Kantakouzenos had himself crowned emperor at Adrianople (Edirne). The coronations are surely linked, but their sequence would be more complicated if there were any grounds to justify Alderson's statement that Dushan had married his daughter (supposedly another Theodora) to Orhan in 1345.[2]

During these events, Kantakouzenos records that he invited Orhan to send a numerous army to escort his bride from Selymbria (Silivri). Orhan sent thirty ships, cavalry, and the most eminent of his followers there in early summer (Doukas's date). Kantakouzenos then describes how he, his empress Eirene, and their three daughters (Maria, Theodora, and Helena) proceeded with his army to Selymbria. The empress and her daughters spent the night in the imperial tent; Kantakouzenos with the army. On the next day the empress, Maria, and Helena remained in the tent. Kantakouzenos was the only person on horseback; apparently even Orhan's cavalry was dismounted. Kantakouzenos had ordered a *prokypsis* platform to be built of wood outside the town. Theodora mounted the *prokypsis*. It was surrounded by silk and cloth-of-gold curtains. They were

---

[1] Kantakouzenos, ii. p. 586.

[2] A. D. Alderson, *The structure of the Ottoman dynasty* (Oxford, 1956), p. 165, table xxii; M. A. Purković, 'Byzantinoserbica', *Byz. Zeits.* 45 (1952), pp. 47–9. I am grateful to Mrs Zaga Gavrilović for this reference.

drawn to disclose the bride encircled by lights carried by kneeling eunuchs. Trumpets, flutes, and all manner of musical instruments were sounded. When they fell silent, encoomia were recited in honour of the bride. Then Kantakouzenos held a feast for Greeks and Turks which lasted for several days.[1]

The Turkish wedding guests at Selymbria apparently took their time to disperse; they were being a nuisance to all parties in Thrace in late summer. But it was Kantakouzenos who now won the race to Constantinople, which he entered on 2 February 1347, for his second coronation on 21 May. On 28 May 1347 he married his third daughter, Helena, to John V Palaiologos; their own daughter was to marry Orhan's son, Murad I, in 1389.[2]

An unusual feature of Theodora's marriage was that it took place on Byzantine, not Turkish, territory: hence there was no call for *nymphopostoloi*, bridal escorts.[3] But the price Kantakouzenos paid for the alliance seems to have been the absence of the bridegroom himself. If this is so, Doukas should be preferred to Kantakouzenos as to who made the first move over the marriage. Kantakouzenos had been helped by Orhan in 1345 and would surely have mentioned his presence at his own wedding in 1346. As it was, the first (and perhaps only) time he seems to have met his son-in-law was when Orhan came to Turkish Skutari (Üsküdar, Chrysopolis), opposite Constantinople, in the summer of 1347. Kantakouzenos describes how he came over to see Orhan for a few days. He and the *emir* ate together, while Orhan's four sons ate at a nearby table. They were not Theodora's children (she probably mothered Halil), but Ibrahim (b. 1310), Sülayman (b. 1316), Murad I (b. 1326?), and Sultan (b. 1324). Even then Orhan would not leave Turkish territory, but Kantakouzenos, Theodora, and the four Ottoman princes

---

[1] Kantakouzenos, ii. pp. 586–8. Orhan was then about 60. He seems to have married another Christian, Asporcha, at about the same time; Alderson, *Structure*, loc. cit.

[2] Kantakouzenos, ii. 591–6; Nicol, *Kantakouzenos*, pp. 62–5, 135–58; Alderson, *Structure*, p. 166, table xxiii.

[3] Michael Panaretos, *Peri ton Megalon Komnenon*, ed. O. Lampsides (Athens, 1958), p. 72.

crossed to Byzantium for further festivities, where Theodora stayed with her mother and sisters for three days before returning to Bithynia.[1]

Theodora Kantakouzene was widowed in 1362, when she may have returned to Constantinople to recount her affairs to her father before 1369; at any rate Kantakouzenos, his empress Eirene, and their three daughters are last found reunited as hostages of Andronikos IV in Galata in 1378–81.[2] Kantakouzenos concluded his account of the marriage of 1346 with a description of the dangers Theodora faced among the barbarians of Bithynia in defence of her Orthodoxy in 1346–62. She not only resisted religious conversion, but managed to persuade many Christian converts to Islam to return to their faith, assisted the poor, gave gold to ransom slaves from the barbarians, and was a haven of salvation to those *Romaioi* who, by God's will, suffered. According to her father, her life among the barbarians had been a shining example of virtue to all.[3]

The context

Among late medieval dynasties, the Byzantine were pivotal: they eventually linked the ruling families of Western Europe with the *kiriltays* of Central Asia and understood (or compromised with) both series of systems. They also brought their new Turkish and Türkmen neighbours into the network. By their alliances from 1352 with local Türkmen chiefs the Grand Komnenoi of Trebizond had a hand in creating territorial principalities out of wandering clans.[4] By his alliance with Orhan in 1346 Kantakouzenos paved the way to the supplanting of one extended ruling family, the Palaiologos-Kantakouzenos, by another, the Ottoman, in 1453, by when

---

[1] Kantakouzenos, iii. 28; T. S. Miller, 'The history of John Cantacuzenus (Book IV): text, translation, and commentary' (The Catholic University of America, unpublished Ph.D. thesis, 1975), pp. 165, 267–8.

[2] Nicol, *Kantakouzenos*, p. 135.

[3] Kantakouzenos, ii. pp. 588–9.

[4] A. Bryer, 'Greeks and Türkmens: the Pontic exception', *DOP*, 29 (1975), pp. 130–2.

Mehmed II had a rather better hereditary claim to the Byzantine throne than had Kantakouzenos in 1347.

Between 1297 and 1461, thirty-four or more Byzantine, Trapezuntine, and Serbian princesses married (in order) Mongol *hans* and *ilhans*, Turkish *emirs*, and Türkmen *begs*. During this period no Orthodox is known to have married a Muslim princess.[1] In Kantakouzenos's youth, when the most important alliances were still Mongol, there was what amounted to an imperial finishing school for such brides:

Realising that they could not defeat the barbarians in battle, the emperors of the *Romaioi* escaped destruction by conciliating them with gifts and courtesies. They were made particularly tractable and friendly towards the *Romaioi* by being given brides from among the ladies of the imperial family. . . . So, maidens of exceptional beauty, not only of the aristocracy but also of lowly origin, were brought up in the imperial palace like the princesses and, as the need arose, were betrothed to the *satraps* of the Mongols.[2]

Kantakouzenos's initiative in marrying Theodora to a Turk in 1346 was surely in the mind of Alexios III Grand Komnenos of Trebizond when he took the plunge and married the first Byzantine princess to a Türkmen in 1352, beginning eleven such alliances. As Chalkokondyles remarked, the Trapezuntines preserved their Hellenic speech and customs, but intermarried with neighbouring barbarians, 'so as not to have trouble owing to the ravaging of their land by the latter'.[3]

---

[1] Marriages listed in G. E. Rakintzakis, 'Orthodox-Muslim mixed marriages, ca. 1297–1453' (University of Birmingham, unpublished MA thesis, 1975). The list of Byzantine marriages in M. Izeddin, 'Notes sur les mariages princiers en Orient au moyen âge', *Journal asiatique*, 257 (1969), pp. 139–56, is less reliable.

[2] Kantakouzenos, i. p. 188.

[3] Chalkokondyles, 461–2; Bryer, *DOP*, 29 (1975), pp. 135, 149 Appendix ii. Cf. the supposed reply of Prince Nicholas I of Montenegro (1860–1918) to a criticism of the meagreness of that country's exports: 'What about my daughters?' W. Miller, *Trebizond, the last Greek empire* (London, 1926), p. 69; H. de Windt, *Through savage Europe* (London, n.d.), pp. 49–50. Defending the Kantakouzene marriage of 1346, D. M. Nicol, *The last centuries of Byzantium*,

The ceremony
Apart from Theodora's betrothal and marriage contract, the only element of her marriage ceremony recognizable from late Byzantine imperial wedding ritual is the *prokypsis*, a sort of illuminated imperial *tableau vivant*, of which Kantakouzenos's description of the sensational performance of 1346 is our best account. The late Byzantine antiquarian spirit encouraged the revival or elaboration of at least three features of imperial ceremony from the twelfth or thirteenth centuries: the raising of the emperor on a shield, his anointing, and his *prokypsis*.[1] *Prokypsis* is in fact, though probably not etymologically, derived from the epiphany of the imperial family in the imperial box, or *kathisma*, of the hippodrome. It was

1261–1453 (London, 1972), p. 210, notes that 'things in Constantinople could still compare favourably with the standards in Trebizond, where the Emperor Alexios II, who died in 1330, had married no less than three infidel wives, and where the Emperor Basil who succeeded him gave two of his daughters as brides to local emirs.' It should be made clear that the sequence of marriages of Trapezuntine princesses to local *begs* (not *emirs*) began six years *after* the Kantakouzenos alliance (and twelve years after the death of the Grand Komnenos Basil in 1340). Furthermore, Alexios II's wife was the daughter of an Orthodox Georgian, Beka Jaqeli. The honorific epithets applied to his children by other alliances (*Ana-Kutlu, Aza-Kutlu,* and *Ak-Bogha*) are certainly Turkic or Mongol, but that is no evidence that their mothers (probably concubines) were Muslim, for Orthodox Georgian princesses (and even one Palaiologine) assumed Turkish epithets, such as *Gülhan* (Eudokia), wife of the Grand Komnenos Manuel III. The only Grand Komnenos known to have taken a Turkish wife (or probably concubine, for he was also married to a Georgian) was John IV, who, rather unconvincingly, explained that he had done so in the interests of piecemeal proselytization. See Panaretos, ed. Lampsides, pp. 63, 64, 66, 67, 70, 78, 81; Pero Tafur, *Travels and adventures, 1435–1439*, trans. M. Letts (London, 1926), p. 131; J. Sauvaget, 'Noms et surnoms de Mamelouks', *Journal asiatique*, 238 (1950), p. 37; Gy. Moravesik, *Byzantinoturcica*, ii (Berlin, 1958), pp. 57, 69, 92.

[1] D. M. Nicol, '*Kaisersalbung*, The Unction of emperors in late Byzantine coronation ritual', *Byzantine and Modern Greek Studies*, 2 (1976), pp. 37–52; C. Walter, 'The significance of Unction in Byzantine iconography', ibid. pp. 53–74; and the same's 'Raising on a shield in Byzantine iconography', *Revue des études byzantines*, 33 (1975), pp. 315–56. Dr Michael Jeffrey, of the University of Sydney, is to publish a convincing demonstration that the *prokypsis* ceremony can be traced back to the marriage of Theodora, neice of Manuel I Komnenos, with duke Henry II of Austria in 1148.

performed on state and religious feasts, such as weddings. By the thirteenth century the term meant not only the display itself, but the platform on which it was held. In Constantinople and Nicaea it was staged near, or in the gallery of, a church. In Trebizond a gallery seems to have been specially built for it in the coronation church of the Chrysokephalos after 1223, but the *prokypsis* may also have been held in the *Epiphaneia* court of the palace and in the main square, the *meidan*.[1] Spatharakis has recently demonstrated that the scene in Cod. Vat. Gr. 1851, fo. 7v, long regarded as an illustration of an actual *prokypsis*, cannot be so identified.[2] But the convention of late Byzantine portrait groups which he studied is surely the pictorial equivalent of *prokypsis*.[3] Such illustrations and actual displays of *prokypsis* served to demonstrate the exact status of each member of a swiftly changing hierarchy of collegiate sovereignty as definitively as any Politburo grouping at a May Day parade: emperors, co-emperors, empresses, princesses, and despots were carefully disposed according to rank. For marriages the *prokypsis*

---

[1] See the lemma to the Planudean Anthology, XVI, 380 in W. R. Paton, *The Greek Anthology*, v (London, 1970), p. 385; A. Cameron, *Porphyrius the charioteer* (Oxford, 1973), pp. 200–1; Pseudo-Kodinos, *Traité des offices*, ed. and trans. J. Verpeaux (Paris, 1966), pp. 171, 181, 183, 195–8, 202–3, 208–9, 226–7, 286–7; A. Heisenberg, *Aus der Geschichte und Literatur der Palaiologenzeit* (*Sitzungsberichte der bayerischen Akademie der Wissenschaften*, philos.-philol. und hist. Klasse, Abh. 10, Munich, 1920), pp. 85 ff.; O. Treitinger, *Die oströmische Kaiser und Reichsidee nach ihrer Gestaltung in höfischen Zeremoniell* (Jena, 1938), pp. 112 ff.; Ph. Koukoules, *Byzantinon bios kai politismos*, iv (Athens, 1951), pp. 134–5; E. M. Kantorowicz, 'Oriens Augusti—Lever du Roi', *DOP*, 17 (1963), pp. 159–62; H. W. Haussig, *A history of Byzantine civilization*, trans. J. M. Hussey (London, 1971), pp. 38, 55, 193, 398, 401, and pl. 32; Panaretos, ed. Lampsides, p. 78; and on the whereabouts of *prokypsis* in Trebizond, A. Bryer and D. Winfield, *The Byzantine monuments and topography of the Pontos* (Washington, D.C., forthcoming), chap. 20.

[2] See Koukoules, *Bios*, iv, pl. 5; J. Strzygowski, 'Das Epithalamion des Paläologen Andronikos II', *Byz. Zeits.* 10 (1901), pp. 553–4, and pl. vi, 2; S. P. Lampros, *Leukoma Byzantinon Autokratoron* (Athens, n.d.), pl. 80; and I. Spatharakis, *The portrait in Byzantine illuminated Manuscripts* (Leiden, 1976), pp. 210–30 and pl. 162.

[3] e.g. the portrait group of Manuel II Palaiologos's family in Lampros, *Leukoma*, pl. 84, and Spatharakis, *Portrait*, pl. 93.

served the function of a modern royal wedding group photograph. But in 1346 Theodora had to stand alone with her eunuchs. She was, however, awarded the *epithalamia* recited at a *prokypsis*, such as had been sung for Theodora Komnene, bride of Henry, brother of Conrad III, in 1147–8, and for Constance, daughter of Frederick II, bride of John Vatatzes in 1244, at their own displays.[1] One can only speculate as to how Kantakouzenos's poets handled their theme in 1346; Gibbon is scornful as to their likely quality.[2]

Rubriquis and Ibn Battuta report on similar Mongol displays, and the Seljuks and Danishmendids had their audience chambers. But there is no evidence for *prokypsis* in the simple early Ottoman custom and Kantakouzenos evidently made two concessions to Orthodox and Muslim sentiment in 1346. First he ordered a secular wooden *prokypsis* stage outside Selymbria. The town and its citadel was then substantial and well-walled; it was probably governed by Phakrases. Its churches included one recently built by Alexios Apokaukos, assassinated in the year before. But even if common sense dictated that Turkish troops should not be allowed into the town, clerical sense surely denied a church as the theatre for the *prokypsis*.[3] Second, as in a Muslim, but not Orthodox, marriage, the mother and sisters of the bride were excluded from the show, even as spectators.

The marriage in custom
Historians of the early Ottomans regularly comment on the debilitating effects on the first *emirs* of their encounter with imperial

---

[1] Kantorowicz, *DOP*, 17 (1963), p. 161; G. Schlumberger, *Byzance et croisades* (Paris, 1927), pp. 63–4.

[2] E. Gibbon, *The history of the decline and fall of the Roman Empire*, vi (London, 1788), p. 317.

[3] William of Rubruck in *Contemporaries of Marco Polo*, ed. M. Komroff (London, 1928), p. 99; *The travels of Ibn Battūta A.D. 1325–54*, trans. H. A. R. Gibb, ii (London, 1962), p. 483; Alderson, *Structure*, p. 93; what appears to be a Danishmendid audience chamber at Neocaesareia (Niksar) is described in Brycr and Winfield, *Monuments*, chap. 7; S. Eyice, 'Alexis Apocauque et l'église Byzantine de Sélymbria (Silvri)', *Byzantion*, 34 (1964), pp. 77–104; and Démétrius Cydonès, *Correspondance*, ed. G. Camelli (Paris, 1930), p. 214.

Byzantine family ceremonial, beginning with the wedding of 1346.[1] This is hard to credit. If Orhan had been a witness of his wife's *prokypsis*, it is difficult to know what he would have made of it. Despite Enveri's conventional account of the splendour of the *Despoina*'s robes in 1344, Kantakouzenos did not have access to the Byzantine imperial regalia in Constantinople (which had anyway been pawned to Venice in 1343) and Gregoras was scornful of the clay utensils and sham vestments which were to be used at his second coronation in 1347.[2] Others would wish to lay the whole question of the status of Ottoman women, and the *harem*, at a Byzantine door, for which there is marginally more justification than the view that the so-called Ottoman 'Law of Fratricide' has Byzantine antecedents.[3]

More important is the question of dowry and bride-price.

P. Magdalino, 'Byzantine churches of Selymbria', *DOP*, 32 (1979), pp. 347, 350, notes two extramural churches, St. Agathonikos and St. Alexander.

[1] Alderson, *Structure*, p. 77 and n. 3, on the 'luxurious ceremonial still surviving at the Byzantine court', which Orhan, for one, 'must have witnessed . . .'

[2] Gregoras. ii. pp. 788–9; T. Bertelè, 'I gioielli della corona bizantina dati in pegno alla repubblica Veneta nel sec. XIV e Mastino II della Scala', *Studi in onore di Amintore Fanfani*, ii (Milan, 1962), pp. 91–177.

[3] See N. M. Penzer, *The Harēm* (London, 1967), p. 288; a popular view is expressed by Selma Ekrem, *Turkey old and new* (New York, 1947), p. 73; 'How, then did the Turkish women lose their ancient freedom? When the Turks conquered Istanbul they discovered veiled women and apartments where they were segregated, for the Byzantine Greeks did not allow their women much liberty. The Turkish men were much impressed by what they saw . . .' In fact urban, rather than ethnic, influences seem to have been more important; see Gertrude H. Stern, *Marriage in early Islam* (London, 1939), and 'Harim', *Encyclopaedia of Islam*, 2nd ed. As for fratricide, it is true that Andronikos III Grand Komnenos executed his brothers Michael and George on his accession to the throne of Trebizond in 1332, before any known cases of Ottoman fratricide. But it was hardly a Byzantine custom, or even a regular Ottoman one before Mehmed II institutionalized the practice, and it would be claiming much for a petty Grand Komnenos to influence a Sultan over a century later. See Doukas, ed. Grecu, pp. 37, 39, 71–3, 235, 287; Panaretos, ed. Lampsides, p. 64; Alderson, *Structure*, 27; but Miller, *Trebizond*, p. 43, reverses the claim and makes Andronikos III follow 'Turkish practice'.

Orthodox and Islamic canons recognize the dowry (*mahr*) but are in direct opposition to Mongol and Türkmen custom, which is a bride-price. When in 1452 Sphrantzes led an embassy to find a bride for the last emperor of Constantinople, he found that the Grand Komnenos John IV of Trebizond (whose family had been marrying Türkmens for a century) still offered a dowry, but George VIII of Georgia (where Orthodox had been marrying Muslims for three centuries) demanded a bride-price. Where, as in the Caucasus, dowries and bride-prices existed side by side, the bride-price tends to drive out the dowry.[1] It was clearly essential to the status of a Byzantine bride in a Muslim land that she have a dowry; equally it was a mark of ownership to pay a bride-price, which Muslim rulers would not wish to forgo. There is evidence that the Grand Komnenoi and their Türkmen allies in the Pontos solved the problem by paying both dowries and bride-prices, leaving each party to interpret the results as it wished.[2] In this ambiguous field Kantakouzenos would naturally offer a dowry: the brideprice was Orhan's military support. But, like the Türkmens of the Pontos, Orhan may well have viewed the marriage of 1346 as a mark of vassalage. His *ulu hatun* (chief wife and mother of Murad I) was Nilüfer, whom he married in 1299. Evidently a convert to Islam, she was the daughter of the Byzantine governor of Yarhisar. Alderson

---

[1] Sphrantzes, pp. 74, 362; Makarios Melissenos makes George VIII say: 'It is not our custom for women to give money to men when they are going to marry, but men to give money to women.' Sphrantzes was surprised and replied: 'I have never heard such a custom and law, as your highness mentions.' The Georgian ruler laughed and went on to speak of other wonders. In 1452 a Byzantine emperor could hardly afford to accept a bride on such terms. But that the Georgian may not simply have been bargaining is shown by the fact that the Orthodox Ossetes abandoned the dowry system in favour of the bride-price (*kalim*) of their Sunni Chechen-Ingush neighbours: see J. F. Baddeley, *The rugged flanks of the Caucasus*, i (Oxford, 1940), pp. 207, 267. Cf. Doukas, trans. Magoulias, p. 272 and n. 51. Dede Korkut, ballad vi, confirms that fourteenth-century Türkmens offered a bride-price to Byzantine fathers-in-law: see Bryer, *DOP*, 29 (1975), pp. 135–6. But that the dowry also survived among the Ottomans is evidenced by *The Turkish letters of Ogier Ghiselin de Busbecq*, trans. E. S. Forster (Oxford, 1968), pp. 28, 118–19.

[2] Bryer, *DOP*, 29 (1975), pp. 135–6.

had no doubt that the marriage 'symbolised the annexation of her father's estates'.[1]

The status of the bride

So far as Byzantines were concerned, the most satisfactory diplomatic marriage was perhaps their last. Theodora Grand Komnene became *hatun* of the Akkoyunlu ruler Uzun Hasan (1449–78) in 1458. Dowry and bride-price had been paid; she had been taken to her husband by a *nymphostolos*. High Commissioner for an empire which expired in 1461, she nevertheless maintained a Christian household with chaplain, and succoured her husband's Christian subjects. Most remarkably, she conducted personal negotiations on behalf of her husband with Western powers.[2] More typical was perhaps the case of a certain still unidentified product of the palace finishing school for Mongol brides. This Palaiologan princess became the third *hatun* of the Kipchak *han* Muhammed Özbeg (1312–41). Like his other *hatuns* she had an impressively large household, and freedom enough to obtain permission to return home for the birth of her child in 1332. Ibn Battuta joined her caravan from Astrakhan to Constantinople. At the Byzantine border in Bulgaria he was disturbed to see that she abandoned her portable mosque and started eating pork and drinking wine: 'Inner sentiments concealed [hitherto] suffered a change through our entry into the land of infidelity.'[3] The Palaiologan princess was evidently a closet Christian.

[1] Alderson, *Structure*, p. 85; Nilüfer (or Lülüfer), apparently the first Greek to enter the Ottoman dynasty, gave her name to a river near Bursa and to the Nilüfer *hatan imareti* in Nicaea, built in 1388. Ashikpashazade in *Vom Hirtenzelt zur Hohen Pforte*, trans. R. Kreutel (Graz, Vienna, Cologne, 1959), p. 39.

[2] An *ulu hatun* was the senior wife, a sort of *Valide Sultan*, probably by right of mothering a designated heir. It is notable that no Byzantine princess is known to have reached this status of considerable authority. But a puzzling Greek ceramic epitaph of 28 September 1342 from Erzincan mentions an unnamed *megale chatouna* who apparently died as a *presbyterissa*: F. Cumont, 'Inscription de l'époque des Comnènes de Trébizonde', *Mélanges Pirenne*, i (Paris, 1926), pp. 67–72; J. E. Woods, *The Aqquyunlu. Clan confederation, empire* (Minneapolis and Chicago, 1976), pp. 101, 135, 158; Bryer, *DOP*, 29 (1975), pp. 137, 149 n. 146 to appendix ii.

[2] Ibn Battuta, trans. Gibb, ii. p. 501.

The most surprising feature of her father's account of Theodora's married life is not that she kept her faith and made no secret of it but that she encouraged Orhan's subjects to revert to Orthodoxy. Kantakouzenos cannot be accused of ignorance of either Orhan's Bithynia or of Islam—or rather anti-Islamic polemic, with which he was to fill over 320 columns of Migne's *Patrologia*, where one naturally looks in vain for any hint that the monk Joasaph had a Muslim son-in-law. The penalty for reversion to Christianity was death, last known to have been paid in that area as late in 1819. One of Kantakouzenos's own protégés, the monk Meletios, could have told him that with some feeling, for Meletios had begun his career as Muslim *ulema* in Orhan's own capital of Bursa.[1] By his own epigraphy and Ottoman historiography, Orhan was a *ghazi*: he could do no other than convert. The question is whether Kantakouzenos was disingenuously trying to justify his alliance with Orhan, or whether he was reporting actual conditions in Bithynia, where it is possible that things were still so fluid that reversion may not have been such a reckless act. Bithynia was the last Anatolian province, apart from the Pontos, to experience wholesale conversion. As a good *ghazi*, Orhan had urged his soldiers to take its Christian women as wives when he captured Nicaea in 1331.[2] Anatolian Greeks commonly lost first their daughters, then their faith, and finally their language. But, aside from marriage, conversion was only the first stage in the process of turning a Greek into a Turk, which elsewhere took three generations or more. Orhan's Bithynia was in the throes of the first stage for a generation after 1331, which (as Kantakouzenos knew) is unusually well documented. By 1338 large numbers of Christians of Nicaea had evidently converted, for Patriarch John XIV Kalekas (1334–47) sent them, then and in 1340,

[1] John VI Kantakouzenos, *Contra Sectam Mahometicam Apologiae IV* and *Mahometem Orationes Quatuor*, PG 154 cols 371–692, probably written in 1360; R. Clogg, 'A little-known Orthodox neo-martyr, Athanasios of Smyrna (1819)', *Eastern Churches Review*, 5 (1973), pp. 28–36; Vryonis, 'Human sacrifice', p. 144.

[2] Vryonis, *Decline*, p. 392 n. 126; Ashikpashazade, trans. Kreutel, pp. 67–8.

letters which are commonly taken as the first evidence of widespread crypto-Christianity (public profession of Islam and private confession of Orthodoxy). He condoned it as the only alternative for those public converts to Islam who did not seek martyrdom. In fact it is not clear from Kalekas's letters whether they are a statement of an existing situation or an incitement to crypto-Christianity—which, elsewhere, appears as a widespread phenomenon much later and not primarily through Muslim pressure.[1] But it is clear that Kalekas knew the risks of reversion. Kalekas was no friend of Kantakouzenos, or of another of the emperor's protégés, (St.) Gregory Palamas, archbishop of Thessalonike (1347–59). But an ill wind drove Palamas on to Orhan's shores and he was able to report on the situation at first hand. He visited the *emir*'s summer palace and Nicaea in 1354 as a prisoner before he was ransomed from Orhan (probably by Kantakouzenos). Palamas had a mixed reception, but was impressed by the theological tolerance of Orhan's grandson and the friendliness of a crowd before which he debated with a *mullah* in Nicaea: 'One of them said, the time will come when we shall understand each other; and I am glad, and pray that the time may come soon.'[2] Palamas and the *mullah* were perhaps able to reason and hope, but others had evidently entered an unreasonable twilight between the two faiths in which there was no hope. Local *Chiones*, apparently Christians who had adopted Judaism as the best of both worlds, found themselves denounced as retrograde by both Palamas

---

[1] H. W. Lowry, 'The Ottoman Tahrir Defters as a source for urban demographic history: the case study of Trabzon (ca. 1486–1583)' (unpublished ULCA Ph.D. dissertation, 1977) for the process of conversion; Vryonis, *Decline*, pp. 341–3; N. E. Meliores, *Hoi Kryptochristianoi* (Athens, 1962), pp. 37–9. The supposed continuity of these 'crypto-Christians' with the later phenomenon described, for example, in M. E. Durham, *The Burden of the Balkans* (London, 1905), pp. 205–8, 291–2, is questioned in A. A. M. Bryer, 'The Pontic revival and the new Greece', *Hellenism and the first Greek war of liberation (1821–1830): continuity and change*, ed. N. P. Diamandouros and others (Thessaloniki, 1976), p. 176.

[2] J. Meyendorff, *A study of Gregory Palamas* (London, 1964), p. 197; Ševčenko, 'Decline', p. 179.

and the Muslims.[1] Palamas's and Kalekas's letters reveal a nebulous area between the two faiths (perhaps bridged by local cults) created by the strain of swift conversion, which had yet to be healed by a generation or two of assimilation. But they do not reveal any evidence of reversion to Orthodoxy: the drift to Islam was inexorable. Even Kalekas had not advocated reversion, for it would have been simply irresponsible. By claiming that Theodora had encouraged reversion, was Kantakouzenos doing no more than putting the best light he could upon her marriage? The political ends had at least justified the means, for Theodora brought the *emir* to see his father-in-law at Skutari in 1347 (the forerunner of at least six similar Türkmen state visits to Trebizond after 1352) and Orhan remained an ally.[2]

The marriage in canon law

So far as Orhan was concerned the events of 1346 constituted a marriage whether he was there or not. Theodora lay outside the degrees of affinity and her people had received the Book before the Prophet, while Orhan himself did not exceed the canonical limit of four wives.[3] This makes Umur's previous rejection of the *Despoina* all the more puzzling. In the second version of his tale, Enveri was following convention in making his *ghazi* hero reject the blandishments of women, particularly Christian. He had already made him reject the advances of the marchioness of Bodonitsa in somewhat similar circumstances.[4] But this is not Umur's argument in the first version of the story, which Lemerle found inexplicable.[5] It was that he was Kantakouzenos's brother and so could not marry his own daughter. Kantakouzenos describes Umur as *symmachos*, but

---

[1] Anna Philippides-Braak, 'La captivité de Palamas chez les Turcs', *Travaux et Mémoires*, 7 (1979), pp. 204–5, 214–18. A satisfactory etyomology for 'Chiones' has yet to be found.

[2] Bryer, *DOP*, p. 29 (1975), p. 135.

[3] A. J. Arberry, *The Koran interpreted*, i (New York, 1955), pp. 58–9, 100–1, 103, 128; N. Daniel, *Islam and the West. The Making of an Image* (Edinburgh, 1960), pp. 135–46.

[4] *Destān*, ll. pp. 531–64; Lemerle, *Aydin*, p. 77.

[5] Lemerle, *Aydin*, p. 175.

Enveri's term for the relationship meant more than that: the *tekfur* was Umur's *kardesh*. The situation is understandable in the surviving Turkish institutions of *kardesh*, not just a brotherhood but a blood-brotherhood. In fact Gregoras had got it right by comparing Kantakouzenos and Umur to Orestes and Pylades. A *kardesh* has an entrée into his adoptive family's household which cannot be abused. In late 1345 Kantakouzenos may quixotically have asked his *symmachos* Umur's permission to marry Theodora to Orhan because he thought he had offered her to him first. But Umur, as *kardesh*, would have interpreted it as a fraternal discussion over the future of a daughter (or niece) who had once been inexplicably offered to him.

So far as Kantakouzenos the emperor was concerned, he bravely describes the *prokypsis* of 1346 as a marriage. Theodora was at least outside the canonical age of twelve years for a bride and Gregoras was enthusiastic about the alliance, whereas he had condemned the notorious case of Simonis, whom Androikos II had given at the age of five years to the mercy of the thrice-married barbarian, but nevertheless Orthodox, Milutin of Serbia.[1]

So far as the Church was concerned, the age limit was perhaps the only canon that the 'marriage' of 1346 did not break: they are too many to list here.[2]

[1] Gregoras, i. p. 243; Nicol, *The last centuries*, pp. 126–7; there is a wall-painting of the unhappy bride at Gračanica.

[2] Byzantine civil and canon lawyers would have found it difficult to know where to begin, if they had wished to condemn imperial marriages with Muslims, because neither law embraced the matter. But impediments to marriage with heretics, infidels, and Jews, and to polygamous marriages, are abundant enough and even betrothal would have been illegal, for that had to be blessed by a priest. The problem had long risen, on a less scandalous level, with the question of Orthodox marriages with Roman Catholics. See (for civil legal objections), K. Harmenopoulos, *Procheiron Nomon to legomenon He Hexabiblos* (Athens, 1935), pp. 319, 348; and (for canon legal objections), G. A. Rhalles and M. Potles, *Syntagma ton theion kai hieron kanonon* (Athens, 1852–59), ii. pp. 251–4, 471, 498 (baptism, sometimes practised by Turks, was invalid because they regarded it as a sort of prophylactic only), pp. 500–1, 505–6; iii. 173, 180, 198–9, 364; iv. 337, 439, 476; D. M. Nicol, 'Mixed marriages in Byzantium in the thirteenth century', *Studies in Church History*, 1 (1964), pp. 160–72; Daniel, *Islam and the West*, pp. 146–8.

So far as ordinary Byzantines were concerned, some had come to the 'Moment of Vision'. Obscure but apparently popular feelings were to make Alexios III, Grand Komnenos of Trebizond, hold off a full seventeen years before he gave Tajeddin *beg* an imperial bride in 1379—although there seems to have been no objection to her marrying an Orthodox Serb later.[1]

So far as Kantakouzenos, monk and Orthodox theologian, was concerned, the 'Moment of Vision' must have been painfully clear, as his defensive account of the events of 1346 hints. He was in a unique position to know that the honeymoon was over before it had begun, and that the alliance was unequal. But it took Doukas to admit that the marriage between Theodora Kantakouzene and the *ghazi emir* had been no marriage at all. Doukas was writing in the same decade as Enveri. His terminology is as conventional as the Ottoman poet's. Whereas Enveri had insisted on the chastity of Umur, Doukas makes Orhan insatiable, following traditional Christian medieval rumour of Muslim behaviour—although he knew Orhan's successors as well as any Greek.[2] But Doukas, unlike Kantakouzenos, had nothing to gloss over, and his later account of the sequence of events in 1346 is probably to be preferred to the emperor's own. Above all, his disgust with 'this abominable betrothal' is authentic enough:

When Orhan heard [Kantakouzenos's] ambassadors proposing this un-expected marriage contract and making promises of infinite treasures, he was like a bull which had been parched by the burning heat of summer, and was with mouth agape drinking at a hole filled from the coldest water, but unable to get his fill; thus was he transformed as he listened because of barbarian incontinence. This nation is intemperate and lustful as no other people, incontinent beyond all races and insatiate in licentiousness. It is so inflamed by passion that it never ceases unscrupulously and dissolutely from having intercourse by both natural and unnatural means with females, males and dumb animals. The people of this shameless and savage nation, moreover, do the following: if they seize a Hellene or Italian woman, or a

[1] Panaretos, ed. Lampsides, pp. 74, 78–80.
[2] Daniel, pp. 141–6, 320–2. For Doukas's other accusations of Ottoman immorality, see ed. Grecu, pp. 87, 123, 201, 211, 381–5.

woman of another nation, or a captive or deserter, they embrace her as an Aphrodite or Semele, but a woman of their own nation or of their own tongue they loath as though she were a bear or a hyena. Orhan, therefore, when he heard of the proposed marriage with Kantakouzenos's daughter (for she was beautiful in form and her countenance was not without grace) and the size of her dowry and the betrothal gifts sent by Kantakouzenos, quickly gave his consent.[1]

[1] Doukas, ed. Grecu, p. 59; trans. Magoulias, p. 73.

List of the published Writings of Richard William Southern

1933
'Ranulf Flambard and early Anglo-Norman Administration' (Alexander Prize Essay), *TRHS*, 4th series, xvi, pp. 95–128 (revised and repr. in *Medieval Humanism and other studies*, 1970, pp. 234–52).

1937
Review: *St. Bernard of Clairvaux* by Watkin Williams, *History*, xxi. p. 367.

1938
'Some New Letters of Peter of Blois', *EHR*, liii. 412–24.

1939
'An Alphabetical List of Dukes, Marquesses and Earls, 1066–1603', *Handbook of British Chronology*, ed. F. M. Powicke *et al.* (Royal Historical Society).

1941
'St. Anselm and his English Pupils', *MARS*, i. pp. 3–34.

1943
'The First Life of Edward the Confessor', *EHR*, lviii. 385–400.

1948
'Lanfranc of Bec and Berengar of Tours', *Studies in Medieval History Presented to F. M. Powicke*, ed. R. W. Hunt, W. A. Pantin, and R. W. Southern, Clarendon Press, pp. 27–48.

1949
Review: *The Religious Orders in England*, by David Knowles, *JTS*, 50, pp. 98–100.

1950

'A Note on the Text of "Glanville", *De Legibus et Consuetudinibus Regni Angliae*', *EHR*, lxv, 81–9.

'View from the Osler Pavilion', *Cross-Section: the Magazine of the Oxford United Hospitals*, Summer 1950, pp. 26–8.

Review: *Ways of Medieval Life and Thought*, by F. M. Powicke, *Oxford Magazine*, 15 June, pp. 558–60.

1951

Review: *Odo of Deuil: De Profectione Ludovici vii in Orientem*, ed. and trans. V. G. Berry; and *Oliver of Paderborn: the Capture of Damietta*, trans. J. J. Gavigan. *Medium Aevum*, 20, pp. 84–6.

Review: *The Episcopal Colleagues of Archbishop Thomas Becket*, by David Knowles, *EHR*, lxvii. 87–90.

1953

The Making of the Middle Ages, London: Hutchinson.

Reviews: *Tithes and Parishes in Medieval Italy and the historical roots of a modern problem*, by Catherine E. Boyd, *Medium Ævum*, 22, pp. 109–10.

Richard of St. Victor: Sermons et Opuscules Spirituels, ed. J. Chatillon and W. J. Tulloch, *EHR*, lxviii. 632–3.

1954

'St. Anselm and Gilbert Crispin, Abbot of Westminster', *MARS*, 3, pp. 78–115.

'Exeter College', *Victoria History of the County of Oxford, iii, The University of Oxford*, ed. H. E. Salter and M. D. Lobel, London and Oxford, pp. 107–18.

1955

' Tenth Century', *Encyclopedia Americana*.

w: *Otto of Freising: The Deeds of Frederick*, trans. C. C. Mierow

R. Emery, *EHR*, 70, 315–16.

1956

Reviews: *The Growth of Papal Government in the Middle Ages* by Walter Ullmann, *EHR*, 71, 635–8.

Richard III by P. M. Kendall, *The Economist*, 21 Jan., pp. 199–200.

An Introduction to Anglo-Saxon England by P. Hunter Blair, ibid. 24 March, 645.

A History of the English Speaking Peoples, i. The Birth of Britain by Winston S. Churchill, ibid. 28 April, 3.

History of the Byzantine State by G. Ostrogorsky, trans. Joan Hussey, ibid. 29 Sept., 1040.

Angevin Kingship by J. E. A. Jolliffe, *Oxford Magazine*, 1 March, pp. 322–3.

Christianity and the State in the Light of History by T. M. Parker, ibid. 1 Nov., 76–8.

From Becket to Langton: English Church Government, 1170–1213 by C. R. Cheney, *TLS*, 17 Aug. 482.

1957

Reviews: *The Eastern Schism* by Steven Runciman, *EHR*, 72, 101–3.

The Letters of John of Salisbury, i. The Early Letters (1153–1161), ed. W. J. Miller, S. J. and H. E. Butler, revised by C. N. L. Brooke, ibid. 72, pp. 493–7.

Theobald Archbishop of Canterbury by Avrom Saltman, *History*, xlii. pp. 218–220.

Ordericus Vitalis: ein Beitrag zur Kluniazensischen Geschichtsschreibung by Hans Wolter, S. J., *JEH*, 8, 232–3.

The Religious Orders in England, vol. 2, by David Knowles. *JTS*, N.S. 8, pp. 190–4.

Analecta Monastica, ii (*Studia Anselmiana*, 31) by J. Leclercq, ibid. pp. 194–6.

A History of Technology, ii. The Mediterranean Civilizations and the Middle Ages, c. 700 B.C. to c. A.D. 1500, ed. Charles Singer, E. J. Holmyard, A. R. Hall, and Trevor I. Williams, *The Economist* 5 Jan., pp. 26–7.

Feudal Britain by G. W. S. Barrow, ibid. 12 Jan., pp. 109–10.
A History of Medieval Europe from Constantine to St. Louis by R. H. C. Davis, ibid. 14 Dec.
Frederick II of Hohenstauffen by Georgina Masson, ibid. 28 Dec. pp. 112–16.

1958

'The Canterbury Forgeries', *EHR*, lxxiii. 193–226.
'The English Origins of the "Miracles of the Virgin" ', *MARS*, iv. pp. 176–216.
Reviews: *Fritz Saxl 1890–1948: a volume of memorial essays, EHR,* lxxiii. 752–3.
Warwick the Kingmaker by P. Kendall, *The Economist*, 4 Jan., 30.
The Sicilian Vespers by Steven Runciman, ibid. 29 March, Spring Books, 6.
Political Thought in Medieval Times by J. B. Morrall, ibid. 30 Aug., pp. 664–7.
The Northern Seas: Shipping and Commerce in Northern Europe, 300–1100 by A. R. Lewis, ibid. 18 Oct., 226.

The Life of Edward II by the so-called Monk of Malmesbury, ed. and trans. N. Denholm Young, *Oxford Magazine*, 27 Feb., p. 333.
Medieval Thought from St. Augustine to Ockham by Gordon Leff, *Time and Tide*, 28 June, p. 802.

1959

'Pope Adrian IV', *The Times*, 1 Sept. 1959 (revised and reprinted in *Medieval Humanism and other studies*, 1970, pp. 234–52).

Reviews: *The Intellectual Heritage of the Early Middle Ages* by M. L. W. Laistner, *EHR*, lxxiv. 713–14.
The King's Two Bodies: a study in Medieval Political Theology by Ernst H. Kantorowicz, *JEH*, 10, 105–8.
Medieval England, 2 vols., ed. A. L. Poole, *The Economist*, 10 Jan., p. 121.

Rural England, 1086–1135 by Reginald Lennard, ibid. 5 Sept., p. 726.
The Origins of Russia by George Vernadsky, *Listener*, 26 Feb.

1960

'The Place of England in the Twelfth Century Renaissance', *History*, 45, pp. 201–16 (revised and repr. in *Medieval Humanism and other studies*, 1970, pp. 158–80).

Review: *Untersuchungen über Inhalt und Datierung der Briefe Gerberts von Aurillac* by Mathilde Uhlirz, *EHR*, lxxv. 293–5.

1961

The Shape and Substance of Academic History. Inaugural Lecture as Chichele Professor of Modern History, Clarendon Press, repr. *The Varieties of History from Voltaire to the Present*, ed. Fritz Stern, 2nd ed., London, 1970, pp. 403–22.

1962

Western Views of Islam in the Middle Ages, Harvard University Press.
The Life of St. Anselm by Eadmer, NMT.
'The Place of Henry I in English History', Raleigh Lecture on History, *Proc. Brit. Acad.*, 48, pp. 127–69 (revised and repr. in *Medieval Humanism and other studies*, 1970, pp. 206–33).
Review: *The Religious Orders in England*, vol. 3, by David Knowles, *JTS*, NS. 13, 469–75.

1963

St. Anselm and his Biographer: a study of monastic life and thought, c. 1059–c. 1130 (Birkbeck Lectures, Trinity College, Cambridge, 1959), Cambridge University Press.
'Commentary', *Scientific Change: a symposium in the History of Science, 9–15 July 1961*, ed. A. C. Crombie, pp. 301–6.
'The Church of the Dark Ages, 600–1000', *The Layman in Christian History*, ed. S. C. Neill and H. R. Weber, pp, 87–110.
'A Wonder of the Victorian Age: Balliol celebrates its 700th anniversary', *Oxford Mail*, 28 June, 8.

Review: *Medieval Technology and Social Change* by Lynn White Jr, *History of Science*, 2, pp. 130–5.

1964

Foreword to *Oxford Studies Presented to Daniel Callus* (Oxford. Hist. Soc., NS. 16, v–viii.

'Sir Maurice Powicke, 1879–1963', *Proc. Brit. Acad.*, 50, pp. 275–304.

'Expanding Christendom, i. Bede, ii. Anselm, iii. Meister Eckhart', *Listener*, 13 Feb., 20 Feb., 20 March, pp. 267–9, 308–10, 425–7 (revised and repr. in *Medieval Humanism and other studies*, 1970, pp. 1–26).

1965

'Medieval Humanism, i. Religious Humanism, ii. Scientific Humanism, iii. Practical Humanism', *Listener*, 20 Aug., 9 Sept., pp. 303–5, 377–80, 412–15 (revised and repr. in *Medieval Humanism and other studies*, 1970, pp. 29–60).

Reviews: *The Historian and Character* by David Knowles, *EHR*, lxxx. 570–1.

The Life of Edward the Confessor, ed. and trans. F. Barlow, *History*, 1, pp. 197–9.

The Martyrs of Córdoba (850–859): a study of the sources by E. P. Colbert, *JEH*, xvi. 228–9.

The York Psalter in the Library of the Hunterian Museum, Glasgow by T. S. R. Boase, *Medium Ævum*, xxxiv. pp. 139–40.

1966

'1066', *New York Review of Books*, 17 Nov., pp. 33–6.

1967

Reviews: *Magna Carta*, by J. C. Holt, *EHR*, lxxxii. 342–6.

The Letters of F. W. Maitland, ed. C. H. S. Fifoot, *History and Theory*, vi. pp. 105–11.

Augustine of Hippo by Peter Brown, *New Statesman*, 22 Sept., 360–1.

1968

'Thomas Aquinas', *International Encylopaedia of the Social Sciences*, i. pp. 375–7.

Reviews: *The Letters and Charters of Gilbert Foliot* and *Gilbert Foliot and his letters* by Adrian Morey and C. N. L. Brooke, *EHR*, lxxxiii. 784–9.
Letters of Peter the Venerable, ed. Giles Constable, *TLS*, 7 March, 234.

1969

Memorials of St. Anselm, ed. with F. S. Schmidt, O.S.B. (Auctores Britannici Medii Aevi, i.).

1970

Western Society and the Church in the Middle Ages (Pelican History of the Church, ii).
Medieval Humanism and other studies, Blackwell, Oxford.
'Aspects of the European Tradition of Historical Writing: 1. 'The classical tradition from Einhard to Geoffrey of Monmouth'. Presidential Address, *TRHS*, 5th series, xx. pp. 173–96.
'A meeting of the ways in Oxford', *The Tablet*, 31 Oct., pp. 1062–3.

1971

'Aspects of the European Tradition of Historical Writing: 2. Hugh of St. Victor and the idea of Historical Development'. Presidential Address, *TRHS*, 5th series, xxi. pp. 159–79.

Reviews: *The Letters of Innocent III (1198–1216) concerning England and Wales: a calendar with an appendix of texts* by C. R. and M. G. Cheney, *EHR*, 86, 796–9.
Hubert Walter, by C. R. Cheney, *EHR*, 86, 829–30.

1972

'Aspects of the European Tradition of Historical Writing: 3. History as Prophecy'. Presidential Address, *TRHS*, 5th series, xxii. pp. 159–86.

1973

'Aspects of the European Tradition of Historical Writing: 4. The Sense of the past'. Presidential Address, *TRHS*, 5th series, xxiii pp. 243–63.

'Dante and Islam', *Relations between East and West in the Middle Ages*, ed. Derek Baker, Edinburgh University Press, pp. 133–45.

1974

Review: *Fontes Harleiani: a study of the Harleian Collection of Manuscripts in the British Museum* by C. E. Wright, *EHR*, lxxxix. 113–16.

1976

'Master Vacarius and the Beginning of an English Academic Tradition', *Medieval Learning and Literature: Essays presented to R. W. Hunt*, ed. J. J. G. Alexander and M. T. Gibson, Clarendon Press, pp. 257–86.

'A Benedictine Monastery in a disordered World' (an address given on the opening of a new monastic library at Mount Angel, Oregon, in May 1970), *Downside Review*, xciv. pp. 163–77.

'A commemoration sermon on William Laud', *The Beauty of Holiness*, ed. Benedicta Ward, Fairacres Publication pp. 57, 1–8.

1977

'The Historical Experience'. The Rede Lecture in the University of Cambridge, *TLS*, 24 June, pp. 771–4.

1979

Platonism, Scholastic Method and the School of Chartres, Stenton Lecture, 1978. University of Reading.

1980

Preface to *Prophecy and Millenarianism: Essays in honour of Marjorie Reeves*, ed. AnnWilliams, Longman.

'Vivian Hunter Galbraith, 1889–1976', *Proc. Brit. Acad.* lxiv (1978), 397–425.

Index

Modern historians (post 1660) are not included in the text.

Index

Index

Index